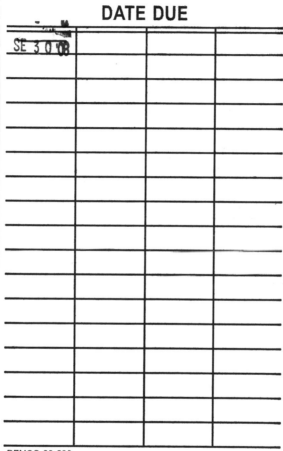

DATE DUE

SE 3 0 08			

DEMCO 38-296

Rhetoric and the Law
of Draco

Rhetoric and the Law of Draco

EDWIN CARAWAN

CLARENDON PRESS · OXFORD
1998

...don Street, Oxford OX2 6DP
York
Bogota Bombay
Town Dar es Salaam
Istanbul Karachi
Kuala Lumpur Madras Madrid Melbourne
Mexico City Nairobi Paris Singapore
Taipei Tokyo Toronto Warsaw
and associated companies in
Berlin Ibadan

Oxford is a trade mark of Oxford University Press

Published in the United States
by Oxford University Press Inc., New York

British Library Cataloguing in Publication Data
Data available

Library of Congress Cataloging in Publication Data
Rhetoric and the law of Draco / Edwin Carawan.
Includes bibliographical references and index.
1. Homicide (Greek-law)   2. Trials (Homicide)—Greece—Athens.
I. Title.
KL4388.M87C37   1998   345.495'120252—dc21   97-45972
ISBN 0-19-815086-5

1 3 5 7 9 10 8 6 4 2

Typeset by Hope Services (Abingdon) Ltd.
Printed in Great Britain on acid-free paper by
Biddles Ltd., Guildford and King's Lynn

For
Alison Parker

δάμαρτι κριτῇ τ᾽ ἀδαμάστῳ

PREFACE

This book is a study of how the Athenians came to terms with the killer—how the lawgivers of the ancient democracy devised their various remedies against bloodshed and how the citizens themselves decided the inevitable disputes at trial. It is a study of primitive law and the way of reasoning about guilt and innocence that grew out of it. But Athenian justice may seem remote from modern concerns, and the reader who is curious enough to open to this preface but wary of proceeding any further may well ask, 'Why should this matter to us?' To that wary reader, I suggest, the ancient problems matter because they teach us about our own most troublesome assumptions.

In the Anglo-American tradition—indeed in the broader currents of modern law in the West—there are two aspects of a homicide that we consider most important: the wrong to the community and the agent's state of mind. In our understanding of the wrong, the criminal aspect predominates: the hurt to the victims has become part of a deeper violation against us all. And in our reckoning of guilt—who is to blame and how much—we tend to be preoccupied with inner motives: what distinguishes murder most foul from culpable negligence or unavoidable mishap is a matter of the killer's intentions or expectations. These principles enter into our deepest convictions, stir the most impassioned debate about the gravest social ills, and guide the remedies we devise in the legislature and the courtroom. This way of thinking takes on a certain inevitability; and so, when we venture into another way of justice, we are likely to carry these principles with us or to regard any alien typology as irrational or inferior. But let us ask ourselves, how well do we understand our own way of judging the killer?

In Athenian justice the criminality of homicide, the wrong to the greater community was a rather dim concept, largely overshadowed by the wrong to the family. And *mens rea* itself—the presumption that the real source of guilt is the inner mind—is an even murkier notion. But Athenian justice was based upon a way of arguing things out before a jury of the people, a discursive process for collective decision that is perhaps closer to the Anglo-American tradition than any other system ancient or medieval. Their way of reasoning about the guilt in other minds and the wrong it does to the community may prove to be much closer to the concepts embedded in our own way of justice than the popular misconceptions we often labour under.

Consider for the moment a perspective even more remote in cultural difference, though closer to us in time. A perfectly rational system for distinguishing degrees of guilt in a homicide may be constructed upon the *means* of killing and the *relationship* between killer and victim. Such is the prevailing pattern in early Chinese law, beginning with the T'ang code of the seventh century (AD) and perpetuated in the Ming recension for centuries thereafter.[1] These medieval codes differentiate as distinct crimes such killings as murder by serpent or other venomous animal; placing something lethal in an orifice; murder and mangling the body for magical purposes; starvation or exposure; killing by arrows or other missile weapon; mortal wounding by horse or vehicle; killing by trap or snare; and driving a person to suicide. This sort of list-making predominates over any articulation of criminal wrong in more abstract terms. There is a distinct provision for 'premeditated homicide', but there is little more than a glimmer of true intentionality: the crime is differentiated not by any measure of motives or expectations but purely by the outward conditions—prior preparations, plotting with others, and the like.

Interwoven with these criteria of means is a set of rules about the relationship violated: thus, alongside the usual rules regarding adultery that ends in violence, we find fairly elaborate rules regarding parricide, the widow who kills her husband's surviving relations, any killer who murders three or more persons in one family, killing a son or other dependant and falsely blaming another, and concealing the killing of an elderly relative. For each of these degrees of homicide, the Chinese codes prescribe specific penalties: a hundred blows with a cudgel, or three hundred; imprisonment for shorter or longer terms; and for the most serious violations, strangling or decapitation (depending on gender and status).

Now we may be inclined to distance ourselves from this way of justice, secure in the assumption that our own way of coming to terms with the killer is more rational or humane, or that our system

---

[1] See G. MacCormack, 'T'ang and Ming Law of Homicide', *RIDA* 35 (1988), 27–78.

of justice evolved from the the will of the people whereas the dynastic justice of medieval China had no such source. But other cultural differences aside, is our way of justice any more valid? How can we be certain of the wrong in the killer's mind? And why should the crime against the community at large outweigh the violation of family or other social ties?

The origins of our 'murder' lie deep in the Norse justice that the Danes brought to Britain. In essence, a murder is a killing by stealth: a murderer is a killer who does not reveal himself in the customary way.[2] There is a presumption that he plotted to ambush his victim to escape unwitnessed. But intentions *per se* were not always at issue: even intentional killings were once settled by compensation. It is the concealment and deception, with the threat it poses to a rather precarious social order, that marks the more heinous crime.

In saga the killer must promptly announce the killing and prepare to make suitable compensation to the victim's kinsmen. If there is some dispute, the parties routinely submit their differences to recognized arbiters whose knowledge of the customary law and past history of the adversaries enables them to make a compelling judgement. In troublesome cases the dispute may go before the assembly of peers, the Althing. But in the homicide disputes of saga, the issue is more a matter of the respective rights than of some objective fact. The arbiter is likely to tally up past grievances and kinship obligations, he does not investigate what happened, he does not speculate about inner motives, and he does not make findings about the wrong or the threat to the community. It is ordinarily assumed that no member of this honour-bound society would try to conceal what he did or why he did it, although often there is no authority that can impose a sentence, in despite of the parties, to preserve public order.

But when the Danes imported Teutonic justice among the Anglo-Saxons, it had to be adapted to the interests of a ruling class, and at this point murder took a surprising turn. It was regularly assumed that any killing by stealth, where the killer was undetected, was the work of rebellious subjects and the local community

---

[2] See esp. Thomas Green's classic study, 'The Jury and the English Law of Homicide 1200–1600', *Michigan Law Review*, 74.3 (Jan. 1976), 413–501; followed by Jeremy Horder in the very useful *Provocation and Responsibility* (Oxford, 1992). The most intriguing source for Norse/Icelandic homicide disputes is, of course, *Njal's Saga*.

was conspiring to conceal his identity.[3] The whole village or 'hundred' might therefore be held liable for the killing! Once again, *mens rea* is little more than a glimmer, overshadowed by the outward conditions. And the criminal aspect of the killing is altogether lost in a fractured community: the killings that matter most are those that pit the locals against their foreign lords.

Murder in the Anglo-American tradition is ultimately derived from this killing by stealth, and much of its furtive past still haunts us. Our notions of premeditation and malice aforethought were shaped by the persistent menace of robbers who slew their victims: such a killer waits in ambush to take his victim by surprise, perhaps without specific intent to kill, but with every preparation to leave his victim no means of escape. The Athenian conception of murder most foul derived from a very different social dynamic, but as we shall see—if the wary reader perseveres—the makers of the ancient democracy arrived at a way of reasoning about intentions and community interests that is not that far from our own.

From this entrée, the reader will gather that my comparative interests lie mainly in the background of English and American law. There will be comparisons of other modern mechanisms—notably the German law of criminal negligence in Chapters 6 and 7—but by and large, Anglo-American law lends itself more readily to comparison with the Athenian. After all, the other European traditions derive from the Roman law, which was largely maintained by the praetors and their appointed judges; that élite judiciary still prevails on the Continent. But the English law is rooted in the verdicts of layman juries, and in that respect the law of the Athenians may sometimes prove more informative than the Roman. For the Athenians invented this kind of jury trial and it shaped their legal concepts, much as the English jury of the early modern era has shaped our own notions of murder.

But if I must admit to a certain Anglocentrism in this study, I also insist that the book before you was written without prejudice or partisan agenda. I hope the reader will therefore bear with me in the usage of certain loaded terms. In general, I have tried to reduce all such terms to an academic and minimalist sense, or avoid them altogether. Thus I refer to 'the primitive law' and to various 'primitive' remedies and I mean nothing subjective by this: I simply

---

[3] W. Blackstone, *Commentaries on the Laws of England* (1769; facsimile, Chicago, 1979) 4.14.2 (referring to Bracton 3.2.15).

mean that such and such a measure belongs to the rules and remedies that were given a fixed form in the earliest code.[4] 'Ideology' is
another unfortunate but almost indispensable term. It is sometimes
treated as the intellectual property of a certain school of thought.
But in this study it means nothing more than the connected body of
beliefs and values that so profoundly define a community—this is
not a book about class struggle. 'Liberalism' is another tarnished
term that I should like to use in something approaching its proper
sense. After all, teachers of political theory routinely speak of liberalism to describe the formative doctrines of Locke and thinkers like
him. Modern liberalism asserts that people should define their lot
by what they themselves decide: claims of justice, of rights and
remedies should not be circumscribed by 'necessary' conditions of
gender, race, disability, or inherited disadvantage.[5]

Let me also assure the wary reader that I have done all I could to
remove any barriers of jargon, legal or rhetorical. When a new principle is introduced I have tried to make its meaning clear from paraphrase, context, and example. Indeed, I have given priority to
renderings that should be self-evident to the non-specialist, while
indicating for the student of that specialty the corresponding term
of art. So, for instance, where we come to the earliest rhetorical
devices for transferring blame from the agent to the victim, the
theoretical term *metastasis* is relegated to a parenthesis (as a
reminder to the reader whose interests are primarily rhetorical).

In order to give access to supporting documents without unduly
burdening the reader who wants to move on, I have generally given
translation in the text and put whatever Greek seems indispensable
in the notes. The reader who wants to look more deeply into problems of text or translation will have to consult her own sources; I
have simply tried to provide a few crucial citations—this is not a
sourcebook. The most important sources are readily available. The
full text of the extant fragment of Draco's law is presented in recent
works by a number of scholars, so I have chosen not to reproduce
it here in full but to treat each provision in its place.[6]

---

[4] Similar usage was adopted by A. S. Diamond in the influential study *Primitive
Law Past and Present* (London, 1971).

[5] See Bernard Williams's recent study, *Shame and Necessity* (Berkeley, 1993),
128–9: 'Modern liberal thought rejects all necessary social identities.'

[6] *IG* I³ 104. For text and commentary, I cannot improve on Ronald Stroud's pre-
sentation in *Drakon's Law on Homicide* (Berkeley, 1968). Stroud's text is reproduced

As a further aid to the reader I give a synopsis of the homicide speeches in the Appendix. Even the expert will sometimes stumble over Lysias 1 and Lysias 12—*The Slaying of Eratosthenes* and *Against Eratosthenes*. In the body of the book, each speech is treated in detail in its chapter, and elsewhere I have tried to give sufficient context to make clear to the non-specialist which speech is which. But when in doubt, you have the synopsis for quick reference.

in full by M. Gagarin, *Drakon* xiv–xv; *E.* Cantarella, *Corso di Diritto Greco* (Milan, 1994), 210. For the main provisions, see Ch. 2 §1 n. 3.

ACKNOWLEDGEMENTS

This is a first book, it has been rather long in the making, and I am therefore deeply indebted to friends and teachers who have persevered in the endeavour. There are three who have prodded this rough creature from its very first steps: Michael Gagarin, George Kennedy, and Martin Ostwald. Anyone familiar with their work will recognize that they approach this material from very different perspectives. No one of them will agree with all of it—they may yet have much to quarrel with. But over the past eight years they have given much hard labour to the shaping of this work. They bear no blame for any errors that remain, but they must share a good measure of the credit for anything useful that is in it. George Kennedy, who was my teacher and adviser, editor, and critic long before this book began, deserves a special acknowledgement. For whatever sense I have made of the ancient trial comes from an abiding fascination with the way argument works that he taught us at North Carolina.

My heartfelt thanks to those who have laboured over the various drafts for Oxford University Press, in particular to Douglas MacDowell, the first reader, who gave this work his encouragement and guidance, and to Tom Chandler who copy-edited the typescript.

There are a number of others who have criticized or otherwise contributed to preliminary studies and various parts of the work in progress. In particular I wish to thank Thomas Cole, David Mirhady, Laura Oaks, GailAnn Rickert, Zeph Stewart, Ron Stroud, and Bob Wallace.

To others who have given me support moral and more tangible but who will have to be content without an exhaustive list of names, I am none the less grateful: to the Fellows and Staff of the Center for Hellenic Studies, where this project began; to colleagues in the Department of Politics at The Catholic University in Washington, who invited me to visit while the book was getting under way, and who helped me get a sense of what the ancient law might mean in the broader scope of political thought; to the colleagues here at Southwest Missouri who have looked kindly on my efforts—especially to our valiant seekers after text in Interlibrary Loan—I am much obliged.

CONTENTS

Abbreviations   xix

1. Reading the Laws 'Written in Blood'   1

   Introduction   1
   §1. Dividing the Issues: The Evolution of the Separate
       Courts   6
       1.1 Mythic Foundations of the Courts   10
       1.2 Solon's Amnesty Law and the Ancient Regime   13
       1.3 Blood Price and Bloodguilt   17
   §2. Proof and Probability   20
       2.1 Early Rhetoric and the Irrational   21
       2.2 Legalism and Rationalism   25
       2.3 Prospective   28

PART I. *Historical Reconstruction of the Homicide Law*

2. Draco's Law and the Killer's Intent   33

   §1. The Terminology of Intentions   33
       1.1 Volitional Terms in the Text of Draco's Law   36
       1.2 Intentionality in Homer   45
   §2. The Archaic Method of Judgement (*Dikazein*)   49
       2.1 Homeric Judgement and Achilles' Shield   51
       2.2 Judgement in the Law of Gortyn   58
       2.3 Witness, Oath, and *Istōr*   61
       2.4 The Issue before the Elders   64
   §3. Intentionality and Procedure in Draco's Law   68
       3.1 The Judgement of the Tribal Kings   69
       3.2 The Issue before the *Ephetai*   71
   §4. Conclusions   79

3. The Five Courts of Homicide   84

   §1. The Basis for a Reconstruction   84
       1.1 Straight Judgement: *Euthydikia*   84
       1.2 Authenticity of the Laws in Demosthenes 23   88
   §2. The Origins and Development of the Five Courts   99
       2.1 The Prytaneum and Phreatto Court   99

2.2 The Areopagus and the Palladium 108
2.3 The Delphinium Court 118
§3. Justifiable Homicide and the Amnesty of 403/2 125
3.1 Restriction of *Dikai Phonou* 126
3.2 *Mnēsikakein*, Self-help, and Summary Arrest 128
§4. Summary 133

4. Preliminaries, Out-of-court Remedies, and Trial 136
§1. *Prodikasiai* 137
1.1 *Diōmosia* 138
1.2 Perjury in Homicide Proceedings 143
§2. Execution and Settlement 147
2.1 Execution by the *Polis* 147
2.2 *Aidesis* and Compensation 150
§3. The Judges at Trial: Areopagites and *Ephetai* 154
3.1 Dicasts and *Ephetai* 155
3.2 Special Competence of the Homicide Justices 160
3.3 Decline of the *Ephetai* 162
§4. Conclusions 167

PART II. *Commentary on the Homicide Speeches*

5. The *Tetralogies* and the Court Speeches 171
§1. Invention in the *Tetralogies* 177
1.1 Questions at Issue 177
1.2 Known Parallels 180
1.3 Use of Probabilities 184
§2. Miasma Doctrine in Legal Argument 192
§3. The Law Prohibiting Justifiable Killing 198
3.1 The Issue in *Tetralogy* 3 199
3.2 Justifiable Response against 'Error' 203
3.3 Plato's *Laws* 859–76 206
§4. Conclusions 208

6. Antiphon 1 and the Concept of Malice 216
§1. The Charge and the Question at Issue 219
1.1 The Facts Admitted 221
1.2 Malice Aforethought: *Pronoia* 223
1.3 Acquittal for Innocence of Malice 226
1.4 Judgement for the Plaintiff 227
§2. The Opposing Arguments 229

2.1 The Case for the Defence   230
2.2 The Case for the Plaintiff   232
2.3 Anticipation and Rebuttal   238
§3. Conclusions and Parallels   242
    3.1 Proof and Probability (*Tetralogy* 1 and Lysias
         Against Mikines)   242
    3.2 Malice and Popular Morality: The Stepmother
         and Deianira   247

7. Antiphon 6: Causation and the Law   251

§1. *Bouleusis*: 'Planning' and Decision   255
    1.1 Historical Usage   257
    1.2 The Causal Argument in Antiphon 6   260
§2. The Question of Law and the Contest of Oaths   270
§3. The 'Contest of Oaths' as an Organizational Principle 280

8. Justifiable Killing and the Problem of Lysias 1   282

§1. Lysias 1 (*On the Slaying of Eratosthenes*)   284
    1.1 The Question of Law in Lysias 1   287
    1.2 The Question of Entrapment   293
§2. *Tetralogy* 3 and the Notion of Provocation   299
    2.1 *Tetralogy* 3   301
    2.2 The Case against Euaion (Dem. 21. 70–6)   308
§3. Conclusions: Euthyphro's Case against his Father   310

9. Warrant and Arrest for Homicide: Antiphon 5 and
    Lysias 13   313

§1. Antiphon 5 (*Herodes*)   314
    1.1 The Method of Proof   316
    1.2 The Question of Law   331
    1.3 Immediate Incrimination and Arrest ep'
         autophōroi   351
§2. Lysias 13, *Against Agoratus*   354
    2.1 The Question of Intent   356
    2.2 The Question of Legality   362
§3. Conclusions and Parallels   370

10. Legalism and Lysias 12   373

§1. Old and New Reasoning in Lysias 12   376
§2. Reinventing the Ancestral Law   382
    2.1 Draco's Law and the Discovery of the Mind   383

2.2 Ancient Rationalism and Modern Law   386

Appendix: A Synopsis of the Athenian Homicide Speeches   390

Bibliography   393

Index of Passages Cited   403

General Index   407

ABBREVIATIONS

Blackstone, *Comm.* W. Blackstone, *Commentaries on the Laws of England. Book the Fourth, Of Public Wrongs*. Facsimile of 1st edn. 1769 (Chicago, 1979)

Blass, *Att. Beredsamkeit* F. Blass, *Die attische Beredsamkeit*, 2nd edn. (Leipzig, 1887–98)

Bonner and Smith R. Smith and G. Bonner, *The Administration of Justice from Homer to Aristotle*, 2 vols. (Chicago, 1930–8)

Busolt and Swoboda G. Busolt and H. Swoboda, *Griechische Staatskunde*, 2 vols. (Munich, 1926)

Davies, *APF* J. K. Davies, *Athenian Propertied Families 600–300 B.C.* (Oxford, 1971)

Gagarin Michael Gagarin, *Drakon and Early Athenian Homicide Law* (New Haven, 1981)

—— *EGL* *Early Greek Law* (Berkeley, 1986)

Hansen, *Apagoge* M. H. Hansen, *Apagoge, Endeixis and Ephegesis against Kakourgoi, Atimoi and Pheugontes* (Odense, 1976)

Heitsch, *Antiphon* *Antiphon aus Rhamnous*, Mainz, *Abh. Akad. Wiss. Mainz*, 1984.3

Kennedy, *Persuasion* G. Kennedy, *The Art of Persuasion in Ancient Greece* (Princeton, 1963)

Latte, *Heiliges Recht* K. Latte, *Heiliges Recht. Untersuchungen zur Geschichte der sakralen Rechtsformen in Griechenland* (Tübingen, 1920)

MacDowell, *AHL* D. H. MacDowell, *Athenian Homicide Law* (Manchester, 1963)

Maschke, *Willenslehre* R. Maschke, *Die Willenslehre im griechischen Recht. Zugleich ein Beitrag zur Frage der Interpolationen in den griechischen Rechtsquellen* (Berlin, 1926)

Parker, *Miasma* R. Parker, *Miasma: Pollution and Purification in Early Greek Religion* (Oxford, 1983)

Philippi, *Areopag* A. Philippi, *Der Areopag und die Epheten* (Berlin, 1874)

Ruschenbusch '*ΦΟΝΟΣ*'   E. Ruschenbusch, '*ΦΟΝΟΣ*. Zum Recht
                           Drakons und seiner Bedeutung für das
                           Werden des athenischen Staates', *Historia*,
                           9 (1960), 129–54

Solmsen, *Antiphonstudien*   F. Solmsen, *Antiphonstudien* (Berlin, 1931)

Stroud, *DL*   R. Stroud, *Drakon's Law on Homicide*
                           (Berkeley, 1968)

Wallace, *Aeropagos Council*   R. W. Wallace, *The Areopagos Council to
                           307 BC* (Baltimore, 1989)

Wilamowitz, *AA*   U. von Wilamowitz-Moellendorff, *Aris-
                           toteles und Athen*, 2 vols. (Berlin, 1893)

I

Reading the Laws 'Written in Blood'

Introduction

Draco's laws of bloodshed occupied a singular place of reverence among the laws of the ancient democracy at Athens—'the noblest and most hallowed of all . . . forever unaltered' (Ant. 5. 14 = 6. 2). Enacted in the seventh century BC (*c*.622) to resolve conflict among the ruling families, they were retained virtually intact as the democracy emerged and evolved, down to the end of the democratic regime some three hundred years later. Against other offences the law of Athens underwent prodigious changes beginning with Solon (*c*.594): the second lawgiver recognized the right of any concerned citizen to prosecute for a multitude of misdeeds, and this involvement awakened a sense of wrong to the community. But against homicide the burden of prosecution continued to rest almost exclusively with the aggrieved parties themselves, the victim's kinsmen. In this respect Draco's law was a legacy of the archaic *polis* where noble families held sway. Yet it became an icon of the democratic ideology in which loyalty and legitimate authority belonged to the *dēmos*. This paradoxical conception had a profound and still unfathomed effect upon the early development of rhetoric at Athens. Rhetoric emerged as the voice of democracy, but our earliest rhetorical texts are speeches for homicide trials, proceedings largely dictated by laws inherited from the era before a broader citizenry assumed sovereignty. The record of Draco's law is therefore of great importance for the history of ideas not simply for its value as a document of primitive law but because it preserves the first imprint of the most fundamental devices of rhetoric as a technique of public discourse. Here we can see how the Greeks came to define 'issues in dispute', to differentiate questions of intent, liability, and legal cause, and how they learned to prove by outward signs the source of wrong that lies in the inner mind.

In later tradition, of course, 'Draconian measures' have come to symbolize the severest remedies of a ruthless authority; they are the very antithesis of reasoned argument. This image was created in the age of Aristotle and Demosthenes, when Demades made his famous complaint that 'Draco's laws were written in blood.'[1] Plutarch, who recorded the complaint four hundred years after Demades made it, readily explained that Draco prescribed the death penalty for almost all offences. Plutarch was a creature of a very different world from Draconian Athens, and his explanation is anachronistic. For most offences in the archaic *polis* there was no state intervention, certainly no state execution. Draco constructed his code upon an ancient foundation of self-help and private settlement: against the thief, the adulterer, or the killer, let the injured parties exact retribution for themselves and they may slay the offender with impunity. These conventions gave a decided advantage to the most powerful families who could easily reconcile those whom they injured and forcibly punish those who injured them. Bothered by such inequities, some Athenians of Aristotle's era began to regard Draco's laws as unjust and undemocratic. And the ingrained character of sanctioned violence is probably what Demades meant when he spoke against 'the laws written in blood'.

But there is a meaning to these words that Demades himself may not have fully appreciated. For at their inception Draco's laws signalled the end of heroic remedies meted out by gods and mighty lords, and marked the beginning of a way of justice more accessible to ordinary men. The long-standing rules of engagement had proved inadequate in many instances, and in response to these defects Draco instituted his one profound innovation, a grand jury to decide by majority verdict those disputes that the parties themselves could not settle. Draco made his laws on the pattern of heroic justice and to a great extent they perpetuated those violent remedies; but they also captured the antithetical principle, that justice be decided by reasoned argument before a body representing the community. Thus the laws written in blood set the stage for that most characteristic social drama of the ancient democracy, the jury trial. This book is a study of that development, from the primitive law to the earliest art of legal argument. This first chapter introduces the mythic antecedents and the scholarly problems.

[1] Plut. *Sol.* 17 = Demades fr. 23; cf. Joannes Tzetzes, *Chil.* 5. 342. Popular sentiment that Draco's laws are 'unjust' is indicated in Dem. 23. 64. In late antiquity Libanius, *Decl.* 1. 1. 145 protests, perhaps too much: 'Who has spoken ill of Draco or declared his laws invalid, however harsh the rule that death must come before justice be done?'

The legendary traditions tell us much of quarrels that could not be resolved by the customary rules. The most famous of these tales are Orestes' vendetta against the murderers of his father, and the vendetta against Odysseus for the slaying of the suitors. Each tale ends in a charter for some god-given means of settlement. The prospect of peace for Odysseus is somewhat uncertain, but there is at least the suggestion that Athena imposed a binding resolution (*Od.* 24. 528–48). And the plight of Orestes supposedly inspired Athena to install the court on the Areopagus. But to appreciate the lawgiver's task, let us consider the kind of case that even the gods could not resolve: such was the murder of Iphitus by Heracles.

In all of the ancient tradition on Heracles' doom, the slaying of Iphitus is represented as an especially heinous crime.[2] It begins innocently enough: the hero was denied the prize of princess Iōle at the archery challenge of Eurytus; he drove off some horses to requite his loss. The missing mares were soon tracked by Eurytus' son, Iphitus. Heracles slew him by guile: he welcomed Iphitus to Tiryns and led him to the ramparts to scan the plain for his mares; then, from the cyclopean walls the hero threw his unsuspecting victim to his death. For this killing by treachery, Heracles was at first denied purification. In time the hero was absolved at the hands of one lord or another, but the ritual did not suffice to end the torment of 'defilement'; so, at last, he turned to the oracle at Delphi. Here again he was denied purification, and, so the legend tells, he seized the tripod and wrestled with Apollo. Ultimately, the god, under duress, decreed an especially demeaning form of living death for Heracles' expiation: he must sell himself into slavery in Asia. There he was purchased by Omphale to be her body servant (to the delight of the ancient artists).

At the end of this humiliating penance, is Heracles cured of his rage? No, he returns to take vengeance for his shame and seize by force the prize for whom the trouble all began. He lays siege to the citadel of Eurytus, kills the king, and takes Iōle as a bride-of-war. Of course, the long-neglected wife Deianira soon brings about his death, and in tragedy this doom is presented as the will of Zeus. But for our purposes the lesson of the story is this: heroic justice had no means of deciding the very crimes that most threatened the peace,

---

[2] Along with Sophocles' *Trachiniae*, see esp. Diodorus 4. 31; cf. J. March, *The Creative Poet: Studies on the Treatment of Myth in Greek Poetry* (London, 1987), 49–77.

those for which no arbitrary penalty could end the cycle of vendetta. Athena's judgements for Orestes and Odysseus were inspired by the same predicament.

The immediate setting of Draco's legislation was a similar failure of justice, the cycle of conflict that followed Cylon's coup.[3] Ten years before Draco made his laws, Cylon seized the Acropolis and was there besieged. The instigator himself escaped, and his followers were persuaded to come down from the Acropolis to stand trial. They came down from their asylum clinging by a cord to the goddess's protection (as Plutarch tells it); but the lifeline broke as they neared the Areopagus shrine of the avenging Furies, and there many of them were put to death. The survivors and kinsmen of the slain sought retribution for decades to come. Now the killing of the Cylonians would have been regarded as a justifiable action against tyranny, were it not for the religious constraints the killers had violated. The Alcmeonidae, who led the reprisals, were eternally accursed for this crime.

In this historical case we have a religious complication that parallels the breach of sacred guest-friendship in the legendary killing of Iphitus. In both cases the religious rationale represents a harsh reality: the plaintiffs are convinced that the killers plotted against their kinsmen and used the pretended sanctuary as a place of ambush. And for this most damnable wrong they refuse any settlement short of death.

These notorious quarrels illustrate the problem that confronted the lawgiver. In the face of such complications, how is a solution to be devised that both sides will have to accept? The killer may claim that he deserves some consideration because he acted by necessity or in frenzy of the moment. The plaintiffs will claim that he plotted to kill by deception and in violation of sacred law. The killer may claim he acted in justifiable retribution against the traitor, the thief, or the assassin. The plaintiffs will claim that his jusfication is only a pretext. Before any such dispute is decided, the very question at issue must first be defined. This is perhaps the most fundamental task of reasoned argument for a collective decision: how are we to define the dispute in such a way that a third party can decide between the two sides? Only when the issue is thus defined can we take on the second task, to convince the judges that ours is the rightful claim on that issue in dispute.

[3] Herodotus 5. 71; Thuc. 1. 126; Plut. Sol. 12.

These are the quintessential functions of the discursive technique the ancients later called *rhetorikē*—to persuade our audience that the issue we raise is paramount, and then to convince them to take our side. The earliest documents of this technique are the speeches written for homicide disputes. In them we find that homicide trials two and three hundred years after Draco were still argued by rules implicit in the ancient law. In the century from Antiphon to Aristotle, the issue must still be defined in terms that the parties themselves will swear to, and the arguments will proceed largely upon the basis of these commitments, validated by religious conviction and social conscience.

Out of these conditions rhetoric as we know it arose. This is not to say that there was no 'rhetoric' in the broader sense, beginning before Draco. Surely there were certain strategies adapted to the courts of kings or councils, and some devices to sway assemblies of the people; these tactics were recognized and somehow taught or demonstrated by one practitioner to another.[4] But in the archaic proceedings before kings and councils of elders, so far as we can judge, justice was to be found in the wisdom or inspiration of the judges themselves. Perhaps they looked to the god for some sign or consulted their recollection of ancient precedent; but no fixed standard that all parties might consult existed. Decision-making was largely the prerogative of an élite and its rationale was not nececessarily accessible to all observers. Even the decisions of a citizen assembly were probably governed by a few authoritative voices, leaders who prevailed by their known character or standing more than their reasoning. And certainly, from all that we know, simple homicide and other matters of injury to the family were never submitted to the full citizen assembly to decide. When Draco codified the homicide law and established a grand jury to decide such inter-family disputes, he created a new social reality. What constitutes right and wrong is now defined by a fixed standard to which all members of the community have access—justice is no longer dependent on the wisdom or the whim of 'bribe-devouring kings' (as Hesiod called them, *WD* 39). The jury that Draco empanelled cannot simply look to their own insight or their own interest. They are called upon to decide the dispute by criteria set forth in the law.

---

[4] See e.g. Kennedy, *Persuasion*, 35–40, on 'Homeric rhetoric'.

Draco's law and the social drama that derived from it have much
to tell us about our own way of justice, how we arrived at our
notions of rights and wrongs and what juries of the people must
decide. The two tasks of primitive rhetoric are the keys to this
inquiry. (1) How did the lawgiver first divide the killer's intent
from his actions, thus to define the one or the other as the *question
at issue*? And (2) what stood for *proof* on these first defined issues in
the earliest jury courts? The following sections outline the scholarly dispute on each of these two elements of the art.

§1. Dividing the Issues: the Evolution of the Separate Courts

Suits for intentional homicide and wounding are tried at the Areopagus, as
well as poisoning and arson; only these cases are judged by the council.
Unintentional homicide even in cases of planning, or if one kill a slave, a
metic, or foreigner, those at the Palladium court (decide). If the killer confesses to the killing but claims to have killed lawfully—as in apprehending
an adulterer, or mistakenly in war, or in athletic contest—for this they
judge at the Delphinium.   (*Ath. Pol.* 57.3)

In the Aristotelian *Athenian Constitution*, roughly three hundred
years after Draco, we find this short and uncomplicated explanation of a division of jurisdiction among the three principal courts of
homicide: the court of the Areopagus, manned by the full council
of former archons, heard charges of intentional homicide, wounding, and arson; the Palladium court heard charges of unintentional
homicide and any homicide charges in the deaths of slaves and non-
citizens; the court at the Delphinium heard pleas of lawful or justifiable homicide in specific instances defined by law. In addition to
these, we are also told of a court at the harbour shrine of Phreatto
where a defendant already in exile might return to plead against
charges of murder; and finally at the Prytaneum, the ancient head-
quarters of the executive officers, a tribunal consisting of the tribal
kings and the king archon heard charges against unknown
assailants and inanimate instruments. This elaborate structure
holds the key to much of our inquiry. How, in the course of history,
did the various issues come to be divided among the several courts?
On this question we have no straightforward evidence; the standard
theories have been based largely upon charter myths of the

Areopagus such as we find in Demosthenes' more complicated account.

Among many institutions of ours that are not found elsewhere, there is one unique to us and held most sacred among us, the court at the Areopagus. . . . First, long ago, as tradition tells, in this court alone the gods determined that homicide charges were to be brought and the penalty paid, and the gods themselves would be the judges; that Poseidon, so the story goes, demand justice of Ares for the death of Halirrothius, and that the twelve gods judge between the Eumenides and Orestes. These are ancient legends; there are other tales more recent. This court alone no tyrant or oligarchy nor even the democracy ever dared to strip of its jurisdiction for homicide; but all men agree that any justice of their own finding would be weaker than the justice found in this court. And beyond these other proofs, here alone no defendant convicted or plaintiff defeated has ever proven the verdict unjust. (23. 65–6)

Here Demosthenes articulates a basic tenet of Athenian ideology, the primacy of the Areopagus court as a symbol of inherited law—the most ancient of all courts, once occupied by the gods themselves. Where Demosthenes hails the Areopagus, even sceptics have tended to follow. From such material scholars generally assume a certain model of jurisdiction—let us call it 'the Areopagite model': it assumes that the aristocratic council on the Areopagus was also the original homicide court, going back before Draco; the later jurisdictions of the several courts for unintentional, justifiable, and other categories of homicide were somehow derived from the powers of this primordial body.

The modern Areopagite model goes back to Georg Schömann's work early in the nineteenth century.[5] The Athenian notion of an ancestral constitution founded upon a council of nobles had a special appeal for German scholars of that period. Thus Schömann assumed rather uncritically that the Areopagus council once held undivided jurisdiction for homicide, that Draco took that authority from them, divided it among the five courts and assigned

---

[5] G. F. Schömann, 'De Areopago et Ephetis' (Greifswald, 1833); *Griechische Alterthümer*, 2nd edn. (Berlin, 1860), 336; cf. M. H. Meier and G. F. Schömann, *Der attische Process* (Halle, 1824), 10–12. Schömann's article of 1833 came in response to K. O. Mueller's case for the *ephetai* in *Aeschylos Eumeniden* (Göttingen, 1833; translated as *Dissertations on the Eumenides of Aeschylus*, Cambridge, 1835). For earlier bibliography, following this issue back to the 1600s, see esp. Philippi's preface, *Areopag* (Berlin, 1874), vi–x. Cf. L. Lange, 'Die Epheten und der Areopag der Solon', *Abh. der königlichsächsischen Gesellschaft der Wiss.* (1879).

jurisdiction to the fifty-one judges known as *ephetai*. The Areopagus remained a council of state. Solon later reconstituted the Areopagus as a council of former archons and gave them special jurisdiction for murder.

Adolf Philippi challenged this model in an influential work of 1874—*Der Areopag und die Epheten*. He found no reliable evidence that the Areopagus court antedated Draco, and he identified the *ephetai* as, in fact, older authorities both in homicide trials and as a council of state. These *ephetai* were representatives of the noble clans, the Eupatrids.[6] Draco simply established a rule for trial by a larger body of fifty-one, rather than allowing final verdict by the smaller committee of chiefs (*prytaneis*). The council of the Areopagus proper was first established by Solon and entrusted by him with the special jurisdiction for intentional murder and related offences.[7]

But fifty years after Philippi, the Areopagite model was revived.[8] In this more recent incarnation, the aristocratic council of the Areopagus was once again the ancient homicide court before Draco, and (unlike Schömann's model a century before) the Areopagus now supposedly retained jurisdiction for intentional murder when Draco instituted the *ephetai* as juries in the other courts. In roughly this form the Areopagite model has been standard to this day.[9]

---

[6] The meaning of the term ἐφέται is still disputed. Philippi himself concluded with Lange, 'De ephetarum Atheniensium nomine' (Leipzig, 1873), that the term is approximate to 'chieftains over the clans' (ἐπὶ τοῖς ἔταις), as Aeschylus, *Persae* 79 would suggest. Perhaps as plausible is the folk etymology in Pollux 8. 125, that the term derives from *ephesis*, 'appeal'. For the tradition on Draco himself, largely apocryphal, see now T. J. Figueira, 'The Strange Death of Draco on Aegina', in R. Rosen and J. Farrell (eds.), *Nomodeiktes* (1993), 287–303 (= *Excursions in Epichoric History* (Lanham, Md., 1993) 231–54).

[7] J. H. Lipsius, *Das attische Recht und Rechtsverfahren* (Leipzig, 1905), 1: 14–20; cf. J. Miller, 'Drakon' in *RE* 5 (1905), 1651–2. In more recent work arguing priority of the *ephetai*, promising approaches have been offered by Ruschenbusch, 'ΦΟΝΟΣ' (1960), R. Sealey, 'The Athenian Courts for Homicide', *CP* 78 (1983), and Wallace, *Areopagos Council* (1989).

[8] The Areopagite model was generally assumed (often without comment) by e.g., Wilamowitz, *AA* (1893), ii. 199; G. Glotz, *La Solidarité de la famille dans le droit criminel en Grèce* (Paris, 1904), esp. 301–2; *Histoire grecque* (Paris, 1925), i. 420–4; Maschke, *Willenslehre* (1926), 42–3. The current version of the Areopagite model is found in Busolt and Swoboda (1926), ii. 804 n. 4 (with a summary of earlier positions), and 811–19; Bonner and Smith (1930), i. 97–9.

[9] See H. J. Wolff, 'The Origin of Judicial Litigation', *Traditio*, 4 (1946), esp. 74; E. Heitsch, 'Der Archon Basileus . . . ', *Symposion 1985* (1989).

It is perhaps difficult at first to see how such theories have shaped modern interpretation of homicide trials two hundred years after Draco and Solon. Why should we bother with the old question of which came first, the Areopagus or the *ephetai*? But if we follow out the implications in the scholarship, we can see that the Areopagite model has fostered certain assumptions about what was at issue and how it had to be argued.

If the Areopagus council was indeed the ancient homicide court with undivided jurisdiction before Draco, how do we account for the historical division of jurisdiction with separate courts for each of several charges? Schömann supposed that *separate venues* for intentional, unintentional, and justifiable homicide were in existence before Draco: the body identified with the Areopagus would convene at each of several shrines to judge the case proper to that venue.[10] But this rationale assumes that intentional, unintentional, and justifiable killing were recognized as separate issues for trial even before the first lawgiver. Yet the extant remains of the law suggest no such division of homicide before Solon; there is certainly nothing to indicate that the Areopagites were a 'circuit court' responsible for different crimes at different court sites.

The more natural hypothesis is that the divided jurisdiction corresponds to a division of authority between the principal court and some secondary body. This second alternative is therefore generally assumed by advocates of the Areopagite model: at one time the Areopagus court decided all types of homicide without distinction.[11] The *ephetai* were then established as the community acknowledged that the unintentional or justifiable killer was entitled to some consideration. This court was inspired by compassion for the fellow tribesman who acted without malice.[12] Such disputes required greater discretion in weighing the evidence. Cases before

---

[10] Schömann, 'De Areopago', 195. Even Wallace does not question the notion that the separate venues go back before Draco: see *Areopagos Council*, 7–47 (esp. 19 at n. 64 and p. 46).

[11] Cf. Wolff, 'Origin of Judicial Litigation', 74: 'We may further take it for granted that the court of the ephetae in the Palladium . . . was of more recent date than that of the Areopagus. Since the conception of unpremeditated homicide at one time emerged from the originally undivided homicide delict, which was tried by the Areopagus, it is a fairly safe assumption that the court in the Palladium split away from the Areopagus.'

[12] The most persuasive rationale along these lines was given by L. Gernet, *Recherches sur le développement de la pensée juridique et morale en Grèce* (Paris, 1917), 339–88.

the Areopagus would then be those where intent and justification were *not* at issue, and a verdict might be virtually dictated by sworn testimony or torture of slaves.

Thus the Areopagite model makes certain assumptions about the original issues in homicide cases: unintentional killing was set aside for special consideration and murder with malice emerged by contradistinction, as the remnant of a wrong that was once judged simply as 'guilty or not'. This model has greatly affected the interpretation of the extant speeches. But, as we shall see in the second part of this study, it is not what the speeches themselves would suggest.

And, as the next few chapters will show, the record of the law itself suggests a more straightforward development: it begins, as Philippi supposed, with the *ephetai*. The Areopagus was later established as a special court for those cases where the plaintiff swore unrelenting enmity for deliberate murder. It is to the Areopagus, then, that the task of greater discretionary judgement is given, to decide subtle questions of the killer's intentions. The *ephetai* continue to judge cases where intent is not at issue, and such cases are more likely to be decided by direct testimony, without calculating probable implications of motive and circumstance. To clear the way for this development, let us here reconsider the evidence so often adduced for the Areopagite model.

1.1   The Mythic Foundations of the Courts

The view that the Areopagus was once the site of all homicide trials relies upon legendary material, such as Demosthenes recalls in *Against Aristocrates* (cited above), and even these tales give no clear indication that the pre-Draconian homicide court was identified with the aristocratic council that later convened at that site. There are four cases prominent in the tradition: these were reported by Hellanicus and they are attested by various other sources.[13] (1) The etiological myth of the court's founding is mentioned by Demosthenes and was known to Euripides: Ares slew Halirrothius for the rape of Alcippe, and Poseidon brought him to justice on the hill later called *Areios Pagos* (hill of Ares). (2) Cephalus was tried there for the accidental slaying of his wife Procris; (3) and Daedalus

---

[13] Hellanicus F22 (= schol. Eur. *Or.* 1648). For the myth of Ares' trial, cf. Eur. *El.* 1258–65, and Hellanicus F1; Dinarchus 1. 87; Apollodorus 3. 180 (14.2).

there faced charges for the intentional murder of Talos. And of course there is the most famous example: (4) Orestes was tried for the slaying of his mother, Clytemnestra, at Athens on the Areopagus. These tales involve what later law would regard as two or more separate categories of homicide, to be tried by separate courts—at least one case of intentional murder, one of unintentional, and at least one case of justifiable killing. Hellanicus' report therefore indicates popular belief that all homicide trials were once tried on the Areopagus, but it is of little value as evidence on the historical events. It certainly does not prove that the aristocratic council once held jurisdiction for several differentiated categories of homicide. After all, the gods were supposed to have judged at these trials, not a jury of men.[14]

The only part of the tradition that clearly conceives of a trial jury manned by mortal judges rather than judged by the gods is the Aeschylean version of (4) Orestes' trial for the retributive killing of Clytemnestra. The claim that the gods themselves once judged such cases appears to be integral to the older tradition. The version that Aeschylus immortalized in the *Eumenides*, with a jury of Athenians empanelled by Athena, is likely to be his own invention.[15] There are many interpretations of Aeschylus' charter myth and it is beyond the aims of our inquiry to follow out all the implications.[16] But it is clear enough that Aeschylus recognized earlier trials in legend and did not mean to contradict the tradition of Ares' trial. The distinctive innovation that he finds in the trial of Orestes is the elevation of mortal jurors to shoulder the burden once borne only by the gods.

The drama focuses upon the movement from pre-legal remedies of blood vengeance toward rule of law. The Furies are eager to usurp the power that gods have held over the settlement of homicide

---

[14] Cf. Jacoby on Hellanicus (323a) in *FGrHist* 3b, Text pp. 22–5, Notes, p. 22; Wallace, *Areopagos Council,* 8–10, argues rightly against the Areopagite model and the view that the mythic trials derive from an era when all homicides were tried on the Areopagus. See also L. Pearson, *The Local Historians of Attica,* 2nd edn. (APA Monographs; Philadelphia, 1942), 15–17, for the view that these were all inventions of the 5th cent.

[15] With Dem. 23. 66 (cited above) cf. Eur. *El.* (produced 413), 1258–60, describing the site of Ares' trial οὗ πρῶτον θεοὶ | ἕζοντ᾽ ἐπὶ ψήφοισιν αἵματος πέρι. Jacoby himself (see the previous note) follows the view that Aeschylus' tale of Orestes' trial on the Areopagus was the tragedian's own invention. Homer apparently knows of no trial of Orestes.

[16] Cf. Sommerstein's commentary, *Aeschylus: Eumenides* (1989), esp. 19–25.

(360–6), and so they have challenged Orestes to a test of oaths (429). Athena establishes her jury of men so 'that injustice not prevail by oaths'.[17] Thus Aeschylus and his audience seem to have supposed that homicide disputes were once settled solely by oath, self-help, and divine retribution, before the founding of the Areopagus court. The drama does not dispute the tradition that there were earlier trials on the Areopagus in which the gods gave judgement, nor does it give much support to the common assumption that the primitive homicide court was to be identified with the aristocratic council of state.

The mythic foundings of the other homicide courts are reported by Pausanias (1. 28) six centuries after Hellanicus. These late inventions are even more contrived than the Areopagus legend. Pausanias tells us that the Palladium court was founded when Demophon seized Athena's Palladium, as the Argives returned from Troy, and he accidentally killed some innocent bystander (cf. Pollux 8. 118–19). In the Delphinium court Theseus was first acquitted for the lawful slaying of the rebel Pallantids (though Euripides' *Hippolytus* shows him condemned to exile). And there is the tale that the Phreatto court was modelled on the hearing that Telamon gave Teucer, when he pleaded innocent of complicity in the death of Ajax. These reports are probably of little value even for Athenian ideology in the fifth and fourth centuries; they certainly lend no substantive support to the view that the fivefold division of jurisdiction was more ancient than Draco.

Demosthenes treats the laws for the separate jurisdictions (23. 63–79) as the work of unknown lawgivers—'whoever they were, whether heroes or gods'.[18] This comment at least takes us back within a generation of Hellanicus, and it clearly contradicts the traditions in Pausanias. It also shows in itself that the rules of jurisdiction—which case went to which court—were likely to be later, not earlier than Draco. We know that Solon took over the

---

[17] *Eum.* 429–32: κλύειν δίκαιος μᾶλλον ἢ πρᾶξαι θέλεις . . . ὅρκοις τὰ μὴ δίκαια μὴ νικᾶν λέγω. Apollo in turn offers judgement by oath of Zeus (620–1). There may also be some reflection upon this historic shift from divine to mortal judgement in the problematic lines, 482–3, where the probable reading, δικαστὰς ὁρκίων αἰδουμένους θεσμόν, seems to emphasize the transfer from θεοὶ ὅρκιοι, gods 'invoked by oath' to a jury of men 'respectful of the oath ritual'.

[18] In §22 the law defining the separate jurisdiction of the Areopagus is grouped with the laws of Draco and (cf. §51) implicitly attributed to him, but the phrasing of the jurisdictional rules seems unsuited to the archaic lawgivers: thus Ruschenbusch, 'ΦΟΝΟΣ'. See Ch. 3 §§1.2 and 2.2.

Draconian homicide laws substantially unchanged, and we can only suppose that if these laws were Draco's they would be identified as the work of one lawgiver or the other.

The myths that were made to account for the several courts are also at odds with simple considerations of how such rules would have functioned in practice. Before the separate jurisdictions were prescribed by statute, we can only assume that accused homicides took refuge at whatever shrines afforded safety. It is certainly possible that there were customary rules by which the defendant would want to take refuge at one shrine if he claimed to be innocent of malice, another if he claimed to be justified in killing. But even the legends offer little support for such a theory, and there is no obvious reason why an unintentional killer must take refuge at a certain shrine of Athena and a justified killer must take refuge with Apollo. Such a differentiation requires that innocence of malice and legal justification be generally recognized as deserving special treatment, and in Draco's law such distinctions do not seem to make much of a difference.

1.2   Solon's Amnesty Law and the Ancient Regime

The only documentary evidence for the early development of the homicide courts consists of Draco's law itself and Solon's amnesty law (reported in Plut. *Sol.* 19). To supplement these texts we have a few testimonia from writers of Athenian history in the late fifth and fourth centuries BC, when they apparently had access to documentary sources. The bearing of Draco's law itself will be taken up in detail in Chapters 2–3.[19] Here it will suffice to clear away some of the preconceptions that have been fostered by Plutarch's report of Solon's law and by the fragments of the atthidographers preserved in later commentators. Let us begin with the latter first, with the few limited conclusions that can be drawn from the testimony of late antiquity and medieval times.

Against the Areopagite model we have two testimonia that the *ephetai* were the older body, one by the ancient lexicographer Pollux (2nd c. AD) and another by the Byzantine commentator Maximus (7th c. AD). Pollux tells us that Draco founded the *ephetai*

---

[19] A glance will confirm Plutarch's comment that the text of the law made no mention of the Areopagites: for text and description, see Stroud, *DL* 1–7; *IG* I² 115 = *IG* I³ 104.

with jurisdiction for all homicides and Solon established the Areopagus council to share jurisdiction with the *ephetai*.[20] And Maximus, citing Androtion and Philochorus (4th c. BC), indicates that the Areopagus council somehow originated in the body of fifty-one judges. That is to say, the body of fifty-one *ephetai* was established prior to the Areopagus council, as a court with full jurisdiction for homicide.

The note in Maximus is garbled and difficult to interpret, but by this account Androtion would appear to have identified the early 'Areopagite judges' with the body of fifty-one *ephetai*.

For from the nine elected archons at Athens it was necessary to convene the Areopagite judges, as Androtion says in the second book of the *Atthides* ; and later the council of the Areopagus became greater in number—that is, the [council] of fifty-one men of more notable standing—but only of Eupatrids, as we said, and those distinguished by wealth and prudent character, as Philochorus reports in the third book of the same [*sic*] *Atthides*.[21]

Maximus seems to suggest that the original Areopagite court was a much smaller body of incumbent archons (nine or fewer) and this body later *grew into* a college of fifty-one; presumably the Areopagus later grew to historic proportions as it was joined by the new archons of each term.[22] Maximus may have misunderstood Androtion; the parenthetical connective 'that is' (*toutestin*) would

---

[20] Pollux, *Onomasticon* 8. 125: ἐφέται τὸν μὲν ἀριθμὸν εἰς καὶ πεντήκοντα, Δράκων δ᾽ αὐτοὺς κατέστησεν ἀριστίνδην αἱρεθέντας· ἐδίκαζον δὲ τοῖς ἐφ᾽ αἵματι διωκομένοις <u>ἐν τοῖς πέντε δικαστηρίοις. Σόλων δ᾽ αὐτοῖς προσκατέστησε τὴν ἐξ Ἀρείου πάγου βουλήν.</u> The term προσκαταστῆσαι is ordinarily used of appointment or cooptation of new colleagues to an existing body, and it would appear to mean that the new council supplemented and shared the duties of the standing *ephetai*. Pollux supposes that the five sites were already designated in Draco's time, but that is likely to be his own inference from Demosthenes.

[21] Maximus (Conf.) schol. Dionysius Areopagiticus (Migne, *Patrologia Graeca* 4. 167) = Androtion [*FGrHist* 324] F4: ἐκ γὰρ τῶν ἐννέα καθισταμένων ἀρχόντων Ἀθήνησι τοὺς Ἀρεοπαγίτας ἔδει συνεστάναι δικαστάς, ὥς φησιν Ἀνδροτίων ἐν δευτέραι τῶν Ἀτθίδων· ὕστερον δὲ πλειόνων γέγονεν ἡ ἐξ Ἀρείου πάγου βουλή, τουτέστιν ἡ ἐξ ἀνδρῶν περιφανεστέρων πεντήκοντα καὶ ἑνός, πλὴν ἐξ εὐπατριδῶν, ὡς ἔφημεν, καὶ πλούτωι καὶ βίωι σώφρονι διαφερόντων, ὡς ἱστορεῖ Φιλόχορος διὰ τῆς τρίτης τῶν αὐτῶν Ἀτθίδων (= 328 F21). Cf. Wallace, *Areopagos Council*, 14–16.

[22] Wallace, *Areopagos Council* 14–15; cf. Jacoby's Notes, *FGrHist* 3b, 2:105–11, on Androtion F3–4. Curtius, *Ber. d. Berlinische Ak.* 1873, pp. 288–90, regarded the kings in Solon's amnesty law as the archons and *prytaneis*, supposing this usage of the term 'kings' was a relic of transition from decennial archonship to annual office; Philippi, *Areopag*, 236–8, rejects this view.

certainly suggest that what follows was his own inference.[23] But we cannot entirely discount the implication that Androtion identified the *ephetai* as early 'Areopagite judges'.

Solon's amnesty law is quoted by Plutarch apropos of this problem, which of the two courts could claim priority. This question was evidently much debated in ancient times, and Plutarch cites as 'the majority' those who claim that Solon in fact established the Areopagus. The biographer also correctly notes that the text of Draco's law nowhere mentions the Areopagites. He hastens to add, however, that the thirteenth axon of Solon's code contains the amnesty law referring to the Areopagus as a judicial body. He then quotes the law verbatim.[24]

Those outlawed before the archonship of Solon are restored to their citizen rights, except those exiled by the Areopagus or those exiled by the ephetai or by the Prytaneum, condemned by the kings, for homicide or slaughter or for tyranny, at the date of this statute.

Plutarch himself reads the law proleptically: 'those exiled by the Areopagus' refers to those who had been convicted *previously* (by whatever court) on charges that were to be decided *henceforth* by the Areopagus. Disregarding this lame suggestion, Wolff supposed that the courts and their respective jurisdictions are parallel: the Areopagus and the *ephetai* heard cases of homicide and factional 'slaughter' respectively; and those accused of seeking a tyranny were tried by the Prytaneum court, where the aristocratic council was led by the archons; the role of the kings was, supposedly, only to proclaim the verdict.[25]

---

[23] His purpose in this comment is to identify his author Dionysius as 'the Areopagite' (however mistakenly): 'Those among the Athenians foremost in lineage, wealth and prudent character . . . deliberated in the Areopagus council.' To this he adds: 'For from the nine elected archons it was necessary to convene Areopagite judges, and later the Areopagus council became a body of greater numbers.' The added inference—'*that is*, the body of fifty-one'—hardly makes for compelling evidence that Androtion saw Draco's jury evolving from an even smaller 'Areopagus'. From Pollux and Plutarch, it seems as likely that Androtion reported the historical council of the Areopagus (numbering *c.*200) was formed on the model of the older body of fifty-one *ephetai*, and Maximus misunderstood.

[24] Plut. *Solon* 19. 4: ὁ δὲ τρισκαιδέκατος ἄξων τοῦ Σόλωνος τὸν ὄγδοον ἔχει τῶν νόμων <u>οὕτως αὐτοῖς ὀνόμασι γεγραμμένον·</u> "ἄτιμων ὅσοι ἄτιμοι ἦσαν πρὶν ἢ Σόλωνα ἄρξαι, ἐπιτίμους εἶναι, πλὴν ὅσοι ἐξ Ἀρείου πάγου ἢ ὅσοι ἐκ τῶν ἐφετῶν ἢ ἐκ πρυτανείου καταδικασθέντες ὑπὸ τῶν βασιλέων ἐπὶ φόνῳ ἢ σφαγαῖσιν ἢ ἐπὶ τυραννίδι ἔφευγον ὅτε ὁ θεσμὸς ἐφάνη ὅδε."

[25] 'Origin of Litigation', 74–6; cf. Wallace, *Areopagos Council*, 7–28. For the meaning of 'slaughter' (*sphagai*) as killings in factional strife, see below n. 28. We

But if we are to reconcile the documentary texts and the fourth-century tradition, we must assume that the Areopagus had once held some jurisdiction by which it condemned criminals to exile before Solon, but that this jurisdiction was separate from the ordinary homicide jurisdiction. The ancient tradition that Solon founded the Areopagus council is consistent with this conclusion, if this charter accounts for the founding of the council as it was constituted historically, as a body of former archons, officials who had risen to that rank by vote of the people. It is pushing Plutarch's testimony too far to suppose that *no* aristocratic body had ever deliberated on the ancient site of the Areopagus court, since the Aristotelian *Constitution* and the *Politics* report received opinion that the Areopagus held *political* authority before the time of the lawgivers.[26] Whatever body preceded Solon upon the Areopagus, it was chosen by some means other than democratic election and evidently it functioned in other capacities than as a homicide court.

The most cogent rationale for the pre-Solonian jurisdictions was offered by Ruschenbusch, taking carefully into account the phrasing of the statute that Plutarch took pains to copy verbatim.[27] The lists of courts and jurisdictions would appear to be arranged chiastically: (*a*) those exiled by the Areopagus or (*b*) those (exiled) by the *ephetai* or by the Prytaneum; (*b*) for homicide or slaughter or (*a*) for tyrannny. Thus the Areopagus court (*a*) was assumed to be the court that condemned those who had conspired against the aristocratic regime (as most scholars would suppose on other grounds);

have no evidence that an official body at the Prytaneum held authority to deal with tyrannical conspiracy.

[26] See *Politics* 1274[a], for the controversy regarding Solonian institutions: against Solon's title as founder of a mixed constitution, Aristotle observes that the Areopagus preceded him; cf. *Ath. Pol.* 3 and 8. The Draconian constitution in *Ath. Pol.* 4 is a late intrusion, contradicted by *Politics* 1274[b], but it indicates 4th-c. controversy. In order to maintain that the pre-Solonian council met with the archons at the Prytaneum, Wallace explains away the mention of the Areopagus in Solon's amnesty law as a mere redundancy; by his view 'Areopagus' refers to the *ephetai* who judged some homicides on the Areopagus. Wallace finds a similar redundancy in Patrocleides decree (405), referring to the *ephetai* and the Delphinium court ; but as we shall see this later instance has its own explanation in the special procedures regarding 'justifiable homicide'.

[27] '*ΦΟΝΟΣ*' 132–5. For Plutarch's testimony, see above n. 24. Gagarin, *Drakon*, 128–32, follows Ruschenbusch in this reading and adds a very useful note on the function of chiasmus in archaic usage, 155–8: Subject/Verb chiasmus in Draco's law (SVVS or VSSV) is a structural device marking the beginning and end of clauses in connected sequence.

the *ephetai* and the kings at the Prytaneum court (*b*) judged cases of homicide and 'slaughter' respectively. This sort of phrasing is congenial to the archaic laws, where chiasmus often functions as a structural device. And the division of cases that emerges by this interpretation is certainly better supported by other evidence on the primitive jurisdictions: the Areopagus is identified with the aristocratic council, which would naturally oppose an attempt at tyranny; and the *ephetai* remain the principal homicide judges before Solon.[28]

1.3 Blood Price and Bloodguilt

The Areopagite model assumes that intentionality emerged as an issue for the lesser court: separate penalties were established for unintentional homicide when Draco assigned that jurisdiction to the *ephetai*. The emergence of miasma doctrine and the abolition of *poinē* are therefore seen as prime motives for Draco's innovation. Because pollution of bloodguilt indiscriminately endangered the community even in unintentional killings, Draco supposedly created a court to address that threat. And to ensure that the unintentional killer should not purchase his redemption at the community's peril, financial compensation, *poinē*, was eliminated even in these less grievous homicides.

The doctrine that any killer brings defilement upon the community supposedly emerged in the early seventh century, propagated by the cult of Apollo as the purifier of homicides.[29] The law of the

---

[28] The ancient tribal kings held an authority corresponding to their later jurisdiction against the unknown killer: they would pass sentence against the unidentified assailant in feud or factional 'slaughter'; see Chs. 2 §3.1 and 3 §2.1. For *sphagai* as killing in factional violence; cf. Xen. *Hel.* 2. 2. 6; 4. 4. 2; Isoc. 5. 107; 8. 96; see also Gagarin, *Drakon*, 129 n. 49.

[29] U. von Wilamowitz-Moellendorff, *Die Glaube der Hellenen* (Darmstadt, 1955), 36; H. J. Treston, *Poiné: A Study in Ancient Greek Blood Vengeance* (London, 1923), with elaborate speculation on the spread of 'Apollinism', 123–275; M. Nilsson, *History of Greek Religion* (Oxford, 1925) 190; Bonner and Smith, i. 53–5 (favouring Treston's contention that *miasma* invalidated *poinē*); Busolt and Swoboda, 805; R. Moulinier, *Le Pur et l'impur dans la pensée grecque* (Paris, 1952), 43–6. Ritual purification is first attested in the Homeric *Aithiopis* (7th c.). Crucial to Treston's view is the clause μηδὲ ἀποινᾶν in the law cited Dem. 23. 28; but, as we shall see, this clause is unlikely to be an authentic Draconian provision. Glotz, on the other hand, *Solidarité* esp. 314–21, held that blood price persisted into classical times. MacDowell, *AHL* 1–5, 141–50, and Gagarin, *Drakon*, 164–7, question the impact of pollution doctrine.

homicide courts was dictated by this religious movement: the Prytaneum court was established to condemn and expel impersonal objects tainted by the killing; and the special trial at Phreatto harbour was arranged so that the tainted killer should not even set foot on Attic soil. But this theory runs afoul of the evidence on many points, and Robert Parker has recently given the problem a sound and systematic reassessment.[30]

Parker concludes that the developing conventions regarding pollution grew in tandem with the law; they are not to be explained away as rationalization of customary rules, nor to be invoked as a cause or inspiration of Draco's code. Apollo's part in purifying the killer was perhaps exaggerated by inventive treatment in drama; Zeus *katharsios* never relinquished this role.[31]

The extant homicide law of the Athenians contains, it is true, provisions dictated by fear of pollution (Dem. 20. 158; 23. 72), but whether these are indeed authentic Draconian provisions is another question. The special remedies at the Prytaneum and Phreatto courts were no doubt interpreted by Athenians of the classical era as safeguards against miasma.[32] But in origin these courts were probably designed for quite a different purpose (Ch. 3 §2.1): the Phreatto court provides special protections against vendetta; the original purpose of the Prytaneum court had more to do with practical measures against unidentified killers than purely religious formalities. The threat of miasma certainly intruded upon homicide proceedings at some point, but as we shall see, the implications of this threat in the extant speeches are quite different from what is usually assumed; and the era when this threat became a major preoccupation appears to be later than Draco.

The peculiar feature of homicide pollution (as distinct from other forms of miasma in birth, disease, and natural death) is the wrath of the victim's ghost, intent upon demonic retribution, haunting his tainted killer as though on the scent of blood—as

---

[30] *Miasma* (1983), 104–43, and 367–92; on the Homeric evidence, 130–43.

[31] Parker, *Miasma*, 134. One underpinning of the old miasma theory is the apparent absence of pollution doctrine in the Homeric poems, as compared with the miasma obsession of tragedy. But there is a fundamental difference in perspective between the two genres—the killings that heroes commit are necessarily treated differently in epic than in drama. Second, all of the *elements* of classical pollution doctrine are to be found in the Homeric poems; even the notion of physical defilement is perhaps suggested by the epithet of Ares, *miaiphonos*. On the priority of Zeus *katharsios*, against the arguments of Nilsson, see *Miasma*, 139 with n. 143.

[32] Cf. Treston, *Poiné*, 195–7 and 257; Parker, *Miasma*, 119–20.

Clytemnestra's ghost roused the Furies against Orestes. Because the real danger comes from the victim's wrathful spirit, the fear of miasma is particularly aroused by the *intentional* killer. Such is the pattern of the extant speeches.[33] In the two documents relating to unintentional homicide, the threat of miasma and avenging spirits is all but absent.[34] If miasma had any effect upon the development of jurisdiction, it is more likely to have influenced the creation of a special court for murder; and this development, I shall argue, came after Draco's law.

It is still commonly assumed, however, that such religious scruples ultimately put an end to settlement by blood price, *poinē*.[35] But, as we shall see, the preponderance of the evidence weighs heavily against this sort of progress (Ch. 4 §2.2). A law that Pollux attributes to Draco himself *limits* financial settlement but clearly recognizes the practice.[36] And such was clearly the intent of the Solonian amendment prohibiting extortion of ransom: abuses were penalized but the customary compensation was accepted and allowed to persist.[37]

In sum, the mythic foundings and the historical law do not lend much substance to the Areopagite model. And if we cannot rely on this model for dividing the questions at issue among the various courts, neither can we proceed on the usual assumptions about the methods of proof. How then are we to understand the peculiar uses of sworn testimony and 'probabilities' in homicide trials? What are the litigants trying to prove and how are the judges supposed to decide?

[33] Fear of *miasma* is prominent in *Tetralogies* 1 and 3 and acknowledged in Antiphon 1 and 5, where the killers are charged with intentional killing or with complicity in a murder (as also in Lys. 12). For this theme in the court speeches, as compared with the *Tetralogies*, see Ch. 5 §2.

[34] Antiphon 6 (*Choreutes*) and *Tetralogy* 2. One could argue that the defendant in Ant. 6 ignores the issue only because it would prejudice the judges against him. But *Tetr.* 2, giving both sides of the case, recognizes that *miasma* does not have the same effect as in a murder: the victim of unintentional killing rouses no wrath in the dead but in the living (1. 2); cf. Parker, *Miasma*, 104–6.

[35] Cf. MacDowell, *AHL* 9, arguing prohibition in classical times; see n. 29 above.

[36] Pollux, *Onomasticon* 9. 61: κἂν τοῖς Δράκοντος νόμοις ἔστιν ἀποτίνειν εἰκοσάβοιον. The reference ἐν τοῖς Δράκοντος νόμοις probably means no more than ἐν τοῖς φονικοῖς. Cf. E. Ruschenbusch, ΣΟΛΩΝΟΣ ΝΟΜΟΙ. *Die Fragmente des Solonischen Gesetzeswerkes* (Wiesbaden, 1966), frs. 9–12 regarding *poinē*. For the view that the rule of twenty head is restrictive, setting an *upper* limit on compensation cf. E. Heitsch, 'Aidesis im attischen Strafrecht', *Abh. Akad. Wiss. Mainz*, 1984. 1, 12.

[37] For the general practice: schol. D to *Iliad* 18. 497, ποινῆς οὖν λέγει τῆς καλουμένης παρὰ τοῖς Ἀττικοῖς ὑποφόνια . . . λέγεται δὲ κοινῶς ἀνέκτισις, ποινή.

We moderns look upon the men and women of the jury as the 'triers of fact', and we are predisposed to see the ancient jury in much the same light. We readily presume that the jury's essential task was to get at the truth of what happened, that the earliest murder court would look to direct evidence to establish 'the facts', and in the absence of such proof, they would ponder the circumstantial evidence of means and motive as another way of getting at that same objective reality. But the argumentation of the extant speeches calls all of our assumptions into question.

§2. Proof and Probability

The logic of probability was the defining feature of classical rhetoric. The *enthymeme*, as Aristotle called it, was a peculiarly Greek invention; it has had profound effects upon the later development of law and social ethics in western civilization.[38] It is, indeed, the very substance of the modern verdict. However much we insist upon what we call 'the facts' in evidence, the determination of a jury is ultimately a matter of *the probable facts*.[39] And when we have to determine the defendant's inner intentions, our jury is almost entirely dependent on probable signs of malice or guilt revealed in his actions. We know or readily presume that men are likely to resort to violence from various motives: if the circumstances show that a defendant had the desire and the opportunity to do what he is accused of, even without an eyewitness—perhaps even in utter disregard of such witnesseses—we may conclude not only that he did it but also that he did it with a certain intent. And even if our defendant did not specifically intend to injure, we are likely to hold him accountable for the harm he should have anticipated. This realm of virtual reality is the home of that quintessential creature of the modern law, 'any reasonable person', whose expectations and standards of judgement have come to define what is blameless and what is culpable. This reckoning of probable intentions and reasonable expectations assumes a model of the

---

[38] The Greek development is, so far as we know, unique among the societies of primitive law: see George Kennedy's study *Comparative Rhetoric: an Historical and Cross-cultural Introduction* (New York and Oxford, 1997), 205.

[39] See esp. R. H. Gaskins, *Burdens of Proof in Modern Discourse* (New Haven, 1991), 21–9.

mind that is accessible to everyman. With this device the Greeks forever altered the course of justice: probability would ultimately prevail even over the judgements rendered by the gods.

2.1 Early Rhetoric and the Irrational

In his defence of the ancient courts, Demosthenes claims that the Areopagus followed a special procedure of infallible proof; and we find, in fact, that the extant homicide speeches rely heavily upon formalistic instruments of proof—oath, witness, and the letter of the law—less on the kind of circumstantial reasoning that prevails in later argument. From this feature, scholars sometimes find in the earliest speeches a naive and irrational standard of judgement.

The older methods of proof, including testimony of witnesses under oath and slaves under torture and the wording of the law itself, Aristotle described as non-technical—*atechnoi*—lacking or deficient in the artful reasoning that defined the classical technique (*Rhet.* 1. 15). Artful or technical arguments—*entechnoi*—reasoning from probability and the patterns of human experience, had become the decisive mode of judgement in the sophistic enlightenment of the fifth century. In the fourth century, Aristotle's terminology reflects this priority. His contemporary Anaximenes went further, regarding the formal means of proof—oath, witness, and so on—as secondary or supplementary to the *main* proofs from probability (*Ars Rhetorica* 14–17). The earliest extant speeches, however, seem strangely preoccupied with these supposedly secondary proofs.

The work of Antiphon in the fifth century, the earliest of the major speech writers and one whose surviving corpus is almost entirely devoted to homicide speeches, is crucial to our understanding of this development. Friedrich Solmsen argued that Antiphon stands at the transition from the older non-technical proofs to the artful reasoning from probability.[40] This progressivist principle—that unsophisticated proofs are early, artful proofs late—has influenced much of the scholarship on these texts: it is even adduced in dating the extant speeches.[41] But some of the

---

[40] The influence of Solmsen's *Antiphonstudien* (Berlin, 1931) is evident in Kennedy's *Persuasion*, 131–3; cf. *Cambridge History of Classical Literature*, i. 501. For fair comment on Solmsen's theory, see F. Zucker, *Gnomon*, 12 (1936) 442–4.

[41] On the dating of Antiphon's speeches, see K. J. Dover, 'The Chronology of Antiphon's Speeches', *CQ* 44 (1950), 44–60; on *eikos* as a stylistic feature, pp. 47–9 *et passim*.

assumptions that Solmsen and his predecessors made about the workings of law are now discredited, and his basic model of the transition from one mode of reasoning to the other has proved doubtful.[42] Solmsen followed his teacher, Wilamowitz, in the view that the art of rhetoric that developed at Athens was a native product and not a borrowed art from Sicily, as tradition would have it.[43] In the oldest speeches (Ant. 1, 5, 6) he found an inherited defect: what we would regard as important evidence, both direct and circumstantial, seems to be treated in a disconnected manner, without a sense of the logical implications. The testimony of witnesses, oaths of the principals, and the other forms of evidence often seem to prove nothing substantive, yet the argumentation is clearly structured around them, as though the speaker and his audience are drawn by a force of implicit adherence to them. These 'barycentres' of belief (*Gravitationszentren*) attract 'everything that is in any way relevant to them'.[44]

From this pattern Solmsen deduced that Antiphon was still guided or constrained by pre-rational modes of argument—from the self-evident meaning of oath or testimony itself—even as he pioneered the probabilities of circumstance and character. But there are indications that reasoning from probability was more advanced than Solmsen's theory would allow. In the Homeric *Hymn to Hermes*, perhaps a hundred years before Antiphon's work, we find reasoning from probability parodied: the baby Hermes protests that a newborn is an unlikely cattle rustler. And Solmsen's approach proves especially awkward when we turn to Antiphon 5, *On the Murder of Herodes*, a more sophisticated product of the art, with much more elaborate argument from probability than in Antiphon 6, though the two speeches cannot be more than a few years apart.[45]

---

[42] For critiques of Solmsen, see G. Goebel, 'Early Greek Rhetorical Theory and Practice' (diss. University of Wisconsin, Madison, 1983), 49–55; and now M. Gagarin, 'The Nature of Proofs in Antiphon', *CP* 85 (1990), 22–32.

[43] On this issue see Goebel, 'Early Rhetorical Theory', 85–6, 270–2, 356, *et passim*; cf. E. Schwartz, 'Commentatio de Thrasymacho Chalcedono', *Index scholarum in academia Rostochiensi* (1892), esp. 7–15.

[44] *Antiphonstudien*, 22–6. Regarding Ant. 6, Solmsen concludes: 'Offenbar sind wie die ὅρκοι so auch die μάρτυρες ein natürliches Gravitationszentrum der rednerischen Ausführungen . . . Sie sammeln aber auch—und das ist das Wesentliche—unter ihrem Zeichen alles, was nur in irgendeinem Sinn mit ihnen zu tun hat' (26).

[45] Gagarin, 'Proofs in Antiphon', 31; see also F. Scheidweiler, 'Antiphons Rede über den Mord an Herodes', *RhM* 109 (1966), 332–8; Goebel, 'Early Rhetorical Theory', 225–30.

Antiphon 5 is a speech for the defence in a case prosecuted by the summary procedure of 'warrant and arrest' (*endeixis*/*apagōgē*) rather than the traditional suit for homicide, *dikē phonou*. The speaker himself suggests that the method of argument is dictated by the procedure, that he must rely upon circumstantial reasoning because his accusers have evaded the oaths and sanctions of the traditional *dikē* (11–12). It is true that much of the argument and the narrative are connected, at least superficially, with the handling of non-technical proofs; but in the overall arrangement of the speech and sheer weight of argument, the probabilities predominate. To take a simplistic but suggestive measure of the difference, the very language of probability, *eikos*/*eikota*, is found 22 times in Antiphon 5, only 3 times in Antiphon 6.[46] More significantly, the actual substance of the formal proofs is given surprisingly little weight in Antiphon 5, though it would appear to be greatly to the defendant's advantage to give a more substantive explanation of the testimony on both sides—particularly the testimony of a free man under torture that establishes the defendant's alibi. Instead, the formal proofs are subordinated to probabilities of means and motives: did he have a plausible opportunity to take part in the killing? Is it likely that he planned or anticipated the circumstances?

Solmsen's theory is also undermined by a dubious model of the religious origins of justice. Kurt Latte had argued that the archaic settlement of disputes was based upon automatic procedures and 'irrational' proofs, including ordeal as well as oath and witness.[47] Such irrational proofs rely upon divine intervention to prove a man's innocence or guilt. Thus the watchman in *Antigone* 264–7 affirms, 'We are ready to walk through fire, hold molten metal in our hands, and call the gods to witness.' Latte concluded that such

---

[46] The language of probability (εἰκός/εἰκότα/εἰκάζειν) is also comparatively rare in Ant. 1, five times of which three are parenthetical: 2, 17, 18 (οἷον εἰκός in narrative).

[47] Disputed by Gagarin; *EGL* 19–50. Against Gagarin's model, see Ruschenbusch in *CP* 84 (1989), 342–5; R. W. Wallace and R. Westbrook in *AJP* 110 (1989), 362–7. Against Latte's model, *Heiliges Recht*, esp. 5–47, cf. S. Humphreys, 'Social Relations on Stage: Witnesses in Classical Athens', *History and Anthropology*, 1 (1985), 313–69. The primacy of 'processual acts' in archaic Greek law was argued by J. W. Headlam, *JHS* 13 (1892–3), 48–69; this approach is followed by G. Thür (beginning with 'Zum *dikazein* bei Homer' *ZSS* 87 (1970)). Gagarin disputes Thür's findings: he has argued for 'accidental' testimony (i.e. to facts in dispute) at Gortyn, in *Symposion* 1985 (1989), and in *GRBS* 25 (1984), 345–9. He finds some exceptions but by no means disproves the rule that witnesses at Gortyn *primarily* attested to 'processual acts'. See Ch. 2 §2.

references attest to a superstitious spirit of the law, one that continued to haunt the courts of classical Athens; it was because of this conviction of divine justice that formal proof from oath and torture so long prevailed. Latte's model has, as we shall see, a fundamental flaw in the way it presents the ancient reasoning from oath and ordeal.

Solmsen's basic observation, however, that the arguments in the earliest speeches seem to be dictated by formalities rather than rational implications, remains a valid insight and one for which a better explanation should be found.[48] Solmsen supposed that Antiphon dwelt upon the non-technical proofs because the artful technique of argument from probability was in its infancy. But the difference between Antiphon's arguments and those of later authors is not entirely a matter of maturing art. The other evidence on homicide trials, including speeches of Lysias whose relevance Solmsen did not fully consider, suggests that there may be important procedural criteria. The early emphasis upon formal representations in sworn testimony as superior to reasoning on facts and circumstances may have something to do with rules of evidence that are peculiar to homicide procedure rather than unique to Antiphon. Just as we see a reversal in technique from Antiphon 6 to Antiphon 5, so, too, in the homicide speeches of Lysias a generation later— one by *dikē phonou* and another by summary arrest—we find a remarkable difference in the weighing of non-technical proofs and artful probabilities (Chs. 8–9).[49] In the traditional *dikē* the older means of proof prevail. But in trials by summary arrest the litigants take full advantage of circumstantial reasoning on means and probable motive. The rules of procedure seem to dictate the mode of argument, and we must therefore heed the formal requirements of law if we are to make sense of the peculiar uses of proof.

[48] Goebel, 'Early Rhetorical Theory', argues that systematic argument from probability at Athens derived from the Sicilians, against the views of Wilamowitz, Schwartz, Solmsen, *et al.* For Goebel the arguments that Solmsen sees as disconnected *atechnoi* follow a method πρὸς τὸν ἀντίδικον: everything aims at discrediting the conviction of the adversary through probable signs (*tekmēria*). His arguments against Solmsen prove generally successful on Antiphon 5 (225–30) but seem little better than special pleading on Ant. 1 and 6 (on which see Chs. 6 and 7).

[49] In Lys. 1, in a *dikē phonou*, εἰκός is found only once, and that in parenthetical ὥσπερ εἰκὸς ἦν (5); twice in Lys. 13 (1, 40) but six times in Lys. 12, all proper probabilities. In Lys. 1 much of the argument is based on relevant laws. In Lys. 12 and 13 (special accounting and summary arrest), the argument focuses on probable intent. See Chs. 8, 9 §3, and 10 §2.

2.2 Legalism and Rationalism

These are the most hallowed of laws . . . , the most ancient . . . and forever
unaltered, and this is the surest sign of laws well-founded . . . So you must
not judge the worth of the laws by [the litigants'] arguments . . . *but you
must judge their arguments by the laws.*   (Ant. 6. 2 = 5. 14)

When Antiphon called upon the judges to weigh the arguments by
the laws and not the laws by the arguments, he was invoking a fundamental principle of legalism: the authority of law resides in the
law itself—it is not derived or transferred from the will or interpretation of the people.[50] This way of justice attaches pre-eminent
importance to formal acts of due process prescribed by the laws.
Indeed these 'processual acts', as demonstrations of the claimant's
right, tend to overshadow the actual events of the crime; the early
speeches thus take on a certain formalistic or artificial character.
But let us beware of misconstruing this primitive legalism.
Antiphon is not calling for the judges to decide the outcome
mechanically, without reasoned judgement: the verdict is not
determined by 'automatic proof' of prescribed oath or a specified
number of witnesses, such as we find in other systems of primitive
law. He is rather insisting upon the requirements of the law, the
oaths and other commitments, as a guarantee of the litigants' convictions. They are bound by religion and social conscience to swear
in deadly earnest and honour the consequences of their oath as a
categorical imperative.

This mechanism is an inheritance from the era when the verdicts
of chiefs and elders were not commands of a sovereign but instruments of consensus, means by which the principals themselves
might resolve their disputes in self-help or private settlement. In
later rhetorical theory, of course, these instruments were treated as
subordinate or secondary, but from a historical perspective they are
better understood as the primary means of proof, as they were once
decisive in the settlement of disputes according to primary rules of
customary obligations. The remains of archaic Greek law will give
us a picture of early justice in which the judges attempt to render a
ruling for the parties to assert their claims by retribution or reconciliation. The wisdom of such arbiters lay in their insight into the
underlying motives and limitations of human character—they were

---

[50] Cf. J. Shklar, *Legalism*, esp. 1–18.

not ignorant of what later legal reasoning would call 'the probabilities'. But officers of the archaic *polis* had feeble powers of investigation and enforcement: they had no objective means of establishing what happened and who is to blame, independent of what the claimants themselves had to say; and the archaic authorities would rarely attempt to impose a judgement in despite of the claimants themselves. Much depended upon framing the judgement in such a way as to compel one party or the other to confront the consequences of his claim more squarely, before god and community: let the claimant present his proof of the claim and act upon it. The proverbial judgement of Solomon works upon much the same principle. The plaintiffs' subjective grievance and what they intend to do about it are of more immediate importance than the objective reality of what the defendant actually did. The chief concern of those who sit in judgement is to formulate a decision whereby the claimants themselves must give proof of their convictions and face the full consequences.

Statute law, by contrast, defines liability in abstract and objective terms—'if a man kill, even without malice, let him be exiled'. The art of reasoning from probability comes into greater demand in the era of such 'secondary rules', when statute law calls upon the judges to decide for themselves which of the two claims is closer to the truth. It is no longer left to the litigants to decide on their own conviction who is ultimately to blame. At Athens the questions of legal responsibility that statute law defined were ordinarily submitted to citizen juries to decide for the community the objective reality of who has done wrong. In the courts of the people, the patterns of human experience naturally prevail over the blunt instruments of oath and slave torture.[51] Ultimately a claimant must show that his claims conform to a standard model of motives and actions that the judges will recognize for themselves.

Max Weber described a similar pattern of development in legal reasoning: it is essentially a movement from external forms and outward demonstrations—*extrinsic formal* rationalism—to a more direct reckoning of the intrinsic values and interests of the commu-

---

[51] Automatic resolution by oath and divine intervention seems to be presupposed in Aesch. *Eum.* 439, ὅρκον οὐ δέξαιτ' ἄν, οὐ δοῦναι θέλοι; cf. 365, 432: the gods disdained to judge (i.e. to have settled on oath) homicide disputes, hence the court of mortal judges was founded. I have adopted H. L. A. Hart's 'primary' and 'secondary rules' (*The Concept of Law* (Oxford, 1961), 77–96) simply as a useful distinction, without entering into the wider debate on the positivist model.

nity—*substantive* rationalism.[52] Weber's typology was largely based upon comparative evidence of other legal systems, and perhaps Weber himself did not fully appreciate the Athenian phenomenon. But his paradigm is remarkably accurate in describing the evolution of homicide trials in the ancient democracy. The homicide proceedings are the most conservative part of Athenian justice, and the homicide judges are peculiarly preoccupied with formal standards of oath-taking and other processual acts. In time they will have to weigh the probable facts and social consequences— 'who done it' and who is hurt by it? But they do not take on such questions lightly. In fact they seem to arrive at this kind of reasoning by a slow and circuitous route.

Now a modern reader will naturally presume that such questions of fact—'who done it' and who is hurt by it?—have always been the most important issues for the judges to decide. But in the absence of any semblance of forensic method—when physical evidence is not even presented—it is only through the reckoning of probabilities that the facts of the crime—who struck the blow, with what weapon, and with what aim—can be treated as a reality apart from the representations. And it is only when the judges are called upon to render a verdict as a matter of public interest, outweighing the private wrongs, that they must decide for themselves the deeper questions of what wrong was done and who is to blame. Homer and the legendary traditions, tallying a good many homicides, never mention a 'who-done-it'; and comparative evidence confirms that this is not an issue that societies of primitive law readily take to court. It is only in the time of Antiphon that we meet with such a case that only conjecture can solve, and it is even then presented as something of a paradox.

The beginnings of this evolution, much as Weber described it— from external representations to the inner logic—can be found in the documents of Draco's law. The prominence of oath and challenge to torture derives from entrenched rules for consensual judgement, principles that prevailed in homicide disputes long after they were outmoded in other areas of the law. This formal rationalism persisted because of the special social dynamics of the crime, and because the select body of judges saw their duty in a different light from that which guided the other citizen juries.

---

[52] See *Max Weber on Law in Economy and Society*, ed. and trans. M. Rheinstein and E. Shils (1954), 224–55, with Rheinstein's introd. xlii–xlvi.

Reasoning from probability arose, as we shall see, with the reck-oning of intentions, not as a way of determining the facts or physi-cal reality of what happened. And the evidence suggests that the probabilities were originally brought to bear not as a means of determining what the killer wanted or anticipated in the course of the killing but rather as a test of what the litigants truly believed at trial. The plaintiffs had to adduce some outward evidence to justify their claim under oath to 'know well' the defendant's intent, and the defendant would try to show that his accusers had not acted as they would if they truly believed in his guilt. This kind of moral calculus entered into the trial proceedings at a very early stage, long before the Greeks began to speak of 'the probabilities' as a special-ized term. This method for validating or disproving the oath pro-vided the basis for a true rationalism, and out of it ultimately the reckoning of community values and interests entered into the Draconian courts.

2.3   Prospective

The first part of this study, Chapters 2–4, takes up the reconstruc-tion of the homicide procedure from its archaic origins to the time of Demosthenes. This procedural investigation should give us some answers to the most basic questions of rhetorical art: what is at issue, for the judges to decide, and how is that crux of dispute determined? Much of the reconstruction is theoretical, but a great deal of work has been done in this area and some perspective on the recent findings is now in order. The second part, Chapters 5–9, will analyse the argumentation in the extant homicide speeches in a case-by-case commentary; we shall reconsider Solmsen's theory and weigh other explanations of the peculiar reasoning that emerged from the primitive law. The conclusion (Ch. 10) offers a final perspective on the laws of bloodshed as they affected demo-cratic thinking and rhetorical art in ancient Athens and as they reflect upon similar developments in the modern law of the western democracies.

As we turn to the first stage of historical reconstruction, let us beware of the usual assumptions. It is often supposed that the founding of the homicide courts and the complex division of authority among them indicates a movement of political interven-tionism, aiming at greater central authority in the early *polis*; this mechanism of official justice emerged somehow fully armed from the Dark Age. Thus we are told that Draco's law represents 'a legal development far advanced from that of Homeric times', that 'prosecution of murder and manslaughter is no longer left to the bloodvengeance of the victim's kinsmen but was now subject to a procedure regulated by statute' and presided over by officers of the state.[53] But like democratic government, the law developed by adaptation: customary rules proper to the dominant families were rendered into statute in the early *polis*; these secondary rules became an instrument of justice for the greater community of the *dēmos*.[54] Inevitably something was lost in the translation from aristocratic values to a broader social order; but the essential features of primitive judgement remained in force. Draco undertook to strengthen the rules of the old regime, not to replace the prerogatives of the families and phratries with some higher authority. The limited intervention by the judges that Draco empowered was one small step; Solon's reform was a greater stride; further changes would follow. But the archaic apparatus remained, indeed, largely unaltered down to the time of Demosthenes, however inscrutable the laws 'written in blood' might prove to the layman.

[53] Busolt and Swoboda, 808.

[54] For the translation of aristocratic values into democratic rhetoric see Josiah Ober's very useful study, *Mass and Elite in Democratic Athens* (Princeton, 1989), esp. 251–66.

PART I

Historical Reconstruction
of the Homicide Law

2

Draco's Law and the Killer's Intent

The extant fragment of Draco's law refers to the killer's intentions three times in the first ten lines, but it gives no clear indication of how those intentions were to be weighed. Scholars have readily supposed that the trial judges were called upon to decide precisely this question of whether the killing was intentional or not, and because our fragment seems to apply only to unintentional homicide, intentional murder must have been treated elsewhere. But those who maintain this theory have had to treat as late intrusions any terminology that seems out of place in an archaic law for unintentional killing.[1] This chapter is largely devoted to these matters, intentionality in Draco's law and the authenticity of the relevant provisions. In the first section we shall re-examine the key volitional terms describing the killer's involvement and state of mind (§1). The following sections take up the reconstruction of procedure with particular regard to questions of malice (§§2–3). As we shall see in the chapters ahead, this aspect of the primitive procedure greatly affected the division of jurisdiction—how murder and other homicides were divided among the several courts—and the weighing of probable intentions ultimately offered the greatest scope for rhetorical art.

§1. The Terminology of Intentions

First Axon:
  Even if without malice aforethought [one man kill another], let him be exiled; and the kings shall give judgement (*dikazein*). Guilty of homicide

---

[1] For the view that the extant statute represents a later redaction, see esp. W. Dittenberger, *Sylloge inscriptionum graecarum*, 3rd edn., 4 vols. (Leipzig, 1915–24), i. 111; R. Dareste de la Chavanne, *Recueil des inscriptions juridiques grecques* (Paris, 1895), ii. 1–2; Miller, 'Drakon' in *RE* (1905), 1650–4; cf. Busolt and Swoboda, 808; Heitsch, *Antiphon*, 14–20; and most recently, T. Figueira, 'The Strange Death of Draco on Aigina' in R. Rosen and J. Farrell (eds.), *Nomodeiktes* (1993) 237–8. On the problem of intentionality, see esp. Maschke, *Willenslehre*, 28–63; Ruschenbusch, '*ΦΟΝΟΣ*', 139–45; Gagarin, *Drakon*, 11–16.

[is either the perpetrator] or the planner; and the justices (*ephetai*) shall decide (*diagnōnai*).[2]

Let them make settlement (or 'be reconciled' with the killer) if there is father, brother, or sons surviving, all in agreement, but he among them who opposes shall prevail. If there are none of these (nearest kin) surviving, let (right of settlement) extend to cousins and sons of cousins, if all are willing to be reconciled; but he who opposes shall prevail. If there are none of these kinsmen surviving—if the killing was unintentional and the fifty-one justices decide that the killing was unintentional—let ten kindred (*phratores*) grant pardon, if they are willing; and let the fifty-one choose them by rank. And let those also who were earlier guilty of homicide be subject to this statute.[3]

What was preserved in the fifth century as the first 'axle' or turning-table (*axōn*) of the ancestral laws apparently begins with the penalty and procedure for unintentional homicide; intentional killing appears to be nowhere directly addressed in the extant fragment. It has long been assumed therefore that a separate provision

[2] For the text and many of the supplements I have followed Stroud, *DL* (see n. 3). The problematic term *pronoia* I have rendered as 'malice aforethought', as this phrase conveys both the sense of 'harmful intent' that scholars have recently preferred and the notion of foresight implicit in the base meaning. A defence of this interpretation will be given below (§1.1.1). *Aidesis/aideisthai* indicates the end of *atimia* and the exile's formal reinstatement in the community; this procedure is ordinarily more of a transaction than an outright reprieve: hence *aidesis* is rendered 'reconciliation' or 'settlement'. In the special case of 'pardon' by the phratry the law says literally 'ten phratores shall admit him', with no specific reference to *aidesis* (see §3.2.1). *Phratria/phratores* (an ancient subdivision of the tribe supposedly descended from a common ancestor) I render as 'kindred' (to lend a similar archaism); *ephetai*, as 'justices', to distinguish them from ordinary judges.

[3] Stroud's text, *DL* 5 (= *IG* I³ 104. 10–20), reads as follows:

πρ͂οτος ἄχσον.
καὶ ἐὰμ μὲ ʼκ [π]ρονοί[α]ς [κ]τ[ένει τίς τινα φεύγ]ε[ν· δ]ι-
κάζεν δὲ τὸς βασιλέας αἴτιο[ν] φόν[ο] E . . . . . . -17- . . . . E [β]ολ-
εύσαντα· τὸς δὲ ἐφέτας διαγν[ο͂]ν[α]ι. [αἰδέσασθαι δ᾿ ἐὰμ μὲν πατέ]ρ ἔ-
ι ἒ ἀδελφὸ[ς] ἒ hυε͂ς, hάπαντ[α]ς, ἒ τόν κο[λύοντα κρατε͂ν· ἐὰν δὲ μὲ] ho͂υ-
τοι ὀσι, μέχρ᾿ ἀνεφ[σι]ότετος καὶ [ἀνεφσιο͂ ἐὰν hάπαντες αἰδέσ]ασ-
θαι ἐθέλοσι, τὸν κο[λύ]οντα [κ]ρα[τε͂ν· ἐὰν δὲ τούτον μεδὲ hε͂ς ε͂ι, κτ]έ-
νει δὲ ἄκο[ν], γνο͂σι δὲ hοι [πε]ντ[έκοντα καὶ hε͂ς hοι ἐφέται ἄκοντ]α
κτε͂ναι, ἐσέσθ[ο]ν δὲ h[οι φ]ρ[άτορες ἐὰν ἐθέλοσι δέκα· τούτος δ]ὲ ho-
ι πεντέκο[ν]τ[α καὶ hε͂ς ἀρ[ι]στ[ίνδεν hαιρέσθον. καὶ hοι δὲ πρ]ότε[ρ]-
ον κτέ[ν]α[ντ]ε[ς ἐν το͂ιδε το͂ι θεσμο͂ι ἐνεχέσθον . . .

In the lacuna, line 12, the precise restoration is disputed, but some contrastive term indicating the actual slayer seems certain: the planner is opposed to 'the perpetrator' (*ergasamenos*), 'one who struck with his own hand' (*autocheir*), or simply 'the killer' (*kteinas*). For earlier reconstructions, cf. Dareste, *Recueil*, ii. 1–24; Bonner and Smith, i. 110–25.

for the trial and punishment of intentional murder once stood at the head of Draco's law, and this murder law was then superseded by a new provision in the Solonian code. By this theory the provisions for settlement or reconciliation (*aidesis*) apply only in cases where the killing is judged unintentional, and intentional murder was subject to more serious penalties. If this is so, then obviously the main issue in many cases before the 'justices', the *ephetai*, was likely to have been precisely the question of the killer's intent.

But the law as we have it indicates no separate penalty for murder as opposed to unintentional killing, and if the difference was of no consequence in punishment, the very concept of intentionality may have been of little relevance to the justices' verdict. Gagarin has recently argued that the opening provisions of the extant inscription implicitly apply to intentional homicide as well as unintentional killing—'even if without malice . . . let him be exiled'. There was no distinct provision for murder separate from the procedure and penalty for other killings. The provisions for settlement (*aidesis*) apply equally to the wilful murderer and to one who has killed unwillingly or in error. The most provocative implication of this argument is that the opening of our law is complete, and that conclusion has met with much scepticism. To some of us it seems certain that a clause or heading has been lost or deleted.[4] If we assume that the Areopagus council was later established as a special court for intentional homicide, then any heading or opening provision of the earlier law that had assigned such cases to the *ephetai* would presumably have to be omitted in the later recension. On the other hand, if there was a lost heading, it is just as likely the original would have indicated, as the extant fragment seems to imply, that the provisions for trial, exile, and *aidesis* apply to all homicides, intentional as well as unintentional killing.[5]

There is a good prima-facie case for the latter interpretation. First of all, there is the clear implication that the general provisions for exile and settlement apply equally to the 'planner' as the perpetrator, and the most natural inference would be that planning a

---

[4] Among the sceptics: Sealey, 'Athenian Courts for Homicide', 292; Wallace, *Areopagos Council,* 16–18 (with a list of others unpersuaded, n. 61, p. 234); P. J. Rhodes, 'The Athenian Code of Laws', *JHS* 111 (1991), 91 at n. 24, is also 'not one of those who can persuade themselves' that the extant beginning is original.

[5] The surviving *axōn* would have some designation of the offence, presumably with the genitive of the charge, φόνου. The natural implication would be that the provisions apply generally.

homicide implies intentional involvement. Those who suppose that
the extant fragment applies only to unintentional killing have had
to import a rather sophisticated notion of 'planning' an unintended
outcome, and for that very reason they conclude that late interpolations have contaminated the ancient law. Second, there is the special provision for pardon by the phratry in cases where there were
no eligible kinsmen surviving. In such cases the justices were to
make a specific determination whether the killing had been intentional or unintentional, and the fact that a special ruling was needed
naturally suggests that the justices' verdict ordinarily entailed no
such determination.

The question of the law's integrity—whether the extant provisions for trial, exile, and *aidesis* are substantially complete or a
Draconian murder law has been deleted—can be better answered
when we have a broader picture of archaic justice, when we have
determined the roles of the judges and the litigants and the nature
of the process. That broader picture we must reserve for the later
sections (§§2–3). To lay the groundwork for this reconstruction we
first examine the crucial terms of intentionality and guilt as they are
used in our inscription (1.1), and then compare the relevant usage
in other archaic material, particularly the Homeric poems (1.2).

1.1   Volitional Terms in the Text of Draco's Law

The text of the law itself involves what some have regarded as
ambiguous and redundant terminology for guilt and intent. This
feature is problematic in a document which by its nature would
seem to require clear and definitive terms. Maschke thus supposed
that the provisions suggesting a more advanced conception of
intentionality belong to later interpolations, and this basic
approach has been followed in a number of influential studies. In
this school of thought the extant fragment refers to 'planning' an
unintentional homicide, a concept subject to subtle reformulation
in the later period. Ernst Heitsch has given the most recent and
perhaps the most cogent explication of the text by this approach
and it will be useful here to follow his outline.[6]

---

[6] Heitsch, *Antiphon*, 50–62. For πρόνοια as 'intent to kill' and μὴ ἐκ προνοίας
equivalent to ἄκων, see W. J. Loomis, 'The Nature of Premeditation in Athenian
Homicide Law,' *JHS* 92 (1972), 86–95; followed by Gagarin, *Drakon*, 30–7. Cf.
Maschke, *Willenslehre*, 50–62, supposing *pronoia* an anachronistic interpolation.

There are two sets of terms where redundancy or discrepancy would seem to suggest interpolation of more advanced phrasing alongside the original terms. First, the initial phrase 'without malice aforethought' (*pronoia*) is evidently equivalent to 'unwilling' (*akōn*) later in the document (17), and Heitsch quite reasonably supposes that *pronoia* is a concept of the later period. Second, he interprets *aitios*, generally 'guilty', in one context as roughly equivalent to *bouleusas*, 'planner' (26–9); whereas, in the initial, general provision the same term encompasses both indirect agency and direct—'guilty is the planner or the perpetrator'. Therefore, Heitsch reasons, the initial provision involves a later interpolation: the sophisticated concept of 'planning' an unintended death was necessarily introduced in the later period.

This solution involves several difficulties. There is perhaps a certain circularity in supposing that the terms in question must involve a more advanced conception and therefore concluding that they must belong to a later recension. This approach also assumes that the language of the earliest laws observed a rigid and well-defined terminology, without overlap or redundancy. The legalistic pronouncements of Demosthenes may imply such a view in the fourth century, but it is misleading to impose a rigid terminology upon the seventh-century lawgiver. And the apparent equivalence of such qualifiers as 'without malice aforethought' and 'unintentional' involves its own set of problems. It is true that these terms often seem to be equivalent in classical usage.[7] But that is not to say that there was no distinction at the time of enactment. There are very clear indications, after all, that *pronoia* retained something of its base meaning of forethought or prior design even in classical times, and killing with prior design is sometimes treated as a more serious wrong. Finally, and perhaps most telling, aside from these supposed interpolations there is no internal evidence whatever of tampering with the text. On the contrary, there are clear indications that the Draconian core of the homicide code was indeed preserved verbatim, without change: the retroactive provision, 'let those also who were (found) guilty [before enactment] . . . be subject to this statute' (lines 19–20), would have been otiose at the time of

---

[7] This is the finding of Loomis (see above, n. 6). Maschke, however, *Willenslehre*, 53–4, observed that *pronoia* retains a sense of premeditation as late as Sophocles and Herodotus, and he therefore assumed a distinction between ἄκων and μὴ ἐκ προνοίας.

reinscription. If the inscribers were inclined to bring their text up to date at any point, they would most likely have omitted this clause.[8] The burden of proof falls to those who would argue to the contrary, that the text as we have it is riddled with deletions and interpolations.

If we start with the more economical hypothesis, that the extant fragment is a faithful copy of the original law, then it is reasonable to suppose that it preserves a set of terms that do not imply advanced conceptual distinctions but necessarily involve a degree of ambiguity and overlap, such as we would expect to find in the first statutory formulation of what had been customary rules. Draco's legislation, in order to formalize current practice, made the most meaningful use of the relevant terms to encompass as wide a range of pleas and charges as was foreseeable.

1.1.1 'Without Malice Aforethought' and 'Unintentional'

Now it is true that the abstract noun *pronoia* is not found in Homer, but its absence from the epics does not prove that it was unfamiliar to the seventh-century audience. In hexameters the noun is metrically awkward, but we do find the more versatile verb, *pronoein*, and it clearly indicates forethought or prior deliberation. Homeric usage thus attests to this value for the term in the age of Draco.[9] The moral bearing of intentionality in Homer is a more complicated problem and we shall take up this broader issue in the next section. But here let us consider the more specific question of whether the Homeric value of *pronoia* as foresight or prior design may apply to Draco's law.

The generally prevailing view is that *pronoia* in the law was synonymous with harmful intent: a killing *mē ek pronoias* was simply unintentional (= *akōn*). We are therefore to conclude that there was no meaningful distinction of premeditation or forethought such as *pronoia* conveys in ordinary language. The most influential author of this opinion, Louis Gernet, supposed that the Greek conception of legal wrongs evolved from a primitive religious notion of transgression against god or sacred order; in such *délit objectif* the

---

[8] The *anagrapheis* were certainly not beyond tampering with the text where possible; on the process of codification see esp. N. H. Robertson, 'The Laws of Athens, 410–399 BC', *JHS* 100 (1990), 43–75, and Rhodes, 'Athenian Code'. But in this, perhaps best known of the ancient laws such tampering seems less likely.

[9] *Il.* 18. 526, 'they foresaw no deception'; *Od.* 5. 363, 'there was no better (plan) to devise'.

wrongdoer's intent was largely irrelevant.[10] The lesser guilt of unintentional wrongs was first recognized within the cult and kinship community of the *genos*, and this principle was then transferred to the *polis*. Thus *mens rea* evolved from religious identity and kindred sympathy, and there was no functional distinction of premeditation.

There have been sporadic attempts to differentiate *pronoia* from simple intent, particularly in regard to reconciliation or pardon, and when Stroud re-edited the inscription he suggested that *mē ek pronoias* in the initial provision for exile and *aidesis* and *akōn* in the special rule for pardon by the phratry might refer to two distinct categories.[11] Along the same lines Eva Cantarella concluded that *pronoia* indeed indicated a categorical distinction with serious consequences for determining the killer's return: any killer who had not acted with prior design might be absolved by the victim's family, but only he who was judged *akōn* might be pardoned by the phratry.[12]

There are, after all a good many cases where *pronoia* unequivocally indicates forethought—defendant brought a weapon, was discovered in ambush, or was found concocting a poison.[13] And we are told that prior design or deliberation constitutes a more serious wrong (Plato, *Laws* 9. 866d–67b). We shall examine this evidence more closely in regard to the one extant speech where malice aforethought appears to be the principal issue, Antiphon 1 (Ch. 6). But for the moment let us simply consider a passage that is often overlooked in this connection, one where we are told explicitly that the language of the law entails precisely this distinction between *pronoia* and simple intent: *Eudemian Ethics* 1226ᵇ30–1127ᵃ2.

As for those actions that are within our own control whether we act or act not, if someone commits an act or refrains for his own purpose and not through ignorance, he acts or refrains voluntarily; but many such actions

[10] *Recherches sur le développement de la pensée juridique et morale en Grèce* (1917), 310–88.

[11] *DL* 41. Loomis, however, 'Premeditation', rejected this distinction, without invoking Gernet's model but not without inferring profoundly religious inspiration in the law.

[12] *Studi sull'omicidio in diritto greco e romano* (Milan, 1976), 87–111.

[13] Premeditation shown in bringing a weapon: Lysias 3. 28 and 4. 6–7, 10–11. Concocting a poison: F62a Thalheim (= F41 Blass), from *Against Lysitheos*. The argument that the meaning of *pronoia* in wounding with intent to kill is irrelevant to the meaning in murder is special pleading: see Ch. 6 §1.2. Wallace, *Areopagos Council*, 98–100, also finds Loomis's thesis unconvincing.

we commit *without deliberation or premeditation*. For all that is done by choice (*proaireton*) is necessarily voluntary; but not all that is voluntary is a matter of choice . . . *and from this it is clear that the legislators rightly distinguish between what is intentional and unintentional and what is done by* pronoia. . . . For clearly deliberate choice (*proairesis*) is not simply the will nor [simply] the expectation (or opinion, *doxa*), but it is the expectation combined with the desire.[14]

From this passage we would naturally conclude that there was a distinction in the law between 'malice aforethought' and simple intent. The fact that the two are often paired in common usage means very little, especially in contexts where any distinction is irrelevant to the argument. And even if we suppose that there was no longer any special consequence to malice aforethought in the age of the orators, we cannot conclude that it was already a distinction without a difference at the enactment of Draco's law. After all, the original legislation is addressed to immediate social needs at a time when disputes were settled by customary rules and the bargaining terms had no statutory definition.

The later evidence would suggest that *pronoia* entailed an especially important distinction for the oath of the plaintiffs: an accuser can readily swear to the malice revealed in prior overt acts when he cannot otherwise claim to 'know well' the inner state of mind of the killer ('know well' appears to be the conventional language of the oath). As rhetorical argumentation developed, state of mind became more readily accessible, as the litigants and their judges came to accept the virtual reality of probable motive as deduced from circumstantial indications. But as we shall see, the traditional procedure revolves around the formal validity of the plaintiff's oath, and in this system prior design, as revealed in overt acts, is the most accessible measure of *mens rea*.

By contrast the language of simple intent, *akōn/hekōn*, is naturally suited to the defendant's oath: he can certainly swear to his own internal motivation more convincingly than his accuser. Thus in a revealing Homeric paradigm, which we examine in more detail below, the accused wrongdoer is challenged to swear that 'he did not willingly prevail by fraud'.[15] It is therefore highly suggestive that the one passage in the extant fragment of Draco's law where the term *akōn*, 'unwilling', is clearly preserved is the one provision

---

[14] Cf. M. Woods, *Aristotle* 'Eudemian Ethics', 2nd edn. (Oxford, 1992), 146.
[15] *Il.* 23. 585, μὴ ἑκὼν . . . δόλῳ. See §2.1.

where the *defendant's oath* is likely to be decisive: the special provision for pardon by the phratry. This procedure will require deeper investigation (Ch. 3 §2.1), but the special circumstance suggests a natural explanation. Since this procedure was available only when there were no surviving kinsmen eligible to prosecute, it looks as though the justices' determination would be based largely upon the oath and supporting evidence of the defendant—it does not appear to be an adversarial process. It is therefore all the more appropriate that the terminology of acquittal should reflect the stronger affirmation of innocence that only the defendant himself could swear to. When surviving family members resolve to prosecute or settle with the killer, they would base their decision upon what they themselves knew of overt acts revealing 'malice aforethought'.

There is thus an important distinction affecting the validity of the litigant's oath. And there is also a distinction that must have been meaningful in weighing the blood price. *Hekōn*, after all, is a much broader volitional term than *pronoia;* it may describe an attitude, 'favouring,' 'yielding', or 'consenting' even to an event or condition that may *not* be the subject's deliberate intent.[16] The negation of this form of volition, *akōn*, is thus a stronger affirmation of innocence than 'without malice aforethought'. In Draco's day therefore it is quite understandable that the victim's family might be willing to reconcile with a killer who pleaded convincingly that he acted *akōn*—under compulsion, accidentally, or unwittingly—and yet be unrelenting in their hatred toward a killer who acted spontaneously in anger, though without *pronoia*. To regularize this distinction Draco prescribes exile for all killers, even those who are not accused of the more serious malice aforethought; he allows pardon by the phratry only in those cases judged unintentional.

1.1.2 'Guilty is the Planner'

In regard to the second apparent discrepancy—where *aitios* 'guilty' in one context seems equivalent to *bouleusas* 'planner', but elsewhere is more general—we should beware of a similar tendency to interpret distinctive ethical terms as 'functionally opposite' when that opposition is not in their base meaning nor suitable to the context. Now since Heitsch supposes that the initial provision for exile and *aidesis* pertains only to unintentional killing, he assumes also

---

[16] See Rickert's study, Ἑκών and Ἄκων in early Greek Thought (APA, American Classical Studies 20, 1989), esp. 71–8.

that *bouleusas* must imply 'planning' or determining an unintended death (such cases as attested in Ant. 6); and since this subtle concept would appear to be a late formulation, he concludes that the term 'planner,' *bouleusas*, must be a later interpolation in the Draconian text. Older usage, he supposes, would have described the instigator or initiator of a killing by another's hand simply as *aitios*.[17] Such usage is apparently demonstrated in the provision, lines 26–9 (= Dem. 23. 37), against the vindictive killing of an exiled homicide who abides by the terms of his banishment: 'if anyone kill . . . or be *aitios* for the killing', he is subject to punishment on the same terms as the killer of an Athenian. Here we are to interpret *aitios* as functionally opposite to the perpetrator, hence equivalent to *bouleusas*. But in the initial provision—'guilty (alike) is the perpetrator or the planner'—*aitios* has the broader meaning. Thus in one passage *aitios* means simply 'guilty'; in the other (26–9), it means '*indirectly* responsible'.

This analysis is open to the same objections that we raised in regard to malice aforethought. Draco framed the law from customary rules based upon private settlement; when he came to address guilt and innocence, he inevitably resorted to a terminology that had not yet evolved the kind of functional opposition that later legal reasoning would construct. And in this instance the evidence is even more conclusive that the two terms are simply not equivalent in the law. The base meanings of *aitios* and *bouleusas* derive from wholly different conceptions, and in fact an implicit distinction between the two is clearly evident in the very passage where Heitsch has found them equivalent.

Aitios, after all, looks to the consequences of guilt—liability—rather than to the initial cause. As ethical reasoning becomes more sophisticated in its reckoning of indirect and remote causes, the instigator or planner of an act is recognized as *aitios* because he set the causal sequence in motion; but *aitios* is not in itself synonymous with 'initiator' (*arxas*, lines 33–4). In origin *aitios* and *aitia* have to do with retribution and compensation. The most probable etymology derives *aitios* from *aisa*, 'share' or 'portion'. Other cognate terms similarly indicate loss and restitution: particularly suggestive is the adjective *aisimos*, as in Poseidon's promise to Hephaestus to

---

[17] See n. 6 above. Maschke, *Willenslehre*, 89, reasoned conversely, that *bouleusas* was the *older* term for indirect agency, later replaced by *aitios* in this sense; and that Dem. 23. 37 represents a late interpolation in the law.

pay ransom for Ares, 'all that is due'—*aisima panta*.[18] Archaic usage confirms that in many instances *aitios* by implication means 'liable' for damages more than morally blameworthy. Thus in *Iliad* 1. 152 ff. against the arrogance of Agamemnon, Achilles protests that he came to Troy out of loyalty, not to settle any score of his own with the Trojans, 'since they are in no way *liable* to me (οὔ τί μοι αἴτιοί εἰσιν), for they have never driven off my cattle or horses . . . or plundered my land'. There is a similar implication in Agamemnon's protest in *Iliad* 19. 85 ff., that he offers compensation to Achilles as a gift, not as a payment of liablity (ἐγὼ δ' οὐκ αἴτιός εἰμι). And in *Odyssey* 22. 47–9, when Odysseus has struck down Antinous with his first arrow of vengeance against the suitors, Eurymachus pleads that the others should be spared for ransom since Antinous was responsible, *aitios*, for all the suitors' offences and he has fully paid.[19]

Thus in the settlement of disputes the causal term *aitios* carries the clear implication that compensation or retribution is owed. It would therefore appear to be implicit in the order of the opening provisions in Draco's law (lines 12–13) that the defendant who is judged *aitios* is liable for his wrong and will pay with exile or death if not by financial settlement.

Draco's legislation belongs to the aftermath of the coup led by Cylon and reprisals led by the Alcmeonidae (Hdt. 5. 71; Plut. *Sol.* 12). The immediate aim of the lawgiver was to give recognition and greater effectiveness to the customary rules of retribution and settlement, thus to eliminate conflicting expectations that might lead to irresoluble vendetta. Thus in the passage where Heitsch finds *aitios* equivalent to the planner, *bouleusas* (26–9), Draco prescribes that he who kills or is any way liable for the killing of an exile 'be subject to the same terms' of compensation or reprisal that applied in the killing of an Athenian resident. The emphasis here is upon the full equivalence of remedies against anyone implicated in the unlawful killing of an exile, just as in the death of a fellow citizen in Athens. He who is 'liable for the killing' is not simply the planner or instigator, but anyone subject to any remedy or sanction resulting from the killing. The provision is clearly crafted so as to include

---

[18] *Od.* 8. 347–8. Cf. Chaintraine, *Dictionnaire étymologique* s.v. αἴτιος, connecting the term also with δίαιτα and αὔνυμαι, probably also αἰτίζομαι, 'beg'.

[19] Cf. *Hymn to Hermes* 274–6 and 382–3, where the infant cattle rustler offers an oath that he is not *aitios* for the lost cattle of Apollo.

those who claim to kill justifiably but who arguably violated the laws protecting the exile; it might also include those who undertook to abduct or drive off the exile or otherwise acted against him without intending to kill, but whose actions had unintentionally led to his death. In either case it was open to the family of the slain exile to charge that the killer was indeed liable, *aitios*, for whatever remedies law or custom allowed. Available remedies against the *aitios* might include seizure of property if he were unwilling to agree to settlement; conversely, the exile who lawfully abides by the terms of his banishment has his property protected by law (Dem. 23. 44). Liability might also extend to hostage-taking, *androlēpsia*, which was evidently an acknowledged remedy against a killer who refused to come to justice (Dem. 23. 82). Thus in the Draconian context, the phrasing 'if anyone kill or be liable for the killing . . . he is subject to the same remedies' hardly suggests that *aitios* is in any way equivalent to *bouleusas*.

'Planning', like *pronoia*, is a concept suited to the plaintiff's sworn claim as a measure of liability. A plaintiff cannot easily swear to 'know well' the defendant's state of mind, but he may be able to swear in good conscience to the planner's liability in a fatal undertaking that he authorized or initiated. In all periods the verb *bouleuein* ordinarily implies intent or purpose, but, again, that is not to say that it is functionally opposite to unintended mishap or accident. Its essential meaning is 'to make a plan or design of action' (*boulē/bouleuma*). The emphasis evident in most patterns of usage is not upon the intent or purpose *per se*, but upon the decision that sets a sequence of events in motion. That decision is most clearly revealed in plotting or instructing another agent.[20]

The self-evident meaning of the law—taking each of the key terms in its essential, non-oppositional, value—is that exile and *aidesis* are prescribed for all homicides, even if the killing was without any degree of malice; liable alike is the perpetrator and the planner. The latter clause applies to all homicides regardless of intent. In the historical context in which this legislation arose, it seems likely that *bouleusas* in the initial provision would allow for certain kinds of unintentional killing that were likely to be all too common a consequence of violent reprisals: it should include those cases where X orders Y to take some action against Z—whether vindictive attack,

---

[20] We shall examine the evidence for 'planning'—including the decision or determination of an unintended outcome—in detail in regard to Antiphon 6 (Ch. 7).

seizure of property, or abduction of persons. In any case, an unintended death was a likely result, and in such cases, X might plead that he was not the killer and did not intend to kill; but he would be none the less liable by the rule 'guilty is the planner as the perpetrator'.

Thus the terminology of guilt and intent in our inscription suggests that the lawgiver was attempting to articulate a complex set of ethical problems. The very persistence of these overlapping terms in the later era, when much of the original relevance was lost, attests to the conservatism of the legal tradition. It is hardly proof against authenticity. The specific volitional terms in our copy of Draco's law involve no inconsistency sufficient to suggest abridgement or interpolation. What anomalies there are derive in large part from the transitional character of the document: the lawgiver must not only institute new procedures with binding force thereafter but also allow for earlier settlements and reassert the validity of pre-existing conventions. The provision for retroactivity—'let those also who were earlier guilty of homicide be subject to this statute'—and the special provision for pardon by the phratry—the one passage where *akōn* is clearly read and to which the retroactive clause is especially relevant—attest to the document's transitional character. These provisions were largely obsolete at the time of reinscription but they were none the less faithfully recorded in the text.

Perhaps the most persistent doubts, however, have been prompted by the general emphasis in our law upon intentionality and the apparent indifference to intentions in the other archaic material, particularly the Homeric poems. Those who suppose that the law implies a separate treatment of intentional murder as a more serious offence find it obviously inconsistent with the remedies we find in Homer and conclude that the language of our law cannot be the original wording of the seventh century. But if we proceed from the most natural implications of the law as we have it, that the lawgiver recognized intentionality but did not presume to dictate how it would be weighed by the victim's family, then we have an arrangement of primitive law that is entirely consistent with the customary rules that preceded it.

1.2   Intentionality in Homer

In the Homeric poems we find more than two dozen references to the treatment of homicide and these are generally seen as conclusive evidence against intentionality.[21] In the great majority of examples, it is true, the killer goes into exile without trial and apparently without any attempt to reconcile with his pursuers, and we have no single instance where we are told explicitly that innocence of malice would count in the killer's favour. But the essential elements of such a system are in place. The custom of accepting compensation in settlement is well established: this is shown by the trial scene on the shield of Achilles (which will require more detailed discussion below); and Ajax' counsel to Achilles in the embassy scene (*Il.* 9. 632–6). In the latter passage it is remarked as an established remedy that in some cases a man will take payment and relent from his vendetta against the killer even in the slaying of a son or brother (so much the more readily should one accept a settlement in such minor offences as the taking of a slave woman). We are not told how those who accept a settlement come to that decision, but presumably there was *some* principle or convention whereby settlement was to be granted or denied. Ajax does not expressly plead that Agamemnon's offence is the more forgivable because it was unintended; but we know that Agamemnon himself now claims that divine delusion led him to do wrong.[22]

There are only two examples where we are expressly told that a killing was unintended or believed to be unintentional: the case of Patroclus (*Il.* 23. 85–90) who, as a youth, killed a companion at a game of dice 'in anger, not meaning to kill him'; and the scene in Odysseus' hall, when disguised as a beggar he shot down Antinous and the other suitors threatened to kill him though they assumed he had killed in error (*Od.* 22. 1–33). Both passages show that there was no binding rule that guaranteed settlement in such cases, but neither case is proof that intentionality had no bearing in a settlement. The suitors' threat to Odysseus proves nothing: they believed him to be a beggar, whom they would gladly abuse without provocation; as a known felon (*kakourgos*) and one without aristocratic ties or citizen rights, he could expect none of the customary protections that the suitors themselves would claim. And in the

---

[21] Conveniently assembled by Gagarin, *Drakon,* 6–10; cf. Maschke, *Willenslehre,* 1–10.

[22] Cf. *Il.* 9. 115–20; 85–91. For Agamemnon's ἄτη and the supposedly deficient sense of human agency, cf. E. R. Dodds, *The Greeks and the Irrational* (Berkeley, 1951), 1–18; A. W. H. Adkins, 'Values, Goals and Emotions in the *Iliad*', *CP* 77 (1982) esp. 307–12 and 324–6 (against Lloyd-Jones, *The Justice of Zeus* (Berkeley, 1983), 15).

case of Patroclus, on the other hand, the very emphasis upon state of mind is a strong indication that intentionality was a recognized factor in the calculus of guilt.

The character of Patroclus and his relationship to Achilles were reworked in a late stage of the poem's composition.[23] Earlier tradition had treated him as a kinsman of Achilles and one whose killing must therefore be avenged by customary obligation. In the *Iliad* as we have it, Patroclus has become the archetypic comrade, for whose death the tie of friendship is the sole bond of vengeance. Thus the fateful decision of Achilles is made the more heroic. The poet has recast the relationship to involve the sympathies of his audience more directly, and to the same end, I suggest, he has enhanced the tragic stature of Patroclus by involving him in the epic problem of recklessness, of wrongs done without specific intent.

Such is the context in which the ghost of Patroclus recalls his coming to the court of Peleus, in exile for the killing of a boyhood friend: as a child, in anger at a game, he had killed though not meaning to kill. The poet expected his audience to share the hero's compassion. Their natural feeling would be that an outcast like Patroclus somehow deserved redemption, that in such circumstances, where the killing was done with the utmost diminution of responsibility, those factors should have some bearing upon the fateful decisions of kinsmen and community, whether to reconcile with the killer or unleash a vendetta to the death. In any event, unless the qualifier 'not meaning to kill' is a meaningless formula, it suggests that intentionality was a consideration.[24]

This interpretation goes against the influential view of A. W. H. Adkins, that intentions were ethically irrelevant.[25] But there is

---

[23] See R. Janko, *Iliad Commentary* (Cambridge, 1992), iv. 309–14, esp. 313, on the *Patrokleia*.

[24] Similarly in the lost *Epigoni*, Cephalus fled for the accidental killing of Procris and was purified by the Cadmeans: *Suda* s.v. Τευμησία: τ. 429 (Adler). Again in the tale of Adrastus, Herodotus reports that Croesus forgave his son's killer because the killing was not his intentional act but the god's doing 1. 45. It is perhaps misleading to adduce here (as Gagarin, *Drakon*, 32) the categories recognized in classical procedure, where Patroclus' offence might not have qualified as unintentional; he would have been none the less eligible to make settlement for a killing in anger. On the relevant argument in *Tetralogy* 3 and Plato's discussion of killing in anger in the *Laws*, see Ch. 5 §3. Cf. Cantarella, *Studi sull'omicidio*, 43–9

[25] *Merit and Responsibility*, 30–57, esp. 50–2. Against Adkins's view, see esp. A. A. Long, 'Morals and Values in Homer', *JHS* 90 (1970), 121–39, esp. 124 n. 9. Further insight is offered by Rickert, Ἑκών *and* Ἄκων, 45–78, with examples of

ample evidence that an agent's volition determined blame or approval to some degree: *Il.* 6. 522–3, Hector rebukes Paris because he willingly (*hekōn*) withdrew from battle (i.e. not because of a wound or other necessity); *Il.* 18. 434, Thetis claims sympathy from Hephaestus for her sorrows, among which she counts her marriage to a mortal, to which she was subjected 'though unwilling' (*ouk ethelousa*). Intentionality is clearly at issue in the oath that Menelaus demanded from Antilochus: if he is to claim the prize, he must swear upon it that he did not *willingly* prevail by fraud.[26] Telemachus will rouse resentment if he *willingly* sends away Penelope (*Od.* 2. 133). Again, Nestor asks of Telemachus whether he is *willingly* subjected to ill-treatment by the suitors or overwhelmed by a hostile community (*Od.* 3. 214–15). Thus already in Homer intentionality appears to influence blame or acceptance. In time a strongly felt social convention arose that tended to ensure the right of settlement to an unintentional and repentant killer.

Now I conclude that the ghost of Patroclus belongs to such an era of ethical revision, when the killer's intent was coming to be a factor in reaching a settlement. There was obviously no binding rule to guarantee to the repentant killer the right of reconciliation, but there was a certain onus upon the victim's kinsmen to accept a settlement if the repentant killer convincingly pleaded innocent of malice. A similar expectation seems implicit in the general provisions of Draco's law for exile and *aidesis*. Intentionality had entered social conscience but it was not yet prescribed that innocence of malice entitled a killer to make his peace.

With this understanding of the ethical concepts let us turn to the questions of procedure, how the participants were to proceed. What was the function of the 'kings' and what was at issue before the *ephetai*? Here again the specific provisions of our law have been often found inconsistent with prevailing models of archaic justice.

ἄκων and οὐκ ἐθέλων not 'functionally opposite' in meaning 'against one's will' but more broadly describing the agent's attitude, whether favouring or disinclined to the act or consequence. And see now B. Williams's very valuable reassessment of agency, intentionality, and responsibility: *Shame and Necessity* (Berkeley, 1993), 21–74.

[26] *Il.* 23. 573–9; cf. line 434, 'he himself willingly' (αὐτὸς ἑκών) drove his team to cut off his opponent. On this passage see further §2.1. Similarly the formula *Il.* 11. 55 = 17. 666, 'he gave ground unwillingly for he feared', suggests that retreat is less to the hero's shame; at *Od.* 13. 277 sailors are not to blame for going off course if driven by the wind, 'much against their will.'

But if we take the inscription as we have it, giving the most natural meaning to the clauses as they stand without importing anachronistic assumptions, we find that Draco's law is largely consistent with the conventions in Homer and other archaic evidence.

§ 2. The Archaic Method of Judgement

The opening provision of our law calls for the kings to give judgement (*dikazein*) and the justices to decide the dispute (*diagnōnai*). In the time of Antiphon and of our inscription, final judgement in homicide cases was the role of the justices, the *ephetai*. The tribal kings, *basileis* (or *phylobasileis*), were largely restricted to the peculiar jurisdiction of the Prytaneum court, for homicide by an unknown assailant or impersonal instrument (Ch. 3 §2). Yet the most natural reading would be that the lawgiver refers to this body when he calls for 'the kings to give judgement'.[27] The prominence of the tribal kings in the opening provision is all the more surprising as they are never elsewhere mentioned in the various clauses of our inscription. These provisions include the verdict of the justices for unintentional homicide in cases calling for pardon by the phratry (16–19), the trial of those who illegally put to death the exiled homicide (29), and the special cases of self-defence and the killing of an assailant (33–6). These are all cases in which the *ephetai* will be called upon to give a decision, and in none of these provisions is there any specific role for the kings. Given the state of the evidence, we should not overemphasize this feature. Perhaps the orginal audience would assume that the kings should exercise the same function in these cases as well. But it is also reasonable to suppose that the sequence of the extant provisions represents a logical order. Since the initial provision on exile and *aidesis* is essentially a rule of recognition validating customary procedures, the function of the kings in the opening clause was probably adapted from earlier practice. They may have had little or no authority in the special cases treated later in the law.

---

[27] It is sometimes supposed that this phrase refers to the *archon basileus*, the chief magistrate who conducted preliminary hearings and presided at the trial in *dikai phonou*. But it is uncharacteristic of the law for 'the kings' in the plural to encompass a succession of magistrates, each acting individually; the lawgiver speaks of the abstract instance in the singular, 'if a man kill'.

Wallace has recently identified the pre-Draconian homicide court as a jury of kings or chief officials—the *phylobasileis* and *archon basileus* (perhaps joined by other archons *ex officio*).[28] This body was then superseded by the jury of fifty-one justices that Draco established. This part of Wallace's reconstruction is based largely upon broader historical development and the sometimes dubious evidence of late commentators, but it agrees with the most natural reading of the law as we have it. The judgement of the kings was an ancient authority that Draco adapted to more complex decision-making. The view of the kings' jurisdiction that has long prevailed, however, relegates them to a mere formality. So long as it was supposed that the Areopagus council was the ancient homicide court before Draco, it was also presumed that the role of the kings must have been no more than a ceremonial pronouncement of the verdict that the high court had given.[29] But if we set aside the Areopagite model, we are presented with a view of the kings that is more consistent with the Homeric evidence and the later historical development.

The chief evidence for the ancient jurisdiction of the tribal kings consists of Solon's amnesty law (Plut. *Sol.* 19. 4) and the classical jurisdiction of the kings in the Prytaneum court.[30] Solon's amnesty law indicates that there were still, a generation after Draco, homicides in exile who had been condemned by the court of the tribal kings at the Prytaneum. Amnesty is denied to (among others) those exiled by the Prytaneum court, 'condemned by the kings, for homicide or "slaughter"'. The kings' classical jurisdiction in cases of slaying by an unidentified killer or inanimate instrument clearly derives from the more ancient issue of 'slaughter', mayhem, or indiscriminate vendetta. Thus the amnesty law indicates that the tribal kings once gave final verdict in a specific jurisdiction.[31]

---

[28] *Areopagos Council*, esp. 27–8; see Ch. 1 §1.2.

[29] For the view that the Areopagus court antedated Draco and the *ephetai* were instituted as a special court for *unintentional* homicide: Wolff, 'Origin of Judicial Litigation', 74; Maschke *Willenslehre*, 49–51. For the opposing view: Sealey, 'Athenian Courts for Homicide', esp. 85–92.

[30] For assigning homicide jurisdiction to the justices and kings, tyranny to the Areopagus, see Ch. 1 §1.2; cf. Wallace, *Areopagos Council*, 7–28, with my review in *AJP* 111 (1990), 410–14.

[31] It is perhaps likely that even before Draco, in cases of great consequence the kings might defer to an assembly or council; but the old assumption that the pre-draconian Areopagus was the homicide court is contradicted by Aristotle's testimony that Draco made no constitutional revision (*Pol.* 1274[b]) and the evidence that

The initial provision of Draco's law assigns to the tribal kings a general function of judgement apparently affecting most homicide disputes, and the natural implication of the law would be that this function of the kings precedes that of the *ephetai*, both in the order of procedure and in historical development. From these indications I assume as a working hypothesis that the court of the tribal kings was once the principal homicide court and with the institution of the special court of fifty-one *ephetai* the jurisdiction of the tribal kings was accommodated to the new procedure. Now the usual view of the kings' function in Draconian proceedings—that they were merely to make formal pronouncement of the justices' verdict—derives from the Areopagite model; it assumes that the kings played the same limited role before Draco as did the *archon basileus* in a much later period. But if we dispense with this anachronistic approach, it is reasonable to suppose that the judgement of the tribal kings in Draco's law was in some ways analogous to the judgement of chiefs and magistrates such as we find in other records of archaic society. Let us begin with the Homeric material, for what it may tell us about the antecedents of Draconian procedure.

2.1   Homeric Judgement and Achilles' Shield

Those who give judgement in the Homeric poems propose a means of resolving the dispute, ordinarily by oath or payment, and it is generally a solution that must be mutually acceptable to the interested parties.[32] Thus in *Il*. 23. 574, where Menelaus disputes the prize for the chariot race with Antilochus, he calls upon the assembled leaders to 'give judgement' among them, seeking the middle ground, partial to neither side.[33] He then resolves the dispute by challenging Antilochus to affirm his right to the prize on oath: the claimant must swear by Poseidon that he has not willingly

---

Draco himself assigned homicide jurisdiction only to *ephetai*. See Ch. 1 §§1.1–2 (on the Areopagite model) and Ch. 3 §2.1 (on the Prytaneum).

[32] Cf. G. Thür, 'Zum δικάζειν bei Homer', *ZSS* 87 (1970), 426–44. This model is largely discounted by S. Humphreys, 'The Discourse of Law in Archaic and Classical Greece', *LHR* 6:2 (1988), 465–93, and Gagarin, *Drakon*, and *EGL* (esp. 29–30).

[33] Cf. *Il*. 23. 573–9: ἡγήτορες ἠδὲ μέδοντες | ἐς μέσον ἀμφοτέροισι δικάσσατε, μηδ' ἐπ' ἀρωγῇ . . . εἰ δ' ἄγ' ἐγὼν αὐτὸς δικάσω. On evidentiary oath cf. Bonner and Smith, i. 28.

prevailed by fraud (ὄμνυθι μὴ ἑκὼν . . . δόλῳ, 585). As Antilochus refuses to swear and no competing proposals are forthcoming, the matter is decided. This is a simple 'oath-challenge', a straightforward means of settling disputes within the archaic aristocracy. Menelaus' challenge to Antilochus, to swear to his claim, is not a second solution, but the beginning of the 'judgement' that he has invoked: he himself, as chief among the lords assembled, will be the first to put the rival claims to proof. In this case, the first judgement proves decisive, but if it had not, the other lords would have proposed similar means of resolving the dispute.[34]

The trial scene on the Shield of Achilles suggests a similar mechanism (*Il*. 18. 497–508). This case involves a dispute over *compensation* for a homicide. There is no dispute of the fact that the defendant was responsible for the killing. The roles of the various participants, judges and litigants, are still much debated, and it remains uncertain what precisely is at issue in this symbolic trial scene. The poet seems to say that the defendant claims to have paid full compensation, and the plaintiff, that he has received none; but the means of deciding the case suggests in itself that the dispute involves more than the mere fact of payment.

Both sides seek a settlement and each man has pledged a talent. The sum of two talents, rather in excess of the usual blood-price, will go not to the successful litigant but to one among the judges 'who speaks straightest judgement'. This arbiter does not appear to arrive at this verdict by discovering undisclosed facts in the case or by invoking an arcane body of rules. Those who give judgement are neither investigators nor 'lawsayers'. The dispute will be resolved by a judgement that the litigants themselves must acknowledge as a straight and unswerving answer to their pleas, worthy of the talent each has pledged. To put the problem squarely before us, I offer the following interpretation. The phrasing in parentheses represents what I think to be the most probable implications of certain disputed terms.

The people crowded the market-place, for there a quarrel had arisen: two men quarrelled over the price of a man slain. One claimed (the right) to make full payment, declaring (payment) before the people; the other refused to accept any settlement. Both were eager to reach an end before a witness (to their oath). The crowd shouted support for them both—

---

[34] Thus Thür, 'Zum δικάζειν bei Homer', 426–44; A. Primmer, 'Homerische Gerichtsszenen', *WS* 83 (1970), 5–13, noting the connective phrase εἰ δ' ἄγ' ἐγὼν.

partisans on both sides—but the heralds held back the throng. The elders sat upon polished stones in the shrine circle; they held in their hands the sceptres of far-voiced heralds, with these then they sprang up and gave judgement, (for) each side in turn. There lay before them two talents of gold, a prize for him who among them spoke straightest judgement.[35]

The Shield of Achilles is, of course, a symbolic device. It becomes, in Lessing's famous phrase, 'a quintessence of all that goes on in the world'.[36] But despite the highly artistic character of the text, the trial scene is rightly regarded as crucial evidence on archaic procedure. It represents the settlement of disputes in Homer's own day—by a sort of 'prophetic fallacy', Hephaestus in the age of heroes is made to depict the justice of the poet's own era. It is puzzling testimony because, by the nature of the ecphrasis, the poet attempts to convey a sequence of proceedings as a single tableau, and he relies upon his audience to recognize the scene and visualize the figures in their proper roles.[37] Because the poet may assume that his audience is familiar with the workings of contemporary justice he is content to sketch in the participants without explaining the issue or the procedure.

[35] λαοὶ δ' εἰν ἀγορῇ ἔσαν ἀθρόοι· ἔνθα δὲ νεῖκος | ὠρώρει, δύο δ' ἄνδρες ἐνείκεον εἵνεκα ποινῆς | ἀνδρὸς ἀποφθιμένου· ὁ μὲν εὔχετο πάντ' ἀποδοῦναι | δήμῳ πιφαύσκων, ὁ δ' ἀναίνετο μηδὲν ἑλέσθαι· | ἄμφω δ' ἱέσθην ἐπὶ ἴστορι πεῖραρ ἑλέσθαι. | λαοὶ δ' ἀμφοτέροισιν ἐπήπυον, ἀμφὶς ἀρωγοί· | κήρυκες δ' ἄρα λαὸν ἐρήτυον· οἱ δὲ γέροντες | ἥατ' ἐπὶ ξεστοῖσι λίθοις ἱερῷ ἐνὶ κύκλῳ, | σκῆπτρα δὲ κηρύκων ἐν χέρσ' ἔχον ἠεροφώνων· | τοῖσιν ἔπειτ' ἤισσον, ἀμοιβηδὶς δὲ δίκαζον. | κεῖτο δ' ἄρ' ἐν μέσσοισι δύω χρυσοῖο τάλαντα, | τῷ δόμεν ὃς μετὰ τοῖσι δίκην ἰθύντατα εἴποι.

[36] G. E. Lessing, *Laokoön* (1766) § 19. On the Shield, its place in the epic and overview of the bibliography, see now M. W. Edwards, *Iliad Commentary* (Cambridge, 1991) v. 200–9; P. R. Hardie, 'Imago Mundi', *JHS* 105 (1985), 11–31; Stanley, *The Shield of Homer* (Princeton, 1993), 186–90. Among earlier works: W. Schadewaldt, 'Der Schild des Achilles', *NJb* 113 (1938); M. Schrade, 'Der Homerische Hephaistos', *Gymnasium*, 57 (1950); J. T. Kakridis, 'Erdichtete Ekphrasen', *WS* 76 (1963), 7–26; and K. Fittschen, *Der Schild des Achilles* (1973), 1–17.

[37] Edwards aptly describes the technique, *Iliad Commentary* v. 207. The breach of verisimilitude was noted by Eustathius (iv. 236, van der Valk), who judged that the phrase 'sceptres in hand . . . .' (505–6) is 'harshly expressed' (στρυφνῶς πέφρασται), as *each* elder is to take the sceptre as he rises to speak. Rather than give a representation of one image in a series, the poet gives a panorama of the whole sequence, in the manner of the visual arts. This is evident in the treatment of the heralds' 'sceptres', where the plurals indicate literally that each elder is shown with a staff in his hand—presumably some rising, others seated—in order to indicate the sequence of judgement, as the one herald's staff passes from one speaker to the next. The herald's staff, of course, indicates who has the privilege to speak, and it would defeat the purpose if each participant had his own.

The view that the central issue of our dispute is a question of rights—whether the defendant can reclaim his status in the community or the plaintiff is to have his revenge—goes back to the 1820s and generally prevailed in the nineteenth century.[38] Thereafter, however, the current of opinion shifted to what was felt to be a more literal reading, that the proceedings were essentially a voluntary arbitration to decide whether the defendant had paid or had not paid; this is, after all, the view of the ancient scholia.[39] Then in 1946, in what was to be the most influential work on this problem for forty years, H. J. Wolff dismantled the façade of arbitration.[40] Wolff relied, however, upon a broad array of material from later Greek procedural law, particularly the statute law of Hellenistic and Roman times; and he tended to retroject these later procedural mechanisms into archaic times. The method is questionable and the conclusions are virtually untenable.

First of all, relying perhaps too much upon the view then prevailing, Wolff assumed that the question at issue must be the simple matter of payment or non-payment in fulfilment of an earlier composition.[41] The only evidence that he adduces on this point is the very term 'payment' (apodounai), which he finds 'decisive', since in later procedure it is a technical term 'for paying a debt already incurred'. For such terminology, however, the Hellenistic evidence is of doubtful validity for the Homeric context. And the

---

[38] See esp. W. Leaf, 'The Trial Scene in Iliad XVIII', JHS 8 (1887), 122–32; for further references cf. A. Steinwenter, Die Streitbeendigung durch Urteil, Schiedsspruch und Vergleich nach griechischen Rechte (Münchener Beitrage 8, 1925), 34 n. 3; Bonner and Smith, i. 31 n. 5.

[39] Cf. schol Il. 18. 497–8, 499–500 (Erbse 4 (1975), 535–6): ἔστι δὲ στάσις καταστοχαστική, τοῦ μὲν λέγοντος δεδωκέναι τὴν ποινήν, τοῦ δὲ ἀρνουμένου εἰληφέναι. This view is followed by Lipsius, attische Recht, i. 4; Busolt and Swoboda, i. 332–3; Bonner and Smith, i. 31–41. H. Hommel advanced the arbitration thesis in a review of Steinwenter (1925) in PhW och 48 (1928), 359–68; see esp. 365–8; forty years later he defended it in 'Die Gerichtsszene auf dem Schild des Achilles', Palingenesia, 4 (1969), 11–38, with a very useful review of earlier scholarship on this question, pp. 11–12 nn. 2–5.

[40] 'Origin of Judicial Litigation', 31–87; later published in German, in Wolff's Beiträge zur Rechtsgeschichte Altgriechenlands und des hellenistisch-römischen Ägypten (1961), with a 'Nachtrag 1960' rebutting M. Bohacek's then recent revival of the arbitration theory, IURA 3 (1952) 191 ff.

[41] Wolff rightly rejects the argument, going back to S. Maine's Ancient Law (Boston, 1861), 363–5, that the procedure is analogous to the old Roman legis actio and the two talents are pledged by way of sacramentum to the state. Lucian's parody, Piscator 41, suggesting that the two talents are a wager, to be awarded to the victorious litigant, is also of doubtful relevance.

evidence of Homeric usage itself, though inconclusive on many points, clearly indicates a meaning for the plaintiff's position that would seem to contradict Wolff's interpretation: the plaintiff *refused* (*anaineto*) to accept anything.[42] That the issue is phrased in absolute terms—that one claimed to make '*full* payment' (*pant' apodounai*) and the other refused *any* settlement—suggests that more was at issue than simply the fact of payment or the amount.[43] The defendant, after all, appears to be invoking a natural implication of retributive justice: he has not only the obligation but a certain entitlement to make settlement, to be reconciled, to have his outlawry ended, and thus to return to his community. His plea is therefore translated, 'he claimed *the right*' to make full payment.[44]

The Homeric value of 'full payment' is indicated by a similar context in *Odyssey* 8. 347–8. Poseidon promises to pay compensation for Ares, whom Hephaestus caught in adultery: he vows before the gods to pay the claim in full, 'all that is due'—*aisima panta*. The latter phrase involves the same sense of 'liability' that we saw in *aitios*. By the very nature of the concept it is understood that this compensation, payment of 'what is due' for the man 'liable', properly remedies the wrong. Poseidon's offer, like that of our defendant, appeals to a sense of intrinsic obligation on both sides to resolve the dispute in this way. But in the shield scene, the plaintiff *refused* to accept *any* compensation; evidently he intended either to take vengeance upon his enemy or to drive him into exile. Thus, rather than merely a matter of the fact or amount of payment, the elders are to decide an issue of grave consequence to the

---

[42] The value of ἀναίνετο is reasonably clear and consistent: as Leaf argued, 'the regular homeric sense of the verb is *refuse*. In two places only is it possible to translate it *deny*, *I* 116, ξ 149; and in both of these it is used absolutely, not of denying a fact, but of repudiating an idea.'

[43] Cf. Steinwenter, *Streitbeendigung*, 34 n. 3. Wolff, 'Origin of Litigation', 37 n. 18, passes off this objection by invoking the 'rigidity of primitive procedure' which 'does not allow qualified assertions'. Wolff's conclusion on ἀποδοῦναι is based upon an earlier study of procedure and usage in Hellenistic and Roman times, *TAPA* 72 (1941), 427. The scholiast (above n. 39) may be disregarded, as he misinterprets the setting as a formal trial on the classical model.

[44] For the value of εὔχετο, 'claim the right,' Leaf, *Iliad*, App. I, p. 611, cites *Od.* 5. 450, ἱκέτης . . . εὔχομαι εἶναι, meaning 'I claim the right of a suppliant'. Bonner and Smith object (i. 33) that 'one who insisted on the right [to pay] could scarcely be said to pay all'—but the parallel at *Od.* 8. 347–8 proves that this may be precisely the case. In support of this interpretation—that the killer may 'claim the right' to make settlement, see now R. Westbrook's study based on Near Eastern and Mycenean parallels, 'The Trial Scene in the *Iliad*', *HSCP* 94 (1992), 54–76, esp. 71–4.

community. Does the outcast retain some vestigial right to reclaim his place within the group? Is the plaintiff obligated by the prevailing conventions of retributive justice to weigh certain factors toward reconciliation?

Disregarding these questions, Wolff assumes rather much about the roles of the various participants: (1) There stands behind the scene the figure of a magistrate who first intervened to protect the defendant from his pursuer and then submitted the case for judgement, much as a magistrate might do in the historical period. (2) The assembled folk (*laoi*), 'partisans on both sides', are none the less to be final authority in our primitive trial. Also doubtful is (3) the role that Wolff assigns to the *istōr* : this figure will decide the case based upon his knowledge of the facts, and his wisdom will be recognized by the people's acclamation. The first assumption is plausible, perhaps, but unsupported by the Homeric evidence. And the role that Wolff assigns to the 'jury of the people' as the ultimate authority seems a gross exaggeration of their informal participation.[45] There is no suggestion that the people's acclaim is to be decisive. On the contrary, the people are divided, 'partisans on both sides' (*amphis arōgoi*), whereas Homeric judgement requires a solution that is non-partisan (*mēd' ep' arōgēi*, *Il.* 23. 574). The fact that the defendant makes his declaration before the multitude does not necessarily mean that the multitude will decide.

The council of tribal elders is the only body to whom judicial competence is attributed, and their role seems proper to the aristocratic regimes of the Homeric world, where Mycenean monarchs no longer held sway but broader polities had yet to evolve. Thus at the centre of the tableau are the elders seated within the shrine; the voices of partisans have been heard, but the herald's sceptre is passed among the elders.

Their method of 'judgement'—*dikazein*—is likely to be much the same as that indicated by the same term in the dispute of Menelaus

---

[45] In *dikai phonou* the *dēmos* had no corresponding role (unless we accept the view that juries of the people replaced the *ephetai*). And in the trial-scene, 'declaring to the people' apparently implies 'full payment' (from the preceding line): i.e. defendant presents before the assembly of elders and people the payment (in sum or in token) that he is prepared to make. Leaf, *Iliad*, 305, notes parallels at 12. 280, 15. 97, and 23. 333–4. Similarly, in response to Menelaus' oath-challenge (23. 573–9), Antilochus must lay his hand upon the horse that is at stake if he is to claim it by oath. Westbrook, 'Trial Scene', 74, concludes from Mycenean parallels that the *dēmos* in fact refers to the council of elders as official authority for the community, distinct from *laoi*.

and Antilochus in book 23. In that case Menelaus called for the lords to give judgement, and he himself, as foremost in rank, began the process by challenging Antilochus to assert his claim under oath. In the same way the elders in the shield-scene will challenge the rival claimants to make formal proof of their claims by oath or testimony of witnesses or conceivably by some other test. The tribal elders do not deliberate as a body to decide the outcome by vote or decree; rather, each in order (by rank or other priority) will propose a means of proof that should be self-evident from the claims themselves. The prevailing elder's judgement, like the judgement of Solomon, will defer to the claims of the litigants but challenge their good faith. Thus the litigants themselves, by their willing agreement or implicit consent, will determine the author of 'straightest justice'. This interpretation has been persuasively argued by Gerhard Thür; it is not without its difficulties, but in sum it appears to be the most workable model of archaic judgement.[46]

Thür's theory relies upon a distinction in the methods of resolving disputes indicated in archaic texts by the terms *dikazein*, which I render as 'give judgement,' and *krinein* or *diagnōnai*, 'decide' or distinguish between conflicting claims. *Dikazein* in archaic legalistic contexts regularly seems to denote a method of judgement that is largely dictated by a decisive oath or body of witnesses. *Krinein* and *diagnōnai* usually involve what we might rather call discretionary judgement (*freie Beweiswürdigung*).[47] This long-standing distinction was challenged by Talamanca, and Thür's theory has been somewhat eclipsed.[48] Talamanca points to other passages in Homer where *dikazein* apparently involves discretionary judgement; and in the laws inscribed at Gortyn, Talamanca insists upon a broader, more complex value for the key term. But the principal Homeric evidence consists of two passages where *dikazein*

[46] Thür, 'Zum δικάζειν bei Homer', 426–44; cf. Primmer, 'Homerische Gerichtsszenen', 5–13; Hommel, 'Gerichtsszene', 30 n. 84. The view that the litigants will choose straightest judgement was anticipated by M. Gelzer, *PhWoch* 42 (1922), 900. For the opposing view see M. Talamanca, 'Δικάζειν e κρίνειν nelle testimonianze greche piu antioche' in *Symposion 1974* (1979), 103–33, with Thür's response, pp. 133–5; cf. Humphreys, 'Discourse of Law', 466–7.

[47] This is a view going back to Latte, *Heiliges Recht* (1920), 39–41; V. Ehrenberg, *Die Rechtsidee im frühen Griechentum* (Leipzig, 1921), 96–8; followed *inter al.* by Maschke, *Willenslehre* (*passim*); Steinwenter, *Streitbeendigung*, 45–8. Wolff also adopted this basic distinction.

[48] 'Δικάζειν e κρίνειν', 103–33. Gagarin, *EGL* esp. 29–30, also rejects Thür's arguments.

designates the judgement of Zeus and a third describing arbitration.[49] The two instances describing the judgement of Zeus may mean nothing for the special context of the trial scene, where the author emphasizes legal process. The *dikē* of Zeus is a function of his autocratic power: his judgements are absolute, without reference to opposing views. And the last passage, describing the parties to an arbitration as *dikazomenoi*, in the middle voice, offers little proof that *dikazein*, in the active, is synonymous with the arbitrator's 'decision'. The evidence of the laws at Gortyn are more decisive and here Thür's thesis is in principle confirmed.

2.2   Judgement in the Law of Gortyn

The Law Code of Gortyn, like the extant copy of Draco's Law, is an inscription of the fifth century that preserves statutes of an earlier time, perhaps going back to an era not much later than the final composition of the *Iliad* and certainly comparable in legal development to the social order of Homer's audience.[50] The archaic character of these ordinances, inscribed in an out-of-the-way corner of Crete, should surprise no one: in law as in linguistics the most isolated outpost of a culture is likely to be the most conservative. Here, none the less, Talamanca disputes Thür's thesis that archaic 'judgement' requires the parties to prove their claims by oath or other formal proof; *dikazein* in the Gortyn Code, he argues, sometimes implies discretionary judgement; the specific instances that he cites are, however, misconstrued.[51]

---

[49] The judgement of Zeus: *Il.* 1. 536–43, κρυπτάδια φρονέοντα δικάζεμεν; 8. 425–31, φρονέων ἐνὶ θύμῳ δικαζέτω. Arbitration of private suits: *Od.* 12. 437–41 (simile) κρίνων νείκεα πολλὰ δικαζομένων. So too Hesiod's complaint against the 'crooked *judgement*' of 'gift-devouring kings' (*WD* 39, 221) offers little support to Talamanca's argument, as it may as easily be construed as precisely the kind of automatic judgement that Thür supposes (so Humphreys also reads the Hesiod passages, 'Discourse of Law', 466–7); conversely abuse of discretionary judgement is indicated in *Il.* 16. 387–8, as σκολίας κρίνωσι θέμιστας. Talamanca also adduces *Od.* 11. 547 (judgement for the arms of Achilles) παῖδες δὲ Τρώων δίκασαν καὶ Παλλὰς Ἀθήνη. But this passage was bracketed by Aristarchus for good reason (though Talamanca protests, 108–9 n. 10).

[50] The archaic character of the Gortyn Code (though not 'primitive' in the sense of earliest legislation) is generally acknowledged, e.g. by Diamond, *Primitive Law* 22. Its provisions are readily paralleled in the early lawgivers; see, for instance, Gagarin, *EGL* 69, 74.

[51] Thus Talamanca, 'Δικάζειν ε κρίνειν' 124–5, argues that the phrase in col. 1. 35–6, 'a year after *the judge has given judgement*' (καταδικάκσει ὁ δικαστάς), refers

The Great Inscription at Gortyn (*IC* 4. 72) shows a remarkably consistent distinction between the magistrate's 'judgement' (in dialect *dikaddēn* or *dikaksai*), and his 'decision under oath' (*omnunta krinēn*): 'judgement' is required in cases where formal proof, by oath of the principals or testimony of witnesses, determines an automatic resolution prescribed by law; 'decision' by the magistrate under oath is required where there are conflicting claims and the law prescribes no automatic resolution. Thus in case of unlawful seizure of persons (col. I. 1–14), where the charge is not disputed, 'let the judge *give judgement* for release'; but if the defendant denies it and there are no witnesses, the law prescribes 'let the judge *decide* under oath'. Regarding seizure of a slave, if a witness testifies, 'let [the magistrate] *judge* in accord with the witness' (19–20); but if testimony is conflicting or inconclusive, 'let him *decide* under oath' (22–4).[52] The general principle is recognized in column XI: 'In matters where it is written to *give judgement* in accord with witnesses or for oath of denial, let him give judgement as it is written; otherwise let him *decide* under oath.'

There are, moreover, a number of provisions in particular that tend to substantiate Thür's model of archaic judgement. In a divorce dispute where the claims are irreconcilable, if the husband denies that he is to blame, 'let the judge *decide* under oath'. In division of property, if the husband claims that the wife has taken property to which she is not entitled but she denies it, 'let the judge *give judgement* that she swear an oath of denial by Artemis'; if she does so, her right to the property is confirmed; if she does not, the property evidently reverts to the husband (col. II. 52–III. 7). Thus the magistrate is to act just as Thür would imagine the elders proceeding in the

back to rulings described as 'decision under oath' (ὀμνύντα κρίνεν, 23–4); but the immediate reference is to the 'judgement' of default in lines 28–9 (δικάκσατο).

[52] A similar automaticity is indicated in property disputes (col. V. 31–4), where the magistrate is instructed to judge in favour of those willing to accept a division of property, and against those who refuse; but he is to decide under oath in case of conflicting claims (39–44). Again, in case of inherited debts or obligations (col. IX. 29–31), 'let the judge give judgement in accord with testimony . . . let him give judgement for the plaintiff if he and witnesses swear' (cf. 50–1). This aspect of early judgement as Beweisurteil, an order for the plaintiff to assert his claim under oath (at Gortyn δικάκσαι ἀπομόσαι), Latte regarded as a common feature of Hellenic law: *Heiliges Recht*, 8–17. Gagarin disputes this model, and seems to have established some instances of 'accidental', non-formal witnesses at Gortyn (i.e. verifying facts rather than formal claims): see esp. 'Witnesses in the Gortyn Laws', *GRBS* 25 (1984), 345–9.

shield scene: each will call for one litigant or the other to assert his claim by oath or other formal test. This principle is further illustrated by the rule for settling a breach of partnership (col. IX. 43–54): 'if witnesses testify . . . let the judge give judgement according to the testimony'; but without decisive testimony the judge is to give *judgement for the plaintiff to choose* the means of resolution, whether by exculpatory oath or other proof. This provision indicates that beneath the formulae of the extant law there is embedded an even more fundamental consensual principle, whereby the litigants themselves are to acknowledge the 'straightest judgement'.

There is no direct treatment of homicide in the Great Code at Gortyn—it is not unlikely that homicide was left largely to private settlement.[53] But the principle of automatic resolution by oath and oath-witness is clearly demonstrated in the one situation that most closely approaches the question of the respective rights of the parties in a homicide. In cases of adultery the plaintiff is to seize the offender and demand payment from his family in the presence of witnesses; if the offender's family fail to ransom him within five days, 'his captors may do with him as they wish'. But if the accused or his kinsmen object that he was taken by deception or entrapment, then his captors must swear, with witnesses to their oath, that he was taken in adultery and not by deception (*IC* 4. 72, col. II. 27–45)—that is, they must swear to the rightness of their claim, disavowing malicious intent or any contributory responsibility on their own part. This purely formal process assures an automatic resolution without intervention by the state, even though a retributive homicide may be the result.[54]

Thus in the Gortyn Code we have all of the elements required in Thür's reconstruction: the role of the magistrate is to propose resolution by oath or other proof test; alternative means of resolution are proposed; final settlement is for the parties themselves to

---

[53] Homicide is mentioned in an early fragment, *IC* 4. 9, but there is no sign of a law of homicide like Draco's. Similarly in the Code of Hammurabi there is no general provision for homicide, though there are no less than six special provisions relevant to homicide disputes, from which G. R. L. Driver and J. C. Miles conclude that blood feud was still anticipated, with settlement ordinarily involving compensation: *The Babylonian Laws* (Oxford, 1952), 314–17.

[54] Automatic resolution by oath, in the absence of other evidence, is also indicated in Solon, F42 Ruschenbusch: τὸν ἐγκαλούμενον, ἐπειδὰν μήτε συμβόλαια ἔχῃ μήτε μάρτυρας, ὀμνύναι. The law is cited, with doubtful relevance, where the scholiast has glossed the term δοξασταί at Ant. 5. 94, 'judges are they who decide which of the litigants swears rightly' (εὐορκεῖ).

decide; and this consensual arrangement functions even in cases where a retributive homicide is the likely outcome. It is true that the extant statutes at Gortyn generally prescribe specific means of settlement, and the open-ended judgement that Thür has described has only the one parallel (col. IX. 43–54). But statute law by its very nature would tend to specify the procedure. Otherwise the judges at Gortyn played much the same role as did the elders in the Homeric trial scene. Their method is, in fact, consistent with the principle that Wolff himself defined: the judges are to 'state the right', to recognize the formal conditions for legitimate exercise of self-help. The outcome is not a verdict imposed by sovereign command upon one party or the other. Its social function is rather to reconcile the hostile parties: each is to recognize the claims of the other, thus disavowing the cycle of vendetta that would inevitably arise if one side were faced with an unacceptable outcome.[55] Contrary to Wolff's reconstruction, the archaic judges are not called upon as experts in the facts of the case; they might perhaps have incidental familiarity with the circumstances, but they are expert only in the procedures of settlement. Judgement prevails by reducing the litigants' claims to a formulation they cannot dispute.

2.3   Witness, Oath, and *Istōr*

The elders constitute the sole judicial authority in the Homeric trial scene, there is no supernumerary magistrate and no verdict of the people such as Wolff suggested. The final figure in Wolff's scenario is the *istōr* who supposedly rendered straightest judgement by firsthand knowledge of the case. *Istōr* in archaic and archaizing usage sometimes means 'expert' or 'skilled practitioner'. But the *istōr*'s expertise does not appear to consist in knowledge of specific facts but in mastery of a general area of endeavour. Thus the Muses in the Homeric *Hymn to Selene* 1–2 are 'skilled at song'; and the

---

[55] Thus reasons Latte, *Heiliges Recht*, 10–11. I cannot follow Gagarin's objection that we know of 'no homicide in the epics [giving] rise to vendetta' (*Drakon*, 18). Surely the aftermath of the suitors' slaying in the *Odyssey* would indicate that such consequences were expected and only averted by extraordinary means. Similarly in the Orestes saga, that 'the killings of Aigisthos and Klytaimnestra are not avenged in turn' is the exception proving the rule and making precedent for the special case. The sacrifice of Iphigenia—cause for Clytemnestra's revenge—is not found in Homer because, in context, he emphasizes Orestes' righteous vengeance: J. March, *The Creative Poet* (London, 1987), 85.

Amazons are, in the words of Bacchylides (*Epinician* 9. 43–4), 'skilled in spearmanship'.[56] The more prominent meaning of *istōr*, however, is 'witness'. In some instances *istōr* appears to mean no more than 'witness' to the fact, but even here the *istōr* has an enabling function, guaranteeing some implicit claim of right or obligation. More common and of particular interest for our inquiry are those passages where *istores*, divine and mortal, are invoked as witnesses and guardians of an oath or claim. Thus in the Hippocratic Oath, to cite the most famous example, the gods of healing are invoked as *istores* (or, rather, in dialect, *histores*).[57] In drama the gods are invoked as 'joint witnesses' or guarantors, *synistores*, when mortals are to witness a vow or an act that implicitly asserts a claim.[58] The mortal role of *istōr* as a recorder and guarantor of such 'processual acts' asserting some legal claim or status is indicated in an inscription at Orchomenos, where one *istōr* is witness in each of several contracts.[59] Again, at Thespiae, in a record of emancipation, several citizens are named as *istores*. The balance of the evidence would suggest that the Homeric *istōr* was a witness of this kind: his function was to validate acts of legal process.

What was later to be the ordinary term for 'witness', *martys* (Homeric *martyros*), was commonly used of gods as witnesses and guardians of oaths, but in the Homeric poems *martyros* is nowhere used of a mortal witness to oath or other proof in settlement of a dispute.[60] Mortals are called *martyroi* to witness acts of injustice—

---

[56] Heracles in *Od.* 21. 26 is 'mightily skilled (*epiistōr*) in great deeds'. Cf. Plato, *Cratylus* 406b: (of Artemis) ἀρετῆς ἵστορα τὴν θεόν; 407c, Ἥφαιστον . . . φάεος ἵστορα.

[57] So, too, in the ephebic oath, by which young men upon eligibility for military service affirmed their loyalty: καὶ τὰ ἱερὰ τὰ πάτρια τιμήσας. ἵστορες θεοί, κτλ. (Pollux 8. 106).

[58] Thus in Eur. *Supp.* (1165–76; cf. 1188–94) Theseus calls the gods as *synistores* to witness his service. In Soph. *Ant.* 542, Hades and the gods below are divine witnesses, *synistores*, not simply of the burial but of Antigone's devotion; they are implicit guarantors of whatever honour she may have in this world or the next based upon that claim.

[59] For the Ϝίστωρ as witness to agreements at Orchomenos, *c.*222–200 BC, cf. E. Schwyzer, *Dialectorum Graecarum exempla epigraphica potiora* (Leipzig, 1923), 523. 64, p. 255; at Thespiae, *IG* VII. 1179 (date uncertain). See now R. Connor's study 'The *Histor* in History', in R. Rosen and J. Farrell (eds.), *Nomodeiktes* (Ann Arbor, Mich., 1993), 3–15, esp. 6–12: the historian, in origin, fulfilled 'a crucial social role, the development of fair judgements and the formation of social consensus' (12).

[60] Cf. *Il.* 3. 277–80, where Agamemnon invokes Zeus, Helius, and the gods below to witness the agreement for single combat between Menelaus and Alexander;

that is, to witness the facts of a case rather than processual acts: thus Achilles says to the heralds who come to take Briseis from him, 'You two shall be witnesses before gods and men' of the wrong in the act (9. 338–9).

Conversely, it is a consistent feature of the Gortyn Code that the role of witnesses (in dialect *maityres*) is not to testify to the facts of the main issue but to the 'performance of processual acts'. In the settlement of adultery charges, for instance, the witnesses are not called upon to vouch for the fact of adultery but rather that the plaintiff has properly made his claim to the family. Then if ransom is not duly paid, they are to witness his oath, that he has taken the culprit righteously and not by entrapment, thus establishing his right to execute his claim upon the adulterer.[61]

In the Homeric poems, however, there is no clear instance where *martyros* identifies mortal witnesses serving in this role; the rare word *istōr* appears to be a specialized term for this function, as witness and guarantor of oath and other processual acts.[62] Such is the meaning in the only other Homeric passage where *istōr* occurs: *Iliad* 23. 486–7. In the middle of the chariot race (to which Antilochus' dispute with Menelaus is sequel), Ajax the son of Oileus boasts that his countryman Diomedes was first to round the turn, and Idomeneus in anger suggests what we would call a side bet: 'Come, let us both pledge a tripod or a cauldron, and make Agamemnon our *istōr*, which team of the two was ahead (at the turn).' Agamemnon is not called upon to resolve the fact in dispute by keener sight or better vantage, since the teams would long since

22. 255, Hector, facing Achilles, pleads for a covenant that neither defile the body of the other; 'the gods be best witnesses and overseers of agreements'; 7. 76–86, Zeus as *epimartyros; Od.* 16. 422–3, Zeus, *martyros* of suppliants.

[61] This feature of the code was long ago noticed by J. W. Headlam, 'Procedure of the Gortynian Inscription', *JHS* 13 (1892–3), 51; cf. *IC* 4. 72, col. 2. 28–45, for witnesses in adultery cases. Gagarin, again, argues against this processual function in 'The Function of Witnesses at Gortyn', *Symposion* 1985 (1989), 29–54; cf. *GRBS* 75 (1984), 345–9.

[62] The term derives from the root Ϝιδ-, from which derive εἶδον and οἶδα ('saw' and 'know'), and we would therefore expect the *istōr* to affirm what he has witnessed at first hand. This function is perhaps reflected in the familiar formula by which the parties to homicide disputes will affirm their claims on direct knowledge, εὖ οἶδα (see esp. Ch. 6. §2.3). There is also a suggestive cognate term found in the archaic material by the lexicographers and commentators: *iduos* (or *iduios*). Eustathius (12th c. AD) commenting upon the Homeric *istōr*, notes that Draco and Solon used as a corresponding term *iduos*; Hesychius (5th c. AD) gives the puzzling explanation s.v. ἰδυῖοι· μάρτυρες ἢ οἱ τὰς φονικὰς δίκας κρίνοντες, οἱ δὲ συνίστορας.

have rounded the turn. The matter will be decided by the chario-
teers when they have finished the race—the first-hand witnesses
will be *martyroi*. The chief lord among those present will serve as
witness of the oaths and guarantor of the wager.

The most probable role of the *istōr* in the trial scene is such as we
find in later usage and in the role of witnesses in the laws of Gortyn:
he was witness to claims and processual acts rather than the facts
of the crime. And it is reasonable to suppose—as Wolff himself
supposed—that this witness, at whose hands both parties are 'eager
to reach an end' (*peirar helesthai*), is also to be identified with the
elder who speaks straightest judgement. It is clear that the *istōr* is to
be in some way responsible for the solution, and the term describing this 'end' or limit—*peirar*—may be especially appropriate to
the elders' function. Similar language describes the tools of the
bronze-smith's craft, *peirata technēs* (*Od.* 3. 432–4).[63] The means of
resolving the dispute that the elders devise are 'instruments of
judgement'—as it were, *peirata dikēs*. They do not impose a verdict; they provide a device for the litigants themselves to choose.
Each party gives a talent in 'consideration' of this service, to bind
the author of straightest judgement as a witness of their settlement
in any future dispute.

2.4   The Issue before the Elders

Such is the procedure described in the Homeric trial scene. The
role of the elders is to devise tests of the litigants' convictions in
order to reconcile otherwise irreconcilable claims in a dispute that
threatens the community. In this role, as we shall see, they prefig-
ure the kings who gave judgement in archaic Athens. And in both
settings the very nature of the procedure tells us something about
the kinds of issues anticipated in homicide disputes.

We have seen that the language of our text tends to disprove
Wolff's explanation that the point in dispute was a simple question
of whether the defendant had fulfilled an earlier agreement for settlement, and the nature of the procedure makes his explanation all
the less likely. A financial dispute of this kind could easily have

---

[63] This is Thür's suggestion, 'Zum δικάζειν bei Homer', 439. The large amount
is consistent with Hesiod's complaint against 'gift-devouring kings' who give
'crooked judgement', and Herodotus' tale of Deioces (1. 96–103), who ruled the
Medes through skill in judgement.

been resolved without invoking the assembled elders, with the body of the community in attendance. If the terms of settlement had been decided by an earlier agreement, then payment should have been guaranteed by pledge of security or bond (*enguē*), just as Hephaestus demands that Poseidon give surety for compensation of his claim against Ares (*Od.* 8. 347–56). If the defendant failed to make good on the agreement, the surety would have been forfeit. If an earlier composition had been made without surety, then witnesses should have been required, and any later dispute could have been settled by their testimony, just as property disputes were decided in the Gortyn Code. Thus I conclude that the promise of 'full payment' has to do with claims of liability yet to be resolved.

Now Gagarin has suggested one plausible interpretation that allows for an earlier agreement, and his explanation makes a likely connection between the Homeric trial and the issues anticipated in Draco's law.[64] The Homeric scene readily suggests a dispute where settlement was accepted by *other* members of the family, but this plaintiff vowed that *he* would not abide by it. This sort of problem appears to be a major concern in Draco's legislation. The general provisions describing who is eligible to prosecute and make settlement are clearly intended to resolve such disputes: settlements are declared invalid if there is any disagreement among the eligible kinsmen—'he who opposes shall prevail'. Gagarin's scenario does not answer all the questions, but it has the advantage of taking the Greek at face value and it is especially suited to the symbolism of our Homeric trial. The emblem on Achilles' shield focuses upon the *process* of judgement. The negotiated settlement of disputes in the City at Peace stands opposite the mayhem of the City at War. From this singular perspective we wonder at the very viability of that process and the social pressures that sustain it.

The operative principle of retributive justice suggests an intrinsic obligation on both sides. When the plaintiff declares the offender *aitios*, 'liable', there is the natural expectation that the latter should be able to resolve the claim by paying 'all that is due', *aisima panta*. As Ajax counselled Achilles, even a man whose son or brother has been slain will accept compensation and be reconciled. The issue that looms large in the paradigm of judgement before the elders is the validity of this very principle. The plaintiff refuses to

[64] Gagarin, *Drakon*, 15–19.

accept any settlement. Can he in good faith, before the gods and the assembled community, deny the killer's plea for peaceful resolution? The moral onus upon the plaintiff becomes all the more compelling, if, as Gagarin supposes, even his own kinsmen are willing to reconcile. Can he defy the overwhelming force of custom and community interests that even his kinsmen have acknowledged?

The question we would like to have answered, since volitional terms are so prominent in Draco's Law, is whether the weight of malice and moral innocence entered into the Homeric dispute. In the Homeric trial scene there is no straightforward indication that the killer's intent was even a matter for consideration, and the apparent disregard of *mens rea* in other archaic material has made scholars all the more suspicious of our inscription. But we must not conclude that the proceedings familiar to Homer's audience had no place for such considerations. A plea for reconciliation by its very nature implies repentance, and repentance after the fact may be very near to denying malice in the act. The decision to grant or deny settlement lies ultimately with the injured party: he may rightfully disregard state of mind. But the elders may challenge him to confront the issue, to acknowledge or deny the killer's plea of innocence under oath. We have seen the moral weight of intentionality not only in the pathos of Patroclus but also in the oath-challenge that Menelaus addresses to Antilochus: he may exercise his claim if he swears that he did not *willingly* defraud. Similarly the archaic procedure preserved in the Gortyn Code requires that those who apprehend an adulterer must swear that they have taken him in the act and without entrapment—that is, without wilful deception—if they are to execute their claim. The consequences are much the same: a failure of settlement may lead to a retributive homicide. The elders, unconstrained by statutory prescriptions, would therefore address every conceivable consideration, calling upon the plaintiff to answer any claim of innocence or justification the defendant may offer. Thus the elders give judgement to 'each side in turn'.[65] This alternation is not a sign of rivalry among the elders; they are not characterized as 'partisan' like the bystanders. It suggests that they will address the oath-challenge or other test of conviction first to one, then to the other of the two litigants. And in

---

[65] The adverb ἀμοιβηδίς suggests alternation, 'each side (of two) in turn,' rather than simply 'one after the other'; thus Eustathius glosses ἀμοιβηδίς as ἐναλλάξ.

this process innocence of malice or other mitigation may have easily entered in.[66]

The audience of the *Iliad* probably assumed that the judgements of the elders, addressed to 'each side in turn', would be challenges such as these. (1) Let the plaintiffs swear that defendant is guilty of their kinsman's slaying. (2) Let the defendant swear that he did not willingly kill. (3) The plaintiffs may then be challenged to swear that the killer acted with malice aforethought, in the literal sense of *pronoia*. As we have seen this primitive measure of intentionality is especially suited to the plaintiffs' oath: they should be able to swear to their conviction of malice revealed in overt acts of prior design. Otherwise (4) they may be called upon to swear that the defendant is liable for the killing 'even if he killed without malice aforethought'. In the latter case terms of settlement might be formulated as a judgement for the parties to affirm under oath: (5) let the killer vow to abandon his homeland for a prescribed period and arrange suitable payment; (6) the plaintiffs shall renounce further vendetta and reconcile with the defendant on these terms, thus ending his outlawry. But if a plaintiff absolutely refuses to reconcile with the killer—as our plaintiff in the Homeric trial appears to do—he may then be called upon to affirm explicitly that he will deny settlement and show no mercy, even though his kinsman was slain without malice. Against the last proposition, social conscience may have weighed heavily. But the elders have no authority to *enforce* a settlement. It is only by such tests of conviction that the plaintiff is made to reckon with the killer's intent.[67]

Before procedures were devised to define the question at issue, such as evolved historically in Athens, the process of judgement must necessarily have comprehended a range of possible issues. The plaintiff is likely to insist upon one aspect of the case; the defendant, on another. The method of alternating judgements in the form of challenges to oath or other test of conviction was a natural device for identifying and addressing the issue that was crucial to the parties themselves. As we turn to examine the method of judgement in Draco's law, let us bear in mind the Homeric prototype.

[66] See Westbrook, 'Trial Scene', 71–2, for comparative evidence of the distinction between aggravated homicide and a killing with mitigating factors.

[67] Thür, assuming only questions of fact can be at issue, suggests that the focus of the elders' deliberation would be such issues as which gods to invoke or whether combat or ordeal should decide the case: 'Zum δικάζειν bei Homer', 436.

Primitive judgement is by its very nature discursive, not constrained by statutory prescription or formalistic conventions. The social dynamics dictate the method. The process that we have described is not, strictly speaking, 'judicial' litigation such as Wolff supposed. It is a more essential and direct method of resolving disputes, designed to assure that the litigants acknowledge the moral burden of their claims, constrained by social conscience when coercive command of the state was ineffectual. The historical procedures for homicide originated in a tribal aristocracy whose factions retained considerable autonomy, and the rules devised for that context persisted, as we shall see, long after the social premises of that system had lost validity. In the following section we shall reconstruct the workings of the court that Draco devised, to determine the questions at issue and the nature of the argument in the earliest procedure for jury trial.

§3. Intentionality and Procedure in Draco's Law

The common view of Draco's trial procedure has been greatly influenced by H. J. Wolff's study 'The Origin of Judicial Litigation among the Greeks' and I have therefore treated him as a hostile witness—and one all the more troublesome because his contributions in other areas of ancient law have been so profound. This received opinion of Draconian procedure relies upon two problematic assumptions that Wolff's study fostered. There is first the notion that the aristocratic council on the Areopagus was the ancient homicide court before Draco, holding jurisdiction over an 'undivided homicide delict'. By this view the Draconian justices were established specifically to hear cases in the newly defined category of unintentional homicide, a division of what had been previously the undivided jurisdiction of the Areopagus. This assumption is, as we have seen (Ch. 1 §1), unsound: we have no evidence beyond the charter myths to suggest that the Areopagus council was an ancient homicide court before Solon, and we have credible testimony to the contrary. Second, assuming that the Areopagus court had given final verdict in homicide cases before Draco, scholars generally follow Wolff in supposing that the role of the tribal kings must therefore have been subordinate to that verdict even before Draco—that the role of the tribal kings 'to give judgement' was then merely a formal pronouncement of the verdict that the *ephetai* or Areopagus had voted. The opening provisions are thus understood to mean, 'The kings shall judge guilty either the perpetrator or the planner' (*vel sim.*). This interpretation strains the syntax: the verb *dikazein* is not found in comparable usage with indirect statement or predicate accusative ('judge him guilty').[68] And Wolff's reconstruction runs counter to the archaic parallels, whereas the arrangement of Draco's law itself suggests a natural connection.

3.1 The Judgement of the Tribal Kings

In the archaic material that parallels Draco's law, 'to give judgement'—*dikazein*—ordinarily describes a function that resolves the dispute in and of itself. In the Homeric context as in the Gortyn code, he who gives judgement calls upon the litigant to establish his claim of right by oath or affirmation of witnesses. And it is the more natural assumption that Draco's 'judgement' had much the same meaning as it has in the parallel material nearest to it in time and legal development. The burden of proof should rest with those who would argue to the contrary, that Draco's 'judgement' must mean something other than what it means for Homer and at Gortyn.

It is inherently more likely that the seventh-century lawgiver envisioned a procedure whereby many, perhaps a majority of cases were to be settled solely upon the judgement of the kings: the Draconian *basileis*, like the Homeric elders, attempted to devise a means of consensual resolution by oath or other test of conviction. If this judgement was accepted or unopposed, then the case was settled.[69] Consensual resolution was an abiding principle in settlement of homicide disputes among the Greeks. The state was slow to enforce a verdict in disputes between the victim's kinsmen and the killer's kin where a ruling unacceptable to either side would not long delay the cycle of violence.

---

[68] Δικάζειν is occasionally used with internal accusative (= δίκην/δίκας), but accusative of persons is not used with the simplex (as opposed to the compound καταδικάζειν = 'condemn').

[69] Gagarin, *Drakon*, 47–8, allows for a verdict of the *basileis* in cases of voluntary exile but seems to assume their ordinary function was to pronounce the verdict of *ephetai* (*EGL* 89); cf. Bonner and Smith, i. 79. For final judgement by the *basileis*, see Ch. 3 §2.1, on the Prytaneum; and §2.3, regarding Andoc. 1. 78 on those condemned by the kings at the Delphinium.

The opening provision in Draco's law itself suggests that the judgement of the kings preceded jury trial, and, if uncontested, was to be the final resolution: 'even if without malice [a man kill] let him be exiled; and the kings shall give judgement.' The lawgiver expects that in most cases the killer would go voluntarily into exile, whether the killing had been intentional or not (as in the Homeric examples). The kinsmen of the victim would then formalize their claim upon oath by judgement of the kings. Having thus established their right, they could then deal with the killer on their own terms, either by putting him to death if he were apprehended or by confiscating his property if his family could not persuade them to accept a settlement. In some cases, perhaps very few even into the seventh century, the defendant might take refuge at a shrine and invoke a hearing by the tribal kings, perhaps pleading some excuse or justification. At their prompting he might declare his readiness to pay compensation, as did the defendant in the shield-scene: he would undergo a period of exile and otherwise satisfy the plaintiffs' claims. If the parties accept such an arrangement, then the judgement of the kings is final. If, however, the claims of the kinsmen and the plea of the defendant are irreconcilable, then the archaic mechanism of justice falters, the defendant refuses to abandon his home and the prosecutors seek vengeance. It would appear to be precisely at this juncture, where conflicting claims could not be resolved by consensual judgement, that a more authoritative body was invoked by Draco. The kings would exercise the same judicial competence they had previously in those disputes where a consensual settlement could be arranged. Their judgement was therefore not subordinate to the decision of the *ephetai* but was a prior and alternative means of resolving the dispute and one that was often sufficient in itself.

This mechanism of judgement suggests a solution to the most puzzling difficulty in Draco's law: how could intentionality enter into the reckoning if the same rule of exile and *aidesis* governed the unintentional killer and the intentional murderer? The opening words of the law itself seem to reflect a standard formulation of the kings' judgement calling upon the litigants to acknowledge intentionality—if a man kill, with or without malice, the kings shall give judgement to that effect. They will call upon the plaintiffs to swear to their conviction of malice aforethought or to affirm that the defendant is liable for the killing though he killed without malice.

The question of the killer's intent was thus put to the plaintiffs. *Mens rea* remained essentially a criterion of private settlement. It was not ordinarily an issue for the justices to decide.

3.2 The Issue before the *Ephetai*

In this section we shall draw what conclusions we can about the original issues before Draco's justices. This inquiry is fraught with its own problems of authenticity, and it involves us once again in the question of how intentionality entered into legal reasoning. The inscription includes varying forms of reference to the *ephetai*, and some commentators have regarded this variation as a sign of interpolation or abridgement. The judges are sometimes named by their formal title as 'the justices' (*ephetai*, lines 13, 29, 35–6); sometimes, by their title and number, as 'the fifty-one justices' (17), or by the number alone as 'the fifty-one' (19–20, 24–5). This variation has led some to suppose that two different groupings are meant; others have argued that the full reference to 'the fifty-one ephetai' belongs to the original statute, when the office was first established, and the shorter reference must belong to a later period, after the justices were a familiar institution.[70] But even at the original institution of Draco's court the term *ephetai* itself would need no explanation, as it had been used of homicide judges and tribal leaders even earlier.[71] And the full designation, 'the fifty-one ephetai', belongs to a special context, where, as we shall see, there was a pressing need that the justices arrive at a consensus in their verdict and a quorum of fifty-one be in agreement.

3.2.1 The Quorum of Fifty-One

The surviving rules calling for decision by 'the fifty-one' have to do with the special provision for pardon by the phratry, and it is this set of rules in which public officials first take upon themselves the weighing of the killer's intent. In the event that there are no surviving relatives—and apparently only in such cases—the justices will give a special determination on the question of malice. It is only when the family are unable to make this determination for

---

[70] For two bodies of *ephetai*, see G. Smith, 'Dicasts in the Ephetic Courts,' *CP* 19 (1924), 353–8; cf. Stroud, *DL* 48–9. Ruschenbusch regards the variation in terms as a sign of interpolation in his review of Stroud in *Gnomon*, 46 (1974), 815–17; but see further discussion in Ch. 4 §3.

[71] Philippi, *Areopag*, 203; Wallace, *Areopagos Council*, 11–22; cf. Ch. 1 §1.

themselves that the *ephetai* are to intervene in this decision. Otherwise the lawgiver acknowledges the family's traditional right to decide upon settlement without interference by officials of the *polis*. The special procedure for pardon by the phratry is a singular infringement of that autonomy, and it is therefore expedient that the full authority of this body be brought to bear.

By contrast, in disputes prosecuted by surviving kinsmen the main issue before the justices does not appear to be a question of malice but simply a question of whether the defendant is responsible for the outcome and therefore liable to the family. The agent's intent may be seen to affect his role in the causal sequence, but motives and intentions are not in themselves an issue for the justices to decide. We have seen that the rule 'guilty (alike) is the perpetrator or the planner' indicates that the justices' jurisdiction encompassed some intentional killings, but so far as we can see there is no viable mechanism for making separate determinations of malice or innocence of intent. The latter defect is of special relevance here, as we try to reconstruct the role of the *ephetai*.

The distinctive feature of *decision* or discretionary judgement (*diagnōnai*) such as the justices are assigned is that the verdict lies between two mutually exclusive claims, either for the plaintiff or for the defendant. It is quite unlike the open process of *judgement* whereby the tribal chiefs devised a means of consensual resolution, embracing the conflicting claims. In archaic *judgement* such issues as intent might be easily addressed—just as Menelaus challenged Antilochus to claim his prize upon oath that he did not *willingly* do wrong. But a jury of fifty-one, giving a decision between two irreconcilable claims, cannot be expected to deliberate upon secondary issues such as malice. Rather they must decide the issue before them by a straight vote, either for the plaintiff or for the defence.

Now the parties presumably come before the *ephetai* reiterating the same positions they have taken in judgement before the tribal kings, and these claims may certainly involve a dispute about the killer's intentions. The plaintiffs may have sworn to their conviction that defendant did the killing with malice aforethought. But the justices are not called upon to decide state of mind *per se*, to determine whether the killing was intentional or not. They will simply decide whether the defendant is liable. The *ephetai* probably arrived at their decision following a mechanistic model of causation, such as we find in other primitive jury trials. Motives and emotional states are reduced to external causes. Thus in cases where we would identify provocation as a factor affecting state of mind and diminishing responsibility, medieval juries in England distorted the known circumstances to construct a physical barrier: in a case where the killer is plainly driven by inner impulse of rage or fear, not compelled by external force or constraint, he is found none the less to have fought 'with his back to the wall'—though direct evidence has indicated nothing of the kind.[72] By a similar principle the Draconian justices seem to have submerged intentionality within a mechanistic framework. A killer who retreated from his assailant until he had no escape may be acquitted on the grounds that the effective author of the killing was the assailant who drove him to it. Conversely, a defendant who has shown deliberate purpose by overt acts leading up to the killing—bringing a weapon, attacking in ambush—is more easily declared to be 'the killer'. In certain circumstances a defendant could argue that an apparently unintended and accidental act was simply *not his doing*, especially when accident may be construed as divine agency—as Croesus acknowledged that Adrastus was not to blame for the slaying of his son. We shall examine the evidence for this causal model below and investigate the method of argumentation that arose from it in due course. But at this point the archaic procedure itself is sufficient to suggest that intentionality was not ordinarily treated as a separate issue for the justices.

If we have to assume that the justices were required to give a verdict on the question of intent, then I think we shall find them enmeshed in procedures that would probably have been unworkable and practically unparalleled in the Athenian judicial system. Either the justices must (*a*) choose among three or more verdicts— not guilty, guilty with intent, guilty without intent, and perhaps others—or (*b*) they must first decide guilt, and then by a second vote decide the question of intent. A choice among several verdicts (*a*) is unacceptable, as in many cases the vote would be divided three ways and there would be no majority verdict—a plurality verdict, which the majority opposed, would sometimes prevail.

---

[72] For the ingenuity of medieval juries in resolving questions of *mens rea* as mechanical causation, see Horder, *Provocation*, 7–9; cf. Green, 'The Jury and the English Law of Homicide'. For classical argument on provocation, see Chs. 5 §3 and 8 §§2–3.

The second scenario (*b*), where intent is decided by a second verdict, is also unlikely, though there is perhaps a procedural parallel to be found in the classical arrangement for some cases to have the penalty decided by a second vote (*agōnes timētoi*).[73] This would be the most plausible rationale for those who insist that Draco prescribed separate penalties for intentional and unintentional killing. In fact, this kind of solution, with a separate hearing on the second issue, is essentially what Draco devised for the special case of pardon by the phratry. But in ordinary cases this explanation is all but untenable. First of all, we have in the extant homicide law no indication of such double proceedings. Second, if we are to assume that one court of homicide once decided all cases in this way, assigning separate penalties by a second vote, then it is difficult to see how or why the division of jurisdiction among several courts—one for charges of intentional killing, another for unintentional, and so on—was ever to emerge. Why would later procedure dispense with the straighforward mechanism of a second hearing in favour of a much more elaborate arrangement of divided jurisdiction?

The special rule for pardon by the phratry is, to my mind, the decisive evidence on this point. This provision makes it all but certain that the ordinary verdict of the justices was not in itself a determination of intent or a decree for settlement. Only in the special case will the justices give a ruling of unintentional killing. The *phratores* are then to act on behalf of the victim's family to determine whether the exiled homicide will be allowed to return; their authority derives from their kinship (however tenuous). Even in this special instance the officers of the state, the *ephetai*, will not have the last word as to settlement. Though the killer be pronounced innocent of intent by verdict of the justices, the phratry members are not bound by that verdict: they grant pardon only 'if they are willing'. The ordinary presumption and weight of community feeling would be perhaps strongly in favour of a defendant judged innocent of intent, but the justices had no authority to *order* that the phratry grant pardon. They had only authority to *forbid* pardon for intentional murder, and only in this special case. The lawgiver thus allowed an opportunity for those who had gone into exile without trial to return to their homeland when the usual

---

[73] With the exception of certain public suits (*graphai*), these were primarily cases in settlement of contractual obligations. The parallel is intriguing, but see further on this question, Ch. 3 §1.1.

arrangements for settlement were no longer available.[74] Under ordinary circumstances, for those who had gone into exile either voluntarily or by judgement of the kings, a formal verdict by the justices on the question of intent was unnecessary. If there were surviving kin with the power of settlement, only they could absolve the killer. But if there were no eligible kin surviving, then the justices take part with the phratry in a decision that would otherwise have been made solely by the family. The justices will decide whether the killing was unintentional; and even then, if the killer is declared innocent of intent, it is not the justices but the 'kindred' *phratores* who have the power to grant or deny pardon.[75] It is because the justices are here taking upon themselves a power that belonged to the family, that the lawgiver makes the arrangement conditional upon a vote of 'the fifty-one *ephetai*', requiring consensus among the full body, just as he required unanimity for settlement among the eligible kinsmen.

The role of the justices in deciding for or against special pardon is historically significant on two counts: (1) by their verdict, though restricted to exceptional cases, the state might intervene to *forbid* settlement; (2) to justify this intervention the community recognizes by statute the principle of intentionality. It is likely to be the first marginal intervention by officers of the state in a decision that was otherwise entirely a matter of private settlement.

3.2.2 Causation and Retributive Justice

The question of whether the defendant is liable, *aitios*, was for the justices to decide in cases that could not be resolved by the kings' judgement, especially cases involving some question of who is ultimately responsible in a sequence of action. Any considerations of intentionality were subordinate or incidental to a more mechanistic question of retributive justice. The surviving phrase 'guilty of homicide is . . . the planner' looks to the causal sequence. As we

---

[74] If we assume that the determination of innocence in this special case was to be based upon the original charge at an earlier trial—the plaintiffs had then charged the killer as unintentional, and at the later hearing the *ephetai* make their determination on this background—we encounter a host of difficulties. How were the justices to reconstruct the original charge without an official record or verification from next of kin? And this procedure would offer no relief to the more pressing predicament of those who had gone into exile without any sort of trial. See Ch. 3 §2.1.2.

[75] The provision for pardon by the phratry may have served as a safeguard against any attempt to exterminate the rival clan; so guesses Gagarin, *Drakon*, 51. For further arguments on this provision for special pardon, see Ch. 3 §2.1.2.

have seen (§1.1.2) the 'planner' or instigator, *bouleusas*, initiates the causal sequence by his order or decision and is thus indirectly responsible. His intention may be presumed, but that is not the emphasis of the term. The meaningful opposition in this opening provision lies between direct and indirect agency.

There are two further provisions of the extant inscription that point to a fundamental question of causation of this sort: the two surviving rules governing defence against violent attack. The issue is cast in mechanistic terms: the defendant must show that he is not the initiator of the causal sequence, that he acted in immediate response to impetus of another agent.

Cases of homicide arising from brawls and quarrels would regularly require the justices' decision, since by the nature of such events consensual judgement would prove less viable. In the fragmentary provisions on violent quarrel or 'affray' (lines 33–36), it is clear that causal responsibility is assigned to him who first struck or laid violent hands on another. One of the two clauses evidently treated those cases where the aggressor is the killer; the other presumably weighed the responsibility of one who kills in defence.

He who kills in defence against assault is *not* simply acquitted in all cases: this is evident from later legal argument, as we shall see in regard to *Tetralogy* 3, and it is indirectly confirmed by the clauses that follow the law on affray. The lawgiver devoted a special provision (lines 36–8) to defining certain cases where self-defence was indeed grounds for full acquittal: he who kills another 'in immediate defence against violent and unjustified confiscation or abduction' was to suffer no penalty.[76] That a separate statute was required to declare the killer guiltless in this special case shows that otherwise self-defence was not in itself grounds for acquittal, just as a killer who acted 'even without malice aforethought' would expect to suffer the consequences of exile and *aidesis* if he could not show that the killing was not his doing.

In order to acquit the killer outright in the special case of defence against seizure (36–8), it is particularly clear that the justices are to look to specific causal conditions. The killing must come in *immediate* response to an attack that is both *violent* and *wrongful*. In other words, they are not asked to consider state of mind—reasonable fear or outrage—but only the violent impetus that brought on the fatality.

---

[76] *IG* I³ 104. 36–8 = Dem. 23. 60: καὶ ἐὰν φέροντα ἢ ἄγοντα βίᾳ ἀδίκως εὐθὺς ἀμυνόμενος κτείνῃ, νηποινεὶ τεθνάναι.

Thus the provisions on affray and defence against violent seizure (33–8) indicate that the justices were primarily concerned with matters of causation. There are other clauses of Draco's law, however, that have been thought to indicate special protections for the unintentional killer and hence that the distinction between intentional and unintentional killing must have been part of the justices' verdict.

The first of these is the provision that protects the exiled homicide from vendetta (26–30): if one kill or be responsible for killing an exiled homicide who has abided by the terms of his exile, not venturing into the border markets or the athletic and religious gatherings of the Greeks, then the murderer is to be subject to the same penalty, 'on the same terms as in the killing of an Athenian; and the justices shall decide'.[77] But this provision is part of a series of Draconian rules regarding the exiled homicide: homicides who abide by the terms of banishment until they reconcile are protected in various ways; those who violate the terms of exile and trespass in Attica may be put to death with impunity.[78] In these provisions there is no reference to intentional or unintentional killing, and from later law it is clear that even the intentional killer was entitled to some protection in exile.

The other protections that are thought to apply only to unintentional killers are attested in citations by Demosthenes that cannot be restored in the inscription. We shall weigh the authenticity of these citations in the next chapter, but it will be helpful here to anticipate some of the implications. The Draconian law cited in Demosthenes 23. 44 would indicate that the property of some exiled homicides was protected from confiscation, and it is sometimes argued that this protection can only have been given to unintentional homicides.[79]

---

[77] *IG* I³ 104. 26–30 = Dem. 23. 37: ἐὰν δέ τις τὸν ἀνδροφόνον κτείνῃ ἢ αἴτιος ᾖ φόνου, ἀπεχόμενον ἀγορᾶς ἐφορίας καὶ ἄθλων καὶ ἱερῶν Ἀμφικτυονικῶν, ὥσπερ τὸν Ἀθηναῖον κτείναντα, ἐν τοῖς αὐτοῖς ἐνέχεσθαι, διαγιγνώσκειν δὲ τοὺς ἐφέτας. Figueira, 'Death of Draco', 292, concludes that this provision belongs to the era of the first Sacred War (*c.*590); cf. Jeffery, *Archaic Greece* (1976), 73–5.

[78] The Solonian law cited in Dem. 23. 28 contains this cross-reference to earlier, Draconian statute: τοὺς δ' ἀνδροφόνους ἐξεῖναι ἀποκτείνειν ἐν τῇ ἡμεδαπῇ καὶ ἀπάγειν. The phrase ἐν τῇ ἡμεδαπῇ is almost certainly the reading in lines 30–1 of the inscription, and there is an obvious connection of thought between this clause and the one preceding; cf. Stroud, *DL* 54–6; For analysis of Demosthenes' citations see Ch. 3 §1.2.

[79] Ruschenbusch, 'ΦΟΝΟΣ', 140, assumes this provision and the one against vindictive killing of the exiled homicide applied only to the unintentional killer; but cf. Gagarin, *Drakon*, 60–1.

If anyone seize, drive or convey across the border any property belonging to homicides in exile, of those whose property is protected (or not subject to confiscation, *epitima*), he shall owe an equal amount as though he had done so in [Attica].

This provision, though it cannot be restored in the extant inscription, is generally and rightly assigned to Draco's law: shortly after the citation (51) the speaker adds as a general reference that the homicide laws he has cited are indeed Draco's; and this particular provision (44) also involves the archaic conception of *atimia* as 'outlawry'. The law is therefore reasonably treated as an authentic Draconian statute. It does not say, however, either explicitly or by implication, that the legal protections belong only to unintentional killers. If we assume, as the other evidence would indicate, that the precise terms of exile and compensation were originally a matter for private settlement, then the most natural conclusion is that this clause once safeguarded the property of *any* exiled homicide who had arranged a settlement by which his property was protected.

The law of justifiable homicide cited in Demosthenes 23. 53 is often treated as Draconian, and here apparently we find cases where the judges are to decide a question of intent: 'if one kill in athletic competition unwillingly, . . . or in warfare mistakenly.'[80] But the authenticity of the text that an ancient editor inserted in the manuscript is here exceedingly doubtful, as we shall see (Ch. 3, esp. §2.3). And even if we assume that this law derives from a Draconian original, it offers no proof that intent was at issue in ordinary proceedings, as it applies only in specific instances protected by law— some of which are unintentional killings, others obviously quite wilful. The statutory protections serve to safeguard socially valued conventions of competition, common defence, and integrity of the *oikos*. From the surviving texts it would appear that cases prosecuted under this law were argued on the same principle of causal liability that governs other proceedings before the *ephetai:* he who kills another accidentally in competition or in a lawful act of

---

[80] Before Stroud re-examined the inscription of Draco's Law it was generally supposed that this law on justifiable homicide is to be restored in lines 36 ff. (Bonner and Smith, i. 123); but this restoration is now disproved. For the assumption that this law derives from Draco (whether it is to be found in the inscription or not), cf. Ruschenbush, *'ΦΟΝΟΣ'*, 145, 150. For the distinction between Draco's statute and the laws of the several courts indicated in Dem. 23. 63–70, cf. Busolt and Swoboda, 813 n. 1; and see Ch. 3 §2.

vengeance must show that the victim himself is responsible for his own death. Innocence of malice was no defence.[81]

The last and most crucial evidence indicating a criterion of intent is the law cited in Demosthenes 23. 72: if convicted of *unintentional homicide*, the killer must depart within a specified period and by a prescribed route, and continue in exile until the victim's family is reconciled.[82] In large part because of the credibility of the earlier citations by Demosthenes, it is often supposed that this provision is also an authentic Draconian law. But this clause, like the law of 'justifiable killing', probably belongs to the later division of jurisdiction, not to Draco's legislation. In fact Demosthenes himself gives every indication that this law is *not* drawn from the same text as the citations from Draco. This provision granting safe exile to the unintentional killer is cited *after* the closure or seal against altering the Draconian laws (62). The seal against revisions has a reasonable claim to authenticity, as the nature of the penalty it imposes—outlawry extended to the household—belongs to the Draconian setting. But the law assuring a safe path of exile for the unintentional killer (72) is cited specifically among the laws of the Palladium court, along with the many rules and 'unwritten conventions' governing homicide jurisdiction, for which Demosthenes himself knows not the author, 'whether gods or heroes' (70). In Demosthenes' day there was probably no reliable evidence on the origins of these rules; he can only invoke the tradition that homicide jurisdiction was established by the mythic trials of Ares, Orestes, and the others. In fact, as we shall see in the next chapter, the division of homicide jurisdiction was probably a product of Solon's reforms.

§ 4. Conclusions

Draco's law is sometimes looked upon as a monument to the discovery of *mens rea*. Maschke and others after him supposed that the lawgiver instituted the grand jury of fifty-one *ephetai* to allow for the kind of discretion required in weighing the killer's intent. But

---

[81] For the causal arguments in such cases, see Ch. 5 §3, on *Tetr.* 2–3; and Ch. 8 on *Lys.* 1.

[82] For the view that Dem. 23. 72 is an authentic Draconian law, cf. Ruschenbusch, '*ΦΟΝΟΣ*', 139, arguing that the other protections, Dem. 23. 37 and 44, extended and elaborated this rule.

proceeding on this assumption, scholars have concluded in somewhat circular fashion that the extant copy of the law is defective. Read as a judicial guide for rulings of unintentional homicide, the inscribed text seems full of intrusions inspired by more evolved concepts. The findings of this chapter contradict Maschke's model on both counts. The lawgiver's principal concern was not to ratify a new criterion of guilt for officers of the *polis* to impose but to reinforce the customary rights of the surviving family to weigh the killer's liability as they saw fit. The only official intervention in the weighing of intentions comes as a limited solution to a marginal problem. The justices were to determine the killer's intent only in cases where there were no surviving kinsmen eligible to exercise their right. If we see that the law as we have it is a document of this profoundly conservative purpose, then we have no good reason to doubt its authenticity. In its volitional terms and procedural rules the law that survived in 409 is entirely consistent with the archaic context.

The lawgiver's chief purpose was to render the customary rules of kinship and social obligation more systematic and secure. He therefore made the following refinements. (1) The immediate family are given uncontested priority over cousins and collateral kin for prosecuting and making settlement with the killer. Only if there are none of the nearer kin surviving may the cousins assert their right. (2) There is also a clear commandment that only in the event of unanimous agreement by the eligible kinsmen is settlement to be valid. Thus the family retained an autonomous right to retribution but they are also called upon to resolve potentially disruptive disputes among themselves. In judgement before the tribal kings any dispute among the plaintiffs would have to be resolved as they are called upon to swear to their claim of right. This procedure would often suffice as a basis for settlement between the plaintiffs and the defendant. But in cases where one or both parties dispute the kings' judgement the dispute was now to be decided before the new body of fifty-one justices.

The justices would appear to be the earliest trial jury, in the sense of a representative body constituted specifically for the task of deciding disputes by majority vote.[83] Judgement by the tribal kings

---

[83] There were presumably older 'trial' proceedings before the full assembly or aristocratic council, especially in regard to urgent wrongs to the state; see my study 'Eisangelia and Euthyna', *GRBS* 28 (1987), 167–208.

or elders was a different kind of procedure, one that relied upon consensual resolution by oath-challenge or other proof test such as we find in other archaic evidence. This older procedure now serves as a preliminary device to define the issue at trial in such a way that the justices may give a straight verdict for the plaintiff or for the defendant. If the kings had judged for the case to be decided upon the plaintiffs' oath that defendant was liable to them for the slaying of their kinsman, under whatever conditions, but the defendant swore that he was not such a killer, then the conflicting oaths would be the focus for arguments at trial.

In this way, as judgement is handed down from the kings to the justices to decide, the substantive consequences are clearly defined as a matter of retribution. If the justices find for the plaintiff, they have validated his claim to compensation or self-help against the defendant. The latter is liable, *aitios*, regardless of his intentions. This much we can deduce from the archaic evidence itself. The killer's state of mind is not something that the judges will try to determine. If a man kill, the law prescribes exile and *aidesis*, regardless of his intent. It remains uncertain whether the term of exile was subject to any limit or qualification.[84] In all probability the term of exile was subject only to the dictates of the family and was decided in *aidesis*. Ordinarily it was a matter solely for the family to decide whether and on what terms the defendant's repentance or innocence of intent entitled him to make peace.

There is one last provision that is plausibly assigned to Draco and which perfectly illustrates the conservative character of his legislation as a set of secondary rules that define the methods by which more primitive obligations can be met. We have found that the life and property of an exiled homicide are protected so long as he abides by the terms of his exile. Somewhere alongside this provision stood an ordinance for the opposite case: if the killer returns to Attica without *aidesis*, he may be put to death. A Draconian rule for execution or arrest is mentioned in a later statute cited by Demosthenes (23. 28): plaintiffs may seize the offender and put him to death on sight or bring him before the magistrate for execution, 'as it states on the ⟨first⟩ axon'. But this traditional remedy had

---

[84] Stroud, *DL* 57, notes a possible reference to confiscation or prescribed terms of exile in lines 39–41 (ἀπόστασιν . . . δεκάτες), but this section probably applies to the special cases, violent altercation and retributive killing, treated in the preceding lines.

evidently proved inadequate, and Draco therefore sought to strengthen it.[85] If the right to self-help is uncertain, if the exile resists arrest and is killed in the struggle, then the family of the slain homicide may find grounds to seek retribution. It was evidently in answer to this predicament that Draco introduced what I shall call 'warrant' (*endeixis*) as a safeguard for one who undertook to arrest or execute an exiled homicide trespassing in Attica. The law of warrant is cited by Demosthenes, 23. 51, shortly before the closure, and the orator here affirms that he is indeed citing from laws of Draco: 'There shall be no prosecution for homicide whatever against those who obtain "warrant" against an exile, if he should return where prohibited.'[86] The significance of this law was long disputed, but its pragmatic purpose, as yet another device to break the cycle of vendetta, now seems secure. Inevitably, in some cases where an exiled homicide was found in Attica and put to death by his victim's kinsmen, his execution would invite reprisal. The law of warrant, however, guarantees freedom from prosecution and affords the protections of law to those who would apprehend an illegal returnee if they first identify him as an exiled homicide before a magistrate. Thus the secondary rule affirms and enables the fulfilment of primary obligations.

The laws for warrant and arrest were to be of particular significance in the classical era as an alternative to the traditional suits for homicide, but in origin they were part of the same mechanism of self-help and private settlement. In both procedures the original intervention of the *polis* would appear to be motivated not by an ideological aim to advance official authority as an end in itself, but

---

[85] The law of warrant and arrest probably extended the right of self-help against the homicide beyond the family to other members of the community: Hansen, *Apagoge*, 100–3 and 111–12. Cf. Democritus, B257–9: members of the community have the obligation to slay the outlaw just as they would slay a marauding beast—'to kill by ancestral law the hostile creature'.

[86] Dem. 23. 51: Φόνου δὲ δίκας μὴ εἶναι μηδαμοῦ κατὰ τῶν τοὺς φεύγοντας ἐνδεικνύντων, ἐάν τις κατίῃ ὅποι μὴ ἔξεστιν. Cf. Hansen, *Apagoge* 113–18. I render *endeixis* as 'warrant' in the sense of informed 'authorization', as it is analogous to a modern warrant issued by a magistrate upon reasonable suspicion for law enforcement officers to act. Cf. Blackstone, *Comm.* iv. Ch. 21. §1; H. Potter's *Historical Introduction to English Law and its Institutions* (London, 1958), 270. In British law the justices' authority to issue a warrant on probable suspicion was confirmed by legislation of 1848 and 1952. Of course the ancient warrant authorized forcible arrest by a private citizen rather than an official (the variation known as *ephēgesis* approximates the latter).

as an expedient to maintain and strengthen the pre-existing social order of tribal loyalties.

In the generation after Draco the officers of the *polis* at last assume an authority in resolving homicide disputes that had been previously exercised only by the surviving kinsmen. It will be tempting to see the Solonian innovations as, at last, an ideological restriction upon the autonomy of the ruling families in favour of the *dēmos*, or at least a triumph of legal process over self-help. But we should bear in mind Hansen's caveat, that all such models of moral development in the criminal law must be regarded with the utmost scepticism.[87] In fact, the rules that Solon imposed also appear to be largely conservative in spirit, remedies to persistent defects in the system of traditional rules, defects for which Draco's remedy had itself proved deficient. By Draco's original arrangement there would still be instances, perhaps many, when a homicide defendant might plead innocent of malice, win the sympathy of many among the community and sway some among the victim's family, but still be denied any hope of returning to his homeland by one holdout among the victim's kin, who refused to be reconciled out of vindictiveness or hope of some material advantage in the defendant's absence. The rules for private settlement would sometimes prove grossly inequitable to defendants of lesser means, as the wealthy could purchase absolution for even the most malicious murder, yet they might disdain any offer of compensation for the killing of a kinsman, no matter how innocent of malice they knew the killer to be. And the most powerful plaintiffs themselves would sometimes find fault with Draco's arrangement, as the killer was now afforded the prospect of safe return *without consent* of the immediate family, either by agreement of the cousins once the nearer kin had died out, or by pardon of the phratry when no eligible kinsmen survived—no matter how vehemently they had refused to be reconciled while they lived.

[87] *Apagoge*, 117.

3

The Five Courts of Homicide

If we set aside the Areopagite model that Demosthenes articulated and modern scholars have generally followed, and look instead to the direct evidence, we should conclude that the earliest homicide jurors were the *ephetai*; the jurisdiction of this body was not divided by intentionality or other criteria; ordinarily they made no ruling on the killer's intent but only did so when special hearings were required for pardon by the phratry. It was Solon who first authorized the Areopagus council to determine malice aforethought, and it was this reform that led to the classical division of jurisdiction. In this chapter we proceed on this hypothesis to construct a new model of how homicide was divided among the five courts.[1]

§1. The Basis for a Reconstruction

In any reconstruction of this kind we make certain assumptions about the value of the evidence and the practical realities. Much of what we assume depends upon the account of the homicide laws in Demosthenes 23: the authenticity of this material is by no means certain, though some passages are often accepted without question; this problem will be taken up in the next section. The practical realities of procedure—how a plaintiff actually went about prosecuting his kinsman's killer—also involves uncertainties that are all too often ignored. Let us begin by acknowledging these practical limitations.

1.1 Straight Judgement: *Euthydikia*

Athenians of the fourth century used the term *euthydikia* to describe trial on the main issue, as opposed to the various prelimi-

---

[1] A similar approach was taken by Sealey, 'Athenian Courts for Homicide'.

naries that might delay or derail the proceedings.[2] It also implies a fairly self-evident and universal principle of the Athenian system: without extended deliberation a grand jury can only render a single, 'straight' verdict; it cannot easily decide secondary issues. A large body of jurors cannot ordinarily be asked to decide among three or more possible verdicts if they are to reach a *majority* decision (as we have noticed, Ch. 2 §3.2). Now if the jurors are allowed to deliberate among themselves to seek consensus, then several possibilities may be considered, but we have no indication that Athenian juries ever proceeded in this way. And in a body of fifty-one, evidently voting without discussion among themselves, it is unreasonable to suppose that the judges could consider three or more verdicts—unless, of course, these several alternatives could be treated seriatim. If a jury of fifty-one (or, for that matter, twelve or nine) attempt to decide among several verdicts, without the kind of extended deliberation that is allowed in American jury trials, inevitably in many cases there will be no clear majority. Thus if one jury of *ephetai*, in one hearing were to decide among 'guilty', 'not guilty', 'unintentional', and perhaps 'justifiable' homicide as well, then all too often the vote would be split and a plurality would prevail *against the majority*. This outcome was unacceptable to the Athenians. We know of no instance in any Athenian court where one vote decided among three or more propositions or where a mere plurality prevailed—indeed, Aristotle ridicules the notion.[3]

If there are several propositions to consider, a procedure must be found to divide the questions so that each may be decided in turn by a straight, majority vote. Thus when the question of proper procedure was recognized as a separate issue, it was tried separately (*paragraphē*), before trial on the main issue. In cases where the penalty was not prescribed by law but had to be determined by the jurors (*agones timētoi*), there were two successive ballots: one to decide guilt or innocence; a second to decide between the penalties proposed by prosecutor and defendant—the condemnation of Socrates is a familiar example.

---

[2] For this value of the term, see Wolff, *Paragraphe*, 138: ' "direktes Streiten" . . . εὐθυδικία, wie der prägnante Ausdruck lautet'; cf. Isoc. 6. 43; 7. 3; Dem. 34. 4.

[3] That such 'straight judgement' was the rule is shown by Arisotle's reaction to the scheme attributed to Hippodamus of Miletus, that jurors be allowed each to record a *qualified* verdict (*Pol.* 1268a–b). The only apparent exception is inheritance disputes, where the court has to decide among several claimants (Dem. 43. 7–10).

Now it is highly unlikely that the archaic homicide court regularly rendered a similar double verdict, first deciding guilt or innocence, then, if they convicted, deciding questions of intent or justification and thus determining the severity of the sentence. If such double verdicts were at one time the standard procedure, then it is hard to see how or why the issues were later divided among the several courts. The classical division of jurisdiction rather suggests in itself that, when the questions of intent and justification came to be differentiated, each was defined as *the* issue for a jury to decide.

This very basic point is often overlooked, yet it is crucial to the historical problem before us. It will also prove instrumental in our understanding of legal argumentation in the homicide courts. If we suppose that the Areopagus or the *ephetai* once weighed the separate questions of intent and legal justification along with the straight issue of liability, then we must also reckon with the rather awkward consequences. If indeed the judges were to decide a case in which the verdict may be either intentional or unintentional homicide or yet again outright acquittal, then they are likely to be split three ways, with no majority.

The most straightforward means of considering several possible verdicts—and one that seems most congenial to the Athenian way of justice—was to divide one question from another and give each a separate hearing. In classical homicide procedure this principle is embodied in separate venues: the *archōn basileus* directed the parties to one site if they wished to raise the issue of intent, another if their dispute focused on the question of causal responsibility, a third if the issue was legal justification. This system reflects a fundamental respect for the autonomy of the litigants, for they themselves decide by their claims what is to be treated as *the* issue for straight judgement.

The opening provisions of Draco's law suggest that the tribal kings would continue to decide many cases, as they had previously been called upon to 'give judgement,' *dikazein* (Ch. 2 §3.1). The kings would propose that one party or the other demonstrate the righteousness of his conviction by oath and other tests. In cases where that direct judgement was disputed, Draco now provided a further remedy: a grand jury of fifty-one tribal representatives would decide the one question of strict liability—is the defendant *aitios*? The question of malice or moral innocence was still solely for the plaintiffs to weigh, so long as there were eligible kinsmen surviving. The lawgiver evidently presumed that in most cases the family would reconcile with the killer if they accepted the plea that he was innocent of intent to kill; ordinarily that question was not for the judges to decide. Of course, what would later emerge as separate pleas of innocence of intent or legal justification were considerations that might well be treated as factors in causation and thus enter into the judges' decision: there might be a fine line between striking back in anger (intentionally), and acting in desperate self-defence or under compulsion (arguably an unintentional or justifiable act). But the archaic judges were not free to render a verdict of 'unintentional homicide' *per se*, as distinct from intentional murder, nor could they assure any preferential treatment to one they judged to be liable though innocent of malice. That distinction was present to the mind of the lawgiver and recognized by his constituents, but it was not one that they wished to have decided by official intervention, when the parties themselves could decide. Only when there are no close kinsmen of the victim surviving does Draco call for an official intervention on this issue: if the killer is to be entitled to special pardon by the victim's 'kindred', the phratry, he must stand trial on the issue of intent. This awkward solution was dictated by the principles of *euthydikia* and autonomy: wherever possible the parties themselves must decide by their oaths what is at issue and what the consequences of judgement will be.

We have noticed that Draco's remedy has its defects. The defendant who claims that he was innocent of malice may none the less be denied a consideration that many of his countrymen might feel he deserved, so long as his victim's kinsmen survive to oppose him. But the immediate family of the victim, those most likely to be overwhelmed with grief and the urge for vengeance, were also faced with an unwelcome prospect, that even the most savage and malicious killer of their kin might someday return to Attica, if he outlived them and was able to reconcile with their cousins or with the phratry. In these respects Draco's solution ultimately failed to satisfy the principles of consensual judgement. Defects such as these prompted revision of Draco's law a generation after it was enacted, but the later draftsmen of the law aimed to remedy these defects, not to depart from the ancient principles of autonomy and *euthydikia*.

1.2   Authenticity of the Laws in Demosthenes 23

Demosthenes' account in *Against Aristocrates* 22–81 is our single most important source for the development of homicide procedure. Unfortunately there is a great disparity between some sections and others. Demosthenes generally assumes as common knowledge that Draco was the author of the entire body of law regarding homicide.[4] Some of the laws he cites as Draconian are almost certainly authentic; but other citations are demonstrably later than Draco, possibly later than Solon.[5] But there is an orderly arrangement to this digression on the homicide laws, and understanding that arrangement will help us to evaluate the evidence he gives us.

Demosthenes' account appears to be arranged in three segments. (1) The first of the homicide laws cited, §§22 and 28, can be reasonably assigned to a later period by terminology and reference to Solonian institutions. (2) In §§37–60 some of the laws cited can be restored with reasonable confidence in the extant copy of Draco's law. The laws in this central segment are all characterized by terminology suitable to the Draconian era. It is in this portion at §51 that Draco is introduced as the author of certain laws and, by implication, not of all such laws. And at the conclusion to this segment Demosthenes cites verbatim what appears to be the authentic closure or seal against altering the Draconian laws, §62. (3) The laws cited after §62 deal specifically with the respective jurisdictions of the five courts (63–81). None of the latter can be credibly restored in the inscription. Demosthenes refers to these laws of the several courts as the creation of unknown gods and heroes. From these guideposts I think it reasonable to suppose that Demosthenes takes his material from three distinct but connected texts and he presents them in an arrangement that reflects that relationship. Consider the first two segments.

---

[4] Thus in *Against Leptines' Law* (20) 157–8, Demosthenes describes as Draconian the whole corpus of homicide law, from the founding of the Areopagus to the least detail of the religious sanctions. There is nothing in the extant inscription to indicate the latter provisions, and nothing in the primitive procedure to call for a statutory requirement along these lines—the religious sanctions appear to require no prescription.

[5] E. Drerup, 'Ueber die bei den Attischen Rednern eingeleten Urkunden' *Jahrbücher für Klassischen Philologie* (1898), 264–80, concluded that the documents in this speech are substantially accurate, reasonably free of interpolation and fabrication. For the law of the Delphinium court, however, Drerup believed that the ancient editor inserted the wrong document; see below, §1.2.2.

1.2.1 The Laws of Draco and Solon's 'Preamble' (§§22–62)

The law with which Demosthenes begins his digression, §22, is the statute that defines the Areopagus' jurisdiction: 'The Council of the Areopagus shall judge homicide and wounding with malice aforethought, arson and poisoning, if one kills by giving the drug.'[6] As we have seen (Ch. 1 §1.2), it was most probably Solon who founded the historical Areopagus as a council of elected archons and instituted their special jurisdiction as a murder court. And the statute cited by Demosthenes seems out of character with the primitive rules in the Draconian inscription: the successive clauses specifying various charges to be tried at the Areopagus—arson, poisoning, and wounding, in addition to murder, and the specific condition that a defendant accused of poisoning be charged with directly administering the drug—all suggest incremental refinements.

The law is described in the manuscripts as 'A Law from the Homicide Laws of the Areopagus'. This is undoubtedly a heading provided by the ancient editor and it probably indicates that he found this document among statutes specifically relating to the Areopagus' jurisdiction. It is clearly a statute framed to fix the competence of the high court, rather than a general statute on homicide such as we find in the inscription of Draco's law. A later date for the law of the Areopagus is further indicated by the term describing their function as 'to give judgement'—*dikazein*—rather than to 'decide' or 'render a verdict' (= *diagnōnai* or *krinein*). In the archaic usage, as we have seen (Ch. 2 §§2–3) *dikazein* describes a process that it is fundamentally different from an ordinary jury verdict: it describes a proposal for consensual judgement at the hands of a chief or magistrate, a judgement that the parties themselves will acknowledge and execute. Such appears to be the sense of *dikazein* in the opening to the inscribed law, 'the kings shall give judgement'. The jury of *ephetai* renders a verdict in cases where 'judgement' is disputed; their function is 'to decide', *diagnōnai*. How it came about that *dikazein* was introduced as the proper term to describe the verdict of the Areopagus, with its special implications for execution, will be taken up below, §2.2; but here it is enough to

---

[6] *ΝΟΜΟΣ ΕΚ ΤΩΝ ΦΟΝΙΚΩΝ ΝΟΜΩΝ ΤΩΝ ΕΞ ΑΡΕΙΟΥ ΠΑΓΟΥ.*
Δικάζειν δὲ τὴν βουλὴν τὴν ἐν Ἀρείῳ πάγῳ φόνου καὶ τραύματος ἐκ προνοίας καὶ πυρκαϊᾶς καὶ φαρμάκων, ἐάν τις ἀποκτείνῃ δούς.

recognize that the language of Demosthenes' law does not appear to be the language of Draco.

For the law cited in §28 we have, again, reasonably conclusive proof that it is not a Draconian statute. It is a later amendment giving what appears to be an accurate cross-reference to the original Draconian table: [7]

It is lawful to put to death manslayers (if apprehended) in the homeland, and to arrest them, as it directs in the [first] axon; but not to torture nor hold for ransom, or (the offender) shall owe damages in twice the amount. Let anyone willing bring charges to the archons, to each for his jurisdiction; and let the court of the people decide.

The provisions for prosecution by 'anyone willing' and trial before a court of the people show that this law is a product of Solon's reform. And the rule not to torture or hold for ransom is consistent with other restrictions on the plaintiffs' claims in the age of Solon.[8] This law was framed as a safeguard against attempts by the plaintiffs to extort a higher settlement from an exiled homicide. By contrast, the earlier provision 'on the axon' to which this later statute refers, a provision allowing self-help execution or summary arrest of an exiled homicide who returns without settlement, is almost certainly an authentic Draconian law: it can be restored with reasonable confidence in the fragmentary inscription; the terminology is consistent and the practice itself entirely in keeping with the archaic mode of resolving homicide disputes.

These two examples demonstrate how we must approach the laws that Demosthenes cites, if we are to determine their value for a reconstruction of the authentic Draconian statutes and the later jurisdictions. These first two citations also contribute something to our understanding of the grouping of laws in Demosthenes' argument. Unlike the incidental references in other speeches, the citations in *Against Aristocrates* appear to follow the framework of the homicide code. Demosthenes probably expected his audience to recognize that he was following the arrangement of the law itself.

---

[7] Τοὺς δ' ἀνδροφόνους ἐξεῖναι ἀποκτείνειν ἐν τῇ ἡμεδαπῇ καὶ ἀπάγειν, ὡς ἐν τῷ ⟨α'⟩ ἄξονι ἀγορεύει, λυμαίνεσθαι δὲ μή, μηδὲ ἀποινᾶν, ἢ διπλοῦν ὀφείλειν ὅσον ἂν καταβλάψῃ. εἰσφέρειν δ' ἐ⟨ς⟩ τοὺς ἄρχοντας, ὧν ἕκαστοι δικασταί εἰσι, τῷ βουλομένῳ. τὴν δ' ἡλιαίαν διαγιγνώσκειν.

[8] See Heitsch, 'Aidesis'; my studies, 'Νηποινεὶ Τεθνάναι· A Response', *Symposion 1990* (1991), 107–14; 'Tyranny and Outlawry' in R. Rosen and J. Farrell (eds.) *Nomodeiktes* (Ann Arbor, 1993), 305–19.

The citations at §§22 and 28 probably belong to a separate table of statutes consisting of later modifications. This table was probably a Solonian preface or preamble to the Draconian laws: its provisions embody the changes that followed from Solon's reforms.[9] By ideological convention, this 'Solonian preamble' would be regarded as a coherent part of the Draconian corpus, as all homicide laws were ascribed to Draco. Thus, where Demosthenes names Draco specifically as the author of the law for *endeixis*, he also invokes his name as author of 'the other statutes that I have cited from the homicide laws' (23. 51). The law of *endeixis* or 'warrant' was probably cited directly from Draco's *thesmos*. The law of the Areopagus (22) and the law against torture and extortion (28) have no such title.

The laws with which Demosthenes began his account are not likely to have been taken at random, from any odd sections of the code. Rather, they embody two fundamental changes: the law of the Areopagus court (22) is the single most important revision in the homicide law, qualifying Draco's general provision for hearings by the kings and justices; the law against torture and extortion (28) is a crucial restriction upon the Draconian law of arrest (*IG* I³ 104. 30–1). It is therefore likely that the two laws derive from the same section of the code, and probably from the section preceding the Draconian 'axones'.

The laws cited thereafter, §§37–60, generally agree with the extant fragment of Draco's law. These include provisions for the protection of life and property of an exiled homcide, without distinction of intentionality (37, 44); the law for warrant and arrest of an exiled killer who trespasses in Attica (51); and the law for justifiable killing in defence against violent seizure or abduction (60 = *IG* I³ 104. 37–8). The latter is closely followed by the closure, fixing the law against alteration (62): 'Any officer or citizen guilty of confounding or altering this statute (*thesmos*) shall be outlawed (*atimos*), himself, his descendants, and property.' Here the archaic

---

[9] Cf. Stroud, *DL* 54–6, on *IG* I³ 104. 30–1. The cross-reference to 'the axon' shows that this text is a later addendum. It is generally supposed therefore that this statute was found in a later axon that Solon placed after the Draconian laws; for this reason the text is emended to designate the *first* axon. But if this statute belonged to a stele serving as preface to Draco's law, it would perhaps refer simply to 'the axon' to indicate the older laws that followed.

terminology tends to support the authenticity of the law as belonging to the Draconian era.[10]

1.2.2 The Law of Justifiable Homicide (53–6)

In the midst of the authentic Draconian documents there is one of doubtful authenticity: the law that has made its way into the text at §53 differs markedly from the law that Demosthenes expounds in the following sections. Let us re-examine the key terms.[11]

If one kill in athletic contest unintentionally, or in warfare in case of mistaken identity, or slaying upon the road, or acting against assault of wife or mother, or sister, or daughter or concubine kept for freeborn children—on none of these counts is the killer to be exiled.

Against the authenticity of this text as a Draconian law, consider first of all the curious clause, 'slaying upon the road'.[12] Various interpretations and ingenious emendations have been offered,[13] but no satisfactory explanation has yet been given. It has even been suggested that what we could call 'vehicular homicide' was embraced by this clause; but it is hard to see how any one of the usual hypotheses suits the ends of public policy in the same way that athletics, military service, and defence of the *oikos* against sexual violation obviously called for legal safeguards. It is, of course, a dubious practice to assume an interpolation where we cannot explain what the interpolator thought it should mean. But the

---

[10] There is of course the apparent contradiction between this seal upon the laws and subsequent revisions, and it is partly for this reason that I am inclined to suppose that the revisions in Dem. 23. 22 and 28 were part of a Solonian preamble rather than appended in later axones. The seal provides 'closure': there will be no alterations or additions; the revisions were therefore put *before* the laws under seal and treated as explication.

[11] Dem. 23. 53: ἐάν τις ἀποκτείνῃ ἐν ἄθλοις ἄκων, ἢ ἐν ὁδῷ καθελών, ἢ ἐν πολέμῳ ἀγνοήσας, ἢ ἐπὶ δάμαρτι ἢ ἐπὶ μητρὶ ἢ ἐπ' ἀδελφῇ ἢ ἐπὶ θυγατρί, ἢ ἐπὶ παλλακῇ ἣν ἂν ἐπ' ἐλευθέροις παισὶν ἔχῃ, τούτων ἕνεκα μὴ φεύγειν κτείναντα. Cf. *Ath. Pol.* 57. 3: ἐὰν δ' ἀποκτεῖναι μέν τις ὁμολογῇ, φῇ δὲ κατὰ τοὺς νόμους, οἷον μοιχὸν λαβὼν ἢ ἐν πολέμῳ ἀγνοήσας ἢ ἐν ἄθλῳ ἀγωνιζόμενος, τούτῳ ἐπὶ Δελφινίῳ δικάζουσιν.

[12] Perhaps the most plausible explanation is indicated by Harpocration, *Lex.* 217 (Dindorf): 'Demosthenes . . . says "apprehending on the road" instead of "in ambush or waylaying" (ἐν ὁδῷ καθελών ἀντὶ τοῦ ἐν λόχῳ καὶ ἐνέδρα); similarly they use the Homeric expression "going the road" (ὁδὸν ἐλθέμεναι).' The phrase thus suggests retributive killing, describing the action of the attacker, not of one acting in defence.

[13] Drerup, 'eingelegten Urkunden' 277, suggested ἐν ὅπλῳ, 'in arms', for ἐν ὁδῷ, 'on the road', thus linking this phrase with the following provision on friendly casualties.

silence of Demosthenes himself is telling: in the body of his argument, he makes no mention of the suspect phrase where he would surely have found some conflict with Aristocrates' decree, if indeed it was to be found in the law he had read to the court.

The term crucial to our inquiry, 'unintentionally' (*akōn*) is equally suspect: it is not to be found in Demosthenes' commentary on the law, and the explanation he gives would seem to imply that intentionality was not at issue. He does, indeed, refer obliquely to the killer's 'purpose' (*dianoia*)—'to defeat his opponent alive and not to kill him'. But rather than justify a killing in competition upon this principle, Demosthenes reduces the legal justification to a matter of the victim's just deserts: 'If he was too weak to bear the struggle for victory, the lawgiver regarded [the victim] responsible for his own misfortune, and therefore allowed no retribution for his death.'[14] If the law that Demosthenes had read to the court treated the killing as justifiable because it was unintentional, then this rationale would seem superfluous. The document at §53 was probably inserted by an editor who assumed too much from the comment on 'purpose'. It is at best doubtful whether the qualifier 'unintentionally' was the wording of the statute that Demosthenes cited.

In explicating the clause regarding killing in warfare, however, Demosthenes himself verifies the condition, that such a defence rests upon 'mistaken identity' (*agnoēsas*). The parallel text in *Ath. Pol.* 57. 3 also indicates that mistaken identity was essential to the plea. If it could be shown that this was indeed the wording of a Draconian statute, then we would have evidence of another instance where Draco instructed the *ephetai* to decide a question of intent. But considering the dubious authenticity of this citation, we cannot conclude with confidence that Draco himself set aside casualties of friendly fire and sword as a special case where the issue at trial was essentially a matter of *mens rea*. It is of course entirely in character for Demosthenes to read Draco's laws in the light of current applications. And if a false document or the wrong document was inserted into the text, it was easy enough for a spurious term to make its way from that document into the main argument at the hands of an over-helpful scribe.

---

[14] Dem. 23. 54: ἐσκέψατο . . . τὴν τοῦ δεδρακότος διάνοιαν . . . ζῶντα νικῆσαι καὶ οὐκ ἀποκτεῖναι. εἰ δ᾽ ἐκεῖνος ἀσθενέστερος ἦν τὸν ὑπὲρ τῆς νίκης ἐνεγκεῖν πόνον, ἑαυτῷ τοῦ πάθους αἴτιον ἡγήσατο, διὸ τιμωρίαν οὐκ ἔδωκεν. On the concept of justifiable retribution for the victim's unintentional wrong, see Ch. 5 §3.

Drerup long ago accounted for the discrepancies by supposing
that the text of the law, which a later editor brought into the
manuscript tradition, was a different statute from the one that
Demosthenes had read to the court and to which he directed his
comments.[15] Drerup resisted any attempt to explain away the discrepancies as interpolation or fabrication, and he makes a good case
for the overall accuracy and authenticity of the legal documents in
this speech; glosses and piecemeal intrusions are minimal. He concluded, however, that Demosthenes' argument on this particular
law represents a later statute, while the manuscript document is an
earlier version which the editor inserted intact. The reverse, I suggest, is the more likely solution: the editor in fact inserted a *later*
version of the law. Demosthenes himself seems to be referring to a
reliable documentary source for Draconian laws in sections 37–62.
And we can reasonably conclude that there was indeed a later
statute recasting the substance of Draconian laws on justifiable
killing to be found in the enabling ordinance for the Delphinium
court.

There is one last discrepancy between the clause that concludes
the manuscript document and the conclusions that Demosthenes
draws, and this also suggests that a later law was wrongly placed
among the Draconian *thesmoi*. The manuscript document ends
with a general rule regarding the defendant's immunity: 'the killer
shall not be exiled' (literally, 'not to flee', *mē pheugein*). In his own
comment Demosthenes absolves the killer in somewhat different
terms. 'Consider how righteously and fairly [the lawgiver] has *distinguished each instance*' (*hekasta dieilen*, 54): he who kills in athletic
contest is innocent (*ouk adikein*); he who kills mistakenly in warfare
is pronounced 'free of guilt' (or 'untainted', *katharos*) and not subject to prosecution (*ou dikēn hupekhein*); he who acts against sexual
violation may kill the offender with absolute impunity (*athōios*). It
is usually supposed that Demosthenes' words are merely variations
on the guarantee of acquittal that the document provides: *mē
pheugein* is taken to mean that the killer will not face trial, 'will not
be defendant', because that is precisely what Demosthenes seems
to interpret *his* law to mean. But this goes against the actual application of the law in such cases: he who kills the adulterer caught in
the act certainly could be made to stand trial. And it is clearly not

---

[15] See Drerup, 'eingelegten Urkunden', esp. 276–8.

what the Draconian statute would have meant by such a phrase: to judge from the opening lines of Draco's law, *mē pheugein* would mean literally that the killer is not subject to exile, though he may yet be required to reconcile with the victim's family. In the first two instances, athletics and warfare, Demosthenes supposes not simply that the killer shall not be exiled but that he faces no legal proceedings or sanctions whatever.

Demosthenes' commentary §§54–6 probably refers to an authentic Draconian statute. After all, it falls squarely between the law of *endeixis* (51), expressly attributed to Draco, and the closure fixing the Draconian laws against change (62). The arrangement of Demosthenes' paraphrase—taking each category separately and treating the consequences as somehow distinct—suggests that the text of the law presented a similar sequence of three or more separate sentences. For killing in warfare the law apparently absolved the killer from legal proceedings (*ou dikēn hupekhein*). For killing in response to sexual violation Demosthenes paraphrases the status of the killer as 'free from penalty,' *athōios*. This is the same gloss that Demosthenes uses for the archaic penalty in the Draconian law in §60, *nēpoinei tethnanai*—more literally '[the offender] be slain with impunity'. The latter was a remedy quite distinct from immunity to prosecution; it was indeed the customary remedy againt sexual violation, and we may reasonably conclude, such was the wording of Draco's law.[16]

Plato's treatment of justifiable killing in *Laws* 874c, follows a similar arrangement: he who kills a thief in the night shall be guiltless (*katharos*); he who kills in defence against a mugger likewise is guiltless (and so on); but in case of sexual violation of a free woman or child, let the offender be slain with impunity (*nēpoinei*).[17] This similarity in the arrangement of the two accounts would suggest that the original statute that inspired both versions was not a general rule connecting all three categories (or however many), but a

---

[16] See my studies on this remedy, '*Νηποινεὶ Τεθνάναι*' and 'Tyranny and Outlawry'.

[17] Plato places two other instances after the clause on sexual violation: retributive killing for rape of a wife or acting in defence of immediate family; in these instances also the killer shall be *katharos*. Plato assigns the two conditions, *katharos* and *nēpoinei tethnanai*, to the same category: he introduces this section as 'cases where the killer should rightly be *katharos*'. Killing in athletic contest or in warfare he treats separately as 'involuntary homicide' (865a), in a clear departure from Athenian law (cf. Ch. 5 §3).

list of offences, each with its penalty—even where the penalties overlap.

The evidence is indirect and not altogether conclusive, but in sum it weighs heavily against the manuscript document as a Draconian law. The law that Demosthenes had read to the court, which apparently belonged to the body of statute designated as 'Draco's Law', specifically excluded legal recourse or private claims in killings of these categories seriatim: if one kill in athletic competition he is not liable (perhaps *ouk aitios*); if one kill in warfare he is not subject to judgement (perhaps *dikas mē eínai*); if one kill in defence against sexual violation, he is free of any claim by kinsmen of the offender (νηποινεὶ τεθνάναι). The document in the manuscript, on the other hand, is probably the law of the Delphinium court, a somewhat later statute which reformulated these separate categories as a single jurisdictional rule, just as was done in the law of the Areopagus (§22). It was promulgated sometime after Draco's legislation as an amendment to it. In homicide disputes of this kind the killer is not automatically sent into exile, as Draco's law would ordinarily require; but if charges are brought by family of the victim, disputing the legality of the killing, then trial will be held at the Delphinium.[18]

The ancient editor probably assumed that the Draconian law of justifiable homicide that Demosthenes had read to the court in §53 was the same as the law of the Delphinium court to which he alludes in §74. Thus he added what he thought was the relevant document, though some of its wording was not reflected in Demosthenes' argument. So long as it was believed that the classical division of jurisdiction was at least as ancient as Draco's law, there was no reason to suppose that the law defining the Delphinium jurisdiction was distinct from Draco's laws on justifiable killing. But if we set aside this assumption, it seems a necessary conclusion that the law of the Delphinium court was a later statute and was bound to reflect some revision in legal concepts.

---

[18] The full text probably ended not at the words μὴ φεύγειν κτείναντα, but with a provision for trial at the Delphinium (δίκας δὲ διδόναι ἐν τῷ Δελφινίῳ, vel sim.) The editor who inserted this text would assume that the provision for trial was separate, since he interpreted μὴ φεύγειν to mean that the defendant would *not face trial*.

1.2.3   The Laws of the Several Courts (§§63–81)

The final segment, §§63–81, describes the workings of the several courts, and here Demosthenes seems to have drawn his material from a separate source, distinct from the homicide laws attributed to Draco. In the previous sections, from the point where the speaker invokes the name of Draco to the closure (§§22–62), it is clear that the laws cited form a unified body of statute. Now a transition marks a new body of material distinct from the foregoing: 'Not only these laws has he transgressed but also others too numerous to cite'; in sum, 'the laws concerning the homicide courts', the rules for 'summoning, giving testimony and taking the oath, and any other requirements of law' (§63). Aristocrates has violated all such rules by allowing immediate execution if anyone is *accused* of killing Charidemus.

In the juristic discourse that follows, Demosthenes sometimes suggests that the same basic rules govern all the courts equally, but elsewhere he makes clear that there are separate statutes governing the preliminaries and rules of procedure for each of the five courts. Thus at §§63–4 he seems to treat the rules for summoning, testimony, and oath-taking as the same for all five courts; but later he treats the preliminaries for Areopagus trials as a unique ritual (67); he refers to the rules governing Palladium trials as a specific set of statutes (71);[19] and for each of the three major courts—Areopagus, Palladium, and Delphinium—he refers to distinct and specific rules (73, τὰ διορισθέντα).[20] Among such specific ordinances is the rule that a defendant may depart into voluntary exile before the last speech; this clearly applies only in trials for intentional homicide, where the defendant is subject to execution if convicted—therefore at the Areopagus and, presumably, the Delphinium—but not in

---

[19] He refers to the law of the Palladium court as τοὺς παρὰ τούτῳ νόμους; these require (as in Areopagus trials) 'first *diōmosia*, second the argument, and then, third the judgement of the court'. The ritual preliminaries for Areopagus trials, involving the sacrifice of a boar, a ram, and a bull are evidently not the same as those in Palladium preliminaries, but constitute an oath-ceremony 'which no man swears for any other purpose' (68). The protocol for this religious observance was not simply dictated by unwritten custom but specified in statute (70): there are rules prescribing the wording of the oath and the calendar for preliminaries and trial. There is also a special penalty for perjury in the Areopagus: one false oath disqualifies the swearer and his descendants from any further action on oath (68); elsewhere the offender was disqualified only upon a third count of perjury, and the *atimia* was probably not hereditary (A. R. W. Harrison, *The Law of Athens* (Oxford, 1971), ii. 78).

[20] Cf. §74, for the Delphinium court, οἱ περὶ τούτων ἐν ἀρχῇ τὰ δίκαι' ὁρίσαντες.

cases of unintentional homicide at the Palladium, where safe departure is guaranteed by law (72). Again, the rules of summoning, testimony, and oath of both parties governing the three major courts are obviously meaningless at the Prytaneum hearings for killings by unknown assailants, and probably also irrelevant at the Phreatto hearings for exiled homicides, as we shall see. It is clear then that there were certain rules defining jurisdiction and procedure peculiar to each of the five courts; these were recognized by statute. It is in this sense that he speaks of 'the laws of the Areopagus' and, we may assume, he would also distinguish 'the law of the Palladium', 'the law of the Delphinium', and 'the law of Phreatto'.

Demosthenes himself, of course, regards these sets of rules as 'ordinances of primeval antiquity', and he refers to their unknown authors as 'those in the beginning who instituted these rules—whoever they were, gods or heroes'.[21] But there is no doubt he is referring to statute law and not simply to unwritten custom. He regards these as primordial rules, older than Draco, that were recorded in statute at some later date. Draco was the earliest identifiable lawgiver; that these ordinances had no known author suggests that they were, in fact, rendered into statute sometime *after* Draco—otherwise these laws would be attributed to the ancient legislator to whom all other homicide laws were attributed (however inaccurately). If these rules of jurisdiction were codified in Draco's time, there should be some allusion or connection to them in the extant remains of Draco's legislation; and they would be known thereafter as 'Laws of Draco' rather than the laws of the several courts. But Demosthenes expressly regards the rules of procedure and jurisdiction that he summarizes in §§63–81 as distinct from the 'Laws of Draco'. It is therefore reasonable to suppose that these laws were the work of Solon or a successor, whose work could not readily be acknowledged without violating the Draconian closure. They were thus honoured as primordial ordinances of mythic origin, though the workings of the courts themselves argue for a more recent evolution.

---

[21] Dem. 23. 70, οἱ ταῦτ' ἐξ ἀρχῆς τὰ νόμιμα διαθέντες, οἵτινές ποτ' ἦσαν, εἴθ' ἥρωες εἴτε θεοί; cf. 73, νόμιμ' ἐκ παντὸς τοῦ χρόνου; 81, ἃ θεοὶ κατέδειξαν καὶ μετὰ ταῦτ' ἄνθρωποι χρῶνται πάντα τὸν χρόνον.

§2. The Origins and Development of the Five Courts

With this understanding of Demosthenes' account, we turn now to
an archaeology of the five courts—one in which we can learn very
little from the physical remains of the court sites. And we cannot
rely upon the legalistic model that Demosthenes and his contemporaries have handed down to us. We must rather look to the formative concepts and practical consequences of the Draconian
foundation.

2.1   The Prytaneum and the Phreatto Court

The earliest of the five courts are the two that were of little practical significance in the classical era and are therefore least studied in
modern work: the courts at the Prytaneum and the Phreatto. These
are both institutions of the era of vendetta and voluntary exile—
when the killer was sometimes unidentified, often untried. As com-
pulsory adjudication superseded the older means of settlement,
these courts became little more than curiosities.

(i) Prytaneum. It is often supposed that the principal function of
the Prytaneum court was to give formal condemnation of impersonal objects whose impact resulted in an accidental fatality; this
ceremonial function was meant to purify the city of an object
tainted with miasma.[22] But again it is largely the legalistic perspective that Demosthenes has given us that has fixed this belief in
received opinion. Demosthenes introduces the law of the
Prytaneum court precisely because the legal nicety contrasts so well
with the summary procedure of Aristocrates (23. 76): 'If it is not
right to deny a trial even to a lifeless thing . . . surely it is awful and
unrighteous to banish a human being . . . without trial or verdict.'

---

[22] On the 'punishment' of inanimate objects, see Holmes's first lecture in
Common Law, 'Early Forms of Liability': he derives the Roman *noxae deditio* and
Germanic deodand (whereby the object is forfeit to the ruler as agent for the god) to
a desire for vengeance upon the immediate cause or instrument; he assumes the
Prytaneum procedure is of the same type (12–13). But see above Ch. 1 §1.3, on the
workings of miasma. Aeschines 3. 244, mentions expulsion of inanimate objects but
does not connect it with the Prytaneum; he may be referring simply to religious convention, as his other example—casting out the severed hand of a suicide—would
suggest. One revealing example is given in *Suda* N. 410.7 (Adler): the people of
Thasos cast into the sea a statue that fell and crushed its assailant.

We should not lose sight of the fact that our sources also define the homicide jurisdiction of the Prytaneum as those cases where the assailant is unidentified; this is likely to be the principal and original function of the court.[23]

The Prytaneum court is the one site of the five for which we have documentary evidence for a special jurisdiction before Solon. As we have seen, Solon's amnesty law refers to the court of the tribal kings in the Prytaneum.[24] Those exiled by the kings' verdict were probably those charged with 'slaughter' or 'mayhem' (*sphagai*)— indiscriminate killing in factional strife or vendetta. It is such circumstances as these that provide the most likely occasion for proceedings against a killer whose precise identity could not be established, who would have gone into hiding rather than come forward. The ritual condemnation of the weapon is an obvious act of symbolism for which the doctrine of miasma provided a rationale. In origin, however, it is likely that no taint attaches to the object in and of itself but only by contact with the murderer whom the spirit of the dead pursues.[25]

The extant fragment of Draco's law refers to the 'judgement' of the kings, and (I have argued Ch. 2 §3.1) this is more likely to be a preliminary judgement that would prove final in many cases, rather than merely formal pronouncement of a verdict that the *ephetai* had previously reached. Draco's law assumes the principle of *euthydikia:* the kings will first propose consensual settlement by oath-challenge, based upon the self-evident claims of the two parties; if that resolution is unacceptable, the *ephetai* will decide the dispute on the issue that the parties themselves have defined in their oaths. When Draco authorized the jury of fifty-one *ephetai*, the older court of the tribal kings was left with much the same competence it had previously held: in most cases the defendant would go voluntarily into exile but seek to obtain by the oaths of his accusers some

[23] On the general functions, see S. G. Miller, *The Prytaneion* (Berkeley, 1978), 18–24. The ancient texts referring to the homicide court include Harpocration 128. 11–14 (Dindorf) and Pausanias 1. 28. 10. Harpocration says explicitly that the 'stone, stick, sword, or such' is charged when the one who threw or struck it is unidentified.

[24] Plut. *Sol.* 19. 4 (see Ch. 1 §2.2). There is also reference to those exiled by the kings in the Prytaneum in the text of Patrocleides' decree in Andoc. 1. 78. This difficult text will be treated below in discussion of the Delphinium court §2.3.

[25] The practice is neither analogous to deodand nor rooted in vengeance against the instrument itself, as Holmes supposed. See above n. 22; cf. Parker, *Miasma*, 104–43.

guarantee of his claim to eventual settlement and return. There would also be cases in which the defendant failed to come forward; in these cases, whatever claim the plaintiffs urged against him was likely to be upheld by the kings. In those cases where the killer could not be precisely identified, he could be designated by his weapon or other attribute, found guilty and thus condemned to lifelong exile or death by verdict of the kings at the Prytaneum.

It remains uncertain what connection if any there may be between the primitive authority of the tribal kings, led by the *archōn basileus*, and the historical office of the *basileus* as president and preliminary investigator in homicide hearings (see Ch. 4 §1). It is still sometimes argued that the tribal kings regularly convened at preliminaries and at trial alongside the *archōn basileus*. Whether this is so we cannot determine; there is no clear evidence and perhaps little probability that the kings convened in all cases. But there is an inherent plausibility to the notion that the court of the tribal kings continued to meet to render a formal verdict in those cases *where the accused failed to come forward.* In cases where a known defendant had gone into voluntary exile rather than face trial, just as in cases where the killer could not be precisely identified, it is not unlikely that the tribal kings were called upon to support the *archōn basileus* in issuing the condemnation. After all, the competence of the *basileus* was severely restricted in classical times: he would be reluctant to give judgement on his own authority in favour of a plaintiff who clearly intended to take vengeance on the accused. If there continued to be cases of uncontested judgements against accused homicides, then it would seem necessary that some greater official and religious authority be given to the *archōn*'s verdict, if he were to sentence a man to death or lifelong exile. And there is, as we shall see, an intriguing indication that the tribal kings played a role in condemning defendants at the Delphinium court as late as 403 (§2.3).

(ii) Phreatto. The court at Phreatto is an even more puzzling relic. Demosthenes tells us that this court was set aside for those cases where a killer 'exiled for unintentional homicide, not yet reconciled to his prosecutors, faces charges of a second, intentional slaying'. It is this special case that accounts for the venue.[26]

---

[26] Dem. 23. 77: ἐάν τις ἐπ' ἀκουσίῳ φόνῳ πεφευγώς, μήπω τῶν ἐκβαλλόντων αὐτὸν ᾐδεσμένων, αἰτίαν ἔχῃ ἑτέρου φόνου ἑκουσίου. This clause is put in quotes in most major editions (e.g. Dindorf and Blass, Butcher, but not by Gernet in the Budé of 1959), but it is probably a paraphrase involving at least one misleading gloss.

[The lawgiver] convened the jurors where the defendant could face them, designating a certain venue at the sea, 'in Phreatto' as it is called. The defendant comes then and makes his plea on shipboard, without reaching shore; the others hear and judge on land. And if convicted, he rightly pays the penalty for wilful murder; but if acquitted, of this charge he goes free, though he yet faces exile on the earlier count.

The other ancient authorities give a somewhat different account of the procedure. Aristotle in the *Politics* observes that cases such as were heard at Phreatto were likely to occur 'rarely in the whole history of even great states', and his observation is all the more striking as he seems to have assumed a somewhat broader jurisdiction than Demosthenes had defined. In the *Politics* Aristotle speaks simply of a fourth class of homicide charges, 'such as are brought against those exiled for homicide *upon their return*' without specifying that the second charge be intentional murder (1300^b27–30). Thus on the narrow grounds that Demosthenes defined for trial at Phreatto—where a convicted man, exiled for unintentional homicide, is charged with a second count of homicide that must be intentional murder—there would hardly seem to have been much need for a special court. The other ancient testimonia are also at odds with Demosthenes on this point, and on the preponderance of the evidence alone it is reasonable to conclude that the Phreatto court was originally intended for a broader purpose.[27]

In origin the hearings at Phreatto would certainly appear to be a safeguard of the exile's right to seek reconciliation (*aidesis*) and return to Attica, and on this assumption Heitsch has recently proposed a very persuasive explanation for the rationale that Demosthenes gives. He connects the law of Phreatto with other Draconian safeguards against vendetta—notably the law against vindictive slaying of a homicide who abides by the terms of his exile.[28] By the law of Phreatto the exiled homicide who used lethal force against unlawful pursuers and faced a charge of murder on this second count could plead innocence or justification in the court

---

[27] For a more detailed account see my study 'Trial of Exiled Homicides and the Court at Phreatto', *RIDA* 37 (1990), 47–67; cf. Sealey, 'Athenian Courts for Homicide', 285–7.

[28] 'Archon Basileus'; on Phreatto, see esp. pp. 77–8. Heitsch would also include the guarantee of a safe escape for the homicide whose crime is judged unintentional (Dem. 23. 72); and the rule that a defendant accused of *intentional* homicide be allowed to go safely into exile before the final speech at trial.

at Phreatto.[29] This was probably the chief function of the Phreatto court as Demosthenes understood it. But there are a number of considerations that tend to disprove the hypothesis that this was the *original purpose* of the special court.

There is first the obvious question why this procedure is to be available only in cases where an exiled homicide is charged with a second, *intentional* killing. If the principle of fairness that Demosthenes extracts from the law—that a man, once convicted, not be prejudged on a second count—were indeed the aim of the lawgiver, it is difficult to see why a similar trial should not be available also in cases where a second count of unintentional killing was alleged.[30] Presumably, any homicide eligible for *aidesis* should be allowed a hearing on *any* charge that might jeopardize his rightful hopes of a safe return. Yet Demosthenes assumes that *only* a second count of murder is to be tried in this way. This objection applies equally to the rationale that Heitsch has offered: if it were lawgiver's intent to safeguard the rights of the homicide who lawfully abides by the terms of exile, in the event that he must kill in self-defence, then the law should allow for a defence against *any* charge of homicide, whether intentional or not. After all, if the family of the victim were intent upon barring the exile's return they could still do so by charging him with unintentional killing.

Furthermore, if as Demosthenes supposes this procedure applies only in cases of intentional murder, the special precautions at Phreatto seem inconsistent with the law of the classical era. In principle, convicted murderers were to be executed, yet the position of the defendant on shipboard would allow him an avenue of escape even after the verdict had been rendered.[31] These contradictions suggest that the law of Phreatto was originally devised in the era before intentional murder was regularly assigned to a separate court with separate penalties and rules of procedure.

---

[29] For self-defence prosecuted as intentional homicide, see M. Gagarin, 'Self-defense in Athenian Homicide Law', *GRBS* 19 (1978), 111–20; cf. Heitsch, 'Archon Basileus', 78. The lines on defence against assault and seizure in Draco's law, 33–8, do not seem to envision outright acquittal.

[30] A second charge of unintentional homicide could be just as damning, as there would be a judgement against him *in absentia*, and without *aidesis* for this second charge he could be arrested and put to death upon his return.

[31] Murder defendants were allowed to go into exile before the last speech (Ant. 5. 13; *Tetr.* 3. 4. 1), but were executed if they awaited the verdict and were convicted.

In the Aristotelian *Athenian Constitution*,[32] there is no suggestion that the second count of homicide must be intentional murder to qualify for trial in the Phreatto court. The later commentators, moreover, though often dependent on Demosthenes for their knowledge of the homicide courts, generally follow a tradition similar to that in Aristotle: they apparently assume that charges before the Phreatto court need not be intentional murder.[33]

In the fragmentary copy of Draco's law we have clear reference to a trial procedure prescribed for homicides already in exile, in the event there are no eligible kinsmen surviving, 'if the killing was unintentional and the fifty-one justices decide that the killing was unintentional'.[34] It is often assumed that the justices' decision on the question of intent belonged to a previous verdict in response to charges lodged soon after the killing. But this can only be so if in fact intentionality itself was regularly at issue in trials before the homicide judges. The findings of our study thus far tend to prove the contrary, that in the major provisions of Draco's law, for ordinary cases prosecuted by the victim's family, there is *no statutory distinction* between intentional and unintentional homicides.[35]

Among several points in the law that strongly tend to this conclusion must be counted the very provision in question. Pardon by the phratry is allowed only in cases where there are no eligible kinsmen of the victim surviving; and in such special cases pardon is forbidden only if the killing is judged intentional. The natural implication of this exceptional restriction is that under ordinary circumstances the kinsmen were free to accept a settlement or to deny it, regardless of the killer's guilt or innocence of intent. If in ordinary cases prosecuted by immediate kinsmen it was also

[32] *Ath. Pol.* 57. 3: 'If one in exile, under conditions for which pardon is allowed, be subject to a charge of slaying or wounding (ἐὰν δὲ φεύγων φυγὴν ὧν αἴδεσίς ἐστιν αἰτίαν ἔχ[ηι] ἀποκτεῖναι ἢ τρῶσαί τινα), for this they hold trial in Phreatto.'
[33] Thus the entry in *Lexicon Seguerianum* 311. 21–2 tells us that defendants at Phreatto were 'those in exile for unintentional slaying but tried on some other charge' (ἐπ᾿ ἄλλῳ δέ τινι κρινόμενοι). Hesychius, s.v. ἐν Φρεάτου (E 3450 Latte), says simply 'in the court in which they judged cases of unintentional homicide (ἐν τῷ δικαστηρίῳ ἐν ᾧ ἐδικάζοντο ἐπὶ ἀκουσίῳ φόνῳ.). In Pollux 8. 120, discrepancies in the manuscript tradition suggest that the lexicographer found a rather different account than Demosthenes gave, though a later hand attempted to reconcile the two accounts. Harpocration *Lex.* 115. 7 (Dindorf) quotes Dem. 23. 77, but adds that Theophrastus gave another treatment in *Peri Nomon.* Pausanias 1. 28 speaks of 'another charge,' ἕτερον ἔγκλημα.
[34] Dem. 43. 57 (= *IG* I³ 104. 16–20). Text is given Ch. 2 §1.1 n. 3.
[35] See Ch. 2 §3.2; cf. Gagarin, *Drakon,* 65–79.

required that the *ephetai* judge the killing unintentional before settlement were to be allowed, there would be no need of a special rule to this effect in the case of pardon by the phratry.

If the separate penalties of classical procedure—for intentional murder, execution and confiscation; for unintentional killing, exile and *aidesis*—were not yet recognized or enforced by Draco's Law, then ordinarily the verdict of the *ephetai* would have made no meaningful distinction on the question of intent; and therefore the verdict of the *ephetai* on the question of intent must have been given in a special hearing, separate from ordinary trial. Further evidence pointing to this conclusion is to be found in the clause for retroactivity that immediately follows the provision for special pardon and would appear to be most strictly relevant to it. The lawgiver assumes that there are homicides in exile who have not stood trial but will some day seek to return.[36] For the untried killer already in exile, if there are surviving kinsmen of the victim, the terms of settlement are entirely in their power—nothing in Draco's law alters that basic arrangement. But when there are no eligible kinsmen surviving, now the lawgiver provides a means by which the killer may someday return, if he is then judged innocent of malice. Now for the first time and only in these special cases, officers of the *polis* will participate in this decision and make the determination whether the killing was wilful or innocent of intent.

The case of an exiled homicide who would return to Attica to plead innocent of intent would require special arrangements for trial. It is perhaps possible that there were some cases tried at Phreatto while there were yet surviving kinsmen of the victim eligible to prosecute and they wished to deny him the right to return even if he should survive them. They would also attempt to take their vengeance upon him if he could be apprehended in Attica.[37]

---

[36] Heitsch himself, '*Aidesis*', 17–20, suggests that the aim of this provision was to allow for settlement by those homicides who had gone into exile without trial, especially relevant to the transitional period when Draco's law came into effect. In support of the view that the verdict on the question of intent belongs to a later hearing, it should be noticed that the crucial clause belongs to the conditional—'if there be none of these (kin surviving) . . . and the *ephetai* decide . . . '—and that the series of conditionals specifying who is to be eligible to participate in settlement all obviously refer to the period after the trial.

[37] None of the ancient sources mentions the prosecutors at Phreatto, though they specifically account for the positions of the defendant and the judges. The absence of kinsman-plaintiffs at Phreatto would be, in fact, consistent with the nature of the hearing for special pardon: in all likelihood the proceedings would be initiated by family or friends of the defendant, in his behalf, not as an adversarial process.

But most cases would come to trial only when there were no surviving kinsmen who were eligible to prosecute: in those cases the defendant, if he returns without settlement, is still in danger of vindictive attack by other relatives beyond the circle of those eligible to prosecute; he may have been subject to arrest by any concerned citizen.[38] The hearing for special pardon would therefore require precautions to assure the defendant a safe avenue of escape, such as the arrangements at Phreatto.

The special arrangements at Phreatto—with the judges on shore and the defendant aboard ship—have often been interpreted as dictates of miasma-doctrine, but it is more reasonable to suppose that the original purpose of these precautions was not simply to avoid defilement, which could be managed at other border sites, but to ensure that a fair hearing could be given to a defendant whose life was in jeopardy *wherever* he could be apprehended by his pursuers.[39] From these special precautions it is clear that the law of Phreatto assumes much the same conditions as the law cited in Dem. 23. 37, against the vengeful murder of homicides in exile. This provision can be confidently restored in Draco's Law (*IG* I³ 104. 26–9). The law of Phreatto would appear to be subsequent to it. Both statutes clearly address the danger that the victim's kinsmen may pursue their vendetta even at the frontiers and safe areas where traditional sanctions should protect the exile.

In Draco's law the close connection between special pardon and retroactivity—'And let those . . . earlier guilty of homicide be subject to this statute'—suggests that special pardon was especially significant in the period of transition from customary rules, ordinarily involving voluntary exile, to the full application of statute law. The lawgiver expected the traditional arrangement to persist, that those involved in homicides would continue to go voluntarily into exile without trial and later seek to reconcile and return; but he now prescribed procedural rules for trial by an official body of the *polis*, which would tend to restrict private claims and vendettas. The exiled homicide was not to be eternally banished from his homeland, beyond the lifetime of his victim's kin, if he could establish

---

[38] The right of self-help, to seize and put to death wrongdoers, was recognized by Draco (Dem. 23. 28, 51, 60). For the view that this right extended beyond the family to any citizen, see Gagarin, *EGL* 113 n. 35; cf. Hansen, *Apagoge*, 99–108.

[39] Cf. Plato, *Laws* 9. 867e, prescribing special hearings at the border to determine whether the conditions of exile and settlement have been duly met. For the tenuous connection between miasma doctrine and these rules, see Parker, *Miasma*, 104–43.

his innocence of wilful murder. If these were the original aims of the law for special pardon, the Phreatto court would seem suited to the purpose. There is nothing in the authentic Draconian material that would indicate statutory rules for holding such a trial at a specific site, but the need would be immediately obvious. It is therefore likely that the Phreatto court was instituted soon after Draco's law was enacted.

These considerations suggest that the issue before the Phreatto court was not a second, separate count of homicide, as Demosthenes supposed, but a formal question on the original homicide for which the defendant had undergone voluntary exile; he had thus implicitly acknowledged liability but he would now plead innocence of intent in order to qualify for pardon by the phratry. The wording of later commmentators, in fact, suggests that the Phreatto court was not concerned with charges of a second, separate homicide (*heterou phonou*, as Demosthenes insists), but with a *second charge* (*deuteran aitian*, Pollux 8. 120; *heteron enklēma*, Pausanias 1. 28. 11).

Consistent with this reading is the entry in *Lexicon Seguerianum* regarding Zea, the supposed site of the harbour court 'at Phreatto':[40] the defendants were 'those in exile for unintentional homicide but subject to *charges* for intentional homicide'.[41] We are not told that the defendant was charged with a separate *crime* in any of the testimonia independent of Demosthenes.[42] Even the charter myth in Pausanias follows a tradition that the Phreatto court was the proper venue for hearings in which an accused homicide who attempted to return to his homeland might answer charges not on a second count of homicide but on the original charge that barred his return: 'Teucer was the first to make his defence in this manner, pleading to Telamon that he had done nothing to cause the death of Ajax.'

---

[40] *Lex. Seg.* 311. 17–20: ἐν Ζέᾳ· τόπος ἐστὶ παράλιος. ἐνταῦθα κρίνεται ὁ ἐπ' ἀκουσίῳ μὲν φόνῳ φεύγων, αἰτίαν δὲ ἔχων ἐπὶ ἑκουσίῳ φόνῳ. Against identifying the court at Phreatto with the site at Zea, see A. L. Boegehold, 'Ten Distinctive Ballots: The Law Court at Zea', *CSCA* 9 (1976), 8–17.

[41] In legalistic contexts, *aitia* ordinarily means '(formal) charge' rather than 'crime' or actual 'culpability': Antiphon 5. 38, 55, 69, 85; 6. 16–18, 26–7, 34; and note esp. the parallel in Ant. 5. 89–90, where the speaker protests against the form of the charge (*aitiasis*) as an abuse of procedure.

[42] The texts are quoted above nn. 32–4, 40; Harpocration simply follows Dem. 23. 77.

If such was the original purpose of the Phreatto court, it is likely to have been of much greater importance in the development of judicial proceedings for homicide than Demosthenes and his contemporaries realized. Draco's provision for special pardon—'if the killing was unintentional and the fifty-one justices decide that it was unintentional'—opened the door on the question of intentionality and first allowed for official intervention in matters that had previously been solely for the victim's family to weigh. If, as this reconstruction supposes, the Phreatto court was founded to decide precisely such cases as these, it was the immediate predecessor of the Areopagus court itself, as a place of trial on the question of intent. After the founding of the murder court at the Areopagus, the Phreatto court eventually became all but obsolete. The homicide jurisdiction was divided, and it was prescribed by law that much more serious and irrevocable penalties were to be assessed for murder than for unintentional killing. It became necessary at the outset to charge the accused either as an intentional killer or as one innocent of intent; and from then on, the unintentional killer was much less likely to go voluntarily into exile without a judgement to confirm his plea and his right to return. Other Solonian reforms restricting the family's right to retribution are consistent with this model, as we shall now see.[43]

2.2   The Areopagus and the Palladium

(i) Areopagus. We have seen that the law of the Areopagus that Demosthenes cited §22, giving jurisdiction for murder and related offences of premeditation, probably belongs to a later addendum or what I have called a 'Solonian preamble' to the Draconian laws. This conclusion is indicated by the anachronism of the language; it is supported by connection with the law against torture and extortion that follows (28), where the role of 'anyone willing' and trial before a court of the people attest to Solonian authorship.

In the speech *Against Aristocrates* Demosthenes treats the murder court on the Areopagus as an ancient institution of the gods themselves (Ch. 1 §1.1). But there is other testimony on the law of the Areopagus in Demosthenes' speech *Against Leptines' Law* (20. 157–8; cf. §1.2); and in this earlier speech we find the notion that it

---

[43] For reform of *aidesis* restricting the plaintiffs' claims, see Heitsch, '*Aidesis*', esp. 3–10.

was Draco who codified the body of inherited, previously unwritten law, and appointed the Areopagus as the chief court to administer it.

From what crime would we most pray for deliverance, and what is treated with most seriousness among all the laws? That there be no murder against one another, to which end the council on the Areopagus was specially appointed. Now even among the laws on these crimes Draco—though he made it heinous for one man by his own hand to kill another, and prescribed that the killer be barred from the water of purification, from the bowls of libation, from temples and marketplaces, tallying all the other prohibitions that he thought would deter anyone from doing such a thing—none the less he did not deny the claim of justification but established conditions under which it is lawful to kill and, if one do so, he is absolved.

In this passage Demosthenes seems to invoke the name of Draco as a conventional and convenient way of referring to the broad body of law on all aspects of homicide. But it is not unlikely that he is also calling to mind, for many among his audience, a specific text of law—the one legal text, other than their own oath as jurors, with which they were most likely to have certain knowledge: the beginning of the most ancient of the laws, those attributed to Draco. If as I have suggested the official text of the *axones* stood beside a Solonian preamble stating the major modifications, then it is likely that Demosthenes means to evoke precisely that text. This stele would record the general statute for Areopagite jurisdiction (reported in 23. 22), various provisions regarding the outlawry of those convicted (23. 28). Alongside these there stood the prohibitions that Demosthenes lists here: that the killer be barred from rites of purification, that he shall not share in religious observance or set foot in the temples or city centre. In connection with these prohibitions there was evidently some provision for justifiable homicide against violators. The aim of the various prohibitions, Demosthenes concludes, is deterrence; and if the lawgiver expected these prohibitions to achieve that end, he undoubtedly relied as much upon threat of forcible arrest and summary retribution as upon religious conviction.[44]

[44] Lysias 1. 30–1 also indicates that some part of the law on justifiable homicide was to be found among 'the laws of the Areopagus': the Areopagus was not to condemn a man for the killing of an adulterer caught in the act; this provision was probably followed by the rule that such cases should go before the Delphinium court. See §2.3 n. 58, and Ch. 8.

The text of Draco's homicide law that the inscribers followed in 409 appears, after all, to have lost its original heading: the copy begins abruptly, 'even if without intent'. In substance the initial provisions are intact, but the framework has been altered. The original heading had been replaced by some other, formally distinct material. But we must also accept the validity of the law in Dem. 23. 62, the closure against changes in the Draconian *thesmoi*. It is therefore likely that later revisions regarding the Areopagus court were grouped together as a preamble to the axones proper; and this arrangement of the homicide laws would have encouraged popular belief that Draco was indeed the author of them all.

This suggestion—that the allusion to Draco's law in the *Leptines* refers in fact to a Solonian preamble—is a hypothesis and no more. But it is clear in any event that the institutions attributed to Draco are most probably not Draconian. Chief among these is the Areopagus' jurisdiction for intentional murder.[45]

We have direct testimony of ancient authors that Solon was indeed the founder of the Areopagus court of homicide, and we have the resounding silence of Draco's law itself, which so puzzled Plutarch. Neither in the extant fragment nor in any of the authentic citations in Demosthenes do we find mention of the Areopagites or 'the council'.[46] The extant speeches also imply that the question at issue before the Areopagus was precisely the question of malice aforethought. This special jurisdiction is more likely to be an outcome of purposeful reform than merely the odd remnant of what was once an undivided jurisidiction.

Aristotle had addressed the tradition that Solon founded the Areopagus council, and he took exception to it. By this view the Areopagus was the oligarchic element of a mixed constitution that the lawgiver devised; the elected magistrates served as the aristocratic element; the courts of the people, the democratic. It is to this conception that Aristotle objects, arguing that 'two of these ele-

---

[45] G. Thür, 'The Jurisdiction of the Areopagos in Homicide Cases', *Symposion* 1990 (1991), 53–72, argues that *autocheir/bouleusas* was the original division of jurisdiction (the former belonging to the Areopagus as the more serious offence). Wallace (responding to Thür in *Symposion* 1990) rightly takes issue. But there are certainly some passages (e.g. Isoc. *Panegyr.* 111) where (*auto*)*cheir* means more than 'by his own hand', and seems naturally to suggest wilful murder.

[46] *Sol.* 19. 3: 'The majority claims that Solon . . . founded the Areopagus council, and the fact that Draco nowhere mentions the Areopagites seems to confirm their view'; see Ch. 1 §1.2. Cf. Pollux 8. 125 (text given Ch. 1 §1.1 n. 14).

ments, the council and the elected magistrates preceded Solon' (*Politics* 1274ᵃ). Aristotle's objection, however, does not preclude the hypothesis that Solon founded the council as it was historically constituted, assigning to it powers and obligations that no previous body had held. Such would be a plausible basis for the traditions that Plutarch and Pollux report. The Aristotelian *Constitution* reports that Solon altered the duties and qualifications of those who belonged to the ruling body. Assuming they were previously co-opted among the noble clans ('chosen by rank', *Ath. Pol.* 3. 6), we have now to reckon with a body of a different character, to a greater degree responsive to the *dēmos* who elected them and before whom, Aristotle insists, their accountings will finally come. On the strength of this legitimacy, I suggest, Solon authorized the Areopagus council as a special court for crimes of premeditation.[47]

The practical consequences of Draco's legislation suggest that his successor would be called upon to deal with the issues of intentionality more squarely. We have seen that Draco largely preserved the autonomy of the family in private settlement; the law for special pardon was his one clear concession to the compelling sense that punishment should be somehow measured by the wrongdoer's intentions. Draco's modest remedy evidently proved inadequate, and various reforms of Solon's agenda seem to be designed to make up for Draco's deficiencies. It was evidently Solon who limited the period of exile for unintentional killers and regulated the sum of compensation to be arranged in private settlement.[48] These measures amount to a restriction upon vindictiveness and financial aggrandizement by the plaintiffs. The law against torture and extortion of exiled homicides (Dem. 23. 28) serves a similar purpose. The effect of these reforms would be to diminish the lure of *poinē* and turn the plaintiff's attention to other measures of justice, absence of malice, and other mitigating factors.

The concerns of the victims' families would also be more squarely addressed. The new jurisdiction of the Areopagus with specific authority to decide the question of malice aforethought paves the way for the ultimate measure of intervention by the state,

---

[47] Cf. Wallace, *Areopagos*, 39–47, on the 'Solonian constitution' in *Ath. Pol.* 8.

[48] Schol. *Iliad* 2. 665 (= *Solonos Nomoi* [Ruschenbusch] F7): 'It is Hellenic custom . . . to demand lifelong exile, which Solon limited to five years.' Other fragments, F9 and 11–12, attest to some treatment of financial settlement; see Ch. 1 §1.3 nn. 36–7. In general Solon seems to have prescribed specific sums: see fragments 23a–d, 26, 30a–b.

execution of the death penalty by officers of the state.[49] He who is charged with intentional killing and convicted of it will be henceforth sentenced to death or eternal exile; his property will be confiscated by the state and can no longer be bargained in compensation to the victim's family. Where the family demands the ultimate penalty against one whom they accuse of wilful murder, the new high court will decide. And the execution of this judgement, to assure that the offender will be irrevocably removed from the community, is no longer left to the plaintiffs themselves.

The wording of Solon's statute in Dem. 23. 22—'the council of the Areopagus shall give judgement' (*dikazein*)—probably reflects precisely this connection between the new judicial function and the new remedy of state execution. In earlier usage, as we have seen, the role of chiefs and elders 'to give judgement' consists in an order or proposal for the parties to resolve their dispute by asserting their claims under oath and executing those claims in their own right. As a magisterial function, archaic *dikazein*, 'to state the right', was in effect an order for execution, originally to be carried out by the plaintiffs themselves; conversely, the role of the *ephetai* was 'to decide' disputed cases (*diagnōnai*). The law of the Areopagus maintains this distinction: the role of the new high judges 'to give judgement' differs as a magisterial function from that of the *ephetai*. The latter simply decide between the conflicting claims of the two parties, and it remains for the plaintiff himself to exercise his claim. But when the Areopagites find for the plaintiff, their judgement *demands* execution; retribution is no longer left to the plaintiff's discretion. This abrogation of autonomy and self-help is consistent with the force of the law against torture and extortion of ransom for exiled homicides who are captured. Rather, the order for execution that 'judgement' entails will now be carried out by officers of the *polis*.

This reconstruction suggests that there was in origin a profound distinction between the function of the Areopagites in deciding cases of intentional murder and that of the *ephetai* in the other courts. In the Areopagus the ultimate issue is whether the defendant will be put to death: by his insistence upon charges of wilful murder, the plaintiff refuses private settlement. Only if the plaintiff insists that the killer acted with malice aforethought and there-

[49] Cf. G. Thür, 'Die Todesstrafe im Blutprozess Athens', *Journal of Juristic Papyrology*, 20 (1988), 142–56.

fore demands the full penalty does the archon appoint a date for trial at the Areopagus. The outcome will be a straight verdict, either for the plaintiff or for the defendant. A conviction will lead to execution upon the person and property of the defendant; an acquittal will release the defendant from execution by the state. If the defendant can prove that he did not act with malice afore-thought, a verdict of the Areopagus in his favour will amount to a reprieve from state execution. It does not necessarily acquit him of all liability. Ordinarily a defendant before the Areopagus would categorically deny that he committed the act as charged. But in some cases he might be forced to acknowledge culpability as an unintentional killer and to this degree incriminate himself under oath, if he wished to preserve his property and prospects of a safe return to his homeland. In such cases he must either go voluntarily into exile and arrange settlement, or risk the vengeance of his victim's kinsmen; he has, after all, condemned himself to this sentence by his own oath.

To understand this mechanism we must bear in mind the principle of *euthydikia*. The dispute is defined by the oaths themselves in such a way that a decision can be given by a single straight vote, for the plaintiff or for the defendant. In cases where the conflict of oaths centres on the question of malice, the Areopagus will judge on that issue. They will sometimes hand down a verdict in favour of a defendant who is none the less culpable—a verdict of 'guilty though innocent of intent' is for another court, the Palladium, to render.

That the single issue of intent was precisely the question before the Areopagus is attested by the case cited in *Magna Moralia* 1188ᵇ31–7: a woman who caused the death of her husband by a potion was tried before the Areopagus on a charge of intentional murder but acquitted on the grounds that she had acted out of love. The full implications of this case will be treated in a later chapter (Ch. 6)—the anecdote is certainly no proof that a verdict for the defendant was a full reprieve from all penalties. But one fairly certain implication is that the Areopagus did *not* render a verdict of 'guilty though unintentional'.[50]

---

[50] Sealey, 'Athenian Courts for Homicide', 282, briefly considers this explanation and decides 'though not conclusively, that by the time of Aristotle the Areopagus could reach a finding of involuntary homicide', apparently tantamount to full acquittal, but see Ch. 6.

That the issue of malice aforethought was the one issue before the Areopagus is also indicated by the arguments in cases of wounding with intent to kill, which also came before that court. Thus in Lysias' speech *Against Simon*, 42–3, the defendant argues on intent:

Clearly those who framed these laws did not think it warranted to exile those who happened to break some heads in a fight . . . but those who wounded others, intending to kill . . . for such cases they established such severe retribution believing it right for offenders to pay the penalty for what they planned or premeditated. . . . And often in the past you have rendered just such a verdict regarding malice.

Such characterizations of the court's jurisdiction would seem to encompass intentional homicide (Ch. 6 §1.2). We would therefore assume that the high court will not vote for the plaintiff who cannot prove his conviction that death was caused with malice aforethought. We find a further indication that intent was the issue before the Areopagus in the murder case mentioned in the anonymous *Life of Thucydides* §6 (regarding Thucydides the son of Melesias, not the historian). Here we are told that one Pyrilampes was acquitted by the Areopagus for killing his lover in jealous anger.[51] This report cannot be relied upon as historical evidence but it is probably a fair reflection of popular belief that the issue before the Areopagus was precisely the question whether the defendant acted with malice aforethought. On this point it is at least consistent with what Lysias and Aristotle tell us, that the main issue before the Areopagus—in homicide as in wounding, presumably also in arson and poisoning—was the question of *pronoia*. The extant homicide speeches will bear this out.

This special jurisdiction was a natural product of the political development. The Areopagus as a body was first charged with deciding homicide disputes when Solon reconstituted the council as a college of former archons and put the election of archons to a vote of the assembled *dēmos*. Previously the Eupatrid clans had held council among themselves, but now the governing body would be open to those elected by the people. This democratic innovation was to change the character of the ruling council profoundly. Although at the outset the body of former archons would continue

---

[51] See my study 'The Trials of Thucydides "the Demagogue" in the Anonymous *Life of Thucydides the Historian*', *Historia*, 45 (1996), 405–22.

to be dominated by Eupatrid interests, in time other sectors of the *dēmos* would achieve an equal or greater voice. And it was to this body, with at least the promise of broader authority, that Solon entrusted the new jurisdiction, arrogating to them a decision that had been formerly a matter solely for the family of the victim to weigh—whether the killing was unintended and emendable, or malicious and punishable only by death.

(ii) Palladium. The special jurisdiction of the Areopagus represents the first stage of an historical divison of authority among the three major courts of homicide. It was in some respects a profound innovation, but it was also a gesture of supreme deference to the older lawgiver. The *ephetai*, whom Draco had constituted as a committee of fifty-one from among the ruling body of Eupatrids, would now derive from the new ruling council of elected archons; there need be no change in the formula for constituting this body. And the court of the *ephetai* would essentially retain its ancient jurisdiction; only those cases centring on the new issue of intent would go before the full council. If the plaintiff did not wish to dispute the defendant's innocence of malice but only sought suitable retribution for unintended death, he would make his charge accordingly; and if the defendant denied even this involvement, the *archōn basileus* would direct the litigants to the Palladium. A defendant who was there found liable was entitled to all of the old arrangements and protections. Thus Solon abided by the seal upon Draco's *thesmos:* there was nothing in his reforms that overtly altered the composition or diminished the authority of the traditional jury and nothing that infringed upon the autonomy of the parties themselves.

Thus the law of the Palladium represents the *original* authority of the *ephetai* as defined and limited by successive legislation: 'Unintentional homicide even in cases of "planning", or if one kill a slave, a metic, or foreigner, those at the Palladium court (decide).'[52] Just as in the law of the Areopagus, the law of the Palladium contains several refinements upon the basic area of jurisdiction: not only is the court to hear cases where cause of death is attributed to a defendant's unwitting actions, including cases of indirect agency, but it will also hear all cases where the victim is a non-citizen. The killing of non-citizens—slaves, metics, or foreigners—was

[52] *Ath. Pol.* 57. 3: τῶν δ' ἀκουσίων καὶ βουλεύσεως, κἂν οἰκέτην ἀποκτείνῃ τις ἢ μέτοικον ἢ ξένον, οἱ ἐπὶ Παλλαδίῳ.

probably first recognized as a special category under the law sometime after the original division of jurisdiction. But this later statutory distinction simply gave official recognition to what was
implied in that first division of authority: only cases of the *intentional* killing of an *Athenian* were reserved for judgement of the
Areopagus; all other cases remained for the *ephetai* to decide.[53]

Similarly the specific clause of statute assigning to the Palladium
certain cases of 'planning' a homicide is probably to be understood
as a later specification of the original jurisdiction assigned to the
ephetai in Draco's law (*IG* I³ 104. 12–13). By the Areopagite model,
however, this was a Draconian innovation transferring part of the
ancient Areopagite jurisdiction to a lesser court. Along these lines,
it is usually supposed that Palladium jurisdiction encompasses *all*
cases of 'planning' a homicide—all those originally covered by the
meaning of Draco's law, obviously including intentional homicide.
Since 'planning' seems to be treated by later authors as a distinct
criminal category rather than simply a subset of homicide, it is
sometimes supposed that the term also denoted *attempts* at murder
(other than wounding). The latter notion—that the Athenians recognized criminal intent without injury—was rightly dismissed by
MacDowell; but even he held on to the notion that the Palladium
tried all cases of 'planning'—including *intentional* homicide. This
long-standing view has been recently disproved by Gagarin.[54]

The jurisdiction of the Palladium included all cases of unintentional homicide, *even* those cases involving 'planning'—determining events or instigating actions that inadvertently lead to death.
Full discussion of this legalistic concept is best reserved for a later
chapter (Ch. 7) on the major evidence, Antiphon 6. But for now we
should proceed on the natural assumption that the Palladium jurisdiction for 'planning' is consistent with the fundamental division
between intentional and unintentional homicide; it represents a
legalistic refinement upon that basic distinction rather than a
departure from it.

[53] Sealey offers a similar reconstruction, 'Athenian Courts for Homicide', esp.
290–3.
[54] See M. Gagarin, '*Bouleusis* in Athenian Homicide Law', *Symposion* 1988
(1991), 81–99, and MacDowell, *AHL* 60–9. Where the Aristotelian *Constitution*
(*Ath. Pol.* 57. 3) and later tradition (cf. Harpocration 127. 13, Dindorf) report that
the Palladium jurisdiction included charges μὴ ἐκ προνοίας καὶ βουλεύσεως, we
should understand that καὶ βουλεύσεως does not designate a separate jurisdiction
but a subset within the general category of unintentional killing.

Thus the various provisions of the Palladium law are not simply an assortment of petty jurisdictions that were delegated piecemeal from the Areopagus to the lesser court. Rather these provisions represent what remained of the original undivided jurisdiction, after the Areopagus council was called upon to judge the intentional murder of an Athenian. The law of the Palladium court itself, formally defining the jurisdiction as it was known in classical times, must therefore belong to the era of Solon's reform.[55]

There is one provision of the Palladium law, however, that is often treated as evidence that a separate jurisdiction for unintentional homicide goes back to Draco: this is the law cited in Dem. 23. 72, guaranteeing to the convicted homicide a safe departure to exile.

What then does the law say?—that one convicted of unintentional homicide depart within a specified period, by a prescribed route, and abide in exile until he is reconciled with [the family]† of the victim.[56]

This is a paraphrase of the law, but it appears to be substantially accurate. Thus the speaker refers to reconciliation with 'one' or 'some' among the family of the victim, where we can be reasonably certain that the statute either specified who was eligible to grant pardon, or made cross-reference to the rules in Draco's law. Similarly he speaks of 'a specified period' of time and 'a prescribed route', where surely the statute must have been more specific as to how, by whom, or by what rule the time and place were to be determined. Again, 'convicted of unintentional homicide' is Demosthenes' rendering of a context he thought his audience would find obscure. The 'conviction' was simply a ruling for the plaintiff; since the Palladium court was set aside for those cases where the question of intent was not at issue, a defendant who

---

[55] The archaeological evidence is not much help. Travlos, 'The Lawcourt ΕΠΙ ΠΑΛΛΑΔΙΩΙ', *Hesperia*, 43 (1974), 500–11, identifies the building excavated south of the Acropolis at Diakou and Makri streets as the Palladium court; he concludes (505) that the structure that stood there in classical times was built at the end of the 6th c. (or beginning of the 5th). There are remains of an older structure at the site. The identification is by no means certain; A. L. Boegehold, *The Athenian Agora*, vol. 28, *Lawcourts at Athens* (Princeton, 1995), 47–8, discounts it and locates the Palladium at Phaleron.

[56] For the MS reading αἰδέσηταί τινα, most editors suppose αἰδέσηταί τις, but given the older usage of αἰδεῖσθαι, that change seems unwarranted. And it does not remove the more serious difficulty: it was not sufficient for the defendant to reconcile with *one* among the family of the victim; there must be unanimous agreement among all eligible kinsmen—'he who objects shall prevail'.

failed to impress the justices with the righteousness of his plea was said to be 'convicted of unintentional homicide'.

By this reconstruction, the statute prescribing a safe avenue of exile for those convicted of unintentional homicide belongs to the laws of the several jurisdictions (§1.2.3). These were framed after the homicide jurisdiction was divided between the *ephetai* and the Areopagus; only then was it meaningful to charge a killer specifically with unintentional homicide. The arrangement of Demosthenes' account suggests that this statute belongs to a body of law separate from the Draconian original. And the prescriptive character of this law also sets it apart: among the laws directly attributed to Draco (23. 37–62) there is no suggestion of precise rules for executing judgement, such as this paraphrase suggests. The next provision in Demosthenes' paraphrase, following the law for the convicted killer's departure and apparently joined closely to it in Demosthenes' source, similarly prescribes specific performance (72):

Then [the lawgiver] defines in what manner [the exile] is to return—not left to chance, however he happens to arrive, but after sacrifice and purification, the other requirements that he has specified must be done.

Such statutory prescriptions probably developed through historical usage, and not simply by lawgiver's *fiat*.[57] These provisions are quite different in character from the ordinances preserved from Draco's *thesmoi*, but they are typical of Solon's reform: precise, prescribed remedies tended to replace the open texture of self-help and private settlement.

2.3   The Delphinium Court

There is a third court, . . . the most hallowed and awe-inspiring of them all, for those cases where a man confesses to the killing but claims to have acted lawfully: this is the court at Delphinium. For those who originally defined these jurisdictions . . . considered that Orestes confessed to having killed his mother and was acquitted by a jury of gods, and they reckoned that there *is* some justifiable killing—for the gods would not have rendered an unjust verdict. They therefore defined by statute the circumstances in which it is lawful to kill.   (Dem. 23. 74)

---

[57] Elsewhere Demosthenes mentions similarly precise rules prohibiting aid or purification of the homicide among the laws of the Areopagus court, and these he attributes to Draco by ideological convention: Dem. 20. 157–8. See above §1.2.

The court at the Delphinium, where the defendant would plead that the killing was justifiable by law, is perhaps the most problematic of the three major courts. What precisely was at issue before the Delphinium court? Was it a question of whether the killing conformed to certain legal categories, as Demosthenes seems to suggest? Or was it more a question of motivation and legal cause, as we might suppose from the argument of Lysias *On the Slaying of Eratosthenes*? The topic in the *Tetralogies* on 'the law prohibiting [even] justifiable killing' suggests that the principle of legal justification had long been a subject of controversy.[58] Demosthenes' exercise in popular jurisprudence suggests that the controversy was not yet resolved. In his earlier account of the law relevant to this jurisdiction (53–9), he has treated the very concept of 'justifiable' homicide as a difficult one that must be explicated point by point. Here he confuses the issue by treating the trial of Orestes on the Areopagus as a charter myth for the Delphinium jurisdiction.

But the legendary paradigm is not so remote from the workings of this court as it might at first appear. The slaying of a homicide who trespasses where prohibited by reason of bloodshed—such as the slaying of Clytemnestra—was indeed among those cases in which ancient custom deemed the killing righteous and historical law afforded the killer certain safeguards. The mythic precedent suggests perhaps that unwritten law might be invoked as legal justification. The other available evidence suggests that the defendant's plea must be based upon some statutory protection, and Demosthenes' explanation is in fact consistent with that principle. We have no indication whatever (apart from the legendary precedent) that a defendant could base his plea upon unwritten law. If we assume then that a valid defence before the Delphinium must invoke specific provisions of written law, we are faced with the necessary conclusion that the Delphinium jurisdiction was itself a product of historical legislation. This seems to be, after all, what Demosthenes was trying to explain—that primitive claims of religious or customary justification were in time reduced to statute,

---

[58] On the rule 'prohibiting even justifiable killing' in *Tetr.* see Ch. 5 §3; and on Lys.1, Ch. 8. On the nature of the cult see F. Graf, 'Apollon Delphinius', *MH* 2 (1979), 2–22. The shrine in Athens was located south of the Olympieum near the Ilisus. Andocides 1. 78 mentions those condemned to exile by the Delphinium court alongside those condemned by the *ephetai* and therefore excluded from the amnesty (below).

and the Delphinium court was established to maintain the legal protections embodied in statute.

Because the plea of justifiable homicide must have some basis in specific law, it is sometimes supposed that the distinguishing feature of Delphinium trials was the strictly legal question of whether the protections of law formally applied. But this view must be rejected on several counts. In such cases as athletic contest or friendly casualties in warfare, it seems unlikely that there would be any question before the court whether the killing indeed took place in those circumstances. The prima-facie validity of the plea, whether it indeed conformed to the conditions prescribed by law, was determined by the *basileus*, along with other questions of admissibility, at the preliminary hearings (Ch. 4). But most importantly, the direct evidence gives no indication that questions of legal definition were at issue. Demosthenes' explanation (54–6) would suggest that the *victim*'s role in the events was the crucial factor. The defence in Lysias 1 suggests again that the legal criteria were not disputed: the issue at trial is whether the defendant in fact initiated the fatal events of his own motivation, or the victim himself is responsible (Ch. 8).

There is one distinctive feature of these proceedings that will help us to understand this approach: whether a case will go before the Delphinium rather than elsewhere is determined not by the plaintiff's charge but by the defendant's plea. In cases going before the Areopagus or Palladium it was the plaintiff who determined which court would decide the issue. In most cases the *archōn basileus* would be obliged to let the proceedings go forward to whatever tribunal the charge would indicate, so long as charges were admissible prima facie on the basis of preliminary proceedings. If the plaintiff charged that the killing was intentional and thus demanded the extreme penalties, then the case would ordinarily go before the Areopagus; if he believed the killing unintentional and was willing to accept a lesser penalty of exile with the prospect of settlement, the case went to the Palladium. But if the plaintiff contends that the killing was wilful and the defendant pleads that his actions were justified by law, then the case will go before the Delphinium court.[59] So long as the question of intent was *not* defined as a separate criterion, there was no reason to treat a plea of

[59] On the Delphinium jurisdiction see MacDowell, *AHL* 70–81; on choice of venue, Heitsch, 'Archon Basileus', esp. 72–4.

justifiable homicide as a separate issue. If intent was not regarded as a separate question, then in all cases the issue was essentially the same: was the defendant liable or was some other factor to be regarded as cause of death? Only after it is established that plaintiffs charging wilful murder and demanding execution will go to one court and those willing to accept a lesser penalty for an unintended killing proceed to another, is it necessary to set aside yet a third venue where the defendant will acknowledge that he willingly committed an act of violence but plead that he is exonerated by the law.

As we have seen (§1.2.2), it is evidently the law of the Delphinium that is entered in the text of Demosthenes' *Against Aristocrates* among the laws of Draco, at §53. It is probably the same law to which we have brief reference in the *Athenian Constitution* 57. 3. From the specific instances listed in the two accounts, it is sometimes supposed that a verdict of guilty in the Delphinium court could amount to *either* intentional *or* unintentional homicide. In those cases where the defendant acts against sexual assault, the case would certainly centre on his motives. Our only surviving speech in such a case—Lysias 1—shows clearly that the charge was likely to amount to entrapment. If the defendant is found guilty in such a case, his crime amounts to murder and he must suffer the same punishment as those convicted at the Areopagus. On the other hand, killings in athletic contest or in combat seem approximate to accidental death and thus resemble cases at the Palladium; one might therefore suppose, a verdict against the defendant would amount to exile for unintentional killing. But this latter inference is mistaken. In these two instances—death in competition or combat—the issue again involves intentionality: whether the killing is committed with malice upon the pretext of legal cause. This implication is at least consistent with the relevant arguments in the *Tetralogies*. The second Tetralogy, involving a fatal accident in athletic training, with no suspicion of malice, was set before the Palladium as a case of unintentional killing. The third Tetralogy, however, focuses upon the killer's motivation in using lethal force against an assailant; a conviction would entail the death penalty; and this text, I argue, represents a case for the Delphinium.[60]

---

[60] This is crucial but problematic evidence on a number of points and will be reviewed in detail, Ch. 5 §§1 and 3.

By this reconstruction, the law of the Delphinium is to be understood as a further amendment to Draco's procedural rules, subsequent to Solon's reform. There was no need for a separate court of
justifiable homicide until Solon set aside the Areopagus as a special
court for crimes of malice aforethought against Athenian citizens.
The earlier lawgiver had prescribed that the killer, whatever his
plea, should seek refuge in exile until reconciliation could be
arranged. Exile was not itself a penalty but part of the mechanism
of private settlement. Draco certainly pronounced the killer free
from claims to compensation in some cases (in defence against violent seizure or abduction, for instance); but his solution to the
problem of legal justification seems to have taken the direction of
'warrant' (*endeixis*). Those who would avail themselves of justifiable retribution must first inform the magistrates and arm themselves with the authority of law; there can then be no dispute of
their right. In many instances, however, Draco's 'warrant' would
not suffice: grieving and vindictive kinsmen might make it dangerous for a killer claiming justification to remain in Athens until the
matter could be decided. The Delphinium law then provides precisely the rule that is needed: in those cases where the defendant
claims legal justification, he has the protection of law until such
time as the tribal kings or *ephetai* pass judgement against him—he
need not take refuge in exile (*mē pheugein*).

Evidently the defendant might appeal to any law providing a
basis for justifiable killing; he was not limited to the instances specified in the Delphinium law. The description in the Aristotelian
Constitution (57. 3) suggests that all cases involving legal justification would be tried before this court, not simply the few standard
instances—athletic competition, warfare, and retribution against
adultery. Thus presumably, in cases of killing a subversive or other
public enemy or in defence against illegal seizure—where the law
provides *nēpoinei tethnanai*—if legal justification were disputed, the
defendant would be tried at the Delphinium. In cases of killing a
thief or adulterer caught in the act, or other instances where immediate self-help is allowed, then presumably the plaintiffs must
charge that the killing was *wilful* beyond legal justification. The
defendant must plead that he is not the killer, that other causal factors—the recklessness of the offender and the command of law—
brought about the killing. He must show that the events were not
his doing, that he had no independent motivation. This, as we shall

see, is precisely the case that Lysias attempts to make in the speech *On the Slaying of Eratosthenes*. This was the most viable defence at the Delphinium, to blame the victim and maintain the fiction of legal cause.

The homicide court at the Delphinium is logically the last in the sequence: cases going before the Delphinium were those in which the defendant would invoke protections of statute law; this jurisdiction therefore developed as a consequence of written law rather than a relic of unwritten rules. And the very nature of this jurisdiction presupposes that another special court was already assigned the separate issue of intent. This last court of the *ephetai* was conceived as a solution to a persistent problem, a generation after Draco first codified the customary rules of self-help. The special court for justifiable killing was probably instituted soon after Solon assigned jurisdiction for murder to the Areopagus, as a further consequence of *mens rea*: this court of last resort would hear those cases where the killer could not deny hostile intent but would justify his motivation by the law. Where this plea of legal cause was disputed by the victim's kin and could not be vindicated in judgement before the tribal kings, it would go before the *ephetai* for a decision at the Delphinium.[61]

Draco had opened the door on the question of intent with his provision for pardon by the phratry in those cases where there were no surviving kinsmen of the victim eligible for *aidesis*. Draco's half-measure evidently proved inadequate, and Solon sought to remedy the failings of his predecessor: henceforth if the kinsmen were determined to deny the killer any opportunity for settlement, they must charge him with intentional homicide and prosecute before the newly empowered court of former archons; if convicted, the killer would be subject to execution and confiscation of property by officials of the state.

The Delphinium jurisdiction represents a second question of intentionality, one that arises only after this first question of malice

---

[61] Draco undoubtedly recognized justifiable homicide—or rather denied retribution—in such cases as immediate defence against violent theft or abduction, apprehension of exiled homicides returning illegally, self-help against sexual violation of the *oikos*, and against attempted tyranny. Where legal justification was disputed, the *ephetai* would decide the straight question of liability, as in any other case. A separate jurisdiction for such cases was later established and a number of instances were recognized where, in the interest of public policy, the killer could claim legal justification.

aforethought has been asked and answered. In the Areopagus court
the defendant would answer that he did not intend to kill. But in
cases before the Delphinium this is not a viable defence: the answer
to the first question is that the defendant did indeed intend to use
lethal force—this is true in all the instances defined by statute and
contemplated in Demosthenes' commentary. Even in an athletic
contest the killing is *not* considered 'excusable' as an accident:
Demosthenes explains that the killing will be found justifiable on
grounds that the victim himself is at fault, 'as he proved unequal to
the struggle'. It is thus the second question of motives that must
now be answered—whether the killer's intentional act of violence is
strictly in obedience to the law. It might yet be found that his wilful act was proximate cause in a wrongful death: it might be argued
that he had used the legal protections as a pretext and thus murdered by premeditation (as in the case of Lysias 1). At the very
least, it must be shown that it was his intentional act of violence that
initiated the causal sequence, a reckless act beyond the dictates of
law. The latter rationale is demonstrated in the third Tetralogy:[62]
the defendant cannot deny that he intended to injure his opponent,
and it is not enough to show that he did not specifically intend to
kill; he must show that his intentional act of violence was not the
cause of death. If convicted, in either of these examples, defendant
would be guilty of intentional homicide and, presumably, subject
to the same penalties of execution and confiscation handed down by
the Areopagus.

The nature of proceedings in the Delphinium court is of special
significance for the role of the *archōn basileus* and the tribal kings in
the complex preliminary process of *prodikasiai* (Ch. 4 §1). For it
was probably the function of the *basileus* himself to determine
whether in fact the defendant's plea of legal justification was valid
prima facie—that is, whether the wording of the law that he
invoked could in fact apply to the case at hand. This juristic question does not appear to be at issue at trial before the *ephetai*. By the
very nature of this special jurisdiction, it is reasonable to suppose
that whenever the victim's kin disputed the legal grounds of a
defendant's plea, the kings themselves—the *archōn basileus* supported by the tribal kings—would decide on their own authority
whether defendant's plea was admissible. If the *basileis* gave judge-

---

[62] So I conclude, Ch. 8; but cf. Gagarin, 'Self-Defense'.

ment for the defendant, then the usual sequence of proceedings
went forward; but if they disallowed the defendant's plea, their ruling would amount to a verdict of exile or self-help execution. The
defendant must necessarily seek refuge in voluntary exile or face
the threat of vendetta. As he has admitted under oath that he is
implicated in a violent death, he faces the same automatic consequences that would attend any other verdict or admission of guilt.

There is an intriguing testimony to the authority of the tribal
basileis in such cases: in the amnesty law cited by Andocides (1. 78)
we find reference to 'those under sentence of exile or death from the
Delphinium, condemned by the kings'. It is sometimes supposed
that the Delphinium court is mentioned here simply as one among
the courts of the *ephetai*, who are mentioned in the previous
clause—the redundancy belongs to official jargon. But the natural
inference would be that *these* exiles, condemned by the kings at the
Delphinium, *were distinct* from those exiled by verdict of the
ephetai. And this distinction would suggest that even in the late
fifth century there were some homicides exiled from the
Delphinium court by the ancient power that Draco had recognized
in his initial provision: 'let the kings give judgement.'

Such was the division of jurisdiction that emerged with Solon's
reforms. From this formative era the homicide courts appear to
have remained, true to tradition, largely unchanged down to the fall
of the democracy and its restoration in 403. A number of the refinements that are found in classical procedure appear to have developed in the intervening period, and we shall retrace some of these
developments in the following chapter. But the fundamental rules
of jurisdiction, determining what issue was to be decided before
what court, appear to largely unaffected—even, so far as we can
judge, when the Areopagus' political jurisdiction was abolished in
461.

§3. Justifiable Homicide and the Amnesty of 403/2

There was, however, one final stage in the evolution of the courts
that requires brief notice here to complete the outline of historical
development and lay the groundwork for the closing chapters of
this study. We know that the settlement that ended civil conflict in

403/2 involved some revision of rules affecting both *dikai phonou* and the alternative procedures, warrant and arrest (*endeixis/ apagōgē*). The effect of these changes has been often misinterpreted. It is generally assumed that the citizen's oath 'not to remember past wrongs' (*mē mnēsikakein*) was meant as a general prohibition against partisan litigation.[63] Thus, it is supposed, the broad principle of amnesty itself constituted one of the chief legal complications in Lysias 13, *Against Agoratus*, where the defendant is charged with complicity in political murders—precisely the sort of case the oath would seem to disallow. On the same assumption, one might conclude, the oligarch Eratosthenes, who is attacked at his accounting in Lysias 12, could not have been otherwise prosecuted for the killing of Polemarchus because of the pledge 'not to remember past wrongs', if by this rule partisans were prohibited from legal action for wrongs committed under the oligarchic regime. The ancient evidence clearly shows, however, that homicide procedure was subject to specific restrictions under the new regime; these rules affected both the traditional *dikai phonou* and those cases, like Lysias 13, prosecuted by warrant and arrest.

3.1   Restriction of *Dikai Phonou*

The Aristotelian *Constitution* listing the main provisions of the agreement, reports that *dikai phonou* were to be prosecuted 'according to ancestral law, if a man kills or wounds another *by his own hand*' (*autocheiria*; 39. 5). The latter clause is a very important qualification: cases other than direct agency—complicity or any other indirect involvement—were not actionable under the traditional procedure. That is to say, the amnesty excluded those cases which would have been prosecuted on grounds of 'planning' (*bouleusis*). This concept encompassed many degrees of indirect agency, including cases of unintentional involvement; in legalistic terms it is the opposite of killing by one's own hand (for full discussion, see Chs. 6–7). Some restriction of prosecution on grounds

---

[63] Thus A. Dorjahn, *Political Forgiveness in Old Athens* (Evanston, Ill., 1946), 24–33, treats the oath as a broad prohibition against vindictive legal action, but he must make room for numerous exceptions; the same basic approach is followed (though with better insight) in Loening's study, *Reconciliation*, 133–200. For this approach to Lysias 13, cf. F. Blass, *Die attische Beredsamkeit* (Leipzig, 1887–90), 555; and see further critique of received opinion in Ch. 9 §3.

of 'planning' was probably a welcome revision in view of the juristic difficulties that had arisen from this ill-defined concept in the late fifth century. And there was an urgent need that these difficuties be resolved in the situation after 404: there were undoubtedly many who were known or supposed to have acted as informants or accessories in the executions, and upon whom the kinsmen of those slain would readily have taken vengeance.

The Thirty routinely enlisted others, sometimes including non-partisans, to take part in the arrest of their victims: thus we learn that Socrates himself was called upon to join in the arrest of Leon of Salamis; and Meletus, the accuser of Andocides, actually took part in the arrest. Similarly Eratosthenes, who took part in the arrest of Polemarchus but avowedly opposed his execution, might have been prosecuted for his complicity were it not for the special restriction against this kind of homicide prosecution.[64] Under the traditional procedure such involvement (even unwilling) would have been actionable as planning or determining. This situation threatened an avalanche of litigation and, undoubtedly, of extra-judicial remedies as well—hence the qualification that traditional proceedings for homicide were available only against the direct agent, who killed 'by his own hand'.

This restriction formally applied only for the amnesty, but it inevitably affected popular understanding of permanent legal principles. Andocides (1. 94) assures us that the ancient principle 'guilty alike is the planner as the perpetrator' continued to be valid; and the report in *Ath. Pol.* 57. 3 shows that planning was still recognized in law as a basis for prosecution in the later fourth century, 'even in cases of unintentional killing' (Ch. 7 §1). But there is some indication that the problematic concept of 'unintentional planning' was permanently devalued by the revisions of 403. We know of no case after Antiphon 6 (419/418 BC) where a defendant is charged with homicide in a *dikē phonou* on such grounds. Given the paucity of evidence, this gap may mean very little. But there is a telling remark in Plato's treatment of causal agency in the *Laws*: apparently the concept of killing by one's own hand, *autocheiria*, had come to encompass some degrees of indirect involvement that once

---

[64] Most commentators recognize that Lysias' case against Eratosthenes could not have been prosecuted by *dikē phonou* because of the new restrictions; Loening, *Reconciliation*, 92–112, to the contrary.

were described as *bouleusis*.[65] The outmoded concept of 'planning' had given way to an even more awkward fiction.

We see perhaps the beginnings of this development in the immediate post-revolutionary era, in Lysias 12 (*Against Eratosthenes*) and 13 (*Agoratos*) where the prosecutors portray the defendants as the immediate authors of the killings, not as accomplices or accessories, though they were merely instrumental in executions that they did not design. The provision against guilt by planning is also indicated in the hypothetical case against Meletus that Andocides describes in 1. 94: Meletus had been one of those enlisted by the Thirty in the arrest of Leon, and Meletus admits as much; the law recognizes the principle that the planner is subject to the same penalty as is he who acts by his own hand; on this principle Meletus is surely liable to the sons of Leon for their father's murder. But 'one must abide by the laws in effect since [403/2]' and for this reason—because of the recent restriction of *dikai phonou*—Meletus had not been charged.[66]

3.2 *Mnēsikakein*, Self-help, and Summary Arrest

The citizen's oath 'not to remember past wrongs' is often construed as a general restriction against partisan lawsuits: this is, supposedly, the legal basis for Meletus' immunity and for certain complications in the arguments of Lysias 12 and 13; it is even mistakenly brought into the case against Socrates.[67] Supposedly the oath itself was intended to disallow or discredit any vindictive court action to settle the score for wrongs done under the oligarchy.[68] But that

---

[65] *Laws* 9. 865–72, esp. 865b–c: in cases of killing 'either by one's own person or through the persons of others' the killer is wholly responsible as *autocheir*. See T. J. Saunders, *Plato's Penal Code* (Oxford, 1991), 236–8; cf. Ch. 7 §2.

[66] It is commonly supposed that Meletus was not charged simply because of the amnesty, either by reason of the oath μὴ μνησικακεῖν, or because one must apply the laws as of 403/2 (i.e. disregarding earlier offences): cf. MacDowell, *Andokides on the Mysteries* (Oxford, 1962), 133, taking issue with Bonner and Smith, ii. 82. But see Ch. 9 §3 and cf. Loening, *Reconciliation*, 102–8.

[67] T. Brickhouse and N. Smith, *Socrates on Trial* (Princeton, 1989), 72–4 and *passim*, suppose that Socrates' association with Critias and Alcibiades could not be grounds for the charge of corrupting the youth, as the amnesty barred legal action for wrongs of the earlier era.

[68] Thus Dorjahn, *Political Forgiveness*, 32–3, interprets μὴ μνησικακεῖν as a bar against vindictive legal action, but makes a list of stipulations: '(1) informers were not subject to prosecution . . . ; (2) confiscated property was restored; (3) actions to recover money were permissible'; but '(4) suits for damages were prohibited; (5) at

assumption is based largely upon the prologue to Isocrates 18, *Against Callimachus*, where we are apparently told that the new procedure for *paragraphē* was instituted expressly to combat vindictive litigation. This interpretation has led to serious misreading of the other cases, but it is a matter that will require detailed discussion in connection with broader legal developments, and that discussion must be taken up elsewhere.[69] Our purpose here is to follow out the implications of the oath *mē mnēsikakein* in the workings of homicide law. Whatever its relevance *in court*, the oath clearly had certain consequences for *out-of-court* remedies.

'To remember past wrongs'—*mnēsikakein*—in its most familiar usage, describes the reprisals of national or tribal hostility *without sanction of law*: thus Plato in the Seventh Letter speaks of those victorious in factional violence 'who remember past wrongs in wanton bloodshed'.[70] Similarly, in an inscription of about the same era (363/2), we find the Athenians and the people of Iulis (on the nearby island of Ceos) pledge reconciliation, 'I shall not remember past wrongs, . . . nor shall I kill or drive into exile.'[71] The negative, 'not to remember past wrongs', affirms reconciliation between two states or two parties in civil conflict; it is an affirmation that neither side will take unilateral retribution in redress of wrongs done by groups or individuals on the other side.[72] It is the clear intent of the

a candidate's *dokimasia*, acts committed under the Thirty could be made an issue; and (6) in any prosecution, conduct under the Thirty might be treated in proof of character.'

[69] Some of my arguments on *paragraphē* were presented at a meeting of the American Philological Association, Dec. 1993, 'Archinus and the Violator of Amnesty: *Ath. Pol.* 40. 2'. I argue that the original aim of this procedure was not to block *partisan* lawsuits *per se* but allow a procedural challenge against any legal action in violation of specific covenants of the amnesty (*synthēkai*). This position is based upon the early cases prosecuted by *paragraphē* and procedural parallels, together with the more common application of *mē mnēsikakein* as a seal upon covenants of arbitration (cf. [Dem.] 59. 46–7). It will be argued more fully elsewhere. On pronouncements of the orators regarding the amnesty as a bar against partisan litigation, see for now Ch. 9 §3.2.2.

[70] *Ep.* VII. 336e–337a: σφαγαῖς μνησικακοῦντες. For similar usage, cf. Diodorus 15. 40. 2 (probably following Ephorus) of civil conflict in an Arcadian town, Phialeia (375/4), ὁ δημοτικὸς ὄχλος . . . ἐμνησικάκει . . . πολλοὺς ἀποσφάξαντες.

[71] *IG* II² 111 (= Tod 142), lines 58–60, 82; the meaning of this pledge as a disavowal of violent reprisal is all the more evident as it stands in contrast to the persecution of pro-Athenian citizens of Iulis by compatriots who had seized property and taken lives in direct contravention of earlier agreements (lines 27–41).

[72] Cf. *IG* I³ 76 (= Tod 68) line 15, a decree of 422: Athenians come to terms with the rebellious Bottiaeans; the generals, council, and other officials are to pledge no reprisal, οὐ μνησικακήσω. Herodotus 8. 29, reporting the Thessalians' message to

oath of 403 that the Athenian people as a body shall not victimize the oligarchs or their sympathizers, as often out of civil conflict the defeated party became victims of reprisal. The most immediate effect of such a provision is that there would be no unilateral *group* action to settle the score (i.e. decrees of council or assembly for confiscations, banishment, etc.). But clearly it also extends to the actions of individuals who seek redress of their own personal grievances. What then does it mean for an individual to 'remember past wrongs'?

Mnēsikakein, of course, sometimes simply describes an *attitude*— 'to bear a grudge'—without implying immediate action. But where *mnēsikakein* is used of individual *action*, there is the clear implication that the action involves retributive self-help. Thus Andocides, inveighing against his accusers (1. 95), calls Epichares 'the very reminder of his own wrongs' (ὁ μνησικακῶν αὐτὸς αὑτῷ). He cites the decree of Demophantus declaring outlaw anyone who serves in council with an oligarchic regime—'Let him be slain with impunity . . . and the killer keep his property'—as an example of the traditional justice against collaborators that his accuser has escaped by the amnesty. The evident implication is that if 'remembering past wrongs' were allowed, Epichares would be subject to summary execution and confiscation by anyone willing.

In the aftermath of civil conflict the natural implication of the oath *mē mnēsikakein* was not that a litigant was prohibited from taking partisan claims to court, but that he could not in good conscience resort to *out-of-court* remedies in violation of specific covenants. This principle is crucial to the case mentioned in the Aristotelian *Athenian Constitution* (40. 2): we are told that Archinus, the amnesty activist who later authored the *paragraphē* legislation, first enforced the amnesty by arresting an unnamed citizen who had begun 'remembering past wrongs against the returnees'. Archinus brought him before the council and per-

their inveterate adversaries the Phocians, 'though it is in our power to seize your land and enslave you', οὐ μνησικακέομεν; Thuc. 4. 74. 2–3, of Brasidas' settlement between the parties at Megara, μηδὲν μνησικακήσειν, followed by violation of the oath as those in power engineered the execution of a hundred leaders of the opposition. For the Athenians' oath of reconciliation, cf. *Ath. Pol.* 39. 6; Xen. *Hell.* 2. 4. 38 and 43. The oath is conceived as a covenant between the two parties; in Lys. 13 (*Agoratus*) 78 and [Lys.] 6 (*Andocides*) 39, it is argued that defendant is not party to 'the covenants'. Loening, *Reconciliation*, 135, 195, condemns the argument as specious, but see Ch. 9 §3.2.

suaded them to have him put to death without trial as an example
to others. The example seems to have served its purpose: we are
told, 'no one ever thereafter remembered past wrongs'. This
vaunted eradication of vindictiveness is contradicted by quite a few
court cases involving patently partisan issues. Yet scholars generally suppose that what is meant by *mnēsikakein* in this context is
precisely that—vindictive litigation on partisan claims.[73] The
Athenian Constitution gives no indication that the punishment was
disproportionate or illegal, and in light of the general usage it is
reasonable to suppose that it was a fitting response: the offender
had been prosecuting his claims by extrajudicial means—seizing
property or attacking persons.[74] In other words, the offender was
prosecuting his claims by retributive violence, by self-help and
summary execution. Such actions were traditionally recognized as
legitimate remedies, but legal justification for violent self-help was
cancelled by specific covenants regarding property and status.

And such, after all, is the natural implication of the report of the
amnesty provisions in *Ath. Pol.* 39. 5–6. Here we find the injunction 'not to remember past wrongs against anyone' excepting the
Thirty and other oligarchic principals, and even these are protected
if they submit to accountings. This provision follows immediately
upon the ordinance for homicide procedure, restricting prosecution for complicity. The oath 'not to remember past wrongs' is
immediately relevant to the problem of resolving homicide
charges: by traditional retributive justice, kinsmen of the victim
were entitled to take summary action against an accused homicide
who ignored the proclamation or an exiled homicide who trespassed where prohibited. By this traditional mechanism there were
likely to be many instances where the victim's kinsmen would
forcibly seize or kill the accused. The most immediate and self-
evident intent of the oath *mē mnēsikakein* was to renounce this
mechanism of vendetta. And that is clearly its intent in the special
provision protecting the most hated public enemies. The rule that

[73] See e.g. P. J. Rhodes, *A Commentary on the Aristotelian 'Athenaion Politeia'*
(Oxford, 1981), esp. 471–2 and 477–8, suggesting that the cessation of vindictive
suits was brought about as much by the new procedure for *paragraphē* as by execution of the unnamed *mnēsikakōn*; supposedly the meaning of *Ath. Pol.* is that no legal
action thereafter came to court in defiance of the amnesty. But surely the author of
Ath. Pol. or his source was acquainted with such partisan cases as the suits against
Andocides, Menestratus, and Agoratus (Ch. 9 §3.2).
[74] Cf. *Tetr.* I. I. 6: defendant 'remembering past wrongs . . . plotted murder'.

the Thirty and other principals are themselves protected by the amnesty 'only if they submit to special accountings' clearly implies that otherwise they would be subject to *mnēsikakein*. From what measures of vindictiveness are they now protected? The record of Athenian legislation on tyranny and subversion shows emphatically that the ordinary remedy against such offenders would be immediate execution by 'anyone willing' (as Andocides in fact remarks, 1. 95). The provision that the Thirty and their most trusted henchmen be protected from *mnēsikakein* so long as they submit to public reckoning is a significant advance toward due process, but the threat of violent retribution is unmistakable.

The pledge *mē mnēsikakein* also affected the ordinary operation of summary procedures, warrant and arrest (*endeixis/apagōgē*) for the prosecution of homicides and public enemies. By traditional justice anyone who had first given information before a magistrate or official body and had been given warrant for forcible arrest, was not legally accountable if the alleged offender were killed or injured in the arrest. And on the same principle, a concerned citizen might attempt to make a forcible arrest without warrant, confident that the magistrate would authorize execution without trial. Such events were clearly anticipated by those who drafted the agreement, as we may judge from the councillor's oath, cited by Andocides 1. 91: 'I will sanction no warrant or arrest regarding past wrongs (except in the case of those exiled).'[75] This restriction goes hand in hand with other measures to thwart vendetta. In the case of Lysias 13 (*Agoratus*) we learn that the Eleven, who held jurisdiction in the arrest, required that the plaintiffs affirm that they had apprehended the accused killer upon immediate incrimination (*ep' autophōrōi*): this condition implies direct agency (*autocheiria*), and it thus approximates the rule for *dikai phonou* disallowing homicide charges for mere complicity. It is clear in any event that the ancient formula was no longer a criterion for summary execution but was now interpreted as a condition of arrest for trial.[76]

---

[75] The exception applies to those duly exiled by legal process, including homicides, who were regularly excluded from amnesty; cf. Solon's amnesty law, Plut. *Sol.* 19.

[76] See Ch. 9 §3.2. In the record of 4th-c. procedure we find other indications that homicide arrest was fully adapted as an initiating procedure .for trial: like other *graphai*, it carried a penalty for failing to win one-fifth of the votes, and the death penalty was prescribed in lieu of *timēsis*.

The special provisions that came into effect with the restoration of democracy undoubtedly affected later understanding of the fundamental workings of homicide law. What was traditionally viewed as justifiable homicide could no longer be so easily justified simply as retribution for wrongdoing. And the difficult conception of planning, which had once implicated informants and accomplices, was no longer so readily invoked. These singular exceptions notwithstanding, the traditional concepts of liability and principles of jurisdiction were remarkably persistent. In the chapters ahead we shall see that the workings of the homicide courts continued to rely upon the ancient mechanism of oath and self-help: each participant is bound by fear of god and shame of social conscience to follow the consequences of his sworn claims; and the threat of vendetta hangs over him who does not abide by this judgement.

§4. Summary

From the findings of this chapter and the chapter preceding, the historical development of the homicide courts from the era of Draco to the time of Demosthenes may be outlined as follows.

1. The earliest homicide court of the Athenians probably consisted of the tribal *basileis* with the *archōn basileus* presiding. Their 'judgement' (*dikazein*) took the form of oath-challenge or demand for other proof test. Homicide disputes were ordinarily resolved through voluntary exile, self-help, and private settlement. There was no state enforcement: performance was guaranteed by the automatic consequences of oath and tribal loyalty. The Prytaneum court, with historical authority against unidentified killers, was a vestige of this early court of the tribal kings.

2. Draco established a larger body of fifty-one tribal representatives as *ephetai*. This committee was drawn from the ruling body of Eupatrid clans; the precise composition remains uncertain, but the most likely configuration is that twelve members were admitted from each of the four tribes (with perhaps some representation from each phratry), joined by the three chief archons. This larger body, more broadly representative of the community, was convened to 'decide'

(*diagnōnai*) the question of liability and to render a straight verdict upon that question—either for the plaintiff or for the defence. Ordinarily these 'justices' made no determination as to the killer's intent or justification; they weighed such considerations only as causal factors. Only in cases where there were no surviving kinsmen eligible to prosecute were the *ephetai* to decide the question of intent: they would then select members of the phratry to decide upon settlement. The Phreatto court was a relic of this historic advance in the legal implications of intentionality.

3. Solon reconstituted the Areopagus Council as a college of former archons, and to this body he assigned special jurisdiction for the intentional killing of an Athenian. It is most probably in connection with this reform that the state assumed a role in execution. In those cases where the plaintiffs charged the killer with malicious intent and therefore refused to consider settlement, it was now required that officers of the state perform the execution and see to the confiscation of the killer's property, a part of which reverted to the state; plaintiffs were thus restrained from vendetta and from aggrandizing their claims to compensation.

4. The older body of *ephetai* held what remained of their original jurisdiction—cases other than intentional killing of an Athenian. The *ephetai* themselves would continue to be a committee of the ruling council, though the membership of that body would change. These judicial committees would continue to decide those cases where strict liability was the single issue for the judges' 'decision'. Trials in such cases were assigned a venue at the Palladium shrine of Athena.

5. In connection with Solon's reform, whereby intentionality was defined as a separate issue for the court of the Areopagus, it was also necessary to establish a special court for those cases where the killer must acknowledge hostile intent but could claim justification in the law. Such was the court at the shrine of Apollo Delphinius. The plea of legal justification was extended to certain areas where the danger of a wrongful death was balanced by the interests of the community; killing in warfare or athletic competition was thus pardoned by public policy. But the original jurisdiction of this court was prob-

ably directed largely to cases of justifiable self-help, where the family of a victim of reprisal could claim that the killing was in fact maliciously designed and therefore without legal cause. This crime thus amounted to wilful murder, and, like cases at the Areopagus, convictions at this court would also lead to state execution.

6. Under the amnesty of the restored democracy homicide prosecutions were restricted by certain provisions of 'the oaths and covenants'. In regard to killings in civil conflict, there were to be no prosecutions for indirect involvement—complicity or conspiracy—as had been allowed under the old interpretation of the rule 'guilty alike is the planner as the perpetrator'. In *dikai phonou*, homicide was to be prosecuted by the ancestral law only in cases of direct agency—*autocheiria*. Charges of killing by 'planning', *bouleusis*, were not allowed. This rule was originally directed solely to the regulation of homicide prosecutions for political murders committed during civil conflict, but the antiquated concept of *bouleusis* seems to have been permanently devalued. A similar restriction also affected the alternative procedures, 'warrant and arrest' (*endeixis/apagōgē*). Traditional out-of-court remedies—self-help and summary execution—were disallowed.

This reconstruction is necessarily hypothetical and it does not pretend to the certainty which in outline it may suggest. But I submit that it is more logically consistent and more true to the ancient evidence than the Areopagite model that received opinion has maintained. By the prevailing view it is sometimes supposed that there was yet a final evolution of the homicide jurisdiction, perhaps connected with the revisions of 403, whereby the ancient authority of the *ephetai* was transferred to ordinary juries of the people. But as we shall see in the next chapter, the preponderance of evidence inclines to the opposite conclusion, that in keeping with the arch-conservatism that sustained *dikai phonou*, the official authority of the Draconian justices remained unaltered.

4

Preliminaries, Out-of-Court Remedies, and Trial

The questions at issue in homicide trials were largely defined by the division of jurisdiction among the three major courts in the generations after Draco's law. At trial the judges were asked to decide for the plaintiff or for the defendant on one of three issues: whether the killer acted with malice aforethought; whether one who acted without malice was none the less responsible for the fatality; or whether some threat or compelling circumstance recognized by law was seen to cause and justify an intentional act of lethal force. We have no evidence that a question of the killer's identity, for instance, was ever a principal issue until the late fifth century, and then it was treated as highly exceptional and paradoxical; special procedural devices were employed to bring this question in (Chs. 5 §1 and 9 §1). We now turn to examine the procedural rules that shaped the arguments, rules governing the preliminaries, the trial, and the consequences. These rules first of all enabled the *basileus* to determine the admissibility of the charges and the plea, and thus to decide which court would hear the case. There were rules regarding the oaths and evidence to be submitted in preliminary hearings, and these, too, put some constraints on the arguments offered at trial. The aim of this chapter will be to discover the general parameters of this process. How were the respective positions of the litigants established? What sort of evidence was allowed and at what stage? What means were available to challenge the statements of one's opponents, and how were the various means of proof that were advanced in preliminaries later to be treated at trial? We must also determine the competence, the formal powers and limitations, of judges and presiding magistrates. Who, after all, were the *ephetai*? And what authority did the *basileis* themselves retain in the age of Antiphon? In this chapter we examine these practical constraints on the argument, first considering the preliminaries (§1) and then the consequences of prosecution for homicide (§2), before we try to define the role of the judges at trial (§3).

§1 *Prodikasiai*

Draco's law begins with reference to the role of the kings, the ancient college of tribal *basileis* led by the *archōn basileus*. They are to give judgement, *dikazein*. The usual view has been that this provision refers to a formal pronouncement by the *archōn basileus* of the verdict rendered by the justices at trial. In the preceding chapters, however, I have argued that the judgement of the Athenian *basileis* corresponds to the judgement of kings and elders in other archaic settings: their duty was to find an 'instrument' to which the parties themselves would consent. The issue in dispute was thus ordinarily decided by oath or other test of conviction; a 'decision' by the fifty-one *ephetai* was required only in those cases where judgement of the kings was disputed. The evidence suggests that the *basileis* retained that fundamental competence into the fourth century. The amnesty law of 405/4 excluded 'those under sentence of exile or death from the Delphinium, condemned by the kings': the natural implication of this clause is that in preliminary hearings where the defendant pleaded legal justification the *basileis* retained the right to disallow his *plea* on prima-facie grounds and thus to condemn him to exile without trial.[1]

Conversely, we know that in other cases the *archōn basileus* alone could reject the *charges* on purely procedural grounds, even where the case had sufficient merit to go to trial. Thus in their first attempt to bring charges against the defendant in Antiphon 6, the prosecutors were unable to proceed: (38, 42)

The *basileus* read them the laws and showed from the calendar that it would not be possible to enter the charge and call the witnesses (on schedule) as the law requires . . . For the *basileus* was required, once charges were brought, to hold three preliminary hearings in three months, and then bring the case to court in the fourth month; and there were only two months remaining in his term of office. Thus he was unable himself to bring the case to court, and he was not permitted to hand the case over to his successor, as no *basileus* in this land has ever done so.

Despite such evidence—or by a misreading of it—there is a common assumption that by the late fifth century the whole preliminary process was largely a matter of formalities, that the role of the *basileus* was merely to prepare the case for trial, and that there was

---

[1] On Patrocleides' decree, reported in Andoc. 1. 78, cf. Ch. 3 §2.3 (*ad fin.*).

little opportunity for final resolution before the case went to court—some three months after the initial charge. Thus, it is assumed, whatever proof was offered in preliminaries had no binding force until it was heard by the judges. In many cases, for all practical purposes, perhaps this was true. But there is clear evidence that private settlement was still possible even after formal charges had been made. And it was also apparently possible to impeach the sworn statements of the prosecutors and thus resolve the case without trial, perhaps even as late as the third and final *prodikasia*. Even in those cases that would go to trial, the oaths of the principals and witnesses were entered in definitive form at some point in the preliminaries, and any dispute of the facts or the technicalities was ordinarily settled there, before the main issue was submitted to the judges.[2]

It was in preliminary hearings that such conditions as 'malice aforethought' and 'planning' must be grounded in sworn testimony to overt acts or utterances. And if there was any question of the killer's identity it must be resolved ordinarily at this stage; if the plaintiffs did not have some unequivocal means of incriminating the accused, on their own direct knowledge of the crime or by sworn testimony of other first-hand witnesses, then most plaintiffs would abandon their case rather than risk the social and religious stigma of having their oath discredited.

1.1   *Diōmosia*

Latte argued that the oath by which a plaintiff initiated homicide proceedings in classical Athens had once been automatically decisive: a plaintiff who could secure a prevailing number of supporting witnesses all swearing to his claim would thus guarantee judgement in his favour; in time, however, this procedure became merely a ceremonial commencement of legal action—the sworn claim by which a plaintiff asserted his right to retribution became

---

[2] For oaths in *dikai phonou*, see Dem. 23. 67–8; [Dem.] 47. 72, and Aeschines 2. 87. MacDowell, *AHL* 96–8, argues against the view that oaths were sworn in *prodikasiai*, but see Philippi, *Areopag*, 80, 84–8; Lipsius, *Att. Recht*, i. 831; Bonner and Smith ii. 167–70. The findings of A. Dorjahn, 'Anticipation of Arguments in Athenian Oratory', *TAPA* 66 (1935), 274–95, and 'On the Athenian Anakrisis', *CP* 36 (1941), 182–5, explaining advance knowledge of the adversary's case by way of gossip, are dubious. On plaintiffs' eligibility, see now Alexander Tulin, *Dike Phonou* (Stuttgart, 1996).

an initiating formality.[3] This model is now much disputed, and I have argued that the decisive mechanism of archaic judgement was somewhat different from the automatic judgement upon oath that Latte and others imagined. Draconian judgement is not an irrational reckoning by arbitrary test of formulaic oath or magic number of witnesses; it relies upon the formulation of an oath-challenge or other test of conviction whose justice could not be denied by either party and which was thus to be the basis for consensual settlement. And in this sense the oath of homicide proceedings continued to be a principal instrument of proof in the classical era.

Such statements as we find in Dem. 23. 71 are sometimes taken for evidence that the oath-taking itself was postponed until the trial: 'Here also [at the Palladium] the established procedure is first the oath-taking (*diōmosia*), second the argument (*logos*), and third the decision of the court (*gnōsis*).' This outline of the proceedings supposedly suggests that the decisive oath-taking, whereby the plaintiff swore to the charge and the defendant to his plea, was part of the same hearing in which they made their arguments and were given a verdict by the judges. But we must not push this schedule too far. Demosthenes is simply arguing that all stages of the procedure are essential for its validity, and Aristocrates, by allowing summary execution, has disregarded the law; it does not mean that there was no *diōmosia* until the case came to court. There are clear indications, after all, that the oaths of the *antidikoi* were finalized in the preliminaries: in each of the three speeches in *dikai phonou*—Antiphon 1 and 6 and Lysias 1, all 'prepared speeches', written in advance of the trial—the speaker knows the wording of his opponent's oath verbatim.

The courtroom scene in Antiphon 6. 14 is often cited as evidence that the adversaries affirmed their statements under oath at the outset of the trial, but this formality in no way diminishes the decisive function of oath-taking in the preliminaries: 'Many of those present know all of the events full well, they hear the "oath-official" (*horkōtēs*) and pay close attention to whatever I say in my defence.' An officer of the court had administered the oath at the start of proceedings, but what precisely he had said is uncertain. The same passage reveals a written indictment, so that we know the substance of the plaintiff's oath was fixed. It is still perhaps conceivable that

---

[3] *Heiliges Recht*, esp. 19–25. Latte refers to this initiating oath as 'prozeßbegründender Eid'.

the oath-official simply pronounced a formula regarding the consequences of perjury and that the adversaries then for the first time swore to their claims. But why then does the speaker not say 'those present have heard *me* pronouncing my oath', rather than the oath-official? The natural implication of his words is that the oath-official read out or recited the wording of the *diōmosiai*, and then called upon the *antidikoi* to affirm what they had previously sworn.[4] Such appears also to be the procedure for the testimony of chief witnesses: ordinarily the testimony was established under oath in preliminaries and affirmed at the trial.

A passage crucial to our understanding of the function of oath-taking is the description of proceedings at the Areopagus in Demosthenes' speech *Against Aristocrates* (23) 67–8:

Surely you all know that at the Areopagus, where the law prescribes that homicide charges be tried, he who accuses another of such a crime must first swear an oath of annihilation upon himself, his house and kin, and that oath he swears not in the ordinary way but as no one swears on any other occasion—standing over the entrails of a boar, a ram, and a bull, slain by the competent officials and *in the proper period of days*; so that both in regard to the calendar and regarding the participants, everything is done as ritual requires. And even afterward he who has sworn such an oath is not yet unchallenged, but if he is proved false in his accusations, he gains nothing but condemnation for perjury to hand down to his descendants.

Demosthenes suggests that this elaborate oath ritual was peculiar to murder trials at the Areopagus, but obviously some parallel procedure would be necessary at the other major courts.[5]

If we assume that this oath ritual and all the formalities connected with it took place at the outset of the trial, then we may

---

[4] R. Bonner argued, 'Evidence in the Areopagus', *CP* 7 (1912), 450–3, that written affidavits were not required for trial at the Areopagus, even late into the 4th c.; but the only positive indication of oral evidence that he can offer is [Dem.] 40. 32, which proves only that an especially outrageous instance of *fabricated evidence* could be contested by *new evidence*, apparently without a written deposition previously submitted (the word εἶπε is certainly not decisive). Even if written depositions were not used in the Areopagus when they became standard elsewhere, the substance of the claims could easily be fixed in some standard and memorable phrasing for the oath-official to recite.

[5] For this 'greatest and strongest of oaths' in homicide proceedings, incumbent both upon the principals and their witnesses, cf. Antiphon 5. 11–12. The Delphinium proceedings, where the penalty was much the same as at the Areopagus, probably involved much the same ritual. The scholia to *Iliad* 15. 36–7 record popular belief that the custom of swearing by three gods—Zeus, Poseidon, and Athena—goes back to Draco.

suppose that Demosthenes is simply alluding to this commencement. But a number of indications prove otherwise. This oath-taking is sanctified by an especially awe-inspiring ritual for which only certain religious officials and certain days of the calendar are approved. It is possible that the reference here to certain dates upon which the ritual is permitted—'in the proper period of days'—implicitly refers to the requirements for setting a date for the trial itself, and that the ritual would be performed on the trial date immediately before the arguments began. But the most natural reading of this passage would be that the oath-ritual is to take place on a separate date within a prescribed period before the trial, and it is surely reasonable to suppose that the sequence of dates to which Demosthenes here refers is the same sequence described in Antiphon 6. 38, 42 (cited above): the oath-ritual belongs to one of the three *prodikasiai*.

Practical considerations would suggest that this elaborate and irrevocable ritual must be performed at a date set prior to the trial. At the Areopagus the plaintiff is asking, after all, for a sentence of execution and confiscation, rather than exile and *aidesis;* and to validate his claim to this extreme remedy he must invoke vengeance from the gods upon himself and his family if he should swear falsely, as he stands over the freshly slaughtered offerings of three victims.

It is perhaps somehow possible that this ritual would be performed before the full court of the Areopagites themselves; but it seems more likely that it took place on a separate date, with only the appropriate officials and interested parties present. We know of course that official business in other bodies began with a sacrifice—the assembly ritual is parodied by Aristophanes in *Ecclesiazousae* 128. But if a sacrifice of this sort began the proceedings at the Areopagus, it only complicates the agenda. A sacrificial commencement on behalf of the deliberating body is not at all analogous to the oath-taking of homicide litigants. The latter would require a lengthy protocol for preparation of the several victims and purification of those involved in the ceremony (by contrast to the cursory ritual that Praxagora mocks). It seems awkward and improbable to suppose that the plaintiff would then turn immediately from the sacrifice to address the court—that this ritual with all its requirements would be duly and methodically performed, all the other formalities be met, the full sequence of four speeches delivered, with testimony of witnesses and other evidence presented to the court, and the votes of the judges cast and tallied, all on the same day. We know, of course, that the trial itself was completed in one day; it seems the more likely conclusion that the oath ritual was performed earlier.

Let us suppose then that the oath-taking in its decisive form belonged to an earlier stage of the proceedings and was not postponed until the trial itself. At the trial the parties were simply called upon to reaffirm their oath before the jury and 'those present', some of whom had presumably witnessed the original oath-taking. The *horkōtēs* would read out or recite the oath and call upon the parties each to affirm the statements that they had sworn in *prodikasiai*.

The agenda at trial would seem to require that the oath be taken in *prodikasiai*, and the functional character of the preliminary hearings would also indicate as much. They were not simply formalities to prepare the case for court but were rather intended to allow every possible means of resolving the case without trial. Otherwise the rules of procedure, requiring a delay of some three months or more before trial, seem entirely inconsistent with the fundamental belief that the very presence of the killer posed a serious threat to the community. Thus, even in the age of Antiphon, the *prodikasiai* allowed for the *basileus* to resolve the case in some instances: he would disallow the plaintiffs' charge if technical requirements were not met; and he surely sought to bring about a settlement, if that could be managed, without trial. In such cases as Antiphon 6 the evident assumption is that the parties will settle out of court—and that appears to be what had indeed happened before the turn of events led the plaintiffs to reopen the case (§38). Financial compensation was still a viable means of settling the case, though sometimes treated as not entirely reputable (§2.2). The defendant might still avail himself of exile at any point in the preliminaries, if it became obvious, in the course of oath-taking and sworn testimony, that he had no defence.

The oaths of the parties themselves were instrumental in the pretrial proceedings, and if the dispute were not resolved there, these binding claims would then define the issue for trial and thus determine which court would hear the case. The law dictates wording of the oaths by which this determination is made: the plaintiff would have to swear that defendant is liable as the killer, and that the killing was done with or without malice aforethought and planning

(Ant. 6. 22). He should have direct knowledge or first-hand witnesses to implicate the defendant. And in charging malice aforethought or planning, the plaintiff would swear to 'know well' the killer's state of mind from overt acts prior to the crime. Considering these procedural and evidentiary implications, I conclude that the *diōmosiai* must have been finalized in the preliminaries. Any challenge of perjury against the oaths of the principals or testimony of witnesses would also be lodged at this stage.

1.2 Perjury in Homicide Proceedings

The witnesses in homicide proceedings were of a special character: in other procedures the witnesses might testify without oath; but in *dikai phonou* the witnesses swore to their statements. Much as the principals themselves swore to their claims, the supporting witnesses swore to the validity of those claims—not to specific facts or circumstances. Latte and other scholars of the Germanic tradition have generally regarded these homicide witnesses therefore as the Hellenic counterpart to the *Eidhelfer* of early Germanic law: originally a prevailing number of such witnesses would be decisive in itself (or, if not, a stronger oath-challenge or ordeal was prescribed); in time this automatic mechanism gave way to the judges' discretion (*freie Beweiswürdigung*), to determine 'which party swore rightly'.[6] We cannot, of course, rely upon this Germanic model in all particulars, but the chief point of comparison—that witnesses swore to the righteousness of the claim, not to specific facts—certainly appears to be true of *dikai phonou*. As a consequence of the witnesses' special function, false testimony—in these cases, true perjury—appears to have been subject to a special remedy.[7]

In all cases punishable by death or enslavement it would appear to be the rule that charges of false witness be tried before execution

---

[6] See Latte, *Heiliges Recht*, 24–5, regarding the gloss in Hesychius, s.v. δοξασταί· κρῖται εἰσιν οἱ διαγινώσκοντες, πότεροι εὐορκεῖ τῶν κρινομένων; and 26–33, for automatic judgement upon prevailing witnesses (Arist. *Pol.* 2. 5, 1269ᵃ; cf. Ch. 10 §2.2). That homicide witnesses swore to the gist of the claim is shown by Ant. 5. 12, 15; Lys. 4. 4; Isoc. 18. 53.

[7] Perjury in proceedings at the Areopagus (presumably hearings before the *basileus* as well as trial before the whole body) constituted a special category: *Ath. Pol.* 59. 6 refers to τὰ ψευδομαρτυρία ⟨τὰ⟩ ἐξ Ἀρείου πάγου in the court of the Thesmothetes (cf. Pollux 8. 88).

on the main issue.[8] As there are also indications that no challenge for perjury could be entered at trial for homicide, it seems certain that challenges to testimony were lodged in preliminaries and tried before the main issue. This is the most likely interpretation of the evidence in the two cases known to us, in which homicide charges led to convictions for perjury against the plaintiffs and their supporters: these are the cases mentioned in Isocrates 18. 52 and in the Demosthenic speech 59. 10.[9] Both passages indicate a sequence of proceedings that ended at trial before a dicastic jury of several hundred; from various indications it is clear that these hearings were not *dikai phonou* before *ephetai*. The sequence of proceedings is of special importance for our inquiry here as it suggests the prescribed order for oath and testimony in *prodikasiai*.

In the earlier of the two cases, one that Isocrates reports (soon after 403/2), Callimachus gave testimony in support of his brother-in-law, charging one Cratinus in the death of a slave-woman—who was actually found alive. The perjury of Callimachus and his role in instigating the perjury of others is the focus of the speaker's argument, and his insistence upon that point should leave little doubt but that Callimachus was in fact convicted in a suit for false witness (*dikē pseudomartyriōn*), rather than merely discredited in a homicide trial.[10]

The passage indicates a sequence of proceedings, evidently including the hearings in *prodikasiai* and the subsequent suit for perjury (53–4):

Cratinus kept quiet *the rest of the time* so that [Callimachus and his supporters] might not change tactics and invent other arguments, but be caught in the act. When the brother-in-law had made his charges and Callimachus had sworn to the woman's death (ἦ μὴν τεθνάναι), [Cratinus and friends] entered the house where the victim was concealed, took her by force, and brought her before *those present* at the court. As a result, when 700 were sitting in judgement, though fourteen other witnesses gave the same testimony as he, [Callimachus] received not a single vote.

---

[8] Cf. E. Leisi, *Der Zeuge im attischen Recht* (Frauenfeld, 1908, repr. New York, 1979), 120–41.

[9] For full discussion of these two passages see my study 'Ephetai and Athenian Courts for Homicide' in *CP* 86 (1991), 3–6.

[10] The speaker dwells upon the charge of perjury at some length: cf. 51, 56–7 ἐπιορκῶν ἐξελέγχεται . . . τὰ ψευδῆ μαρτυρῶν . . . ψευδῆ τολμᾷ μαρτυρεῖν. Evidently witnesses confirmed the earlier conviction (54–5). For oaths to the fact of the killing, cf. [Dem.] 47. 70; on the latter case and oaths of plaintiffs and witnesses, see MacDowell, *AHL* 94–109.

In this sequence it seems highly unlikely that the initial charges, the discovery of the 'victim', and the verdict of the 700 all belong to the same hearing. It appears rather more probable that the false charges were sworn at an earlier hearing, these charges were disproved by the discovery of the living victim at a later stage of the proceedings; that singular discovery effectively quashed the homicide proceedings and led to a perjury trial before 700 jurors.

On the opposite assumption that the 'victim' was brought into court before the homicide judges, this case is sometimes cited as proof of the admissibility at trial of new evidence, material not discovered in preliminaries.[11] The principle that crucial new evidence would not be excluded is certainly credible and does not depend upon this tenuous proof. If we insist upon this case as an instance of new evidence at trial, then we must imagine that the defendant was prepared to risk everything on a very unlikely sequence of manœuvres. If in fact the defendant waited until the trial was under way before seizing the victim and bringing her to court, he would have needed a recess (*anabolē*), and it is doubtful whether the *basileus* could be relied upon to grant a delay once the trial had begun. Even supposing the victim was suddenly dragged into court, at this late stage of the proceedings there was nothing to prevent the prosecution from disputing her identity. It seems unlikely therefore that the defendant would have waited until after the first speech at trial to present surprise evidence.

It would seem necessary for the plaintiff to swear to his charges and present witnesses to the fact that death had indeed occurred (ἦ μὴν τεθνάναι) and that the defendant was the killer, at the earliest stage of proceedings. The sequence that Isocrates describes suggests further that some formal confirmation of the charge was to follow, at a later stage of the hearings, and it was then that the sworn statements on both sides were finalized.

The later case mentioned in pseudo-Demosthenes 59. 10 indicates a similar sequence—and indeed there is a remarkable parallel between the two cases, half a century apart. In this case, we are told, Stephanus as prosecutor had sworn that Apollodorus (the probable author of the speech) had struck and killed a slave woman, and that

---

[11] Bonner, 'Evidence in the Areopagus', 452–3; F. Lämmli, *Das attische Prozeßverfahren* (Paderborn, 1938), 96–7; M. Lavency, *Aspects de la logographie judiciaire attique* (Louvain, 1964), 131–3; Leisi, *Zeuge*, 81 n. 2, treating this as rare 'autopsy'.

he suborned the perjury of others to support him in this charge: Stephanus first provided himself with witnesses, then made proclamation of the homicide and began the *prodikasiai;* in the hearings he swore to the fact of the killing, 'which had neither happened nor been witnessed nor reported'. Then, *'having been proved a perjuror and instigator of false charges and exposed as a hireling . . . he ended up winning few votes out of 500, convicted of perjury'.* The last phrase is superfluous unless we are to understand that the conviction for subornation of perjury before a jury of 500 followed an earlier hearing where the sworn charges of homicide were challenged and disproved.

The precise order of proceedings is uncertain, but taken together with the other indications that the decisive proof was entered in preliminaries and that every opportunity was given to resolve the case without trial, these two cases suggest that charges of perjury against statements sworn in *prodikasiai* would be decided before the main issue could go to court for *euthydikia.*

The date and historical circumstances in which suits for false witness were first instituted have not been securely determined, yet we can reasonably suppose that some form of 'challenge' (*episkēpsis*) was an ancient remedy against flagrant perjury. Aristotle attributes this device to Charondas, the lawgiver of Catana, probably in the sixth century (*Pol.* 1274[b]). At some point in the parallel development at Athens it was decided that the question of perjury be tried separately, either as a secondary issue to be tried after trial on the main suit, or as a preliminary issue to be settled before trial. Before this procedure was devised, the archon himself was probably left to decide what statements, if any, could be thrown out on the strength of an opponent's challenge; he would make this determination by the same discretion that enabled him to throw out the charges if formal criteria were not met, or to disallow the plea of legal justification if it had no basis. In the rare cases where 'real evidence' could be adduced—such as the person of the alleged victim, as in the case of Isoc. 18. 52—the archon's ruling would have been self-evident. By all indications, of course, the Athenians put little faith in physical evidence, and most charges of false testimony would have been much more difficult to decide—hence the institution of a special hearing before a dicastic jury (probably no earlier than the mid- to late fifth century).

The Athenian magistrate was naturally reluctant to invoke a

hearing for perjury in homicide proceedings except in the most flagrant instances. In *dikai phonou* the litigants retained much of their ancient autonomy for self-help and private settlement. The tests of conviction by which the parties themselves determined the issue were therefore pivotal to the argument at trial. The role of the court was to decide the superior validity of one man's oath over the other.

§2. Execution and Settlement

In principle, execution and enforcement were left to the litigants themselves to fulfil as commitments of their oaths. In cases before the Palladium the law prescribed that the condemned man go into exile by a certain route within a certain period (Dem. 23. 72), but there was no officer of the state who would assume responsibility to enforce this decree. It is primarily the threat of lawful retribution at the hands of the plaintiffs that guaranteed the defendant would comply. In recognition of these dire consequences, the successful plaintiff at the Palladium court was called upon to swear again to the righteousness of his claim *after the verdict had been rendered* (Aeschines 2. 87).[12] The plaintiff must swear this 'final oath' that the verdict is just and his claim is true, precisely because he is empowered to take retribution in his own hands if the convicted manslayer should violate his banishment.[13]

2.1   Execution by the *Polis*

For convictions by the Areopagus and Delphinium courts, on the other hand, the death penalty was prescribed, and in classical times this sentence was carried out by executioners for the state. The murderer's property was also confiscated and disposed of by officers of the state, though a large portion of the proceeds may have reverted to the plaintiffs if they availed themselves of further

---

[12] Commentators have generally found it puzzling that Aeschines should refer specifically to the Palladium court as one where a final oath of this sort was sworn after the verdict. Philippi, *Areopag*, 93–4 n. 33, simply deleted the offending phrase, ἐπὶ Παλλαδίῳ as an intrusive gloss; cf. MacDowell, *AHL* 93.

[13] In this instance the Athenian mechanism for execution recalls the standard 'judgement' of the Gortynian code, 'Let the magistrate judge for the plaintiff to swear' and the plaintiff will then proceed to execute his claim; so reasoned Latte, *Heiliges Recht*, 11.

remedies. The precise rules regarding confiscation in homicide cases are nowhere clearly stated, but if we follow the most natural assumption, that similar rules applied in homicide confiscations as in other *apographai* (for impiety, etc.), we should conclude that the plaintiff stood to gain considerable compensation from the killer's estate.[14] The penalty of death and confiscation, without possibility of settlement, was probably established by the same Solonian reform that transferred cases of intentional killing to the Areopagus, as Thür has argued.[15] These reforms go closely together with the restriction of self-help against homicides, forbidding torture and extortion for ransom (Dem. 23. 28). Rather than risk charges for violating this restriction, some plaintiffs who had apprehended the killer would call upon officers of the state to carry out the execution; and in time it came to be prescribed that all executions for murder should be handled in this way; the plaintiff himself was permitted only to stand by (Dem. 23. 69).

Thür has made a very convincing case that Solon was the author of state execution, but he has also made a rather unconvincing connection between the archon's role in execution and the function described as *dikazein*. In the *Athenian Constitution* 57. 4 we learn that 'the *basileus*, when he gives judgement (*dikazei*), removes his crown'. Thür here follows Wolff's old assumption that 'to give judgement' means formal pronouncement of the verdict, after the jury has rendered its decision. He therefore supposes that the magistrate removes the symbol of his office because the king's judgement is in effect the order for execution. But where Thür supposes that this judgement is a formal pronouncement after the verdict, the context of the testimony itself suggests that the king's judgement belongs to the *prodikasiai*:

---

[14] For the sale of property confiscated from those sentenced by the Areopagus, cf. *Ath. Pol.* 47. 3; Harrison, *Law of Athens*, ii. 178–9, 211–17. For profit from confiscation by *apographē*: Dem. 8. 69–71, political profiteering; 49. 45–7, profit from surplus. U. Kahrstedt, *Staatsgebiet und Staatsangehörige in Athen* (Stuttgart, 1934), 134, argued that *apographē* was the only ordinary means of confiscation; after all, Athenian procedure relies as far as possible on private initiative. The statutory limits to private profiteering remain uncertain: Dem. 53. 2, as we have it, would indicate 'three-quarters' of the proceeds (τὰ τρία μέρη); but this seems extravagant, and an inscriptional parallel suggests perhaps 'one-third' (τὰ τρίτα μέρη) is right. See D. M. Lewis, 'After the Profanation', in *Ancient Society and Institutions* (ed. E. Badian, Oxford, 1966), 188 and n. 67.

[15] 'Todesstrafe', *JJP* 20 (1988), 142–156; see Ch. 3 §2.2.

The king introduces the case and [the judges] give judgement (*dikazousin*) both in the open air; and the king, when he gives judgement (*dikazei*) removes his crown. The defendant *at other times* is prohibited from holy ground, nor is he permitted to enter the agora, but on this occasion (only) he enters the shrine to make his defence.

This passage has to do with the general precautions to avoid defilement by the killer, and it clearly refers to the prohibitions that apply in the period before trial. It is reasonable to suppose therefore that the requirement for the king to remove his crown 'when he gives judgement' also applies to proceedings before the trial, in order to avoid defilement of the sacrosanct symbol of his office when he confronts the accused killer. In the hearings the king calls for the oaths that will decide the defendant's fate: the archaic parallels would suggest that the king's judgement is in essence a challenge to the parties to assert their claims under oath. The 'order for execution' is effectively contained in the oath-challenge: the parties must abide by the implications of their oaths. It was therefore unnecessary for the *basileus* to give a formal order for execution after conviction. The jury's verdict is, in essence, a validation of the plaintiff's claim and it was for the plaintiff himself to demand execution. In a case of capital murder those who would carry out the execution for the state (presumably the Eleven) would be on hand, and if the defendant had not already fled into exile before the final speech, then upon hearing the verdict the plaintiff would call upon the authorities to apprehend the killer and execute judgement upon him.[16]

State executions for murder were evidently quite rare—we know of no single instance where execution is certain. Much more commonly, a defendant accused of intentional killing would have gone voluntarily into exile, and a judgement *in absentia* would entitle the plaintiff to exercise his claim of retribution in the event that the defendant returned to Attica.

A verdict in favour of the defendant at the Areopagus could have one of two consequences. If the defendant swore categorically that

---

[16] The original implementation of state execution was probably modelled on the ancient procedure *ephēgēsis*, whereby an informant called upon the authorities to apprehend an offender: on this procedure, see Hansen, *Apagoge*, 24–5. The one known case of *ephēgēsis* against a homicide is reported in Dem. 23.31 (arrest in the assembly by the Thesmothetes); presumably the killer was put to death, but we are not told so explicitly.

he was not 'the killer', he would go free if the judges decided for him. But if he must admit to some measure of responsibility in the killing in order to plead more convincingly that he was innocent of malice aforethought, I conclude that he would be none the less subject to the automatic consequences of his oath—exile and *aidesis*—just as if the plaintiff had won a verdict to that effect in the Palladium. If he has, in effect, admitted liability, he must then arrange settlement with the victim's family if he was to be assured of a safe return to his homeland.

2.2 *Aidesis* and Compensation

We have noticed considerable evidence that payment of 'the blood price'—*poinē*—was not eliminated but rather regularized by the laws of Draco and Solon (Ch. 1 §1.3). The text most often cited in evidence against *poinē* is the rule against extortion of ransom, *mēde apoinan*, in the Solonian amendment to the law of arrest and execution cited by Demosthenes 23. 28.[17] But the rule *mēde apoinan* here applies specifically to those instances where an exiled homicide is caught in flagrant violation of his exile; it says nothing about arrangements for compensation before or during exile when the killer lawfully abides by its terms. This rule was probably intended to limit or discourage efforts of the victim's kinsmen to aggrandize their claim, and not expected to end financial compensation altogether. A similar aim is evident in the supposedly Draconian law cited by the lexicographer Pollux, which limited the value of *poinē* to 'twenty head of cattle'. If such was the intent of the special rule *mēde apoinan*, we can only assume that the general practice was accepted and allowed to persist.

The very term that defines lawful homicide as a killing 'with impunity', *nēpoinei*, also suggests an original restriction against *poinē*. Thus Draco's law prescribed that killing in response to seizure of property or abduction of persons would involve no penalty or compensation, *nēpoinei* (Dem 23. 60 = *IG* I³ 104. 37–8). Presumably in the settlement of other cases no such restriction applied.[18] The property of an exiled homicide was therefore pro-

---

[17] On this provision, see Glotz, *Solidarité*, 319; Ruschenbusch, 'ΦΟΝΟΣ'; cf. Gagarin, *Drakon*, 24–6.

[18] On killing 'with impunity', see my response to Velissaropoulos in *Symposion* 1990.

tected: he who seizes the exile's lawful property (*epitima*) was as liable as if he had seized property of a citizen in Attica.[19] Demosthenes, who cites this provision, makes no mention of financial settlement, and he assumes that Draco meant for this protection to apply only in cases of unintentional homicide, as it did in his own day. But it is more likely that this law originally also applied to intentional killers in the era before special penalties and state execution were prescribed. The aim of the law was to guarantee that the exile who submits to lawful settlement not be deprived of the means to do so.[20] Confiscation of the murderer's property by the state belongs to a later era, when at last central authority intervened to prohibit private settlement for intentional homicide—and even then financial motives were not entirely eliminated.

In Demosthenes' day the murderer's property was indeed seized, but there is ample evidence that other homicides were sometimes resolved by private settlement, ordinarily involving financial or other compensation. Thus the lexicographer Harpocration refers to *hypophonia* as 'the money given in homicide to the relatives of the slain man, so that they do not prosecute their claim'; he indicates that Theophrastus discussed the practice in his work *On the Laws* and there gave reference to two speeches of the younger contemporary of Demosthenes, Dinarchus.[21] Now it may be argued that this note refers simply to bribes given to avoid legal proceedings, and thus to a practice quite distinct from archaic *poinē*; but the wording requires no such distinction. The ordinary means of 'prosecuting' an offender certainly encompassed extrajudicial remedies. In principle the outcome of legal proceedings was a judgement authorizing the plaintiff to act in self-help. The plaintiff who has a judgement rendered in his favour is thereby authorized to execute his claim upon the person or property of the homicide if he returns

[19] Dem. 23. 44. On the authenticity of this provision, see Ch. 3 §1.2; that the rule originally applied to all exiled homicides, see Gagarin, *Drakon*, 60 n. 83. The statute implies another class of homicides whose property may be confiscated (*atima*); cf. Ruschenbusch, 'ΦΟΝΟΣ', 142–5.

[20] For *aidesis* in Draco's law involving financial settlement, see Heitsch, *Aidesis*, esp. 5–12: in Homeric usage the verb *aideisthai* ordinarily involves financial considerations; cf. Eustathius, *Comm. ad Iliadem* 779. 60. Heitsch himself believes that *aidesis* in Draco's law was initially available only to the unintentional killer, but see Ch. 2.

[21] Harpocration 297 (Dindorf) s.v. ὑοφόνια· τὰ ἐπὶ φόνῳ διδόμενα χρήματα τοῖς οἰκείοις τοῦ φονευθέντος, ἵνα μὴ ἐπεξίωσιν· Δείναρχος ἐν τῷ κατὰ Καλλισθένους καὶ ἐν τῷ κατὰ Φορμισίου, Θεόφραστος Νόμων ιϛ'.

without reconciliation. Voluntary exile without trial continued to be a common resolution of homicide disputes even in classical times, and Harpocration's paraphrase of Theophrastus would also apply to financial compensation in such cases. Financial settlement in an age of more advanced legality is none the less equivalent to *poinē*.[22]

Demosthenes 58. 28–9 explicitly refers to a case where the brother of a homicide victim accepted compensation to reconcile with the killer, yet this passage is sometimes discounted as evidence for financial settlement.[23] Thus, MacDowell insists that the passage proves only that such practices were disgraceful. But, as Glotz argued, if the practice were actually illegal or unparalleled, we would expect the speaker to say so. We should not press the argument from silence too far, but this passage at least serves to support the implication of Harpocration's note, that financial settlement was not prohibited by law or binding custom but continued in practice.

MacDowell argues instead that *failure* to prosecute was itself a criminal offence, to be prosecuted by a suit for impiety, *graphē asebeias*. He finds evidence for this legal mechanism in the prologue to Demosthenes' *Against Androtion* (22) 2: the speaker, Diodorus, recounts how his uncle had been prosecuted for impiety by the unscrupulous litigator Androtion; the charge of impiety was based upon the claim that the uncle had consorted with Diodorus though he was his father's killer.[24] As proof against financial settlement, this is dubious on several counts. Financial compensation is never mentioned; rather the uncle was charged with impiety for 'consorting' with the killer. We know that false allegations of parricide were one of the few slanders actionable by Athenian law (Lysias 10), yet Diodorus says nothing of such a suit. And we must remember that Diodorus means to *discredit*

---

[22] Schol. D *Iliad* 18. 497, ποινῆς οὖν λέγει τῆς καλουμένης παρὰ τοῖς Ἀττικοῖς ὑποφόνια . . . λέγεται δὲ κοινῶς ἀνέκτισις, ποινή. Cf. *Solonos Nomoi* F9–12 (Ruschenbusch).

[23] Dem. 58. 28–9: ἀργύριον λαβὼν ἀπηλλάγη . . . διελύσατο πρὸς τοὺς τὴν αἰτίαν ἔχοντας. Cf. MacDowell, *AHL* 9; Bonner and Smith, ii. 196–7. For financial settlement in the fourth century, cf. Glotz, *Solidarité*, 306–21; esp. 314–15.

[24] This passage is certainly evidence that suit for impiety could be brought against a kinsman of the victim who consorted with the killer. Diodorus makes a point of the prosecutor's failure to win one-fifth of the votes (3) thus indicating a *graphē asebeias* (against his uncle) in which such failure cost the prosecutor 1,000 drachmas (cf. Dem. 24. 8, referring to the same case).

Androtion for abusing legal procedures to serve his own ends; he does not imply that suit for impiety was a regular remedy against failure to prosecute. Finally, perhaps most important here, there is the simple fact that the killing alleged in this case is a *parricide*, for which far greater stigma attaches to the killer and to those who associate with him than for other homicides. Though we have no evidence of a statutory distinction between kin-slayings and other homicides, it is not unlikely that the former were generally barred from private settlement by sheer force of public feeling, and an interested third party was all the more likely to prosecute for impiety any family members who knowingly consorted with a kin-slayer. This special case certainly gives us no proof of a general bar against mercenary settlement.

Private settlement is also indicated in the narrative of Antiphon 6 (*Choreutes*), where the defendant tells us in rather cryptic fashion that the prosecutor had previously reconciled with him; he makes no mention of financial considerations, but some financial advantage is implied in his charge that the victim's kin sought a reconciliation only after they had lost hope of reward from the defendant's political opponents (38). Though he claims that his accusers had initiated the settlement to make up for their improper charges, this is probably a misrepresentation, and it is obviously to his advantage to pretend that the settlement had little to do with the homicide and that he had not sought reconciliation to clear himself of the killing. This is a complex argument which will require detailed treatment (Ch. 7), but for now it is at least prima-facie evidence that a homicide that could be brought to trial could also be settled privately. And although it seems to be a somewhat disreputable practice, there is at least the implication that settlement was secured by financial consideration.[25]

The principle behind private settlement is suggested by the legalistic commonplace in Demosthenes 37. 59 = 38. 22: the victim himself, if he survives long enough to speak, has the power to absolve even the intentional killer; otherwise—*without* the victim's express absolution—settlement would appear to be prohibited for

---

[25] Heitsch assumes financial motives in three cases: in Ant. 1 the defendant's stepmother was implicated by Philoneus' slave, and private settlement was arranged with his relations; the plaintiff himself, excluded from the father's estate, was probably motivated by some expectation of financial advantage; *Antiphon*, 29–30 and *passim*. Cf. Chs. 6–7 and 9 §2.2.

intentional murder in the fourth century. In cases of unintentional killing, however, some arrangements for settlement were anticipated. The period of exile and ritual purification was seen as part of this appeasement of the victim's wrathful spirit, and there is no reason to doubt that material compensation continued to be a regular and accepted condition of *aidesis* well into the classical period. There can be no question that payment involved some ethical liability, as any such settlement might be *construed* as a cynical and mercenary transaction. Given the ethical implications and the rhetorical possibilities, it is perhaps surprising that we have only the one note of righteous indignation against it (Dem. 58. 28–9). In all, we have no indication that financial settlement for homicide was prohibited by law or custom (except perhaps in kin-slaying), and clear evidence that it persisted in practice. This conclusion will be of considerable significance as we analyse the extant speeches: financial incentives sometimes affect the argumentation, particularly in regard to the probable motives of the plaintiffs.

These aspects of the procedural mechanism—oath-taking in the preliminaries and the fulfilment of oath in execution—would serve to define the positions of the adversaries in *dikai phonou*. We shall follow out the workings of this mechanism in the chapters ahead. But for an understanding of the practical constraints upon argumentation in the extant speeches, there remains one final and crucial consideration: the competence of the judges.

§3. The Judges at Trial: Areopagites and *Ephetai*

In murder trials before the Areopagus court, we know that the judges as Areopagites possessed a special competence by virtue of their tenure as archons and their experience thereafter as a permanent jury. But the qualifications of those who judged homicide cases in the Palladium and Delphinium courts are nowhere clearly defined in our sources. It was once generally assumed that the courts of the *ephetai* were given over to ordinary juries of the people at some uncertain point in the long evolution from Solon down to the end of the fifth century. In a study on precisely this problem I have argued against this 'dicastic model': all the arguments in favour of dicastic juries in the ephetic courts are essentially groundless, while there is considerable evidence identifying the *ephetai* with the Areopagites.[26] It is beyond the scope of this chapter to reargue the matter in detail, but it will be useful to review the major points that affect our understanding of the argumentation.

The problem revolves around three points in dispute—one of which we have already raised and answered (§1.2). Often cited as the clearest evidence of what we may call the dicastic model are the two cases where homicide proceedings were concluded before juries of several hundred, hence dicastic juries: Isoc. 18. 52, and [Dem.] 59. 10. In these two passages, however, the procedural details clearly indicate that the cases were resolved in hearings for perjury and not at trial on the main issue of homicide. On the other hand, there are a few passages where the speaker appears to identify the *ephetai* with the ordinary juries of layman dicasts—where he addresses the jury in a *dikē phonou* as a court of the people; or where, in proceedings before dicastic courts, a speaker suggests that the judges are 'the same' jurors who would decide the case in traditional homicide proceedings. These clues will be given closer scrutiny in the following section, §3.1; and in §3.2, we examine the direct evidence of Draco's law and the *Athenian Constitution*, together with the scattered testimonia in Demosthenes' *Against Aristocrates* and elsewhere.

3.1 Dicasts and *Ephetai*

Among various passages where the speaker seems to identify the judges in the homicide courts as juries of the people,[27] the most significant evidence comes in Antiphon 5 and Lysias 1. In the former speech, *On the Murder of Herodes*, in an action prosecuted by warrant and arrest (*endeixis/apagōgē*) before an ordinary dicastic court,

---

[26] '*Ephetai*', *CP* 86 (1991), 1–16.

[27] There are also various passages where the homicide judges are called *dikastai;* these are sometimes cited in evidence that the judges were ordinary 'dicasts', on the facile assumption that *dikastai* is a technical term reserved for this meaning. There is absolutely no basis for this view; cf. Dem. 23. 66, of the original jury on the Areopagus (*theoi dikastai*); Ant. 5. 11. 'All the courts try homicide cases in the open for no other reason but so that the judges (*dikastai*) do not consort with those whose hands are unclean.' Among all the courts that try homicide cases the speaker is obviously including the Areopagus court—indeed he is thinking primarily of the Areopagus. There is also an especially pointed reference to judges as *dikastai* in Ant. 1. 23, in a speech for trial at the Areopagus (Ch. 6); arguments to the contrary rely upon the *petitio principii* that the case must have gone to a dicastic jury at the Palladium 'since the judges are called *dikastai*'!

the defendant argues that the case should properly be tried by the traditional procedure *dikē phonou*, and he refers to the judges in such proceedings apparently as the *same* jury before whom he pleads: 'For [if the case is retried in the proper court] I will not evade your judgement (*gnōmas*), but it will be you who there vote to decide my case; and if you spare me now you can then do with me what you will.'[28]

To understand this bit of popular jurisprudence we must recall that the speaker is interpreting the charges against him as intentional homicide, and he clearly implies that the proper court to hear his case would be the court of the Areopagus. It is precisely the point of the speaker's argument that the court before whom he is being tried, a dicastic court with jurisdiction in 'felony arrest' (*apagōgai kakourgōn*), is not competent to judge the case at hand, and that his accusers have abused procedural rules to have him tried for homicide before this body.[29] Thus he protests against what he labels as deceptive tactics of the prosecution: they have evaded the traditional precautions against perjury, the special requirements for oath-taking in homicide proceedings, and in particular the oath against allegations unrelated to the case itself (§§11–12), all of which are proper to trial at the Areopagus. That he identifies the citizen jurors ideologically with the highest court tells us nothing about jurisdiction.[30]

This passage proves only that the preferred homicide judges, before whom the defendant would be tried in *dikē phonou*, were a body *separate* from the ordinary juries as late as 420/419 (the approximate date of Ant. 5)—otherwise he would not anticipate the accusation that he was merely attempting to elude the court of the people. Of course, there is little doubt that the Areopagus continued to be a court of former archons and it is to this court that our defendant demands a change of venue.

---

[28] Ant. 5. 90 (cf. 94); see Sealey, 'Athenian Courts', 294–5, identifying the homicide courts with dicasts; but cf. MacDowell, *AHL* 56.

[29] On the legalities in Ant. 5, see Heitsch, *Antiphon*, 34–89; Scheidweiler, 'Antiphons Herodes', 319–38; U. Schindel, *Mordfall Herodes* (Göttingen, 1979); Gagarin, *The Murder of Herodes* (Frankfurt, 1989), 17–30.

[30] The defendant is citizen of a subject state that had recently rebelled against Athenian suzerainty; he assures the judges that he would not escape Athenian jurisdiction. He therefore addresses the jury as 'you [sc. Athenians]' (76–80, esp. 76–7). Cf. 8, 19, 42–8, 61, 80: '*your* laws', '*your* magistrates', '*your* state', and 'your populace'.

In the later case, Lysias 1, (perhaps twenty years afterward) the defendant seems to characterize the judges in such a way as to suggest that the citizen juries had assumed jurisdiction in *dikai phonou*. The husband who slew the adulterer pleads justifiable homicide before the Delphinium. The court's verdict is called 'most sovereign of all', and it is sometimes assumed that this phrase could properly refer only to the popular courts in the era after 403.[31] But the argument that concludes with the words 'most sovereign of all' (κυριωτάτη) is *not* meant to exalt the court but to emphasize their power to abrogate the law. The defendant's case depends entirely upon his claim that he acted in obedience to the laws: it was not his own initiative but the laws that led to the death of the adulterer. The argument that concludes 'most sovereign of all' is a warning against a wrongful and irreversible verdict.[32] Against charges of entrapment, the defendant claims to have sworn, as he struck the fatal blow, 'It is not I who kill you but the law that you transgressed' (26). He cites statute for the lawful slaying of adulterers caught in the act (28); and he pointedly refers to the clause that expressly forbids the Areopagus, 'to whom both ancient law and current ordinance assign jurisdiction in homicide cases', to condemn the lawful slayer of an adulterer (30). The verdict of the court, he suggests, embodies 'the highest authority' in that the judges have the power to invalidate the law—'whereas I regarded the law of the *polis* as superior' (κυριώτερον, 29). Now, if the judges were a jury of the people, we would expect the speaker to argue, 'how can this body assume authority to judge a case where the law forbids even the Areopagus to condemn'; but there is no such distinction. In fact, the statute that protects the lawful killer from condemnation by the Areopagus has the greater relevance if the judges are in fact identified with the Areopagites.

Thus, though Antiphon 5. 90 and Lysias 1. 36 are often taken to suggest that the ordinary dicastic panels were also judges in the homicide courts, the argumentation in both speeches in fact suggests quite the opposite. There is yet another set of passages that

---

[31] The court's verdict is called πάντων τῶν ἐν τῇ πόλει κυριωτάτη (36). See Smith, 'Dicasts', 354; Bonner and Smith, i. 271; but cf. Philippi, *Areopag*, 326 n. 218.

[32] For the standard warning to the jury that a wrong verdict (through abuse of procedure) is ἰσχυρότερον τοῦ δικαίου, cf. Antiphon 5. 87 = 6. 3–4. For the categories of lawful or 'justifiable' homicide, cf. *Ath. Pol.* 57. 3, and Dem. 23. 74; and see Ch. 3 §2.3.

suggest a clear distinction between the competence of the homicide justices and that of the dicastic juries. The law against irrelevant charges, 'not to speak outside the issue' (Arist. *Rhet.* 1354ᵃ18–24) clearly applies to cases before the Areopagus and almost certainly in the ephetic courts as well. A similar rule formally applied in dicastic courts: *Ath. Pol.* 67. 1 reports that in suits before the dicastic courts the parties swear to 'speak to the issue'; and the dicastic oath in Demosthenes 24. 149–51 indicates that the judges are to disregard irrelevant arguments. But the rule of relevance in cases before the Areopagus seems to have been more restrictive and more seriously respected than the corresponding rule in the dicastic courts.[33] And Antiphon 6. 9 suggests that the same strict rule of relevance that applied in cases before the Areopagus also applied in the other homicide courts: the speaker in a case before the Palladium protests against irrelevant allegations, which *none* of his accusers had *ever* been able to prove in earlier legal action; 'but in this case, where they are prosecuting for homicide and the law requires that they direct their charges to the issue'[34] they fabricated false charges regarding his duties to the state. The reference to earlier legal action is vague;[35] but given the emphasis of the argument, the key phrase 'where . . . prosecuting for homicide and the law requires . . . ' certainly suggests that a more restrictive rule of relevance applied in the homicide courts than elsewhere.

We know of no penalty or procedure against irrelevant accusations. If there was a stronger rule against irrelevant charges in homicide proceedings than in the dicastic courts, it would appear that the judges themselves were expected to demand a greater respect for the laws and rules of procedure, by which relevance was determined, than did the ordinary dicasts.

---

[33] On the law μὴ ἔξω τοῦ πράγματος λέγειν, cf. Antiphon 5. 11 and *passim*; Lys. 3. 46; and esp. Lycurg. 1. 11–13, emphasizing the strict provision against irrelevance in the Areopagus, in contrast to the popular courts. On *Rhet.* 1. 1. 5, 1354a18–24 see E. M. Cope and J. E. Sandys *'Rhetoric' of Aristotle* (Cambridge, 1887), i. 7–8; Wallace, *Areopagos*, 124. Pollux, *Onom.* 8. 117, reports that proems and emotional appeals were especially prohibited before the Areopagus. Lucian, *Anach.* 19, suggests that the herald would silence the speaker if he violated the rule, but no 5th- or 4th-c. source indicates any overt means of preventing or penalizing irrelevance.

[34] Ant. 6. 9: φόνου διώκοντες καὶ τοῦ νόμου οὕτως ἔχοντος εἰς αὐτὸ τὸ πρᾶγμα κατηγορεῖν.

[35] It is sometimes supposed that this passage refers to the δοκιμασία βουλευτῶν, but see E. Heitsch, *Recht und Argumentation in Antiphons b. Rede* (Abh. Akad. Wiss. Mainz, 7, 1980), 42.

In the extant speeches, as we shall see more fully in the chapters ahead, the argumentation itself indicates that the homicide justices were specially qualified to weigh the *legal* issues peculiar to homicide proceedings. This special competence appears to be directly related to the decisive function of the oaths in the traditional homicide procedure. It is noteworthy in this regard that the statutes cited in Lysias 1 in proof of legal justification are the only direct citations of law in the extant homicide speeches, whereas such citations are a familiar aid to the argument in speeches before the dicastic courts. Evidently *dikai phonou* were decided by judges who possessed some basic, formal competence in the workings of the law. They were *not* jurisprudents or true legal experts, any more than the Areopagites were, nor were they immune to artful arguments on probability and causation, any more than the layman dicast; but the litigants certainly seem to regard these justices as having a better working knowledge of the legal principles and procedural rules proper to homicide disputes than they expect in the dicastic juries.[36]

It may still be argued that the *ephetai* were special panels of fifty-one, chosen from among the dicasts by seniority, rank, or merit, and thus distinguished by their special qualifications.[37] We do, indeed, find other official bodies chosen from citizens above the age of 50, but it is likely that the lexicographers who attribute such qualifications to the *ephetai* have misinterpreted their sources. We find no reference to any special grouping of dicasts by age or rank in any fifth- or fourth-century sources; and in particular, the treatment of dicastic courts in the *Athenian Constitution* 63–6 gives no

---

[36] Noteworthy in this regard is Socrates' reaction to Euthyphro's news that he is involved in homicide proceedings (even before learning that he intends to prosecute his father): most people have no knowledge of how this is done; it is not something for any ordinary person to undertake but requires exceptional skill (4a–b).

[37] Photius, *Lex.* s.v. ἐφέται (i. 236 Naber): ἄνδρες ὑπὲρ πεντήκοντα ἔτη γεγονότες καὶ ἄριστα βεβιωκέναι ὑπόληψιν ἔχοντες, οἱ καὶ τὰς φονικὰς δίκας ἔκρινον. (= Suda E. 3876, 2: 484 Adler); cf. Pollux 8. 125, ἀριστίνδην αἱρεθέντας. We find reference to similar age qualifications for public arbitrators ('in their sixtieth year' *Ath. Pol.* 53. 4) and for special embassies ('over 50 years of age', Plut. *Per.* 17; cf. Aeschin. 1. 23), but there is no mention of a roster of senior dicasts. Philippi, *Areopag*, 138–40, recognized that the report that the *ephetai* were chosen ἀριστίνδην is probably a misinterpretation of [Dem.] 43.57 (= *IG* I³ 104, line 19), ἐσέσθων οἱ φράτερες . . . δέκα· τούτους δὲ οἱ πεντήκοντα καὶ εἰς ἀριστίνδην αἱρείσθων; he suggested (211) that their number was mistaken for an age qualification; he was followed by Lipsius, *Attische Recht*, i. 18 n. 62; but cf. Busolt and Swoboda, 803–4; MacDowell, *AHL* 50; Wallace, *Areopagos Council*, 52.

indication whatever that special juries were chosen for the homicide courts. On the other hand, the special command of the legalities that the orators attribute to judges at the Palladium and Delphinium suggests that they had some experience as magistrates; the body from which such judges were most likely to be chosen was the Areopagus—and, as we shall see, the *Athenian Constitution* and other contemporary sources tend to confirm this connection.

3.2   Special Competence of the Homicide Justices

The decisive evidence regarding the competence of the homicide justices is to be found in Draco's law and the few references in later tradition where the *ephetai* are treated directly. The decree for the reinscription of the homicide code itself, as a valid statute rather than merely of antiquarian interest, shows that the traditional body still held jurisdiction for homicide in 409/8; and the decree of Patrocleides 405/4, which refers to those exiled by verdict of the *ephetai* among those excluded from amnesty (Andoc. 1. 78), would seem to prove that they retained their ancient authority.[38] Those who suppose that ordinary dicastic juries had taken over the duties of *ephetai* must assume that the archaic phrasing is merely a 'survival', preserved for the sake of traditionalism, after an amendment to earlier law had recognized dicastic juries as so-called *ephetai*. In rules of amnesty, however, it seems unlikely that a misleading archaism would be left without an explanation, if those excluded from amnesty were those convicted by ordinary citizen jurors.

There is no doubt that some provisions in the ancient law had indeed taken on new meaning in the course of two centuries, down to the decade of the reinscription and Patrocleides' decree. But we cannot simply assume that the archaic terms were now assigned democratic values. On the contrary, the traditional homicide procedure was apparently regarded in some quarters as an undemocratic relic. Whatever changes had come about in the workings of the courts, the Draconian institutions were not entirely democratized. And in Draco's ancient mandate for the *ephetai* there are two functions in particular that would seem to require superior competence.

---

[38] For the validity of the statutes, see Stroud, *DL* 49; followed by Gagarin, *Drakon*, 22–3 and *passim*; but see also Smith, 'Dicasts', 356, suggesting that a separate group of fifty-one *ephetai* (also dicasts) were involved in *aidesis;* cf. Wallace, *Areopagos Council*, 104.

The special rule involving the *ephetai* in pardon by the phratry would seem, by its very nature, beyond the authorized competence of the ordinary dicasts.[39] In this special case the justices acted for the family, weighing the killer's intent and selecting phratry members to participate in *aidesis*. In this role they acted as magistrates—much as the eponymous archon would act in behalf of orphans and heiresses without *kyrios*—rather than ordinary dicasts. No other known function of the dicastic jurors is precisely parallel to this duty, and the dicastic oath (Dem. 24. 149) does not seem to allow them such authority: 'Neither shall I restore to the city those exiled or sentenced to death.'

A further rule that can be confidently restored in Draco's law, and one strongly suggesting that the *ephetai* were identified with the Areopagus, is the provision for trial of those who unlawfully took vengeance against an exiled homicide. If the exiled homicide who abides by the terms of his banishment is slain unlawfully, his killer is to be tried by the *ephetai* 'just as in the killing of an Athenian, under the same terms'. This measure is often discounted as an archaism, but Demosthenes treats the clause as a valid statute that Aristocrates' bill would violate, and it would seriously undermine his suit for illegality if the ancient law upon which he bases his challenge had been altered by later amendment. Furthermore, we should consider that the most likely occasion for this rule is the vindictive murder of an exiled homicide by his victim's kinsmen, an intentional killing (cf. Dem. 23. 42). But after Solon's reform the murder jurisdiction belonged to the newly constituted Areopagus council; the provision for trial of intentional homicide by the *ephetai*—'just as in the killing of an Athenian'—would make sense only if the *ephetai* were identified with the Areopagus.[40] If, however, later amendments to the law expressly transferred the jurisdiction of the *ephetai* to the dicastic juries, the provision for trial of intentional homicide by the *ephetai*, 'just as in the killing of an Athenian', would be obviously inconsistent. In other circumstances murder trials would go before the high court of former archons, but in this instance murder charges would be tried before

---

[39] On this special provision and the possible connection with the Phreatto court see above Ch. 3 §2.1.2; cf. Gagarin, *Drakon*, 48–51; Heitsch, *Aidesis*, 17–20. For earlier views on the role of *ephetai* in *aidesis*, see Ruschenbusch, '*ΦΟΝΟΣ*', 137–9.

[40] Cf. Wallace, *Areopagos Council*, 17–18, arguing from this very clause (*IG* I³ 104, lines 28–9 = Dem. 23. 37–8) that the Areopagus was occupied by *ephetai* before Solon.

an ordinary layman jury. It is highly unlikely that Demosthenes would have given such emphasis to this clause in his argument on the illegality of Aristocrates' decree if there had been an amendment altering the very body that Demosthenes defends as ancient and unaltered.

There is one further document bearing upon the competence of the homicide judges: the account of the homicide courts in *Athenian Constitution* 57. 3–4. The passage begins as follows: 'Suits for homicide and wounding, if one kill or wound with intent to kill, are judged in the Areopagus, as well as cases of poisoning . . . and arson; these cases alone are tried by the (Areopagus) council.' The author proceeds to list the various courts, Palladium, Delphinium, and Phreatto, each with its jurisdiction. He then concludes, 'These cases are judged by men assigned (their duties) by lot, except for those cases that go before the Areopagus.' It is often assumed that 'men assigned by lot', *hoi lakhontes*, would naturally denote the ordinary dicasts. Greek usage in general, however, and the usage of the *Athenian Constitution* in particular, strongly suggest that this phrase, without more specific designation, ought to indicate men chosen from the larger body implied in the immediate context. 'Men assigned by lot' nowhere automatically indicates jurors of the ordinary dicastic panels, but only has that value where the dicastic courts are the immediate topic of discussion.[41] Now the account of the homicide courts is quite separate from the survey of dicastic courts, and it begins with reference to the jurisdiction of the Areopagus in cases of intentional homicide, wounding, and so on: 'these cases *alone* are tried by the council.' In this context the natural implication of the phrase identifying the *ephetai* as 'men assigned by lot, except for those cases that go before the Areopagus', is that the *ephetai* were a committee chosen from among the Areopagites for cases other than those that go before the full council.

3.3   Decline of the *Ephetai*

The one testimony that is sometimes taken as a direct reference to reform of the homicide courts is found in Pollux, the lexicographer of the second century AD. After a questionable sketch of the courts'

---

[41] The evidence is presented in my '*Ephetai*', 15 with n. 39.

historical development, Pollux makes a curious remark on the *decline* of the ancient justices: 'little by little the court of the *ephetai* became an object of ridicule.' It has been supposed that this passage refers to a period of decline in the late fifth century, leading up to reform of ephetic jurisdiction in 403/2.[42] But Pollux does not refer explicitly to such reform, as he does to the reforms of Draco and Solon. The most likely explanation is that Pollux derives this note on the decline of the *ephetai* from Demosthenes 23, the source of much of the lexicographers' information on the homicide courts.[43] At 23. 64 Demosthenes anticipates that some of his audience will have little reverence for the traditional homicide courts: ' . . . all of the rules governing the five (homicide) courts are prescribed by law—"Yes indeed," someone may say, "but worthless and unjustly instituted."' It may be argued that this objection is not to be taken entirely in earnest; but we know that the foundation of democratic institutions was a subject of some partisan debate in the fourth century, and this remark is not likely to be entirely facetious. Despite the conventional posture of reverence for the ancient laws, it is evident as early as Lysias 1 that trial before the ephetic courts was sometimes regarded as an antiquated and unpopular procedure. The cases mentioned in Isocrates 18. 52–4 and pseudo-Demosthenes 59. 10 show that the oath-bound procedure in *dikai phonou* was notoriously subject to abuse and often ended in trial for perjury. Aside from such litigious devices, the traditional procedure appears to have fallen into disuse.

Evidence of this obsolescence is found in the argument of Demosthenes 23 itself. The survey of the homicide courts concludes with a reference to the alternative and evidently more familiar procedure by warrant and arrest (*endeixis/apagōgē*); these remedies allowed for the prosecution of homicide before a dicastic jury, if the prosecutor 'has ignored all other measures, or [if] the proper time for lodging charges has passed, or [if] for any other reason he does not wish to

---

[42] Pollux 8. 125: κατὰ μικρὸν δὲ κατεγελάσθη τὸ τῶν ἐφετῶν δικαστήριον. Miller, 'Ephetai' *RE* 5 [11905] coll. 2825–6; cf. Wallace, *Areopagos Council*, 104 with n. 42.

[43] For the lexicographers' dependence on Dem. 23 (and Arist. *Ath. Pol.*), see Philippi, *Areopag*, 59–60 and 84; cf. Busolt and Swoboda, 803–4. The specific connection between Pollux 8. 125 and Dem. 23. 63–4 seems to me reasonably secure in view of the lexicographer's ready reliance on Dem. 23 for other particulars of the homicide courts. For 'contempt' of the Areopagus itself, cf. Din. 1. 50–5 and see my study '*Apophasis* and *Eisangelia*: The Role of the Areopagus in Political Trials', *GRBS* 26 (1985), 130–4.

follow these procedures' (80). This passage, though much disputed, certainly recognizes the limitations of the traditional procedure.[44] A *dikē phonou* was cumbersome and often avoided. For all the cases known to have been prosecuted by *dikē phonou* in the era after Antiphon, we know of as many homicide cases prosecuted by alternative procedures, chiefly *apagōgē* and *endeixis*.[45]

The nature of proceedings by warrant and arrest have been thoroughly investigated in recent work.[46] It will be sufficient here to compare these summary procedures in outline with the sequence of proceedings in *dikai phonou*. We know that *apagōgē* was in origin an alternative to self-help, whereby the victim of theft or other injury, or the concerned citizen who discovered an exile or other excluded persons in violation of the prohibited areas, might forcibly seize the offender and take him before the magistrate for execution. *Endeixis* appears to be a Draconian innovation that provided certain guarantees to the plaintiff: if he would first inform the magistrate of the violation, he was then, in effect, given warrant for forcible arrest;

[44] On Dem. 23. 80, ἀπαγωγὴ φόνου, etc., see MacDowell *AHL* 130–40; Hansen, *Apagoge*, 99–112; M. Gagarin, 'The Prosecution of Homicide in Athens', *GRBS* 20 (1979), 301–23; and M. H. Hansen, 'The Prosecution of Homicide in Athens: A Reply', *GRBS* 22 (1981), 11–30. For popular avoidance of *dikai phonou* as a procedure of forbidding complexity, cf. Plato, *Euthyphro*, 4a–b.

[45] In addition to the trumped-up charges in Isoc. 18. 52–4 and [Dem.] 59. 10, we know of only five or six *dikai phonou* after Antiphon, some doubtful: Lys. 1; Pl. *Euthphr.*; Dem. 21. 104 (after an *apagōgē* had been rejected); Dem. 23. 31 (arrest of a convicted homicide); and Dem. 54. 25 (which MacDowell, *AHL* 68, identifies as a charge of wounding rather than homicide). The case against Euaeon cited in Dem 21. 72–4 possibly led to trial before the Delphinium, but we are left without a clear indication of the period or procedure. There is a probable case prosecuted by *dikē phonou* before the Delphinium court, mentioned in Ar. *Rhet.* 1379ᵇ7–10, against one Demosthenes (presumably not the orator) but we have no clue on procedural details or the date (possibly 420s, involving Demosthenes the general of that era?): see G. Kennedy, *Aristotle 'On Rhetoric'* (New York and Oxford, 1991), 192 with n. 174; Hansen rejects the identification of this case with the known charges against Demosthenes the orator (by warrant, *Apagoge* catalogue no. 23). The case against Eratosthenes (Lys. 12) was *not* prosecuted by a *dikē phonou* but would probably have been handled in special accountings of the Thirty (*Ath. Pol.* 39. 6); Lys. 10. 31–2 may also refer to such proceedings. For homicides prosecuted by *apagōgē* and related procedures in the same period, see Hansen's catalogue in *Apagoge*, nos. 4–5, 11–12, 16–17, and 23. The procedure in Lysias' *Against Mikines* is also uncertain and even its authenticity as a speech-for-trial is doubtful; see Ch. 5 §1. There are three other speeches in the corpus of Lysias known only by title or short reference; cf. Lipsius, *Attische Recht*, 902.

[46] See Hansen, *Apagoge*, 1–28 (on the basic procedures) and 99–112 (on the application against homicides); cf. E. Ruschenbusch, *Untersuchungen zur Geschichte des athenischen Strafrechts* (Graz and Cologne, 1968), 57–8 and 64–70; on summary execution see my studies '*Akriton apokteinai*' and '*Nēpoinei tethnanai*'.

and if the wrongdoer were killed resisting arrest, the killer was not subject to legal action. In time, of course, *endeixis* came to be a more flexible instrument; the defendant might ordinarily be left at liberty until the trial, though with the obvious threat of forcible arrest at any time. He was thus given every encouragement to resort to exile or private settlement.

A significant principle of the original proceedings appears to have maintained its validity throughout the historical period: the arrest should be made 'upon immediate incrimination' (*ep' autophōrōi*), that the offender be caught or discovered in commission of the crime, in possession of stolen goods, or in other circumstances that showed self-evident guilt for an obvious and incontrovertible wrong. This was originally a requirement of arrest for execution, not for trial. The prosecutors would swear not simply to the fact of the crime but to immediate apprehension of the wrongdoer in flagrant violation. This aspect of the proceedings—that the plaintiff swears not simply to the fact of the wrong but also to his right to seize the offender— is an obvious relic of self-help. There is inherent in this requirement a principle of automaticity: the offender could be put to death without trial if he could not deny his guilt. In its conception this rule assumes that the compelling power of self-evident proof will force a confession or at least prevent the accused from disputing the indisputable circumstances. In practice, however, warrant and arrest were probably invoked in many circumstances where the defender's guilt was not altogether indisputable; in such cases he was likely to deny the charges no matter how compelling the evidence against him, and the rule that an offender might be put to death *if* he were apprehended *ep' autophōrōi* and *if* he confessed became a safeguard of due process.

The accusers would swear not simply to the fact of the crime but rather to the fact of having seized or discovered the offender *ep' autophōrōi*. This aspect of the original procedure continued to shape the proceedings in classical times: in those cases that were to go to trial there appears to have been very little preliminary discovery of evidence or arguments beyond the original statements of the plaintiffs and denial by the defendant; whatever testimony they offered at trial, as to the probable motives, opportunity, means, and so on, was not bound by oath. Such cases went speedily to trial before an ordinary dicastic court; there was no elaborate sequence of proceedings such as we find in *dikai phonou*.

There were a number of situations in which the summary procedure might be preferable, some indeed where it might be the only viable remedy. Obviously an exile who entered Athenian territory without reconciling with his victim's kinsmen was subject to warrant and arrest. Perhaps more important, though less recognized, was the class of killings which we might call 'felony murder'— killing in the commission of another felony. And at least by the end of the fifth century these procedures also seem to have been specially adapted to the prosecution of political killings.[47] By such applications of the laws for warrant and arrest, these swifter and supposedly more democratic remedies came to overshadow the traditional form of settlement by *dikē phonou*.

The implications of this development, whereby homicides were more often prosecuted by the alternative procedures, must be carefully considered. It is mistaken to suppose that the traditional procedure would be naturally relegated to the dicastic courts—such an assumption misconstrues the nature of procedural change in the Athenian system.[48] Instead the very fact that the traditional jurisdiction became outmoded is a strong indication that it did not yield to democratic innovation.

We have seen that the phrasing and practical implications of the law strongly indicate that the *ephetai* continued to be a body of special competence, distinct from the ordinary dicastic courts, as late as the decade of the reinscription of Draco's law (409/8) and Patrocleides' decree (405/4). It is also a reasonable conclusion, from Demosthenes' treatment of the Draconian statutes as valid and unaltered, that there had been no major revision of the homicide code in recent memory, from the turn of the century down to the time of the speech *Against Aristocrates*. The report in Pollux that the court of the *ephetai* declined in authority probably reflects Demosthenes' response to revisonist sentiment in the 350s. The

---

[47] On the case against Agoratus and the earlier case against Menestratus, see Ch. 9 §3.

[48] The various theories that the ephetic courts were allotted to juries of the people by Solon or by Pericles have at least the advantage of supposing a constitutional crisis to account for the reform. But Smith's view of Periclean reform goes against the common tradition that homicide jurisdiction alone was unaltered; and the more radical views of Ruschenbusch and Sealey rest upon no very secure foundation, since it is still much disputed whether Solon in fact established a system of dicastic panels such as we find in classical procedure. For debate on the establishment of *dikastēria* see esp. P. J. Rhodes, 'Εἰσαγγελία', *JHS* 99 (1979), 104; and M. H. Hansen, 'Athenian Heliaia', *Classica et Mediaevalia*, 33 (1981–2), 9–47.

contempt for the ancient courts that Demosthenes addresses is certainly not the sort of protest that would demand reform. We would perhaps expect reform if the traditional courts were inadequate to deal with current and pressing legal issues; but in this case, traditional proceedings and trial before the *ephetai* had been largely superseded by more summary methods and had simply fallen into disuse. After all, the traditional procedure was originally intended to serve chiefly as an instrument of settlement and a guarantee of safe exile for unintentional homicides. It was not intended to resolve all homicide charges by jury trial.

§4. Conclusions

If indeed the *ephetai* were chosen from the ancient council, they brought to the task considerable legal experience from their tenure as archons and as Areopagite judges. This is not to say that they were unmoved by the artful techniques that fostered litigiousness in the courts of the people; but they were expected to have a better working knowledge of legal principles and procedural rules; and in particular they were required to have a fundamental understanding of the practical implications and religious sanctions involved in the ancient procedure. By the nature of the procedure itself the justices are to act more in the character of a college of magistrates than a jury of the people. Trial before the justices was preoccupied with processual acts. We have seen that the oaths of the *antidikoi* and their witnesses in *dikai phonou* took a peculiar form: not only were the ritual trappings of blood-sacrifice particularly solemn and disturbing, but the content and function of the oaths were treated as a decisive enactment of the dispute for trial—thus Demosthenes treats it, as do the speakers of Antiphon 5 and 6. The parties to homicide disputes were especially enjoined against accusations on extraneous issues: the plaintiffs were required to swear specifically to the fact of death and to their claim of retribution against the defendant. Of course, in cases going before the Areopagus, plaintiffs would swear to malice aforethought and this issue would invite conjecture on probable motive. But the weighing of motives and circumstances was directed, as we shall see, not so much to the defendant's state of mind at the fatal moment of the killing as to his state of mind at the fateful moment of his oath.

PART II

Commentary on the Homicide Speeches

5

The *Tetralogies* and the Court Speeches

Among the documents of homicide law and early rhetoric at Athens the *Tetralogies* attributed to Antiphon are crucial. They have often been the touchstone of received opinion, the indicator by which we are to assess the value of other evidence and the worth of scholarly speculation. They may also have been regarded as something of a philosopher's stone, by which to transmute material of dubious value. Their argumentation shows some suggestive affinities with the demonstration speeches of Gorgias and the paired speeches of Thucydides' history.[1] But there is no other surviving document quite like them, nor any from which their probative value can be easily confirmed. Many of the basic problems remain therefore unresolved.

The question of authorship, whether these speeches are some-how the work of Antiphon, 'the Rhetor', and whether he is one and the same as 'the Sophist', is probably a *non liquet*.[2] The more promising inquiry, whether these speeches are an authentic product of Antiphon's era (either his own work or that of a contemporary), is also a vexed question, but there is now perhaps a growing consensus in favour of period-authenticity. The language and law of the *Tetralogies* are often at odds with the other Antiphontian speeches, those that represent actual arguments for trial; but scholars who favour authenticity generally suppose that the *Tetralogies*

---

[1] For this general characterization see Blass, *Attische Beredsamkeit*, 149–74; Lipsius, *Attische Recht*, 602, 615 (based on a previous study in *Bericht. Leipzig* 56 (1904), 191–204); Gernet, *Antiphon*, 6–16; Dover, 'Chronology' (1950), 56–9; MacDowell, *AHL* 80. The present chapter is a more detailed version of a study published previously in *AJP* 114 (1993), 235–70.

[2] Hermogenes reports the ancient debate whether Antiphon of Rhamnous, whom he identifies especially as the author of *phonikoi* and *dēmēgorikoi*, is also the author of the *Peri Alētheias* and other works attributed to 'the Sophist': *Peri ideōn* B 399 = Diels A2 (see also, beyond the fragment, lines 133–9 where Hermogenes identifies Antiphon 'the author of *phonikoi*', as a pioneer in the 'political genre'). The separatist view was well argued by E. Bignone, *Antifonte oratore e Antifonte sofista* (Urbino, 1974); but a rigorous rebuttal has now been offered by M. Gagarin, 'The Ancient Tradition on the Identity of Antiphon', *GRBS* 31 (1991), 27–44.

reflect the workings of the law courts in the age of the orators with sufficient accuracy to suit their rhetorical purpose. It remains uncertain precisely what the author's purpose may have been, whether the *Tetralogies* were an instructional device or an abstract theoretical essay.

Blass, whose influence has been perhaps most lasting, has led us to suppose that these exercises in homicide argumentation have broad, general application:[3] the same arguments on human nature and probable motives would be applicable in other procedures, and they were intended for an audience of some rhetorical proficiency but still of largely practical concerns. A similar reading contributes to Thomas Cole's recent reconstruction of early rhetoric:[4] he treats the *Tetralogies*, along with the showpieces and lost disputations of Gorgias, as typical of early instructive *technai*—model arguments of general applicability, 'teaching texts' rather than 'reading texts'. On this theory, the *Tetralogies* as *technai* were prior to the logographer's written text for clients to con by memory; and thus Cole's reconstruction upholds the widely-held hypothesis on the dating of the *Tetralogies*, that they belong, whether Antiphon's or not, to the era of his earliest work.

The prevailing assumption of period-authenticity is largely a legacy, however, of the reaction to Dittenberger's arguments a century ago.[5] Against Antiphon's authorship Dittenberger emphasized the apparent discrepancies between the legal framework presupposed in the *Tetralogies* and the actual workings of the law at Athens. Many of the inconsistencies were soon resolved by

---

[3] Thus Blass, *Attische Beredsamkeit*, 149–50, is singularly indifferent to the legal discrepancies, and emphasizes the practical applications; he rejects the analogy sometimes drawn between the *Tetralogies* and the artificial topics of declamation: 'Antiphon's Fälle dagegen sind so, dass sie sich jeden Tag ereignen konnten, und die Gesetze, worauf er sich bezieht, sind die bestehenden. . . . so übte er sich für die Praxis.' Various anomalies can be explained by the didactic aims: the arguments are abbreviated, narrative and witnesses omitted; they show greater sophistication and intensity precisely because of their purpose as instructional devices. Similarly Kennedy, *Persuasion*, esp. 130–1, assumes that theoretical innovation was directly geared to practical technique.

[4] *The Origins of Rhetoric in Ancient Greece* (Baltimore, 1991), esp. 73–8, 80–2 with n. 10, on the 'proto-rhetorical practice and demonstration text'; cf. G. Kennedy, 'The Earliest Rhetorical Handbooks', *AJP* 80 (1959), 169–78, regarding early *technai* as collections of common topics and devices.

[5] 'Antiphons Tetralogien und das attische Criminalrecht', *Hermes*, 31 (1896), 271–7 and 32 (1897), 1–41; and, responding to Lipsius (above n. 1), in *Hermes*, 40 (1905), 450–70.

Lipsius, whose authoritative voice silenced most of the sceptics.
But Gernet was not entirely convinced by Lipsius's arguments, and
taking into account the peculiar, non-Attic terminology of the
Tetralogies, he suggested that they might be the work of an Ionian
student or imitator of Antiphon.[6] And Solmsen, doubting the
authenticity of the *Tetralogies*, excluded them altogether from his
study of the development of artistic proofs in Antiphon:[7] the
Tetralogies, preoccupied with argument from probability, would
appear to be an end product of the evolution from *atechnoi* to
entechnoi pisteis, in which Antiphon stands as a transitional figure.

The presumption of authenticity is again evident, however, in
Dover's chronology of the Antiphontian speeches: he concedes that
the *Tetralogies* are stylistically anomalous but, he none the less
assures us, they are indeed 'consistent with the hypothesis' of
Antiphon's authorship, and he clearly prefers the view that the
Tetralogies are authentic but 'were written in imitation of an Ionic
genre'.[8] This theory accounts for the *Tetralogies*' persistent use of
Ionic terminology (e.g. $\kappa\alpha\tau\alpha\lambda\alpha\mu\beta\acute{\alpha}\nu\epsilon\iota\nu$ 'convict'; $\kappa\alpha\tau\alpha\delta o\kappa\epsilon\hat{\iota}\nu$ 'suspect') that is distinctly at odds with the usage of the court speeches
and with Attic legal usage in general. It is reasonable to assume that
the *Tetralogies* follow the prestige dialect, 'just as Ionic scientific
words appear in the fragments ascribed to the Sophist Antiphon'.[9]
But Dover's hypothesis also suggests an unwarranted inference—
that Antiphon (or a contemporary) found an Ionic exemplar for the
peculiar format of paired court speeches, which he then adapted—
with legal terms intact—to the Attic setting. There is not the least
indication of an Ionic model for this particular kind of exercise—

---

[6] Gernet, *Antiphon*, 15–16, regards linguistic discrepancies as decisive evidence
against Antiphon's authorship, though he accepts the legal competence of the author
('celui que nous appellerons donc le Pseudo-Antiphon'), probably a figure prominent in sophistic schools, perhaps of Ionian origin. Cf. P. von der Mühll, 'Zur
Unechtheit der antiphontischen Tetralogien', *MH* 5 (1948), 1–5.

[7] *Antiphonstudien*, esp. 3 n. 1.

[8] Dover, 'Chronology', esp. 56–9; cf. Wilamowitz-Moellendorf, 'Die erste Rede
des Antiphon', *Hermes*, 22 (1887), 198. Dover discounts Gernet's theory: 'The picture of an Ionian composing three sets of speeches in Attic but forgetting or not
knowing that Attic normally said $\ddot{\iota}\sigma\mu\epsilon\nu$ and $\dot{\alpha}\pi\epsilon\lambda o\gamma\eta\sigma\acute{\alpha}\mu\eta\nu$, is an unrealistic one.'
This objection holds only if we assume that the author's aim was to provide a prac-
tical demonstration text.

[9] The list of vocabulary and phrasing not found in the court speeches is quite significant: in addition to those listed by Dover and Gernet (above, nn. 6 and 8) and of
particular interest for this study are those relevant to miasma-doctrine ($\kappa\hat{\eta}\lambda\iota\varsigma$,
$\pi\rho o\sigma\tau\rho\acute{o}\pi\alpha\iota o\varsigma$, $\kappa\tau\lambda$.) and causation ($\dot{\alpha}\tau\nu\chi\acute{\iota}\alpha$, $\kappa\tau\lambda$.).

neither the *Antilogies* of Protagoras nor the lost disputations of Gorgias seem at all comparable.[10] The *Tetralogies* are, after all, sharply focused exercises in argumentation on issues specific to homicide trials: cause of death, consequences of defilement, justifiable homicide, and so on. To suppose that an otherwise unknown Ionic original inspired Antiphon to devise an Attic version, and hence to conclude that all anomalies may be explained away as vestiges of a lost exemplar, is, to put it generously, an inelegant solution.[11]

Suppose then that the *Tetralogies* are not Antiphon's but a product of his era. The chief evidence to support this hypothesis is the fifth-century perspective that many readers find in the *Tetralogies*: traditional religiosity in regard to defilement and 'justifiable killing' is here joined with sophistic ingenuity in regard to causation, human nature, and probable motives. This outlook seems suited to the fifth-century 'enlightenment'—one thinks of *Oedipus Tyrannus* and *Orestes*. Fernanda Decleva Caizzi, in an extensive discussion of miasma-doctrine and 'the law forbidding justifiable killing', claims that the arguments on these issues reflect the same clash of written and unwritten law that inspired *Antigone*; she thus regards the 'enlightenment' perspective as authentic and consistent with an early theoretical work by Antiphon.[12] Similarly, Michael Gagarin has interpreted 'the law prohibiting both just and unjust killing' as 'a moral comment on the Athenian legal system'; he, too, regards the *Tetralogies* as the work of Antiphon or a contemporary.[13]

---

[10] The *Antilogies* of Protagoras (80 Diels and Kranz, F5) were probably an early dialogue form, evidently prefiguring Plato's *Republic* I. Similar *disputationes* are attributed to Gorgias by Cicero, *Brut.* 46–7; cf. Aristotle, *Soph. El.* 33, 183^{b}38. See Cole, *Origins of Rhetoric*, 75. The Doric antilogy *Dissoi Logoi* (*c.*400) also contrasts with the *Tetralogies*: the former are little more than a list of antithetical views without any formal structure of court trial or other procedure.

[11] This hypothesis seems to rest upon the manuscript attribution and the discrepancies themselves: the manuscripts tell us that these speeches are Antiphon's; their usage is Ionic and at odds with the extant court speeches (which date to a few years before his death); therefore the *Tetralogies* must be an early work following an Ionic model.

[12] Cf. Günther Zuntz, 'Earliest Attic Prose Style', *CM* 2 (1939), 121–44, and 'Once Again, the Antiphontean Tetralogies', *MH* 6 (1949), 100–4, on the treatment of 'judicial murder' in Ant. 5: 'The parallel in the third Tetralogy is wholly dominated by the idea of the avenging spirit . . . [which] fails to reappear in extant speeches. The abandonment of this traditional motif is characteristic evidence of a changed "Zeitgeist".' (*MH* 6 (1949), 102).

[13] *Antiphontis Tetralogiai*, 21–44; cf. M. Gagarin, 'Prohibition of Just and Unjust Homicide in Antiphon's *Tetralogies*', *GRBS* 19 (1978), 303.

Arguing against Antiphon's authorship, however, and in favour of a date in the fourth century, Raphael Sealey has raised various points of law and politics, along with a salutary reminder of the dubious attribution of such texts.[14] There are, after all, grounds for reasonable suspicion. There is no reference to the *Tetralogies* before the Second Sophistic. Neither Aristotle nor Anaximenes anywhere mentions Antiphon as the author of such a work. Of course, there were presumably many sophistic speeches that Aristotle does not mention, but surely, if Aristotle had known of a *technē* such as later tradition attributes to Antiphon and to which the *Tetralogies* presumably belong,[15] he would have found some occasion to allude to it, since the *Tetralogies* certainly encompass important topics for which Aristotle cites other theoretical treatments.[16] From the very nature of the transmission of such texts it is doubtful whether even the small corpus that has come down to us under Antiphon's name is entirely his own.[17] We find speeches that are obviously the work of other authors in the corpora of Lysias and Demosthenes; much the same uncertainty surrounds the collection of prooemia in the Demosthenic corpus, as well as the collection of proems attributed to Antiphon.[18] The manuscript attribution and the scattered indications that the *Tetralogies* were regarded as Antiphon's in the time of Harpocration and Pollux offer us very little assurance that they are indeed his work.[19] And on a number of points of ideology and legal argument there is a significant difference of perspective

---

[14] R. Sealey, 'The *Tetralogies* Ascribed to Antiphon', *TAPA* 114 (1984), 71–85.

[15] L. Radermacher, *Artium Scriptores*, 76–81; see above, n. 4.

[16] On the problematic nature of justifiable killing, see *Rhet.* 1. 13. 2 (1373[b]) and 2. 24. 3 (1401[a]) citing Alcidamas and Theodectes; for argument from probability, as to the more likely aggressor, 2. 24. 11 (1402[a]) citing 'the *technē* of Corax'.

[17] Dover, *Lysias and the 'Corpus Lysiacum'* (Berkeley, 1968), 148–74. I cannot accept all that Dover says regarding composite authorship and 'client copies', but the principle that the corpus of a given author is likely to include anything the ancient editor thought relevant seems indispensable.

[18] *Suda* A 1458, I 352 (Adler) = Fragments 68–70 (Blass).

[19] Harpocration and Pollux cite distinctive words and phrases found in the *Tetralogies*; they do not identify the work unambiguously, but the pattern of such citations strongly indicates that they or their immediate sources had text of the *Tetralogies* and attributed it to Antiphon. Thus Harpocration (*Lex.* 5. 6) attributes the phrase ἀγνεύετε τὴν πόλιν to Antiphon ἐν τῷ β′; it is found in *Tetr.* 1. 3. 11. 'In the second' may of course indicate that the first *Tetr.* was already second in the corpus; but it may also indicate that the *Tetralogies* were in the second book of a *technē*. Harpocration regularly refers to major court speeches by title, to the theoretical works by number.

between the popular reasoning of Antiphon's era and that of the 'restoration' era—the generation or so after 404—and the *Tetralogies* conform more closely to the latter.[20] The latest studies, however, tend to assume period-authenticity and to resolve the discrepancies on a more general understanding of the *Tetralogies* as a theoretical work, influenced by the kind of demonstration in experimental methods that we find in Gorgias' *Helen* and *Palamedes*, and from this influence also marked by Ionicisms.[21] On this reading there is no need to assume that the *Tetralogies* are an adaptation of an Ionic original in trial format, and thus the obvious difficulties inherent in Dover's theory are avoided. But we are left with another puzzling anomaly. The theoretical demonstration that Gorgias perfected made use of mythic cases with little semblance of court proceedings; this genre was carried on in later works attributed to Antisthenes and Alcidamas. Why does the author of *Tetralogies* depart from the pattern of mythic, and hence plainly speculative scenarios, to model his demonstration upon actual court proceedings of a particular type, involving scenarios indeed remarkably parallel to certain known cases? The answer to this question may yet be entirely consistent with the theory of an early, authentic demonstration text from the era of Antiphon. But we must at least recognize the obvious implication that these exercises have something to say about homicide trials *per se*: they are a reflection upon certain methods of reasoning proper to homicide proceedings, and in taking this singular perspective the author's concerns are at least partly legalistic—he is making some comment on the workings of the law.

[20] At *Tetr.* 2. 1. 1 the author seems to assume a distinction between laws and decrees proper to the era after 404: Sealey, '*Tetralogies*', 80–4; cf. F. Decleva Caizzi *Antiphontis Tetralogiae* (Milan, 1969), 211. Also perhaps indicative of a post-revolutionary perspective is the designation of the voters (and the law?) as 'the highest authority in all the state' (cf. Lys. 1. 36); and the line of argument in *Tetr.* 1. 1. 6 and 4. 9—the prosecutors portray the defendant as *mnēsikakōn*, and defendant argues that his very wealth is proof of his innocence, 'for it is those who are not so fortunate who profit from factional strife'. See von der Mühll, 'Unechtheit', 3, and cf. Lys. 25. 10 (*c.*399).

[21] Such seems to be the assumption of Cole, Gagarin, and others. Along similar lines an intriguing solution has been offered by D. C. Innes (*Argumentation*, 5 (1991), 221–31): the rhetorical setting of the *Tetralogies* is not Athens but 'Sophistopolis', much as other showpieces of the era address a broader audience. She goes too far in her arguments that the legal setting of the *Tetralogies* is not recognizably Athenian, with 'no indication that we are in a democracy' (223–5). For the view that the law of *Tetralogies* is fictitious or universal, cf. G. Thiel, *Antiphons erste Tetralogie* (Groningen, 1932), 13–15.

In the following sections we shall compare the *Tetralogies* with corresponding arguments in the court speeches and other evidence on popular reasoning under three headings: first the subject matter of the *Tetralogies*, the kinds of cases that the author has chosen and the framing of specific issues as the foci of his arguments; second, the argument based upon miasma-doctrine; and third, the various propositions regarding 'the law that prohibits (even) justifiable killing'.

§1. Invention in the *Tetralogies*

1.1 Questions at Issue

The traditional homicide procedure involved an exhaustive mechanism for determining the question at issue and limiting the dispute to that question. Antiphon's court speeches suggest that this mechanism goes back before living memory (5. 88 = 6. 6). The *Tetralogies* reveal a singular preoccupation with this aspect of homicide argumentation; indeed, it has long been assumed that the *Tetralogies* are arranged as they are, apparently treating in order cases of intentional killing, unintentional killing, and so-called justifiable killing, in order to parallel the division of jurisdiction among the Areopagus, Palladium, and Delphinium courts. This aspect of the proceedings is easily seen in the first and third *Tetralogies*, in the very scenarios that our author has devised. But the second *Tetralogy* addresses this concern in the most direct and meaningful way: some matters, decided by law, are beyond dispute; 'if there is an issue in dispute (*amphisbētēsimon*), this is assigned to [the judges] to decide.'[22]

The author thus suggests to his audience a basic division of issues as questions of fact, law, or definition. The systematic division of issues—what would later be the province of *stasis*-theory, what this author and Aristotle call 'issue in dispute' (*amphisbētēsimon*) is largely a product of fourth-century rhetorical analysis (*Rhet.* 1374[a], 1417[b]). Yet the author of the *Tetralogies* seems to assume that the

---

[22] Τὰ μὲν ὁμολογούμενα τῶν πραγμάτων ὑπό τε τοῦ νόμου κατακέκριται ὑπό τε τῶν ψηφισαμένων, οἳ κύριοι πάσης τῆς πολιτείας εἰσίν· ἐὰν δέ τι ἀμφισβητήσιμον ᾖ, τοῦτο ὑμῖν, ὦ ἄνδρες πολῖται, προστέτακται διαγνῶναι.

rudiments of this classification are familiar to his audience.[23] The opening statement indicates (1) that the defence will have no basis to dispute the facts, which are agreed upon, and (2) any legal questions have been resolved by 'the laws and by the voters, who are sovereign'. The plaintiff has agreed that the act was unintentional, but he claims that defendant is none the less liable; he cannot dispute the facts or the legalities.

But, of course, there is a defence to be made, and the plaintiff, in his second speech, reacts with dismay: 'he has shown to what extremes dire necessity can drive anyone . . . *I would not have supposed that he would (even) answer the charge.*' The prosecutor contends that he has lost half of his allotted time by virtually dispensing with the first speech when he thought that the trial was a mere formality. This tactic corresponds to a familiar device in the court speeches ('surely my opponent will not have the audacity to dispute . . .' *vel sim.*).[24] But in the court speeches this tactic draws upon what has been discovered in the pretrial hearings, the *prodikasiai* (Ch. 4 §1). Thus in Antiphon 6. 15–17 the defendant is able to make such nonsense of the charges precisely because so much has been established in the preliminaries: he knows the wording of the charge and how the key terms will be interpreted, and he is confident that the plaintiffs cannot dispute the testimony of his witnesses. By the nature of the proceedings, the issue for the jury to decide—whether a question of intent, liability, or legal justification—was clearly defined before the trial.

In the *Tetralogy*, however, there is the clear implication that the prosecution do not know how the defence will argue their case or even the wording of their plea. If this were an actual case for trial, the issues would have been clearly defined in the three preliminary hearings. The statements on both sides would have been attested under the solemnest of oaths (Dem. 23. 67–8). Antiphon 1. 2 refers to a written indictment; Antiphon 6 (§§14–17) shows that sworn statements were read out at the beginning of the trial and each side knew the content of the other's affidavit beforehand.

The author of *Tetralogies* reduces this process to utter confusion.

---

[23] The manuscript hypotheses identify the issues as στοχασμός, question of fact (*Tetr.* 1), or μετάστασις/ἀντέγκλημα, transferred blame (*Tetr.* 2–3). The hypotheses of course do not go back to the author of the *Tetr.* himself, but cf. Cole, *Origins of Rhetoric*, 97–8.

[24] Cf. Ant. 1 (*Stepmother*) 5–7, 28–30.

He treats the case as though the two parties have somehow gone to trial without defining the issue. The plaintiff pretends to have no knowledge of how the defender will plead—indeed, he had supposed that his opponent would abandon the case in desperation and immediately send his son into exile.

In alluding to the provision that allows voluntary exile before the final speech the author is treating the conventions in a provocative way. He has properly exploited this rule in *Tetralogies* 1 and 3, where the charge is intentional killing and the death penalty looms; but it is irrelevant in cases of unintentional homicide such as this, where the defendant is guaranteed a safe path of exile after the verdict. There was nothing to gain by forgoing the trial.[25]

Now discrepancies such as this tend to disprove the notion that the *Tetralogies* were in any sense an instructional device in practical technique for aspiring advocates to imitate. The *ephetai*, who judged *dikai phonou*, were clearly officers of some special competence, probably Areopagus members, former magistrates (Ch. 4 §3); they had at least a good working knowledge of the procedure and probably would not have been much impressed with the tactic in *Tetralogy* 2. Unless we are to suppose that the author was wholly ignorant of this aspect of his chosen format, it is reasonable to conclude that he has intentionally seized upon a case in which the ordinary mechanism for defining the question at issue would prove inadequate.

It is perhaps tempting to suppose that Antiphon or some other thinker of his day ventured upon experimental investigation of 'issues in dispute', which would prove to be more systematically treated in later rhetorical theory; *dikai phonou* with their peculiar mechanism for defining the issue would serve as a suitable model. But it is also possible that a later thinker, in the era when 'issues in dispute' were a recognized subject of rhetorical analysis, transposed the theory into the trial format. Such an essay might well have been prompted by certain controversial cases in which the issues in dispute proved singularly problematic. Each of the *Tetralogies* has, as we shall see, a close analogue among cases of some notoriety, and the correspondence is likely to be more than coincidence.

[25] See Ch. 3 §2.2.2 (at n. 56) on Dem. 23. 72. The confusion about the penalty in *Tetr.* 2 has been often observed: the speaker for the defence refers to the prospect of a verdict against him as though the boy's life were at stake (διαφθορὰ, 3. 2. 10); cf. Sealey, '*Tetralogies*', 77.

1.2   Known Parallels

In the second *Tetralogy* the concise, elliptical approach to the scenario suggests in itself that the author has taken up a familiar paradox, one in which the 'issue in dispute' might well seem elusive. The sole narrative, which must suffice for the four speeches, is the one brief sentence, 'My son was struck by the javelin thrown by this youth in the gymnasium and immediately died.' Compared to the court speeches, this hardly seems an adequate scenario. There are other details that will emerge obliquely in the course of the arguments—such as the suggestion that the boy ran into the target area at the moment when the trainer gave the signal to throw. But the author does not give the full picture at the outset evidently because he assumed that his audience would recognize the case—much as Gorgias could assume that his audience knew the stories of Helen and Palamedes. In fact, Plutarch reports that Pericles and Protagoras debated just such an incident, as to whether the weapon itself or the officials were culpable (*Per*. 36).

If we assume that this case was well known to the audience of the *Tetralogies*, then the initial formulation regarding the 'issue in dispute'—'what is agreed upon as to the facts of the case, the law and the voters have judged; . . . if there is an issue in dispute it is [for the judges] to decide'—suggests that the author intended to discount the familiar solutions. Later in the *Tetralogy* (3. 7) the prosecution expressly discounts one of the verdicts that Pericles and Protagoras supposedly debated, that the officials were culpable; the author sees no need to explore this approach. It was probably also a common assumption that the defendant in such a case might plead that the killing was justifiable by the law of the Delphinium court. But by this rule the defendant may admit to the killing but claim legal justification only if he can invoke a specific provision of statute; among such instances were death in athletic competition—not, as our author has construed the case, in training. In the treatment of 'issues in dispute' with which he begins this case, the author seems rather pointedly to reject a plea of legal justification. What 'the law and the voters have judged' evidently refers to statutory rules that would upon strict construction invalidate a plea of legal justification.

In all three *Tetralogies* we find a similar allusiveness; the succinct, abbreviated narrative seems to presuppose a certain audience

awareness of the issues in the famous or typical case. The second
Tetralogy is again the clearest instance and what we learn of the
controversy surrounding this case tells us something about the
author's inspiration.

If we accept the historicity of the anecdote and assume that
Pericles and Protagoras indeed debated this very theme, then it is
possible that the incident occurred in the 440s (or very soon
after)—probably the era of Antiphon's earliest involvement as legal
counsel. Plutarch's account clearly suggests, however, that
Stesimbrotus was the ultimate source for the tale of Pericles' quarrel with his son Xanthippus; and it is in this context that we are told
Xanthippus exposed the debate with Protagoras.[26] Plutarch himself is sceptical of Stesimbrotus' account, and if, as seems likely, the
tale is a rank fabrication by Stesimbrotus, the story was current no
earlier than the late 420s, probably later.[27] On this assumption the
Tetralogies would belong to the same period as Antiphon 5 and 6,
with which they are so much at odds stylistically. They may yet be
a work of the same author, utilizing the literary dialect and depart-
ing widely from his court practice; or it may perhaps be the work of
a contemporary or 'student' of Antiphon, but if so, it was not necessarily written before his death.[28] And a third possibility is not out
of the question, that the tale told by Stesimbrotus was elaborated
by a later author, and it was this later publication that prompted the
author of *Tetralogies* to write an adaptation. In any case the
Tetralogy was clearly inspired by the *cause célèbre*.

In subject matter the other two *Tetralogies* are similarly preoccupied with extraordinary precedents; both may be linked to common topics in the rhetorical handbooks, and both seem to anticipate
audience interest in certain notorious cases.

The first *Tetralogy*—in which the defendant must argue that he
is not likely to have killed the victim precisely because he is
the most likely suspect—takes up the famous technique that was

[26] Stesimbrotus (*FGrHist* 107) F11; Plut. *Per.* 36. 4–6. Xanthippus reportedly
told the tale to discredit his father as an effete intellectual. The whole anecdote (36.
2–5) probably derives from S.; he is cited by name 36. 6 and a connection with the
previous anecdote is indicated: πρὸς δὲ τούτοις καὶ τὴν περὶ τῆς γυναικὸς
διαβολὴν ὑπὸ τοῦ Ξανθίππου φησὶν ὁ Σ . . . διασπαρῆναι.

[27] Plutarch seems anxious to quash the slanders of Stesimbrotus, *Per.* 13. 16. See
my study, 'Thucydides and Stesimbrotus', *Historia* 38 (1989), 144–61.

[28] For the ancient tradition that Antiphon of Rhamnous was a teacher of rhetoric,
cf. *Menexenus* 236a; Anon. *vit. Thuc.* 1–2; Radermacher, *Artium Scriptores,* B X.
2–3, 5–9.

pioneered by Tisias and, as Aristotle tells us, elaborated at length in 'the *technē* of Corax'. This adaptation of the topic may have been inspired by famous unsolved murders, or by a recent case in which the puzzle of 'who-done-it' roused popular interest.[29] But the one clear parallel, for which we have direct testimony, is the work of Lysias generally identified in antiquity as *Against Mikines*. Though little remains of this intriguing work, it is usually supposed to be an authentic speech-for-trial. From the fragments and testimonia we can surmise that the defendant had allegedly waylaid his victim after a dinner party, and by circumstantial proof he had denied the very fact of his involvement.[30] But the nature of the case, the type of procedure, the date, and even the authorship are uncertain; nor can we decide conclusively whether the speech was written for a client to deliver at trial or as a demonstration of technique. The evidence we have tends to support the latter hypothesis—the *Mikines* was probably an artificial demonstration of technique, much like the *Palamedes* of Gorgias or, indeed, like the *Tetralogy* itself. Such at least is the most natural inference from the hypothesis to *Tetralogy* 1, where the parallel between the two works is remarked: 'Antiphon's skill . . . is revealed most of all in these *Tetralogies* in which he contends against himself; for he has given two speeches for the plaintiff and two for the defendant, by way of demonstration (or exercise), similarly brilliant on both sides. *This speech then resembles Lysias' speech written 'Against Mikines'; the gist is as follows.* . . ' Now the connective particles (μὲν οὖν . . . δέ) would suggest that the basis for comparison between the *Tetralogy* and Lysias' speech lay not only in the scenario but also in masterful demonstration of technique, and there is at least the implication that the brilliance common to both works was similarly demonstrated by argumentation 'on both sides,' whereby the master 'contended against himself'.[31]

---

[29] *Rhet.* 2. 1402ª17 ff.; cf. Plato, *Phaedrus* 273b, attributing the technique to Tisias. Gagarin ('Proofs in Antiphon', 30) aptly calls this method 'reverse εἰκός'. On the identity of Tisias cf. T. Cole in *ICS* 16 (1992). It is also possible that the author was influenced by such celebrated cases as Ant. 5 and the unsolved murder of Ephialtes; see below at nn. 41–6.

[30] Hyp. Tetr. 1: ἔοικε μὲν οὖν οὗτος ὁ λόγος τῷ Λυσίου λόγῳ τῷ πρὸς Μικίνην γεγραμμένῳ. For fragments see T. Thalheim's edition, *Lysiae Orationes* (Leipzig, 1913), 354; Blass, 1. 361.

[31] For the value of μὲν οὖν cf. Denniston, *Greek Particles*, 470–81; Kühner and Gerth, *Grammatik*, 2. 2. 157. Denniston objects (473) to Kühner's view, 'οὖν weist auf das Vohergehende hin, und dient zugleich zur Kräftigung des μέν'; but I find the

There is further evidence that the *Mikines* indeed argued 'on both sides' of the case, though not apparently in the form of paired speeches. It was evidently a speech for the prosecution, but scholia to Hermogenes *Peri Staseōn* indicate that a significant part of the argument was devoted to 'anticipation' of opposing arguments (*prokatalēpsis*, or as the scholiast calls it, ἀντιληπτικόν). The testimony comes in a passage on 'circumstantial proof from the opposite of present circumstances': in regard to 'proof from t he person' one is to argue,

'I would not have employed these accomplices, but those servants less likely to be suspected, or an outside agent'; this method Lysias uses in the speech *Against Mikines*. This is an anticipation of defence arguments, for [the defendant] will say 'it was possible for me to accomplish this through other agents'.[32]

This report treats the *Mikines* as an exercise in conjecture as to the fact, as does the hypothesis to the *Tetralogy*, and in this context the passage clearly suggests that Mikines was implicated indirectly by the involvement of his slaves, who were caught in the act and apparently slain rather than subjected to torture. Another fragment suggests similarly that Mikines was implicated by his *absence* from the family banquet, rather than by eyewitnesses placing him at the scene of the crime.[33] All of the available indications would lead us to suppose that the *Mikines* was an artificial demonstration of technique rather than a speech-for-trial. It is certainly not to be relied upon as evidence that cases of 'who-done-it' were commonplace in the murder courts of the fifth century. If the similarity between the *Tetralogy* and the *Mikines* suggests anything at all regarding

latter more apt in regard to the very passages listed by D. as 'οὖν emphasizing a prospective μέν'. In any event, there can be little doubt οὖν ordinarily refers back to the preceding, and such would be the most natural interpretation in the hypothesis to *Tetr.* 1.

[32] Schol. ad Hermogenis Status, 4. 405. 5–18 (Walz): οὐκ ἂν ἐχρησάμην τούτοις συνεργοῖς, ἀλλὰ τοῖσδε τοῖς ἔλαττον ὑποπτευθησαμένοις οἰκέταις ἢ ξενικῇ δυνάμει· τούτῳ καὶ Λυσίας ἐν τῷ πρὸς Μικίνην χρῆται· ἔστι δὲ ἀντιληπτικόν τοῦτο· φήσει γὰρ, ὅτι ἐξῆν μοι δι᾽ ἑτέρων τοῦτο πρᾶξαι. Such is precisely the nature of the defence arguments in *Tetr.* 1 (see esp. 4. 8, 'more likely not to be present,' i.e. to employ others). The hypothesis to *Tetr.* 1, evidently working in the same tradition as the scholia to Hermogenes, remarks that the 'conjecture' as to the fact is 'partial' or 'incomplete' in that the reverse probability focuses only upon the person.

[33] Thalheim, *Lysiae Orationes*, 354: οἱ μὲν ἄλλοι συγγενεῖς παραγένοντο, μόνος δ᾽ ἀπελείφθη.

authenticity, it is perhaps an indication that the *Tetralogies* belong
to the era of Lysias rather than Antiphon.[34]

There are obvious parallels, again, between the issue in the third
Tetralogy—in which the defendant must plead that he was not the
initiator of a brawl with an older man—and various common topics
of the later rhetorical literature. The theme owes something to the
fact that such brawls were undoubtedly commonplace in all
periods; but the scenario in *Tetralogy* 3 is remarkably similar to the
case reported by Demosthenes, 21. 72–5.[35]

Whatever the date of his work, in his choice of scenarios the
author reveals an interest in problems that are fundamentally legal
or juristic, areas where the rules and principles that shape the
courtroom arguments prove inadequate or suggest problematic
consequences. He is preoccupied with complications that are
largely *legalistic*: he is as much concerned with formal rules that the
law prescribes as with the substantive ethical issues that gained
such currency in the 'enlightenment'—indeed, he seems to fasten
upon the clash of technicalities and verities. Thus in the second
Tetralogy the author has focused upon an incident where accepted
notions of causation and legal justification seem to defy the ordinary procedures, the formal rules and conventions of *dikai phonou*.
The hypothetical 'who-done-it' in *Tetralogy* 1 has similar legalistic
implications.

1.3   Use of Probabilities

There has been a general tendency to emphasize the importance of
argument from probability in the *Tetralogies* and accordingly to
date them to the height of the sophistic era when such tactics were
new and intriguing. But the author's method is not such as to suggest that probabilities *per se* were among his chief interests. He uses
probabilities only in the first and third *Tetralogies*; and in the third,
only in regard to the commonplace that 'the young are more prone
to reckless violence'. *Tetralogy* 1, to be sure, involves a *tour de force*

---

[34] If *Against Mikines* is a speech-for-trial, then it is, I think, more likely for the
Tetralogy to have been written in imitation of it than vice versa (more likely for art
to imitate life). If both are artificial demonstrations on the same theme, it is not
unlikely that they belong to the same milieu.

[35] With the ethical proof in *Tetr*. 3, regarding e.g. youthful *akolasia*, cf. Aristotle,
Rhet. 1389[a]. On the case reported in Dem. 21. 72–5, see below §3.1, and cf. Ch. 8
§2.2.

in conjecture on probable motive; but this exercise in probabilities is secondary to a more provocative purpose.

The probabilities in *Tetralogy* 1 focus upon a question of fact, whether the defendant is the unknown agent who ambushed the victim. From all available evidence, the extant speeches for court cases and the record of statute law, the question whether the defendant or some other unknown assailant was in fact the culprit was rarely (if ever) the issue in *dikai phonou*, at least up until the restoration era. The homicide procedure that Draco devised was intended primarily to facilitate private settlement, providing for exile and *aidesis* or for self-help; trial before the *ephetai* was invoked only where such judgement was disputed. The function of the Draconian trial was not to investigate or make a determination upon the facts, but to give judgement of *liability*, either for the plaintiffs or for the defendant. The argumentation focuses not upon questions of fact or circumstance *per se*, but upon the oaths, witnesses, and challenges as tests of the claimant's conviction. It appears to have been firmly believed or at least a fiction well maintained that a 'known' killer—one whose guilt was witnessed or strongly presumed by others—would be compelled by religion and social conscience to acknowledge his involvement. But if the killer was an unscrupulous character, unaffected by religious and social constraints, and the plaintiffs had no admissible proof beyond their suspicions, they had little prospect of convicting him; this is shown by the predicament of a plaintiff described in Demosthenes 47. 69–70 (below).

Now the author of *Tetralogy* 1 is remarkably attentive to this aspect of the proceedings. He seems to assume that the plaintiff would rely on some, at least minimal proof by the formal instruments: in this case it is the dying testimony of a slave. Bear in mind, if our author had not wished to be at all constrained by court practice, he might have ventured upon a purely circumstantial case. Instead he adapts the conventional arguments on testimony under torture into the framework of his argument: where the prosecutor insists upon the validity of the slave's testimony, the defendant devalues it by comparison to the testimony of free men subject to penalties for perjury.[36] But the author has skewed his scenario in

---

[36] Cf. *Tetr.* 1. 4. 7, 10. Witnesses in *dikai phonou* took the same oath as the parties themselves (cf. Ant. 5. 12). The earliest known perjury suit in *dikai phonou* is reported in Isoc. 18. 52 (Ch. 4 §1.2), possibly treated with greater emphasis as a novel procedure. Indeed, Ant. 5. 95 suggests there was as yet no remedy against perjury in such cases.

such a way as to subvert the ordinary function of the trial. Ordinarily the plaintiff's oath would require either firsthand knowledge or eyewitness testimony of overt actions—otherwise, he could not easily swear to 'know well' the guilt of the accused. In this case the sole basis for the plaintiff's oath is the reported testimony of the dying slave. Hearsay of living witnesses was not allowed, and the testimony of slaves was ordinarily admissible only if properly obtained under torture. Our author has taken pains to evade both restrictions. He has constructed a case that is technically admissible but upon the flimsiest possible foundation.

So far as we can judge, circumstantial evidence alone was not felt to be sufficient grounds to bring a case to trial, though once at trial the probabilities were often decisive. Where there were no qualified witnesses or other evidentiary proof upon which to base the charges, the only accepted course of action for the family of the victim would be to make their proclamation at the Prytaneum against the unknown killer.[37] That proclamation of the unknown killer was sometimes their only recourse, even in cases where the plaintiffs were reasonably certain of the killer's identity, is shown by the case described in the Demosthenic speech *Against Evergus* (47) 69–70. In this case the plaintiff's standing is somewhat uncertain, since the old woman who was killed was simply a former slave, and no longer technically within his *oikos;* that fact would not seem to prevent him from prosecuting in her death if he had adequate proof. But the exegetes told him plainly, 'since you yourself were not present, but only your wife and children, and there are no other witnesses, make proclamation against no one by name but against "the perpetrators and killers" '. Clearly there was no statutory restriction preventing him from prosecuting the man he knew to be the killer, but the religious officials warned him that he would only be inviting social disgrace and suspicion of perjury before the gods, if he prosecuted on the testimony of persons who could neither support him under oath nor give evidence under torture.

For trial before the ordinary homicide courts prosecutors would have to swear, either on their own conviction or on the basis of

---

[37] For judgement against the unknown killer at the Prytaneum, cf. *Ath. Pol.* 57. 4; Dem. 23. 76. The restriction against prosecuting without evidentiary proof should not be construed as a *statutory* rule, nor can we conclude that the basileus was forbidden by law to let such a case go forward: in Dem. 17.70 the exegetes' response suggests a customary rule but one none the less prohibitive; without reasonable evidentiary proof, the plaintiff's oath would only bring discredit upon him.

other first-hand witnesses, that so-and-so was 'the killer'. Before the Areopagus they must also swear that defendant acted with malice aforethought, and it was probably expected that the plaintiff should have some evidentiary basis for even this aspect of the charge.[38] *Tetralogy* 1, by contrast, goes as far as the procedure will allow to dispense with these requirements.

The issue in *Tetralogy* 1 has, indeed, its parallels among Antiphon's court speeches. In both Antiphon 1 and 5 the charges amount to premeditated murder, as in the *Tetralogy*. In one case, Antiphon 5, the principal issue appears to be whether the defendant or some other assailant did the killing, and the case is based largely on circumstantial evidence. But here the similarities end.

Antiphon 1, *Against the Stepmother*, is the only extant speech prosecuted on the same charge in the same jurisdiction as envisioned in *Tetralogy* 1—intentional homicide before the Areopagus. The question of fact, however, as to what the defendant actually did, is not the principal issue. It is evident from the argumentation that the *question of malice* was crucial to the defence.[39] The plaintiff is prosecuting in obedience to his father's dying charge, and he claims that his father had actually caught the woman 'in the act' on a previous occasion, though she claimed to have given the potion for love (§9). The slaves' evidence would supposedly have confirmed the previous incident (thus suggesting she knew the effects of the drug). A similar case is described in the Aristotelian *Magna Moralia* 1188b29–38—indeed, it is possibly the same case (perhaps as notorious as the scenario in *Tetr.* 2): here intent is clearly the issue and we learn that the woman was acquitted on grounds that she acted from love rather than malice. In any event, in Antiphon 1 the question of fact, whether the stepmother was implicated in the poisoning, does not appear to be at issue.

Other than *Tetralogy* 1 we have no reliable indication that questions of fact, as to what precisely the defendant did, were ever at issue in *dikai phonou* of Antiphon's era. Lysias' *Against Mikines*, as

---

[38] *Magna Moralia* 1188b shows that defendant could be acquitted on the issue of intent. The argumentation in Ant. 1 suggests that the plaintiff would offer formal proof on prior knowledge or design (in that case, challenge to torture): Ch. 6 §2.2. Similarly in Lysias 1 witnesses will affirm defendant's claim that he acted without prearrangement.

[39] See Ch. 6 §1. A plea of innocence of intent is anticipated in §§22–3: the defence will admit complicity in the killing but will plead that the killer acted 'without design'.

we have seen, was probably an artificial demonstration of circumstantial proof, and in any event almost certainly a work of the generation after Antiphon. Antiphon 5, *On the Murder of Herodes*, is a case of 'who-done-it' similar in some respects to that of the *Tetralogy* but prosecuted by the procedure for warrant and summary-arrest (*endeixis/apagōgē*). Here the prosecutors rely upon the testimony of a slave under torture, which was evidently handled improperly and discredited by the slave's dying recantation. The defendant argues that he should properly be tried by *dikē phonou*, before the Areopagus; but there is some distortion of procedural rules, evidently intended to deceive the 'layman' dicasts before whom warrant-and-arrest cases were tried.[40] The legalistic argument is certainly not to be treated as reliable testimony that such cases were regularly tried at the Areopagus. Indeed, even as he insists upon remanding his case to the high court, the defendant clearly means for the citizen-judges to conclude that the charge would there be found untenable. Rather than regard *Tetralogy* 1 as an earlier theoretical model for certain arguments in Antiphon 5, it is at least as reasonable to suppose that the celebrated case of Euxitheus in some way influenced the author of the *Tetralogy* in constructing a similar unsolvable case as a hypothetical *dikē phonou*.[41]

The very problem of how to convict a murderer who plots to evade detection is, to be sure, a recognizable topic in the extant court speeches, but there it serves a different function. By the very nature of the proceedings a murder without witnesses could not be proved with certainty but only by conjecture; that fact became axiomatic. We find this topic developed in Antiphon 6 (*Choreutes*) 18: 'in cases where murder is planned and executed without witnesses, judgement can only be rendered on the basis of such claims as the plaintiff and defendant put forward . . . rather upon conjecture than sure knowledge of the facts.' In such cases the judges must weigh the litigant's claim to direct knowledge and 'investigate every least detail of what is said'.[42] Notice, there is no suggestion that the judges would examine other evidence, direct or circum-

---

[40] Cf. Heitsch, *Antiphon*, 44–56; Gagarin, *Murder of Herodes*, 17–29; and see Ch. 9 §1.2.

[41] Political motives, for instance, colour the case of Ant. 5, where he pointedly reminds the court of the unsolved murder of Ephialtes; and the author of *Tetr.* 1 was similarly mindful of unsolved political murders: cf. 1. 1. 6; and 1. 4. 9, 'those . . . not so fortunate who profit from factional strife'.

[42] He is evidently referring to the familiar εὖ οἶδα of the *diomosiai;* see Ch. 6 §2.

stantial; in a murder without witnesses they must make their determination solely upon what the principals have said. Now the defendant has introduced the problem of murder without witnesses as a
worst-case scenario, by contrast to his own case where there are
many witnesses and no dispute on the facts: therefore the judges
must not rely upon the artful conjectures of the prosecutors.[43] The
chief function of the topic is to emphasize by contrast the certainty
of the defendant's proof from sworn witnesses. When we turn from
this usage to the proem of the first *Tetralogy*, it looks as though the
author has chosen his scenario precisely to demonstrate how the
paradigmatic worst case might in fact be won. He has reversed
the situation: assume there are no reliable witnesses, the bare minimum of formal proof for admitting the charges. He follows that
assumption to its ultimate implication—to try the case solely upon
hearsay, probable motive, and prejudicial appeals. In this way the
topic in the court speeches may have served as a model for
Tetralogy 1.[44] The reversal of this argument in the *Tetralogy*, on
the other hand, would not have been much use in the homicide
courts—that is the point of the topic, that such cases were almost
unwinnable. It has left no mark upon the extant court speeches.

In the *Tetralogy* we are told, crimes done on the spur of the
moment are not difficult to prove; but where the perpetrators are
well suited to the deed by nature and experience, foreseeing the
danger and taking every precaution to avoid suspicion, they are difficult even to discover, let alone convict. Upon this principle the
author urges the judges to rely upon the probabilities; he proceeds
to incriminate the defendant by showing that no chance assailant,
presumably killing for theft or other common motive, was likely to
have done the murder. The device is not unlike what we find in
Gorgias' *Palamedes* or, for that matter, the extant fragment of
Antiphon's defence: consider all possible motives and opportuni-
ties, and exclude the alternatives one by one. This similarity is, of
course, no proof of authenticity; the *Tetralogy* may imitate the
other models.[45]

---

[43] This passage should not be construed to suggest that cases of 'who-done-it'
commonly came to trial in *dikai phonou*. Ordinarily the plaintiffs themselves would
claim direct knowledge of the events, or otherwise pursue alternate procedures.

[44] Von der Mühll, 'Unechtheit', 4–5, offers a similar hypothesis.

[45] *Tetr.* 1 is closer to the *Ulysses* attributed to Alcidamas than to Gorgias'
Palamedes; see below §4. We may assume that the extant fragment of Antiphon's
Defence derives from a post-eventum publication rather than a 'prepared text', and

In a case where the evidence is not so clearly stacked in his favour, we might expect Antiphon to reverse the argument, much as the author of the *Tetralogies* has done; but consider the parallel in Antiphon 5 (*Herodes*). In this case we have, indeed, other plausible suspects—fellow travellers on the fateful voyage; we might expect the prosecution to exclude them from suspicion and the defendant in turn to raise a reasonable doubt whether some other assailant did the killing (as the defendant does in *Tetr.* 1). But instead, he simply cites examples to support the conventional topic, murder without witnesses, impossible to prove beyond conjecture (64–9). He reminds his judges of the murder of Ephialtes, for which no one was ever charged (though some were suspected for motive).[46] There was also the unlikely case of a slave-boy 12 years old who attempted to murder his master and would have gone undetected had he not lost his nerve. Rather than answer circumstantial evidence with probable suspects (as in *Tetr.* 1), Antiphon focuses upon the paradox of charging murder without reliable witnesses; his probabilities are addressed to the value of the proof, not to the objective questions of what the defendant actually did or intended.[47]

Compare also the version of this argument in Antiphon 1. 28, against the oath sworn by the defence: 'How can anyone know what he was not present to witness? Those who plot murder . . . do not make their plans and preparations in the presence of witnesses, but with as much secrecy as they can manage, so that no one may know.' The victim was taken unawares but survived long enough to call upon his son, the plaintiff, for retribution; otherwise no one would have suspected. In this passage once again the problem of murder without witnesses is introduced not in regard to the facts of the crime but to the means of proof, the assertory oath that constitutes the basis of the case: it provides an argument against the defence oath and in favour of the plaintiff's. In all three court

it may, of course, bear little resemblance to what was actually said. Von der Mühll, 'Unechtheit', 3, speculated that certain passages in the *Tetralogies* directly imitate Antiphon's *Defence*. For comparison of the *Defence* and Ant. 5, see Solmsen, *Antiphonstudien*, 59–62. This technique is also adapted in Lys. 1. 43–6: Ch. 8 §1.2.2

[46] Plutarch reports (*Per.* 10. 7) a tradition that some suspicion attached even to Pericles; other suspects were undoubtedly more obvious.

[47] Thus in Ant. 5. 43 the defendant attempts to discredit the slave's testimony under torture, by protesting 'Would I have enlisted an accomplice to be a witness to the crime?'

speeches, in fact, the topic is directed against artful conjecture, in favour of the speaker's oath and other formal instruments of proof. But in *Tetralogy* 1 the topic serves as justification for basing the case on circumstantial evidence, disregarding the customary validity of oaths and other instruments.

In general, the *Tetralogies* differ widely from the court speeches in their handling of evidentiary proof. The only treatment of witnesses is found in *Tetralogy* 3, where they are mentioned sporadically and the author seems to assume that witnesses can be found to substantiate any assertion. This method is perhaps unremarkable if we assume that the *Tetralogies* are a purely theoretical essay, but it may also reflect a more cynical view of the traditional rules of evidence. The treatment of testimony under torture is particularly suggestive.

In all three of Antiphon's court speeches the speakers claim to have challenged their opponents to decide certain crucial questions by torture; the opponents, of course, refused.[48] In Antiphon 5 (*Herodes*), the slaves would presumably have established the defendant's alibi; in Antiphon 6 (*Choreutes*), they would have established that defendant had no involvement in the events leading to the victim's death. Again, in Antiphon 1 the plaintiff challenged the defender to submit slaves for torture: the slaves would presumably have established that the stepmother once attempted to drug the victim. These challenges were lodged in preliminaries and, had they been accepted, the procedure would have been administered before the trial, with the wording of the interrogation submitted in writing beforehand and the responses witnessed by both sides.

The author of *Tetralogy* 1 is obviously familiar with the rhetorical uses of such evidence, but he is not constrained by the procedural rules. There is a good deal of argument devoted to the dying servant's testimony, treating it either as crucial or questionable without torture. But in the closing speech for the defence we meet with a direct challenge by the defendant to submit the question of his alibi to his own slaves under torture. At this point in the proceedings there was no longer any practical opportunity for this procedure; the author of the court speeches never even suggests such a ploy. The author of *Tetralogies* evidently ventured upon a surprise

[48] On challenge to torture Thür, *Basanos*, esp. 11, 132–3, on Ant. 1.

tactic, which would have been doubtful of success in court, in order to achieve a sensational effect with another audience.[49] In sum, the author of the *Tetralogies* seems reasonably attentive to the framework of Athenian law. He knows, for instance that the attending physician cannot be charged in the death of his patient; he is also aware that the famous case in *Tetralogy* 2 was not technically within the jurisdiction of the Delphinium court; he is evidently familiar with the language of Draco's law regarding the 'planner' (*bouleusas*) and 'the first to lay violent hands'. All of the details lend verisimilitude.[50] But his handling of 'issues in dispute', evidentiary proof, and probabilities contradicts the very principle of homicide proceedings. His subject matter suggests an interest in peculiarly juristic problems and his method seems to reflect a certain scepticism regarding conventional legal reasoning—How can the case be limited to a foregone decision on the 'issue in dispute'? How can a man be condemned on so flimsy a pretext as hearsay of a dead slave's accusation?[51] This kind of critique belongs to an era when the failings of the traditional procedure were all too apparent.[52]

§2. Miasma Doctrine in Legal Argument

The defilement that a killer brings upon the community is perhaps the most pervasive theme in the *Tetralogies*, but the method of

---

[49] Cf. Lämmli, *Attische Prozeßverfahren*, 106; Thiel, *Erste Tetralogie*, 14–15, taking this divergence from court practice as an indication against authenticity; Thür, *Basanos*, 223–4, suggesting that Aeschines 2. 126–7 imitates the device in *Tetr.* 1. The author of *Tetr.* 1 himself may have been influenced by the exceptional instance in Ant. 6. 23–4, where the challenge declined proves decisive when extraneous charges were injected into a major political trial before the *heliaia*.

[50] A suggestive detail is the date of the crime, during the Dipolieia, which gives defendant his alibi (*Tetr.* 1. 4. 8). The detail was probably chosen for literary interest (cf. *Clouds* 983) and as a legal curiosity: the ritual involved the slaying of a bull and search for the unknown killer, evidently parallel to the proclamation of unknown killers at the Prytaneum; cf. H. W. Parke, *Festivals of the Athenians* (Ithaca, NY, 1977), 162.

[51] Decleva Caizzi, *Antiphontis Tetralogiae*, 50, 69, suggests a conservative polemic against sophistic probabilities; cf. Gagarin, 'Prohibition of Just Homicide', 303, regarding this argument as 'a moral comment on the Athenian legal system'. Those who believe that Antiphon the politician and the author *On Truth* are the same will perhaps see a connection between the critique suggested in *Tetr.* 1 and the treatment of oath-taking in the Sophist's treatise; cf. Gagarin, 'Identity of Antiphon', 27–44.

[52] The only reference to perjury proceedings in *dikai phonou* is *Tetr.* 1. 4. 7, 10; see Ch. 4 §1.2.

treating this topic is virtually unparalleled in the speeches for trial. In the *Tetralogies* the speakers repeatedly call upon the judges to realize the threat to themselves and to the *polis*, and to cleanse the city of this evil.[53] In the court speeches the threat of defilement and avenging spirits is indeed invoked, but properly against the principals themselves: they are the ones who will risk pollution and the spirit's wrath if they fail to honour the victim or to abide by their oath. There is no overt consideration of the threat to the judges or the community. The speaker conjures up the threat of defilement only to prove his own conviction or challenge his opponent's resolve. Thus the defendant in Antiphon 5 (11, 82) argues that trying his luck at sacrifice and safe passage at sea, where a tainted killer would be likely to meet with misfortune, is proof of a clear conscience. In Antiphon 6. 40 the speaker recalls that the prosecutor met with him publicly soon after the death, as proof that his accuser did not then believe him guilty. Again, in both 5 and 6, we find the commonplace that even a man who kills his own slave, with no one to avenge the death, will purify himself as religion requires, without any legal sanction to compel him (6. 4 = 5. 87; Ch. 9 §1.1.4). The prosecutors will claim that they only bring the menace upon themselves if they condemn the wrong man and let the killer go free. The defendant will plead that a killer cannot evade the consequences of his guilt by deceiving the judges, and therefore his oath of innocence has the greater claim to credibility.

Such is the characteristic use of miasma-doctrine as a source of arguments in the court speeches: the fear of defilement and avenging spirits is an assumed premiss in proof of the speaker's conviction and his opponent's deceit. The *Tetralogies*, however, repeatedly invoke the fear of defilement to different effect: it is a matter for the judges to weigh directly as a threat to themselves and to the community they represent. Thus in the first *Tetralogy*, the prosecutors begin with a version of the standard argument—'the defilement falls entirely upon us' if the wrong man is convicted and the real killer goes free (1. 3)—but they quickly proceed to the more ominous implications. In the conclusion to the opening speech we find the threat to the greater community now elaborated as the

---

[53] Cf. Sealey, '*Tetralogies*', 74, against Adkins, *Merit and Responsibility*, 100–6. For the religious sanctions as a parallel mechanism, see Parker, *Miasma*, esp. 104–43; and, against the usual view that the Prytaneum and Phreatto courts were instituted specifically to safeguard the community against pollution, see Ch. 3 §2.1.

peculiar responsibility of the judges: 'It is inexpedient for you to allow this man, tainted and unholy as he is, to enter the shrines of the gods and defile their sanctity . . . for it is from just such desecrations as this that public disasters befall . . . It is rather your personal obligation to effect vengeance, regarding his acts of impiety as your own disaster, and thus absolve the community of defilement' (1. 10–11). In response (2. 11) the defendant claims, it will not be he who pollutes the shrines of the gods but the prosecutors, if they falsely convict him; they will be the cause of calamity for persuading the jury to offend the gods.

It is perhaps reasonable to assume that such beliefs were implicit in Antiphon's court speeches; but none of them expresses this ominous injunction to the jury. The closest parallel comes in the epilogue to Lysias' speech *Against Eratosthenes* (12) 99–100, but even this instance points up the difference between miasma arguments in Antiphon's court speeches and the more provocative version in the *Tetralogies*. Lysias does indeed refer to the defilement of temples and public places by the Thirty and it is therefore all the more striking that he emphasizes his own resolve rather than the responsibility of the judges. In keeping with the standard miasma argument, he defends his earnest conviction against the obvious charge of vindictiveness. He is acting, he contends, in defence of the dead: 'I believe they are listening and will know how you vote, and they regard those who acquit these men as casting a verdict of death upon them, but those who exact punishment take vengeance in their behalf.' Threatening as it seems, there is a significant difference between this epilogue and the miasma argument characteristic of the *Tetralogies*: Lysias does not warn that the judges must condemn the killer to avert disaster to the *polis*, as the *Tetralogies* repeatedly urge. He may suggest to some among them that they themselves will be haunted by the spirits of the dead, but he largely adheres to conventional reasoning on the problem of bloodguilt—the judges are not implicated.

It is perhaps only in a pamphlet such as this, that Lysias could even insinuate a threat of haunting against the judges and defilement hovering over the whole city—to rid Athens of this menace 'is not the work of one man or two, but of many' (Ch. 10 §1). His argument appeals to the people's justice of the restored democracy. The case could not be prosecuted by homicide proceedings where charges of instigation or complicity were excluded by the amnesty.[54] Eratosthenes' complicity in the killing of Polemarchus could only be addressed in the special accountings to which members of the oligarchic regime must submit. By the nature of this forum, homicide could be treated more as a criminal matter, affecting the community, rather than simply a matter of private wrongs and personal liability as *dikai phonou* were traditionally prosecuted. Even in that setting Lysias evidently did not yet feel he could assert outright that 'these men bring damnation upon the *polis* and it is the judges' duty to save her'. Instead he is largely faithful to the conventions of legal argument on these religious matters. It may have been the suggestion, however, of a threat to the jury in this famous diatribe and others of its era that prompted the author of *Tetralogies* to elaborate upon the theme as he does.

Consider the peculiar turn of the argument in the second prosecution speech of the first *Tetralogy* (3. 10–11): 'If the defendant is wrongly acquitted, the avenging spirit of the dead (*prostropaios*) will not trouble us but will haunt you. Realizing this threat, avenge the dead . . . cleanse the city. For thus . . . *you absolve yourselves of defilement* on his account.'

The first speech of the second *Tetralogy*—the singular case of misadventure with the spearcast—also carries on this elaboration of the miasma argument beyond the practice of the court speeches. The plaintiff first observes that the vengeful spirit of the victim is only a threat to the wilful murderer, but the killing none the less threatens the community: the unintentional killer 'has roused no rage of vengeance in the dead but in the living'; the judges have to worry about vindictive plaintiffs rather than the victim's spirit![55] Following this appeal, the author warns the judges to avert the threat of defilement to the city, as their own special responsibility. 'Do not permit the whole community to be defiled by his guilt,' he urges. And in the epilogue of his second speech he threatens, 'The mark of defilement . . . weighs upon you: if you convict and bar him from prohibited areas, you (yourselves) will be free of any claims; but if you acquit him you become responsible. . . Do not share in his defilement.'[56]

---

[54] *Ath. Pol.* 39. 5; Andoc. 1. 91–4. On implications of amnesty, see Chs. 3 §3 and 9 §2.2.

[55] The sentence, 'he has roused no rage . . . in the dead but in the living' (2) was bracketed by Gernet; but, for the older belief that the avenging spirit haunts the 'intentional' killer, cf. Parker, *Miasma*, 105–30.

[56] *Tetr.* 2. 3. 11–12. The 'mark of defilement', *kēlis*, is a poetic word common in tragedy, found only here in Antiphon. Cf. Parker, *Miasma*, 107.

The *mythos* behind these remonstrations is fully articulated in *Tetralogy* 3. 1. 1–4: a man's life is a gift of the god, and the spirit of the dead is roused to vengeance by the theft of what god has given; thus he bequeaths the wrath of avenging spirits as god's retribution, and his curse pursues those who wrongly bear witness for his killers *and those who wrongly judge against him*. The speaker invokes this spectre as a guarantee of his conviction but also as a threat to the judges.[57] The defendant takes up the argument (2. 8), threatening the judges with avenging furies if they should convict him. And in the epilogue of the final speech, those who speak for the defendant urge the judges to fear defilement and avenging furies. (4. 10–11).

By contrast, the standard injunction to the judges emphasizes piety toward the gods and the laws, not the consequences of defilement.[58] Again in the parallel passage Ant. 1. 3–4, there is no reference whatever to miasma or avenging spirits as a concern of the judges; and in this speech, if anywhere, such an appeal for the community would seem fitting since the plaintiff calls upon the judges to act as his kinsmen, inasmuch as his agnate relatives are against him.

The more ominous turn of the argument, particularly the generalized threat of miasma in cases of unintentional homicide (*Tetr.* 2) and the myth of haunting as the spirit's retribution for the theft of what god has given (*Tetr.* 3), has a suggestive parallel, however, in Plato's adaptation of the popular mythology in *Laws* 9. 865d–e:

They say that the victim of a violent killing . . . soon after death, overwhelmed with fear and dread at the violence done him, rages against his killer; and seeing his killer frequent his familiar haunts, the spirit is frightened and disturbed and himself endeavours to wreak havoc with every power he has, with guilty conscience as his ally, upon the perpetrator, both the man himself and all his affairs.

This 'ancient *mythos*' is introduced to justify the rules requiring exile and purification even in cases of unintentional killing. It must

---

[57] *Tetr.* 3. 1. 4–5: ὑμεῖς δὲ . . . ἅπασαν τὴν πόλιν καθαρὰν τοῦ μιάσματος καταστήσετε. So again in the second prosecution speech (3. 3. 7), ἀντὶ τοῦ ἀποθανόντος ἐπισκήπτομεν ὑμῖν, τῷ τούτου φόνῳ τὸ μήνιμα τῶν ἀλιτηρίων ἀκεσαμένους πᾶσαν τὴν πόλιν καθαρὰν τοῦ μιάσματος καταστῆσαι.

[58] The closest parallel is Ant. 6. 3–6: 'Trials for homicide are of great importance for you, the judges, rightly to decide, most of all for the sake of piety to the gods, and also for your own sake' a wrongful verdict is 'a wrong and a sin against god and law'; cf. Ant. 1. 31.

be given due reverence, Plato suggests, not because it conveys a literal truth but because it embodies and enforces a useful rule. We find, I think, a similar perspective on traditional belief in the *Tetralogies*. The author's archaizing piety is a purely formal posture—his evocative language is learned in large part from the drama. His threats of haunting and defilement are no more proof that the *Tetralogies* belong to the era of Sophocles' *Antigone* than Plato's ancient *mythos* proves a similar date for the *Laws*. The treatment of miasma is not in itself decisive evidence against authenticity. It is reasonably clear, however, that the emphasis upon defilement as a threat to the *polis* is uncharacteristic of the court speeches. And on balance, this shift in argumentation should weigh against the views of Zuntz, Decleva Caizzi, and others, who see this feature of the *Tetralogies* as inspired by an authentic, presophistic religiosity. Considering this feature in isolation we might simply conclude that it is yet another indication that the *Tetralogies* are purely theoretical in their aims and largely irrelevant to court practice. But the very notion that the trial is fundamentally concerned with this threat to the *polis*, and that the judges' verdict should be directed against this urgent danger, implies an immediate understanding of homicide as a public wrong, not merely a private offence to be settled by a decision regarding liability, as in the traditional procedure. If, as the evidence indicates, Draco's law was addressed to settlement between the families—imperatives of religion required no secondary rules—then in this feature we have a simple linear development from Draco's trial procedure to the extant court speeches: *dikai phonou* remained quintessentially a means of resolving private disputes about liability. In the *Tetralogies*, however, we find an emphatic declaration that homicide must be judged as a public wrong.

The turn of the century—the fall and restoration of democracy—seems to have brought about a similar awareness (see Chs. 9 §3 and 10 §1). This new rationale represents a departure from the formalism of the traditional procedure in the direction of 'judgement by ideology', based upon shared values and community interests.[59] This evolution was perhaps inspired in part by the complicated legal issues created by the crimes of the Thirty and the amnesty that followed their overthrow. Whatever its inspiration this new

[59] In Weber's typology, 'substantive rationalism'; see further in the conclusions below §4.

legal reasoning is fully represented in the *Tetralogies*, particularly in treatment of 'justifiable killing' to which we now turn.

§3. The Law Prohibiting Justifiable Killing

We have finally to consider the one discrepancy which was never resolved to Dittenberger's satisfaction—the law prohibiting just as well as unjust killing. In *Tetralogies* 2 and 3 the author invokes this prohibition as the basis for a puzzling sequence of argument. It is treated as a rule of statute law, yet it seems inconsistent with what we know of Athenian laws: in phrasing it lacks the characteristic condition (e.g. 'if a man kill . . . let him be exiled'); and in substance it seems to be flatly contradicted by considerable evidence that justifiable homicide was indeed sanctioned in a number of special circumstances.[60] There is also an unlikely ambiguity in the meaning of 'just' or 'justifiable' killing itself: it seems to be synonymous with accidental or unintentional homicide in *Tetralogy* 2, but equivalent to killing in self-defence in *Tetralogy* 3.

To account for these inconsistencies it is often supposed that 'the law prohibiting just as well as unjust killing' is invoked as a principle of popular morality, in essence a rule of unwritten law rather than statute.[61] 'Just and unjust' is a polar expression, and thus the prohibition amounts to a moral absolute—all killing, right or wrong, is forbidden.[62] But this explanation does not account for the fact that the prohibition in question is treated as at least the substance of statute law: in both speeches it is part of the law upon which the plaintiffs base their case (2. 2. 9; 3. 2. 5). It has been suggested that the author intends to show how unwritten law might overturn statute in the courts.[63] But there are no clear parallels for the legal validity of unwritten moral rules. We shall be better able to comprehend the author's purpose if we first determine what is

---

[60] In regard to this problematic formulation, Dover concludes, 'Chronology', 58, 'I am willing to believe the author capable of almost any rhetorical exaggeration.'

[61] Cf. Gagarin, 'Prohibition of Just Homicide', esp. 300–3; he concedes that there is no clear parallel in the most likely sources contemporary with Antiphon.

[62] The Pythagorean commandment, for which Aristotle cites Empedocles, μὴ κτείνειν τὸ ἔμψυχον (*Rhet.* 1372ᵇ6 = Diels and Kranz 31 fr. 135), is a prohibition against killing any animate creature. For the polar expression, 'right or wrong,' cf. Ar. *Ach.* 373; Andoc. 1. 1–2, 135–6.

[63] Decleva Caizzi, *Antiphontis Tetralogiae*, 32–44.

meant by justifiable killing, *phonos dikaios*. The more straight-forward instance is found in *Tetralogy* 3.

3.1 The Issue in *Tetralogy* 3

In the third *Tetralogy* the meaning of *phonos dikaios* seems at first equivalent to killing in self-defence. The defendant claims that the victim struck the first blow, and he was justified in using equal force; indeed, he would have been justified in responding with greater force against the aggressor. He is evidently alluding to a provision of Draco's law. Enough of the wording remains for us to see that there was a specific rule regarding justifiable response against the initiator of a violent altercation (ὁ ἄρξας χειρῶν ἀδίκων).[64] But the defendant cannot simply rely upon the law: he must prove he is not 'the killer', the agent causally responsible. Now the defendant introduces 'the law forbidding just as well as unjust killing' (2. 3) as a form of dilemma: he is surely not guilty of unjust killing, since he responded justifiably to provocation; were he the killer, the killing would be justifiable; but he is not, he insists, the causal agent—that responsibility lies elsewhere. In short: if he were guilty, it must be for either just or unjust killing; his action was justifiable, not unjust; his justifiable response was not in fact the cause of death; therefore he is guilty of neither just nor unjust killing. The law prohibiting justifiable killing is an argumentative device, and we should be wary of reading a moral absolute into it.

From the argument it is reasonably clear that justifiable homi-cide involves an act that the author himself regards as *retributive* violence: 'Had the man died in immediate consequence of the beat-ing, he would have died *justifiably*', for those who start a fight *deserve to suffer* more harm than they do (2. 3). There is no pretence that the defendant was endangered by the victim or acted truly in self-defence; rather he claims to have acted justifiably in meeting injury with retribution.[65]

---

[64] With *Tetr.* 3. 2. 1, cf. *IG* I³ 104. 33–6, and see Stroud, *DL* 56.

[65] *Tetr.* 3. 2. 3: Εἰ μὲν γὰρ ὑπὸ τῶν πληγῶν ὁ ἀνὴρ παραχρῆμα ἀπέθανεν, ὑπ' ἐμοῦ μὲν δικαίως δ' ἂν ἐτεθνήκει—οὐ γὰρ ταὐτὰ ἀλλὰ μείζονα καὶ πλείονα οἱ ἄρξαντες δίκαιοι ἀντιπάσχειν εἰσί. Cf. *Tetr.* 1. 2. 10: 'If I am the probable killer, I am justified (δίκαιός εἰμι); for clearly I would have acted in defence against injury (ἀδικούμενος ἠμυνάμην).'

In the second defence speech (4. 8), those who speak for the defendant return to this argument, but they now link the rule against justifiable killing with the concept of 'culpable error' and 'mischance' (*hamartēma, atychēma*). The law forbidding just as well as unjust killing has been answered, they say, inasmuch as the victim died from ill-effects of medical treatment and not from the blows themselves. Such mischance is the aggressor's doing. The defendant acted entirely unwillingly and suffered misfortune brought on by another's error, while the victim acted entirely voluntarily and brought on his own misfortune.

Now the argument in *Tetralogy* 3 is consistent with that in *Tetralogy* 2 to this extent, that both arguments for the defence ultimately attempt to reduce the issue to one of culpable error for which the victim himself is to blame. The homicide is 'justifiable' in the sense that it was brought on by the victim's mistake. The so-called self-defence thus involves some of the same factors as the unintentional killing: it is the victim himself who set the sequence of events in motion; the justifiable killing is his doing, not the defendant's. Justifiable homicide is not, however, equivalent to unintentional killing.

The original meaning of justifiable homicide as retributive killing is clear in a number of fifth- and fourth-century references. In the fifth century vindictive killing would appear to be the usual, proper meaning of *phonos dikaios;* a certain moral repugnance is sometimes evident, but there is nothing parallel to the notion that it was prohibited by law, written or unwritten.[66] Indeed, the issue before the judges in *Eumenides* is not whether retributive killing is justifiable in the abstract but whether the particular killing in question qualifies for that redemption (611–13).

The clearest parallel to the defendant's position in *Tetralogy* 3 is to be found in Lysias 1. 37. The speaker argues that he would have been justified in luring the adulterer to his doom, in retaliation for earlier injustice: 'I would have thought myself justified (*dikaios*) in apprehending by whatever means the man who had corrupted my wife.' Such 'justifiable' (i.e. retributive) killing must be disavowed,

---

[66] Cf. Aesch. *Ag.* 1604; *Cho.* 988; Soph. *El.* 33–7; Eur. *Hec.* 263; *El.* 1094–6, 1189. Repugnance against this form of 'just killing' is expressed in Eur. *El.* 1050–1, where Clytemnestra challenges, 'Say that . . . your father did not die justly' (ἐνδίκως); and the Chorus answers, δίκαι᾽ ἔλεξας· ἡ δίκη δ᾽ αἰσχρῶς ἔχει. Cf. the fragment of Theodectes' *Orestes* in Arist. *Rhet.* 2. 24. 3, and see below, n. 76.

however, and defendant must base his defence upon an argument from causation, that he did not entrap the victim and was not the initiator of the causal sequence. The argumentation in Lysias 1 will require more detailed treatment (Ch. 8 §1); but here it is sufficient to recognize that the real issue is the question of entrapment and therefore the defendant cannot simply rely upon the statutory provision against adulterers caught in the act. He must show that he did not plot to bring about the fatal outcome, that it was caused by other factors, including the victim's actions. There is, in any event, a singular parallel to *Tetralogy* 3 in the turn of argument, whereby the defendant insists that retributive killing would have been justified but he did not kill even justifiably (Ch. 8 §2).

Now it is reasonable to suppose that problems inherent in the special jurisdiction at the Delphinium court, where such cases as Lysias 1 would be tried, prompted legalistic controversy on the issue of justifiable homicide, perhaps as early as the era of Antiphon but surely by the early fourth century. The Delphinium jurisdiction included retributive killings, as in cases of sexual violation or violent theft or abduction, along with some cases that we would regard as unintentional, such as death in athletic competition or by mistaken identity in warfare. We should not assume from this ambiguity, however, that *phonos dikaios* was in any sense equivalent to unintentional killing. Aristotle, for instance, reflects popular thinking in the *Politics* where he refers to the Delphinium as a court of *phonos dikaios*, but we must not conclude from such references that a defence before this court was open to anyone who might plead that the killing was blameless on grounds of moral justice. It is clear from the Aristotelian *Constitution* that this jurisdiction involved those cases where the defendant admits to the killing but claims legal justification by a specific statutory provision.[67]

Even as late as Demosthenes *Against Aristocrates*, a century after *Eumenides*, it is clear that *phonos dikaios* retained a strong sense of retributive killing. In the section covering the Draconian laws the orator deals with several statutes affecting the Delphinium jurisdiction. Nowhere does he suggest that justifiable homicide was a well-defined legal category. But it is clear that Demosthenes and his audience readily interpreted even unintentional killing in athletic contest as 'justifiable'. In such instances the justification lies in

---

[67] *Ath. Pol.* 57. 3 (κατὰ τοὺς νόμους); cf. Ch. 3 §2.3.

the victim's 'culpable error'. Thus he argues that one who kills in athletic competition is free of guilt, since the victim proved unequal to the contest: 'if he was too weak to bear the struggle for victory, [the lawgiver] considered the victim himself responsible for his own suffering' (53–5). Now there is nothing in the wording of the law to suggest that this was the lawgiver's intent. Demosthenes' legalistic explanation is his own inference. But Demosthenes' understanding of this principle is entirely consistent with the topic in the *Tetralogies*. Justifiable killing includes those fatalities that come as a consequence of the victim's own error.

Demosthenes devotes considerable attention to retributive killing as both 'lawful' and 'justifiable'. Thus, he reports the Draconian law allowing self-help against theft or abduction (60), where the defender may kill with impunity. Aristocrates' illegal measure, by contrast, condemns anyone who might kill Charidemus 'even if justifiably, even if according to law'. Again, in regard to the Delphinium court itself (74–5), though there was apparently no preamble or other text defining 'justifiable homicide' *per se*, the essence of the jurisdiction seems to be retributive killing. From the example of Orestes' trial (on the Areopagus), Demosthenes assumes, the ancient lawgivers once deduced that there are indeed some 'justifiable' killings, 'for the gods would not have given unjust verdicts'. Aristocrates' bill has not exempted such cases but outlaws anyone who kills Charidemus 'even if justifiably, even if according to law'.[68]

In the same period we find further evidence of an ongoing debate on legal justification and a suggestive parallel to the case in *Tetralogy* 3: the case of Euaion reported in the speech *Against Meidias* 21. 72–5 (Ch. 8 §2.2). Euaion struck back in anger against a drunken assailant, who was evidently the weaker of the two (just as in *Tetr.* 3). He was convicted by one vote. The issue, Demosthenes supposes, was not whether the defendant was justified in striking back, but whether his action was proximate cause of death. Those who voted for acquittal evidently judged that even *lethal* force was allowed by law in the case of one who suffered violent insult: the action of his assailant was regarded as the direct cause of his justifiable response, even though death would seem 'excessive retribution', disproportionate to the wrong. Similarly in

---

[68] The same phrase is used as earlier, 60–1: κἂν δικαίως, κἂν ὡς οἱ νόμοι διδόασιν.

Tetralogy 3 the defendant asserts that it is justifiable to respond with equal and greater force against the aggressor.[69] Demosthenes treats the case against Euaion as a famous precedent. It is not unlikely that this case or one like it served as a model for the third *Tetralogy*—just as the case that Pericles and Protagoras debated served as a model for the second. The parallels suggest that 'the law prohibiting just as well as unjust killing' represents the principle that simple retributive killing is wrongful and illegal; only those instances that statutes prescribe are protected by the Delphinium jurisdiction. The legalistic controversy on this issue and the connected problem of culpable error may go back to the era of Antiphon, but there our sources fail us. For a better understanding of the argument in *Tetralogy* 2, we must turn again to the fourth century.

3.2 Justifiable Response against 'Error'

The issue of 'culpable error' is a conventional topic in the fourth century. Aristotle in *Nicomachean Ethics* and in the *Rhetoric* makes a revealing distinction among the key ethical terms: 'wrong' or 'injury' (*adikēma*), 'error' (*hamartēma*) and 'mishap' or mischance (*atychēma*). The report in *Nic. Eth.* 5. 8 is especially helpful as we try to make sense of the reasoning of *Tetralogy* 2:

Of three types of harm (or damage, βλαβή) . . . those done in ignorance are 'errors' (ἁμαρτήματα), as when one fails to affect the (right) person, or effect the (right) outcome, by the means or for the reason intended; for [the agent] either thought he would not hit (the mark), or not with the weapon (that struck), or not the person (that was struck) . . . Now when the error is contrary to reasonable expectation it is a mischance; but when it is not (unforeseeable) yet without malice, it is an 'error', for the agent 'errs' [or 'is at fault'] when the origin of causation is in him, but he suffers mischance when the cause is external. And when he knows the likely consequences but acts without premeditation it is an 'injury', as when one acts in anger or overcome by other emotions. For in these instances in doing harm and committing error [or being at fault] men act unjustly and their acts are injuries.

The phrase 'being at fault' is perhaps the best English approximation to the sense of liability contained here in *hamartēma*. 'Error' is

---

[69] *Tetr.* 3. 2. 2: οὐ ταὐτά ἀλλὰ μείζονα καὶ πλείονα δίκαιοι οἱ ἄρχοντες ἀντιπάσχειν.

causal: it is thus linked to 'injury'. We find a similar distinction in the *Rhetoric* and yet a third version of the commonplace in Anaximenes' *Ars rhetorica*.[70] There is also a similar conception of error and retribution in Plato's *Laws* (as we shall see). In all of these treatments, 'error' is an unintended wrong, yet it is akin to 'injury' and ordinarily involves liability.[71] Bear in mind, these are not the philosophers' own constructs but their rendering of an ethical commonplace.

Such would seem to be the line of reasoning in *Tetralogy* 2. 2. 7–9, where it is usually assumed that justifiable killing is equivalent to unintentional homicide. The defence first establishes that the boy who threw the fatal lance did not himself err but acted precisely as intended: the spear was thrown in the right direction, at the proper moment, and would have struck the target. By Aristotle's model, he neither erred in regard to the act itself, the instrument, or the aim, nor in regard to the person affected. Rather the error lies in the action of the victim, who moved into the weapon's path at the fatal moment. It is he then who erred, causing an unintended outcome from which he himself suffered fitting retribution (2. 2. 8):

and for the error he has been avenged upon himself and has exacted punishment. . . . As the error redounds to him, and the act belongs not to us but to the one guilty of error, as his suffering comes back upon the agent himself, we are acquitted of blame. He has been *justly avenged* upon the agent of his wrong in the moment of his error.

It is at this point (2. 9) that the defendant invokes 'the law prohibiting just as well as unjust killing', as the basis for his acquittal: 'for this boy is acquitted of unintentional killing by the error of the

[70] Arist. *Rhet.* 1374[b]: ' "errors" and "injuries:" are not to be judged on the same scale, nor are "mischances" (commensurate with) "errors". For "mischances" are those events contrary to reasonable expectation and not of malicious intent; while "errors" are those outcomes not unforeseeable, yet without malice.' Anax. *Ars Rhet.* 4. 7–9: 'you regard a wrong done with intent as "injustice" and say that such wrongs deserve the most serious retribution; but to do harm through ignorance must be called "error"; and to fail . . . because of (actions of) others or by chance you regard as "mischance".'

[71] On *hamartēma* as both 'error' and 'fault'—*errore e colpa*—cf. Decleva Caizzi, *Antiphontis Tetralogiae*, 52–8. Ἀτυχία/ἀτυχῆσαι is also extremely rare in 5th-c. sources—nowhere found in the court speeches of Antiphon—but occurs fourteen times in *Tetr.* Decleva Caizzi sees this as yet another instance of Antiphon's formative usage, 'con valore pregnante', *Antiphontis Tetralogiae*, 63–9.

victim himself; and since he is not even charged with intentional killing he is acquitted on both counts.'[72] The same kind of dilemma is utilized here as in *Tetralogy* 3: wrongful death is either just or unjust; the defendant is not even charged with an unjust act of aggression; the justifiable killing is the victim's own doing; the defendant is therefore not guilty of the killing on either count. There is no equating justifiable with unintentional killing; one stands for the other only as a term in the dilemma. What renders the killing justifiable is that the victim's unintended but no less culpable error has been justly punished by his own hand. That this is the thrust of the argument is proved by the reply in the second prosecution speech (3. 7–9): 'I, too, assert that the law rightly demands killers be punished: for it is just that the unintentional killer meet with unintended harm, and the one who has perished . . . would be wronged if he were not avenged.' The plaintiff accepts the notion that retribution for error is justifiable, but he insists, it is the defendant and not the victim who committed the error.

In both *Tetralogies* 'the law prohibiting just as well as unjust killing' serves as the basis for a sophistic dilemma, and in both demonstrations *phonos dikaios* means essentially retributive killing, extended to retribution for culpable error. This device, I suggest, was inspired by controversy regarding the Delphinium jurisdiction. The Delphinium rule amounts to a restriction upon those cases where the defendant can plead legal justification. A plea of lawful homicide is admissible only where the killer can invoke a specific provision of statute, such as the provisions allowing self-help or absolving the athlete or combatant; otherwise even justifiable killing is prohibited. In Lysias 1 the killer of the adulterer must therefore prove that he did not plot the adulterer's murder even justifiably. The author of the *Tetralogies* has adapted this rule in the terms in which it was popularly understood as a device for transferring blame in cases where culpable error may be assigned to the victim: the law prohibits just and unjust killing; all killings are either just or unjust (as Demosthenes insists, 23. 75); if defendant's

---

[72] Gagarin takes this passage as evidence that 'just and unjust' homicide is equivalent to 'unintentional and intentional': 'Prohibition of Just Homicide', 295–7. But in 2. 2. 9 the claim that 'the law [prohibiting just and unjust killing] acquits us' comes as a conclusion or further implication from the preceding argument: 'for [defendant] is acquitted . . . by the error of the victim himself'.

act is neither just nor unjust killing, he is not the killer. By this device for transferring blame (what later theory would call *metastasis*) the author has, in effect, reversed the conventional bearing of the rule that even justifiable killing is prohibited.

Thus in the age of Aristotle and Demosthenes we find the premises for the otherwise puzzling argumentation in *Tetralogy* 2. There is perhaps a further parallel in Aeschines 2. 87–8, though it is difficult to construe what precisely Aeschines means by 'justifiable' killing. He contrasts Demosthenes' unscrupulous charges with the final oath in homicide proceedings where the victor must forswear a 'just' but wrongful verdict. Whatever we are to make of Aeschines' argument, this passage again confirms that it was meaningful in the fourth century to speak of law and procedural rules as prohibiting both just and unjust killing.[73]

3.3   Plato's *Laws* 859–76

There is also evidence of popular reasoning along these lines in the treatment of homicide in Plato's *Laws*, roughly contemporary with Demosthenes' *Against Aristocrates*. The philosophical aims of Plato's treatise must be taken into account, and it is often difficult to determine how far Plato's model goes beyond the laws of Athens. But we can conclude with some confidence that Plato has cast his treatment of the laws of bloodshed in large measure as a response to an ongoing debate upon such principles as 'the law prohibiting justifiable killing'. The laws regarding bloodshed are the most detailed and systematic set of statutes in the whole of Plato's code, and perhaps more than any other part of the *Laws* they seem to be a calculated response to current fallacies of popular reasoning regarding ancient legal principles and institutions. The various preambles and statutes that have to do with what Athenians called 'justifiable homicide' (for trial before the Delphinium court) constitute the outer frame of the homicide code; and in the general introduction we could ask for no clearer statement that this theoretical construct is intended to address popular misconceptions of 'justifiable' retribution (cf. 859d–60c).[74] The lawgiver must recognize two separate

---

[73] Gagarin, 'Prohibition of Just Homicide', 304–6, supposes that here unintentional = justifiable homicide (as he also interprets *Tetr.* 2) though he grants that it is not the best evidence. For the implications of this puzzling testimony on the final oath at the Palladium, see Ch. 4 §1.1.

[74] Cf. Saunders, *Plato's Penal Code*, 243–57.

criteria of judgement: the law is to redress both 'injustice' (*adikia*) and 'damage' or harm (*blabē*); confusion of the two concerns has led to popular misconceptions of justice and justifiable acts. Justice and injustice are matters of a deeper moral order, not simply a measure of the agent's innocence of intent; damage is a wholly separate concern [862b].

Plato makes quite clear that certain acts that proceed from a virtuous character and which are therefore 'just' (in the proper sense) are none the less liable to claims by an injured party: 'The lawgiver must look to both concerns, injustice and harm, and by the laws make good what has been damaged, restore what was lost, and set right what was overturned; killing or wounding he must endeavour to heal, by reconciling the suffering [family of the victim] to those responsible, by compensation for their injuries' [862b–c]. Following these principles, Plato amends the traditional categories of homicide; he dispenses with *phonos dikaios* altogether.

He begins significantly with what the Athenians would have regarded as lawful homicide, to be tried at the Delphinium court, but he defines these offences as 'violent though unintentional'. They include (1) accidental death in athletic competition; (2) accidental death in war or military training, including practice with spear and other weapons.[75] These cases are remedied by ritual purification. A similar remedy applies (3) in cases where a patient dies under a doctor's care.

Defensive or retributive killing is handled under various headings, including some instances where Athenian rules of legal justification seem to be directly addressed or contradicted. Thus we are told that if brother kills brother 'in factional violence or similar circumstances', he is free of guilt: the victim is 'an enemy' to the *polis*; and there is, after all, no assignable claim of damage since the victim's family are also the family of the killer. But there is absolutely no right of killing in self-defence or self-help against parents (869b): 'no law will allow it.'

Self-help killing with impunity (ἀνατί) is granted if an intentional killer returns from exile (871c). And in the final section of the homicide code, there are legal protections for self-help killing

---

[75] There is a problem with the text here (865a–b), all manuscripts reading 'officers' (ἀρχόντων) where editors assume 'spears' (ἀκοντίων). Some reference to lethal weapons is in order since Plato's lawful homicide applies to training both with and without armour.

against (1) theft by night; (2) 'mugging'; (3–4) sexual violation of blood kin or wife; and (5) in defence of kin against lethal threat. These cases and those addressed as 'violent but involuntary', all would come under the jurisdiction of the Delphinium court at Athens if the killer pleaded legal justification. They are nowhere described as 'justifiable' but rather as cases where the killer is 'free of taint' (*katharos*), or 'the wrongdoer be slain with impunity' (*nēpoini*); or as 'those cases where the law allows killing' (876c). In this regard Plato reflects the wording of Athenian law, but he is also following out the principles of moral legislation that he proclaimed in his pre-amble, in answer to the popular notion of justifiable killing.

Plato's treatment of the laws of bloodshed goes well beyond the scope and detail given to other areas of criminal law, and in light of the other evidence it is reasonable to conclude that Plato here enters into an ongoing debate. Demosthenes in the speech *Against Aristocrates*, after all, takes up similar issues. There are also sug-gestive parallels in the fragments of fourth-century thinkers that Aristotle reports as indicative of common topics. The ancient prob-lem of Orestes' guilt came to represent the fundamental paradox of justifiable killing.[76] The traditional procedure that had evolved from customary rules of self-help as a mechanism of private settle-ment was now regarded with a deeper comprehension of bloodshed as a public wrong. Popular controversy on the problem of legal and moral justification is perhaps indicated in Plato's *Euthyphro*. And such issues are plainly a preoccupation of Lysias' speeches in the early restoration era, when he attacks the oligarch Eratosthenes, his brother's killer, as a threat to the *polis*, and the killer of the adulterer Eratosthenes must disavow even 'justifiable' retribution.

§4. Conclusions

The chief aim of this chapter has been to define the relationship between the *Tetralogies* and the court speeches; the connection

---

[76] With Dem. 23. 74, cf. Theodectes' *Orestes* (F5): ' "it is just for the woman who slays her husband" to die, and just for the son to avenge the father; but not for the son to take vengeance upon the mother' (*Rhet.* 2. 24. 3: 1401ᵃ). Again in *Alcmaeon*, Theodectes posed the same problem, viz. that retribution may be justified with regard to the offender, but those who take vengeance may be none the less denied the right. Similarly Alcidamas in *Messeniacus* recast Empedocles' μὴ κτείνειν τὸ ἔμψυχον as a principle contradicting conventional justifications: *Rhet.* 1. 13. 2 (1373ᵇ).

between the two is crucial to our estimation of the *Tetralogies* as evidence for early rhetoric and Athenian homicide law. This line of inquiry has led us inevitably into various considerations that reflect upon the old questions of authorship and authenticity. The conclusions that I would draw in regard to these secondary questions will undoubtedly be met with scepticism, and I will not presume to have proven to the satisfaction of all that the *Tetralogies* are not Antiphon's work nor a product of his era. The substantive findings of this chapter, however, on the difference in outlook and method that separates the *Tetralogies* from the court speeches, I argue with some conviction. The *Tetralogies* are marked by a studied departure from court practice; this is the one fixed parameter in a field of variables; it is the one clear indicator of the author's purpose, in a work that has conjured so many conflicting interpretations. In his treatment of the major topics of *dikai phonou*, where the *Tetralogies* are most clearly parallel to the court speeches, the author has methodically undertaken to confound or reverse the rules and assumptions that governed legal reasoning in the courts. The reversal is perhaps typical of the sophistic demonstrations, but the subject matter is also significant: the author follows the format of *dikai phonou* and deals with notorious cases and problematic con cepts peculiar to that jurisdiction precisely because the legalistic issues are in themselves of some consequence.

This finding contradicts both of the major models. The notion that the *Tetralogies* were designed as 'practice-and-demonstration' texts for aspiring advocates to imitate—embodying certain broadly applicable techniques that 'students' or 'clients' in the courts could adapt to the case at hand—has no basis in the evidence. As a practical guide, the *Tetralogies* would be utterly useless for a litigant involved in homicide proceedings or any comparable legal action. The second, theoretical model—the notion that the *Tetralogies* were experimental or speculative exercises in certain prominent themes of the sophistic 'enlightenment'—may be nearer the mark, but it also founders upon the hard evidence of the court speeches and other extant records. The *Tetralogies* are not an inventive or innovative work, in the sense of an exercise exploring theoretical possibilities that had not been previously demonstrated. There is an unmistakable connection between each of the three scenarios and other notorious cases. Some of these parallels were apparently first publicized in the era after Antiphon. It is, of course, conceivable that the *Tetralogies* were an early speculation on hypothetical cases that later came true; but it is, I think, a more natural assumption that the author took his theme in each case from the *cause célèbre*.

What distinguishes the *Tetralogies* is not their originality in posing a problem or venturing upon an untried theme, but their studied disregard of the old, formalistic method. Now it is not far-fetched to suppose that Antiphon himself composed such a work as a critique of Athenian legalism; but if the *Tetralogies* are in any meaningful sense 'Antiphon's work' they are likely to be a later adaptation or transcription by an author who was not unaffected by developments after 410. This 'student of Antiphon' (for want of a better designation) may himself have been an Ionian, or consciously borrowed from the literary dialect. In either case we can more easily account for the Ionicisms and other stylistic discrepancies by this assumption than by the old theory that Antiphon himself, early in his career, consciously imitated an otherwise unknown Ionic exemplar.

Whoever the author, his method involves a systematic reversal of topics and techniques found in the court speeches. Thus in the second *Tetralogy* we find a virtual parody of the standard *apodeixis*, the exposition of sworn statements and 'issue in dispute' that preliminary hearings had defined. The exercise in probabilities in *Tetralogy* 1 responds to the standard topic that a murder without witnesses cannot be proved beyond conjecture. The treatment of the religious issue, the threat of defilement and avenging spirits, may also be read as a reversal of the traditional court argument. In the court speeches the peril of bloodguilt is invoked as proof of the speaker's conviction—he would not knowingly defy religious sanctions. In the *Tetralogies* the religious consequences are invoked as a matter for the judges to weigh directly as a threat to themselves and to the community, in a legal setting where the capacity for either side to fabricate formal proof is taken for granted. Finally, in the treatment of 'law prohibiting just as well as unjust killing', the author of the *Tetralogies* has extended a concept proper to the Delphinium court into an area where it was never intended. It is properly a rule restricting retributive killing; the author of the *Tetralogies* has adapted this rule as a device for transferring blame to the victim: the killing is either just or unjust; the defendant's action is clearly not unjust (i.e. malicious); the killing is the consequence of the victim's culpable error, and it is therefore his own act and not the act of defendant. In demonstrating this device the author is responding not to the moral conflict of written and unwritten law but to a legalistic issue that seems inherent in the Delphinium jurisdiction and the popular conception of *phonos dikaios* as retributive killing.

Such in brief are the positive findings of this chapter: the subject matter of the *Tetralogies* is largely derivative; their method is essentially a reversal of the court arguments. The further implications of this conclusion should at least convey a caveat against the prevailing and often uncritical assumption that the *Tetralogies* are Antiphon's work or a product of his era. The ancient attribution, after all, tells us very little. We know only that the *Tetralogies* were included in the Antiphontian corpus, along with many works of doubtful authenticity, by the time of Harpocration and Pollux, five hundred years after Antiphon. Hermogenes thereafter suggests that *phonikoi* were given a certain prominence in the collection. Now the prominence of homicide speeches may be due more to the nature of the proceedings than to any special theoretical interest. But as *phonikoi* were not a significant part of any corpus after Antiphon, an ancient editor would naturally attribute to him a theoretical work on that theme that purported to represent a fifth-century perspective. In Antiphon's era, on the other hand, by the nature of *dikai phonou*, a verbatim 'performance text' was more often necessary than in other procedures; and 'client copies' would have tended to assure that *some* copy survive from an era when fully scripted speeches were still an innovation.[77]

A relatively detailed text was especially suitable for preparing the ordinary citizen to deal with Draco's law and the peculiar set of procedural rules and religious sanctions; and a fairly full text of the arguments was all the more workable in *dikai phonou* because the preliminaries assured that the charges, the evidence, and the opposing arguments were known. Such texts would have required a high standard of *ethopoeia*, and it is not unlikely that logographic speeches in homicide proceedings were especially formative in this aspect of early rhetoric. In most other proceedings practice-and-demonstration texts were a better form of instruction for those who were likely to need it—those active in the courts and assemblies.

[77] The other grouping whose authenticity seems to be unquestioned during the Second Sophistic is the set of δημηγορικοί, among which speeches for foreign clients are prominent; here again there were obvious advantages to a verbatim text.

The *Tetralogies* imitate the practice-and-demonstration texts of earlier *technai*, but they are devoted to a type of procedure to which the genre was wholly unsuitable. So far as we can judge, homicide trials were a rare undertaking for even the most litigious of Athenians. Whether the aim of the *Tetralogies* was to illustrate practical technique or theoretical principles, we could hardly imagine a more narrowly specialized study than this treatment of *dikai phonou*, preoccupied as it is with cause of death, defilement, and 'justifiable killing,' and dealing with cases that defy conventional legalities.

The three *Tetralogies* are modelled on extraordinary cases and well-known *controversiae* of the late fifth or early fourth centuries. They have something of the *ethopoeia* of Antisthenes' *Ajax* and *Ulixes*, and the courtroom technique of the *Ulixes* attributed to Alcidamas (in answer to Gorgias' *Palamedes*). But the distinctive feature of the *Tetralogies* is that they are not devoted to the exempla of remote antiquity but to peculiar legal conundrums of recent history. Their approach is not unlike that of the various treatments of the trial of Socrates: they follow the format of court proceedings, they adapt the devices of pathos and ethos that earlier logographers had perfected, and they add various effects intended to recreate oral performance. [78]

The legalistic distortions contribute to this effect: they help to convey oral debate to a literary audience. The threats and emotional appeals to the judges, conjuring miasma and avenging furies, draw upon the conventions of the drama rather than those of the courts. They seem calculated to involve the reader rather than to sway the *ephetai*. The author's preoccupation with the rule allowing the defendant to escape before the final speech is also an indication of this aim. In *Tetralogy* 3 the speakers emerge from the text when we are told in the final speech that the defendant himself has fled and friends concerned for his safety come forward to speak in his behalf. At the same point in *Tetralogy* 1 the defendant remarks that proof of his innocence is furnished by his very willingness to

---

[78] Cf. Cole, *Origins of Rhetoric*, 120, remarking literary rhetoric's 'range of effects commensurate with those available to the best oral performances'. Among these effects were a certain dramatic representation of court proceedings. As we turn from Gorgias' *Palamedes* to Alcidamas' *Ulixes* (Radermacher BVII. 44; BXXII. 16) one is struck by the use of witnesses and the intriguing description of lost documentary evidence—the arrow with hidden winged words (6–7).

remain and risk his life on the verdict. The variation in *Tetralogy* 2, however, where the prosecutor claims he expected his opponent would make no answer to the charge, defies the logic of the procedure: the wording of the plea would be known; safe exile was guaranteed. The author distorts the convention to evoke a more dynamic courtroom confrontation. The dramatic challenge-to-torture in *Tetralogy* 1 has a similar value. The defendant issues his challenge in the midst of proceedings, near the close of his final speech, when it would have done him no good in court. Such theatrics were probably contrived as a device for 'writing out loud' for a reading audience.

The treatment of miasma and avenging Furies also appeals to this same audience, rather than to the *ephetai*. The religious consequences of a killing, so powerfully conveyed in drama, certainly cast a shadow over the legal proceedings; but they were not *at issue* for the litigants to argue and the judges to decide. Neither in Draco's law nor in Antiphon's court speeches do we have any clear sense of a *criminal* aspect to *dikai phonou*, that homicide should be remedied as a public wrong, such as we find in Lysias' treatment of his brother's murder—and in the *Tetralogies*.

In this respect, the *Tetralogies* conform to the same standard that guided the people's juries of the restored democracy. Max Weber characterized this mode of reasoning as 'substantive rationalism' guided by ideology, the expediential and ethical values of the community.[79] Thus in Socrates' defence, Lysias *Against Eratosthenes*, Andocides *On the Mysteries*, and much of the legal record of the early 'restoration' era, the dispute at trial centres not upon formal issues of fact, law, or logic, but upon the interests and avowed values of the newly self-actualized *dēmos*. The speeches for *dikai phonou* clearly indicate an *extrinsic* formal rationalism: the verdict turns upon formalistic criteria of processual acts; this formalism was based upon strict adherence to a traditional procedure and special competence of the *ephetai*.

The *Tetralogies* belong to the legalism of ideology. The fear of miasma is no longer treated as a means of validating procedural acts; it has come to represent the danger that unrequited bloodshed may bring to the community—the danger of vendetta is scarcely

---

[79] In this regard Weber compared the people's justice at Athens and the 'Khadi justice' of Islamic society. See *Weber on Law*, esp. 213, with Rheinstein's introduction xlii–xlvi.

concealed beneath the shadow of divine visitation.[80] 'Justifiable homicide,' retributive self-help, is no longer seen as a straightforward mechanism of law—*the ultimate processual act*—but as a wrong to the *polis*. The ingenious who-done-it in *Tetralogy* 1 reflects a profound disenchantment with traditional justice.[81] In the second *Tetralogy* the plaintiff seems to acknowledge the new distinction of *nomoi* and *psēphismata*, and he addresses the people as lawmakers, 'sovereign in the state'. In the new framework the traditional proceedings before the ancient courts of the *ephetai* were increasingly regarded as antiquated and undemocratic. Since the case proceeded upon the oaths of plaintiffs and witnesses, it was sometimes possible to disable an opponent on largely groundless accusations. A special procedure for trial of perjury charges arising in *dikai phonou* was evidently instituted to remedy such abuses.[82] The *Tetralogies* in fact—alone among the extant homicide speeches—allude to this procedure against perjury in *dikai phonou*, and their very method seems to reflect an utter lack of faith in the traditional rules of evidence and liability. They are in some sense a 'polemic' against the peculiar logic of *dikai phonou*. They are, in all likelihood, the rough product of an era when the workings of law were subject to a new scrutiny and the tools of face-to-face debate were first fashioned into literary technique.

The next section of this study parallels the traditional division of jurisdiction: in Chapter 6, we take up Antiphon 1 and the nature of trials for intentional homicide at the Areopagus; in Chapter 7, Antiphon 6 and unintentional killing tried at the Palladium; Chapter 8, Lysias 1 and trials for justifiable homicide at the Delphinium. In each case we shall review the relevant arguments in the *Tetralogies*, which are generally thought to follow the same division of jurisdiction. But we turn back to the *Tetralogies* with this understanding: they are not to be relied upon in isolation as direct evidence on the letter of the law or the direction of legal reasoning. Where we have corroboration in the court speeches or testimonia on actual cases, they may serve as secondary or supporting evidence on the conventions of court argument, and they some-

---

[80] Cf. *Tetr.* 2. 1. 2: the killer 'has roused no rage of vengeance in the dead but in the living'.
[81] Cf. *Tetr.* 1. 1. 6; 1. 4. 9.   [82] See Ch. 4 §1.2.

times provide further insight or indirect confirmation for matters of law, procedure, and ideology. But we must always bear in mind that the *Tetralogies* give us a somewhat inverted image of the proceedings.

6

Antiphon 1 and the Concept of Malice

The first speech in the corpus was once judged the best of Antiphon's work for its portrayal of character.[1] It is now generally regarded the worst of his efforts for the failings of its argument.[2] It presents us with a set of problems not unlike the puzzle of the *Tetralogies*. The case involves a plot so convoluted that it was once thought to be an artificial scenario for demonstration:[3] the plaintiff, having recently come of age, prosecutes a woman for the murder of her husband, the plaintiff's father; the death occurred some years earlier when the young man was too young to prosecute; the wife allegedly brought about the victim's death by poisoning at the hands of an unwitting accomplice—a concubine who belonged to a friend of the victim and administered the drug to both men. Antiphon's authorship is again in question—though not, in this instance, on grounds of language or law.[4] There are dramatic flourishes that seem out of character with Antiphon's austere style: the plaintiff refers to his 'stepmother' as Clytemnestra and casts himself in the role of a latter-day Orestes. The arrangement of the speech is peculiarly disjointed: the proof (5–13) comes before the narrative (14–20); and after what appears to be the proper epilogue, there is yet a second, rather disconnected, closing statement (28–31). None of these anomalies, however, would have roused so much suspicion were it not that the argumentation seems utterly

---

[1] Wilamowitz, 'Die erste Rede des Antiphon', *Hermes*, 22 (1887), 194–210: 'die beste des Antiphons weil sie am meisten ἦθος hat' (209). Cf. Dover, 'Chronology', 48–9; Blass, *Attische Beredsamkeit*, 187–94; and now Heitsch, *Antiphon*, 21–32 (with earlier bibliography n. 41).

[2] Thus Blass, turning to this work from the *Herodes* (187), remarked that the first speech is far inferior and 'scheint eines Antiphon wenig würdig' (191).

[3] This view goes back to Maetzner's edition of 1838; followed by Meier and Schömann, *Attische Prozeβ*, 311; refuted by P. G. Ottsen, *De rerum inventione et dispositione quae est in Lysia et Antiphonte* (diss., Flensburg, 1847), 4–10. Cf. Blass, *Attische Beredsamkeit* 190; Thiel, *Antiphon's erste Tetralogie*, 22.

[4] The stylistic measures for Ant. 1 fall squarely between those of the other two speeches and Dover therefore dated it after Ant. 6 and before 5. The stylistics at least tend to confirm authenticity.

inadequate. The plaintiff apparently based his charge upon his father's dying word, and the only scrap of corroboration he has is the defence's refusal to submit their slaves to torture. Most of those who have commented on the speech—even those who expressed admiration for it—generally conclude that the plaintiff had no case. The argument seems unworthy of the Antiphon whom later antiquity regarded as the master of homicide disputes.

None the less, this much-maligned document is of singular value for the present study: it demonstrates the focus upon traditional, non-technical proofs that Solmsen found characteristic of early rhetoric.[5] And it is perhaps the best evidence we have by which to judge the kinds of issues that would actually come before the Areopagus in trials for intentional homicide. Contrary to the usual assumptions, the argument in this case centres on the defendant's state of mind and the causal connection linking her 'decision' to the cause of death. There appears to be no real question of what was done or by whom. In this respect the case of the stepmother would tend to confirm what we would suppose from the other evidence on the Areopagus jurisdiction (Ch. 3 §2.2). The trial would turn upon the question of malice aforethought, and in this particular case, as we shall see, that question encompasses the latent guilt of recklessness. This speech may prove to be, after all, a particularly revealing example of the kind of text that was provided to prospective litigants. Whether it was an authentic speech-for-trial preserved for reference and example or was devised even in its conception as a hypothetical model for demonstration, it is clearly a text of far greater value as a guide to argumentation in the murder court than the Tetralogy that affects to treat the same theme.

That very aspect of the argument that once led scholars to suppose that the speech is an artificial showpiece may also be read as an authentic feature of speeches for trial in *dikai phonou*: the lack of real evidence reflects the all-too-real limitations that a plaintiff would often face. The whole of the argument is centred upon the two instruments of judgement, oath and challenge to torture. The plaintiff attacks the defender first for refusing to make use of the only available evidence, viz. the testimony of slaves under torture (6–13), and secondly for swearing on his own conviction—without any way of proving state of mind—that his mother did not plot

---

[5] *Antiphonstudien*, 8–10.

murder (21–4, 28–30). This emphasis upon non-technical proofs conforms to the method that Solmsen found characteristic of the earliest court speeches.

The weakness of the case and apparent inadequacy of the argument, however, remain problematic. What appears to be a fatal flaw in the plaintiff's case, that he does not address the plausible plea of innocence of malice, has led some commentators to suppose that the author failed to appreciate the subtle concept of unintentional 'planning', or indirect agency, as it might apply to this case; others, in order to save the author's argument, have guessed that the concept of *bouleusis akousios* was not yet recognized in the courts of law and popular reasoning—but this is an inference prompted by the arguments of Antiphon 6, to which we turn in the next chapter. Let us first determine what was at issue in Antiphon 1, what were the practical consequences of such a prosecution, what would be the effect of an acquittal or conviction (§1); second, what was the case for the defence, and what case did the plaintiff have (§2). From these findings we should be better able to judge the significance of this document for early rhetoric and legal reasoning (§3).

If the plaintiff against the stepmother patently had no case, then the speech is perhaps more likely to be an artificial showpiece, like the *Palamedes* of Gorgias, prompted by fascination with the legendary lost cause. A similar paradox inspired the first *Tetralogy*, where the author sets out to show how the paradigmatic worst case may in fact be won. It was also undoubtedly part of the appeal of 'Antiphon's Defence'; and it added, no doubt, a rhetorical interest to the various treatments of Socrates' trial. But if this speech is in some sense an artificial model, its aims are likely to be rather different from those of the *Palamedes* and other showpieces. It is devoted to the traditional forms of proof rather than conjecture; and it bears certain marks of logographic authenticity, details of scenario and legal strategy not likely to be invented for purely theoretical purposes. The very anomalies suggest that this speech is a genuine speech-for-trial or a close adaptation. It addresses real-life complications rather than artificial conundrums. The author perhaps kept his original as an exemplar or rough demonstration text from which to extract or illustrate various arguments. The model arguments in such an exemplar would not have been entirely without value even if the client lost his case. Its value would be greatly enhanced, on the other hand, if the prosecution was in some sense successful. And despite its apparent deficiencies there is good reason to suppose that the plaintiff and his counsel had a reasonable expectation of success. The considerations of law and argumentative strategy, to be taken up in the following sections, tend strongly to confirm the simplest and most natural interpretation, that this is indeed an original logographic speech, or at least one closely modelled on arguments for trial—not an artificial showpiece in the impossible case.

§1. The Charge and the Question at Issue

Various problems are posed by the title—*Against the Stepmother for Poisoning*—and the hypothesis that we find in the manuscripts has added to the confusion. These are largely superficial difficulties, however, arising from the inference of an editor in late antiquity; but they may well point to other, more fundamental complications. Thus the charge is indicated in the manuscript as 'poisoning' (*pharmakeias*); yet we learn from Demosthenes' citation of the law of the Areopagus that a charge of poisoning *per se* must allege that the accused administered the drug by his own hand.[6] The most reasonable view is that this case was prosecuted as intentional homicide by 'planning', *bouleusis*. But this interpretation raises its own problems.

It was once supposed that *bouleusis* was treated as a separate offence, to be tried before the Palladium court, and that this charge might even encompass cases of 'attempted murder' without injury (as opposed to malicious wounding, tried before the Areopagus). But Gagarin has now shown convincingly that the passages assigning *bouleusis* to the Palladium court refer to unintentional killing even in cases of 'planning' or determining.[7] In other words, the Palladium jurisdiction expressly includes such cases as Antiphon 6, where the defendant is charged with indirect responsibility for an accidental death and it is clear that *bouleusis* is the technical term for

---

[6] Keil, 'Antiphon κατὰ τῆς μητρυίας', *Jahrbücher für classische Philologie*, 135 (1887), 100, shows to what lengths commentators may go to make a virtue of absurdity: he supposes that the actual charge is poisoning but the author treats it as 'murder with premeditation' because on that count he had a better chance to convict; this trick 'von all sophistischen kunststückchen bleibt das tollste'.

[7] Gagarin, '*Bouleusis*', 81–99. See Ch. 3 §2.2 n. 54; and for full discussion of 'planning' an unintended outcome, see Ch. 7.

this involvement. As for murder by 'planning' or instigation, as in Antiphon 1, there is nothing in the ancient evidence to contradict the most natural assumption that such cases would be tried along with other intentional killings at the Areopagus. And there are indications in the speech itself that would lead us to suppose the case was heard by the high court.[8] The allegation of 'planning' ultimately leads to a serious difficulty in the argumentation, but it does not affect the question of jurisdiction.

The title also raises the problem of 'standing' and the plaintiff's relationship to the victim. The manuscript hypothesis assumes that the plaintiff is a legitimate son of the victim by a previous marriage; but commentators have reached a virtual consensus that the plaintiff is in fact a *later* offspring, probably a freeborn son of the victim by a concubine, possibly non-Athenian.[9] Such an individual's illegitimacy or non-citizen status probably would not hinder him from prosecuting, so long as he was within the circle of eligible kinsmen prescribed in the law. Now the manuscript hypothesis is plainly contradicted by the plaintiff's insistence that he is bringing charges, despite his youth, at the earliest opportunity, some years after the death, as he was previously too young to prosecute. If his half-brothers were younger children of a second marriage, we would not expect the eldest to be old enough to act as *kyrios* for his mother as he does. This implication does not in itself establish the relationship between plaintiff and defendant conclusively, but it is enough to raise a reasonable doubt of the traditional assumptions. In any event, at the time of his death the victim was evidently estranged from the defendant: he was probably involved in a relationship with some other partner, and the other woman is likely to be the mother of our plaintiff.

This question of the relationships leads us to one of the major cruces of the argumentation, that the plaintiff nowhere directly discusses the defendant's motive. This is all the more noteworthy in light of the elaborate arguments on motive in *Tetralogy* 1 and Antiphon 5. Whatever conclusions the jurors are to draw regarding motive in this case, they must evidently form their judgement *from*

---

[8] So Wilamowitz concluded, 'Erste Rede', 196–7 n. 1, *et passim*.

[9] See Heitsch, *Antiphon*, 22. It is usually assumed that the mother was a non-Athenian, perhaps resident in one of the allied states where the father had dealings. It is reasonable to assume that if there were a problem regarding the plaintiff's standing, he would have made some reference to it (as the defendant in Ant. 5 denies anti-Athenian sympathies).

the defence statement. The plaintiff for his part never ventures to explain the background. We are evidently to suppose that the defendant gave the drug because her husband's affections had become more strongly attached to some other partner, presumably the mother of our plaintiff. The speaker himself never says so, although from such a connection he might have proceeded directly to establish a motive of jealousy and vindictiveness. This feature of the argument in itself suggests that plaintiff could confidently expect the defence to acknowledge the situation quite openly, including the victim's relationship with the plaintiff's mother or other partner. And that is likely to be the case only if the defender was prepared to admit that his mother had provided the drug.

1.1   The Facts Admitted

The plaintiff has sworn that the stepmother is responsible for the death and that she acted with malice aforethought and by planning. The latter conditions are clearly the points in dispute. There seems to be very little question of the facts. Whether the events were precisely as the plaintiff reports and the defence conceded as much is doubtful; but from the argument of the speech itself (to which we shall shortly turn) we can conclude with reasonable confidence that the essential fact that the defendant provided the drug that proved fatal was not in dispute. To account for this aspect of the argument Wilamowitz supposed that the concubine who administered the drug had directly implicated the stepmother under torture.[10] The stepmother and her kinsmen had presumably reconciled with the family of the other victim, Philoneos, through *aidesis* and ritual purification. The plaintiff would have been too young at the time to take part. But if this is so, it is puzzling that the plaintiff makes no clear reference to the concubine's testimony to this effect in his reconstruction of the events. Instead, his narrative appears to be based largely on conjecture. On the other hand, it is reasonable to suppose that plaintiff expected the defence to introduce whatever

---

[10] Wilamowitz, 'Erste Rede', 195. Heitsch, *Antiphon*, 25 at n. 37, does not entirely discount Wilamowitz's hypothesis, but rather emphasizes the vagueness of the plaintiff's reference: he has no direct proof of what the woman said under torture; cf. M. Gagarin, *Göttingsche Gelehrte Anzeigen*, 239 (1987), 58–9, supposing the plaintiff persists in a lost cause out of a sense of duty. Thür, *Basanos*, 21 at n. 42, treats the torture of the concubine as execution rather than inquisition.

evidence there was, if the thrust of their case was to deny malice aforethought.[11]

By this theory then the plaintiff calls no witnesses to verify the fact that the defendant provided the drug precisely because the defence would stipulate to it. And if the fact of the defendant's complicity is not at issue, then the plaintiff is at no great disadvantage for his lack of real evidence. In this conclusion we rely admittedly upon the speaker's silence, but the further implications of the argument clearly confirm that the fact of the wife's involvement was not disputed.

There is the rather damning circumstantial evidence that the concubine arranged to administer the drug to both men, to her *kyrios* and to the father of our plaintiff, when she could easily have contrived to drug only her own partner. Now there are any number of possible explanations, but there is also an obvious argument from probability that the plaintiff does not bother to follow out. Were she not acting at the wife's instigation, the concubine was not likely to administer the drug to both men: if her motive was only to regain the affections of her own partner, then she could easily have given him the drug on other occasions, without another man present and thus with less risk. The rhetorical opportunity that our plaintiff has missed, in a speech which does not fail to exploit other probabilities regarding slave testimony, is at least a further indication that the plaintiff expected the defence to concede that the stepmother was somehow involved in the fatal poisoning.

The plaintiff would know what was admitted and what disputed from the *prodikasiai* (Ch. 4 §1). He refers in §2 to written statements for both parties; they swore again to these affidavits at the outset of proceedings. It is clear in the introduction and anticipation of defence arguments (5, 23–6), as we shall see, that the plaintiff knows the wording of the defender's oath and the general direction of his argument. The charge of malice aforethought will be the

---

[11] Blass, *Attische Beredsamkeit*, 189, rejected the possibility that the plaintiff had other evidence (e.g. testimony to his father's dying charge) on the grounds that witnesses in homicide proceedings were required to swear to the righteousness of the plaintiff's claim, and this plaintiff was not likely to find anyone to vouch for him! The case is not quite so unsupportable, but it is unlikely that the plaintiff would not have made some allusion to supporting evidence if he had any. In particular, if there were any witnesses who could confirm the father's dying charge, he would surely have mentioned it in 'the second epilogue', where he rejects the challenge to slave torture on that question (see §2.3).

crucial point in dispute and the plaintiff will have to show that he has sworn to the killer's intent with a moral certainty.

1.2 Malice Aforethought: *Pronoia*

We have noticed that the term of intentionality that is fundamental to the homicide law is also the most primitive approximation to *mens rea*. *Pronoia* naturally conveys a sense of *prior* knowledge or design and thus aptly describes hostile intent as apprehended in overt actions that anticipate the killing (Chs. 2 §1 and 4 §1). It will be helpful here to consider some of the parallel passages that substantiate this value for *pronoia* and serve to explicate the knotted argumentation of our speech.

There is first the evidence regarding charges of malicious wounding (τραύματος ἐκ προνοίας). These passages are often disregarded as irrelevant to homicide procedure, but it is clear that in both procedures *pronoia* refers specifically to intent to kill, and it is therefore unwarranted to discount the evidence in cases of wounding, that *pronoia* involves premeditation or prior design.[12]

Pronoia is clearly distinct from simple and spontaneous intent to harm. Consider first the fragmentary defence speech Lysias 4, where apparently the plaintiff alleged that the speaker planned to kill him with a shard of pottery. The gist is as follows: a dagger would have been a more suitable weapon for murder, but [plaintiff] claims that we made the attack with nothing of this sort—instead he says he was struck with an ostrakon. 'And yet it is clear from what he has said that there was no pronoia, for we would not have gone there without knowing whether we would find an ostrakon or some other lethal weapon but would have brought one with us' (6–7). This defendant proceeds to describe his actions as impulsive and spontaneous, the product of an evening of drunkenness and sexual adventure. It is this set of antecedent events that belies the plaintiff's claim that he was the target of a preconcerted plot (ἐπιβουλευθῆναι). 'Thus council may judge from the sum of

---

[12] Much of this evidence, persuasively presented by Cantarella, *Studi sull'omicidio*, 98–101, is discounted by Gagarin (*Drakon*, 32–3) and others. But if the value of *pronoia* were specific to each offence, we would expect *pronoia* in a case of wounding to mean intent to wound where *pronoia* in homicide means intent to kill. It is quite clear that *pronoia* means intent to kill in both contexts. Therefore we have no reason to doubt that the same sense of prior design applies in both.

testimony and other evidence that there was neither malice afore-thought (*pronoia*) nor wrong' (10–11).

The defendant in Lysias 3 *Against Simon* characterizes the charge against him in very similar terms: 'He claims that we came to his house bringing a potsherd and that I threatened to kill him, and that this constitutes *pronoia*' (3. 28). It is interesting that in both cases the 'weapon' was a piece of broken pottery, a common object that lay ready to hand, and it is not unlikely that plaintiff seized upon this allegation when he could point to no weapon more indicative of murderous intent. But it is none the less significant that the plaintiff has insisted upon this aspect of the attack—that defendant brought a weapon and made an overt threat—as reveal-ing *pronoia*.[13] He has not simply relied upon other circumstantial indicators to reconstruct motivation at the moment of the attack; he has rather built his case upon direct indicators of *prior* design. He says unequivocally that it is this prior demonstration of hostile intent that proves *pronoia* in the legal sense.[14]

And in the closing remarks to this speech we find a fairly straightforward statement that *pronoia* in fact involves prior design and implies intent to kill: it does not apply to spontaneous violence, and by implication therefore it does not apply where the assailant simply attempts to injure his adversary.

Who is so simple-minded as to *premeditate* an attack in advance simply so that one of his enemies may receive a wound? On the contrary, it is clear that those who framed the laws prescribed exile not for those who *happen* to get in a fight and break each other's heads—or they would have sen-tenced many to banishment—but for those who *plotted* to kill but suc-ceeded only in wounding their intended victims, for these offenders the lawmakers prescribed such severe penalties believing that they must pay the penalty *for what they designed and premeditated*.

Our defendant tells us that the law expressly encompasses plotting or preconceived design. And the length to which he is prepared to

---

[13] Another case of wounding with *pronoia* is probably indicated in Dem. 54. 25, and here the *pronoia* consists in instigation; cf. MacDowell, *AHL* 64–9. There is also perhaps an indication that prior design was at issue in a case of wounding, for which we have only a few fragments: Lysias' speech *Against Lysitheos*, F 62a Thalheim (F41 Blass), 'And I caught him mixing earth in a mortar with a stone pestle', pre-sumably for some nefarious concoction.

[14] That prior design constitutes *pronoia* is also shown by the argument from probability, that if he had 'plotted and premeditated' a murderous attack he would not have planned to make the attack when he was sure to be outnumbered and out-manœuvred in the victim's home (29).

go to connect his arguments with this principle shows that it is of paramount importance. Thus he insists that the meaning of *pronoia* excludes ordinary assault and battery 'because no one would premeditate a wounding'! He concludes that a spontaneous attack is not to be construed as 'wounding with *pronoia*' for the very reason that there is no fixed purpose. After ordinary assaults the assailant's remorse is a sign that his act of violence was a spontaneous impulse and not a fixed resolve. And it is fixed purpose or prior design that deserves the death penalty.[15]

From this line of argument we can conclude that *pronoia* indicates more than a generalized 'harmful intent'. There are, after all, other formulations that clearly indicate a recognized distinction between true premeditation and mere harmful intent. Plato's account of killing in anger, *Laws* 9. 866–7, involves just such a distinction, and although he does not use the legal term *pronoia*, it seems reasonably clear from the parallels in Lysias that he is invoking the same concept. There are cases where the killer acts from a sudden impulse, 'there is no previous intent to kill', and the killer immediately regrets what he has done (like those who cause injury on impulse in Lysias' formulation). And quite distinct from these are cases where the killer is driven by long *premeditated* resentment and vindictiveness. In this latter category, the killer plots his revenge long after the provocation and has no remorse after the deed is done.[16] Aristotle confirms that the laws convey a meaningful distinction between 'what is intentional and unintentional and what is done by *malice aforethought*', involving both the desire and the anticipation (*EE* 1226^{b}30–1227^{a}2).[17]

Such is the operative concept of intentionality in the homicide law. Our plaintiff must show that his conviction of prior design is based upon direct demonstration, overt acts, or threats. But if the principle is straightforward, the plaintiff's burden of proof seems all the more burdensome.

[15] 'So you yourselves have judged many times with regard to intent; for it would be a terrible thing if in all cases where a victim was injured in a drunken brawl or clowning around, or fighting over an insult or a girl-friend—for which everyone later comes to his senses and regrets what he did—you should assess none the less severe penalties' (Lys. 3. 42–3).

[16] *Laws* 9. 866d–67b; for translation and discussion, see §2.2 at n. 27. Plato offers no very helpful instruction on how the judges are to make this rather difficult determination on state of mind, beyond the obvious criterion of repentance.

[17] Above, Ch. 2 §1 with nn. 6–16, and 4 §1; see also the analysis of Ant. 5, Ch. 9 §1.

1.3   Acquittal for Innocence of Malice

To answer a plea of innocence of malice the argumentation of Antiphon 1 seems woefully inadequate. Indeed there is a remarkable piece of evidence that might lead us to conclude the plaintiff simply had no case: We are told of a trial in the Aristotelian *Magna Moralia* that is clearly parallel—indeed it is sometimes suggested that this is the very case for which Antiphon's speech was written.

They say a woman once gave a man a potion and he died from it, but the woman was tried at the Areopagus where she appeared and was acquitted by the judges for no other reason but that she had not acted with malice aforethought (*pronoia*). For she gave the drug for love (*philia*) but failed of this purpose; wherefore it was deemed involuntary since she gave the drug as a love potion and not with the intention of killing him.[18]

Here we are told in no uncertain terms that the defendant was acquitted on grounds that she acted out of love rather than malice. But we should not conclude therefore that our plaintiff's case was a lost cause; on the contrary the verdict in *Magna Moralia* seems to have come as something of a surprise. As the text stands, there is perhaps the implication that the defendant unexpectedly appeared before the court; but by the slightest emendation we may improve the connection of thought by reading that the woman had fled into exile when, to everyone's surprise, she was acquitted.[19] In any event, the plaintiff's case was not so precarious as it may now seem.

---

[18] *MM* 1188ᵇ30–37: . . . γυναῖκα φίλτρον τινὶ δοῦναι πιεῖν, εἶτα τὸν ἄνθρωπον ἀποθανεῖν ὑπὸ τοῦ φίλτρου, τὴν δ' ἄνθρωπον ἐν Ἀρείῳ πάγῳ φυγεῖν· οὗ παροῦσαν δι' οὐθὲν ἄλλο ἀπέλυσαν ἢ διότι οὐκ ἐκ προνοίας. ἔδωκε μὲν γὰρ φιλίᾳ, διήμαρτεν δὲ τούτου· διὸ οὐχ ἑκούσιον ἐδόκει εἶναι, ὅτι τὴν δόσιν τοῦ φίλτρου οὐ μετὰ διανοίας τοῦ ἀπολέσθαι αὐτὸν ἐδίδου. There is some confusion in the text apparently arising from the ambiguity of φυγεῖν 'was exiled' or 'was tried'. Most MSS and editors read 'was acquitted' (ἀποφυγεῖν). But Lipsius, *Attische Recht,* 132, adopting the former reading, takes this as an indication that the Areopagus might sentence an offender to exile, if they judged her responsible but innocent of intent. See below §1.4.

[19] The phrase οὗ παροῦσαν, 'where [at the Areopagus court] she appeared', is surprising; she would not have been expected to present herself for trial and execution. In Ant. 1 the woman is never addressed as present in court, and the phrasing suggests otherwise (e.g. §17 . . . τῆς Κλυταιμνήστρας, τῆς τούτου μητρός, where if she were present we might expect ταυτησί). On the absence of women from Athenian courts generally, see now Todd, *Shape of Law,* 201–8. The original reading may have been οὐ παροῦσαν, 'though *not* present they acquitted her': i.e. she had gone into exile, having no expectation of acquittal. The possibility that this person (ἡ ἄνθρωπος) was a slave or concubine does not appreciably affect this point, as she was obviously a person of sufficient value for her *kyrios* to take every measure for her defence.

Since the jury gave a straight vote either for the plaintiff or for the defendant, this report of the verdict cannot mean that the jurors actually specified their reason for acquitting; it can only mean that they voted in favour of the defendant and this was the nature of her plea. There is the clear implication that she admitted giving the drug but swore that she had not intended to harm the victim but meant to regain his affections. It was thus solely on the basis of this claim, not to have acted with malice aforethought, that she escaped execution.

From this report we have confirmation that innocence of malice was a viable plea in the case *Against the Stepmother*. And from the speech itself it is clear that the plaintiff anticipated just such a plea. But he does not seem to have adequately answered it. Are we then to assume that the plaintiff had only the most doubtful prospect of a successful prosecution on this charge? And if so, why did he not prosecute for unintentional killing, on which charge he stood a far better chance of conviction?

1.4 Judgement for the Plaintiff

It is quite possible that the plaintiff stood to gain materially, even in the event of acquittal, if the defendant, though innocent of malice aforethought, was compelled to acknowledge that she contributed to cause of death. That our plaintiff expects such an admission is evident from his treatment of his half-brother's sworn statement for the defence: he will not claim that she is not 'the killer' (5); he will argue that she acted unwittingly and without design (23); but how can he claim that he knows she did not plan the killing, since those who plot murder do not devise their schemes or make their preparations openly? (28–30; see below §2.3). Evidently the son who spoke for the defence was willing to admit that his mother had provided the concubine with the drug that proved fatal, but claimed in his *diōmosia* that the defendant had not intended or instigated murder. Such involvement would certainly be construed as a type of unintentional killing (like the case of Ant. 6): it is an act that would ordinarily have rendered the defendant liable to the plaintiff *if he had prosecuted on such a charge*. Had she been convicted of precisely such unintentional involvement at the Palladium court, her *kyrios* would have been compelled to negotiate a settlement with the plaintiff.

Now it is often supposed that if a defendant were charged with murder at the Areopagus and swore that he was innocent of intent to kill though acknowledging involvement, in the event the verdict went in his favour, he was acquitted outright and free of any consequences from that verdict.[20] But on the contrary, so long as the bond of oath was held inviolable by religious conviction and social conscience, it was likely to be an automatic and practically inescapable consequence of the defendant's oath that he be liable for the unintentional involvement to which he had, in effect, confessed. The natural implication of his oath, which a verdict in his favour would validate, would be that he was willing to undergo exile and *aidesis;* such was the price of acquittal from the more serious charge (such was Lipsius's understanding of the case in *MM* 1188ᵇ). This is certainly a possible consequence of a verdict for the defendant in Antiphon 1, and it suggests a plausible rationale as to why the plaintiff would have prosecuted for intentional homicide when he had a much better case for unintentional involvement.

But if the defendant was willing to admit liability, why then was there any need to proceed to trial? Surely the case could have been resolved without trial, if exile and private settlement were all that the plaintiff might reasonably expect. On the other hand, the plaintiff is bound by his father's dying command, or so he maintains. And, perhaps more compelling, he probably had something to gain by forcing the issue as he does.

The plaintiff probably had some, not altogether unrealistic expectation that he could win the case, and it is reasonable to assume that if the defendant were convicted, some share of the confiscated property would go to the plaintiff. Now in the mid-fourth century Demosthenes refers to the penalty for intentional homicide as execution and 'state confiscation' (*dēmeusis*), as though there was no financial incentive for the plaintiff to proceed to trial. However, the precise rules regarding confiscation in homicide cases are nowhere clearly stated; and if we follow the most natural assumption, that similar rules applied in homicide confiscations as in other *apographai* (for impiety, etc.), we should conclude that the plaintiff stood to gain a third or more of the estate.[21] Of the property that he

---

[20] MacDowell, *AHL* 46–7, considers it possible that the case could be retried before the Palladium. For exile and settlement as a consequence of the oaths, see Ch. 1 §1.3.

[21] For the limits of financial settlement see Ch. 4 §2.1 at n. 14.

would list as belonging to the state by reason of murder conviction, he may have hoped to claim some portion of the property directly as a legitimate heir (by *enepiskepsis*). He might also receive a substantial portion—perhaps a third, possibly more—by *apographē*. And if he could win this case, he might then proceed against his half-brothers for impiety, as knowingly harbouring their father's killer (as in the case mentioned in Dem. 22. 2–3); and by that litigation he stood to profit yet again by private settlement or *apographē*. We have little direct evidence on confiscation in homicide convictions, but we have absolutely no indication that they were handled in any extraordinary way. The usual assumption that the plaintiff in a murder case had nothing to gain but satisfaction is founded solely upon the surface meaning of *dēmeusis*.

Conviction was not a remote prospect. And even if he lost the case he would be in a better position to demand compensation from the defence, if he could force them to concede publicly the defendant's complicity in the death. For these reasons—and of course out of filial devotion—the plaintiff and his counsel had every reason to resist private settlement and proceed to trial.

§2. The Opposing Arguments

Financial liability and private settlement continued to be the expected outcome of *dikai phonou*. For both the plaintiff and the defendant it is primarily the force of religious conviction and social conscience that guarantees performance of whatever resolution they arrive at. The bond of oath was still regarded, at least publicly, as an inviolable commitment. And respecting the sanctity of this commitment, the plaintiff must have some substantive basis when he swears to 'know well' the killer's state of mind. In this particular case these premises of ancient liability suggest the most likely legal strategy. The fact that the defendant provided the drug is not disputed, and the plaintiff has plausible grounds for alleging malice aforethought. He has the prospect of substantial gain if he can win the case and a possible source of financial advantage even should he lose. The argumentation involves a number of problems that can be best resolved by these assumptions. Let us first summarize the defence position as we have deduced it thus far.

2.1   The Case for the Defence

The defence will have sworn a categorical denial of the plaintiff's charge: the defendant's son and defender must affirm on his own conviction (εὖ εἰδέναι) that the woman did not willingly kill, neither by her own hand (χειρουργήσασα) nor by 'plot or premeditation' (ἐξ ἐπιβουλῆς καὶ προβουλῆς). In the *prodikasiai* the defence would have been forced to admit what could not be denied, that the victim's wife in fact gave the drug that was administered; they may also have been willing to admit that she gave the concubine some instruction as to how and when it should be administered—presumably on the very occasion when the two men were to drink together in celebration of a sacrifice. From these premisses it would have been reasonably clear that the defence must base their case on the question of malice aforethought and 'planning'.

The plaintiff clearly anticipates a defence on the question of malice at several points in his argument (5–6, 23, 28). And such is the natural implication of his insistence that the victim met his death unwillingly, at the hands of an intentional killer (25–6; see below §2.2).

The plaintiff also seems to acknowledge, in a passage of the narrative that would otherwise undermine his argument, that the charge of 'planning' will raise a question of proximate cause. Apparently to account for the fact that one victim died immediately from ingesting the poison and the second, his father, died of the effects some twenty days later, the plaintiff suggests that the concubine gave a larger dosage to Philoneos than to the second victim; she did this presumably upon her own initiative in hopes of rousing the stronger passion in her *kyrios*. Now it is unlikely that the author would have failed to appreciate how much this factor might undermine his case: he has carefully and persuasively conjured up a scenario in which the concubine is the unwitting instrument of the conniving wife; he evidently anticipated the argument that the concubine herself initiated the plot and the wife merely provided the drug.

This emphasis appears to be a chief aim of the narrative: the poisoning was supposedly the wife's 'scheme' and the concubine's 'task' (14–15); she simply followed 'Clytemnestra's prescriptions' (17). The poor woman did not realize she had been deceived until the deed was done (19); she was the mere servant of the other's designs and was punished for an act in which she merely had a hand but was not ultimately responsible. It is the defendant who is guilty (20) of 'conceiving and carrying out the crime'.²²

Despite this emphasis, the plaintiff admits that the concubine 'deliberated and decided' (ἐβουλεύετο . . . βουλευομένῃ) how and when to give the drug. It might therefore be argued that the concubine by her own decision had broken the chain of causation connecting the stepmother to the death. The author clearly foresees this argument, that the concubine herself 'planned', deliberated, and decided the fatal turn of events, and thus it was she who was guilty of 'planning'. To answer that argument he insists that the concubine, even in her 'decision', was 'following the [stepmother's] prescriptions'. The concubine's 'decision' was clearly a causal factor, and the plaintiff must somehow show that it does not negate the stepmother's responsibility.

This problem of causation is similar to that of Antiphon 6 (as we shall see), where the defendant is held responsible as 'planner' in the actions of a subordinate, even though the subordinate acted without specific instructions to admininster the drug. A certain preoccupation with the problem of indirect causation and culpability for wrongs in which others were instrumental is evident in the drama of this period, to which we turn in the conclusion to this chapter and the first section of the next. We also find a radical exposition of this topic, as though it had become a notorious crux, in *Tetralogy* 3: here it is debated which of the parties is culpable as 'planner' or instigator in a case where the victim supposedly provoked the defendant's violent response and the plaintiffs themselves may be indirectly responsible for the physician's fatal treatment (Chs. 7 §1.2.3; 8 §2). In the case against the stepmother, the concept of planning is also likely to be crucial to the dispute.

To make the argument that the fatal dosage was decided by the concubine on her own initiative and contrary to any instructions, the defence would have to concede the very facts otherwise in question. To argue that she did not intend to kill, they must admit that she gave the drug with instructions or at least the understanding that it be used to reawaken the men's affections. The fact that the concubine altered the dosage (perhaps her own admission under

---

²² The manuscripts at §20 read καὶ ἐνθυμηθεῖσα καὶ χειρουργήσασα. The latter term, 'carrying out the crime', has been moved up by most editors to modify the concubine rather than the stepmother.

torture) is thus likely to be one of the matters that the defence can be expected to introduce in their own case, as proof that the defendant did not instigate or intend for the woman to kill; what proved to be lethal dosage resulted from the concubine's indiscretion. It is therefore reasonable to suppose that the plaintiff mentioned this detail not because he failed to see its significance but precisely because he anticipated the uses that the defence would make of it, and he therefore set about laying the groundwork for his rebuttal.

If he could not prove the stepmother guilty of wilful instigation on strict construction of the law, he could still make his case by drawing upon ambiguities latent in the legal concept of malice. Thus he portrays the concubine as driven to desperate measures to regain her partner's affection; and he can surely suggest that the stepmother should reasonably have supposed she would endanger the lives of the two men. The case may well turn upon this tenuous causal connection. Is the defendant responsible for the reckless actions of an accomplice whom she aided and encouraged? The plaintiff thus casts his opening narrative in such a way as to conjure in the minds of the jury a vision of the concubine as an instrument of the stepmother's plot. And based upon this image, he intends to refute the defence argument on state of mind, that the defendant is not guilty of intent or instigation. There is, as we shall see, evidence in the text that the second speech would proceed along these lines.

2.2   The Case for the Plaintiff

The most revealing representation of what the defence would argue and how the plaintiff would answer comes after the narrative in the *prokatalēpsis* proper, the anticipation of defence arguments: the defence will admit to complicity but plead that the defendant be spared for innocence of malice:

In behalf of the murderess he will make a plea that is lawless, impious, and unconscionable . . . begging [for a reprieve] for a crime she could not persuade herself not to devise.

. . . He will plead for his mother's life, that she who took life *recklessly* and without fear of god may not pay the penalty for her wrong, if he can persuade you.   (Ant. 1. 22–3)

Gernet saw fit to alter the text: where the manuscripts read 'recklessly' or 'without design' (ἀβούλως), he would emend to 'with premeditation' (ἐπιβούλως). But the emendation is unwarranted. The parallel modifier 'without fear of god' or 'without god's guidance' (ἀθέως) may also suggest that she acted irresponsibly rather than purposefully.[23] Given the emphasis on prior design, it is likely that the plaintiff is here anticipating the argument that the woman acted without planning or premeditation of murder, but was herself a victim of misfortune. Such is the most likely meaning of the plaintiff's insistence upon a point that would otherwise seem superfluous, that the victim 'died unintentionally' or perished 'against his will' (§§25–6). The defence was not about to argue that the victim wanted to die. They would insist that the woman had not intended to harm her husband but to regain his affections. She had herself suffered an unfortunate loss, and was therefore not guilty of 'planning' or malice aforethought.

To answer this argument the plaintiff invokes a concept of recklessness or negligence, *aboulia*. This concept derives from the legal construct of 'planning' or determining an unintended wrong and it involves an interesting approximation to the modern conception of negligence.[24] We shall examine the parallel in detail in the next chapter, but here it is useful to observe certain aspects of negligence that may affect our judgement of the argument. A particularly revealing case, and one which is quite pertinent to our inquiry, became an important precedent for criminal negligence in German law:[25]

In a case decided 1880 the accused left a wine bottle containing a solution of arsenic on the window-sill and left the house, though she should have foreseen that her husband, addicted to drink, might taste it, which he did, with fatal consequences. She was convicted of negligent killing (fahrlässige Tötung), despite the intervening carelessness of the husband, since 'without her act of putting in position and leaving the bottle of poison, the husband of the accused would not have been killed, hence the occurrence of the whole consequence was conditioned by this conduct on her part and therefore her conduct was fully causal'.

Such would be the stepmother's offence, if she did not instigate a murder. If she merely provided the drug unwittingly and it was

<hr />

[23] See *LSJ* s.v. ἄθεος. For the emphasis on prior design in Ant. 1, cf. §§ 3, 5–6, 23, 25–6.

[24] Cf. Maschke, *Willenslehre*, ch. 3, esp. 79–81 on *aboulia* in *Tetr.* 3.

[25] Quoted by H. L. A. Hart and T. Honoré, *Causation in the Law* (Oxford, 1985), 444, from *Entscheidungen des Reichsgerichts in Strafsachen*, 1 (1880), 373–4, regarding 'Condition Theory' and *sine qua non* (442–5).

solely the concubine's initiative to give the drug in lethal dosage, the stepmother's act was none the less causal, *sine qua non*. A similar conception can be detected in the arguments of Antiphon 6 and *Tetralogies* 2 and 3 (Ch. 7 §1.2). Such involvement would be defined as 'unintentional planning'—and in the Palladium court, just as in a modern court, she might have been found liable on grounds similar to those that convicted the German wife.

In the Areopagus court, however, where we have established that this trial took place, the verdict would apparently go in the woman's favour if her action were construed in this way. As we saw in *Magna Moralia* 1188ᵇ (§1.3) the case might well be decided on the question of intent alone. If, on the other hand, it can be shown that the stepmother provided the drug with specific instruction or obvious understanding that the drug be given to her husband in the approximate dosage, *and if she had reason to expect serious injury*, then it is possible to construe her act of recklessness as a kind of voluntary wrong. Such was likely to be a viable case for the prosecution in Antiphon 1, as we may judge from other treatments of the problematic concept.

In Antiphon 6 'planning' ironically describes what we identify as negligence. In Antiphon 1 the author appears to be following another line of reasoning from the same ambiguous concept. In the *prokatalēpsis* he anticipates the argument that the defendant acted without planning or premeditation of murder. In making such a plea, the defence invites a charge of recklessness, *aboulia*, conveying a kind of wilful disregard scarcely distinct from intentional wrongdoing. In the third Tetralogy, *aboulia* is one of the possible degrees of culpability that the defence must answer, in a case where the charge is equivalent to intentional homicide; in that case 'recklessness' describes killing in anger, without restraint (*akolasia*).[26]

Plato's treatment of comparable offences in the *Laws* suggests that killing in anger or passion, even without specific intent, was sometimes construed as a kind of wilful homicide. Plato himself proposes a distinction between a killing in anger that is calculated and analogous to murder and an act of recklessness, in the passion of the moment, that seems closer to unintended death. But he is clearly making a difficult moral distinction where there was no rec-

---

[26] *Tetr.* 3. 2. 4; on this passage, and the following, see Ch. 8 §2.

ognized difference in the law. He attempts to justify this distinction at some length.[27]

We must recognize two types of killing that commonly arise from impulse of emotion but would be more precisely treated separately, as intentional and unintentional acts respectively. Indeed, each is a semblance: the man who guards his anger and takes his vengeance not all of a sudden but afterward, with premeditation, resembles the intentional; but he who without storing up his rage, rather acting (on impulse), on the spur of the moment, without premeditation, conversely resembles the unintentional—though even this is *not entirely without intent* but a semblance of the unintentional. So it is difficult to define killings done in anger, whether they are (all) intentional or some must be considered unintentional. It is most accurate to distinguish between them—by premeditation and without premeditation (*epiboulē* . . . *aproboulia*)—and assign more severe penalties to those who kill in anger with premeditation, but more lenient remedies for those whose act is sudden and uncalculated.

Plato's rather pointed treatment of this distinction suggests that there was no generally accepted criterion for the culpability of wrongs done under the compelling force of emotion. Some cases clearly lacked the more serious element of premeditation but were not altogether free of 'malice aforethought'. Antiphon's case is built upon this undifferentiated notion of reckless wrong, driven by strong emotion: even if defendant gave the drug without *specific intent* to kill, if she foresaw the risk but her passion or jealousy drove her to disregard the danger and thus to participate in a reckless and fatal act, she may be found guilty of malice aforethought.

In modern jurisprudence it remains problematic whether to distinguish between 'specific intent' and malice aforethought in the broader sense—whether we should punish more severely the injury that is done with the specific aim of causing the injury than we do the reckless act, committed without regard for the risk. 'Malice aforethought' certainly encompasses the latter notion. In Sir James Stephen's venerable formulation, it is defined as 'knowledge that the act which causes death will probably cause the death of or grievous bodily harm to some person, whether such person is the person actually killed or not, although such knowledge is accompanied by indifference whether death or grievous bodily harm is caused or

---

[27] *Laws* 9. 866d–67b.

not, or [even] by a wish that it may not be caused'.[28] The difference
between manslaughter and murder lies wholly in the 'degree of
danger'. If, in our case, the stepmother had no reason to expect
death or serious injury from the drug, it is manslaughter; if she
foresaw or should reasonably have foreseen the danger, then it is
murder.[29]

But to understand the ancient reckoning we cannot be overly
burdened by the modern behavioural models. *We* readily assume
that state of mind is an objective reality apart from outward actions
and utterances, and that we have only remote access to this inner
reality through a calculus of outward indications. If we know that
an assailant pursued the victim with a weapon in hand or that the
drug he gave was a known poison, then we may deduce malice from
these circumstances, even if we have no direct evidence of motive.
We may harbour some doubt as to whether it was actually the
agent's intent to murder the victim or merely to do him harm, and
a defendant who can conjure up reasonable doubt may win acquittal. But ordinarily we have no problem with the presumption that
malice aforethought was precisely the inner state of mind of a killer
whose act is by its very nature murderous. In early modern legal
thinking the principle of 'implied malice' was constructed to
encompass such instances, where there are no 'antecedent menaces'
but we assume *mens rea* from the character of the act itself.[30]
Elegant paradigms have evolved from it.[31]

[28] Stephen, *Digest of Criminal Law*, art. 223, followed by Holmes, *Common Law*,
44; W. L. Clark's *Handbook of Criminal Law*[3], ed. W. Mikell (St Paul, Minn., 1915),
ch. 8 §71. Holmes's second lecture is largely devoted to this problem: see esp. 54,
'Acts should be judged by their tendency under the known circumstances, not by
the actual intent which accompanies them'; 61, [in actual crimes, as opposed to
'attempts'] 'mens rea is wholly unnecessary, and all reference to [state of] consciousness is misleading.'

[29] Cf. Holmes, *Common Law*, 50–1. He is sceptical of the doctrine that provocation mitigates the offence and may reduce murder to manslaughter; this point is not
without relevance to the present case but will be more pertinent to the discussion of
Tetr. 3 in Ch. 8 §2.

[30] See Blackstone, defining 'malice prepense' as either express or implied: *Com.*
iv. 199–200. Express malice is found 'when one, with a sedate deliberate mind and
formed design doth kill another: which formed design is evidenced by external circumstances discovering that inward intention; as lying in wait, antecedent menaces,
former grudges, and concerted schemes to do him some bodily harm.' 'Implied malice' is found in such cases as 'where a man wilfully poisons another . . . though no
particular enmity can be proved.'

[31] See R. A. Duff's *Intention, Agency and Criminal Liability* (Oxford, 1990), esp.
the paradigm posed pp. 38–73. Duff offers such criteria as these: an agent's intent

In the ancient model implied malice is a distinction of little consequence. Since the justices are not asked to determine what actually happened, they are not much interested in conjuring up the
killer's state of mind as a virtual reality. They are called upon *to
validate the claim* of one party over the other. For that reason they
are preoccupied with express malice revealed in 'antecedent menaces'. It is those overt acts and utterances demonstrating a preconceived threat that furnish the plaintiff with his grounds for
swearing to 'know well' the killer's mind. Because he looks to the
overt acts rather than the inner mind, he is unconcerned with
implied malice and untroubled by the distinction between recklessness and specific intent.

Instead our plaintiff must prove his own conviction. How has *he*
determined that the death was caused by malice aforethought
rather than unfortunate accident? He must have some basis for his
own conviction that the killing had this distinct character. He
addresses this problem in his one piece of proof beyond the father's
dying words, the challenge to torture.

For I wanted to examine the slaves under torture, since they knew that
even earlier this woman . . . was caught in the act of devising our father's
death by poisoning, and did not deny it, except to claim that she gave the
drug not for his death but as a love potion.   (9)

The slaves were not to be questioned on the fatal incident itself but
in support of the claim that the woman had *previously* tried to drug
her husband and was discovered *ep' autophōroi*. What does this contribute to the plaintiff's case? It suggests *to us* perhaps a probability bearing on the fact of the defendant's involvement: it seems to
establish a pattern. But the ancient text gives no indication that this
was indeed its implication—there is no argument from probability
to the effect that, 'she tried it once; she was likely to do it again'. In
the scheme of the argument, it goes directly to the issue of *pronoia*,
that she knew or should reasonably have anticipated the lethal consequences.

What after all can it mean that she was 'caught in the act' of
devising her husband's death? The ordinary meaning of the legal

is proved 'if, and only if, (1) he would not act thus if he did not have that desire and
that belief; and (2) if he believed that some other possible action would achieve the
desired result more efficiently, he would do that action instead' (59). Cf. 61–3, on the
'test of failure' (if an action would be a 'failure' if it does not achieve a certain result,
then that result is what the agent intends).

phrase *ep' autophōrōi* would tend to exclude the notion that she was merely caught in the *attempt*, preparing the drug or trying unsuccessfully to administer it. In general, the Athenians did not recognize a wrong in the attempt or the intent alone. The technical phrase *ep' autophōrōi* in particular would ordinarily indicate that she was caught in the very commission or consequence of the crime.[32] The likely implication is that she had actually administered the drug on a previous occasion, and her husband had been suspicious of the symptoms, perhaps found the concoction in her posssession, and forced her to confess. The slaves were to testify under torture to this discovery. Their testimony on the earlier incident would prove nothing with regard to the fatality itself. But it would have shown that the serious effects of the drug were known and therefore that the wife knowingly persisted in a dangerous device, with a kind of malice that neither the ancient jurist nor his modern counterpart can easily distinguish from murderous intent.

This means of proving prior knowledge is precisely the kind of method required by the law. The plaintiff is called upon to swear that his kinsmen has died, that so-and-so is liable as the killer, and that he or she acted with *pronoia*. In order for the plaintiff to swear to his own conviction, that he 'knows well' that defendant acted in this state of mind, he relies upon overt acts indicating prior knowledge or expectation of the lethal effects. He does not have to prove specific intent but only that she must have known the mortal peril of what she was doing. At the very least, she co-operated in an act that she knew to be hazardous to her husband. Such recklessness, *aboulia*, is tantamount to malice aforethought. The plaintiff can demonstrate his conviction that the wrong was done with this reckless malice by demanding that the slaves be questioned under torture regarding the previous incident from which the hazardous effects of the potion were known.

2.3   Anticipation and Rebuttal

If we assume that the argument on malice proceeded along these lines, then we can resolve one of the most troublesome discrepancies in the speech, and this solution may give us a rare insight into the earliest speechwriter's art. Consider the plaintiff's first and last

---

[32] See Hansen, *Apagoge*, 48–52, for ἐπ' αὐτοφώρῳ, in discovery of stolen goods (as in Roman *furtum manifestum*); and cf. Ch. 9 §1.3.

formulations of his adversary's position, the introduction to the main proof and the oddly parallel passage in 'the second epilogue'.[33]

I am amazed at my brother, whatever reason he had to become my adversary . . .Yet surely he will not say this, that he knows well his mother did not kill our father. (5–7) I am amazed at my brother's audacity and his reasoning, that he would swear for his mother that he knows well this she did not do. How could anyone know well what he was not present to witness? (28–30)

The second passage is problematic on two counts: it follows what would appear to be the proper epilogue to the speech—already concluding with an appeal to the judges for sympathy toward the victim, righteous retribution toward the guilty. And the plaintiff seems to admit in this 'second epilogue' what he has expressly denied in the introduction.[34]

Now the first passage introduces the challenge-to-torture that the defence rejected: when the half-brother had an opportunity to establish his mother's innocence by the only sure test, he refused. The second passage is directly addressed to the defender's oath. Solmsen therefore explained the disjointed arrangement by assuming that the formal proofs dictate the structure of the argument. Rather than link the two arguments together as proving what we would call 'consciousness of guilt', the two proofs are separate and self-contained, one addressed to the challenge to torture (basanos), the other to the oath itself. There is certainly something to this observation: all of the elements in the speech gravitate around the oath and the challenge to torture. But this organizational principle does not entirely explain the doublet. Unless we are content to alter the text at will, we should look for an important distinction between the first formulation of the defence position and the second.

[33] Θαυμάζω δ' ἔγωγε καὶ τοῦ ἀδελφοῦ, ἥντινά ποτε γνώμην ἔχων ἀντίδικος καθέστηκε πρὸς ἐμέ . . . Καὶ οὐ τοῦτό γ' ἐρεῖ, ὡς εὖ οἶδεν ὅτι γ' οὐκ ἀπέκτεινεν ἡ μήτηρ αὐτοῦ τὸν πατέρα (5–7). Θαυμάζω δὲ ἔγωγε τῆς τόλμης τοῦ ἀδελφοῦ καὶ τῆς διανοίας, τὸ διομόσασθαι ὑπὲρ τῆς μητρὸς εὖ εἰδέναι μὴ πεποιηκυῖαν ταῦτα, Πῶς γὰρ ἄν τις εὖ εἰδείη οἷς μὴ παρεγένετο αὐτός; (28–30).

[34] To resolve the apparent discrepancy it was long ago suggested by Thalheim that we delete the first negative (reading at §6, καίτοι τοῦτο γ' ἐρεῖ, 'he will claim . . . '). But the emendation is unwarranted. The argument that follows clearly demands the negative: he will not (or cannot) claim he knows well . . . for when he had the opportunity to know the truth [by torture] . . . he was unwilling.'

The defence position is summarized in 'the second epilogue' with the vague phrase 'this she did not do'. Such a turn of phrase relies upon the immediate context to make clear what 'this' act might be. If we turn back to the end of the first epilogue (§27), we find very little to help us—'just as she killed him, neither fearing nor feeling shame before gods, heroes, or mankind, so also may she . . . finding neither pity, shame, nor remorse, meet with the retribution she most rightly deserves at your hands.' Somewhat earlier (23) the plaintiff made clear that he expects the defence to admit to complicity in the killing but to plead that the defendant acted without prior design, *aboulōs*. In the second epilogue he is evidently continuing his argument against that plea but answering what his brother would argue in his first speech. The defender could be expected to deny the charge of malice aforethought, and the plaintiff will treat this as the burden of his oath—'*this* she did not do'.

If this is indeed the connection of thought, then the 'second epilogue' appears to convey the speech-writer's outline or précis for the plaintiff's *second speech*, in rebuttal to the arguments anticipated in the first speech for the defence.[35] There are a number of points in favour of this hypothesis. A protest to the same effect, 'I am amazed at my opponent's audacity', is found in most of the second speeches of the *Tetralogies*.[36] As for the brevity of this rebuttal, approximately one-ninth the length of the earlier argument, the evidence of the fourth century indicates that indeed considerably less time was allotted to the second speech than the first.[37] And reading this passage as a focus for rebuttal, it is reasonable to suppose that the speech-writer would have counselled his client in various strategies, considering what the defence might say. The substance of the plea and the direction of the argument they knew, but precisely what wording and what emphasis the defence might use, remained uncertain. For that reason the speech-writer wrote simply, 'I am amazed . . . that he would swear he "knows well", *this* she did not do.'[38]

In what follows, the speech-writer expects the defence to have argued that the defendant did not plot or instigate the killing. He

---

[35] To my knowledge this hypothesis has never been pursued, but cf. Wilamowitz, 'Erste Rede', 209.

[36] Cf. *Tetr.* 1. 3. 1; *Tetr.* 2. 3. 1, 4; *Tetr.* 3. 3. 1, 4.   [37] *Ath. Pol.* 67. 2.

[38] In delivery 'this' may then be elaborated in the very wording that the defence has used, just as the lame εὖ οἶδα of the defence oath is echoed throughout, esp. 6–7, 11, 13, ἔγωγ᾽ εὖ οἶδα.

takes up the conventional worst case of 'murder without witnesses' (Ch. 5. §1) and adapts it to the even more inscrutable problem of plotting and conspiracy (28): 'For how could anyone know well what he was not himself present to witness? Those who *plot* murder . . . do not *devise their schemes and make their preparations* in front of witnesses.'

This adaptation of the common topic brings our plaintiff back to the contest of oaths: the plaintiff is strong in the conviction of his father's dying charge; his brother has refused to confirm his oath by the only available means, submitting the slaves for torture. The final elaboration on that theme now reveals something more of what was anticipated in arguments for the defence: those who are the targets of a murder plot are themselves taken unawares; but if they can, they call upon their nearest and dearest to avenge them— as our plaintiff claims he was charged. 'Thus my father in the throes of fatal illness, charged me, when I was yet a child,' he says pointedly, '—and *not* his slaves.' This turn of the argument probably furnishes more than a touch of pathos: it responds to a likely claim by the defence that *they* had challenged the plaintiff to interrogate slaves under torture, whether the father had in fact made his suspicions known or demanded vengeance in their hearing.[39] As it stands, without further explanation of defence arguments, this reference to the possibility that slaves might have witnessed the victim's statement seems singularly irrelevant. But if it followed a speech for the defence in which an argument based on slave-torture had been developed with some emphasis, then it answers a serious challenge to the plaintiff's conviction: 'Would our father not have revealed his suspicions to others close to him? Why did our brother (the plaintiff) not pursue the available means to corroborate his claim?'

Finally, there is a strong indication that this second epilogue belongs to the second speech, in the closing paragraph itself (31): 'For my part, the tale is told; I have come to the aid of the victim and the law. The rest is now for you to decide for yourselves, to judge what is just. I think the gods below will care for those who are wronged.' This closing is more suited to the second prosecution speech than to the first; it is again paralleled in the second speeches of the *Tetralogies*. And the *Tetralogies*, whether Antiphon's work or

---

[39] So also reasons Heitsch, *Antiphon*, 27.

a product of the next generation, certainly demonstrate a similar technique for clinching the case in the second speech.

The defence is expected to concede that the stepmother provided the drug but to deny that she plotted or intended it to cause the victim's death. They will have challenged the plaintiff's oath that his father swore him to vengeance for a murder *he* knew to be premeditated. In the absence of slave testimony, this hearsay is the only evidence indicating malice aforethought. Had the plaintiff wished to establish his father's charge beyond question, he should have been willing to examine the slaves who were present in the house. To this the plaintiff will answer that the victim of a premeditated plot, if he has but a short time to assure himself of vengeance, will call upon his closest kin and not his slaves to bear witness.

§3. Conclusions and Parallels

In this chapter I have offered a new reconstruction of the puzzling case in Antiphon 1. I have tried to make few assumptions beyond the most likely implications of the argument, and I have avoided emending the text, to which other commentators have often resorted. We cannot entirely discount the possibility that this speech is an artificial demonstration of technique applied to the notorious lost cause. But the most natural interpretation of this document is that it is, as it purports to be, an authentic example of the speech-writer's art, representing arguments for others to deliver in court. Our findings on formative procedures and principles (Chs. 2–5) are consistent with this reading of our earliest speech-for-trial. It will be helpful to summarize these implications and consider a few parallels, first in regard to the method of argument, then the concepts of legal reasoning.

3.1 Proof and Probability: *Tetralogy* 1 and Lysias *Against Mikines*

To a modern reader the most puzzling feature of Antiphon 1 is likely to be the utter lack of any serious investigation of what actually happened or what the defendant specifically intended. Beyond the hypothetical narrative, there is nothing in this speech that attempts to establish what precisely the defendant did to bring about the fatality. Instead the judges are called upon to weigh the ponderous instruments of oath and challenge to torture. This emphasis upon the formal representations, to the virtual disregard of objective facts, was partly a legacy of archaic justice: *dikē phonou* was devised as a means of settling claims, not as a method for discovering the truth. And the preponderance of representation over reality was reinforced by the practical limitations: there was no forensic method to deal with physical evidence and no examination of witnesses to get at the truth.

An oath is, of course, an affirmation about facts—the plaintiff swears to the fact of death, that defendant is the killer, and that she acted in a certain frame of mind. But the oaths are first of all affirmations about what the litigant 'knows well' or honestly believes. And neither our plaintiff nor his adversary seems to be at all interested in getting beyond the representation to discover hidden facts. We might expect the plaintiff to to draw some contradiction between his adversary's claim and the proved or probable circumstances: 'my opponent swears his mother is innocent but circumstances show this is *not the case*.' Instead our plaintiff argues, 'my brother swears "this she did not do", but circumstances show that this is *not his honest conviction*'. Now it is possible that the judges were to reason inwardly from this line of argument, much as we would regard 'consciousness of guilt' as circumstantial evidence on the crime itself. But neither this speech nor the next, Antiphon 6, suggests that the ancient judges were expected to do so. Instead they are called upon to determine which party swears more truly, and they will make that determination not upon a reckoning of the facts but a weighing of the challenges and other demonstrations of conviction.

The plaintiff insists that he is prosecuting at the earliest opportunity. He swears upon his father's dying word. And he has challenged his brother to question the slaves under torture regarding events prior to the fatality. He has also rejected his brother's challenge to torture the slaves regarding the father's command. The whole of the speech focuses upon these formal means of proof. Our plaintiff must show that his conduct in all these processual acts has a logical consistency, that he has steadfastly demonstrated his conviction and has not shirked any opportunity to test his claim.

The first argument (5–13) is entirely devoted to a reckoning of the oath and the challenge as processual acts. Our plaintiff insists that his handling of the challenge proves the justice of his cause, 'that he is righteously prosecuting his father's killer'. As evidence (*tekmērion*) of his conviction, he agreed to a precise written protocol for the interrogation (10). His brother refused. But had the plaintiff refused a challenge on this question, his brother would surely claim it constituted grounds for acquittal (11). How then can he swear that he 'knows well' of her innocence when he has not undertaken the only means of corroboration?

The challenge to torture has no probative value on the *facts* of what happened. It bears upon the plaintiff's *conviction*. The slave torture would have established that the stepmother previously drugged her husband and therefore should have anticipated the injurious effects. This evidence is crucial to the question before the court, whether she acted with malice aforethought and by 'planning'. But there is no behavioural paradigm based upon probable motive such as a modern lawyer might invoke.[40] The previous incident demonstrates at least that the defendant had prior knowledge and proceeded in reckless disregard of the risk. The outcome was therefore the product of her decision. The narrative (14–20) functions largely as a scenario to illustrate this conviction.

The focus of the dispute is upon what the sworn parties themselves have done to prove or disprove malice aforethought as a measure of guilt, not upon what the judges might decide about the defendant's specific intent. The anticipation of defence arguments (21–4) serves to define this contest of conviction: the brother will plead in his mother's behalf that she should not have to pay the penalty for what she did recklessly (*aboulōs*). In the first speech for the defence the brother would attempt to corroborate his oath in his mother's behalf by every means available: he would attempt to impeach the plaintiff's oath on grounds that *he* refused to interrogate slaves under torture as to whether any had witnessed the victim's dying accusation. But in affirming his oath that he 'knew well' of his mother's innocence, the defender would soon find himself all the more inextricably entangled in the causal web. In the 'second

---

[40] See above, n. 31, on Duff's *Intention*. Among relevant criteria, the judges might be asked to consider, 'if [defendant] believed that some other possible action would achieve the desired result more efficiently, [she] would do that action instead' (59). That is, if she truly acted for love rather than malice, surely there were other and less dangerous means to this end; but she chose the known hazard. There is obviously no reasoning along such lines in our speech.

epilogue' (28–31), our plaintiff asks again: How can he swear on his own conviction that his mother is innocent of malice? Now the implications of malice have grown beyond simple instigation to a form of reckless endangerment that the defender did not perhaps fully foresee when he swore 'this she did not do'. And in the face of this unresolved implication the judges are likely to suspect that the oath of the defender, for all his earnest protestation, is worthless.

Thus the argumentation in Antiphon 1 is structured around the formal, non-conjectural instruments of proof—oath and challenge to slave-torture. This arrangement illustrates the organizing principle that Solmsen found characteristic of Antiphon's court speeches. But it is a pattern dictated by the traditional procedure rather than a sign that the author's command of artful argument was limited. In the ritualistic *dikai phonou*, the oaths and other instruments define the orbits of the dispute. The circumstantial proofs are structured around them.

It is quite clear that the traditional proofs are not truly 'irrational': they do not rely upon arbitrary and extraneous indicators. There is no immediate sense that divine intervention would guarantee the outcome. The argumentation is a *systematic* reckoning, not of the facts but of processual representation. The treatment of oath and challenge-to-torture reveals a mode of legal reasoning that Weber described as 'formal rationalism'.[41] This type of justice characteristically develops from the traditional, religious means of resolving disputes: the forms by which gods and spirits were once invoked to decide the case are largely retained, but the focus has shifted from the spiritual agents to the adversaries themselves. Theirs is the right and the burden of proof to establish their claims: they do so by making every effort to arrive at an honest conviction of what they have sworn. They do not expect the judges to make their own determination of what the defendant did or intended.

In this respect the speech differs from the mode of reasoning typical of other Athenian procedures that were tried before ordinary juries of the people. The mode of judgement that prevailed in the people's courts may be characterized as 'substantive rationalism': judgement is dictated by considerations of substantive norms—social justice, community interests, democratic values—rather than formalistic criteria. The *Tetralogies* generally demonstrate this

---

[41] See Rheinstein (ed.), *Weber on Law in Economy and Society*, esp. 227–8. Cf. Ch. 1 §2.2.

form of reckoning. Here the traditional religious concerns are addressed as a matter of social expediency, not simply as a factor confirming the speaker's conviction as it is in the court speeches. Miasma becomes a matter of the judges' duty in the interests of the community; they are to guard against the threat of disaster looming over the *polis*, and they must therefore decide for themselves who is the killer.

In its outlook and method, then, the speech-for-trial is diametrically opposed to the corresponding *Tetralogy*; it also appears to be markedly different from Lysias' *Mikines*, which was probably an essay on a similar theme. In the *Tetralogy* the author has contrived a scenario based upon the bare minimum of formal proof, evading both the restriction against hearsay and the restriction against testimony of slaves without torture. By his scenario he defies the ordinary evidentiary requirements. The whole of his argument is devoted to 'conjecture on the fact', not to the oaths and challenges as tests of conviction.

In the *Mikines* it looks as though even the minimal requirement for formal proof has been evaded: there was no firsthand testimony of either free men or slaves.[42] One fragment suggests that the defendant came under suspicion because he was conspicuously absent from the banquet, not because he was seen pursuing the victim. From another fragment it appears that the defendant's own slaves were somehow directly involved but unavailable for torture: presumably they were caught in the act and slain. The report in the scholia to Hermogenes refers to the argument from reverse probability—'Would I have used my own slaves!' It is possible, of course, that slave testimony was taken and the reverse probability was urged in contradiction to it; but this seems less likely. The hypothesis to the *Tetralogy* and the scholia to Hermogenes agree that the *Mikines* was a *tour de force* in conjecture as to the fact, not reasoning from non-technical proof. Apparently the defendant was implicated only by the involvement of his slaves and other circumstantial evidence. In any event, the *Mikines* would appear to have been an even more daring demonstration of proof from absolute probability than the *Tetralogy*.

The speech-for-trial on the other hand is wholly preoccupied with tests of conviction, and it is this traditional character that

---

[42] See Ch. 5 §1, at nn. 31–5.

accounts for the extraordinary lack of concern for what we would regard as real evidence. The plaintiff bases his case upon his father's dying charge. This is an admissible form of hearsay, and in this respect the case is superficially similar to the evidence in *Tetralogy* 1; in both cases we have the witnesses' dying words reported on hearsay. But the evidence in Antiphon 1 is by its very nature a somewhat more credible source of proof—if we accept that the bond of oath is still binding, enforced by religious conviction and social conscience.[43] To put it bluntly, it was far less repugnant for the plaintiffs in *Tetralogy* 1 to have manipulated, coerced, or simply fabricated the testimony of their slave, than for the plaintiff in Antiphon 1 to swear falsely to his father's dying words. The value of such indirect testimony is directly proportional to the burden of shame if it were found to be false. The author of the speech-for-trial takes this moral calculus seriously; the author of the *Tetralogy* seems to have contrived his scenario as he does because the bond of oath was no longer compelling and the old formalities based upon it were discredited. By contrast, in the case *Against the Stepmother* the issue before the court is ultimately a question of whether the plaintiff himself is properly convinced of his claim and should be entitled to execute it. The judges' verdict is a validation of one claim over the other, not a finding on whether certain actions or intentions occurred. And *pronoia* is an approximation to *mens rea* especially appropriate to this reckoning: it is revealed in overt acts of prior design that a man can swear to or compel his slaves to reveal.

3.2 Malice and Popular Morality: The Stepmother and Deianira

To judge from Antiphon 1 and the other evidence we have, the focus of dispute in a murder case before the Areopagus was likely to involve this conception of malice aforethought. It is not a matter of 'specific intent'—whether the defendant acted purposely to bring about the victim's death—but more broadly whether the defendant's action could be construed as anticipating death or serious bodily harm. Murder *ek pronoias* thus encompassed some of the more oblique aspects of malice.

---

[43] For the close identification of self-worth with the estimation of one's peers in the face-to-face society, involving the effects of 'shame-culture,' see Williams, *Shame and Necessity*, esp. 75–102.

The arguments in Antiphon 1 rely upon a model of causation that is generally consistent with that of Antiphon 6. Contrary to the usual assumption, the author seems fully cognizant of the legal concept of 'planning', comprehending both intentional and unintentional involvement. To counter the plea of innocence of intent, he has devised a double strategy: in order for the defendant to be sure of acquittal on the more serious charge of intentional murder, the defence must, in effect, concede a degree of involvement that would very likely render the defendant liable to some form of settlement; there is also a good chance that the plaintiff can actually win a conviction and profit materially from it. His hopes for a conviction depend ultimately upon the ambiguous concept of 'recklessness', *aboulia*.

In his treatment of this concept Antiphon touches upon an area of ethical speculation that appears to have been of great significance in the last decades of the fifth century—the problems of guilt by intent and indirect causation. It is likely to be more than an accident of the evidence that major dramas of the decade preceding the court speeches, 431 through the 420s, have to do with scenarios illustrating this problem. Thus Euripides' Medea makes use of her children as instruments of her plot and dooms them by their complicity—a notable departure from the charter myth of their cult at Corinth. Phaedra is found guilty of connivance in the vindictive curse upon Hippolytus. And of course the most suggestive parallel is that of the *Trachiniae*, where Deianira is damned for unwitting complicity in her husband's death.[44]

The ambiguities of recklessness and intent have never been easily resolved, and the problem was all the more troublesome in Antiphon's day. The moral lessons of epic and tragedy already attest to a strong sense of the unwitting but no less culpable wrong of recklessness. It is a wrong that goes by many names but its guilt and punishment is a common and easily identifiable theme. Thus in the *Odyssey* the guilt of the suitors is sometimes characterized as reckless indulgence, *atasthalíē*. It is a particularly offensive and

---

[44] On the Deianira legend, see esp. March, *Creative Poet*, 49–77. March would date *Trachiniae* early in Sophocles' career based on supposed echoes in Bacchylides' Dithyramb 16, but see Malcolm Davies, *Sophocles Trachiniae* (Oxford, 1991), xxxii–xxxiii. Another variation on this theme, the poison misdirected, is found (a decade later?) in Euripides' *Ion*, 1205–20. See also Hart and Honoré, *Causation*, 383–4, on the case of the poisoned apple that was unwittingly given to the wrong victim, while the agent, knowing the danger, stood by and did not intervene.

self-serving disregard of social norms and the interests of others, but it often seems to involve no sense of specific intent to harm.[45] And the error of Odysseus himself, which he seems to recognize in the course of his narrative to the Phaeacians, may be similarly characterized as recklessness. The hero and his crew were repeatedly driven by impulse of spirit or will—*thumos*—to acts of adventure, heedless of consequences of which they were forewarned or which a reasonable man would fear. Thus the crew's heedless devouring of the Sun's cattle is repeatedly noticed as the cause of their ruin (first at 1. 7); and Odysseus himself, in telling the story, emphasizes his own responsibility for their suffering at the hands of Polyphemus (9. 213–29), when his *thumos* urged him to adventure. It is this singular lesson he learned in the cave of the Cyclops that strengthens his power of restraint when he bides his time plotting vengeance against the suitors (20. 17–21). The guilt of Oedipus similarly arises unintended from his anger, *orgē*, but he is none the less culpable: the recklessness with which he slew a king is driven by wrath, heedless of the indirect but inevitable consequences of bloodshed—consequences that, from a normative perspective, he should have anticipated.[46]

But the most striking parallel to the case *Against the Stepmother* is the *Trachiniae* attributed to Sophocles, probably a work of roughly the same period. Here Deianira, the wife of Heracles, undertakes a desperate remedy to regain her husband's affections; she is herself the unwitting instrument of the villain who abducted her 'with reckless hands' and died of Heracles' venomed arrow but urged her to save his blood as a talisman against lost love. The blame that attaches to Deianira is ill-defined but undeniable. Hyllus, her son, upon learning after her death that she 'did wrong unintentionally . . . intending to do good', obviously grieves for her and blames himself for her death—he too acted recklessly in condemning her. But she has purchased his remorse with her

---

[45] Of course their attempt to ambush Telemachus shows all-too-specific intent; but consider Odysseus' warning to Amphinomos (clearly a character free of specific intent to harm), 18. 126–51.

[46] For the wrath of Oedipus, cf. *OT* 335–64; 524, ὀργῇ βιασθέν; 687–99; 807, παίω δι' ὀργῆς. On the wrong of excessive violence and recklessness, see further Ch. 8 §2. There are, of course, those who will insist that Oedipus is guiltless, but cf. Williams's interpretation, *Shame and Necessity*, 67–74: the emphasis upon the voluntary as determining what it is to be 'really' responsible is as inaccurate a characterization of the Greek reckoning as it is of our own.

life.[47] Deianira herself clearly comprehends, both in making her decision and after the outcome, that her act is a desperate device of last resort; she fears unforeseen consequences but goes heedlessly on. No sooner has she sent the fatal cloak to her husband than she recognizes the rashness of her act, her 'eagerness, dubious in its outcome'. Upon learning of the disastrous result, she abandons the hope of forgiveness that the chorus offer, that the anger against her will be blunted by her innocence of intent: 'No one who shares in the evil would agree, but only one who suffers no hurt of her own.'[48] Neither she herself nor other kinsmen of the victim could be expected to forgive her reckless act. The ambiguous concept of recklessness—unwitting yet not without blame—is crucial to the tragedy, just as it is crucial to Antiphon's case against the step-mother.

In Maschke's view, it was Antiphon who opened the door on legal applications of negligence (Fahrlässigkeit, *aboulia*), and for this dubious distinction he ranks 'among the greatest jurists of all time'.[49] Maschke's estimation was based largely upon the *Tetralogies* which he thought to be authentic. Certainly from the court speeches I am inclined to share the view that Antiphon dis-covered a paradigm sufficient to answer the old problems of malice and indirect responsibility that were the chief preoccupation of murder trials. Thus in the speech *Against the Stepmother* he seizes upon the latent malice in an act of recklessness. In the sixth speech, *On the Choreutes*, to which we now turn, he will argue from the opposite position, to show how intervening factors negate the defendant's aims and break the causal chain.

---

[47] Hyllus first condemns her as 'the instigator and perpetrator' of his father's death (807–8), then forgives her for her unintended wrong (1123, 1134–9). Heracles, of course, the model of the self-absorbed hero in agony, upon learning the truth, wastes not a word upon her.

[48] *Trach.* 663–70 (προθυμίαν ἄδηλον ἔργου); 727–30.

[49] *Willenslehre*, 75–7, concluding 'So hat der Begriff der Fahrlässigkeit zuerst unter der Denkfigur einer Unterbrechung des kausal Zusammenhanges durch konkurrierendes Verschulden ihren Einzug in das attische und damit in das Recht überhaupt gehalten.' For this breakthrough Maschke places Antiphon 'in die Reihe der großen Juristen aller Zeiten' (77).

7

Antiphon 6: Causation and the Law

The last speech in Antiphon's modest corpus, for a defendant implicated in the death of a choirboy, is the earliest extant speech that can be dated with any confidence: the death occurred in the spring of 419 and the trial was held in late autumn or winter of 419/18.[1] It is also our earliest reliable evidence for the kind of case that was tried at the Palladium. The argument centres upon the peculiar concept of 'planning' or determining in unintentional homicide, and the speech is, again, our best evidence for this peculiar concept. This speech also gives us an intriguing glimpse of internal politics at Athens. There is a consensus going back to Schwartz and Wilamowitz that the defendant in this case was one of those mentioned by Thucydides as relying upon the artful arguments of Antiphon to further their cause in the courts and assembly, and scholars have been inclined to read partisan issues into the arguments. Such matters lie outside the scope of this study. On the questions that most concern us, of law and its rhetorical uses, there has been broad disagreement.[2]

Such basic considerations as the charge itself and the court that would hear it were long misconstrued. From the manuscript title giving the charge as *pharmakeias*, and from the speaker's appeal to the judges as 'most righteous' (*eusebestatoi*), it was once supposed that this case went before the high court of the Areopagus as a case

---

[1] Wilamowitz once dated the speech c.412/11, *AA* ii. 347. Despite arguments to the contrary (esp. B. Keil, *Hermes*, 29 (1894), 34) this date was upheld as recently as 1948 by C. W. Vollgraff, *Mnemos.* (1948), 269. But B. Meritt, *The Athenian Calendar of the Fifth Century* (Cambridge, Mass., 1928), 121–2, and *Athenian Year* (Berkeley, 1961), 209–12, showed that the case belongs to 419/18. This date is accepted by Heitsch, *Recht u. Argumentation*, 48 n. 1.

[2] On the charge and jurisdiction, see Blass, *Attische Beredsamkeit*, 195–6; B. Brinkmann, *De Antiphontis de Choreuta commentatio philologa* (Jena, 1887), 4–21; U. von Wilamowitz, 'Die sechste Rede des Antiphon' (Berlin, 1900), 398–416, esp. 403 (= *Kl. Schr.* iii. 201); cf. Schwartz, 'De Thrasymacho Chalcedonio', treating the *chorēgos* as one who 'molestissimum sycophantum se egisset', 122. For a summary of earlier scholarship, cf. H. Erbse, 'Über Antiphons Rede über den Choreuten', *Hermes*, 91 (1963), 24–6.

of poisoning. More recent studies have recognized that this case does not fit the formal requirement in such cases, that the defendant himself be charged with administering the drug. This case would therefore go before the Palladium as a case of unintentional killing.

Much of the argument has been found specious or irrelevant. Wilamowitz, in fact, argued against the authenticity of 'the first proem' (1–6) partly on grounds that neither the plea of mischance nor the objection to abuse of the laws has any bearing on the case. The proem is now generally accepted as genuine, but other problems of the argumentation, particularly regarding questions of causation and legality, have never been resolved. The view of Wilamowitz still, for the most part, prevails, that this speech is a masterwork of subterfuge addressed to a jury of uninformed laymen. All apparent failings can be explained away by this device. Thus Ernst Heitsch, in the most recent and to date the most thorough study of this speech, *Recht und Argumentation in Antiphons 6. Rede*, has concluded that the author evades the crucial issues and distorts the substance and wording of the charges in hopes of deluding a majority of the jurors. Now I have argued (Ch. 4 §3) that the juries of *ephetai* who heard such cases were not drawn from the ordinary panels of citizen jurors but from the Areopagus council of former archons: though certainly not immune to the artful arguments that prevailed in dicastic courts, they could be expected to have at least a better working knowledge of the laws and procedural rules. From this perspective the argumentation of this case should yield to a new and, let us hope, more coherent interpretation.

The essential facts of the case—what actually happened and what role our defendant played—are once again overshadowed by the formalities. We learn next to nothing of the events leading directly to the death of the victim. We know that a choirboy (*choreutēs*) died of a drug given him while under the supervision of men whom our defendant, the chorus producer (*chorēgos*), had appointed to carry out his duties. He fully reports his preparation for the *chorēgia* and arrangements to delegate his duties to others when that became necessary. But we never learn who decided to give the boy the drug or for what reason. The ancient hypothesis suggests plausibly enough that the drug was to improve the boy's voice, but there is no hint of this in the speech. Instead the speaker describes in detail the sequence of events leading up to the prosecution: the third day after

the victim's death, on the very day of the burial and the day before
the defendant was to prosecute in a case of official corruption, the
family of the victim publicly denounced the defendant as a homicide. They were then obliged to leave off prosecution (apparently
on a technicality). Four months later, fifty days into the new year
(419/18) when the defendant was again about to proceed against
corrupt officials, the brother of the victim, Philocrates, reopened
the case and thus forced our defendant to withdraw from the prosecution he had initiated.

This background is substantially credible, at least in so far as it
could be easily disproved from firsthand experience of the judges
themselves. But it is also likely that the speaker has misrepresented
the actions and motives of his accusers, and he may have omitted
relevant data that would have explained the timing of the prosecution. He protests that the plaintiffs have not availed themselves of
witnesses, that they have refused his challenge to examine those
who were present. This failing has led one ingenious commentator
to suppose that the poisoning was intentionally contrived by the
plaintiffs themselves, and they blocked the investigation in order to
cover their own complicity![3] There is a simpler answer.

The plaintiffs' unwillingness to pursue this evidence indicates
that the prosecutor did not intend to dispute the testimony that the
defendant was absent when the drug was given, and they were
apparently willing to concede that he gave no specific orders for
such treatment. Instead, they would base their case upon the defendant's responsibility for the actions of his subordinates. They
would rely upon a literal reading of the law—'guilty is the planner'—in the conviction that such a case could be decided on this
principle.[4] If this was their strategy, they had no reason to challenge the testimony.

We are presented with two sets of problems, matters of causation
and a question of legality. First (§1) we must try to make sense of
the concept of 'planning' or determining an unintended wrong, as
it applies to this case. Was the plaintiffs' claim that the defendant is

---

[3] K. Freeman, 'The Mystery of the Choreutes', in *Studies in Honor of
G. Norwood* (Toronto, 1952), 85–94.

[4] H. Meyer-Laurin, *Gesetz und Billigkeit im attischen Prozeß* (Weimar, 1965),
took the radical view that Athenian justice was strictly governed by the letter of the
law, with no exception for technicalities that violated principle. Cf. Heitsch, *Recht
u. Argumentation*, 3–12, and Gagarin's review of Heitsch's *Antiphon*, in *Göttingische
Gelehrte Anzeigen* 239 (1987).

liable for the actions of his subordinates, in fact, a radical departure from conventional reasoning? So our defendant argues, and so it is often assumed. But from the defendant's own treatment of the charge and from parallel usage regarding the 'planning' of an unintended outcome, the charge does not appear to be as frivolous as our defendant construes it. On the other hand, the mere fact that he misrepresents the meaning is not, as Heitsch supposes, a sure sign that Antiphon relied upon distortion to deceive a jury of laymen.

It is not the concept of unintentional planning itself that is at issue. The defendant himself seems to acknowledge the viability of this causal mechanism. It is rather the specific application of the concept that he disputes. Can the principle of guilt-by-planning implicate a defendant in a death where his culpability is at most a matter of negligence in official duties? If we follow out the reconstruction of the prosecutor's case, which Heitsch himself has so diligently begun, then I think it will be clear that this is the real question upon which the judges are asked to weigh the oaths and other tests of conviction. The plaintiffs argue that it is the defendant's activism in political trials and his decision therefore to delegate his official duties to others that determined the chain of events leading to the boy's death. It is this causal link to which the defendant so strenuously objects. He calls upon his witnesses not to establish specific facts of what actually happened but to support the substance of his plea, that he did nothing negligent or liable.

From this perspective we can proceed (§2) to the question of legality that occupies so prominent a place in this speech. Is the charge a flagrant abuse of the traditional procedure as our defendant argues, or could it be supported as a reasonable application of the law? This question will require that we evaluate the uses of oath and other instruments of proof. By one line of interpretation, these proofs appear to be largely irrelevant to the issue in dispute— whether the defendant is responsible for the actions of others. The oaths, witnesses, and challenges to torture may seem to have little bearing on this issue. But the nature of homicide proceedings suggests that a litigant's handling of such instruments must furnish proof of his conviction. There must be a moral validity to these public demonstrations of his claim; he must show that he has availed himself of every test to corroborate his oath. The judges are not asked to deliberate upon the meaning of the law: there is no juristic argument about what the lawgiver intended or what value must be given to the crucial terms. The judges are asked to decide 'which of the litigants swore righteously'.[5] The essence of our defendant's complaint is that his accusers have not adhered to the rules of law in such a way as to demonstrate such conviction.

§1. *Bouleusis*: 'Planning' and Decision

The witnesses have testified . . . From these affirmations you must closely consider the sworn statements that they have made and that I have made, as to *which of the two is more true and more righteously sworn*. They have stated under oath that I killed Diodotus by 'planning' his death; while I affirm that I did not cause his death, neither by 'planning' nor by my own hand. They charge me on these grounds, that this fellow* either ordered that the child drink the drug or made necessary or provided the drug. But I shall prove on these very grounds that I am not liable, for I neither ordered nor made necessary nor provided (the drug to be administered)— and, I may add, I was not even present when he drank it.[6]

In this passage the speaker unambiguously defines the task of the judges as a decision between the two *diomosiai*. He also summarizes the charge in terms that some commentators have regarded as a blatant distortion, calculated to deceive and confuse the judges. The chief points of misrepresentation, as Heitsch defines them, are as follows.

1. Though the prosecution have conceded that 'death occurred without malice aforethought and without preparation' (19), they charge that the defendant is guilty of 'planning the death' (βουλεύσαντα τὸν θάνατον, 16). The actual charges undoubtedly held simply that defendant caused the death 'by planning'— *bouleusas* used absolutely, without an object. But the speaker, by giving the 'planning' an object, necessarily suggests a contradiction: 'planning the death' naturally implies intent. By this view,

---

[5] Ant. 6. 16. Cf. Solon F42, and see below §2 n. 33.

[6] Ant. 6. 16–17: Μεμαρτύρηται μὲν οὖν . . . ἐξ αὐτῶν δὲ τούτων χρὴ σκοπεῖν ἅ τε οὗτοι διωμόσαντο καὶ ἃ ἐγώ, πότεροι ἀληθέστερα καὶ εὐορκότερα. Διωμόσαντο δὲ οὗτοι μὲν ἀποκτεῖναί με Διόδοτον βουλεύσαντα τὸν θάνατον, ἐγὼ δὲ μὴ ἀποκτεῖναι, μήτε χειρὶ ἐργασάμενος μήτε βουλεύσας. Αἰτιῶνται δὲ οὗτοι μὲν ἐκ τούτων, ὡς οὗτος * (17) ἐκέλευσε πιεῖν τὸν παῖδα τὸ φάρμακον ἢ ἠνάγκασεν ἢ ἔδωκεν· ἐγὼ δ' ἐξ αὐτῶν τούτων ὧν αἰτιῶνται οὗτοι ἀποφανῶ ὅτι οὐκ ἔνοχός εἰμι· οὔτε γὰρ ἐκέλευσα οὔτ' ἠνάγκασα οὔτ' ἔδωκα· καὶ ἔτι προστίθημι αὐτοῖς ὅτι οὐδὲ παρεγενόμην πίνοντι. * οὗτος AN: αἴτιος ὃς Sauppe.

addressing jurors unfamiliar with the concept of unintentional planning, the speaker hopes to convince a majority that the charges are patently self-contradictory; the plaintiffs themselves are uncertain and insincere in their allegations. This is not an unimportant point and it is certainly reasonable to assume that some among the jurors might be taken in by this phrasing; but it is also likely, as we shall see, that this phrasing was entirely within the range of causal implications involved in *bouleusis*, and it was therefore quite intelligible to the *ephetai*.

2. The second point is doubly problematic because it involves not only the defendant's recasting of the plaintiffs' case but also a somewhat doubtful reading in the text.[7] To take the text as it stands, the defendant suggests that the plaintiffs are charging him expressly with a degree of involvement that his witnesses have denied—that he 'ordered . . . or made necessary or provided'. Heitsch follows Maschke's suggestion that the phrasing 'ordered or made necessary or provided' was simply the defendant's elaboration of the concept implied in *bouleusis:* he misrepresents the charge so as to render it self-contradictory.[8]

Now Heitsch assumes that *bouleusis*, 'planning', in unintentional homicide was a valid application of the law but a somewhat recent conception: the clause regarding *bouleusis* was originally intended to apply in cases of wilful homicide, and it was applied to cases of unintentional killing only as the causal reckoning evolved.[9] Assuming then that it is a novel concept, we should not be surprised to find that a master of legal argument resorts to misrepre-

---

[7] See the note preceding. The MSS read ὡς οὗτος where most editors have followed Sauppe in the reading ὡς αἴτιος ὅς. I grant that the emendation improves the connection of thought, but it seeks to obviate a difficulty precisely where the author may be trying to raise one. The speaker has referred to himself as 'this fellow', τόνδε τὸν ἄνδρα, and this sort of self-reference may have been characteristic of this politician. The ambiguous οὗτος ('this fellow') might also help to confuse the charge of planning: 'They charge that *this fellow* (my subordinate?) ordered [the treatment] . . . but I answer that I am proved innocent by this very charge, since *I* did not order . . . the drug to be given.'

[8] Maschke, *Willenslehre*, 92–8, argued that the case was in fact a prosecution for poisoning as the manuscript title indicates, and that the plaintiffs were attempting to treat any indirect involvement as equivalent to direct agency (αὐτὸς δούς).

[9] Thus far Heitsch and Gagarin agree. In *Drakon*, Gagarin regarded the application of the law against the planner in Ant. 6 as 'abnormal'; he has since accepted the wider applicability of this concept; see his review of Heitsch, *Antiphon*, in *Gött. Gel. Anzeig.* 239 (1987), 57 n. 5. On distortion of the charge, see Heitsch, *Recht u. Argumentation*, 23, 31–2. On the original significance of the *bouleusas*, see Ch. 2 §1.2.

sentation. As Heitsch and others have supposed, the defendant distorts the charge with the expectation that a layman jury ignorant of the legalities would find it paradoxical.

But if the charge were so utterly unfamiliar as to allow for this sort of deception, it is surprising that defendant does not claim that the case had no precedent, as does the defendant in Antiphon 5. In fact, there is considerable testimony that 'planning' an unintended outcome was not an unfamiliar concept, even to the layman. And the preponderance of the evidence suggests that the homicide courts were occupied in the late fifth century by the traditional body of *ephetai*, justices distinguished by some special competence, probably committees of the Areopagus (Ch. 4 §3). This body of former archons acquired a working knowledge of the relevant law in their tenure as magistrates and through continuing service in the homicide courts and other judicial functions of the Areopagus. Antiphon could not expect them to be ignorant of 'planning'.

1.1   Historical Usage

The prevailing view that Draco's law did not envision the 'planning' of an unintentional killing—that this, to our understanding, paradoxical concept was a later extension of the concept for litigious ends—is itself highly problematical. There is no clear indication in the law as to what constitutes 'planning' other than functional opposition to '[acting] by his own hand' (χειρὶ ἐργασάμενος, *vel sim*.). We should be wary of assuming that the 'planner' of a homicide—whose guilt is asserted in the very same provision prescribing exile 'even if one kill *without* malice aforethought'—was a proper culprit only in crimes of intent. Because the verb *bouleuein*, like our 'planning' (German *ersinnen, beabsichtigen*) ordinarily implies a specific goal or aim, we are linguistically predisposed to regard 'planning' an unintended outcome as a late and sophistical semantic change. But what seems paradoxical to us appears, in fact, implicit in the ancient usage. Draco's general provision for exile and *aidesis* made no distinction between intentional and unintentional killing (Ch. 2). In this context, the most natural implication of the text as we have it would be that the crucial clause 'guilty (alike) is the planner or the perpetrator' applies similarly without distinction to all homicides, whether malicious or innocent of intent to kill.

Maschke observed that the archaic mind was reluctant to separate active participation or involvement from the end result;
Antiphon was a leader in this ethical advance. It may be more accurate to say that the break between agency and outcome was still a
distinction without a difference, before Antiphon and the thinkers
of his era made a difference of it. A killer innocent of malice was not
automatically absolved from blame for an injury that he did not
design but none the less brought about—any more than he would
be in modern tort law. The concept of 'planning' in particular
seems to presuppose an unbroken connection between a decision
and the outcome. In essence, *bouleuein* encompasses a plan of action
rather than the end result; the planner, *bouleusas*, may be strongly
disposed (*hekōn*) toward one outcome or another, but whether he
intends it or not is a separate ethical consideration.[10] The event that
he determines may well turn out other than he intended, but it is
none the less what he has decided or 'planned'.

The paradox inherent in this concept of 'planning'/deciding was
a familiar puzzle in archaic and early classical thought. Consider
Hesiod's aphorism in *Works and Days:* 'A man devises ill for himself in devising ill for another, and a wrongful plan is worst of all for
the planner (himself).'[11] The planner of evil devises his own misfortune: the unforeseen outcome is implicitly what he has
'planned'. The paradox implies a concept of 'planning' in which
there is a tenacious link between deciding or 'planning' an act and
its further consequences, even those unintended. Thus in a similar
vein, Theognis vows, 'If I should plot evil for my friend, I would
myself suffer (the harm).'[12]

Now there is no question but that 'planning' a killing *ordinarily*
implied an intended outcome. The locus classicus for the popular
conception of murder by 'planning' or instigation is Aeschylus'
Agamemnon. In the closing scenes Aegisthus emerges as the 'planner' and, as he claims, chief author of the killing though it was
Clytemnestra who struck the fatal blow. Cassandra envisions him
as 'the weakling lion plotting vengeance' in the master's bed
(1223–4). And the chorus condemns him as 'the wilful killer'

---

[10] Again, in light of Rickert's study, Ἑκών and Ἄκων (esp. 128–31, of 'willing;
participation in what is done under compulsion', e.g. Eur. *El.* 1065) we should be
wary of facile equations of volition and purpose. See Ch. 2 §1.
[11] *WD* 265–6: ἡ δὲ κακὴ βουλὴ τῷ βουλεύσαντι κακίστη.
[12] Theogn. 1088–9: εἴ ποτε βουλεύσαιμι φίλῳ κακόν, αὐτὸς ἔχοιμι.

though he plotted a murder he 'could not bear to carry out by his own hand' (1614–34).[13] But the irony of evil planning that brings the planner unintended harm, of which Hesiod and Theognis warned, may also be latent here in Clytemnestra's coup. It is, after all, the stuff of tragedy. Thus in *Medea*, the nurse fears lest the mistress, in her deranged state, may devise some new and unpredictable design, dangerous to herself and those dear to her.[14] So too in *Trachiniae*, Hyllus curses his mother as the 'planner and author' of his father's death (807–8). At this point he cannot know that she did not intend to kill, but even when he realizes that he has mistakenly driven her to take her life, there is no clear sense that either of them is acquitted of guilt because he or she acted unwittingly. Indeed the tragedy seems to presuppose that each is somehow responsible for the actions of others that they brought about through recklessness.[15]

It was not so 'bizarre' as Mashke supposed to speak of 'planning' or deciding an outcome that was unintended.[16] Such usage is indeed paradoxical but it was a familiar paradox. A revealing example is Thucydides 1. 132. 5, where we are told, the Spartans, upon learning of Pausanias' treason, were reluctant 'to decide upon an irremediable act' (βουλεῦσαί τι ἀνήκεστον). They worried that by condemning Pausanias they were determining an event that they might later wish undone.

The most relevant parallel, though surprisingly little noticed, is the argument in *Tetralogy 3*, where we find several references to 'planning' in a case where the defendant struck back without

---

[13] In earlier versions of the myth, the roles appear to have been reversed: it was Aegisthus who struck and Clytemnestra who schemed. In Aeschylus' version Clytemnestra is guilty on both counts, as planner and perpetrator. The innovation somewhat simplifies the problem of Orestes' justification in *Eumenides*. Cf. March, *Creative Poet*, 84–98.

[14] *Med.* 37: μή τι βουλεύσῃ νέον; cf. Cleon's fear or threat, 317, μή τι βουλεύσῃς κακόν.

[15] See Ch. 6 §3.2. The separation of planning and outcome is treated as a rare insight in Herodotus 5. 106, 6. 100. 5, 6. 130. 6, and esp. 7. 10δ. 2, the famous warning of Artabanus, 'to have planned well is the greatest asset' even when the best laid plans are overcome by misfortune. The insight is parodied in Ar. *Eccl.* 474: foolish planning occasionally leads to happier events than those designed.

[16] The perfect middle and passive are regularly used in the sense of 'decided': at [Aesch.] *PV* 998, the Titan laments, 'These things were decided long ago.' For political decision of unintended results, cf. Dem. *Phil.* 1. 41, βεβουλεύεσθ' οὐδὲν αὐτοὶ συμφέρον.

premeditation.[17] In this argument *bouleusis* seems to be synonymous with 'decision'; thus the prosecutor refers to the 'deciding spirit' or will of the defendant (βουλεύσασα ψυχή) as culpable for his reckless act (1. 7). The defendant pleads that the victim who 'plotted' and began the attack is responsible for the death (2. 5, τὸν ἐπιβουλεύσαντα . . . φόνεα). The prosecutor counters (3. 4), 'he claims the victim was 'planner' of the death (βουλευτὴν τοῦ θανάτου) . . . but he who struck without killing is in fact the "planner" of the blow (τῆς πληγῆς βουλευτής); he who struck with deadly force, (is planner) of the death, for the victim died as a result of defendant's wilful act.'

The usage in *Tetralogy* 3 provides at least an approximate parallel to the charge in Antiphon 6 of planning or determining an unintended death (Ch. 5 §3). And the wider usage, from Hesiod and Theognis down to the time of Thucydides, suggests that the Greek moralistic conception tended to link planning to the outcome, whether or not the outcome was specifically intended.

The legal application of the term is largely defined by initial provisions of Draco's law: guilty is the perpetrator or the planner. Culpability is either a matter of direct action or decision. This distinction is fundamental to the base meaning of the term. 'Planning' indicates a crucial choice of action, determining or deciding. This decision is demonstrated either by one's own act or by causing another to act, regardless whether the intent or expectation of that decision is fulfilled.

1.2   The Causal Argument in Antiphon 6

There is nothing in the speech for the *chorēgos* to suggest that 'planning' or decision in this sense was unfamiliar to the homicide judges. In fact Antiphon's argument is not that the concept is invalid but that the plaintiffs have wrongly applied it. This line of argument is found in the treatment of the charges §§16–19, and in the narrative, §§11–14, which focuses on certain causal implications. The argument on abuse of the law will be examined in the second section of this chapter. But here it will be helpful to follow out the treatment of planning and unintentional killing, in order to understand the causal model that is presupposed. It should be clear

---

[17] Gagarin has argued against the usual classification as 'lawful' or justifiable homicide: 'Self-Defense' *GRBS* 19 (1978), 11–20; cf. Ch. 8 §2.

that the paradox of unintentional planning was not in itself at issue, but the plaintiff bases his defence upon a narrower point of causation, one that is perhaps more subtle but also more substantive.

1.2.1 'Planning' and Killing without Intent

The phrase where Heitsch finds distortion of the charge, 'planning the death' (βουλεύσαντα τὸν θάνατον), comes in a fairly straightforward statement of the defendant's plea, and it has more to do with the uses of evidence than the legal concepts. He answers that '*neither* by [his] own hand *nor* planning' did he participate in the killing (16). He has witnesses to affirm that he had no part in the boy's treatment, that he 'neither ordered . . . nor made necessary nor provided [the drug]' (17).

Now the only mention that the charge is unintentional homicide comes thereafter, in connection with a conventional topic such as we found in Antiphon 1 and *Tetralogy* 1 (Ch. 5 §1): in a case of murder planned to avoid detection and committed without witnesses, it is necessary for the judges 'to investigate every least detail of what is said, relying rather upon conjecture'. But the nature of this trial is far different from that hypothetical case: '[here] . . . the accusers themselves admit that the fatality was *not* done with malice aforethought or preparation, and the events took place in full view of many witnesses . . . from whose testimony it would be perfectly clear if there had been any wrongdoing' (18–19). There is no suggestion that 'planning' as a concept does not properly apply; the point is that the plaintiffs' uses of evidence are improper: they are not applying themselves to the instruments by which a case such as this should be resolved. Where the defendant again refers to 'what is planned for death' (ἐπὶ θανάτῳ βουλευθέντα, 18) he is referring not to the case at hand, but *by contrast* to premeditated murder where the killer has taken every precaution to avoid suspicion. Only in such cases as those, with no proof beyond the oaths of the principals, are the judges left to decide the issue by conjecture. The only suggestion that the proceedings are improper for charges of unintentional homicide has to do with the value of formal evidence. In a case such as this where there is no suspicion of stealth or prearrangement but there are sworn statements of firsthand witnesses, the plaintiffs cannot rely on circumstantial proof.

1.2.2 Negligence

Thus by the way he addresses the charges our defendant implicitly concedes that the principle of 'planning' an unintended outcome is valid in other cases. The matter in dispute is rather a question of how that principle is to be applied in this case, whether the concept of indirect and involuntary agency in fact encompasses this defendant's involvement. He repeatedly denies any role in the causal sequence: he neither 'ordered nor made necessary nor provided' the drug to be given. By implication, if he *had* played such a role, he might be presumed guilty of 'planning' or determining the unintended fatality.

Heitsch's interpretation is guided by some suggestive parallels in German law of criminal negligence and it will be useful here to examine these criteria for what they may tell us about the underlying issues in Antiphon 6. There is first the question of whether the *chorēgos* was in any way barred from delegating his official duties to others, in which event his dereliction would be a wrong of outright 'commission'. We have no evidence and little likelihood that there was a specific provision of law restricting such arrangements or imposing any special liability for official duties delegated to others—indeed, there is some evidence that such arrangements were accepted and not uncommon.[18] Since delegating his duties was neither a violation of law nor an unreasonable deviation from the norm, the substance of the charge against the *chorēgos* would appear more or less equivalent to 'negligent omission' (fahrlässiges Unterlassen).[19]

The *chorēgos* would have had a certain responsibilty to see that the production was managed with reasonable safety and competence even after he appointed others to take over his duties. By the modern jurist's construction the case might involve such considerations as (*a*) whether the incident involved unacceptable risk, (*b*) whether the incident could have been avoided by the defendant, (*c*) whether he knew or should have known the risk and means of

---

[18] See MacDowell, 'Athenian Laws about Choruses', in *Symposion* 1982 (1985), 65–77.

[19] *Recht u. Argumentation*, 14–15. In this analysis Heitsch follows H. H. Jescheck, *Lehrbuch des Strafrechts*, 3rd edn. (Berlin, 1978). Negligent omission is determined by 'a normative criterion, that a person, by neglecting to act as expected, has caused injury to certain interests entrusted to his care by the community and otherwise unprotected'. For a more accessible account see F. Bauer and G. Walter, *Einführung in das Recht der Bundesrepublik Deutschland*, 6th edn. (Darmstadt, 1992), 140–3.

avoiding it, (*d*) whether his duties imply a specific obligation to guard against such hazards, and (*e*) whether legal justification or extenuating factors relieve the *chorēgos* of blame. On the question of unacceptable risk (*a*) the defendant says nothing. We have no way of knowing whether the fatal drug was an unusual remedy or given in dangerously high dosage. But such a charge may have been argued from the very fact that the boy died of the drug—*res ipsa loquitur*. It is also arguable (*b*), that the *chorēgos* should have taken precautions to assure that no hazardous treatment was given, at least to order that he be consulted on anything out of the ordinary. Had he done so, he could presumably have avoided the risk. We can assume (*c*), that the general risk of medication was known: the danger of *pharmakeia* was a familiar theme in drama and in court.

Our defendant seems to acknowledge criteria similar to these (*a–c*) where he insists that he exercised reasonable caution and chose men of superlative competence. But there is no direct approach to the most pertinent question in this regard, what precisely the *chorēgos* knew of his subordinate's decisions. Neither does he deal with (*d*), whether his duties expressly required him to take precautions against hazards incurred by his subordinates. Instead he bases his case primarily upon (*e*) the legal or moral justification for entrusting his duties to others: his role in the prosecution of public officials for corruption he treats as a matter of great urgency to the state as well as serious personal obligation, and it was this duty that prevented him from attending to the *chorēgia* in person.

Thus would the questions crucial to this case be defined by the German model of criminal negligence. [20] It is by this model that Heitsch has deduced certain evasions: the defendant evades the fundamental causal issue of 'negligent omission' (*a–c*), whether he is responsible for failing to intervene against foreseeable danger. Was the medication an unusual and unacceptable risk? Would it have seemed a reasonable precaution for the *chorēgos* to warn his subordinates against such risk? Did he, in fact, give his subordinates any such warning? There is no answer to these questions. The witnesses simply affirmed categorically that defendant had no part in the decision to give the drug. Proximate cause is assigned to the intervention of Chance—a device that most commentators have

---

[20] This model of negligence derives from 'Condition Theory' (Bedingungstheorie), based on *sine qua non*. See Hart and Honoré, *Causation*, 442–5, and cf. Ch. 6 §2.2.

found wholly inadequate. And there is no direct approach to (d) the crucial 'juristic problem' of whether the legal concept of *bouleusis* entails official responsibility for duties delegated to others. Did the legal conception of the planner properly extend his responsibility to this kind of connection, the transfer of official duties to others? This question the speaker studiously avoids.[21] Instead the speaker artfully diverts the attention of the judges away from the issues of law and liability by emphasizing (e) the obligation that he incurred in prosecuting major political trials; and it is this tactic that allows him to devote so much of his argument to a tale of political intrigue that is otherwise largely irrelevant.

It is the legal issue (d), the 'juristic problem', that appears to Heitsch ultimately crucial. We must somehow account for Antiphon's silence on this, apparently decisive issue. Why is the defendant not to examine the laws, to deduce the lawgiver's intent and proper applicaton of the law's provisions—as Demosthenes later interpreted the homicide laws? Are we to conclude that so profound a principle of legal conservatism governed the court that the judges would tend to favour the party that made the most direct appeal to the letter of law, that equity and exception against abuse of the law were as yet unavailable?[22] Heitsch is not altogether persuaded. He offers instead an interpretation based upon the rhetorical limitations of the trial setting: (1) citations of law were regarded essentially as a formal 'means of proof', like other documents or instruments; and (2) legalistic dispute over the fine distinctions implied in the language of the law would likely appear over-subtle to the layman jury. Moreover (3) if the defendant were to base his case upon strict construction of 'planning', it would lead him inevitably into a distinction of 'general' and 'specific' instructions. Surely, he would argue, *bouleusas* pertains only to specific orders. This line of reasoning would require him to say more precisely what charge he had given his subordinates and thus entangle him inextricably in the causal web. Therefore, as Heitsch sees it, Antiphon and his client opt for a strategy of evasion.

Heitsch's study of the reasoning in Antiphon 6 from the perspective of criminal negligence offers some valuable insights. But it

---

[21] In regard to the matter of what instruction the *chorēgos* gave to his subordinates, Heitsch himself concludes that this link in the causal chain is simply not at issue. Gagarin differs; see his review in *Gött. Gel. Anz.* 239 (1987).

[22] Such would be the implication of Meyer-Laurin's study, *Gesetz und Billigkeit*.

also suggests certain fundamental differences in the way the case would be tried in modern courts descended from Roman law and the way it was argued in ancient Athens. *Dikē phonou* is, after all, essentially a civil suit, from which the family of the victim ultimately hope to gain some retribution for their loss. It is a matter of negligence perhaps, but not a matter of *criminal* negligence. The trial is not so much a determination upon the defendant's culpability in regard to community interests: it is rather a weighing of the plaintiffs' claim against the defendant's. Therefore we should not resort to the strategy of evasion without considering the case from a more congenial perspective. Since the offence in this case is treated essentially as a wrong to the plaintiffs, the principles of liability in Anglo-American tort law are likely to yield better parallels. In the following paragraphs we shall re-examine Antiphon's causal model from this second perspective. Thereafter we turn to the treatment of various legal manœuvres in the latter part of our speech, a tale that is generally considered irrelevant (§2).

1.2.3 Fair Choice and Last Clear Chance

In his narrative our defendant gives great emphasis to the care he took in preparations and appointment of subordinates. It is reasonable to suppose that this emphasis responds to a charge by the plaintiffs that the *chorēgos* is liable for negligence on this count. There is even a suggestion that they would invoke some general statute requiring that official duties be carried out 'to the best of one's ability'. The defendant seems to address such requirements where he insists that he made arrangements as properly and fairly as he could.

When I was appointed *chorēgos* . . . I undertook the duties *to the best of my ability and with the utmost fairness.* First I had a room made ready for training the chorus, a room ideally suited to the task in my own home, in the very room where the chorus was trained when I previously acted as *chorēgos* for the Dionysia. Then I chose the chorus members *to the best of my ability*, neither fining nor forcing anyone to pay surety nor antagonizing anyone at all. But *in a manner that would be most agreeable and most suitable to both sides*, I, for my part, urged and appealed to them; and they, for their part, sent their sons willingly and gladly. (11)

There is perhaps a further indication of this line of argument in the introduction (9–10), where the defendant protests that he is being prosecuted improperly by private suit for an offence against the *polis* (to which we shall return in §2). The emphasis he puts upon the qualifications of his appointees in §§12–13 also suggests that this was one of the points upon which the prosecutors would attempt to prove negligence.

For I happened to get involved in litigation against Ariston and Philinus . . . I decided that Phanostratus should take charge, if anything were needed for the chorus; he is a fellow demesman of the plaintiffs, and an in-law of mine, to whom I gave my own daughter (in marriage), and whom I expected to take charge *with the greatest care*. In addition [I appointed] two others . . . [one] whom the tribesmen themselves had elected to choose and supervise the chorus on several occasions, thus reputed to be a reliable fellow . . . and the other . . . the very man who regularly recruits the chorus for his tribe. And [I appointed] yet a fourth man, Philip, to whom it was assigned to make purchases and expenditures, if the poet or one of the others indicated a need—*so that the boys would receive the best possible training* and not have to do without anything because of my obligation elsewhere.

There are two concepts familiar from common law that appear to be indicated here in Antiphon 6: the rule of 'last clear chance' and the principle of 'fair choice'. We have also noticed these concepts in the *Tetralogies*. Thus in *Tetralogy* 2, the case of a boy accidentally slain in spear throwing, we meet the rule of last clear chance: 'that the act of a party who failed to take the last clear chance of avoiding the harm is the "proximate cause" or "the cause" of the harm'.[23] The defender argues that the *victim* had the last chance to avoid injury; his recklessness or 'lack of precaution' was fatal (4. 7). The defendant looked and saw no one at his target; had the victim taken such precaution, he would have seen the defendant making his throw; it was thus the victim who had the last opportunity to avoid injury.[24]

The defendant in Antiphon 6 seems to be invoking a similar principle: in narrative (11–13) he lays the groundwork showing his predicament at the time of training the boys for the festival. He was called upon to prosecute an important case, and from that point on he could no longer supervise the *chorēgia* in person. Now the ancient hypothesis claims quite plausibly that the drug was given to improve the boy's singing. Let us suppose then, that the boy had

---

[23] Cf. Hart and Honoré, *Causation*, 219–25: the principle is thought to derive from a ruling of 1842, Davies v. Mann. It is often construed 'as an application of common-sense principles of causation' but is in fact a distortion.

[24] Cf. Hart and Honoré, *Causation*, 221 nn. 7–8 on rulings that plaintiff should have known or foreseen the danger.

some special condition that led the appointees to try a medication. There is no mention of similar treatment for the other boys, and surely if the drug had been administered to others without ill effect, the defendant would have mentioned this. Presumably the victim was ill or had a naturally weak voice; either condition would call for special precautions. But if the boy suffered from a special condition the chief responsibility to invoke precautions lay with the family of the victim, and the defendant insists that they sent the boy 'willingly and gladly'. It is they who had the last clear chance to avoid the risk. Conversely, once the defendant took up other duties he had no opportunity to recognize the risk and prevent harm.

Also relevant to this case is the common-law principle of 'fair choice'.[25] This causal construction is clearly anticipated or assumed in *Tetralogy* 3, the case of killing in response to assault. The victim's decisive act in striking the first blow left the defendant no choice; hence he is not responsible for the fatal blow he struck in reaction to that attack.[26] The causal connection between the attack and the defence must be demonstrated step by step. In the *Tetralogy* it is the physician's malpractice that was proximate cause. By law the physician could not be prosecuted, but since his action would appear to be the direct cause of death and it was the defendant's blow that made medical treatment necessary, the plaintiffs attempt to make the defendant responsible for the death.[27] Then the prosecution in their second speech (3. 5) suppose the defendant will place blame upon them for ordering the physician's fatal treatment; they counter that they were forced by defendant's recklessness and given no 'fair choice' but to employ a physician. The defendant then, in the final speech, follows the causal connection one step further back and argues that if he was responsible for forcing the family to seek medical care, then, on the same principle, he was forced by the victim to act as he did; he was given no fair choice but to strike back.

In the *Tetralogy* fair choice is negated by physical constraint. In Antiphon 6 the defendant argues that it was moral obligation or

[25] See Hart and Honoré, *Causation*, 156–7.

[26] There is no automatic justification for killing in self-defence; see Gagarin, 'Self-Defense', *GRBS* 19 (1978), 111–20, esp. 117–18 on Dem. 21. 72–4; cf. Ch. 8 §2.

[27] In modern tort, physician's negligence would be causal if the treatment were lethal and the original injury not fatal in itself; cf. Hart and Honoré, *Causation*, 352–4.

civic duty that forced him to act as he did. Now the 'normative criterion', the social value put upon the 'concerned citizen' as volun-
teer prosecutor, is difficult to assess in this period, but we have no
reason to doubt that the defendant's obligation to prosecute in the
political scandal he had uncovered would be judged by many
among the jury as necessary and compelling, leaving him no fair
choice but to delegate his duties in the *chorēgia*.[28] It may also have
been argued by the plaintiffs, however, that the defendant liti-
giously overstepped his moral obligation, that his role was self-
serving and unnecessary, and to this charge he will respond, as we
shall see.

These principles, fair choice and last clear chance, are at least a
closer approximation to the underlying model of liability than the
German model of criminal negligence. It is with this principle in
mind that the defendant argues the selection of the chorus was as
fair and equitable as possible: he employed no coercion nor roused
any resentment, neither assessing fines nor demanding sureties
(11). That is to say, he brought no pressure to deny the victim's
family fair choice—if they had feared for the boy's safety they could
have objected. The plaintiffs argued that the *chorēgos* by the exercise of his official authority had left them no choice but to put their
son under his care; he cannot deny that he did indeed 'order' the
boy to participate and it was on his authority that the boy was put
in the care of his subordinates. The plaintiffs may argue that it is
indeed this ordering of others to act that constitutes planning (cf.
§17). After all, the families *were* required to give surety or pay a fine
if they refused to participate. But he can claim conversely that the
families sent their sons 'willingly and gladly', he had only to 'urge
and appeal to them'.[29] By the hendiadys, 'urged and appealed', and
the emphasis upon voluntary compliance of the families, 'willingly
and gladly', he minimizes the implication that he had left the family no fair choice.

But the validity of the defendant's claim that *he* had no fair choice
rests in large part upon the value assigned to his role as a concerned
citizen in the impeachment of public officials for corruption. It is in

---

[28] Cf. Hart and Honoré, *Causation*, 146–57, on moral obligation affecting fair
choice and normative criteria: 'criteria used in settling whether interests threatened
were sufficiently important to justify risk . . . are values believed to be currently set
on them by society.' Cf. Jescheck's formulation regarding 'normative
Gesichtspunkt', above n. 19.

[29] §11: ἐγὼ μὲν ἐκέλευον καὶ ἠτούμην, οἱ δ᾽ ἑκόντες καὶ βουλόμενοι ἔπεμπον.

this connection that Chance intervened. The defendant insists that his involvement in the political trial fortuitously took his attention away from the *chorēgia*. He could not be expected to recognize the risk in delegating the *chorēgia*, and he earnestly believed he could better trust the chorus to the good offices of others than he could withdraw from the prosecution. This claim of moral obligation was largely validated by the people's verdict against Philinus *et al.* The judges may therefore have agreed that he was bound by this duty and had no fair choice but to delegate the *chorēgia*.

But there is the possibility that one or more among the subordinates could actually be impugned as untrustworthy. Our defendant's insistence upon their superior qualifications suggests perhaps that their general competence was under attack. He seems to be especially sensitive to such charges when he characterizes his son-in-law Phanostratus as 'a fellow demesman of the plaintiffs themselves and an in-law of mine, to whom I gave my own daughter [in marriage] and whom I expected to take charge of the *chorēgia* as well as possible' (12). The son-in-law is the one subordinate who had no previous experience. The *chorēgos* could not address a charge against his subordinates without hoisting himself on to the horns of a dilemma. If he admits that his son-in-law or any other subordinate was indeed guilty of reckless endangerment, the prosecution will claim that the defendant was negligent in trusting the chorus to such a character. And if he insists that there was no unusual treatment, that Phanostratus and the others acted precisely as he instructed them, then he as much as admits that he is responsible for 'planning' the fatal events.[30]

Thus he resorts to the plea that Chance intervened. The plea of mischance is often disregarded as special pleading, with no legal basis;[31] and this view is correct in so far as it was not a viable defence to cast blame upon the goddess *Tyche*. But the introduction to the issues in dispute (8–10) and the treatment of the causal sequence in narrative (11–13) strongly suggest that the defendant's case depended upon a more secular conception of Chance, that an

---

[30] Cf. Mashke, *Willenslehre*, 81: the (indirect) agent of a wrongful act or omission is substantially responsible for the damage that another brings about or suffers as a result of acting in conformity to circumstances created by him.
[31] Wilamowitz, 'Sechste Rede' 403–4, insisted that the principle of bloodguilt would not allow for transferring the blame to divine agency of *Tyche* (= *Kl. Schr.* 3: 201). He is followed by Erbse, 'Über den Choreuten', 24–6; cf. Heitsch, *Recht u. Argumentation*, 31.

extraneous factor had intervened breaking the causal connection between his own decisions and the death of the child. He argues that the unexpected coincidence, negating fair choice, relieves him of responsibility. It is this principle to which the speaker refers in his opening remarks, 'by chance rather than wrongdoing' (τύχῃ μᾶλλον ἢ ἀδικίᾳ); in the narrative, 'for it happened that I had other business' (ἐτύγχανε γάρ μοι πράγματα ὄντα, 12); and in the proof proper: 'I insist upon these points not to cast blame upon anyone . . . other than Chance, which in fact has been responsible for the deaths of many others and which neither I nor anyone else would be able to turn aside from whatever must be for each of us' (15).[32]

Thus our defendant evades what would appear to a modern reader to be a crucial question of fact: he refuses to discuss what precisely he said that might have prompted his surrogates to act as they did or what they themselves did by their own decision to break the causal connection. Where the *Tetralogies*, by contrast, analyse the causal sequence directly and self-consciously, the speaker of Antiphon 6 evidently hopes to answer the allegations without entangling himself in the chain of events. The only answer to the causal question comes in the brief narrative where he attempts to show that he himself did not have last clear chance or fair choice in the decisions that proved fatal. Neither does he devote any direct or overt argument to the legal issue—whether the concept of *bouleusis* properly entails such cases as this, where official duties were delegated to third parties. Instead he appears to answer the juristic question only by attacking the conviction of the prosecutors asserted in their oaths. Much of this rebuttal is often regarded as strictly irrelevant, but the argument itself suggests that the defendant is attempting to challeng the legality of the charges in the only manner available in the homicide courts.

§2. The Question of Law and the Contest of Oaths

The *chorēgos* argues that the plaintiffs have made nonsense of their own charges by alleging that he 'either ordered or made necessary

---

[32] A similar principle is evident in the argument on last clear chance and ἀτυχία in *Tetr.* 2. 2. 4, 7 > 3. 6 > 4. 7 (ὁ μὲν γὰρ ἀκουσίως . . . ἀλλοτρίᾳ τύχῃ κέχρηται.). On τύχη as a variable in the causal equation see Edmunds, *Chance and Intelligence in Thucydides* (Cambridge, Mass., 1975), esp. 198.

or provided' the fatal medication where an overwhelming body of testimony confirms that he gave no such instructions and was not even present when the drug was given. He approaches the trial as a decision for the judges to make between the claims that he has sworn and those of the plaintiffs.[33] The judges will decide which of the two litigants has acted upon the convictions of their oaths with the greater integrity. Have the plaintiffs sworn to something they have some way of knowing? Have they sought out the available proofs of testimony and slave-torture? Questions of law, like questions of fact, are largely incidental to this contest of oaths: they are not investigated objectively but as measures of self-verification. Thus our defendant argues that the plaintiffs have themselves indicated, by their own actions, by their indifference to the customary means of proof, and by the spurious grounds of the charge itself, that they have no serious conviction of defendant's guilt. The plaintiffs' oath is unsubstantiated and contradicted by their own admissions.

The 'instruments of judgement', as I have called them, the *atechnoi pisteis*, are given an even greater emphasis in this speech than in Antiphon 1. Indeed, the predominance of reasoning from oath, witnesses, and challenges to torture in this speech, more than any other single source, led Solmsen to conclude that public discourse generally relied upon such proofs down to the very era of these speeches. Antiphon emerges as a transitional figure, who led the way to full utilization of 'artificial proofs' based on generalities of human conduct, but whose technique was still very much shaped by the older conventions. This theory has met with growing scepticism and one of the objects of the early chapters of this study has been to cast a clearer perspective on the rhetorical effects of evolving law.[34]

Draco's trial procedure grew out of an earlier set of customary rules for the resolution of disputes by oath and other tests of conviction, whose consequences were 'automatic' only in the sense that the litigants were bound by religious conviction and social

---

[33] Ant. 6. 16. That such is the nature of the judges' decision is suggested by a gloss on Ant. 5. 94, *Lex. Rhet.* s.v. δοξασταί (Bekker A.G. 242.19 = Solon F42 Ruschenbusch): κριταί εἰσιν οἱ διαγιγνώσκοντες, πότερος εὐορκεῖ τῶν κρινομένων.
[34] Gagarin, 'Proofs in Antiphon', 22–32; cf. *EGL* 19–50; G. Vollmer, *Studien zum Beweis antiphontischer Reden* (diss., Hamburg, 1958), 5–9, 114–17; Goebel, *Early Rhetorical Theory*, esp. 49–55. For this controversy see Ch. 1 §2.

conscience to abide by what they had sworn.[35] Final resolution and enforcement was left largely to the families themselves; the *polis* was slow to intervene. At trial the tribal chiefs 'gave judgement' as a formula rather than a final verdict: they called upon the parties themselves to assert their claims by self-help or private settlement. Judgement was in this sense 'consensual' rather than 'irrational'. The automaticity of proof in the extant speeches is grounded in this idea, that both sides should agree in principle to a settlement based on the automatic consequences of what they themselves have sworn.

The issue before the judges was ultimately a matter of liability: in essence, the judgement of the court validates or disavows the plaintiff's claim of right to exact righteous vengeance against the killer if he does not come to terms. Homicide disputes came to trial only in those cases where the two parties could not agree on compensation. Ordinarily, the lawgiver supposed, the dispute could be settled entirely in family-to-family negotiations, where each side must acknowledge or deny the claims of the other, subject to the imperatives of oath; the dispute would only go to trial in those cases where the consensual framework broke down. The plaintiff, for instance, might be unwilling to accept the defendant's plea that he acted unintentionally (and hence expected a less severe reckoning), or that he was not causally responsible (and hence not liable for compensation at all). But if the plaintiff would demand retribution, he must assert his right to it under oath; and for the judges to decide in his favour he must show that he has proven his conviction by the available tests. The earliest speeches are still very much imprinted with this character.

Now, on the one hand, Solmsen supposed that Antiphon was somehow intellectually constrained by these conventions: 'the composition and arrangement of the speech . . . are only to a very limited degree the work of his art and design . . . the pre-rhetorical, pre-logical organization of objective reality prevails over his own subjective goals.'[36] Antiphon is seen as conceptionally incapable of arguing the case in any other way than by emphasis on the *atechnoi*,

---

[35] See Ch. 6 §3.1, and cf. Williams, *Shame and Necessity*, 75–102.

[36] *Antiphonstudien*, esp. 26: 'Aufbau und Gliederung der Rede sind . . . nur in sehr beschränktem Maße das Werk seiner τέχνη und seiner διάνοια . . . Auch da, wo er die πράγματα im Hinblick auf ein selbstgewähltes τέλος gestalten und die γνώμη τῶν ἀντιδίκων . . . darstellen will, triumphiert die vorrhetorische, vorlogische Gliederung der Objektwelt über seine subjektiven Zielsetzungen.'

from the intrinsic meaning of 'the thing in itself'. This part of the theory cannot bear up against the *tour de force* in reasoning from probable motives and the pattern of human experience that we find in Antiphon 5 (Ch. 9 §1). But in the speeches for *dikai phonou*, particularly in Antiphon 6, the traditional instruments of judgement constitute the ordering principle of the speech. This principle encompasses the law itself as a set of rules governing the prosecution of claims and the tests of conviction to prove them. A summary of the arguments will illustrate this arrangement.

That such is the nature of the contest is announced in the prologue with the conventional appeal to the ancient laws forever unaltered: 'you must not use my adversaries' arguments to discern the worth of the laws, as to whether they are sound or not, but by the laws you must judge their arguments, whether they instruct you rightly and lawfully or not' (2). The defendant has set forth his innocence under oath in phrasing that is logically consistent, and he has made use of every available test to confirm his conviction. The plaintiffs for their part have made a claim under oath that seems logically inconsistent, and they have repeatedly contradicted by their public indifference the procedural rules and social norms for prosecuting a homicide. This theme carries through to the epilogue: 'How could anyone show greater contempt for the law!' (47).

The conventional appeal to religious sanctions (3–6) is also adapted to this end (cf. Ch. 5 §2). The defendant would not knowingly seek an undeserved acquittal, since the consequences of defilement could not be evaded. The threat of miasma is a guarantee of the sanctity of oath: the law holds so powerful a constraint upon the conscience of a killer that even a man who kills his own chattel slave none the less abides by the prohibitions, fearing divine sanction; he who transgresses such constraints abandons all hope, the last, greatest good to mankind; 'and no one would dare to violate the judgement rendered, neither from knowledge of his innocence nor conscious of his guilt.' Even certain of his innocence he must none the less abide by a wrong verdict, should the judges err. The judges themselves must therefore weigh carefully the inescapable consequences of their decision; the plaintiffs obviously are guided by no such scruple. It is in this vein that he condemns the methods of the prosecution (7–10): they slanderously allege public wrongs to distract the judges from the matter at hand, though they pretend to the bond of piety that properly compels kinsmen of the dead to prosecute. The prosecutors have obviously attempted to incriminate the defendant by suggesting his litigious enterprises made him negligent in fulfilling his duties as *chorēgos*. Rather than deal directly with that very pertinent line of argument, he treats it as a flagrant violation of the oath against irrelevant allegations. Rather than abide by the oath, they have attempted to make a public prosecution of a private suit.

The narrative (11–14) is, as we have seen, directed against the allegations of negligence. The defendant's version of the events concludes with the affirmation, 'Many of those present are fully cognizant of all the events, they hear the oath-officer and pay close attention to my response; to them I would certainly want to appear true to my oath (*euorkos*) and honest in my arguments persuading you to acquit.'

In the proof proper, beginning with the treatment of the charges, (15–19) our defendant attempts to discredit the sworn charge of planning from testimony of witnesses that he neither ordered nor made necessary nor was even present when the drug was given. The plaintiffs have shamelessly abused the power of their oath. It is in this context that he takes up the commonplace (§1.2.1), that in cases where a killing is planned and designed to avoid witnesses, the judges must rely upon circumstances and conjecture to test the litigants' claims (18); but in this case there is not the least suspicion of intent or design, and there is an abundance of testimony (19). The purpose of this commonplace is not to suggest that the charge of 'planning' an unintended death is inherently absurd, but rather to emphasize the irregular methods of the prosecution in refusing to avail themselves of the traditional means of proof—testimony of witnesses and of slaves under torture.

The defendant then proceeds to reconstruct the sequence of events leading up to the first accusation and to show how the charge was immediately dismissed on the strength of witnesses and challenges (20–4). The previous hearing thus confirms the validity of traditional tests of conviction over the plaintiffs' devious conjectures (25–6):

these constraints (*anankai*) are the strongest and most secure . . . and convictions that derive from them are the clearest and most trustworthy in determining what is right where there are many men cognizant of the events, both free men and slaves, and it is possible to compel the free men by oaths and pledges, which are of the greatest value to free men, and the slaves by other constraints, by which they are compelled to tell the truth even if they are likely to die for proclaiming it.

Then, with the same emphasis, he reverses the argument (27–9): surely, if they had sworn witnesses on their side they would condemn the defendant if he refused to answer their challenge. By the same token, their refusal to answer his challenges is 'a sure sign (*tekmērion*) that the charge which they have brought is false' (27).

There follows (30–2) what would appear to be an epilogue to the speech thus far, summarizing the evidentiary argument—how else is a man to prove his innocence if he is not to be acquitted on such proof? It bears close reading.

Where a litigant builds his case on mere argument, providing no witnesses to the events, one would say 'his arguments fail for lack of evidence'; and should he provide witnesses but present no circumstantial indications (*tekmēria*) consistent with their testimony, one could make a similar objection. Now I have presented you with reasonable arguments, witnesses to corroborate those arguments, an account of the events consistent with their testimony . . . and finally, the two strongest indications: my *accusers themselves are proved false both by me and at their own hands, while I stand acquitted both on my own reckoning and by theirs.* For when they refused to prove their claim and I was willing to submit the charges to proof, by their refusal they surely acquitted me and turned witness against themselves that their charges were false and baseless. Indeed, if I can treat my adversaries themselves as witnesses in my favour, in addition to my own witnesses, where else must I go . . . to find proof that I stand acquitted of the charge?

I think it likely that this passage marked the conclusion to the first speech, and the 'second proof' that follows it was originally intended for the second speech (as was the second epilogue in Antiphon 1). The conclusion to the first proof serves a function suited to the epilogue in a first speech for the defence:[37] it is an appeal to the judges to weigh what we would regard as a matter of equity—that they do not allow the case to be decided on technicalities without considering the speciousness of the plaintiffs' claim. It is perhaps only in this way that equity can be addressed, and it is therefore best left to peroration.

The second proof that follows this appeal (33–51) is a rebuttal, probably to be delivered after the plaintiffs have put the best face

---

[37] See *Tetr.* I. 2. 13; 3. 2. 7–9; and compare, conversely, the appeal to justice in the *prokatalēpsis* and 'first epilogue' in Ant. I. 23–7.

on their rather irregular prosecution. They delayed some three to four months after the death before pursuing the matter, and the defendant hopes to convince the judges that they were only then persuaded to proceed by bribery rather than earnest conviction of his guilt. This whole passage is sometimes treated with suspicion: it is perhaps technically in violation of the rule against irrelevant arguments; and the speech ends abruptly without the kind of epilogue we might expect. But we must not be misled by the *Tetralogies* where the final epilogues harp upon the killer's defilement as a threat to the community. This preoccupation is uncharacteristic of the court speeches (Ch. 5 §2). The force of religious convictions developed in the second proof to Antiphon 6 is in fact a rather elaborate version of the treatment proper to the courts. These plaintiffs have shown an utter disregard for the constraining threat of defilement and divine vengeance—they would not have delayed fifty days into the new year and often consorted with the defendant had they believed in his guilt.

In the first instance, the defendant begins, the plaintiffs made no accusation whatever until the third day after the death, the very day of the burial—and then acted precipitously, without due observance of ritual (37). Following the boy's death 'they (openly) consorted and spoke with me'. It was only on the third day, the very day of the burial, that his enemies prevailed upon the plaintiffs to proclaim him as the killer and thus exclude him from public places. The timing of the charges perfectly coincides with an important political prosecution, not only on this first occasion but also the second time, fifty days into the new year. On both occasions the apparent aim of the prosecution was to derail the case against Philinus and his associates by removing the chief prosecutor, our defendant: the law requires that whenever formal charges are made in a suit for homicide, the accused is immediately subject to the customary prohibitions, excluding him from public business (36). His political opponents made use of this mechanism in an attempt to have him taken off the case.

The connection is purely circumstantial, but suggestive. There is no evidence offered in support of the contention that the plaintiffs were bribed or that the homicide charges were politically motivated. But there is an intriguing suggestion that incriminating facts were known to the court: the defendant briefly mentions a similar stratagem employed against one Lysistratus, whose case the judges apparently would recall ('as you yourselves have heard'). We know nothing more of this case, and it is perhaps unwarranted to suppose that Lysistratus was excluded from prosecution by precisely the same devise of homicide prosecution; conceivably some other disability was devised in order to prevent him from taking part in the prosecution of Philinus.

In the case against the *chorēgos*, the first attempted prosecution was derailed by the same cumbersome mechanism that made it an attractive snare. The plaintiffs were prevented from lodging their charges by the rule that the sequence of monthly hearings leading up to the trial must be presided over by the same *basileus*. Once this restriction was recognized—and allegedly the instigators withdrew their support—the plaintiffs arranged for a reconciliation. He insists that the reconciliation (*diallagē*) came at their initiative, and that he acquiesced at the urging of his friends. The point of this otherwise irrelevant background is to emphasize the willingness of the plaintiffs to come to terms with the defendant, to reinforce the impression that their sworn charges, now as in the first instance, were utterly without conviction.

The pre-trial settlement was probably more than merely a political arrangement. He makes no mention of financial settlement, but he clearly implies that their conduct was financially motivated throughout: when the defendant got a conviction against Philinus, 'and [the plaintiffs] could no longer help those in whose interest they were paid [to prosecute], at that very point (τότε δή) they approached me . . . and asked for reconciliation' (38).

Now there is an obvious difficulty in this account: if the victim's family and the *chorēgos* have previously arranged a formal reconciliation before witnesses, as he claims, at or near the shrine of Athena and presumably sanctified by oath, why are the plaintiffs not barred from reopening the case? Why does not the defendant at least make more of the previous settlement? There was probably little need to explain the nature of such an arrangement to the justices. And the earlier settlement may have attached greater blame to the son-in-law who had direct responsibility for overseeing the *chorēgia*; a separate prosecution of the *chorēgos* was therefore not excluded. If our defendant acknowledged his own initiative in the earlier settlement he would appear to admit some measure of liability either in regard to his own conduct or in regard to the son-in-law.[38] The brief

---

[38] On this problem, cf. Erbse, 'Über den Choreuten', 29–32.

mention of the reconciliation is entirely suitable for the aims of his argument: here again, in first arranging a reconciliation and then violating the spirit of it, they show clearly their lack of regard for the binding pledges that properly govern the resolution of public claims.

Thereafter they consorted with me and spoke with me in temples and in the agora, in my home and in theirs, and everywhere else. In the end—O, Zeus and all ye gods—this fellow here, Philocrates, stood with me in the council chamber, on the daïs before the full council, shook my hand and spoke to me, calling me by name as I did him. So it was quite a shock to the council to learn that proclamation had been made by these men [excluding me from public places]—the very men whom they had seen consorting and speaking with me the day before!   (40)

The emphasis upon close contact between the plaintiffs and the defendant, 'consorting and speaking', immediately after the death and again for two months after reconciliation, up until the day proclamation was made, all contributes to the argument against plaintiffs' oath as an inviolable pledge of conviction. Threat of miasma and divine visitation ordinarily ensures the integrity of the *diōmosia*, but in this case the plaintiffs have repeatedly shown an utter indifference to such imperatives.

Again in §§41–4, the defendant takes up the implications of the chronology and counters the plaintiffs' complaint against the *basileus* who first rejected their charge. In their indifference to these rules the plaintiffs give 'evidence against themselves, that they are not telling the truth' (41). The *basileus* clearly acted as the laws require, and the proof of his integrity is the fact that the plaintiffs brought no accusation against him at his accountings. Yet they persist in claiming that the first attempt to bring charges was thwarted. The complaint is proved frivolous by the fact that they did not resume prosecution until fifty days into the new year, although the chief plaintiff and defendant found themselves elected to council and frequently in contact.

These men were fully cognizant of the laws and yet saw me taking office as councillor—and there in the very council chamber a shrine to Zeus Boulaios and Athena Boulaia stands, where the members make their prayers, as I did and he did, upon entering council, and as we did upon entering all the other shrines in company with the councillors, making sacrifice and prayer in behalf of the whole city; and where, moreover, I could be seen serving in the prytany . . . [which office involves] sacrifice and dedication of offerings on behalf of the democracy, putting to the vote and stating my views on matters of the greatest and most urgent significance to the *polis*. (45)

During all this time the plaintiffs, if they truly believed the defendant to be tainted with homicide, should have acted to avoid defilement and divine wrath threatening themselves and the city; but they stood by, regularly 'consorting' with the defendant. From this public conduct it is clear that they themselves do not regard him guilty of the killing (46).

Having concluded this second proof, the defendant turns at last to an elaborate peroration upon the perjury of his accusers: 'How could they be more shameless and contemptuous of the laws? These men who could not convince themselves of the very charges of which they expect to persuade you;' they are proved by their devious methods to be the most impious and perjured of men—ἐπιορκώτατοι (48; cf. 33).

What court would they hesitate to deceive, what oaths would they not dare to transgress? These men who lately received thirty minae . . . to remove me from the council, and so swore the hallowed oaths [they have taken in this case] . . . (51) What court would they not enter to deceive, what oaths would they not dare to transgress, these most impious men who have thus come before you, whom they know to be the most just and righteous of all judges among the Greeks, attempting to deceive you, if they can, by swearing such oaths as these?[39]

These are the closing words of the speech as we have it. The last section has been bracketed by some editors; others, who find the epilogue somehow inadequate, have supposed that the original ending was lost. It is, perhaps, in the nature of the logographic text that various sections might not be written out verbatim, or some optional sections included. But there can be little question that the epilogue as we have it brings to a proper close the prevailing argument of the second proof, an argument that has little to do with questions of causation and liability *per se*, but bears directly against the plaintiff's oath.

---

[39] Ant. 6. 49–51. These lines were bracketed by Gernet; cf. Blass, *Attische Beredsamkeit*, 199.

§3. The 'Contest of Oaths' as an Organizational Principle

At the beginning of his proof our defendant asks the judges to consider the two sworn statements (*diomōsiai*) and determine 'which of the two is more true and righteously sworn' (*euorkotera*, 16). This decision is the essence of the trial. The judges are not asked to determine a question of fact, and although the interpretation of legal concepts would seem crucial to the case, the judges are not asked to decide a point of law *per se*. The objective questions of what was done and what the law requires are fundamentally matters for the litigants to investigate and decide for themselves; each party is expected to make proper use of all available means of establishing his own conviction. The judges are asked only to decide between the sworn claims of the two litigants, which of the two has conducted his case with moral certainty.

The structure of the speech is built around this contest of oaths. Each side must shoulder the burden of proof by undertaking the requisite demonstrations, the swearing of available witnesses and challenging the other side to tests of witnesses and slave torture. By these measures of conviction the judges are to decide which of the two adversaries has been the more true to his oath. The substance of the arguments is summarized in the previous section. To demonstrate the organizational principle I offer the following schema.

§§1–6 Prologue: sanctity of the ancient law and its instruments; religious constraints enforcing obedience to the law and the court's judgement.

§§7–10 Introduction (or 'foundation', *prokataskeuē*): initial contrast between the plaintiffs' approach to judgement and the defendant's; the plaintiffs' very allegations suggest indifference to the rules and sanctions governing homicide procedure.

§§11–14 Narrative: allegations of indirect responsibility, extending the legal concept of *bouleusis* to encompass transfer of official duties, are implicitly disproved on the principle of 'last clear chance'.

§§15–29 First Proof (on the evidence)
    15 Presentation of witnesses.
    16–19. Exposition (*apodeixis*): statement of the substance of

the charge and the plea: plaintiffs unwilling to respect the usual standards of proof.

20–9. Proof proper: circumstantial evidence against plaintiffs' oath, indicating political opportunism; plaintiffs are unwilling to avail themselves of testimony by oath and by torture; yet if the testimony were on their side, they would count it decisive.

§§30–2 First Epilogue (summary of evidentiary proof): both witnesses and circumstantial indications contradict the plaintiffs; and they are finally refuted by their own public actions and inconsistent claims.

§§33–46 Second Proof (on the oath)

34–40. Second narrative: circumstantial indications against validity of plaintiffs' oath; freely consorting with defendant they attest to his innocence.

41–6. Proof proper: allegations that the charges were obstructed by the *basileus* turn against the credibility of the plaintiffs; in the new year plaintiffs allowed defendant to take part in official business of the council, where surely religious constraints would have required them to bar the killer.

§§47–51 Second Epilogue: by their disregard of religious concerns, plaintiffs turn witness against themselves; perjury of their oaths manifestly proved.

8

Justifiable Killing and the Problem of Lysias 1

Demosthenes spoke of the Delphinium court as the most dread and awe-inspiring of them all (23. 74). What is it that made the proceedings of this court so disturbing, more so than trial at the Areopagus itself? The verdict of justifiable manslaughter, which the gods themselves had sanctioned, was the most ancient and sacred of legal concepts; it was also the most troubling aspect of the primitive law. How, after all, were the judges to determine what constitutes 'justifiable killing'—to rule that in one case a vindictive killer will go unpunished, in another that the killer be put to death? We know that in the fourth century a defendant must plead that his act was justified by specific provisions of statute law.[1] This legalistic understanding of justifiable killing was undoubtedly strengthened by the reforms of the restored democracy. But the Draconian conception of justifiable homicide as *retributive killing* is remarkably persistent: by this reckoning the justification lies not in the interests of society or moral excuse on behalf of the killer; it is the victim's wrongdoing that brings punishment upon him (Ch. 3 §2.3). The charter myth for this institution is the legendary acquittal of Orestes for avenging the wrong his mother had done his father. And this retributive principle is honoured even in some cases where we might expect a more humane rationale: Demosthenes judges a killing in athletic competition by the same rule that justifies the killing of an adulterer or an outlaw; the victim himself is to blame for his death (23. 54). This principle of Draconian justice persisted even when democratic values might seem to weigh against it. The two ways of justice were sometimes reconciled by rather ingenious constructions.

This accommodation of retribution to legalism is crucial to our understanding of cases before the Delphinium. The emphasis upon

---

[1] Demosthenes and *Ath. Pol.* 57. 3 agree that the killer must claim to have acted 'lawfully' (ἐννόμως, ἐν νόμῳ). We have no evidence that a plea of 'justifiable killing' was ever based upon abstract justice or unwritten law without reference to specific provisions of statute. Even the case of Euthyphro's father seems to involve some appeal to statutory provisions for self-help (below §3).

justification 'in the law' might suggest that such cases would be largely preoccupied with the legalistic question of whether the killer's act conformed to the letter of the statute. But this does not appear to be the issue at trial. Evidently the *basileus* would establish in preliminaries whether the plea was formally valid. The issue before the justices—the one point that the defendant will be most insistent to prove—is that the victim *deserved* what he got, that he brought the killing upon himself. The killer cannot establish justification simply by demonstrating that he has acted in conformity to law; he must show that the blame attaches to the victim. In cases of true retributive killing—the case of the husband who catches the adulterer in the act or of the patriot who acts against the tyrant—a ruling for the defendant amounts to a verdict against the victim. The issue in dispute is not so much whether the killer did right as whether the victim did wrong. To our way of thinking, perhaps, it comes to the same thing. But if we are to understand the logic of the argument, we will have to recognize that the causation is triggered by the victim's wrong.

This approach to the killer's claim of justification dictates the handling of the laws themselves. It is not surprising that the relevant laws will be subject to explication in these cases, though the bearing of the law is *not* subject to debate in other *dikai phonou*. But in the context of legal interpretation at the Delphinium we must recognize that the laws are not treated as an absolute standard by which to judge the defendant's action: the laws are treated much like witnesses and challenges; they are proofs of conviction rather than fact. Our defendant turns to the laws as a test of the righteousness of his claim, that the victim is culpable and brought retribution upon himself.

Now the Delphinium jurisdiction and the very concept of retribution that it embodied were profoundly affected by the revisions of law and procedure under the new democracy, 403/2. By the oath of reconciliation, 'not to remember past wrongs' (*mē mnēsikakein*) citizens renounced violent remedies—vindictive self-help, forcible arrest, and summary execution—that would otherwise have been their ordinary recourse against a known killer or public enemy who trespassed in Attica. By the traditional arrangement, if the victim's kinsmen charged the killer, he would plead legal justification, invoking the relevant statute law before the Delphinium. But by the pledge *mē mnēsikakein*, each citizen committed himself to adhere to the 'covenants' of settlement and not to revert to other remedies. As a consequence of that pledge, they could not plead justifiable killing for retribution against those implicated in the crimes of the Thirty. This was an urgent objective of those who framed the amnesty (Ch. 3 §3).

This restriction of self-help was conceived as a limited safeguard, bearing only upon the events of civil conflict, but it undoubtedly affected popular understanding of the Delphinium jurisdiction. The old rules of retributive justice were no longer self-evident; rather, the law was presumed to prohibit even those retributive killings that had been traditionally regarded as justifiable. It was this or a similar preoccupation, I have suggested (Ch. 5 §3), that prompted the author of the *Tetralogies* to explore 'the law prohibiting just as well as unjust killing'; we shall turn back to the third *Tetralogy* in the later sections of this chapter. But we must begin with the one court speech intended for such a case, Lysias' speech *On the Slaying of Eratosthenes*.

§1. Lysias 1 (*On the Slaying of Eratosthenes*)

The case of Euphiletus for the slaying of Eratosthenes presents the most puzzling problem of stasis of the three speeches in *dikai phonou*.[2] How are we to define the question at issue? Alone of the three, this speech cites the text of statute law and offers interpretation of the relevant provisions; but the question at issue does not appear to be a straightforward question of law. Our defendant cites the text of statute three times in the course of his first proof (27–36). But the laws are treated primarily as criteria of the victim's wrong and the righteousness of retribution; there appears to be no real dispute of legal principles, procedures, or jurisdiction. In this case alone of the three *dikai phonou*, there appears to be some question of what actually happened; but, again, the matters of fact are incidental to the question of convictions.

---

[2] There have been few studies devoted to the legal and rhetorical complications of this speech; scholarly interest has focused on style and ethopoeia. See Blass, *Attische Beredsamkeit*, 571–7; Erbse, 'Lysias-Interpretationen', 51–8; M. Edwards and S. Ussher, *Greek Orators* (Warminster, 1985), i. 220–9. On legal issues, Lämmli, *Attische Prozeßverfahren*, 58–60; J. J. Bateman 'Lysias and the Law', *TAPA* 89 (1958), 276–85; D. Cohen, 'The Athenian Law of Adultery', *RIDA* 31 (1984), 147–65, and *Law, Sexuality, and Society* (Cambridge, 1991), esp. 105–22.

Our defendant, Euphiletus, proceeds as though there can be no dispute that the victim had committed adultery with his wife (on previous occasions, if not on the night in question); indeed, we are told, Eratosthenes was expert at seducing other men's wives.[3] Euphiletus says that he was informed of this by a concerned third party and the fact was confirmed by a slave girl under threat of torture. He then determined to avenge himself when he could catch the adulterer in the act. On the fateful night, he says, the slave told him the man was in the house, and he then called upon his friends and neighbours to assist him in retribution; they caught the man naked in the bed, he admitted the wrong and offered to pay compensation. The defendant rejected compensation and executed the offender on the spot. He has witnesses to corroborate his version of the events: these witnesses not only confirm his claim categorically (28–9) but also later appear to give specific confirmation for the unplanned nature of his reprisal, apparently affirming that he had made no prearrangement with them but came door-to-door rousing assistance (42).

This last point in rebuttal and various points of the narrative suggest that Euphiletus was accused of entrapment. This would appear to be the most serious part of the case against him, but he never answers the accusation directly. Instead he formulates the issue initially as follows:

I think I must show that Eratosthenes seduced my wife and corrupted her, disgraced my children, and committed outrage against me by intruding into my home, that I had no other hostile motive than this, that I did not do it for money—to get rich out of poverty—nor for any other advantage whatever, but only for vengeance according to the laws.   (3–4)

From this formulation we can conclude that two points were considered crucial: the judges must be convinced of the *victim's wrong*; and in order to prove that the victim thus brought his fate upon himself, our defendant will show that he himself had *no ulterior motive*. By this construction the killing came as a consequence of the victim's act; the laws prescribing retribution against the adulterer provided our defendant with his sole motivation. He will

---

[3] The fact that the victim in this case bears the same name and was probably related to the target of Lysias 12 has not been lost upon the commentators. Speculation has gone so far as to identify the two Eratosthenes as one: thus Kirchner *PA* 5035; Blass, *Attische Beredsamkeit*, i. 542–3. But cf. Davies *APF* 184–5; K. Kapparis, *Hermes* 121 (1993), 364–5.

insist that he acted neither by premeditation nor in the passion of the moment but virtually as an instrument of the laws. Thus he relates that he swore, at the moment of striking the fatal blow, 'It is not I who kill you, but the laws!'

It is this formulation that has provoked the sharpest reaction among modern critics: the defendant is relying upon an anachronism in the law to justify a course of conduct that the court of public opinion had long since condemned. The suggestion that the laws themselves are causal determinants seems an intolerable fiction. But, as we shall see, there is more to this line of argument than speciousness. It is an adaptation of the traditional model of justifiable killing—brought on by the victim's wrong—to accommodate the legalism of the new regime. Those who set about rebuilding the Athenian ideology generally seem to have fostered a new-found reverence for statute law as somehow superior to the popular will. Whether the Law is conceived as a fully distinct and 'sovereign' entity is quite another question.[4] It is reasonably clear, in any event, that the workings of law became somewhat objectified, somehow 'other' than the traditional dictates of social conscience. Law is no longer simply a description of recognized norms—*nomos* as *nomima*; it is now more readily seen as an independent and prescriptive standard of what is right.

In the following sections we examine the treatment of law in Lysias 1, beginning with the function of the laws as direct, non-technical proof (§1.1), and turning then to the charge of entrapment and the argument from probability (§1.2). The sophisticated use of conjectural argument is a marked feature of this speech. Indeed, much of the narrative—rightly admired for its action and ethopoeia—lays the groundwork for an argument from probability: the defendant would not have acted as he did if he had planned out and prearranged the killing. It is partly because of the contrast between this method and that of the *dikē phonou* speeches of Antiphon that Solmsen saw the latter as a transitional figure, conceptually constrained by the older, formalistic proof. But there are, after all, some remarkable similarities between Antiphon's method and Lysias'. The formal non-conjectural proofs again form the framework of the argument: in this case the arrangement of this

---

[4] On this controversy see esp. M. Ostwald, *From Popular Sovereignty to the Sovereignty of Law* (Berkeley, 1986), and Ober, *Mass and Elite*. For further perspective, see Ch. 10.

speech is structured around the word of witnesses under oath and the wording of the laws themselves. Indeed, this parallel in method would suggest that the very prominence of such instruments of proof, which Solmsen saw as a technique peculiar to Antiphon, was in fact a traditional aspect of this particular procedure, a convention that other authors would observe when dealing with *dikai phonou*.

1.1 The Question of Law in Lysias 1

Regarding this crime alone, both under the democracy and in time of oligarchy, the same penalty has been assigned, for the weakest to prevail against the most powerful, so that even the lowliest person may obtain the same measure of justice as the highest. (2)

Those who regard this case as a conflict between evolving custom and outmoded law see defendant's arguments as a strategy of 'desperation', clinging to a backward code that democratic society had generally abandoned in practice.[5] We know of no clear parallel for outright execution of the adulterer caught in the act. And there is testimony suggesting that it was either not lawful or at least not acceptable to social conscience for the husband to respond as Euphiletus has done.[6]

There were alternative remedies; our defendant in fact refers to such alternatives only to reject them 'in obedience to the laws'. It was evidently customary for the husband to seize the offender, if he could, and hold him for compensation: if the offender (or his family) denied the charge, they were to bring an action for unlawful detention.[7] We also hear of a 'suit for adultery,' *graphē moicheias*, but it is not altogether certain that this was a distinct procedure.[8] In any event—whether the offender must sue for unlawful imprisonment, or the husband might sue for adultery—such claims were

---

[5] Thus Cohen reasons, *Law, Sexuality, and Society*, 110–22, that the contradiction between the letter of the law and actual practice accounts for Euphiletus' special pleading (esp. 117–18); similarly S. Humphreys, 'A Historical Approach to Drakon's Law on Homicide', *Symposion* 1990 (1991), 19. We may have one indication, however, of another justifiable killing of the adulterer in Lysias fr. 123 (Thalheim) from *Against Philon*.

[6] Plato in the *Laws* allows self-help killing against forcible rape (874c) but adultery is punished by social exclusion (784); cf. Xen. *Mem*. 2. 1. 5; Isaeus 8. 44.

[7] [Dem.] 59. 66, γραφή ἐάν τις ἀδίκως εἴρξῃ ὡς μοίχον; cf. Ruschenbusch, *Untersuchungen Athenischen Strafrechts* (Graz and Cologne, 1968), 35.

[8] *Ath. Pol.* 59. 3; cf. Lipsius, *Attische Recht*, 432. For full discussion, see Cohen's, *Law, Sexuality, and Society*, 98–122; for his doubts regarding γραφὴ μοιχείας, 122–4.

sometimes resolved in court. A conviction would not have allowed for outright execution, but for the husband to 'do as he will' with the offender in the presence of the court 'without a knife' (apparently to prevent killing or castration). And there is of course reference to the punishment of adulterers in Attic comedy, suggesting some form of torture by anal penetration; outright execution is nowhere clearly indicated.[9] Such was ordinarily the extent of violent retribution.

From these considerations we are to conclude that the extreme remedy undertaken by Euphiletus was highly irregular, perhaps of questionable legality, despite the fact that our defendant can quote the laws affirming his justification. Now David Cohen has resolved some of the confusion regarding the legal argument:[10] the first law that our speaker cites is not the law of adultery itself but the law of *kakourgoi* ('known felons' or 'malefactors'). Concluding his narrative our defendant contends (26), '[Eratosthenes] confessed to the crime and begged me not to kill him but to exact payment.' Euphiletus refused payment, he insists, out of reverence for the laws. After the law is read to the court, our defendant asserts, 'He did not dispute it but confessed to the crime, and he begged for his life and was ready to pay compensation.'[11] The speaker's insistence that Eratosthenes confessed to the crime suggests that he is invoking the law of *kakourgoi*, which provided for immediate execution 'if the culprits are taken in the act and confess'.[12]

The second law cited (30) is clearly a statute defining homicide jurisdiction; it is *not* 'the law of adultery' as it has been called.[13] It is introduced as a law recorded on a *stele* on the Areopagus; and

---

[9] For adulterers in Attic comedy, see Cohen's note 'Aristophanes and the Punishment of Adultery', *ZSS* 102 (1985), 385–7. Aristophanes' *Clouds*, 1079–80 suggests that the adulterer caught in the act was at the husband's mercy but would not ordinarily be killed. On the comic 'reaming with a radish', see now Carey in *LCM* 18 (1993), 53–5.

[10] See Cohen's earlier study, 'Law of Adultery', esp. 156–7; cf. *Law, Sexuality, and Society*, 110–22.

[11] Lys. 1. 29: Οὐκ ἠμφεσβήτει, ὦ ἄνδρες, ἀλλ' ὡμολόγει ἀδικεῖν, καὶ ὅπως μὲν μὴ ἀποθάνῃ ἠντεβόλει καὶ ἱκέτευεν, ἀποτίνειν δ' ἕτοιμος ἦν χρήματα.

[12] Aeschines 1. 91: τῶν μοιχῶν . . . ἐπ' αὐτοφώρῳ ἁλόντες, ἐὰν ὁμολογῶσι, παραχρῆμα θανάτῳ ζημιοῦνται, κτλ. See Ch. 4. §3.3; cf. Hansen, *Apagoge*, 44–5.

[13] Thus H. J. Wolff, 'Die Grundlagen des griechischen Eherechts' in E. von Berneker (ed.), *Zur Griechischen Rechstgeschichte* (Darmstadt, 1968), 642, described the statute in Dem. 23. 53 as *the* Ehebruchsgesetz; Cohen correctly observes that this statute 'rather sets out exculpatory or justificatory *conditions*—exceptions to the general prohibition against homicide' (*Law, Sexuality, and Society*, 104).

after it has been read to the court, the speaker offers the following explication.

You hear that the very court of the Areopagus . . . is expressly enjoined from condemning for murder a man who catches an adulterer with his wife and takes his vengeance. And the lawgiver so earnestly approved of this response against violation of wedded wives that he assigned the same penalty in the case of concubines, persons of lesser status. So clearly, if he had had a stronger remedy against violators in the former instance [viz. violation of wives], he would have enacted it.

Here our defendant is evidently referring to the law of the Delphinium court.[14] The correspondence between these provisions and the standard description of the Delphinium jurisdiction is unmistakable. In very similar terms, Demosthenes remarks upon the law of the Delphinium allowing justifiable self-help against the violator of a concubine 'for legitimate offspring'.[15]

Let us consider what it means for Euphiletus to cite this second law. We should not be surprised or misled by the redundancy.[16] After all, Euphiletus is citing these laws as a measure of the victim's culpability and the righteousness of his own claim. The citations of statute are treated *not* as material on a question of law *per se*. There is no procedural question as to whether this case is covered by the Delphinium jurisdiction; and there is no juristic dispute as to the statutory criteria of justifiable killing. In essence the laws are introduced as a means of validating the retributive killing *as a processual act*. Our defendant invokes the laws as a demonstration of his own subjective conviction of the righteousness of his act rather than an objective proof of its legality.

It is from this perspective—recognizing that the laws themselves are treated as proof of conviction rather than procedural criteria— that we must understand the problem that arises with the third law

[14] See Ch. 3 §2.3. By this reconstruction, the Delphinium jurisdiction was first defined by statute after the Areopagus was reconstituted (under Solon). The juries of the *ephetai* would then go as committees of the Areopagus to their appointed venues. Thus what I have called (for convenience) 'the law of the Delphinium' was among the archival 'laws of the Areopagus'.

[15] Dem. 23. 53; cf. *Ath. Pol.* 57. 3. For text and translation see Ch. 3 §1.2.2 with n. 11.

[16] Cohen seems inclined to suppose from the second citation that the law of *kakourgoi* had been somehow restricted; he even thinks it likely that the limitation upon vengeance that applied in court (i.e. *without a knife*) may have been extended to immediate self-help, and Euphiletus must skirt this provision: *Law, Sexuality, and Society*, 113–17.

cited (32). Here the defendant confronts the obvious argument for the prosecution, that compensation was the ordinary remedy 'in the very cases where it is permitted to kill', and it is clear that the latter category refers to cases of adultery—by contrast to *lesser penalties* for forcible rape. The law prescribes that an offender against a freeborn person be liable for double the damages he would owe for violating a slave: this principle applies in the case of forcible rape (βίᾳ) and apparently in cases of adultery, where it is also permitted to kill the offender.

You hear that the law commands, 'If anyone violate by force a free person or child, he is liable for twice the damage (owed for violation of a slave); and if he violate a woman, in the very cases where it is permitted to kill, let him be subject to the same penalty.'[17]

From the law in question our defendant deduces that the ancient lawgiver indeed regarded seduction as a more serious offence than rape, since the rapist violates only the body but the seducer corrupts even the heart and spirit of the wife, alienating her affections from her husband and confusing the paternity of offspring. The defendant gives this principle particular emphasis; his insistence is usually regarded as special pleading, but it was a conventional part of this defence.[18]

Thus [the lawgiver] regarded those who violate their victims by force as deserving a lesser penalty than those who use persuasion: the latter he condemned to death; for the former he prescribed double damages. For he supposed those who act by force are hated by those they violate, but those who seduce by persuasion so corrupt their victims' souls as to make other men's wives more their own than their husbands'. And the whole household comes to depend on *them*—as it is uncertain whose offspring the children may be, the husband's or the adulterer's. To remedy this evil, the lawgiver made death the penalty. So the very laws . . . have not only acquitted me of wrongdoing but ordered me to exact retribution. And it is for you to determine whether these laws are to be valid or worthless.   (32–4)

This entire line of argument on the second and third laws goes to the gravity of the wrong, to prove from the laws themselves that adultery is the most serious violation of the *oikos* and therefore demands immediate and unswerving response.

[17] Lys. 1. 32: ἐὰν δὲ γυναῖκα, ἐφ᾽ αἷσπερ ἀποκτείνειν ἔξεστιν, ἐν τοῖς αὐτοῖς ἐνέχεσθαι.

[18] Against the substance of this claim, see E. Harris, 'Did the Athenians Regard Seduction as a Worse Crime than Rape?' *CQ* 40 (1990), 370–7.

Euphiletus does not confront what would appear to be the procedural implication of this law, that the husband is to demand financial settlement rather than execute the offender; but it is mistaken to assume, without the text of the law before us, that it exclusively prescribed financial settlement and *prohibited* killing the offender. The law in question is likely to be a Solonian addendum, cross-referenced to the Draconian statute: we found a similar method in the amendment against extortion of ransom cited by Demosthenes at 23. 28, where the earlier provision, 'it is lawful to kill or arrest [exiles who trespass]', has the cross-reference, 'as on the ⟨first⟩ axon'. From the record of Solon's law this appears to be the general direction of much of his felony legislation: specific financial penalties were prescribed not to eliminate self-help but *to limit* financial aggrandizement by the plaintiffs, as a safeguard against the abuses of hostage-taking and extortion of ransom.[19]

Is there a legal complication behind Lysias' argument on this point? Cohen once suggested, quite plausibly, that Euphiletus must substantiate the legal grounds of his plea at such length—with such 'desperation'—because of recent restrictions in the law of *kakourgoi*.[20] Any reader of this speech is likely to be struck by the insistence with which our defendant wraps himself in the law, but this emphasis is more a sign of change in the spirit of the law than in the letter. Lysias is mindful of the new legalism and adapts the conventional reasoning to it. He is not clutching at a point of law *per se*. His client is to embrace the command of law as a demonstration of his conviction—much as Antiphon's clients invoked witnesses and challenged the adversary to slave-torture to show that they had undertaken the proper processual means to test their sworn claims.

Without such a show of conviction our defendant might find his judges especially sceptical of 'justifiable killing' under the new constitutional arrangement. The oath *mē mnēsikakein* seems to have inspired a general reaction against retributive violence (Ch. 3 §3). It is with this pledge in mind that Lysias concludes the first proof (37) with a version of the argument we met in the *Tetralogies*, in answer

---

[19] See my studies 'Νηποινεὶ τεθνάναι' and 'Tyranny and Outlawry'.

[20] 'Law of Adultery', 157–9. Cohen seems to have relegated this hypothesis to the realm of speculation in *Law, Sexuality, and Society*, 114–17. In Ch. 9 §2 I argue that the only substantive change in the law of *kakourgoi* was a matter of interpretation, not a revision of statute.

to 'the law prohibiting just as well as unjust killing' (Ch. 5 §3). It *would have been justifiable* (in the traditional sense) to plot murder against the adulterer, but he did not plot or prearrange; rather his actions were dictated by the letter of the law. 'I would have thought myself justified (*dikaios*) in apprehending by whatever means the man who corrupted my wife,' he claims, but he did not, even thus justifiably, devise or prearrange the killing.

Our defendant has explained his conviction of legal cause with a formulation peculiarly congenial to the new ideology (35): 'I believe that all cities make their laws to this end, so that in those actions where we are at a loss [what to do], we may have recourse to [the laws] and thus consider what must be done. It is these laws then that direct the victims of wrongdoing in such cases to take just such retribution.' Antiphon, to be sure, had expressed the conventional legalism by a parallel formulation (6. 2 = 5. 14): the judges must look to the spirit of the long-standing laws to measure the arguments at hand. An abiding faith in oath and the other tests of conviction was essential to this traditional spirit of the law; it was this set of customary obligations that gave authority to the ordinance—without them there was no mechanism of enforcement. Lysias revised this creed to suit the new regime: the loyal constituents of the democracy will now look to the law for guidance not only in deciding lawsuits but also in deciding how they shall conduct themselves as good citizens. And the law that contains this wisdom is clearly the law that cities *make*, law defined by statute rather than the broader spirit of law that once encompassed all those imperatives of social conscience.

In defence of this principle, Lysias argues that a vote for acquittal will effectively abrogate the law of *kakourgoi*. Thieves caught in the act of illegal entry will claim they have come to commit adultery and thus assure themselves of trial and a chance of reprieve, rather than face summary execution. 'All will know that the laws of adultery are meaningless, that they have only to fear your verdict—which is therefore, in this case, the most powerful vote of all decisions in the state.'

Thus in the new climate of legalism our defendant finds ample justification for taking the wording of the ancient law literally—an imperative for an imperative. Where the law reads 'let him die with impunity', Euphiletus insists upon the letter of the law. And in an age defined by the quest for codification, when new laws were literally put on trial for any infidelity, there should be no doubt that Euphiletus' argument was taken seriously.

1.2   The Question of Entrapment

The judges must ultimately decide whether the defendant is causally responsible for the sequence of events which he clearly foresaw, which he did not prevent and may have indirectly furthered. Did our defendant somehow entice and entrap Eratosthenes? Did he perhaps seize the offender outside the house and then drag him in, in order to fabricate the grounds for execution? To make the best sense of these questions let us again consider the case from both sides.

1.2.1   The Case for the Plaintiffs

Euphiletus tells us a good deal about the arguments for the prosecution, both by direct response to those arguments and by his silence on a number of points which, had they been argued by plaintiffs, he must have answered. Their most dangerous allegation is likely to be the claim that Euphiletus 'on that day ordered the servant girl to fetch [Eratosthenes]' (37). The offender then came in response to the servant's invitation. The essence of the charge against Euphiletus thus involves a form of entrapment, that he plotted and premeditated the turn of events (ἐπεβούλευον, 40). It is in answer to this charge that our defendant ventures upon the argument that he would have been justified (*dikaios*) in devising any means to avenge the wrong done him but he did not plot the killing, even thus justifiably. It was evidently crucial to this aspect of the charge that he be shown to have given specific instructions to the slave girl 'on that (very) day'. If he took any action to bring Eratosthenes to his house on the day in question, then he is linked to the causal chain. Euphiletus has suggested in his narrative that he gave no specific instructions to this effect and he clearly implies that he did nothing of the sort on the day of the killing. To support his denial on this point, Euphiletus tells his tale of happenstance, how he went door-to-door summoning his friends and neighbours without any prearrangement, showing that he had not anticipated a confrontation on that night. He recalls his witnesses to verify this point. It is a conspicuous gap in this rebuttal, however, that he neither responds to the allegation of specific instructions nor mentions the possibility of interrogating the slave under torture.[21]

We would ordinarily expect the plaintiffs to have challenged our defendant to have the girl put to torture on the question of whether she was or was not given specific instruction on that day. Assuming he refused, we would expect Euphiletus to address the issue if only to dredge up the conventional arguments against slave testimony. Various explanations suggest themselves: it was implicit in his arrangement with her (18–20) that she would not be put to torture if she co-operated; it is also possible that she enjoyed some special status as a preferred concubine—she has certainly been subjected to his sexual uses (12).[22] But even if the torture were excluded for some legitimate reason, we would have expected the prosecution to raise the issue, if only to suggest what might have been learned had the torture been permitted. And we would therefore expect Euphiletus to seize upon the issue—see how my opponents demand the tortured testimony of a slave girl, when I offer you the willing testimony of free men (*vel sim.*). There is no entirely adequate explanation for this gap and we must perhaps be content with the *non liquet*. Evidently, for whatever reason, the prosecution did not challenge Euphiletus to submit the girl for torture. The plaintiffs would swear that the girl came to get Eratosthenes on the night in question and Euphiletus was not prepared to dispute it.[23]

The natural assumption would be that the wife herself sent the girl, and Euphiletus will be content to have that assumed. But the prosecution would attempt to show by circumstantial indications that the girl acted at the bidding of Euphiletus. What circumstances could be construed as evidence of such planning? Apparently the prosecution would argue that the affair was at an

[21] The break between the first proof and the second once led Wilamowitz to suppose that the latter argument (37–46) was a late addendum, for post eventum publication. Lämmli, *Attische Prozeßverfahren*, 58–69 argued rightly, that this side of the prosecution would have been fully revealed in *prodikasiai*. I am inclined to suppose that the second argument was intended for the second speech. On examination of the slave girl under threat of torture, cf. Thür, *Basanos*, esp. 43–5.

[22] Pomeroy suggests quite plausibly that the girl was naturally allied with her mistress because of the abuse, and could only be made to co-operate by threat of being put to work in the mill: see now *Women in Classical Athens*, ed. Fantham *et al.* (Oxford, 1994), 113–14.

[23] The plaintiffs can suggest that Euphiletus gave specific instructions on the night in question, or that the girl naturally interpreted his words (21) to mean that she should arrange the entrapment. Euphiletus was likely to hurt his case more by disputing the girl's role than admitting it.

end, that Eratosthenes was uninterested or at least would not have gone to the house without an invitation. There is an aspect of the case for the prosecution that leads in this direction: in the conclusion to his narrative (§27), our defendant alludes to the accusation that Eratosthenes was apprehended outside the house and that once inside he fled to the hearth but was dragged from his sanctuary and slain. If the victim was not apprehended *in flagrante delicto*, then the killer's plea of legal justification has no basis. And if there was uncertainty on this point, the prosecution might well deny outright that there had been illicit relations between Eratosthenes and the wife.

But we should not take the latter implication too seriously. The plaintiffs evidently based their case upon their own affirmation that the girl came to fetch Eratosthenes; they cannot very easily admit that he went along with her without conceding that he had some improper purpose. If Eratosthenes were *not* involved with the defendant's wife, why would he have followed the girl to a stranger's house in the dead of night?[24] Euphiletus has witnesses on hand and probabilities to prove that Eratosthenes was not apprehended outside the house nor able to take refuge at the hearth, as the plaintiffs have tried to suggest. He makes no mention of witnesses for the prosecution on this point presumably because the plaintiffs could find none who were willing to swear to this version of the events. I think we can only conclude that this scenario—that the victim was seized in the street and dragged into the house where he fled to the hearth—was offered by the plaintiffs by way of a hypothetical narrative (such as we find in Ant. 1). The plaintiffs' theory can only serve to rouse suspicion that the sworn statements for the defence may be false or misleading. Without some means of demonstrating the plaintiffs' conviction beyond mere conjecture, it does not become an issue at trial. The mere probability is overshadowed by sworn testimony. It is for this reason that a significant point in the sequence of events—which would undoubtedly have been crucial to a modern hearing of the case—is relegated to the realm of virtual irrelevance.

The crucial question at issue is the more complicated matter of planning or prearrangement. Is the defendant responsible for an

---

[24] Todd assumes that the adulterer 'has of course been inside the house all the time': *The Shape of Athenian Law* (Oxford, 1993), 202. This is an intriguing possibility, but entirely ignored by the argumentation.

entrapment that he did not specifically engineer but in which he evidently connived? There can be no question, after all, that the girl herself may have been induced to entrap Eratosthenes by the defendant's promise to spare her punishment for complicity in the affair. His own words may easily be taken as an outright demand that she arrange for the adulterer to be apprehended in the house— 'I expect you to show me this wrong *in the act*' (21).

The scenario posed by the prosecution seems to be that the girl came at Euphiletus' instigation, not at the wife's bidding, but that Eratosthenes was somehow reluctant to continue their liaison: perhaps he had broken it off, they might argue; or quite conceivably he was wary of the outraged husband. He therefore could not be caught in the house, but was apprehended in the street outside the house. This would appear to be an essential point in the causal connection: it is the prosecution's argument that the victim would not have gone to the house without the slave girl's enticement, and even then he was reluctant to enter. And it was the defendant, they contend, who ordered or induced the girl to bring this about.

1.2.2   Case for the Defendant

The defendant never confronts these crucial questions, the exact nature of his instructions to the slave girl (if any) on the day in question, whether he ordered her in so many words or by some understanding to summon Eratosthenes. In response to the plaintiffs' charge that he ordered the girl to fetch his victim (37), he answers equivocally, relying on circumstantial evidence to show they he did not specifically plan to bring about the killing on that night (39–41). Had he so intended, would he have sent away his dinner guest?[25] Would he have found himself so unprepared as to have to go door-to-door rousing his neighbours? It seems perhaps a damning evasion that he does not confront the issue more directly: he should have affirmed that he gave the girl no such instruction at any time. But such a statement would immediately suggest the obvious though evidently awkward means of resolving the issue, testimony of the slave herself under torture. Instead, as we have seen speakers do in the other speeches, this defendant resorts to devices of convention. He and his counsel realize full well that the charge against him involves a more subtle causal connec-

---

[25] Of course, he might have done so precisely to avoid discouraging the intruder.

tion than outright prearrangement. Rather than deal with the complex causation directly, they adhere to the conventional concepts and the traditional instruments of proof—in this case, the witnesses and the laws.

By a tried-and-true method our defendant treats the issue of entrapment in a simplistic but persuasive way. Nearing the end of his second proof (43–6) Euphiletus turns to the question of motive and invokes the device that we have seen demonstrated so often elsewhere.

Consider . . . whether any other grounds of enmity have ever arisen between me and Eratosthenes—you will find none! He had not brought charges against me for profit, nor had he attempted to drive me out of the community, nor was he litigating any private claim; he neither knew of any wrong that I feared to have discovered . . . nor did I have any expectation of making money, if I could bring about [his death]. Some men plot the murder of others for just such motives. But far from having any grievance on grounds of insult or drunken intrusion or whatever, I never even laid eyes on the man until that night. Why then would I willingly risk my life, if I had not suffered *the height of injustice* at his hands? Would I have summoned witnesses to the impious act I was to commit, when I had every opportunity for no one to know, if I had intended to do away with him unjustly?

This is the same device we have seen in Gorgias' *Palamedes*, in Antiphon's *Defence*, and in the first *Tetralogy*, and which we shall see again in Antiphon 5: the alternatives are listed and eliminated one by one, in a manner that appears to be exhaustive. It is a persuasive tactic. It does not, of course, have any relevance whatever to the chief issues in this case.

There is really no question as to what Euphiletus' motive must have been: he knew or suspected Eratosthenes of adultery with his wife. The prosecution seem willing to concede that there was some involvement (§1.2.1). Evidently they attempted to undermine the plea of legal justification by suggesting that the affair was not ongoing, but they could not very well deny that their kinsman had been involved—why else would he follow a slave girl to another man's home in the dead of night?[26]

[26] Of course, *we* can imagine any number of reasons, but it must have been highly suspicious for a slave girl to summon a man to her master's house in the dark of night, in a society where night-time excursions were notoriously difficult or dangerous. And this was a man whom her master did not know, and who was not even a neighbour but from another deme.

The defendant must address the issue in terms that are clearly defined within the legalistic framework. Thus in his adaptation of the conventional defence on motive, he emphasizes the nature of the killing as an act of justifiable retribution, excluding every other motive: 'if I had not suffered the height of injustice at his hands . . . if I had intended to do away with him unjustly.' His sole motive, he contends, is the vengeance that the law itself has pronounced justifiable and *required* of a man in defence of his *oikos*—if one is to read the imperatives of the law at face value. It is this point, after all, that is the fundamental issue in the case, and here it leads him into his conclusion.

In my view this vengeance was not merely for my own satisfaction but in behalf of the whole city. For those who commit such wrongs, when they see what they have to expect from it, will be less likely to transgress against others—if they see that *you* have the same judgement. If not, it would be far better to erase the laws now on the books and enact others, to impose penalties upon those who guard their womenfolk and grant immunity to those desiring to sin against them. This would be much more just than for citizens to be ambushed by the laws that order 'if a man apprehend the adulterer, do with him as he will', when the legal consequences will be more serious for those who are wronged than for those who defile other men's wives against the law. As it is, I run the risk of losing my life, my property, and all the rest, because I was obedient to the laws of the *polis*. (47–50)

This pledge of allegiance to the laws recalls the first proof (29–36), where Euphiletus so fervently wrapped himself in statutes: he refused the offer of compensation because he regarded the laws of the *polis* as more compelling; the laws punish an adulterer more severely than a rapist because his crime undermines the social fabric; the law in fact *orders* execution—it is for the judges to determine whether the laws will be valid; the defendant himself believes that communities make their laws so that good citizens will have rules to guide them.

Thus our defendant portrays himself as a paragon of the law-governed democracy who has been victimized by unscrupulous litigators. He makes his case a challenge against arbitrary changes in the law, much as his fellow Athenians had seized upon legal safeguards against ill-considered legislation. He also respects the implications of the amnesty restricting the Draconian rules of self-help, though these restrictions undoubtedly undermined traditional claims of retributive justice. Euphiletus has alluded to these modifications in his proof, and here, in his conclusion, he suggests that he has been ambushed by those who take unfair advantage of the changes. Had he plotted to entrap the adulterer, he insists, he would have been justified in the traditional sense, but he has acted in obedience to the new legalism: he has seen to it that his justifiable killing is 'justified *in the law*'. He acted precisely as the rules require: he waited to catch the intruder in the act and then demonstrated his conviction of the righteousness of his cause in the very moment of executing his claim, swearing 'It is not I who kill you but the laws'.

Those who conclude that Lysias' argument is itself an unscrupulous distortion of the legalities, perhaps underestimate the conviction with which the Athenians who survived the downfall of their democracy embraced their legalism. The spectre of the laws in Plato's *Crito* suggests that they took it quite seriously. The laws themselves constitute an abstract source of authority independent of divine sanctions and superior to the momentary will of the people. This faith that Antiphon professed a generation earlier, reverence for the 'laws most ancient and forever unaltered', is not something the most conservative court of the new regime could be expected to take lightly.

§2. *Tetralogy* 3 and the Notion of Provocation

But the legalism of Lysias 1 perhaps offends the modern sensibility. In Anglo-American law it is solely the passion of the moment that tends to mitigate—and not to justify—the husband's attack upon the adulterer. Embedded in our reaction is a preconception that may hinder our understanding of the ancient dispute—the notion that 'provocation' should be the true exculpatory factor. Provocation is so familiar and self-evident a concept to us that we are naturally inclined to read it into the ancient example, and we are inclined to be taken aback by Lysias' cynical disregard for what we feel is the true spirit of this ancient rule.

In modern criminal codes such strong provocation translates murder to manslaughter, provided that the killing is done in immediate consequence of the provocation and without rational decision; if the cuckold is not overcome by such immediate provocation he should seek legal remedy rather than act upon his rage.[27] But the evidence we have offers no indication whatever that 'provocation' in this sense was ever at issue in cases before the Delphinium court. The operative principle was retributive justice, even when retribution required the specific sanction of written law. The principle that passion of the moment should be viewed as an exculpatory or extenuating factor is not to be found in Lysias 1. On the contrary, our defendant insists that the sequence of his actions was rational, though not prearranged. He seems determined to quash any implication that he acted recklessly, out of control (*akolasia*). Neither is there any indication that the issue was raised in the opposing speech: the defendant says nothing which would indicate that the plaintiffs had raised the obvious issue of alternative legal remedies, as we might expect them to do. One test of intentionality, after all, is the question whether the defendant had any alternatives; but the options go largely unconsidered. Nor is the principle of provocation found in the *Tetralogy* where we might expect to find it— *Tetralogy* 3, for a killing in response to assault (§2.1).

The evidence suggests that where provocation or crime of passion was at issue, the case would go before the Areopagus, as a case of intentional homicide. The evidence on this point is slim and some of it dubious in itself, but it is at least consistent with the other evidence on the Delphinium jurisdiction. One indication in this direction is the anecdote in the anonymous *Life of Thucydides*, which (in the form in which we have it) attributes to the historian an episode that was originally attributed to Thucydides the son of Melesias.[28] We are told that Thucydides first demonstrated his

---

[27] Holmes, *Common Law*, 51, explained the modern principle as follows: 'According to current morality, a man is not so much to blame for an act done under the disturbance of great excitement, caused by a wrong done to himself, as when he is calm. The law is made to govern men through their motives, and it must therefore take their mental constitution into account.' To Holmes this principle seemed contrary to the purpose of prevention—'the heaviest punishment should be threatened where the strongest motive is needed to restrain.' As for the principle that a violent act must come in *immediate* consequence of overwhelming provocation, Holmes cites Stephen, *Digest of Criminal Law*, Art. 225: 'provocation does not extenuate the guilt of homicide, unless the person provoked is at the time when he does the deed deprived of the power of self-control by the provocation which he has received.' For a lucid account of how the modern concept took shape, see Horder, *Provocation*, esp. 43–110, on the early modern revival of an Aristotelian model.

[28] For the text see L. Piccirilli, 'Alcune notizie su Tucidide di Melesia', *Mus. Helv.* 18 (1985), 259–67, with that author's *Storie dello storico Tucidide* (Genoa, 1985), esp. 176–86. For a summary of the various interpretations and emendations, see my study 'Trials of Thucydides "the Demagogue"'.

brilliance speaking in defence of Pyrilampes on murder charges before the Areopagus: Pyrilampes was accused of killing his beloved in a fit of jealous rage; Pericles was prosecutor, and by defeating him Thucydides rose to political prominence. Such is the tale. It may be worthless as an account of historical events, but at least it tends to confirm that a killing in anger, in the passion of the moment, would be charged as intentional homicide, to be tried before the Areopagus.[29]

A second indication that pleas of provocation would ordinarily go before the Areopagus is found in the fragmentary speech Lysias 3, *Against Simon*. These arguments have to do with another case of violent assault in jealous quarrel, though not fatal in this instance. The defendant is charged with wounding with *pronoia*. Such cases were evidently decided on principles analogous to killing with malice aforethought in the same jurisidiction. It is here, at the Areopagus, that a defendant may appeal to a longstanding principle that violence done in the passion of the moment was distinct from outright intent to kill, and therefore grounds for acquittal (see Ch. 6 §1.2 at n. 15).

From these and other references, we can reasonably conclude that a case of killing or wounding in the passion of the moment was one for the Areopagus to decide, and not for the Delphinium.[30]

2.1 *Tetralogy* 3

The traditional interpretation of the third *Tetralogy*, that as a case of self-defence it would go before the Delphinium court, has been challenged by Gagarin. He argues that a case in which a defendant pleads self-defence would naturally resolve itself into a question of intent, and thus it would properly go before the Areopagus.[31] With regard to the division of jurisdiction, Gagarin's argument is persuasive. But I am not persuaded that *Tetralogy* 3 represents such a case: the central issue appears to be the question of legal justification, not true self-defence. A violent response to assault or insult was traditionally regarded as justifiable on the principle of

---

[29] The problem of weighing cause and intent is suggested by Plato, *Laws*, 866d–e: he attempts to distinguish between crimes of anger with repentance and premeditated vengeance in anger without repentance. On this passage see Ch. 6 §2.2 at n. 27, and cf. Saunders, *Plato's Penal Code*, 225–6.

[30] See Ch. 6 §1.2, on motive in Ant. 1 and *Magna Moralia*, 1188ᵇ29–38.

[31] 'Self-Defense', 111–20.

retributive justice, not of self-preservation. The author's chief pre-occupation appears to be the problem of justifying an act that was blameless by the traditional concept but which was no longer justi-fiable without specific provision in the law.[32]

The pious *mythos*, of which our author makes his prologue in the first speech, serves to rationalize the charge of homicide against a defendant whose justification might not have been questioned by traditional values, and it lays the foundation for 'the law prohibit-ing even justifiable killing': the god desired to make the human race, brought forth our ancestors, and provided us with all the earth and sea for sustenance; 'whoever kills a man unlawfully (*anomōs*) . . . commits an impious act against the gods and confounds the rules customarily honoured among men' (*nomima*). The defendant pleads that he has acted in obedience to the law that allows violent reprisal against him who strikes the first blow; but this can be seen as a mere pretext that the younger and more powerful man seized upon, disregarding the spirit of the law that forbids retributive killing even if traditionally justified. The plaintiffs would not put to death the innocent unjustly (*adikōs*) nor attempt to persuade the judges to render an unlawful verdict (*anoma*). It was an act of wan-ton recklessness for the defendant to attack an older man: for this he must be justifiably punished for confounding the customary rules (*nomima*) regarding the treatment of elders (1. 6–7). Thus they conclude (7), 'the law rightly consigns him to retribution at your hands . . . you must avenge the lawlessness of the injury, pun-ish the wanton violence with a punishment equal to the suffering he caused, and sever from him the soul that decided upon the deed' (*psychē bouleusasa*).

There is an unmistakable emphasis here in the plaintiffs' first speech upon customary rules; implicit in their complaint is an opposition of written law to which the defendant will appeal versus 'common law' and equity, such as Aristotle describes in the *Rhetoric*.[33] There is as yet no overt consideration of the apparent conflict between the statute that the defendant has invoked and the intent of the law; but to judge from the pattern of the *Tetralogies*,

---

[32] By the very nature of such a case, the defendant will plead strict adherence to the letter of the law but the prosecution will contend that his conduct violates the spirit of justice. Cf. Aristotle, *Rhet.* 1. 15. 1–12, 1375ᵃ⁻ᵇ, on argument from conflict in the law.

[33] *Rhet.* 1375ᵃ: ἐὰν μὲν ἐνάντιος ᾖ ὁ γεγραμμένος τῷ πράγματι, τῷ κοινῷ νόμῳ χρηστέον καὶ τοῖς ἐπιεικέσιν ὡς δικαιοτέροις.

the objective of the plaintiffs' first speech is not to confront the
issue directly but rather to introduce the charge and challenge the
defence to respond in such a way as to allow for effective rebuttal in
the second speech.
Now the defendant's first speech begins with a direct appeal to
the provisions of statute by which he claims legal justification (2. 1):
the plaintiffs are attempting to have him put to death wrongfully,
in a case where the victim himself was responsible for his death; 'for
it was he *who first laid violent hands* in drunken assault upon a much
more sober man who is to blame, not only for his own disaster but
also for the indictment against me.' The description 'who first laid
violent hands' follows the wording of Draco's law (36–8). The
interpretation of this phrase is to be a central preoccupation of the
argument henceforth. In the following passage the defendant continues with a further principle derived from Draco's law or its integral amendments (2. 2).

for even if I had defended against him with sword or stone or club, as it was
he who first struck a blow, I would not have been in the wrong; for it is justifiable that those who begin the violence suffer more serious hurt; but,
instead, as I was struck by his hands, and did with my own hands the very
same harm that I suffered, how is it that I did wrong?

The relevant passage in Draco's law cannot be fully restored, but
it looks as though some qualification followed the first rule regarding violent response to the aggressor and this second clause approx-
imated the principle our defendant invokes, that the defender
against aggressive violence is entitled to use greater force (Ch. 2
§3.2.2). It is also likely that the reference to defence 'with sword or
stone or club' is an echo of the wording of law.[34] But I would suggest that this part of the complex argument follows the same
method we have seen in Lysias 1 and in *Tetralogy* 2 in regard to the
law prohibiting even justifiable killing (Ch. 5 §3): the more flagrant
violence *would have been justified* in the traditional sense, but the
defendant did not commit even this traditionally justifiable act.
   In the following sections (3–5) the defendant turns to further
points of law. First he anticipates the charge that 'the law prohibiting just as well as unjust killing' holds him accountable: had the

---

[34] This condition seems parallel to that in the law of adultery allowing the successful plaintiff to do with the offender as he will, 'without a knife': it imposes a limit
upon the retaliatory violence.

man died at his hands, his act would have been justified, as the law allows greater force against the aggressor, but would be none the less culpable by the law prohibiting even justifiable killing. But, he insists, he is not to blame on either count since the proximate cause of death was not his own act but the malpractice of the physician; and as it was the victim's kinsmen who committed him to the physician's care, they bear the responsibility for his death and have brought an unrighteous charge. 'I am (thus) acquitted', he concludes, 'by the very law under which I am prosecuted, for the law requires that he who plotted be held the killer.' In the language of Draco's law, 'guilty . . . is the planner'. The defendant then reverts to the principle that 'the first to lay violent hands' is responsible (6–7). Anticipating the range of constructions that might be put upon his act, he contends: 'if he died by mischance, it was his own doing—for he met his mishap by striking the first blow; if he died by recklessness, it was his own recklessness that killed him, for he was rash in striking the blow.'[35] In conclusion the defendant contends that it is the prosecutors who are unjustly 'plotting' a murder by means of the law and thus confounding the *nomima*.

In rebuttal the prosecutors immediately take up the argument that the guilty party is 'the first to lay violent hands'; they do not dispute the principle that the aggressor is held liable by the law. Rather they dispute the allegation that the victim himself initiated the violence; they refer to the commonplace that young men are more likely to get drunk and start a fight than their elders.[36]

This is a puzzling response: the plaintiffs seem to be treating as a question in dispute whether the defendant or the victim was the first to strike, although witnesses have been called (1. 7) and they evidently indicated that it was indeed the victim who struck the first blow (3. 3). Now one solution to this puzzle would be to assume, along the lines of Cole's interpretation, that each of the *Tetralogies* is to some extent a list of loosely arranged, sometimes unconnected arguments, from which the prospective client might choose points pertinent to his own case: the *Tetralogy* does not represent a single hypothetical dispute but many possible disputes; thus the author demonstrates how each side would argue if the witnesses were in their favour. But this seems to me a rather extreme solution. It is certainly true that our author endeavours to cover a

---

[35] For the degrees of intentionality, recklessness, and mischance, see Ch. 5 §3.
[36] Cf. Aristotle, *Rhet.* 2. 2. 12, 1389ᵃ.

range of possible arguments, but he has presented these arguments as a dramatic unity: he does not leap from one scenario to another.

The solution to this puzzle may be simply that the question of who precisely *initiated* the violence in such a case was often debatable, even if there were testimony that one man or the other struck the first blow. The witnesses are likely to be at odds as to where the taunting left off and the violence began. The law itself, after all, did not define what it meant to be 'the first to lay violent hands'. Thus the plaintiffs' suggestion that the defendant is more likely to have begun the violence may not be in direct contradiction to the testimony of witnesses; it may be simply an attempt to recast the question of liability. Which of the two men actually began the struggle, perhaps by some insulting gesture or other physical abuse, short of coming to blows? The ultimate responsibility might not lie with him who first resorted to his fists. He who *provoked* the quarrel is arguably the more responsible as his behaviour was the truest cause. It is in this vein, then, that the plaintiffs explain: 'the younger are more likely to get drunk and start a fight . . . for they are roused to indulge their emotions by arrogance, youthful vigour, and inexperience of strong drink.'

In the following section (3) the plaintiffs answer the argument that it is lawful to respond to violence with equal force, 'by the same means'—that is, so long as the quarrel does not escalate to lethal weapons, 'sword, or stone, or club'. A young man's hands are by no means equivalent instruments of defence to those of an old man; the proof that the aged victim's hands were no match for his adversary's lies in the fact that 'he didn't leave a mark on him'. And as for the defendant's excuse that he struck with only his hands and without a weapon, the plaintiffs argue that he is all the more to blame inasmuch as his hands are an indivisible part of his own agency. That is to say, if he had struck with a weapon (an external instrument), he might argue that the precise impact of the weapon was beyond his control and not as he intended; but he cannot as easily contend that he did not aim and control his own hands. This point leads the plaintiffs to the crux of the causal argument and one of the crucial testimonia to the concept of 'planning' an unintended outcome: 'He dared to claim that he who struck the first blow without killing is more responsible for the slaying than the killer; for he says that [the first to strike] is the "planner" of the killing . . . [but] if our hands undertake whatever each of us intends, he that strikes with-

out killing is (merely) the "planner"' of the blow he struck, but he
who strikes a fatal blow [is "planner"] of the killing; for as a consequence of what he did intentionally, the man died.'

Finally, the plaintiffs counter the argument that the physician's
treatment was proximate cause, thus absolving the defendant and
implicating the victim's kinsmen themselves who called in the
incompetent physician. The implication of his argument appears to
be that, since the law expressly absolves the physician, the blame
for the physician's misdeed is thrown back upon the next proximate cause. The plaintiffs carry the causal chain back one more step
(7): 'by law the blame reverts to him who struck the fatal blow.' On
the same principle, those who speak for the defendant in the final
speech cast the blame one step further back to the victim himself:
he began the quarrel that provoked the blow that led his kinsmen to
call in the physician whose treatment led to death.

In the final speech of the *Tetralogy* the issue in dispute is treated
as a 'mixed question' of law and of fact, but the crux of the case is
the defendant's plea that his victim was 'the first to lay violent
hands' and defendant himself is therefore guiltless by the letter of
the law. Thus the defender counters the commonplace that the
young are more prone to violence than their elders with the obvious evidence of experience: many young people are self-controlled;
many of their elders, prone to drunken trouble-making. If the
stereotype were a reliable gauge of character, there would be no
need for trial. And the witnesses confirm that the victim himself
struck the first blow (2–3). Taking this point as established, he
treats the overt act of violence as the decisive causal event: if the
plaintiffs are to claim that defendant is responsible for the victim's
treatment at the hands of the physician, because he struck the blow
that caused the injury, they cannot escape the implication that the
victim himself is to blame since he struck the blow that caused
defendant to strike back.

The blame reverts to the first to strike: 'the error' or accident
belongs to him who began the violence (οἰκεῖον δὲ καὶ τὸ ἁμάρτημα
τῷ ἄρξαντι). Even if the defendant's response was more forceful
than the attack upon him, it is not right to convict him, since in all
instances the law lays more serious penalties upon the aggressor
(6–7).

Finally, in regard to the law prohibiting just as well as unjust
killing, the speaker asserts that the charge has been answered

inasmuch as the defendant is not the killer, neither justly nor unjustly: the physician's treatment was proximate cause, and any attempt to cast the blame back to the cause of injury must ultimately hold the victim himself responsible, since he struck the first blow and thus set the sequence of events in motion—he was the author of his own mischance. (8)

Thus the *Tetralogy* illustrates, in its peculiar way, what is likely to have been the central issue in such a case, where a defendant struck back in anger and caused the death of his assailant but appealed to the statutory provision against him who first raised his hand in violence. The dispute will then naturally tend to resolve itself into a question of who was really the initiator of the violence. Some elements of provocation might enter into this determination—the arrogance of youth or the insult of a drunken man—but the consideration of motives and state of mind focuses more upon the aggressor's hostility than the anger it might provoke in his adversary. It may in fact be possible to find witnesses who are willing to identify either party as the aggressor, since it was probably difficult to determine where the taunting and jostling left off and the first punch was thrown. But it is not the killer's outrage that excuses him: there is no attempt to diminish responsibility because abusive provocation supposedly deprived him of self-control. Provocation and passion of the moment may well be a factor in the judges' decision at the Areopagus, where the assailant's state of mind is paramount. But at the Delphinium a killer who acted in anger of the moment and is foolish enough to admit it as much as admits his guilt!

In both Lysias 1 and *Tetralogy* 3 the defendant's action is treated as a mechanistic response, in the one case, to breach of the law against sexual violation; in the other instance, to the first blow struck in violence. There is no delving into the defendant's psyche to show that he was deprived of his wits or driven to do what he did by overpowering rage. Nor is there any rebuttal to the obvious argument for the prosecution that the defendant had other, legal means of redress that he should have preferred. Against the adulterer, as we have seen, there were legal remedies. Against assault or 'outrage' there were also appropriate legal actions (δίκη αἰκίας, γραφὴ ὕβρεως). If state of mind were at issue, it would have been a self-evident test of the defendant's state of mind to inquire why he did not resort to those remedies of law rather than to self-help; but no such test is applied.

In this respect then, the *Tetralogy* is much like the argument in Lysias 1: in neither case is there any serious consideration of the defendant's state of mind, to discover whether passion of the moment deprived him of volition. Such would probably be part of the jury's deliberation in a modern hearing of either case, but it appears to be in the nature of *dikai phonou*, in cases where a defendant pleads legal justification, that considerations of provocation and passion would not weigh in his favour. On the contrary, it is all the more incriminating if he appears to have lost self-control and acted rashly rather than strictly in obedience to the law. That the defendant's act was determined by the law rather than his emotion may seem to us an absurd fiction—and it was perhaps its absurdity that prompted the author of *Tetralogies* to take up this particular demonstration. But it certainly appears to be an *authentic* legal fiction, true to the historical requirements of the Delphinium court.

2.2   The Case against Euaion (Dem. 21. 70–6)

There is one other case reported in sufficient detail to suggest a parallel for the third *Tetralogy*, a case where the defendant struck a mortal blow in anger at a weaker man's assault, but where something approaching the concept of provocation seems to have entered into the judges' decision. Such is the case of Euaion, reported by Demosthenes in the speech *Against Meidias*, 21. 70–6. Now in weighing Demosthenes' pronouncements, we should bear in mind the nature of his own case. He is prosecuting for a violation of rules regarding the choral festival: Meidias had struck Demosthenes in the theatre where he was acting as *chorēgos*.[37] He treats Meidias' offence as 'outrage', *hybris*, and much that he says regarding state of mind is meant to distinguish this more serious offence from simple assault (*aikia*). The orator had sought legal redress rather than strike back in anger, but he cites the case of Euaion, along with another, more obscure instance, to show that the killing is not an unwarranted response against *hybris*.[38] His own

---

[37] The formal charge appears to be ἀδικεῖν περὶ τὴν ἑορτήν; the substantive wrong was an act of *hybris* and *asebeia*. See MacDowell, *Demosthenes* 'Against Meidias', 16–22, and 288–92 on this passage. MacDowell has reservations about the description of *hybris* as an offence against *timē*, but see N. R. Fisher, 'The Law of *hubris* in Athens', in P. A. Cartledge *et al.*, *Nomos* (Cambridge, 1990).

[38] He first mentions the case of Euthynos (71), a wrestler who apparently killed another athlete at a dinner party on Samos. The case was well enough known to

conduct is all the more commendable by contrast to the violent reaction of Euaion.

Here it is clearly the uncontrollable anger that an act of outrage inspires in its victim that gives him justification for striking back with deadly force. It is not, in Demosthenes' estimation, the blow itself that causes the lethal response (as the defendant in *Tetr.* 3 seemed to suggest); it is rather the insult or indignity: οὐ γὰρ ἡ πληγὴ παρέστησε τὴν ὀργήν, ἀλλ' ἡ ἀτιμία. 'For a free man', he continues, 'the mere impact of the blow, though a serious matter, is not so serious as the fact that it is struck in arrogance.' There are many factors that make of the offence an 'outrage' rather than simple injury—'[the assailant's] bearing, the look on his face, the tone of his voice'. The circumstances enter into the equation: Euaion was struck by someone familiar at a private party where both were invited guests; Boiotus was drunk, and he struck the blow in the presence of witnesses who would respect Euaion for his restraint and who might easily have supported him in an action for 'outrage' had he chosen legal redress. None the less Euaion struck back in anger and killed his assailant. Demosthenes, on the other hand, was struck by a personal enemy who appeared to be sober, at a public gathering, in a holy place, where Demosthenes was obliged to be present because of his official duties; and the offence was witnessed not merely by friends but by all the body of citizens and foreign visitors who had come to hear the performance.

Euaion was convicted by the narrowest of margins: nearly half the judges held that he was justified in using deadly force because of the outrage. Demosthenes regards the degree of provocation as the issue crucial to the judges' verdict: those who voted for conviction concluded that his right of defence did not extend to deadly force. But in the eyes of many he was justified. Demosthenes would have been all the more justified in resorting to violence. His restraint is therefore the more commendable and his pursuit of legal remedies all the more worthy of the court's favour.

Thus Demosthenes' interpretation of the case against Euaion serves as an *a fortiori* judgement in his own case; it cannot be relied upon as evidence that such factors were commonly considered in cases of justifiable homicide before the Delphinium court. Indeed, we cannot even be sure that the case of Euaion was tried before the

Demosthenes' audience that he tells us nothing more. It is therefore doubtful whether the case ever went to trial at Athens.

Delphinium. If indeed it was Euaion's plea that he reacted in anger, overcome by emotion, then from the other evidence it seems likely that this case would go before the Areopagus on a charge of intentional homicide.[39] But even if we conclude that Euaion was tried at the Delphinium, we must not be overly impressed by Demosthenes' argument from provocation. The verdict, after all, went against Euaion.

§3. Conclusions: Euthyphro's Case against His Father

The cases of Lysias 1 and *Tetralogy* 3, though quite dissimilar in some respects, are remarkably consistent in their approach to the problematic concept of justifiable homicide. The overriding principle that connects the arguments in both cases is the notion of retributive justice: the killing is the consequence of the victim's wrongdoing. This conception encompassed even unintentional killing. It is with this understanding that Demosthenes explains the law on killing in athletic competition: if the victim proved unequal to the struggle, he is responsible for his own fate. The other evidence on various exculpatory considerations—provocation and passion—yields nothing to contradict this finding, that the Delphinium court was the last bastion of retributive justice.

The traditional causal mechanism, triggered by the victim's wrong, was accommodated to the legalism of the restored democracy by the fiction of legal cause. In order to plead justification, the defendant must appeal to specific statutory rules, and Lysias' speech for Euphiletus reveals how a defendant might maintain the traditional causation by treating the sovereign command of the law as the mainspring of retribution. As in the other proceedings before Areopagites and *ephetai*, the litigant must show that his sworn claim is corroborated by every available test of conviction, that in all the relevant processual acts he has demonstrated his resolve. In this instance the defendant's oath is backed not only by sworn affirmation of witnesses but also by the laws themselves. But what

---

[39] As in the cases of Pyrilampes (anon. *Vit. Thuc.* 6) and the wife in *Magna Moralia* 1188ᵇ; see above §2 at nn. 28–30. It is perhaps possible that such a case could be prosecuted by *endeixis* or *apagōgē*, which apparently became regular alternatives to *dikai phonou*, especially in cases not easily comprehended by the traditional divisions of jurisdiction.

makes these proceedings so disturbing is that *the decisive processual act* by which the defendant asserts his claim of right *is the killing itself*. He therefore claims to have given a singular proof of his conviction as he struck the blow: 'It is not I who kill you but the laws.' And in his argument he looks to the laws not simply to condone what he did, but as a *prescriptive source of moral certainty*—it is by the law that he knew what was right to do. The statutes are not brought in to decide a question of law *per se*—principle, procedure, or jurisdiction—but as proof that the victim's wrong was such as to bring retribution upon himself. The killer therefore acted with absolute conviction of the right.

As one last test of this model, let us consider the strange case of Euthyphro against his father. It is, of course, unclear whether Plato's portrayal was based upon any actual case; but it appears to be an accurate reflection of the kind of legal controversy we might expect after 403/2. Euthyphro certainly seems inspired by a righteous sense of purpose in confronting the complacency of traditional justice. Socrates is surprised, first of all that Euthyphro should be prosecuting in behalf of a victim that was not a member of his household, and second, that Euthyphro is charging his own father. Euthyphro protests, 'It is laughable that you should think it makes any difference whether the victim is a relative or a stranger and not realize that one must only consider whether the killer acted justly or not,' even if the killer is a close relation (4b 7–10). The victim in this case was a hired labourer who in a drunken rage had killed a slave; the killing took place on the family landholding on Naxos. Euthyphro's father had the man bound and left him unattended in a culvert while he sent to Athens to inquire of the exegetes how properly to remedy the first homicide. Meanwhile, the man died. Now it is unclear whether Euthyphro accuses his father of intentional killing or negligence: he says that his father was 'unconcerned and utterly indifferent whether the man might die, thinking it of no consequence since the man was a killer' (4c–d). That the likelihood of death made no difference to the father 'since the man (himself) was a killer', and that the question of intent seems to make no difference to Euthyphro, strengthen the impression that this is a case in which only the question of justification, 'whether the killer acted justly or not', will be at issue. It was probably a case for the Delphinium court. Euthyphro's father would appeal to the ordinary rules prescribing how to deal with the killing of slaves; these remedies probably involved a good measure of self-help.[40] He could probably make a plausible case that he was in the right, at least initially, to take forcible action against the killer. That the culprit died as a result of rough treatment would be laid at his own door: death is fitting retribution for the victim's own wrong.

[40] Plato's arrangements for homicides involving slaves and others of non-citizen status, Laws 869–72, include nothing that precisely covers this situation, but the general tenor suggests that a kyrios would ordinarily take into his own hands the punishment of bloodshed involving menials within his household. The hireling evidently had no citizen status or family to prosecute in his behalf. As for the actual proceedings against Euthyphro's father (if any): Loening, 'Reconciliation', 108–10 with nn. 123–5, accepts the implication that the actual killing took place some six years before the hearing (since Athens presumably lost control of Naxos after Aegospotami in 405); others have supposed either that Athenian citizens might still refer their disputes to Athens, or that Plato committed an intentional anachronism.

9

Warrant and Arrest for Homicide: Antiphon 5 and Lysias 13

The traditional homicide procedure, *dikē phonou*, was a cumbersome, ritualistic remedy. The elaborate sequence of preliminaries and the special rules of evidence and oath-taking were designed to facilitate private settlement. It was a reasonably effective means of deciding a dispute over liability where the fact of the defendant's involvement was not contested and the parties themselves were bound to resolve the grievance by ties of custom and social conscience. But those who prosecuted by the traditional *dikai* found themselves at a serious disadvantage in other respects. If there were no firsthand witnesses that the accused did indeed participate in the fatal act—if the case was one of those that so inspire the modern imagination, a 'who-done-it'—then the plaintiffs had practically no case in the courts of the *ephetai*, no matter how conclusive the circumstantial evidence. It was this limitation of the traditional procedure that inspired the author of the first *Tetralogy*. The traditional *dikai* were also unwieldy for prosecuting outsiders, not bound by ties to the community. Foreign nationals with no particular standing at Athens and 'common criminals' without civil rights were less likely to respect the obligations of oath that made the verdict binding upon citizens and metics. In such circumstances, the plaintiffs sometimes invoked the ancient procedures for warrant and arrest of felons, *endeixis* and *apagōgē kakourgōn*.[1]

Those who prosecuted by this route went to trial with a different set of criteria. In the traditional *dikai* the plaintiffs swore to their

---

[1] For the basic procedures in *endeixis* and *apagōgē* against homicides, see Hansen, *Apagoge*, esp. 99–112; MacDowell, *AHL* 130–40; Lipsius, *Attische Recht*, 317–38; H. D. Evjen, '*Apagoge* and Athenian Homicide Procedure', *Revue d'histoire du droit*, 38 (1970), 403–15, rightly emphasizing the conservative character of this ancient remedy; Ruschenbusch, *Untersuchungen Athenischen Strafrechts*, 67–9, treating *endeixis* as a primitive advance in the archon's authority over self-help. As a concise rendering of *kakourgos*, I have resorted to the common 'felon', as approximate to 'wrongdoer, malefactor', and an inclusive term that comprehends homicide as well as lesser crimes. On the rendering of *endeixis* as 'warrant' see Ch. 2 §3 at n. 86.

'claim of right'—*dikē* in its quintessential sense—and they called upon the judges to validate that claim and thus recognize their right to self-help, much as plaintiffs had done ever since the era of Homer and Draco. But in prosecuting by warrant or arrest, the plaintiffs claim to have caught the wrongdoer in the immediate consequences of his act. They must therefore prove that they have acted on what we would call 'probable suspicion' or 'probable cause'. This criterion gives a more direct approach to the question that would preoccupy a modern jury in a murder—'Did he do it?'

We now turn to the two speeches that survive from such proceedings: Antiphon *On the Murder of Herodes* and Lysias *Against Agoratus*.

§1. Antiphon 5 (*Herodes*)

First I shall show that I am brought to trial in these proceedings in an entirely wrongful and illegal manner . . . For, first of all, though I am indicted as a felon, I stand trial on a charge of murder—a travesty that no one in this land ever before suffered.   (Ant. 5. 8–9)

Thus the defendant begins his challenge to the legality of the proceedings in what has been the most studied of the Greek homicide trials. The speech that Antiphon wrote for the defence was justly praised by the ancient critics; and the questions of law and fact have been more thoroughly disputed by modern scholars than any of the other homicide speeches. Aside from its legal significance and rhetorical interest, this speech is also important for its political ramifications. The defendant, Euxitheus, is a citizen of Mytilene charged in the murder of Herodes, an Athenian citizen who had apparently received a landholding from the property of rebellious subjects on the island of Lesbos. The trial comes only a few years after the revolt of Mytilene, in which our defendant's father was involved, and he must argue at some length against inevitable prejudice on that account. On that count Antiphon has certainly succeeded in winning the sympathy of modern commentators, some of whom suspect that the wealthy Mytilenean was the victim of a frame-up.[2] But there is still no consensus on some of the most basic

---

[2] Schindel, *Mordfall Herodes*, esp. 22–5 and 39–41; Scheidweiler, 'Antiphons Rede', esp. 330–2; Heitsch, *Antiphon*, 33–89; Gagarin, *Murder of Herodes*, argues to the contrary, esp. 111–15.

questions: What grounds does the defendant have for his objection to the procedure? And how has the procedural issue shaped the argumentation in this model of reasoning from probability? The present study will be confined to these two lines of inquiry. I offer no speculation whatever on the guilt or innocence of Euxitheus. The defendant protests that his case should properly be tried by a *dikē phonou*. A case of this kind would have encountered certain obvious limitations, but there is no good reason to doubt that non-citizens could be prosecuted by the traditional *dikē*, if the plaintiffs chose to do so and the accused would come to trial. In this case, however, the proceedings were initiated by warrant (*endeixis*): Euxitheus was served a summons in Mytilene and upon arriving in Athens was promptly arrested and held for trial. He claims that there was some irregularity on this account.[3] Was our defendant perhaps formally charged as accessory to a theft or other lesser felony but then accused of capital murder? Was this, as he seems to be claiming, the very first application of this procedure in a case of homicide? These questions will be taken up below (§1.1.2). It will be helpful first to analyse the argument, to outline the evidence, the proof, and the points in dispute.

In Antiphon 5 the argument centres on the circumstantial evidence.[4] Solmsen himself acknowledged the greater weight given to probabilities in this speech, and he saw it as a sign that the traditional forms of proof—oath and slave torture—were already undermined: this speech is a document of the new technique that Antiphon had only begun to master. But if we look closely at the way probabilities and direct evidence are used in this speech, by contrast to Antiphon 1 and 6, I think it will be clear that the difference in method is not simply a matter of evolving technique. The arguments were largely defined by the initiating procedure.

---

[3] On the procedure in this case see esp. Hansen, *Apagoge*, 14–16, 124. Before Hansen's study, it was sometimes thought that the *apagōgē* served as initiating procedure for some other form of action, perhaps *graphē phonou* (cf. MacDowell, *AHL* 136), perhaps some form of prosecution for theft (Wolff, *Paragraphe*, 112–19; cf. M. Sorof, 'Über die *ΑΠΑΓΩΓΗ* im attischen Gerichtsverfahren', *Jahrbücher für klassischen Philologie*, 128 (1884), 13).

[4] Cf. Scheidweiler, 'Antiphons Rede', 334–8; Goebel, 'Rhetorical Theory', 228–32; Gagarin, 'Proofs in Antiphon', esp. 31–2. Cf. Solmsen, *Antiphonstudien*, esp. 48–53.

1.1 The Method of Proof

Antiphon's speech for Euxitheus differs markedly from the first
and last speeches in the corpus. Here the speaker persistently refers
overtly to 'probability', *eikos/eikota*,[5] and in many other instances
he relies upon circumstantial reasoning on means and motives.
This is not to say that this speech is deficient in traditional evidence. On the contrary, there is actually more of such material than
in either Antiphon 1 or 6. For the prosecution there is testimony by
a slave under torture that he acted with Euxitheus in the killing,
and a brief letter reporting the murder to another supposed conspirator, Lycinus. And there were, presumably, statements by various witnesses: the defendant has witnesses that he never left ship
on the night in question, and he can cite testimony of a freeman
who was put to the torture but in no way incriminated him. There
is an important distinction, however, between the traditional uses
of witnesses and challenges and their use in this case.[6] By the traditional method they serve as demonstrations of the litigant's conviction, that he 'knows well' or earnestly believes in the affirmation of
his oath. But in the *Herodes* the slave's testimony under torture, the
incriminating letter, and the testimony on the alibi are treated
largely as circumstantial evidence on the question of probable
cause, whether the defendant was apprehended in immediately
incriminating circumstances.

1.1.1 Probabilities and Direct Evidence in Warrant and Arrest

By the very nature of the procedure, circumstantial evidence was
often essential to summary arrest. Forcible, potentially deadly
arrest was sanctioned because it was assumed that the culprit would
be apprehended, if not in the very act of committing the crime, at
least in circumstances that clearly and directly incriminated him. If
apprehended in such circumstances the offender could be executed
without trial. At some point early in the development of this procedure it was written into the law that plaintiffs must seize the
offender 'upon immediate incrimination'—*ep' autophōrōi*—if they

---

[5] *Eikos/eikota* 22 times in Ant. 5, against very few instances in Ant. 1 and 6, and
these mostly parenthetical (e.g. Ant. 1. 2, 17, 18, οἷον εἰκός, 'as one would expect').

[6] See *Antiphonstudien*, 43–7, on *modus procedendi*, οἴῳ τρόπῳ ἔρχονται ἐπὶ τὰ
πράγματα.

were *to demand summary execution*.[7] This requirement does not
mean that the offender must be 'caught in the act': it is rather analogous to the Roman *furtum manifestum:* a thief is to be discovered
in possession of the stolen goods (Just. *Inst.* 4. 1. 3). In fact it
implies that the plaintiffs can identify the culprit from the physical
means or proceeds of the crime; they are not dependent upon such
direct evidence as an eyewitness to the crime itself. Now at the time
of proceedings against Euitheus it is doubtful whether it was
required that plaintiffs arrest the accused *ep' autophōrōi* in this strict
sense, *if* they were *not seeking summary execution*—that is, if they
expected to go to trial or to to coerce some settlement by their warrant. But it is clear in any event that the underlying principle of
immediate incrimination was none the less valid, even in cases such
as this, initiated by warrant, where the plaintiffs have been authorized to make forcible arrest of the accused sometime after the
crime. It is readily assumed that guilt should be proved by the
immediate circumstances or consequences of the crime. If the
plaintiffs could not seize the culprit in the very act, they would have
to catch him with the weapon or stolen goods in his possession,
bearing the marks of a struggle, or in some way directly linked to
the killing.

The same principles that shaped *dikē phonou* as an instrument of
private settlement, based upon tests of conviction, cannot hold
true. It would naturally be assumed that the offender subject to
violent arrest would be a person of no standing, whether petty thief
or banished homicide.[8] He may deny his guilt to assure himself of
trial, but this denial is a purely procedural hurdle; it is not an
instrument of proof. In these proceedings neither the parties

---

[7] Hansen, *Apagoge*, 48–53: the essential meaning of the term derives from φωρᾶν
in the sense of 'search for theft'; thus I have resorted to the phrase 'immediate
incrimination'. Harris, '"In the Act" or "Red-Handed"', 182, has recently concluded, that *ep' autophōrōi* in cases of theft 'appears to relate to the manner of acquir-
ing the stolen object'; he bases this conclusion largely upon the distinctions drawn
by Roman jurists regarding *furtum manifestum*. But I have to conclude with Hansen,
that in Athenian practice the distinction is largely a matter of *the manner of discovery*. Hansen, however, sometimes assumes that *ep' autophōrōi* was required in all
apagogai kakourgon. It was clearly not required in the case against Euitheus. For
the view that *ep' autophōrōi* was originally required only in cases seeking execution
without trial, and later extended to cases for trial, cf. Sorof, 'Über die ΑΠΑΓΟΓΗ',
11–12; and see below, §2.2, on the case against Agoratus.

[8] Hansen insists that arrest *ep' autophōrōi* was not required against exiled homicides who trespassed in Attica, but only against ordinary *kakourgoi;* on this point see
§§1.2.1 and 1.3.

themselves nor their witnesses swear the oath of annihilation that defined *dikai phonou*. This difference has great importance for the argumentation. Antiphon elaborates upon it at some length.

All the courts try homicide cases in the open for no other reason but so that the judges do not consort with those whose hands are unclean and the prosecutor does not share the same roof with the slayer of his kinsman. But *you* have violated this law and done precisely the opposite. And, what is more, *whereas you would be required to swear an oath of the greatest and most binding power—invoking annihilation upon yourself and your house—that you truly charge me on no other grounds than the homicide itself,* so that no matter what other wrongs I had done, however many, I should not be condemned on any other grounds than the case itself . . . these rules you have transgressed, making up your own laws of your own devising; you make your accusations *not under oath* and your witnesses testify *not under oath*, whereas they too should have been required to swear the same oath as yourself, clutching the offerings of sacrifice as they made their statements against me. (11)

The fact that the plaintiffs and those who support their accusation are not under oath makes a crucial difference in the way the case is to be argued. In *dikai phonou* the trial focuses upon the oaths of the principals, testimony, and challenges, as tests of conviction: the objective question of what happened is not directly at issue; the dispute centres upon the subjective question of the litigant's conviction of his claim of right—what he earnestly believes and has some way of knowing. In the trial by warrant and arrest, however, the plaintiffs have not sworn to the righteousness of their claim but to the righteousness of the arrest.[9] Have they apprehended the culprit in circumstances that clearly and unequivocally incriminate him? The facts and circumstances of the crime itself are thus directly relevant to the validity of the arrest, and these questions naturally open the door to conjecture on probable motives, means, and opportunity.

And the formal proofs, the *atechnoi*, become circumstantial evidence on the validity of the arrest. Thus in the central sections of his argument our defendant examines the conduct of his accusers in obtaining the confession under torture. The slave's testimony itself—the strongest direct evidence the plaintiffs have—has relatively little weight at face value. What the judges have to weigh,

---

[9] Presumably the plaintiffs were required to affirm their affidavit under oath, but this formality is nowhere mentioned, and Euxitheus implies that there was no oath on the substance of the charges.

after all, is the *report* of that testimony by the plaintiffs and other witnesses, none of them subject to the daunting oath of *dikai phonou*. The prosecutors themselves therefore, rather than rest their case upon the slave's testimony and the letter that supposedly corroborated it, evidently devoted a great deal of their argument to rousing suspicion of Euxitheus' anti-Athenian motives and constructing an elaborate conspiracy theory, to show that his involvement in the events and the actions they took to discover it were sufficient to give probable cause for arrest. Conversely, the testimony of witnesses in support of the alibi, though it might seem to us decisive, is given remarkably little treatment.[10] The value of such testimony is not what it proves about the crime but what it proves about the arrest.

On this reading, then, the focus upon the *atechnoi* in the first half of the speech is not a sign of the intellectual tyranny of traditional, pre-rational methods of proof. On the contrary, if we look to the probative function of this evidence—what it is intended to prove – it is clear that these instruments have become, as Anaximenes described them, supplementary to the rationalistic arguments. Circumstantial proofs as to motive and means emerge as the organizing ideas.[11]

1.1.2 Probable Cause

First and foremost, the procedural challenge itself, beginning with sections 8–19, is fundamentally an argument against what we would call 'probable suspicion' or probable cause for the arrest.[12] It has little to do with the events in question and it does not invoke the text of law as an instrument of proof (as law is treated in Lysias 1).[13] Our defendant rather attacks the prosecutors' handling of the case itself as 'evidence' that the arrest is unfounded: 'First, I shall show that I am brought to trial in these proceedings in an entirely wrongful and

[10] Both pieces of evidence are subject to conflicting interpretation: on the slave testimony and the letter, see below §1.2.3; on the alibi, §1.1.4.
[11] With the following outline see Solmsen's sketch of the argument, *Antiphonstudien*, 13–17; cf. Goebel, 'Early Rhetorical Theory', 225–33.
[12] On the modern foundations of arrest and probable suspicion, see Blackstone *Comm.* iv. ch. 21. The American version is handily defined in Ballentine's Law Dictionary s.v. 'probable cause for arrest' (with case law cited): 'A reasonable ground for suspicion, supported by circumstances sufficiently strong in themselves to warrant a cautious man in believing the accused to be guilty.'
[13] Against the old view that this case involved a formal challenge on the legalities, a form of *paragraphē*, see below, §1.2.

illegal manner . . . [not to evade the jurisdiction of the Athenian peo-
ple] but so that the *prosecutors' violation and contempt of law . . . may
serve as evidence* (*tekmēria*) of the nature of their actions' (8).
Euxitheus insists that his accusers have resorted to an irregular procedure in order to extort some financial advantage: their motives, he
assures the jury (10), will be clear in the course of his argument.

To impress upon the jury the implications of this contempt of
legality, Antiphon invokes the commonplace on the sanctity of the
ancient laws—'the finest and most hallowed of [all] . . . forever unaltered'.[14] The plaintiffs' violation of these laws constitutes the greatest 'testimony' (*marturia*), our defendant claims, in his favour;[15] for
neither the plaintiffs nor their witnesses would swear to the 'oath of
annihilation' that is required in *dikai phonou*. The chief prosecutor's
lack of conviction in the arrest (οὐχ ὡς πιστεύων, 16) is further indicated by the fact he has allowed himself a second means of prosecution (*dikē phonou*), thus ensnaring the defendant twice in jeopardy;
and by imprisoning the defendant he has hindered him from preparing his defence (17). In the sections that follow, our defendant takes
up the various criteria for probable cause, circumstantial evidence on
the questions of motive, means, and direct involvement.

The narrative (20–4) emphasizes the chance turn of events that
brought Herodes and Euxitheus together on the night in question, in
order to dispel any suspicion of prearrangement: the defendant was
on his way to visit his father in Ainos; the victim was conveying some
captives to Thrace for ransom, accompanied by those who were to
pay the ransom. They ran into a storm and happened to anchor near
Methymna, where they met another vessel better outfitted for the
weather; and so they took shelter in the second ship and proceeded to
drink. All of this is confirmed by witnesses. The testimony furnishes
a probability that Euxitheus could not have planned or premeditated
what befell his fellow traveller. Against the implication that
Euxitheus plotted against Herodes, there is also the report that, when
Herodes was discovered missing, it was Euxitheus who sent his com-

---

[14] Ant. 5. 14 = 6. 2. The common passages are still sometimes regarded as interpolations in Ant. 5, hence of no bearing on the substance of the argument: cf.
Scheidweiler, 'Antiphons Herodes', 329 n. 9. Wilamowitz, on the other hand,
'Sechste Rede', 411, supposed that the stock argument was originally devised for
cases of intentional homicide and then adapted (rather imperfectly) to the argument
in Ant. 6. Against the notion that the doublets are the work of a later redactor, cf.
Lavency, *Logographie*, 149–53.

[15] Ant. 5. 15: ἃ δὲ σὺ παρανομεῖς, αὐτὰ ταῦτά μοι μέγιστα μαρτύριά ἐστιν.

panion to Mytilene to report his disappearance—'though surely I did not knowingly send someone to inform against me!' Thus the immediate circumstances contribute nothing to probable suspicion.

The section immediately following the narrative (25–8) addresses 'the probabilities' directly: 'Such were the events; now consider the probable implications'—*ta eikota*. The sequence of thought here is problematic. Solmsen saw in it the gravitational effects of the *atechnoi* that follow (§1.1.4). But these 'probable implications' weigh heavily against immediate incrimination: the plaintiffs voiced no suspicions of Euxitheus until he had departed; they speculate that the victim was killed on land, but witnesses affirmed that Euxitheus never left the ship; they have no plausible account of how the body disappeared without a trace (οὐδενὶ λόγῳ εἰκότι . . . οὐδενὶ τρόπῳ εἰκός, 27–8).

The central section, (29–56), deals with the direct evidence—the slave's testimony under torture, the incriminating letter against the defendant, and the freeman's testimony in his favour—as measures of probable suspicion. Did those making the arrest act properly upon immediate incrimination? Of course our defendant recites the commonplace on the fallibility of slave torture (32–5), but he is more interested in the plaintiffs' handling of this evidence. They kept the slave in their custody and did not allow the defendant or his supporters to have proper access. And although it is customary to reward with freedom a slave who aids in avenging his master, 'they seized him and put him to death—the informant upon whom they base their case against me!' (34). 'For if he remained alive and submitted to the same test of torture at my hands, he would have turned informant against their conspiracy, but with him dead, I have no opportunity to . . . establish the truth' (35). Freed of torture and facing death, the slave recanted and declared Euxitheus innocent; this second statement is the more likely (ἐκ τοῦ εἰκότος, 37). As a rule it is those who are implicated by an informant that do away with him; in this case it is the plaintiffs themselves, 'those making the arrest and trying to make a case' that have done away with the informant.[16] If the defendant had acted as they have done, they would be treating his conduct as the strongest evidence against him (*megista tekmēria*).

---

[16] Ant. 5. 38, αὐτοὶ δὲ οὗτοι οἱ ἀπάγοντες καὶ ζητοῦντες τὸ πρᾶγμα, is often misconstrued as 'those who seized [the slave], investigating what happened'; cf. 34, ἄγοντες τὸν ἄνδρα.

Now there follows an intricate line of argument in which the defendant is to draw contradictions between various points in the evidence and the plaintiffs' scenario, and there is undoubtedly a good deal of misrepresentation. We shall try to reconstruct the plaintiffs' case more systematically below (§1.2.4), but here we should notice a remarkable device in the defendant's version. Where the plaintiffs claim that the slave confessed to '*taking part* in the killing' (*sunapokteinai*), the defendant attempts to recast the testimony to suggest that the slave only admitted 'helping to dispose of the body': the slave had meant that Euxitheus himself killed Herodes and only required assistance in removing the corpse.[17] This device strikes us as surprising, but it relies upon an implicit probability of human character: the slave would more likely have admitted the less serious offence.

The slave's testimony, 'upon which the plaintiffs . . . claim to "know well" [the defendant's] guilt' (52), is treated as a source of implications against probable suspicion, not as probative on the substantive questions of the defendant's involvement. This pattern is remarkably consistent, *even where the direct evidence is in the defendant's favour*. Thus in regard to the testimony of the free man who was put to torture and apparently supported Euxitheus (42), we might expect him to emphasize this testimony, at least to go into it in some detail; but he passes over the substance of this material and treats it as yet another point on which the plaintiffs have acted improperly in the arrest. The testimony of a free man, subject to the same torture as the slave, should have greater value; and the free man stuck to his story whereas the slave recanted; yet the plaintiffs chose to act upon the less trustworthy evidence. The reasonable probability, Euxitheus insists, is 'on his side' (τὸ εἰκὸς σύμμαχόν μοι, 43). Was he, indeed, so misguided as to plot and commit the killing alone, and then run the risk of involving some accessory who might later inform against him?[18] Assume Herodes was killed on shore and the body was then disposed of at sea: how could this have

---

[17] This turn of the argument relies upon an ambiguity in a synonymous term: Euxitheus says that what the slave confessed to was συνανελεῖν—which may mean either to 'help in removing' or 'help in destroying'. This recasting was probably dictated by the legal issue; see below, §1.2.

[18] In this argument (43-4) the defendant is assuming that he is charged with having done the killing himself, single-handed: the plaintiffs contend that Herodes was slain on shore near the ships; surely he would have been able to cry out, if he were the victim of but one assailant; see §1.2.4.

been done, as the plaintiffs contend, without drawing any attention or leaving any trace? (45) Is it reasonable for the plaintiffs to disregard such indications and prosecute the defendant none the less on tenuous evidence? Thus he asks the jury to consider 'what is probable and right (to conclude) from the statements of the two men under torture . . . Which of the two is more probable grounds for suspicion?'(49–52)

The incriminating letter is treated in similar fashion (53–6): there is no examination of the letter itself such as we would expect in a modern court. In fact there is nothing to suggest that the document was actually presented to the jurors: apparently the substance of it was simply described by witnesses.[19] Its value is therefore all the more subject to conjecture. The plaintiffs found the letter on a second search of the ship, after an earlier exploration proved unsuccessful; presumably the letter incriminated the slave, who was then put to torture as the intended bearer (56). But this contention opens the door to another reversal of the evidence: Why was it necessary to send a letter by this carrier? The man 'who had done the deed' could be relied upon to tell the tale himself; the purpose of sending a written message was obviously not to conceal from the bearer what he himself had done.[20] On the other hand the discovery of the letter, like the handling of the torture, tends to disprove immediate incrimination as grounds for arrest: the letter was found only after the first search failed to produce any evidence and the torture of the free crewman also proved unproductive. At that point, in desperation, they planted the letter and then proceeded to torture the slave. But the slave would not corroborate what they had fabricated in the letter: for the letter implicated Euxitheus as the killer, but the slave confessed that he himself was the killer!

---

[19] Such a procedure appears consistent with the ordinary rules of evidence. Thus Bonner observed that even in contract disputes of the 4th c., when the value of written evidence was well established, 'No great importance was attached to the production of the original document' (*Evidence in Athenian Courts*, 62). He cites this case as an instance of the rule that no attempt was made to authenticate a document by handwriting (79). Cf. Leisi, *Zeuge*, 81–3.

[20] Here the defendant reverts to the view that the slave was the actual killer, ὁ εἰργασμένος, in contradiction to his earlier handling of the slave's testimony, in which he concluded that the slave accused him, Euxitheus, as the actual killer and admitted only to being an accessory. In the Loeb translation Maidment glosses εἰργασμένος as 'accomplice', but see §§1.2.3–4.

1.1.3 Probable Motive

The arguments against probable cause have provided the organizing idea of the narrative and proof thus far. Antiphon now turns to the question of motive. He follows a standard method, much like what we find in the first *Tetralogy*, in Gorgias' *Palamedes*, in the fragment attributed to Antiphon's *Defence*, and in the concluding argument in Lysias 1: list the probable motives and exclude them, one by one. If defendant committed the offence he must have done so for reasons X, Y, or Z. Neither X, nor Y, nor Z is likely; therefore defendant did not commit the offence.[21]

So why did I kill him? There was no quarrel between us. They claim that I killed him to oblige a friend. Yet who has ever done *this* crime as a favour? . . . There has to be a serious quarrel for a man to do such a thing; and as he plots against his victim his malice will be obvious (πρόνοιαν . . . φανεράν). But in my case there was no quarrel at all. Was it that I feared for my life at *his* hands? . . . There was nothing of this sort. Was I likely to get rich by killing him? He had no riches. In fact I would have a more plausible charge (μᾶλλον . . . εἰκότως) against you, on the grounds that you were seeking my death to make money. And (in the event of my death) you would be far more justly condemned for my murder . . . For I have clearly revealed your obvious malice (φανερὰν τὴν πρόνοιαν) against me.   (57–9)

In this adaptation, the standard disclaimer of probable motive leads to another piece of circumstantial evidence against the plaintiffs: not only is there no plausible motive for Euxitheus to have done the killing, but, by the same rule that eliminates him from suspicion, the plaintiffs themselves become suspect. Malice aforethought is shown be a deliberate plot; Euxitheus is guilty of none; but his accusers have shown obvious malice in building the case against him.

Now with this turn of the argument Antiphon also dismisses what appears to be the plaintiffs' most plausible allegation as to motive, that Euxitheus hoped to gain some financial advantage by Herodes' death: most probably, the plaintiffs alleged that Herodes was killed in order to free his captives (§1.2). Whether the captives actually escaped is unknown to us, but the prospect provides the plaintiffs with plausible grounds for suspicion; they would surely have argued that this was a probable motive in the plot against Herodes. Euxitheus first answers this allegation simply by denying

[21] Cf. Ch. 5 §1 at n. 47.

that he himself, a more wealthy man, had anything to gain from Herodes.

But the charge is more complicated: it was Lycinus who stood to gain from Herodes' death; it was he who instigated the plot—the incriminating letter is addressed to him. Euxitheus must therefore eliminate Lycinus as well from suspicion (60–3). Lycinus evidently had had some quarrel with Herodes, but had he wished to punish his adversary he could have done so by litigation in the Athenian courts; instead he had actually released Herodes from an earlier claim (as witnesses confirm, 62).[22] This earlier incident is taken as circumstantial evidence that Lycinus bore no malice against Herodes; it also suggests that there was no financial motive. Euxitheus does not address the obvious objection that Lycinus may have settled the case under threat of some more serious legal action. But he does dissociate himself from Lycinus: he had not even helped his supposed comrade by paying the modest fine of seven minae when Lycinus was jailed pending payment. This incident is evidence (*tekmērion*, 63) that Euxitheus would not have done murder to oblige Lycinus. He thus concludes the disclaimer of probable motives: he killed neither from enmity, nor for money or favour.

Having cleared himself and Lycinus, our defendant next answers the obvious argument, 'If not he, then who?' (64–71). It is here that Antiphon elaborates upon the axiom that 'murder without witnesses cannot be proved beyond conjecture'.[23] He mentions the famous case of Ephialtes, whose murder remained unsolved; he recalls the case of a slave who would have gone unpunished had he not panicked and fled the scene; and he reminds the jury of the miscarriage of justice by which the imperial treasurers were wrongly condemned. This pattern provides an answer to the question, 'If not he, then who?': premeditated crimes often remain unsolved.

Next Euxitheus defends his father's involvement in the Mytilenean revolt (74–80). This section serves to dispel prejudice but it is also an argument against probable motive. He then proceeds with a proof from divine favour: safe passage at sea and propitious sacrifice argue his innocence (81–4). This passage will be treated more fully below (§1.1.4). In the epilogue Antiphon returns

---

[22] Lycinus was, like Herodes, most probably an Athenian citizen and cleruch on Lesbos; see esp. Schindel, *Mordfall Herodes*, 213–14.

[23] Cf. Ch. 5 §1.

to the commonplace on sanctity of the laws and sanctions governing homicide (87–9) as an injunction to the jury to weigh the seriousness of their verdict.

In this outline the traditional non-technical proofs have no particular prominence as organizing ideas, as they do in the speeches for *dikai phonou*. The argumentation is structured around two central issues, the conduct of the prosecution and the question of the defendant's motive.

1.1.4   Irrational Proof and the Sanctity of the Law (§§81–9)

The special gravity of these issues in this speech is particularly evident in the otherwise puzzling passage that links the commonplace on the laws (5. 87–9 = 6. 3–6) to a rare proof from divine witnesses. In §§81–4 Euxitheus, speaks of 'signs from the gods' in his favour: the gods reveal the doom of a blood-tainted man in portents and mishaps at sea or at sacrifice; if there had been any such manifestation the prosecutors would treat it as the surest sign of his guilt; but no such sign had befallen him. He has mortal witnesses to affirm that his passage at sea was uneventful and his offerings showed no sign of the gods' displeasure.

This divine evidence is closely joined to the conventional argument on the sanctity of the laws; indeed, the divine evidence makes up for the one significant omission from the commonplace. If we plot the parallel texts in detail, it is clear that the one substantive difference has to do precisely with the element of religious conviction.[24] The speech for the *chorēgos* (Ant. 6) includes the full standard version:[25] we are told that the law of homicide is so compelling that (*a*) an innocent man, wrongly condemned, must irrevocably abide by the judges' verdict and obey the law that excludes him 'from city and shrines, contests and offerings—the greatest and most ancient institutions among men'. And (*b*) even a killer who has no fear of retribution will abide by the automatic

---

[24] Ant. 5. 88–9 is repeated almost verbatim from 6. 6 (sanctity of homicide oath and procedure; special responsibility of the judges to make no mistake, over and above the burden upon the plaintiffs). One point developed in Ant. 6. 4–5 but omitted in Ant. 5 is largely irrelevant to the case of a non-Athenian: exclusion from city centre and sacred ground.

[25] Wilamowitz, 'Sechste Rede', 411, argued that the original from which these two versions are derived would have been especially designed for cases of intentional homicide before the Areopagus. For authenticity of the common passages, cf. Lavency, *Logographie*, 149–51.

sanctions: 'so great is the law's power to compel that even a man who kills his own slave, *with no one to avenge him*, will none the less seek purification and stay clear of the areas prohibited to him in the law, in awe of what custom and religion require'; his only hope lies in reverence for the rules regarding the gods. Pious conventions aside, the inviolable authority that the law holds over a man *wrongly convicted (a)* is largely a matter of fear for his own life: no matter how innocent in his heart, once he is condemned by the court, if he is apprehended in Attica he can be forcibly seized and put to death.[26] But the compliance of a man who kills his own slave *(b)* comes from religious conviction that he must rid himself of defilement.[27]

In the speech for Euxitheus Antiphon has deleted this second example of the law's inviolable power. The proof from divine manifestations takes its place and serves a function more in keeping with the nature of this dispute. The standard version in the *dikē* goes to prove *the defendant's own faith* in his innocence: the man who kills, even with no one to avenge the victim, cannot escape his guilt (6. 4–5). But in the trial by warrant Euxitheus invokes signs from the gods *to convince the jury* of his innocence, not simply as proof of his own conviction. It also raises some doubts as to 'probable suspicion': the plaintiffs waited long after the events to incriminate Euxitheus, even while the gods were affirming his innocence.[28]

1.1.5　Alibi and Immediate Incrimination (§§23–9)

In the passage linking the narrative and proof proper the defendant introduces his alibi (23–4)—which he largely ignores thereafter.

---

[26] This rule applies to exiled homicides generally, intentional or unintentional. A man accused of intentional killing might go voluntarily into exile at any point up until the final speech.

[27] In principle, even the killer of a victim 'with no one to avenge him' could be arrested in violation of prohibited areas by anyone willing, but the duty would usually fall to the *kyrios* of the victim.

[28] He also avoids reinforcing the presumption of religious conviction on the part of plaintiffs whom he accuses of wrongly putting the slave to death (§1.2.3). Antiphon none the less retains the condition 'with no one to avenge him', but with an entirely different implication. He now asserts, 'No one would dare to transgress a judgement that the court has rendered [though confident in his own innocence] but he must abide by the verdict . . . *especially with no one to avenge him.*' This phrase now describes Euxitheus' predicament: he must abide by the verdict, right or wrong, especially since *he*, if convicted, has no one to defend him against vindictive pursuit.

Here he treats the circumstantial evidence directly (25–8): 'Such were the events; now consider the probable implications.' But rather than follow the events in a logical sequence or weigh the probabilities systematically, the argument seems oddly disconnected.

That the defendant gives so little scope to his alibi is one of the most puzzling features of this case. He has witnesses to affirm that he did not leave the second ship on the night of Herodes' disappearance, when the plaintiffs evidently allege that the victim was taken ashore and there met his death. After introducing this point along with other details of the narrative (23–4), he mentions it only once (27) and then it is an almost incidental comment among various reflections on the inherent improbability of the plaintiffs' scenario. In modern proceedings, of course, the alibi alone might be decisive, if the scene of the crime were known and there were convincing witnesses that the defendant was elsewhere at the time. Why then in an Athenian court is this point given so little emphasis? This problem has provoked much speculation, some of it quite plausible but none altogether convincing. Those who treat this case as a document in imperialism have supposed that the defendant must simply realize the overwhelming prejudice against him and his witnesses: an Athenian jury is likely to regard the testimony of these rebellious subjects as mere collusion.[29]

It has also been argued that the alibi is not exploited because the Athenian judges had no Theory of Proof, no objective standard by which to assess the relative value of different forms of evidence.[30] For Heitsch this defect is inherent in the character of Athenian dicastic juries as 'Laienrichter'. It is true enough that the argument seems to assume somewhat less command of the procedural rules than we have come to expect in the speeches for *dikai phonou* before the *ephetai*. And certainly Athenian citizen-judges had no objective theory of proof by modern standards. But this observation is ultimately misleading if it is to suggest that the jurors did not recognize some measures of guilt as more weighty than others. In fact the jury are repeatedly asked to consider what constitutes sufficient grounds for a reasonable person to conclude that the defendant is the culprit—Was there probable cause? And our defendant persistently

---

[29] Schindel, *Mordfall Herodes*, 39.
[30] Heitsch, *Antiphon*, 69–70; cf. Leisi, *Zeuge*, 46–7, 106–19.

reminds the jury of the higher standard of proof in *dikai phonou*, a standard that his accusers have evaded.

In these proceedings there is no compelling oath to validate the testimony, as there was in *dikai phonou*. The testimony of witnesses can only be corroborated by the probabilities. The alibi is therefore valued not so much as evidence on the question of fact, disproving Euxitheus' involvement, as it is another blow against probable cause. The plaintiffs have shown that they themselves had no suspicion of him until quite some time after the events, and they disregarded the witnesses who were at the scene at the time and placed him elsewhere.

And there is perhaps another, more important reason not to make too much of the alibi: it may be entirely irrelevant! Consider the parallel in Antiphon 6 (*Choreutes*).[31] The defendant has witnesses to confirm that he was not present when the fatal drug was given (12–17). But *the defendant's whereabouts have nothing to do with the charge*. The *chorēgos* is charged only with indirect responsibility for the actions of those he authorized to act in his place. Rather than deal directly with the question of what instructions he gave that might have induced his subordinates to make the fatal mistake, he insists upon the alibi.[32]

The alibi in Antiphon 5 serves a similar function: it has little probative value on the factual questions of what he actually did, but it has great value for the procedural objection. Euxitheus claims that he is being prosecuted by a procedure wholly unsuited to the charge: felony warrant and arrest naturally imply immediate incrimination (as in apprehending a common thief); but the plaintiffs have invoked this procedure without the ordinary grounds for probable suspicion, indeed, in disregard of witnesses. Rather than deal with the subtle and all too plausible implications of their scenario he proceeds upon the ordinary assumption, that felony arrest must have probable cause.

The circumstantial reasoning connected to the alibi (§§25–9) covers several points relevant to this line of argument: (25) the defendant was not implicated at the scene when Herodes was reported missing; (26) plaintiffs claim that the killing was done on shore,

---

[31] Heitsch and others point to the parallel in *Tetr.* 1 as proof that alibis in general carried little conviction. But the *Tetralogies* are not to be relied upon as evidence of the practical realities; in the Tetralogy the alibi is introduced by the defendant in his closing remarks, with a dramatic challenge to torture his slaves, at a point where the test was no longer viable. See Ch. 5 §1, at nn. 50–1.

[32] See Ch. 7 §2.

whereas defendant never left the ship; (27) no physical evidence was found at the scene, despite a two-day search, and (28) plaintiffs have no explanation of how the body was disposed of, except speculation that the body was dumped at sea; (29) the only immediate physical evidence they found was a bloodstain aboard the second ship (when it arrived at Mytilene), but even this has nothing to do with the defendant as it was determined to be blood from a sacrificial animal. Thereupon, we are told, the two men were seized for torture (30), and the defendant turns to this part of the proof.

Now Solmsen regarded this passage as typical of the dislocation that results from conventional arrangement of the argument and the gravitational effects of the traditional means of proof.[33] Rather than proceed in logical sequence, the argument is drawn to the testimony under torture. Of course, Antiphon may be simply taking up the points in his adversary's argument, as he has promised to do (8), in the order he anticipates.[34] But the connecting thread is the natural implication of warrant and arrest proceedings, that the culprit should be discovered in patently incriminating circumstances.

The first point is precisely this, that the plaintiffs have not acted upon immediate, self-evident incrimination: 'For first of all, no one made any accusation against me before I departed for Ainos, although Herodes had disappeared and it had been reported to them . . . but *in the immediate circumstances* (εἰς τὸ παραχρῆμα) the truth and the facts were stronger than their accusation.'[35] Second,

---

[33] *Antiphonstudien*, 26–8: 'Wie is die merkwurdige Zerreißung von offenbar Zusammengehörigen (§25, §29f.) und Zusammenstellung von offenbar nicht Zusammengehörigen zu erklären?'

[34] Thus Scheidweiler, 'Antiphons Herodes', 333–8; Goebel, 'Early Rhetorical Theory', 228.

[35] Euxitheus exaggerates this failing. The plaintiffs were probably unable to investigate the site at Methymna before the first ship sailed on to Aenus; thus reasons Schindel, *Mordfall Herodes*, 32. And apparently the second ship was not searched by the plaintiffs until it reached Mytilene. The speaker never says (*pace* Gagarin, *Herodes*, 43) that *they*, the plaintiffs, took part in the initial search at the site; he says only that *a search was made* and no evidence was found. When he says at last, 'they have found neither the vessel itself nor any trace' (28), he is referring to the whole investigation. Where he says earlier at §25 'no one made any accusation . . . although they had *learned of the disappearance*', we would expect him to make a point of it if they had searched the scene for themselves. It seems reasonable therefore to suppose that the two-day search consisted of the first day after the disappearance, when word was sent to the family, plus a second day (or part of a day) after the disappearance was reported. The plaintiffs made inquiries in Mytilene before making their way to Methymna. Thus they had little opportunity to accuse Euxitheus before he departed.

there was no immediate physical evidence or first-hand witness at the scene (οὔτε ὀπτὴρ . . . οὔθ' αἷμα οὔτ' ἄλλο σημεῖον οὐδέν, 27). They therefore conjectured that the victim was slain on shore and his body dumped at sea, so as to avoid detection. They have offered a detailed scenario—'they [claim to] know precisely what happened' (26)—but cannot give a plausible explanation of how the body disappeared. They insist the body must have been thrown from a boat, but 'why was the vessel not discovered, when there would surely be some trace if the body were disposed of by night?' (when the handlers could not see the marks left behind). But 'they have discovered neither the vessel itself nor any trace' (οὔτε σημεῖον οὐδέν, 28). When the second ship arrived at Mytilene they conducted a search and found bloodstains, but these turned out to be unrelated to the crime. They then resorted to torturing the slave, who finally gave them grounds to arrest Euxitheus, 'many days later' (30), 'long after' the events (31).

These several points make one connected argument in the legal challenge. The defendant objects to the prolonged process of discovery that separated the allegations from the immediate circumstances of the crime. There is *viable* evidence—and the defendant must soon deal with it—but the plaintiffs have evaded the ordinary rules of evidence. In *dikai phonou*, by contrast, there was no such requirement for immediate incrimination; plaintiffs and their witnesses swore to the righteousness of their claim rather than to specific facts. But in warrant and arrest plaintiffs should have probable suspicion from direct evidence or immediate circumstances. In this case they have been forced to rely instead upon a dubious discovery long after the events and remote from the scene.

1.2 The Question of Law

Euxitheus' claim that he was 'indicted as a felon' but made to 'stand trial on a charge of murder—a travesty that no one in this land ever before suffered' (9)—has been a focus of controversy on two counts. What basis does he have, beyond the lack of immediate incrimination, for his complaint that the warrant is procedurally improper? And what could have been procedural consequences to this challenge on the legality?

It was once supposed that the procedural challenge was brought forward in the preliminaries as a formal objection and was then introduced, along with the charges and the plea, by the presiding magistrate at trial. By this view the procedural challenge was formally recognized as a distinct and possibly decisive issue; the formal challenge was the logical antecedent to the *paragraphē* procedure that developed in the early fourth century. This reconstruction was demolished by H. J. Wolff and it is now generally abandoned.[36] There was no dividing the question at trial before Archinus instituted such hearings. In this case the procedural challenge was not treated separately but seems to have occupied much of the debate at trial. As a document of legal reasoning, it is none the less significant: the procedural objections in this case appeal to a growing concern that the framework of laws had become all too often an instrument of injustice. This concern is reflected in the contemporary drama of Aristophanes, and it would soon find its remedies.

Wolff's magisterial study effectively disposed of one problem, but his interpretation of the case opened up an even more perplexing one: What precisely is Euxitheus' complaint?[37] He appears to be claiming categorically that the warrant under which he has been charged is not a proper procedure against homicide, and that the use of this procedure for such a charge is unprecedented. In recent work it has sometimes been concluded that the formal charges indeed amounted to some lesser felony and not homicide *per se*. But this solution is not without its difficulties; and commentators are still at odds as to whether this could have been the first instance, as our defendant claims. It is the purpose of this section therefore to reconsider the substance of Euxitheus' cryptic complaint, not as a measure of guilt or innocence,[38] but as a gauge of the workings of the law. The legal question is in itself no trivial matter, since the

---

[36] Wolff, *Paragraphe*, esp. 112–19. For the view that this case involves a formal objection, prefiguring classical *paragraphē*, cf. Wilamowitz, *AA* ii. 369; U. E. Paoli, *Studi sul processo attico* (Padua, 1933; repr. 1974), 99–100; Dorjahn, *Political Forgiveness*, 36. The ancient hypothesis contributed to this misunderstanding, as it remarks that the speaker refutes the charge παραγραφικῶς.

[37] Wolff supposed that the formal charge amounted to some form of theft and he made the subtle distinction that the nature of Euxitheus' complaint is not that the charge is inadmissible (which is the nature of *paragraphai*) but that it 'does not conform to the statutory provisions': *Paragraphe*, 118.

[38] Schindel, after detailed examination of 'distortions' in the argument, concludes that they were prompted by the prejudice that Euxitheus would encounter in an Athenian jury (*Mordfall Herodes*, 39–41). Gagarin (*Murder of Herodes*) argues the distortions might just as well prove Euxitheus guilty.

treatment of legalities in this case and in the later parallel, Lysias 13, give us a singular insight into the legalism that emerged in the restored democracy.

In the following sections we shall first examine the question of whether a specific form of warrant and arrest was available for such cases (§1.2.1), then the problems relating to proposed penalty (*timēsis*, §1.2.2) and the treatment of the tortured slave (§1.2.3). Finally, in the conclusion to this section (§1.2.4) we shall attempt to reconstruct the case for the prosecution.

1.2.1 *Apagōgē kakourgōn* and *Apagōgē phonou*

Euxitheus appears to argue that the procedure under which he has been indicted—under the law of felons (*kakourgoi*)—is proper only for such lesser felonies as theft and mugging. His accusers have argued that 'homicide itself is a great felony', and he would agree that it is indeed among the greatest felonies, like treason and sacrilege. But likewise homicide is addressed by specific laws.

He then lists the procedural safeguards that the plaintiffs have evaded by resorting to felony warrant (10–12). These include the burdensome ritual and awe-inspiring oath of the traditional procedures, with the pledge against allegations unrelated to the homicide (§1.1.1). By avoiding the proper homicide court and bringing the case into the city centre, they have put the citizens at risk from the killer's taint (if they truly believe him guilty). By the felony procedure they have allowed for an alternative penalty to be assessed, in contrast to the automatic penalties for homicide. And they have left themselves the option of a second prosecution by *dikē phonou*, if the felony verdict should go against them—thus subjecting the defendant to double jeopardy. Finally, they have put Euxitheus in official custody without bail, and thus denied him freedom of movement: he should have been able to withdraw into exile, if he chose, or at least had the liberty to prepare his defence effectively.

It is clear enough that the proper procedure, as our defendant sees it, would be the traditional *dikē phonou*, and since this case involves the intentional murder of an Athenian, he envisions a trial before the Areopagus.[39] It is not so clear whether the summary

---

[39] Some scholars suppose that trial before the Areopagus was not a real option; cf. Heitsch, *Antiphon*, 54–6, 80. But there was no obstacle to prosecution of non-Athenians. The law for hostage-taking, *androlēpsia*, (Dem. 23. 82) might in fact be used to coerce the non-Athenian killer to submit to legal proceedings: *Lex. Seg.* 213–14; cf. MacDowell, *AHL* 28–30.

procedure was in fact irregular and improper for prosecuting homicide, as he insists. None the less, the substance of Euxitheus' complaint has been taken largely at face value, and it has been generally assumed that there was as yet no warrant and arrest against homicide proper (*apagōgē phonou*) at the time of Euxitheus' defence. Two generations thereafter we have Demosthenes' explicit testimony on the use of summary arrest against homicides in *Against Aristocrates* (23. 80).

There is yet a sixth remedy . . . if one is uncertain of the other procedures or the time is past in which each of these requirements must be met, or for some other reason one does not wish to prosecute by these means but he sees the killer entering the temples and the agora, he may seize him and take him to jail . . . And if convicted, the killer is sentenced to death; but if the prosecutor does not receive one-fifth of the votes he is fined a thousand drachmas.

In Demosthenes' day this 'homicide arrest', *apagōgē phonou*, was a recognized alternative to the traditional *dikē*. It is generally supposed that this was the procedure invoked against Agoratus (Lys. 13), and hence that homicide arrest was in practice as early as the turn of the century.

But the procedure that Demosthenes describes appears to be distinct from that employed against Euxitheus: in the latter we are told an alternative penalty has been proposed, but in *apagōgē phonou* the death penalty is prescribed. Homicide arrest appears to require that the accused be apprehended in open violation of prohibited areas, but there is no mention of this detail in Euxitheus' case. Relying largely upon these two documents (Dem. 23 and Ant. 5), Hansen has concluded that there was as yet no distinct *apagōgē phonou* in Antiphon's day.[40] The only available remedies, short of *dikē phonou*, were felony warrant and arrest, *endeixis* and *apagōgē kakourgias*.

In any event, it is the felony procedure that is used against Euxitheus—he tells us as much. Was this, as Euxitheus suggests, an irregular, perhaps unprecedented application of it? Gagarin and Edwards seem inclined to take him at his word.[41] But it is argued

---

[40] *Apagoge*, 99–107. Hansen regards the case against Agoratus as *apagōgē kakourgōn*, in default of a specific procedure for homicide; *apagōgē phonou* was not instituted until sometime after 400.

[41] See Gagarin, *Murder of Herodes*, 18–20; 'Prosecution of Homicide', 317–19; cf. Edwards, *Greek Orators*, i. 27–8. Despite explicit testimony that *androphonoi* were

by Heitsch and others that felony warrant and arrest would have become *de facto* the proper remedy against non-Athenians accused of homicide. Euxitheus' complaint that the proceedings were a travesty 'that no one in this land ever before suffered' would be valid only in the sense that no Athenian had ever had to endure it.[42] Now the differentiation of various procedures for homicide as distinct from ordinary felony warrant and arrest has very much complicated the problem, perhaps needlessly. There is no question that summary arrest was an ancient remedy against *convicted* homicides as exiles (*pheugontes*) who trespassed in Attica. The difficulty lies in determining when and under what conditions summary arrest was also allowed against those *accused* or *suspected* of homicide, but who had not been tried and sentenced. Euxitheus' complaint leads Hansen to suppose that a procedure such as Demosthenes describes was not available against untried, suspected homicides in Antiphon's day. It belongs to the set of fourth-century procedures, with distinct penalties and procedural requirements for (1) *accused* homicides, banned from the *agora* and other prohibited areas by proclamation, (2) *suspected* homicides, who had not been formally banned, alongside (3) the traditional remedy against exiled homicides who trespass in Attica.[43] In the earlier period, we are to suppose, there was no immediate remedy against those accused or suspected other than felony warrant and arrest.

Gagarin has disputed Hansen's model on various points.[44] He argues that the two testimonia regarding 'accused' and 'suspected' homicides refer in fact to 'the same or very similar types of *apagōgē*'. What these two applications have in common with the third type (against convicted homicides) is that the real grounds for legal action is not the killing itself but the trespass, 'the crime of being in a place from which one is prohibited'. Gagarin is sceptical of the distinctions that may be deduced from an argumentative account emphasizing due process, and he cautions against expecting the

counted among *kakourgoi* (Aesch. 1. 90–1; *Lex Seg.* 250. 4) Gagarin insists (18 n. 3) 'the laws about ἀπαγωγή did not contain any explicit reference to homicide and . . . we cannot talk of an ἀπαγωγὴ φόνου'; cf. Hansen, *Apagoge*, 36–44, 'Prosecution of Homicide', 21–30.

[42] See Heitsch, *Antiphon*, 50–6, treating *apagōgē* as the regular remedy against non-Athenians.
[43] Hansen, *Apagoge*, 99–107; see Dem. 24. 60, 105; cf. MacDowell, *AHL* 139–40.
[44] 'Prosecution of Homicide' esp. 316–17; further refs. n. 41 above.

kind of systematic categories that we might expect in a modern code of law. His caution is well taken, and I think he is right in supposing that the first two categories (against those accused and suspected) may be scarcely distinct. But, by the same token, it is probably mistaken to insist that these forms of arrest were essentially actions against trespass and no true remedy against homicide—this is to confuse a condition of the arrest with the crime itself. The case against Agoratus (Lys. 13) was surely a case of *apagōgē* against a suspected homicide of the type Demosthenes describes (*pace* Hansen); but the extant speech gives no indication whatever that trespass of the prohibited areas was anything more than a formal condition (see §2 below).

From the evidence we have, we can conclude with reasonable confidence that some form of prosecution by warrant and arrest was available against accused or suspected killers, who had not been convicted by trial, as early as the era of Draco's law.[45] The Draconian secondary rules assume that most homicide disputes would be resolved without trial; self-help and forcible arrest are accepted methods of assuring that the killer come to terms with the family of his victim. The workings of the trial procedure that evolved from Draco's law depended upon the threat of summary action: should the accused killer trespass where prohibited, he could be forcibly seized. Now the Draconian provision, 'It is lawful to kill or arrest the homicide in the homeland' (Dem. 23. 28), was originally intended to apply to voluntary exiles who had not been formally tried; it would naturally apply also to accused killers who would neither avail themselves of exile nor come to terms with their accusers.[46] Similarly the Draconian law of *endeixis*, that he who first secures warrant cannot be prosecuted if the banished killer is killed in the arrest (Dem. 23. 51), originally applied to homicides who had not been tried and sentenced but were, in effect, automatic exiles; it was meant to halt the cycle of vendetta that would otherwise erupt from self-help retribution against known killers. Finally, the Solonian amendment 'not to abuse or hold for ransom' shows that such treatment *had been* a prerogative

---

[45] See Ch. 2 §3. Cf. Evjen, '*Apagoge* and Athenian Homicide', 413.

[46] Demosthenes (ad loc.) treats the law as though only convicted killers are affected, but *androphonos* has no such specificity. Lysias 13. 82, for instance, reports that Agoratus was shunned and nearly executed without trial as a known homicide (ἀνδροφόνῳ ὄντι).

of the prosecutor himself, and it naturally implies that forcible arrest to the magistrate, carried out with potentially deadly force, would still be available against accused or suspected killers who did not seek refuge or legal resolution (so long as they were not subjected to abuse and ransom). In view of the historical development, there is no basis for the common notion that arrest of accused homicides was a late innovation. It was on the contrary an ancient and generally accepted remedy. It was especially applicable against voluntary exiles who returned without reconciliation, against those who were formally banned by *prorrhēsis* but flagrantly defied the ban, as well as those whom we might rather call 'known killers', those whose crimes were witnessed at first hand and universally condemned by social exclusion. Demosthenes of course assumes that the Draconian arrest applies only against *convicted* homicides—and modern scholars readily share the legalistic assumption. But we must recognize that the orator complacently treats the procedural conventions of his own day as embodying the original intent, and in this he is often mistaken.[47]

The procedure against 'known' or suspected homicides that Demosthenes describes (23. 80) is a direct descendant of the ancient remedy. Undoubtedly there were procedural refinements in the era after 404, in keeping with the legalism of the time: the penalty for failing to win one-fifth of the votes, and elimination of penalty-assessment (*timēsis*) in favour of the death penalty are presumably articles of fourth-century revision. But Demosthenes suggests that the contemporary procedure was grafted on to the ancient law for arrest of homicides: it was governed by the same Solonian provision, for the accused to be held in official custody, *not to be abducted by the prosecutors at will.*[48]

The procedure against accused killers that Demosthenes describes follows a logical progression from the Draconian procedure. And in the intervening period, it is reasonable to assume, there was nothing novel or irregular in prosecuting homicide by

---

[47] Thus Demosthenes assumes that the ancient provision 'It is lawful to kill or arrest the killer' (28) refers to arrest by the archons themselves (*ephēgēsis*); he cites an example (31) from the previous year, when the thesmothetes arrested a killer in the assembly and presumably put him to death.

[48] Dem. 23. 80: ἀπάγειν ἔξεστιν εἰς τὸ δεσμωτήριον, οὐκ οἴκαδ' οὐδ' ὅποι βούλεται. Cf. 23. 31: '"It is lawful to kill or arrest"—but abduct to one's own house or however one wishes?'

warrant and arrest. The procedural details to which Euxitheus objects are in fact also attested for the later procedure. One of his objections has to do with penalty assessment (which we shall examine in more detail below §1.2.2); and he repeatedly protests that he is threatened with double jeopardy, that he will be forced to stand trial by *dikē phonou* even if acquitted on the warrant. This complaint is generally discounted, but the attested procedure against accused homicides (those banned by *prorrhēsis* but who violated prohibitions) clearly allowed for a separate penalty assessment (*timēsis*) and could be followed by a *dikē phonou*—it was a device to enforce the prohibitions up until the time of trial.[49] In principle the *dikē* might yet go to trial, regardless of the verdict on the *apagōgē*. In practice, however, the hearing on the arrest would be decisive, and we can reasonably assume that the case would not ordinarily go to trial on the *dikē*. Thus in principle Euxitheus might yet be subject, as he claims, to prosecution under the traditional *dikē* even if acquitted in *apagōgē*, though in actuality the case for the prosecution would probably be untenable at the second trial. Whether we choose to call it arrest for homicide or felony is of little consequence—the Athenians were not much concerned with such categories.

After all, as Wolff himself observed, the substance of Euxitheus' complaint is not categorically that arrest of homicides is improper, but rather that it does not properly apply to his case. The wording of Antiphon's speech does not in itself imply that felony warrant and arrest was never a proper remedy against homicide: Euxitheus' complaint appears to be that he was indicted on the basis of one procedure and tried on the basis of another; he does not say that no form of summary arrest was allowed against homicides. He seems rather to suggest that the case against him is *the kind of case* that could only be tried properly by *dikē phonou*.

With this understanding it is sometimes suggested that there was a discrepancy between the original grounds for the warrant against him and the actual charges that have been brought at trial, and this is the substance of Euxitheus' complaint. Some scholars have pursued the theory that Euxitheus was in fact originally charged with some form of theft or crime against property but then accused of what we would call 'felony murder' (e.g. killing in commission of a

---

[49] Cf. Hansen, *Apagoge*, 100.

theft).[50] The most promising hypothesis along these lines holds that the captives whom Herodes was taking to Thrace escaped without ransom, and the plaintiffs charged Euxitheus for the loss of their property. Thus Heitsch explains the discrepancy between the original warrant and the charges at trial: Euxitheus was indicted for complicity in the captives' escape, but as this charge seemed the more difficult to prove, the prosecutors shifted their ground and tried to make a case for murder.[51] Now Euxitheus tells us nothing of what happened to the captives. But, on balance, it is not unreasonable to suppose that some suspicion of theft or *attempted* theft—whether of slaves or of other valuables—may have figured in the original allegations upon which the warrant was based: on the strength of this warrant, the family of Herodes summoned Euxitheus to trial at Athens, and he came, expecting to face charges of theft or abduction and assuming that at worst he could pay off his accusers. On arriving in Athens, however, he was arrested, jailed without bond, and charged with felony murder. The arrest was not in itself irregular: it had become the ordinary remedy against non-Athenians accused of homicide; but Euxitheus objects because this is not the original charge.

This is an ingenious and attractive theory, but it involves a crucial inconsistency. If some form of warrant and arrest (whether *apagōgē phonou* or *apagōgē kakourgias*) was in fact an accepted instrument of imperial justice against the killing of Athenians by non-Athenians, and the injustice of which Euxitheus complains is only a discrepancy between the original accusations and later charges, then his procedural challenge seems exceedingly and needlessly vague. There is no apparent reason why he should not have said outright, 'They charged me with theft and now accuse me of murder.' And if some form of warrant and arrest for homicide was a regular and recognized remedy against non-Athenians, how can Euxitheus pretend that *dikē phonou* was the only proper

---

[50] Thus Wolff, *Paragraphe* 115, supposed theft or 'stripping the body' (κλοπή, λωποδυσία); Schindel, *Mordfall Herodes*, 25, supposed *andrapodismos*, followed by Heitsch (see the next note). This approach is discounted by Gagarin, *Murder of Herodes*, 18.

[51] *Antiphon*, esp. 57–60; but see Gagarin's review in *Gött. Gel. Anzeiger*, 239 (1987), 60–4. Gagarin objects largely on the grounds that Euxitheus says nothing of the slaves' escape, and that, by Gagarin's own reconstruction (cf. *Murder of Herodes*, 42–3), Herodes' companion on the voyage and his kinsmen (arriving at the scene before the ship departed) would have prevented escape.

procedure? For Heitsch this inconsistency is entirely within the range of distortion that could be successfully perpetrated in the courts of the layman judges. But while I agree in principle that the popular courts would allow a good deal of latitude in legalistic argument, I find it unreasonable to suppose that the jury were expected to be utterly ignorant of the ordinary uses of warrant and arrest for homicide. If we grant that *some form* of summary arrest was a recognized remedy *in some cases* of homicide, then we can only conclude that Euxitheus' complaint was based on a fundamental distinction between the *kinds* of homicide cases that could be prosecuted by warrant and arrrest and those that could be properly prosecuted only by the traditional *dikē phonou*. He has clearly emphasized such a distinction in the argument on immediate incrimination and probable suspicion (§1.1), and he will elaborate upon it in regard to the obvious implications of planning and conspiracy (§1.2.3–4).

1.2.2   The Penalty-Assessment

And though the law requires that the slayer be slain in return, they made a penalty-assessment (*timēsis*) against me—not for my benefit but for their own gain—and in this they would have given the dead less than is due him in the law.   (10)[52]

One of the crucial procedural points in the legal challenge is the objection that the plaintiffs have, at some point in the proceedings, allowed for a lesser penalty. Now by one reading, eliminating the counterfactual aspect of the last clause ('they [would] have given less than is due'), our defendant seems to be claiming that by using warrant and arrest the plaintiffs have invoked a procedure that automatically allows for a penalty assessment as a separate decision of the jury after the main verdict (as in the trial of Socrates). This is one of the principal distinctions that Hansen deduces between *apagōgē kakourgias* and *apagōgē phonou*, that in the latter the death penalty is prescribed, whereas some alternate penalty was apparently allowed in the case against Euxitheus.[53] But the most natural

[52] In the phrase 'they *would* have given . . . less than his due' (ἔλασσον ἔνειμαν ἄν), a corrector in one manuscript has deleted the particle ἄν, and this reading is followed in some editions.

[53] This is one of the difficulties in Hansen's distinction between *apagōgē phonou* and *apagōgē kakourgias*, as he seems to accept the reading ἔνειμαν ἄν, and yet not allow for the possibility that Euxitheus is in fact being tried by a procedure that does not allow penalty assessment.

interpretation of this passage as it stands is that the plaintiffs previously made some proposal by way of penalty-assessment but this proposal is no longer viable—'they *would* have given the dead less than is due . . . ', but their proposal is rejected. In line with this interpretation, the defendant proceeds to treat the penalty that awaits him as nothing short of death.

Now there have been a number of alternative hypotheses based upon this reading. On the one side this detail seems to confirm that the plaintiffs have shifted their ground from one charge to another: the original charge of theft or the like would involve a penalty assessment; the actual charge of murder would involve the death penalty.[54] On the other side Edwards, who accepts Euxitheus' claim that the procedure is unprecedented, supposes that there was some confusion over the procedural rules: the plaintiffs originally proposed a penalty in the preliminary hearing, only to have it set aside by the Eleven.[55] Gagarin, who also assumes that the procedure is novel and irregular, supposes that the earlier assessment was in fact a proposal for private settlement, but that this earlier proposal was automatically cancelled when legal proceedings were undertaken. In the latter inference he may be mistaken. It is commonly supposed that no form of settlement other than execution by the state was a possible outcome of such a case once Euxitheus was arrested and brought before the Eleven; for Edwards financial settlement is 'unthinkable'. But let us consider what Euxitheus seems to suggest, without any preconceptions—that a murder trial might well end in some form of financial settlement, even in the later fifth century.

Euxitheus himself more than once accuses his accusers of litigating for profit. Again, in the consideration of possible motives (59), he counters that he would have a better claim against the plaintiff for 'trying to put [him] to death for money'. And in his closing remarks he seems to suggest that the plaintiffs have still some expectation of considerable financial advantage: he urges the jurors 'to show the sycophants that they are not more powerful than you [the jury] yourselves' (80). The plaintiffs have undertaken legal action in hopes of enriching themselves at Euxitheus' expense and, unless the verdict goes against them, they will not be disappointed.

---

[54] Thus Heitsch, *Antiphon*, 58–9.
[55] Edwards and others assume (counter to Hansen) that *apagōgē kakourgōn* ordinarily required the death penalty, without alternate assessment: *Greek Orators*, ii. 26–7; Gagarin, *Herodes*, 26–8.

Assume then that the plaintiffs have offered an assessment of damages as a pre-trial proposal for settlement: they have perhaps demanded a period of exile and confiscation of some portion of the defendant's property. The accused was not immediately amenable. But even when the warrant was issued and the defendant was summoned and arrested, if he then agreed to the damages, it seems to me unthinkable that the case would go to trial.[56] The counterfactual 'they *would* have given . . . less than is due' implies '*if* I had accepted their pre-trial proposal'. Of course, since the matter has come to trial, the old bargain is no longer on the table. If Euxitheus is convicted, the plaintiffs will then propose a penalty for the judges to consider. They are not bound by any previous negotiations; they would probably demand *execution* as well as confiscation of whatever properties could be seized. With this understanding Euxitheus proceeds to treat the punishment that awaits him as death.

In any event, the matter of penalty assessment does not appear to be a damning procedural manœuvre on the part of the plaintiffs, as Heitsch and others suppose. It is certainly no proof that they have shifted their ground and accuse the defendant of murder after initially charging him only with theft or abduction. Neither can we conclude from this crucial point in the legal challenge that the plaintiffs would have profited from an earlier settlement but now have nothing to gain from a conviction at trial—that they thus prove the sincerity of their charge by forcing the issue without ulterior motive.[57] The view that the plaintiffs had nothing to gain from a murder conviction has no basis in the ancient evidence. On the contrary, financial gain continued to be a motive in homicide prosecutions of both types.[58] We have no reason to suppose that confiscation of property and *apographai* were handled any differently in a murder case than a case of sacrilege: those who initiated an action to confiscate property would expect to receive a substantial share of the proceeds.

[56] There was probably no penalty for dropping the charges or failing to win one-fifth of the votes before the restored democracy, of which such measures were characteristic.

[57] Thus Gagarin, *Herodes*, 27–9: we are to suppose the plaintiffs solely motivated by a desire for vengeance at the trial though willing to settle for financial compensation before trial. Gagarin concedes that the plaintiffs may have anticipated some indirect financial gain from a conviction.

[58] See the discussion of *hypophonia* and confiscation in Ch. 4 §2.2. Gagarin, *Herodes*, 26 n. 28, rejects the implication of *Laws* 866c that confiscated property would devolve to the family.

1.2.3 The Slave Torture (*basanos*)

The one piece of evidence that is most crucial to the plaintiffs' case is the testimony of the slave under torture. Aside from this, they have only the letter to Lycinus to implicate Euxitheus in the killing of Herodes, and the letter is of little consequence in itself.[59] It is the word of the tortured slave, more than any other factor, that directly incriminates Euxitheus. It is a prime focus of the legal challenge, and aside from the general objections to summary arrest, Euxitheus devotes more of his argument to this point than to any other procedural matter. He challenges both the *manner* in which the torture was handled and the very substance of the slave's testimony: the plaintiffs have not only violated the ordinary rules of evidence but also misrepresented what was actually said.

It is just as likely, of course, that the defendant is misrepresenting what the plaintiffs have said: he is clearly distorting what they have made of the slave's testimony.[60] Here, indeed, we encounter the kind of artful deception of layman jurors that Heitsch finds so pervasive in Antiphon. But rather than dismiss the discrepancies as mere distortion, it is perhaps more constructive to interpret the defendant's challenge as we might consider a debatable point of law in a modern court: if a prosecutor must invoke an ill-defined concept in order to make his case, the defendant is certainly entitled to make the most of the ambiguities.[61]

Such is the strategy we discovered in Antiphon 6 (*Choreutes*), where the plaintiffs have claimed that the *chorēgos* is responsible as 'planner' or determiner of what is admittedly an unintended fatality. Because the causal connection is ambiguous and ill-defined, the

[59] See §1.1.3 above, at nn. 20–1. Such evidence could be easily fabricated and there is no indication that plaintiffs attempted to authenticate it. On the face of it, Euxitheus' argument against the letter is quite cogent (cf. Gagarin, *Herodes*, 80–1). But we are entitled to be sceptical of the notion that there was no reason to write out what 'the perpetrator himself' could report. At some point the message might have to be handed on to some third party before it came into the hands of Lycinus.

[60] I cannot follow Gagarin's contention (*Herodes*, 67–8) that 'the slave must have provided a detailed account of the events'. The speech reveals only that the slave confessed to taking part in the killing and also implicated Euxitheus. The very fact that so much depends upon the interpretation of one word, συναποκτεῖναι, clearly confirms what we would expect, that a brief interrogatory was put to the slave for him to answer either in the affirmative or the negative; cf. Thür, *Basanos*, 48–55.

[61] For instance, some state codes in the United States include a rule that a killer who pleads self-defence must show that he had no opportunity to 'retreat', but it is debatable what attempts at escape are required; for a concise account see Clark's *Criminal Law*[3], 181–2.

defendant may succeed in confusing the issue by insisting upon other, extraneous matters; in particular, he makes much of *his* alibi, which is quite irrelevant to the case against him.

Antiphon has devised a similar strategy for the case against Euxitheus: the plaintiffs' case depends upon an involved chain of events; the defence will disregard the subtle mechanism of causation and proceed upon a more straightforward premiss. Now I am supposing that this speech, like Antiphon 6, was the speechwriter's 'prepared text'; the significance of the slave torture and the scenario built upon it would be known from the preliminaries.[62] From the evidence submitted it would be clear that the plaintiffs intended to construct a scenario in which the slave took part in the actual killing and Euxitheus was implicated only as an instigator or planner.

The case for the defence depends upon cutting through this nexus. The defendant will first try to establish that the slave was purchased for the purpose of fabricating evidence; the proof of this is that he was then put to death wrongfully and illegally. This point has been treated extensively elsewhere, and there is no need to belabour it: we can conclude with reasonable confidence that there was no illegality in putting the slave to death, if in fact he confessed to the killing.[63] The conduct of the plaintiffs is questionable only if the slave did not confess to an active part in the murder.

For this reason the defendant challenges the very substance of the slave's testimony: he argues that the slave confessed only to assisting in disposal of the body, an aspect of the crime which the plaintiffs cannot adequately explain. But because he argues sometimes on this assumption, sometimes assuming that the plaintiffs' report is accurate, there is a glaring inconsistency in his representation of their case. Euxitheus first reports the slave's testimony as follows: they say (*a*) that the slave under torture admitted *taking part in the killing* (39); but he then insists (*b*) that the slave actually confessed to helping dispose of the body, and that he, Euxitheus was named as the killer. In rebutting the plaintiffs' arguments on the slave torture itself, the defendant proceeds on the assumption

---

[62] There is no need to suppose that this is a 'client's copy' that has been revised to record what was actually said, a device to which Dover resorts in *Lysias and the Corpus Lysiacum*, 148–74.

[63] Cf. Heitsch, *Antiphon*, 73; Schindel, *Mordfall Herodes*, 34; Erbse, 'Antiphons Herodes', 211–14; Gagarin, *Herodes*, 73–4.

that the latter version (*b*) is in fact what the slave confessed: 'he said that I left the ship and did the killing, and he merely disposed of the body when [the victim] was already dead' (42); 'they bought him and put him to death for their own ends—the informant . . . not the actual killer' (*autocheir*, 47). But when he comes to treat the incriminating letter, he shifts his ground and speaks as though version (*a*) is established, that the slave is 'the perpetrator', the one who had done the killing (*eirgasmenos*, 53): 'the tale could be told more clearly by the one who had done the killing, and there was no point in concealing the message from him!' Again (54), 'the man under torture said that he himself did the killing, but the letter implicated me as the killer'.

The justification for executing the slave outright was that he had confessed to the actual killing. Therefore our defendant attempts to persuade the judges that what the slave admitted was not the killing itself but mere complicity. He expects the jurors to accept that it is inherently more probable the slave would confess to a lesser wrong. And in order to argue that the slave only admitted disposing of the body, Euxitheus contends that the slave actually accused *him* of doing the killing. Thus to prove that the slave was wrongly executed and his reported testimony therefore suspect, our defendant is willing to claim that the slave named him as the actual killer!

This is the most likely explanation of the discrepancy and it has been readily grasped, but the legal implications have not been followed out. It was the plaintiffs' contention that the slave himself did the killing, acting in concert with others (*sunapokteinai*): they did not accuse Euxitheus as the actual perpetrator, 'who slew by his own hand', but as implicated in a conspiracy against Herodes—as, in a sense, the 'planner'. The slave's testimony must have been introduced at the pre-trial hearing in order to establish probable cause. Realizing its implications, Antiphon framed a strategy around the weak link in the causal chain by much the same method he devised for the *choregos*.

1.2.4 The Case for the Prosecution

The slave's testimony under torture is the crucial evidence in this case and it must therefore be the starting point of our reconstruction. We certainly cannot take Euxitheus at his word for what the plaintiffs asserted; we must rather rely upon the aims and emphases of his argument to deduce the nature of the case against him. From the treatment of the slave's testimony we can conclude that the defendant was not charged with direct agency but with some indirect involvement.

Euxitheus, however, among his various representations of the plaintiffs' case, suggests that the charge against him is nothing short of 'murder by his own hand'. Thus in his reckoning of the probabilities he claims, 'they say that [Herodes] died on land, and I (presumably) threw a stone and struck him in the head—I who never left the ship the whole time!' (26). Given the obvious irony of this utterance, it is likely to be an inference *ad absurdum*. The plaintiffs could only have made such an assertion from the content of the slave torture, from the letter, or from pure conjecture. The bearing of the slave torture was to the contrary, that the slave himself was the perpetrator. This imputation is arguably contradicted by the letter: 'the man under torture said that he himself did the killing, but the letter implicated me [Euxitheus] as the killer' (53–4). But it is quite clear that the wording of the letter, as the plaintiffs reported it, was not nearly so explicit as to identify who struck the blow: apparently it said little more than '[our enemy] is done for'.[64]

If the plaintiffs made any suggestion that Euxitheus struck the fatal blow by his own hand, they can only have done so as a conjecture. Such conjecture was insufficient grounds for arrest and it might have made the proceedings quite suspicious to a jury at trial.

But the plaintiffs had no need to make Euxitheus the perpetrator to make him culpable. They had a much stronger case that Euxitheus was responsible by planning or prearrangement. By this strategy the alibi became irrelevant. They had only to establish that Euxitheus was somehow involved in a plot against their kinsman: with his assistance the victim was taken from the ship, conveyed by the very slave who confessed. Herodes was probably taken ashore and slain there, presumably with a stone or other instrument that could not later be identified (after the blood and signs of a struggle were erased by storm or tide).

Euxitheus persists in the ordinary assumptions of warrant and arrest—that he is charged as the sole perpetrator, on probable cause—because these assumptions run contrary to the plaintiffs' rather ingenious construction and he has witnesses to affirm that he

---

[64] Ant. 5. 54: 'If it were too long a story for the messenger to report from memory, one might be compelled to write it out; but this was quite a short message, (simply) that the man is dead.'

never left the ship. Thus he recasts the allegations, to the effect that 'they say the killing was done on shore and I am "the killer"—so I suppose I, who never left the ship, must have thrown the stone that struck the victim a fatal blow!'

Of course, this is not what the plaintiffs maintained. They constructed a scenario in which Herodes was taken ashore and there put to death at the instigation or at least with the connivance of our defendant. The substance of the charge against Euxitheus was not that he was the perpetrator, who killed by his own hand, but that he was responsible as the planner who arranged or facilitated a killing done by others. This is the natural implication, as we have seen, of the treatment of the slave torture, and it is clearly implied by a number of other points in the case for the defence that he is suspect not as *eirgasmenos* or *autocheir* but as *bouleusas*.

The first section of the narrative is cast in such a way as to answer charges of planning and premeditation. The defendant explains that he and Herodes found themselves on board the same ship bound for the same destination through an entirely unsuspicious coincidence. Euxitheus himself was to visit his father, who had taken up residence in Ainos, and Herodes was bound for the same vicinity for his own reasons: 'it was not by my intention but rather by chance, for neither did I persuade him [to make the journey] nor was I [making the journey] for no good reason' (21).

Nor was it by his devising that they put in near Methymna and moved to another vessel to ride out bad weather. The severity of the storm and the measures they took to find shelter were unforeseeable: 'it was not by my prearrangement but by necessity . . . by no devious contrivance of mine, but sheer necessity' (22). Euxitheus has arranged for witnesses to support this assertion, and he clearly anticipated that he would be accused of somehow contriving the situation in which Herodes met his death. It is in answer to such allegations that Euxitheus turns upon his accusers—'It is they who have "contrived and devised" these charges "by malice aforethought" against *me*.' And the ironic turn, 'they say I cast a stone—I who never left ship', follows upon this line of argument. The report of the slave's testimony, again, clearly indicates that the slave had done the killing in concert with others (39, 47). The message to Lycinus implicated him in the conspiracy. And if we grant the natural suspicion, that this attack upon Herodes had something to do with an attempt to liberate his captives, then the web of conspiracy extends to other unnamed persons, the Thracians who had promised ransom and thus induced Herodes to make the journey.

These considerations all point to the conclusion that the plaintiffs' scenario is substantially different from Euxitheus' version of their case. He alters the substance of the slave's testimony in order to discount its more damning implications. He persists in the presumption that it was one person alone who did the killing, where the plaintiffs reconstructed a conspiracy involving at least three persons, probably more. He establishes an alibi that was probably irrelevant, fostering the assumption that arrest implies direct agency, because the real charge is more subtle and difficult to refute.

From the pattern of evasion centring on this very point, I conclude that the plaintiffs have based their case upon the principle of guilt-by-planning in Draco's law. It is because of this construction that the procedure itself comes into question, and it is in direct response to this tactic that Euxitheus protests, 'indicted as a felon, I stand trial on a charge of murder'. By invoking a provision of the law of homicide in a procedure to which it does not strictly apply, the plaintiffs have as much as invited a challenge to the legality of their case.[65]

This principle is the prime target of the legal challenge, but Antiphon must attack it obliquely by conventional tactics. We should not expect the ancient counsel to delve directly into the causal nexus as we might expect his modern counterpart to do. There is, after all, no authoritative interpretation for him to consult. Instead he must proceed from the ordinary assumptions of the jurors. Among such assumptions is the ancient premiss that warrant and arrest must be based upon probable suspicion grounded in immediate incrimination. This premiss is admirably suited to ordinary felony arrest in which the culprit is seen or apprehended with the means or proceeds of the crime upon him. The accusation against Euxitheus, that he was involved in a killing for profit, certainly fits the category of felony murder. But the prosecution is

[65] There is an apt parallel in the case of *United States* v. *Jenkins*, popularized by defence counsel Vincent Bugliosi in *The Sea Will Tell* (New York, 1991). The murder (on a desert island) was done by another person for his own benefit (theft of a vessel). The question is whether defendant Jenkins knowingly co-operated, though without direct participation. The count of felony murder was found inconsistent with the nature of the alleged involvement.

entirely deficient in the kind of immediate incrimination ordinarily
required for felony arrest. In fact, the only grounds for probable
suspicion implicate Euxitheus not in the act but in facilitating a plot
executed by and for others. This is precisely the kind of liability for
which *dikai phonou* provided a time-honoured remedy. Arrest on
probable cause seems absurd.

Consider how Antiphon has gone about exploiting this weakness. He has, indeed, drawn up a list of grievances based upon the
specific differences between the summary procedure and the more
methodical *dikē phonou* (10–12). But he does not confront the juristic principle. He cannot very easily explain: 'my accusers have
implicated me only as an accessory or by connivance, but in fact the
procedure they have used requires that the culprit be caught with
the goods on him.' If he were to attempt a juristic challenge of this
sort he might appear to indulge in the subtle distinctions of which
Athenian juries were sometimes notoriously impatient.[66]

Instead, the method that he adopts is superficially simplistic but
subtly quite effective: he proceeds as though his accusers themselves must be relying on the ordinary principles—as though there
can be no question of prosecuting an arrest in any other way. Thus
where the plaintiffs have accused him of planning or facilitating the
murder rather than striking the blow, he proceeds as though the
latter must in fact be their contention. And where they probably
made no specific claim of any financial advantage to Euxitheus himself (suggesting rather that his motives were political), he proceeds
as though financial gain is precisely what they have alleged—and of
course they are unable to show, as they should, that he is caught
with proceeds of the crime in his possession.

This is much the same method of legal reasoning we found in
Antiphon 6 (Ch. 7). We would identify the real issue as a juristic
question of the *chorēgos*' responsibility for harm done by those to
whom he delegated his duties; but he never deals directly with that
issue. Instead he proceeds as though his accusers must abide by the
ordinary principles.[67] Thus he assumes that to be guilty of planning a fatality he must have either 'ordered or compelled or provided [the drug]'. He denies all counts—and what is more, he

---

[66] Cf. *Tetr.* 2. 2. 2: defendant apologizes for fine distinctions, ἀκριβέστερον ἢ
σύνηθες ὑμῖν.

[67] Similarly Lysias 1 does not attempt to define legal justification but simply proceeds upon the most popular interpretation. See Ch. 8 §1.1–2.

insists, he was not even present! If he were to examine the causal nexus more precisely to extricate himself from it, it would only serve to substantiate a connection that should otherwise seem tenuous. Similarly, if Euxitheus attempted to refute the notion that he induced or assisted others to do the killing, he would have to do some of his accusers' work for them: he would have to examine their scenario step by step and thus render the sequence of events more vivid.

However evasive the tactic, the underlying argument is not without merit. The traditional *dikē* was especially suited to resolve complex disputes of liability, particularly those cases where one party is held liable for the actions of another. The real issue in the case against Euxitheus is whether he is liable for assisting in a scheme that ended in the death of Herodes. The elaborate proceedings in *dikai phonou* were developed to facilitate settlement in just such disputes. Summary arrest allows for none of the safeguards and consensual solutions that availed in the traditional *dikai*. The arrest naturally implies that the offender is discovered in circumstances of immediate incrimination. Now 'guilt by planning' was a *viable* construction and it would again be invoked at trial in a case initiated by summary arrest—Lysias 13 (below, §2). But by its very nature the summary procedure was an unwieldy remedy against more remote involvement, 'planning' a crime without direct participation in the act.

If we conclude that this was the basis of the legal challenge, then the major cruces of this text are resolved: the irregularity against which Euxitheus protests—a travesty 'that no one in this land ever before suffered'—is not that warrant and arrest were not proper remedies against homicides *per se*, but that it was not the proper remedy for this kind of charge, remote involvement by 'planning' or connivance. The evidence clearly indicates that some killers were counted among the *kakourgoi* subject to warrant and arrest, and it seems inevitable that these procedures would have become the ordinary remedies against non-Athenians for the killing of an Athenian (see §1.2.1). This device was not an abuse of imperial power. It is true to the conservative character of Athenian justice that an ancient procedure, originally intended for other purposes, would be made to serve as the best available remedy in a social context that the lawgiver could not foresee.

1.3 Immediate Incrimination and Arrest *ep' autophōrōi*

Warrant and arrest evolved as a sanctioned form of self-help: under certain conditions the officers of the *polis* would recognize the rights of victims or their relatives to take forcible action for recovery of property or retribution for injury. With this warrant, the plaintiffs could not be charged for acting against their adversaries. When the injured parties themselves were unable or unwilling to execute their claims, they could resort to the archons for summary execution; and when the archons were reluctant to provide for execution on their own authority, the plaintiffs' claims would come before the court for a decision. Thus the trial procedure evolved from self-help, and we should not lose sight of that aspect of the proceedings when we interpret the legal arguments in these cases.[68]

It is commonly supposed that one of the conditions for prosecuting a felon by this procedure was that the offender be apprehended *ep' autophōrōi*.[69] This condition was originally equivalent to *flagrante delicto* but later took on a more abstract value of 'self-evident guilt' (§1.1.1). Often cited in proof that this was a condition of prosecution is Lysias' speech *Against Agoratus* (§2): in this case the plaintiffs were required to affirm that they arrested the culprit *ep' autophōrōi*, in order for the presiding officers, the Eleven, to accept the arrest and allow the case to proceed to trial. This text is hardly compelling evidence on this point, however, for, as we shall see, Lysias' argument itself suggests that the procedural requirement was not anticipated when the plaintiffs brought charges. It is therefore likely that the plaintiffs have given this term the broadest possible construction, beyond its ordinary value as a term of law, in order to resolve an unforeseen complication. Before this case I can find no clear instance where *ep' autophōrōi* as a procedural term is given an abstract value.[70]

---

[68] Cf. Hansen, *Apagoge*, 48–53; Evjen, '*Apagoge* and Athenian Homicide Procedure'.

[69] Cf. Lipsius, *Attische Recht*, 318–20; Harrison, *Law of Athens*, ii. 221–4. Lipsius supposed that this condition did not apply in homicide cases (325). Harrison and others assume the contrary, inasmuch as the condition of arrest is trespass in prohibited areas.

[70] By the time of Dem. 19. 132, an abstract sense of 'self-evident guilt' or 'obvious' wrong seems standard legalistic usage; cf. Harris, ' "In the Act" or "Red Handed" ', 177–80. In earlier material the strong sense prevails: Herodotus 6. 72, of Leotychidas discovered in possession of a gauntlet full of silver; 6. 137 of Pelasgians caught in the act of insurrection (hence deserving execution); Eur. *Ion* 1210, of

We have, of course, a good many other passages confirming that it was a matter of special significance in summary-arrest cases that the offender be taken *ep' autophōrōi*, but none of these so clearly indicates that this was a *condition of trial*. On the contrary, the sum of the evidence would suggest that this requirement was originally a *condition of arrest for summary execution*—that is, in those cases where the plaintiffs are demanding that the culprit be put to death without trial, at the hands of the magistrate himself, they must affirm that they have made the arrest in circumstances that would seem to allow no dispute of the charge. Thus Isaeus 4. 28 indicates that felons must be arrested *ep' autophōrōi* as a condition of summary execution, not as a prerequisite for trial. Aeschines speaks of those apprehended *ep' autophōrōi* as subject to immediate execution 'if they confess to the crime', in contradistinction to those cases proceeding to trial.[71] Demosthenes 45. 81 refers to the requirement for arrest *ep' autophōrōi* specifically in connection with summary execution; and from this passage we may reasonably infer that 'confessing to the crime' need not require a direct admission of guilt. Evidently the accused might be put to death without trial if he *could not deny* the wrong: an accused thief, apprehended in possession of stolen property, could be put to death if he could not name a legitimate source from whom he had acquired it.[72] It is therefore all the more imperative that he be arrested *ep' autophōrōi* (i.e. in possession of stolen property) if the plaintiffs are to demand that the magistrates put him to death without trial.

Thus we conclude that the provision for the offender to be taken *ep' autophōrōi* was one of the conditions of immediate execution. This requirement goes closely together with the rule that he be put

---

forced confession (cf. Lys. 13. 30). Ant. 1. 3 is sometimes read in the abstract sense, but the wife was discovered in possession of the drug by a husband suffering from its effects; Ch. 6 §2.2 (n. 32).

[71] Aeschines 1. 91. Hansen, *Apagoge*, 52, supposes that *ep' autophōrōi* was originally a general condition for felony arrest but later 'no longer a condition for the arrest of the offender but only for his instant execution without trial'. But this line of development is contradicted by Lysias 13, where Hansen can only suggest that the plaintiffs 'must have been prevented from [demanding execution] by the fact that the accused was not literally caught ἐπ' αὐτοφώρῳ'.

[72] Dem. 45. 81: if Phormio were arrested as a thief *ep' autophōrōi* and taken before the Eleven, 'with all the goods loaded on [his] back', if he denied the theft, he would then have been asked 'whence [he] obtained them'. As he could give no credible answer, Phormio would then be one 'who deserved public execution' for his ill-gotten gains.

to death 'if he confesses': it is assumed that a culprit confronted with immediate incrimination by the facts at hand will be unable to deny his guilt. This is obviously not a requirement for prosecution at trial, despite the usual inference from Lysias, *Against Agoratus*. It is unsound to reconstruct a general rule from one instance and it is particularly dubious to do so when the one instance obviously involves an exception or recent innovation.

Aside from Lysias 13, there is no evidence that the arrest must be made *ep' autophōrōi* in order for an *apagōgē* to go to trial. It is certainly not a requirement for warrant (*endeixis*); and if it were essentially a condition for trial, there is no reason why it should apply in the one procedure and not in the alternative. In Antiphon 5 there is no suggestion that the offender could not be prosecuted at trial unless apprehended *ep' autophōrōi*, where clearly if there had been any irregularity on that point, Euxitheus would have addressed it. In fact much of the argumentation shows (as we have seen) that arrest *ep' autophōrōi* was indeed the ordinary assumption but there was *no legal barrier* to prosecuting at trial even without immediate incrimination. Euxitheus does refer obliquely to the rule that a killer caught in the act may be put to death, but this comes in an argumentative passage regarding the treatment of the slave: even when a slave is caught *ep' autophōrōi* in killing his master, he is ordinarily brought to the authorities for execution (48). This claim has little value as evidence on legal requirements or actual practice, but it suggests that many among the jury would have regarded the plaintiffs' action as improper: the slave certainly did not murder his own master as he was not Herodes' property at the time of the killing but probably acted at the instigation of another master; and he was not discovered *ep' autophōrōi* in the strict sense, yet they put him to death without reference to the authorities. Having once referred to the condition *ep' autophōrōi*, Euxitheus would surely have made a similar protest in his own behalf if it applied.

In ordinary arrest for trial the original condition *ep' autophōrōi* was not a procedural hurdle. It is, however, an unavoidable implication of summary-arrest procedures that the offender be directly incriminated in the immediate circumstances, and such would be the natural assumption in the arguments at trial. Euxitheus makes much of this presumption of immediate incrimination because the actual charge amounts to a rather remote involvement discovered quite some time after the events. This dispute at trial was a natural outcome of the historical development from self-help. If the plaintiff lacked the formal condition for summary execution, it was then for the jury to decide whether the incriminating circumstances were sufficient to validate his claim. Thus the argument centres on circumstantial evidence. It is precisely this feature that distinguishes the argument for Euxitheus from that of the *dikē phonou* speech with which it shares so much common material, Antiphon 6.

This aspect of the proceedings is also crucial to the one case by summary arrest for which we have the prosecution speech, Lysias 13. The very fact that the case is to be decided by trial rather than summary execution naturally implies that the formal condition of arrest *ep' autophōrōi* has not been met. Yet in the case against Agoratus, the Eleven, who authorized the arrest, insisted upon including the phrase *ep' autophōrōi* in the indictment. This is a move of some juristic significance: the magistrates have put to the court a question that they themselves ordinarily resolved. In the next section we shall try to determine what inspired this innovation, how it happened that a formula once required only for summary execution was added to the indictment for trial.

§2. Lysias 13, *Against Agoratus*

If we were to regard it as proof of a defendant's guilt that the prosecutors persist in their case with vehement conviction of the righteousness of their cause, in defiance of ordinary procedural rules, and with no expectation of material gain, then we would have to render an unqualified verdict of guilty in the case against Agoratus. But of course the plaintiffs' resolve for vengeance is no reliable gauge of the defendant's culpability. In this instance, on the contrary, although the plaintiffs were earnestly determined to punish the man they blamed for their kinsman's death and apparently had no ulterior motive, their case was largely groundless.

There appears to be no question of the events themselves. Much of the sequence of events was documented by the text of decrees and testimony of firsthand witnesses. It is clear that Agoratus informed against certain generals and tribal commanders, implicating them in allegedly subversive activity, in the months before the fall of Athens (in the year 405/4); on the basis of this information a decree was passed for trial to be held before a dicastic jury of 2,000. After the democracy was overthrown and the Thirty came to power, those accused in the people's decree were tried before the council that had been appointed by the new regime; they were condemned and put to death.

For his role in these events, Agoratus was brought to trial sometime after democracy was restored. Now under the amnesty agreement the traditional homicide procedure was allowed only against the actual perpetrator 'who killed by his own hand', *autocheir*.[73] By this provision those who might be held responsible for indirect involvement or 'planning' were categorically exempt from *dikai phonou*. Moreover, we learn that those 'who informed or denounced' were expressly given immunity from prosecution.[74] These protections did not extend to the actual 'author of the crime', as *autocheir* came to be interpreted, but were clearly intended to prevent vindictive action against those who had been involved, often unwillingly, in proscriptions under the Thirty. A similar aim is evident in the pledge sworn by new members of the council, which sometimes authorized summary action against political criminals, not to authorize any warrant or arrest in regard to the recent troubles.[75]

Despite these restrictions the plaintiffs managed to pursue their case against the informant who marked their kinsman for death. Agoratus was arrested and jailed by summary arrest to the

[73] On the date, cf. Loening, 'Reconciliation', 96–7; Blass, *Attische Beredsamkeit*[2], i. 555; Hansen, *Apagoge*, 131. Loening is inclined to date this speech before *IG* II[2] 10 of the year 401/400 when citizenship was granted to non-citizens who had served with the men at Phyle. But this dating relies too much upon inference from the plaintiff's handling of Agoratus' status. It is perhaps as reasonable to date the trial (with most commentators) to the decade after 401/400, since Agoratus was expected to emphasize that he joined the men from Phyle and claimed citizen rights on that count (77).

[74] Isocrates 18. 20. On restrictions of homicide prosecution generally, see Ch. 3 §3.

[75] Andocides 1. 91. For *apagōgē* authorized by council in cases of political bloodshed, cf. M. Tod, *Greek Historical Inscriptions* (Oxford, 1946–8; repr. 1985), 142. 34–41 (= *IG* II[2] 111); Hansen, *Apagoge*, 135–6, on the case reported in Dem. 21. 116–17. The case of Archinus against a violator of the amnesty, *Ath. Pol.* 40. 2, is another instance of summary arrest with execution on the council's order. The bouleutic oath contained the pledge not to order execution on their own authority, 'without vote of the people' (*IG* I[3] 105. 36); and the case *Against the Grain Dealers*, Lys. 22. 2, shows that councillors sometimes took the oath seriously. But the other instances show that council sometimes resorted to extreme measures against public enemies.

Eleven—that is, by much the same procedure invoked against Euxitheus, except that in this instance there was no preliminary warrant.[76] The plaintiffs contend that Agoratus is directly responsible for judicial murder. They argue that the council of 405/4 was already acting in collusion with the oligarchs, since the councillors readily acted against defenders of the democracy and many were reappointed under the Thirty. They accuse Agoratus of being a willing instrument of this conspiracy, though, they admit, he was not actually privy to the plot.

The jurors are thus presented with two versions of the issue: the plaintiffs emphasize a question of intentionality; the defence insists upon a question of legality. But a finding on the first question will largely resolve the second. If Agoratus did not give the information willingly, then he is not the 'author of the crime'; he is then protected by the amnesty and the plaintiffs have no case against him.

2.1   The Question of Intent

The plaintiffs must show that Agoratus took part in the conspiracy willingly and by prearrangement; yet they cannot easily prove or persuade a jury that Agoratus himself instigated the plot against the generals. The substance of their allegation is therefore that Agoratus was presented with an opportunity to enrich or advance himself at the expense of others,[77] and he took the opportunity, neither unwillingly nor unwittingly. He acted in his own interest and on his own initiative; he is thus an active agent and hence the author of the crime, the killer.

The plaintiffs claim to have witnesses to the prearrangement, the deal between the oligarchs and Agoratus. But in the text as we have it there is no indication that witnesses testified on this point. The only witnesses indicated in our text would testify to the victim's charge to his kinsmen demanding vengeance upon Agoratus, and to the treatment of Agoratus during the democratic resurgence, that he was shunned as a known killer. Modern editors have attempted to salvage some basis for the prosecution by introducing the lemma '*marturia*' into the text at §28, where neither the ancient editor nor the author saw fit to indicate direct testimony. The speaker says

---

[76] The MS title wrongly identifies the procedure as *endeixis*. It is clear from the speech itself that there was no preliminary warrant; cf. Hansen, *Apagoge*, 131.

[77] Cf. §53, μέγα τι . . . διαπράξεσθαι.

simply, 'That everything was prearranged . . . *there are witnesses*, and the decree itself . . . will confirm to you'; thereupon in the text we find only the lemma 'Decree', *psēphisma*.[78] Elsewhere in the speech, wherever witnesses are called, they are indicated by such formulae as 'I shall provide witnesses' (42, 66), or 'You witnesses come forward' (64). Where the speaker says simply 'there are witnesses (present?)' we are hardly justified in introducing them into the text in order to remove what seems to have been a very real and unavoidable difficulty in the case.

After all, how would witnesses have confirmed prearrangement except by telling that they saw evidence of a transaction or heard a deal being made between Agoratus and the conspirators? But if he had other evidence, it is astounding that our speaker did not go into it. Instead he relied upon the implication of the decree in which Agoratus was given a grant of immunity and perhaps other considerations. Immediately following the decree, our speaker insists that Agoratus left the altar where he had taken refuge 'willingly, though he now contends that he was removed by force'. And without arguing the point, the speaker passes on to the next scene in his narrative. Because the decree that had just been read to the jury contained a promise of immunity and some material advantage, the speaker can assume that this point needs no further argument.

From this passage and from the utter lack of any direct and specific treatment of evidence on prearrangement anywhere in the speech, and indeed from the speaker's own acknowledgement that '[Agoratus was] not . . . at all privy to their plot', I conclude that the plaintiffs had no firsthand witnesses to substantiate their claim that Agoratus actively and willingly entered into the conspiracy.

The plaintiffs are therefore driven back upon circumstantial reasoning to prove that Agoratus must have acted of his own will. Much of the argument on intent is introduced in the course of the narrative by way of conjecture from probability. The plaintiffs are at something of a disadvantage. They want to establish a presumption that Agoratus was eager to betray the democratic regime, but he would undoubtedly cite the decree in which he was *honoured* alongside those who assassinated Phrynichus, one of the instigators

---

[78] Lys. 13. 28: ὡς δὲ παρεσκευάσθη ἅπαντα ἃ ἐγὼ λέγω, καὶ μάρτυρές εἰσι καὶ αὐτὸ τὸ ψήφισμά σου τὸ τῆς βουλῆς καταμαρτυρήσει. ⟨ΜΑΡΤΥΡΕΣ⟩ ΨΗΦΙΣΜΑ.

of oligarchy in 411.[79] Since they cannot implicate him directly as a party to oligarchic conspiracy, they offer a rather ingenious formulation:

[Theramenes and his backers] *devised the following scheme*: they persuaded this fellow Agoratus to turn informer against the generals and taxiarchs— *not that he was at all privy to their plot*, for they were certainly not, so misguided and lacking in support as to call in Agoratus as a firm ally in undertaking so momentous an endeavour . . . but they decided he would be useful as an informer. And they wanted him to *appear* to be giving his information *unwillingly* rather than by choice, so that the information would seem the more trustworthy. But that he did inform willingly, you will see for yourselves from the course of events. [80]

Agoratus acted willingly, then, in giving information, though he was not a partisan of the oligarchs. The reason for this formulation will be indeed apparent as we follow out the sequence of the narrative, but for the moment it is enough to raise the suspicion that Agoratus must have anticipated the dire consequences which, in hindsight, would seem inescapable. The new council was already suborned to serve the oligarchs' design, and one Theocritus, an associate of Agoratus, was sent before the council to warn of a counter-conspiracy. Theocritus himself refused to name the principals but apparently referred to Agoratus as a further source. Here the plaintiff insists (22), 'Yet if his information had not been prearranged, how is it the council did not compel [Theocritus] to give the names but allowed him to make his allegations against persons unnamed?'

More persuasive is the probability of prearrangement that the plaintiff deduces from the events that follow. The council sent a committee to arrest Agoratus, but certain sympathizers persuaded the councillors to accept their surety and leave Agoratus at liberty. Then those who had posted his bail took refuge with Agoratus at the altar at Munychia and arranged for him to make his escape, so that he could not be compelled to reveal the names of the democratic opposition. He refused to flee.

---

[79] *IG* I[3] 102 = Tod *GHI* i. 86. 26–7; defence on that count answered in Lys. 13. 70–2.

[80] Lys. 13. 18. Note the language of planning: ἐπιβουλὴν οὖν τοιαύτην ἐπιβουλεύουσι. πείθουσι γὰρ Ἀγόρατον τουτονὶ μηνυτὴν . . . γενέσθαι, οὐ συνειδότα ἐκείνοις . . . οὐδέν.

Yet, Agoratus, if there were no prearrangement to guarantee that no harm would come to you, why would you not make your escape when the vessels were made ready and those who gave surety for your release were prepared to sail with you?—You still had the chance, before the council had you in their power. (26)

The consequences of arrest were more serious for Agoratus and exile involved far less sacrifice for him than for those who had given surety, unless it had already been arranged that he would come to no harm. As he did not have citizen status, he could be put to torture, whereas those who urged his escape, as citizens, had no reason to fear torture. And those who gave surety were willing not only to write off their property but also to abandon their homeland, whereas Agoratus, it is argued, would suffer no such loss. Thus there was no apparent motive for Agoratus to face arrest and interrogation before council, unless he had some guarantee of safety and material advantage: 'Though you now pretend it was unwilling, at the time you put to death many good men all too willingly' (28).

It is at this point in the narrative that the speaker introduces the decree that offered immunity and reward, as a proof 'that everything was prearranged'. Thereupon he discounts Agoratus' claim that he was removed from the altar by force, since a more plausible rationale is indicated in the council's decree. It is not unlikely, however, that the council also provided for a guard at the altar to force his surrender and other measures to ensure his compliance. There was probably the threat that penalties for conspiracy would fall not only upon Agoratus but also upon his family if he failed to comply.[81] There is nothing inherently implausible in Agoratus' claim that he was coerced, and his accusers appear to have no witnesses or other direct evidence to the contrary.

The plaintiffs contend that Agoratus' willingness is shown by a second information, naming other conspirators, that he gave to council 'under no compulsion'.[82] And in special session of the assembly at Munychia, he reaffirmed the information he had given. Thus it was decreed that those he had named were to be tried before a dicastic jury of 2,000.

We are entitled to be sceptical of the plaintiffs' contention that this was all part of an oligarchic plot. The plaintiffs contend that

---

[81] Hereditary *atimia* was a regular remedy in such cases; see my study 'Tyranny and Outlawry'.

[82] Lys. 13. 31: ἑκὼν ἀπογράφει, οὐδεμίας αὐτῷ ἀνάγκης οὔσης.

the council members who tried the case, newly appointed by the Thirty, were largely hold-overs from the previous council that drew up the decree. Thus by a connected scheme the information that Agoratus had given in the final months of the old democracy now served as a pretext for judicial murder under the oligarchic regime. But the plaintiffs themselves readily admit that the accused generals might easily have been acquitted if the case had been properly tried before the people—as prescribed in the original decree. Yet despite this break in the causal sequence—despite the fact that the councillors of 405/4 could not have foreseen how events would unfold in summer 404 and did not anticipate trying the case themselves—the plaintiffs hold Agoratus responsible for executions that were ordered and carried out under the Thirty.

The rise of the oligarchs and the changes that they brought about, particularly the change of venue that brought the officers to trial before a partisan council, constitute an outright break in the causal chain connecting Agoratus to judicial murder.[83] Of course the plaintiffs maintain that the councillors who took Agoratus' information and those who passed sentence on his victims were led by the same group and the outcome was much as originally intended. But this is at best a very weak link, and without it Agoratus' involvement cannot be construed as instigation of the murders.

The plaintiffs themselves or their speech-writer evidently recognized this weakness in their case: they therefore fell back upon a second line of attack in the anticipation of defence arguments.

Perhaps he will say that he did not intend to do so much harm. But if a man does you such irreparable harm, however much he may not intend to do the harm he does, I do not think that you must therefore refrain from acting against him.[84]

The speaker then recalls the earlier arguments on intent.

Remember that Agoratus had the opportunity to save himself before he was brought into the council; for the ships were ready to sail and those who

---

[83] Lysias treats the outcome, §38, as though Agoratus stood trial with the other defendants and 'only [he] was acquitted'; this suggests that the whole sequence of proceedings was rigged. But surely Agoratus was spared by grant of immunity and was not on trial with the others.

[84] Lys. 13. 52. It is clear from the context and earlier argument that ἄκων τοσαῦτα κακὰ ἐργάσασθαι refers to the outcome rather than the act: thus I have rendered, 'did not intend so much harm'. It is also clear from context and parallel usage that ἀμύνεσθαι does not mean 'protect yourselves' here, but is used in a hostile sense, 'act against' or 'take vengeance'.

had posted his bail were willing to go with him. If he had obliged them and decided to sail with them, he would not have put to death so many Athenians, *neither intentionally nor unintentionally*.

The plaintiffs have already answered Agoratus' plea that his *act* was unintentional, that is, that he gave the names under duress. Here they suppose that Agoratus will plead he did not contemplate the *outcome*. He is none the less responsible for the remote consequences of his *decision*. The plaintiff is appealing to the jurors' sense of 'fair choice' and 'last clear chance': Agoratus brought about the disaster by his own decision, whether he intended the outcome or not; once he had named certain individuals as opponents of the oligarchic movement, their fate was sealed. He is therefore to be held responsible for consequences that a reasonable person would have foreseen and avoided.

This second line of rebuttal suggests that the plaintiffs might expect many among the jury to accept Agoratus' plea that he acted unwillingly and unwittingly, that he surrendered under duress and submitted to the demands of council without foreseeing the consequences of his compliance. For those jurors our plaintiffs conjure up the spectre of guilt-by-planning. This principle, already problematic in Antiphon 1 and 6, was expressly disallowed by the amnesty of 403/2. The rule allowing homicide prosecution only in cases of 'killing by one's own hand' was intended to block precisely such charges as this, as a wall against the tide of vendetta that would otherwise have inundated all those who had yielded to intimidation and served as accessories under the Thirty.

It is because of this restriction that the plaintiffs could not proceed by the traditional *dikē phonou*, formally charging Agoratus with planning. They have therefore resorted to summary arrest, although it was not strictly suited to charges of this kind. Once they have brought their case before the dicasts, they might cast the ancient net of planning to entangle their adversary; and, despite the abuse of amnesty, they might well appeal to the resentment of many among the jury. They are formally excluded from charging Agoratus as an 'informant or denouncer' and must therefore charge him as the author of the crime. On a narrow interpretation of intent their case is exceedingly weak; it is only by conjuring the more subtle sense of malice that they have any hope of persuading a majority. But it is this imputation of malice in 'planning' that invites the legal challenge.

2.2   The Question of Legality

I hear that he will dispute the charge on grounds that the condition of 'immediate incrimination' (*ep' autophōrōi*) was added to the affidavit of arrest. This seems to me the most simple-minded objection of all, as much as admitting he would have been liable to arrest, had the phrase 'immediate incrimination' not been added. . . . I think the Eleven who accepted this arrest—with no intention of favouring Agoratus!—were quite right in requiring Dionysius to add the phrase 'immediate incrimination'. For how could he not be [immediately incriminated], since he named his victims first before the Five Hundred in council and again before all the Athenians in assembly, and was thus obviously responsible for their death? . . . I have also learned that he intends to argue about the oaths and covenants, claiming that this charge violates the oaths and covenants that we entered into . . . (85–6, 88)

This case is one of many that apparently violated the spirit of the amnesty, and that aspect of the legal complication has tended to overshadow other more substantive questions of law. It is often assumed that a case such as this, involving partisan wrongs of the revolutionary era, was properly excluded by the pledge 'not to remember past wrongs'—μὴ μνησικακεῖν. Therefore it is sometimes supposed that the formal issue in this case was not the murder itself but the trespass: Agoratus' role in the killings was excluded from prosecution by the amnesty, but his return to Attica, from which he was automatically banned by his act of bloodshed, was obviously an offence that fell outside the amnesty. It is this violation after 403 that constitutes the formal criterion for his arrest.[85] This interpretation neatly fits the theory that 'homicide arrest' constituted a distinct procedure, since Demosthenes' description seems to suggest that it was precisely the violation of prohibited areas that was grounds for arrest of an accused homicide.

But this reconstruction of the case against Agoratus—treating the trespass as the formal charge and thus evading the amnesty—is built upon a very flimsy foundation. First of all, there is absolutely nothing in the speech itself to suggest that the trespass is considered the substantive wrong. That omission is especially significant inasmuch as the procedural requirements, particularly the ruling for arrest *ep' autophōrōi*, seem to be a focus of dispute. If the trespass were indeed the basis of the charge, we would expect that to have some bearing

---

[85] Loening, 'Reconciliation', 104; MacDowell, *AHL* 134–8.

upon the question of whether the formal criterion for arrest *ep'* *autophōrōi* had been met; the criterion would amount to a require-ment that the accused be caught in open violation of the prohibited areas. The fact that the plaintiff makes no attempt to answer the pro-cedural requirement on these terms nor offers any evidence that Agoratus had violated the prohibitions must weigh heavily against the theory that trespass was the nature of the charge.

It is reasonable to suppose from Demosthenes' account (23. 80) that 'homicide arrest', so-called *apagōgē phonou*, required that the accused killer be apprehended in open trespass of the prohibited areas, but it is doubtful whether the same condition applied at the turn of the century. And it is mistaken, in any event, to regard this as the substance of the charge rather than *a condition of arrest*. Elsewhere Demosthenes regards the arrest of accused homicides who violate the prohibitions as equivalent to other remedies against persons deprived of citizen rights, *atimoi*, who violate their restric-tions; and this ancient legalism has greatly shaped modern schol-arly opinion.[86] But the procedures against *atimoi* were essentially a means of enforcing sanctions against offenders who had already been sentenced, not a remedy against the original wrong. The homicide arrest that Demosthenes describes is directed against *untried suspects*. In such instances the rule for arrest in prohibited areas amounts to a restriction on self-help by the plaintiffs and not a penalty in itself.[87]

Now our speaker does endeavour to establish that Agoratus was treated as a known homicide. Such is the bearing of his report on the events at Phyle (77–9): we are told that Agoratus was seized and taken to the place of execution, 'where they slew the others, when-ever they apprehended a robber or *kakourgos*'. And such is the effect of the report that Agoratus was excluded from the triumph when the men of Phyle came marching home (81–2), on the

---

[86] This seems to be the underlying assumption of MacDowell and Hansen; and even Gagarin, who categorically rejects the notion of *apagōgē phonou* (*Herodes*, 18 n. 3), does so on the grounds that this type of procedure is not a remedy against homi-cide *per se*, but, like other remedies against violators of *atimia*, is directed against violation of sanctions.

[87] Just as kinsmen of the victim were not allowed to pursue the killer beyond the borders of Attica (Dem. 23. 37), they were also barred from private homes within Attica. Demosthenes finds it reprehensible for council to enter the house of Aristarchus to arrest him: 21. 116–17. The ancient provision for taking hostages from the killer's household, if he would not answer charges (Dem. 23. 82–4), also implies that prosecutors would not ordinarily pursue the killer into his own home.

grounds that 'a murderer must not be allowed to join in the procession to Athena'. For the same reason, 'no one would speak to him, recognizing that he was a murderer', and it was only because Anytus intervened that he was not put to death.[88] Witnesses are called to affirm these reports. But in these passages the speaker makes no connection with the question of trespass. This evidence gives implicit justification for the summary arrest: it shows that Dionysius and his kinsmen believed they were within their rights to arrest Agoratus as a non-citizen and a known homicide; but whether he was apprehended in the prohibited areas (the temples, agora, etc.) is not mentioned. We can certainly conclude that Agoratus had at some point violated such areas since he usurped citizen rights and not only attended the assembly and served in the courts, but also himself initiated legal action—for which he was convicted of malicious prosecution, *sykophantias* (67, 73). But these details are not treated as having any relevance to the questions of immediate incrimination and violation of the covenants.

From these considerations we can conclude that trespass of prohibited areas did not constitute the substance or legal basis for the charge. Demosthenes clearly regards this procedure as a proper remedy against homicide, not merely a recourse against the trespass. And if it were only because the formal charge had to do with the later trespass that the plaintiffs were able to evade the amnesty, then we would expect to find some treatment of this issue—the trespass and circumstances of arrest—where our speaker directly addresses the defendant's objection that the case against him is a violation of 'the oaths and covenants'. If trespass in prohibited areas provided the plaintiff with legal justification on both counts, he would hardly have neglected to make the point at least once.

It is sometimes supposed the nominal plaintiff, Dionysius, would have addressed this point in the first speech.[89] But there is no cross-reference to such arguments, and the speech that we have addresses all other major issues, enters all available evidence, and runs to a length suitable for an unsupported defence.[90] We have no

---

[88] These two passages show that *androphonos* (here translated 'murderer') regularly refers to a suspected homicide and does not automatically imply that the killer has been tried and convicted, as assumed in Demosthenes' treatment of the law on summary arrest and execution, 23. 29 *et passim*.

[89] Loening, 'Reconciliation', 96.

[90] Lys. 13 runs to 97 sections, 31 pages in the Teubner edition; Ant. 5 has 96 sections, 34 pages.

reason to assume that Dionysius made anything more than a brief formal statement, if indeed he was even required to speak. We cannot rely upon his hypothetical arguments to remove the real difficulties in this case. And we must not conjure up lost speeches to answer a false problem. The usual assumption that the oath 'not to remember past wrongs' was a broad barrier against all vindictive litigation is based largely on argumentative constructions (Ch. 3 §3). The plaintiffs in our case anticipate no such obstacle.

The legal challenge that they have to answer appears to be quite specific. Our speaker takes up the several points in their logical order: the long delay before prosecution; the rule for immediate incrimination; and violation of specific provisons of 'the oaths and covenants'.

Agoratus will protest against the long delay between the events in question and legal action, and our speaker answers that there is no statute of limitations on murder (83). Of course Agoratus' argument was not so simple as this: he probably argued that his only offence was in the nature of 'false information'. Prosecution for such offences may indeed have been time-barred.[91] And he could certainly claim immunity under the provision for 'informants and denouncers' in the amnesty (our speaker alludes to such protections, 88–9). But in objecting to prosecution so long after the events Agoratus was likely to make much the same argument we discovered in Antiphon 5 (§1.3): Euxitheus emphasized that he had not been incriminated at the site, that no physical evidence or immediate circumstances linked him to the crime, and that direct evidence was only much later produced. Similarly Agoratus will argue that his accusers have none of the elements of immediate incrimination: they made no claim against him at the time of their kinsman's death (though this is understandable); prosecution was probably delayed for some time even after the oligarchic regime was overthrown;[92] and there is no physical evidence or immediate circumstance to link Agoratus to the actual execution. The lack of immediate incrimination is the crux of the legal problem (85–7).

Agoratus would argue that the dubious legality of the arrest was in fact underscored by the magistrates who insisted that the

---

[91] Loening, 'Reconciliation', 100 with n. 102, rightly recognizes the misrepresentation, and he suggests quite plausibly that Agoratus would attempt to reduce the charges against him to some other crime which might indeed be time-barred, e.g. *sycophantias*.

[92] I am assuming a date soon after 401/400; see above, n. 73.

affidavit include the phrase *ep' autophōrōi:* that is, they had required the plaintiffs to assert that they apprehended the defendant in circumstances that clearly and directly linked him to the crime—circumstances as immediately incriminating as possession of stolen goods—when in fact his involvement in the crime was remote and his responsibility uncertain.

The fact that the plaintiffs did not at first stipulate that they had made the arrest *ep' autophōrōi* suggests in itself that this had not been previously recognized as a lawful condition of arrest-for-trial. Evidently it was not a statutory requirement nor a customary rule of long standing; otherwise the speaker would surely have answered that the Eleven were merely observing formalities of which the chief plaintiff, unschooled in litigiousness, was unaware. Since the plaintiffs did not originally make the arrest *ep' autophōrōi*, and they did not expect it to be a condition of prosecution at trial, the one fairly certain inference that we can draw from this omission is that the plaintiffs made *no motion for immediate execution.* Why then did the Eleven require this phrase?

The speaker suggests that the Eleven actually intended to strengthen the case for the prosecution, but this cannot be taken seriously.[93] Evidently the Eleven would not accept the charge without this qualification; it represents a hindrance to the prosecution, an obstacle intended to limit abuse of the procedure. The magistrates were surely mindful of the covenant prohibiting homicide prosecution in cases other than 'killing by one's own hand'. They realized that for this reason Agoratus could not be prosecuted by the traditional *dikē,* and in resorting to summary arrest the plaintiffs attempted to evade the spirit of this restriction. The magistrates must have seen the danger of this innovation—particularly in the glare of other dangerous precedents (§3). They therefore saw fit to extend the rule against guilt-by-planning. They found a basis for this restriction ready to hand in the law of arrest: the condition that originally applied to arrest-for-execution, that the offender be caught *ep' autophōrōi,* was now extended to arrest-for-trial. This restriction was functionally equivalent to the rule in *dikai phonou:* cases of indirect agency or complicity should be excluded.

Whatever the magistrates' rationale, the defendant clearly bases his legal challenge on precisely this point, that indirect involve-

---

[93] MacDowell puts it well, *AHL* 133: 'Executive officials can hardly have outheroded the accusers by saying that Agoratus deserved a severer charge.'

ment, remote complicity, such as Agoratus' role in the execution of the officers, was excluded from prosecution. This is the argument that the plaintiffs anticipate (87).

For surely you do not think that *ep' autophōrōi* only applies if someone strikes and kills his victim by sword or staff—by that reasoning it would appear that no one killed the men you implicated for no one struck or cut them down.[94] But they were compelled to die by your deposition. Is not he then 'immediately incriminated' who was responsible for their death?

To order or compel the action of another falls within the range of indirect agency described by the *bouleusis*, 'planning' or determining. Thus in Antiphon 6 the defendant is guilty by planning if he 'either ordered, or compelled . . . the drug to be given'. Striking by sword or staff amounts to the antithesis, 'killing by one's own hand'—*autocheiria*. Agoratus insists that only killings of this kind were subject to homicide proceedings; there is a specific covenant to that effect.

In this way Agoratus could be expected to link the objection on immediate incrimination to a broader legal challenge based upon the amnesty: in §88 the speaker warns that Agoratus would 'claim that he is being tried in violation of the oaths and covenants that we [the democrats] in Piraeus concluded with [the oligarchs] in the town'. The plaintiffs' answer to this objection may at first seem specious, but it was evidently a familiar line of argument in such cases.[95]

I do not think the oaths and covenants have anything to do with our actions toward him. For the oaths were pledged between those in the town and those in Piraeus. If he had been among the party in town, while we were in Piraeus, the covenants would have some relevance. But as it is, since he was in Piraeus and so were Dionysius and I and all those seeking retribution, the oaths and covenants are no obstacle [to legal action].

At last we see why the plaintiffs refused to align Agoratus with the oligarchs. The oaths and covenants of amnesty offer no protection to those among the demos who wronged their own party. This claim may not be strictly valid in regard to the specific legal provisions, but we must not dismiss out of hand the principle that this

---

[94] That is, all were executed by hemlock poisoning.

[95] Loening, 'Reconciliation', 135, recognizing the parallel in [Lys.] 6. 39, remarks, 'This argument appears to be as specious as that used by the accusers of Agoratus.'

speaker finds in the covenants. We meet with much the same construction in the speech *Against Andocides* attributed to Lysias, 6. 37–41.[96] It was evidently a standard line of argument against non-partisans who claimed protection under the amnesty, to insist that the covenants properly applied only to those who were party to them. Thus Andocides, who was exiled for an offence previous to the civil conflict, was not party to the settlement and (arguably) could not claim protection. By the letter of the agreement, this argument appears unfounded: there was a general provision for restoration of 'those absent' to be included in the registration of citizens, and no clear exclusion that would affect Andocides.[97] But we cannot deny the appeal of this argument: 'covenant' (*synthēkē*) by its very nature has to do with the claims and obligations of the consenting parties themselves and only incidentally affects third parties. After all, the amnesty agreement seems to have fostered some serious thinking about covenants and social conscience.[98]

The formulation of this principle in *Against Agoratus* touches upon the original and essential meaning of the pledge *mē mnēsikakein*, and it was likely to strike a chord among the jury. *Mē mnēsikakein* was not a bar to legal action for all wrongs committed under cover of civil conflict. This formula naturally retains something of its ordinary sense of quitting grievances in private arbitration. Thus in regarding the oath as the seal of a covenant whereby the people as a body would quit their grievances against former adversaries who are now their partners in the agreement, the plaintiff has a point. In so far as Agoratus identified himself not with the

[96] This document is generally thought unworthy of Lysias, and its authenticity as a court speech is doubtful. The argument is based largely upon the religious conviction that the tainted man brings doom upon the community; the misfortunes that befell Andocides in exile are proof of divine disfavour (cf. Ch. 5 §2 on Lysias 12 and the *Tetralogies*). W. R. Lamb, in the Loeb edition *Lysias* (Cambridge, Mass., 1930), 113, supposed that this speech was in fact a post eventum pamphlet. MacDowell, *Andocides*, 14 with n. 4, follows the more straightforward view of Lämmli, *Attische Prozeß*, 43–9, that this is probably the clumsy work of one of the prosecutors (Meletus or Agyrrhius).

[97] Loening, 'Reconciliation', 36, 135, 195. Given the record that such figures as Andocides did indeed return, we have no reason to doubt that this was the usual interpretation.

[98] One thinks of Glaucon's formulation in *Republic* 2. Aristotle reports the sophistic formulation in *Rhet.* 1. 15. 21–2 (1376^{b}8–13): 'law itself is a kind of covenant' (νόμος συνθήκη τις ἐστίν). Without contractual agreement all commerce and social interaction would fail: Isoc. 18. 27–8. Aristotle himself rejects the notion that the *polis* is an alliance of disparate elements (*Pol.* 1280^{a-b}).

party of the town but with the party of Piraeus and the men of Phyle, he could not claim protection under that covenant. There was no blanket immunity for all who wronged the people.[99]

Thus the basic argument that Agoratus is not protected by the oaths and covenants because he was not party to them was probably regarded as an honest interpretation of the underlying principle. It may be contrary to the letter of specific provisions but it is not altogether alien to the spirit in which many entered into the agreement. And it is in the nature of Athenian law, of which the covenants became an important source, that the legislator's intent and the underlying principles that guided him are not made explicit but a proper rendering of law and equity is for the jury to do.[100]

Agoratus' objection is based upon *specific* covenants, not upon the broad pledge to quit old grievances. He would challenge the arrest (1) for failing to meet the ordinary condition of immediate incrimination, (2) as a violation of the rule against homicide prosecution for complicity, and also (3) as a violation of the rule absolving 'informants and denouncers'. These were the legal grounds of his defence. The oath *mē mnēsikakein* had no bearing on the legality of the charges. Indeed we have no indication that Agoratus was expected to invoke that pledge in so many words. In fact our plaintiffs had adhered to the oath, in so far as it affected these proceedings, quite scrupulously.

Whatever its effect upon litigation, the oath to quit old grievances certainly required the parties to disavow retribution by *extrajudicial* means. The greatest threat to public order lay in the unrestrained exercise of self-help by individual claimants for recovery of property or retribution for bloodshed. The oaths and covenants of amnesty therefore clearly entailed the exclusion of Draconian provisions for self-help and summary execution in cases arising out of the civil conflict. That exclusion has a direct bearing upon the law of arrest, as summary arrest was based upon legitimized self-help: traditionally the plaintiffs could forcibly arrest a criminal upon immediate incrimination. In some instances immediate retaliation constituted 'justifiable killing'; in other cases, if the offender could not deny the charges, he could be put to death

---

[99] [Lys.] 6. 41: 'For it is no violation of the agreements if Andocides pays the penalty for *his own* wrongs, but (only) if one seek personal retribution on grounds of public disaster.'

[100] Cf. Arist. *Rhet.* 1. 15 (1375^{a-b}).

summarily by the magistrates. A known killer or public enemy whose guilt was assured by similarly inevitable incrimination could also be put to death without trial, as the men of Phyle intended to do with Agoratus (77–9).

In the fully formalized procedure of the fourth century, execution without trial appears to have been quite rare. The departure from traditional exercise of such remedies was probably at least in part a product of the amnesty reforms. The restrictions of the restoration era strictly applied only to events of civil conflict, but their principles undoubtedly shaped the thinking of a generation. It is implicit in the nature of summary procedures that if the culprit is killed in the arrest, his killers may claim justifiable retribution, and if they first obtained warrant for the arrest they were entirely free from prosecution. The pledge *mē mnēsikakein*, however, barred arrest by lethal force and execution without trial. It was thus entirely in keeping with the spirit of the oath that the plaintiffs against Agoratus did not at first include the phrase *ep' autophōrōi* in their affidavit of arrest. Far from violating the amnesty, they were adhering to it by forgoing the demand for immediate execution.

§3. Conclusions and Parallels

The case against Agoratus represents the mature development of felony arrest as an alternative remedy against homicide. It is not, as often supposed, an abuse or aberration. Instead it appears to be an accurate and representative document of changes in procedure and legal reasoning whose beginnings can be traced back at least a generation earlier to the case against Euxitheus.

Felony arrest (*apagōgē kakourgōn*) was an ancient alternative against certain types of homicide: it would apply in those cases where the killer was known and could be apprehended in the immediate consequences of his crime. The charge that Euxitheus answers in Antiphon 5 represents an early extension of this procedure to those cases without immediate incrimination, where the defendant's involvement was indirect—where his guilt was a matter of planning or complicity rather than killing by his own hand. It was this novel application against which Euxitheus protested: he was indicted by a procedure that presupposed immediate incrimination, but he was to stand trial upon a principle of indirect liability that properly belonged to *dikē phonou*. However irregular the case against Euxitheus, at the turn of the century, perhaps twenty years after Antiphon 5, we find two parallel cases where defendants who were only remotely involved in the outcome, by planning or complicity, were brought to trial by this ancient remedy against felony murder. The case against Agoratus is one such case; another was the case against Menestratus that preceded it. Menestratus also had given information that led to executions under the Thirty; he was brought to trial by *apagōgē* and executed (Lys. 13. 55–7). Whatever the proper meaning of the oath *mē mnēsikakein*, it certainly did not prevent the people from bringing to justice those who had wronged them.

These cases are not so remarkable for the apparent violation of amnesty (there were many such 'violations') as for the more serious threat that was averted. The truly remarkable implication of these trials is that even in a climate of patriotic fervour these two cases actually went to trial: they were not resolved by self-help or summary execution, as might have been done in an earlier era. This was perhaps the most important procedural implication of the oath *mē mnēsikakein*, that parties to the agreement refrain from settling grievances by acts of retribution that were traditionally justifiable (Ch. 3 §3).

It was violation of this restriction that prompted Archinus to take extreme measures. The author of the *Athenian Constitution* found that Archinus persuaded the council to make an example of the *mnēsikakōn* and thus put an end to violations of the amnesty (*Ath. Pol.* 40. 2). There is also a report in Nepos' life of Thrasybulus that depicts him in a similar role intervening against vindictiveness; and this episode clearly reveals the nature of such violations as partisan bloodshed (8. 3, *caedem facere*).[101] The imminent peril lay not in vindictive prosecution at trial but in other, traditional forms of retribution outside the courts. It is only in this sense of *mnēsikakein* as retributive violence that there is any plausibility to the report that 'no one ever again remembered past wrongs'.

The two subsequent cases, against Menestratus and against Agoratus, prove the efficacy of the example that Archinus made of the *mnēsikakōn*. Under customary rules regarding public enemies,

---

[101] This anecdote probably derives from a tradition honouring Archinus and was wrongly assigned to the better-known figure: cf. Wilamowitz, *AA* ii. 223 n. 7; P. Funke, *Homonoia und Arche* (Wiesbaden, 1980), 17 n. 3.

the two could have been subject to execution without trial—as indeed the men of Phyle had intended to punish Agoratus. With a similar understanding of the ordinary remedies, Andocides reminds his accusers of their complicity in the wrongs of the Thirty, warning that they too might be put to death by anyone willing, if traditional retribution were allowed.

The great significance of the case against Agoratus is not that the plaintiffs evaded the spirit of the amnesty but that they were bound by the letter of it. In this case the outraged plaintiffs have submitted their claim for a decision by a jury of the people, in a matter where formerly they might have acted alone or with only the magistrate's compliance. This case thus represents the culmination of a movement that began with Draco whereby the *polis* gradually asserted the right to intervene in these potentially disruptive disputes: it began with tribal representatives undertaking to resolve a quarrel between the family of the victim and the family of the killer by tests of their respective convictions, when questions of fact or state of mind were left largely to the families to decide for themselves; it arrived at a stage where juries of the people would decide even the question of proper procedural form. Community decision has wholly superseded clan autonomy. Juries of the people will now decide even the question of whether felony arrest is formally admissible as *ep' autophōroi*, a decision that was once put to the magistrate when plaintiffs brought a felon for execution.

Legalism and Lysias 12

Wasn't he who made the law in the beginning
A man like you and me, who by his reasoning persuaded men of old?
So why can't I make law and precedent for the future?
—For sons to pay their fathers back with a beating!

(Ar. *Clouds* 1421–4)

In the finale to Aristophanes' *Clouds* we find this climactic reversal
of the rules. The violence that a son might do his father was condemned by current statute and ancient taboo. Then as now, domestic violence all too often ends in death, and kin-slaying holds a
special horror.[1] Parricide was so heinous an offence that even the
allegation was actionable under Athenian law (which recognized
few slanders). But either the crime or the allegation was common
enough for Aristophanes to make comedy of it more than once.[2]
Thus to overturn the most hallowed of laws, Pheidippides appeals
to the harsh reality.

In this proof of the right to filial retribution, Aristophanes paro-
dies the ultimate triumph of the new reasoning: Pheidippides has
mastered the method by which Sophistry vanquished Philosophy,
the knack of 'making the weaker argument the stronger', of revers-
ing what appeared to be self-evident truth. The most basic principle of this democratic method is that popular usage is the surest
proof of rights and wrongs; this is the implicit rule of recognition,
the key to determining what is law. By this rule Sophistry proved
that adultery must be no great offence since the painful consequences are no worse than all the lawyers, poets and politicians, all

---

[1] Plato, *Laws* 869b, absolutely rejects 'justifiable' violence against the parent—
'No law can allow it.' Bloodshed within the household was especially problematic
because ordinarily it remained for family members to prosecute. For possible remedies against failure to prosecute a domestic homicide, see. Ch. 4 §2.2. Lysias 10 is a
document of the slander law against allegations of parricide.

[2] In *Clouds* 904–11, the *patroloias* is vindicated by the example of Zeus himself;
cf. 1327. For the value reversal, cf. *Birds* 755–9; 1337–9. *Patroloia* encompasses
battery (potentially fatal) and other cause of death; cf. Lys. 10. 8–13, 28; *Frogs* 274,
773, 1191.

the people in the audience endure![3] Of course Pheidippides' con-
version fulfils a stock comic irony. The son has come to this revela-
tion by pursuing *ad absurdum* the very study that his father had
insisted he should learn. But the principle caricatured in *Clouds* is
neither absurd nor trivial: valid norms are rooted in nature, not
convention. The law is no longer respected simply as *thesmos*, an
external standard imposed by god or god-endowed lawgiver; it is
now seen as a covenant among men.[4] The true measure of what is
just and what is not is in the eyes of the citizen judges.

Society with its system of rules is a device that human beings
have made for their own advantage, and if the device proves defective it can be retooled.[5] This is the implicit understanding of the
Antiphon who wrote *On Truth*, who advised his followers to honour their oaths only when it could do them some good. And it is
part of what Thrasymachus meant when he argued 'justice is the
interest of the stronger': in all societies the dominant factions make
the rules to their own advantage; justice is what they make it. This
argument was not the raving of an alienated few; it had great appeal
among the well-to-do because it seemed to affirm a natural hierar-
chy over the arbitrary limits of convention. And this creed evidently shaped Athenian policy of the 420s and 410s, if Thucydides'
account of the debate over Mytilene and the conference at Melos is
at all repesentative. By an inevitable law of nature the strong will
dominate and the weak submit; this rule is established by a pattern
of behaviour accessible to all men's reasoning.

---

[3] *Clouds* 1085–102. (ἦν δ᾽ εὐρύπρωκτος ᾖ, τί πείσεται κακόν; κτλ.) I suspect that
the *reductio ad absurdum* in Plato, *Apologia* 24e–25a (Who is it that makes the young
people better? The jurymen . . . the councilmen . . . all the citizens in assembly!) also
responds to this convention.

[4] Democritus' theory of social evolution was influential in this development; see
T. Cole, *Democritus and the Sources of Greek Anthropology* (Chapel Hill, NC, 1967;
repr. 1990), esp. 75, 84 n. 11. On covenant as a fundamental concept, see Ch. 9 §2.2
at n. 98. Aristotle cites Lycophron for the standard formulation of this view, *Pol.* 3.
9, 1280ᵇ8 (= *Frag. d. vorSokratiker* 83 F3). Cf. E. Schütrumpf, *Aristoteles Politik*
(Darmstadt, 1991), ii. 485.

[5] This movement has been loosely characterized as the birth of liberalism: see
E. Havelock, *The Liberal Temper in Greek Politics* (New Haven, 1957), esp. 272 on
the respective 'contract theories' of Antiphon *On Truth* and Democritus; but cf.
I. D. A. Larsen's review, 'Liberalism in Greek Politics' *PR* 68 (1959), 103–9. It
remains doubtful whether these thinkers fully conceived of rights intrinsic to the
individual, beyond inherited status. For a theory of individual autonomy in
Protagoras, see C. Farrar, *The Origins of Democratic Thinking* (Cambridge, 1988),
15–43, 103–6.

Such was the 'enlightenment' that challenged the sanctity of the ancient laws, and nowhere was the change in thinking more disturbing than in disputes of bloodshed where Draco's *thesmoi* were still the law of the land. This concluding chapter brings our reconstruction of law and rhetoric to bear upon this crisis. The extant homicide speeches, spanning a period of little more than twenty years, provide a rare documentary record for such a pivotal change in thinking. It is a fragmentary record, but enough survives to show a surprising range of arguments and assumptions. Some of these speeches are grounded in the sanctity of ancient laws and the self-evident truth of oaths and witnesses. Other speeches in this corpus seem wholly devoted to the artful technique demonstrated by Sophistry and his student Pheidippides. But this divergence cannot be simply characterized as a quantum leap in reasoning, from the irrational to the ingenious. Even the most conservative of the speeches are documents of a thoroughgoing rationalism. And even the most innovative essays are constrained by ancient legalities.

The traditional suits for homicide, the *dikai phonou*, conform to that mode of reasoning that Weber described as 'extrinsic formal' rationalism; to use a more current catchword, it is a kind of 'legalism'.[6] The criteria of judgement are contained in the laws themselves and not to be deduced from some overarching societal norms. This legalism requires that the judges decide the claim based on rules embodied in the law itself, not with regard to abstract principles of justice or common interest—it is not for the judges to decide what *they* think is right or good for society. The speeches for *dikai phonou* are documents of an abiding faith that the law itself constitutes an objective reality independent of what people may say about it—'you must judge their arguments by the laws and not the laws by the arguments'.

So striking is the disparity between these speeches and the main currents of popular reasoning, between Antiphon *Against the Stepmother* and Pheidippides against his father, that we may be inclined to exaggerate the difference, to suppose that there has been some great leap of understanding or failure of faith within a very few years. But the findings of this study should caution us against making too much of a very modest progress. The disparity between one speech and another may be largely a matter of what the

---

[6] Cf. Shklar, *Legalism*, esp. 20–2, on the conflict of liberalism and legalism.

inherited procedure dictates or enables (§1). And even the most formalistic reasoning of the earliest speeches is not so remote from the premises of the modern jury courts (§2). These two cautions provide the outline for this concluding chapter, as we turn back to a document we have touched upon in many connections, Lysias *Against Eratosthenes*.

§1. Old and New Reasoning in Lysias 12

In the corpus of Lysias we have encountered a number of speeches representing much the same range of methods that we found in Antiphon. Lysias 1, on the slaying of the younger Eratosthenes, is a product of the same legalism that shaped Antiphon 1 and 6: the dispute is largely a matter of the *litigants' convictions* about guilt and innocence and the processual acts by which they demonstrate their convictions. Lysias 13, in the arrest of Agoratus, certainly reflects a shift in legal reasoning in the direction of social justice: the jurymen must decide on their own convictions whether the defendant is to blame for grievous injury to the *polis*. Lysias 12, against the oligarch Eratosthenes on a similar imputation of guilt by complicity, represents the most radical departure from the traditional legalism. But we must not lose sight of the practical limitations: the difference in the way the case is argued is largely a matter of what the procedure demands. Lysias 13 is circumscribed, as we have seen, by the principles of Draconian arrest procedure: it is the requirement for immediate incrimination of the malefactor that calls for the arguments from common experience and community interests. Similarly in Lysias 12, the change of method is prompted by the special procedural setting.

Despite recent pronouncements to the contrary, Lysias' speech *Against Eratosthenes* was not a speech for homicide proceedings, and it is probably not an authentic speech for trial but a hypothetical indictment for publication.[7] It is written in the manner of a complaint at the special accountings that any member of the Thirty would have had to undergo if he were to return to Athens. But even in this forum, even if we suppose a grant of citizenship enabled him to prosecute, it is highly unlikely that Lysias ever presented his

---

[7] See Ch. 5 §2 at n. 54.

argument as a plaintiff.[8] Aside from this document there is no indication that anyone of the Thirty ever returned to Athens to stand his accounting before the people; and in view of the overwhelming odds against them, the absolute silence of other sources seems rather conclusive. In fact, the speech *Against Eratosthenes* is, if anything, a compelling proof of the demands for justice that any of the Thirty would have faced upon his return. If Lysias himself was ineligible, there were certainly others who would take up the cause. And that, I suggest, is precisely the purpose of this speech, to show how the web of traditional liability could still ensnare the Thirty and their henchmen even under the amnesty.

Let us follow out two strands of the argument, one that reverses the old legalism and one that overturns the new rules. These involve (1) the religious consequences of homicide, and (2) the imputation of guilt by 'planning'.

1. There is a persistent notion that homicide proceedings were directly concerned with eliminating the threat of miasma, the defilement that a killer brings upon the *polis*. But the elaboration of this theme in tragedy has probably had more to do with shaping scholarly opinion on the homicide courts than have the court speeches themselves. There is, of course, a provocative treatment of this theme in the *Tetralogies*, but these texts represent a marked departure from the practice of the court speeches. Among the speeches representing arguments for trial, the conjuring of miasma as a representation of bloodshed threatening the community is found only in Lysias 12, not in the ancient courts of the *ephetai*.

In the traditional proceedings we find the firm belief that miasma and avenging spirits will haunt the killer or the perjured plaintiff; there is no apparent threat, certainly no preoccupation with the danger to the judges or the community they represent. With this understanding, the claimants invoke divine retribution to prove their own convictions: the defendant would not knowingly deceive the court since the more damning consequences of his crime could not be evaded; the plaintiff can only antagonize the spirit of the dead if he prosecutes the wrong man and lets the killer go free.

---

[8] On the unlikelihood of prosecution, see Ch. 3 §3 at n. 64, but cf. Loening, 'Reconciliation', 92–112 (supposing prosecution by *dikē phonou*). Todd, *Shape of Law*, 173, follows the view that Lysias was eligible to prosecute as a metic, but see my review in *AJP* 116 (1995), 141–3.

Divine intervention or lack of it is not treated as direct proof of guilt
or innocence. Fear of such intervention may reveal what we would
call 'consciousness of guilt', but signs of a guilty conscience are not
treated as evidence on the truth of what happened so much as proof
that the claim lacks conviction. The *dikē* remains quintessentially a
private matter of liability: it does not allow much scope for the
judges to determine the deeper wrong to the greater community.

In Lysias 12, as in the *Tetralogies*, the defilement of bloodshed
does indeed take on this criminal aspect. In the *Tetralogies* the
judges are repeatedly warned 'to absolve the community of defilement'; they must not allow 'this man, tainted and unholy as he is,
to enter the shrines of the gods and defile their sanctuary'. They
must beware the peril they bring upon themselves: 'Do not share in
his defilement.' It is in this spirit that Lysias in his peroration (12.
99–100) proceeds beyond the commonplace to conjure the spectre
of avenging furies, to threaten his audience with an abiding sense of
the danger that a man so tainted with bloodshed must bring upon
the community.

[To prosecute these wrongs] is not the work of one man or two but a task
for many. None the less I have done all I could for the sake of the temples
that they pillaged and defiled . . . and for the dead whom you could not
defend while they lived but whom you must now come to aid in death. I
believe they are listening and will know how you vote, and they regard
those who acquit these men as casting a verdict of death upon *them*, but
those who exact punishment take vengeance in *their* behalf.

The old reasoning looked upon homicide proceedings as a dispute for two parties to settle between themselves. What is important is that each side come to terms with what he and his adversary
'know well'. But out of the crisis of civil war, this formal rationalism, with its focus upon external demonstrations of conviction,
yields to a more democratic justice. The litigants of this era invoke
a body of jurors who will judge for the people rather than simply for
the plaintiff or for the defendant. And these officers of the imagined
community are called upon not simply to decide which of the litigants has sworn true to his convictions, but to judge the probable
facts of what happened and what was intended or anticipated: they
must determine what role the defendant played and what his motivation must have been, based upon the events they know for themselves (33).

2. The case against Eratosthenes relies upon the ancient nexus of instigation and complicity, of guilt by 'planning' (*bouleusis*), and its treatment of this principle is a revealing index of the change in thinking. The guilt of planning is signalled in the opening provision of Draco's law—guilty alike is the planner as the perpetrator. The issues in all five of the speeches for trial involve this concept, and two of the three *Tetralogies* are also preoccupied with it. Now, in Lysias' *Against Agoratos* we found that the primitive conception of indirect agency was greatly circumscribed by the covenants of amnesty: the speaker must identify the collaborator as the author of the crime; in order to prove this subtle causation, the plaintiff must delve into desires and expectations. The companion piece, *Against Eratosthenes*, proceeds from the same fiction: he who participates in a plot expecting to profit from the outcome is himself 'the killer'.

The primitive conception of *bouleusis* derived from the social order of the early *polis*: it was natural to suppose that a kinsman, slave, or other dependent acted at the instigation of his *kyrios*; and it was thereore reasonable to hold the master himself accountable in the reckoning of settlement. Intentions were incidental to this nexus of complicity—bizarre as it may seem to us, a man might be guilty of 'planning' or deciding an unintended death. From this principle Antiphon and the author of the *Tetralogies* developed a viable concept of negligence, that an agent may be held responsible for remote consequences of his decision that any reasonable person would foresee—it was for this breakthrough that Maschke ranked Antiphon 'among the greatest jurists of all time'. As we have seen, this juristic advance was apparently conceived as an argumentative device for transferring blame (*metastasis*): thus in the third *Tetralogy* the plaintiff demands vengeance upon the defendant's 'deciding spirit'—his was the wilful and decisive act that led others to act as they did; the defendant counters that it was the victim himself who decided the outcome, as he caused the defendant to act as he did (2.5). In the fifth century this principle of 'planning' readily served as a means of entangling a more prominent adversary in the fatal errors of his underlings, as we saw in the case of Antiphon 6 (Ch. 7).

But the problem of assigning guilt by planning is more complicated in the post-revolutionary documents, Lysias 12 and 13. In the latter, the speech *Against Agoratus* (Ch. 9 §3), the case could not

be prosecuted by the traditional homicide procedure because guilt
by complicity was expressly excluded in the covenants of amnesty.
The plaintiffs therefore prosecuted by summary arrest, but they
ran up against a similar obstacle in the burden of 'immediate
incrimination'. The officers in charge, the Eleven, had insisted that
the plaintiffs affirm they made the arrest *ep' autophōrōi*. This condition originally applied to arrest-for-execution: if the offender
were arrested upon immediate incrimination and if he were unable
to deny the charge—caught like a thief with the goods on him—
then he could be put to death without trial. But under the amnesty,
arrest-for-execution was also disallowed. The case against
Agoratus shows that the condition of immediate incrimination was
therefore extended to arrest-for-trial as a way of adhering to the
spirit of the rule against guilt by 'planning'. The magistrate's ruling in that case is likely to be a reaction against recent abuses of
summary arrest, such as the case against Menestratus, where the
defendant was condemned as 'the killer' for his role in political
executions in which he had only the most remote involvement.

The complicity of Agoratus was even more tenuous: he had been
compelled to inform against certain defenders of the democracy
before the oligarchic coup, and his information was later used after
the Thirty came to power as grounds to convict and execute their
opponents. Lysias made a compelling case of it, but we should not
lose sight of the fact that Agoratus was implicated by 'planning' or
deciding the fatal events, in an era when such charges were
expressly barred in homicide suits, and his accusers have therefore
resorted to the Draconian remedy against thieves and malefactors
caught in the act.

The principle of immediate incrimination naturally allowed
greater scope to the reckoning of circumstantial evidence, the probabilities of means and motive. Thus Lysias contradicts Agoratus'
pleas that he acted under compulsion, without intending the harm
that was to come of it: if he had truly wished to avoid harming his
victims he had opportunity to escape. And even if he did not foresee the doom he brought upon his victims he is none the less
responsible, by a principle that seems scarcely altered from the traditional guilt-by-planning: he whose decision leads to inevitable
disaster that a reasonable man would foresee is the author of the
crime. In this and other respects the summary procedures were
more congenial to democratic justice. Here justice is based on the

patterns of human experience, measured by the reasoning of every-man in the interest of the people.

But the most perfectly suited forum for democratic justice is the official accounting. Here the ordinary exclusions of the amnesty did not apply. And this forum naturally invited any considerations of public interest and equity, even where the letter of the law might offer no remedy. Thus for his indictment against Eratosthenes, Lysias chose an arena that imposed no formal restrictions and allowed him to confront the tainted killer in direct examination, as he could never do in the traditional *dikē*. As we saw in the case against the *chorēgos* (Ant. 6), a plaintiff who sincerely believes a man is responsible for his kinsman's death must never speak or consort with him. But in this special forum Lysias contends, 'I want to put him on the stand for interrogation . . . If it were to his advantage, I think it would be wrong *even to converse about him*; but in order to punish him, it is righteous even to confront the man himself.'

Yet with all the advantages of this format, Lysias largely relies upon the old conventions: his argumentation is characterized by the kind of 'layman's legalism' that Antiphon pioneered: where the adversaries resort to sophisticated concepts or ill-defined legalities, the speaker will proceed upon the simplest layman's understanding. He takes the letter of the law at face value; he who is party to the killing is guilty as 'the killer'.

Thus Lysias proceeds to treat Eratosthenes' involvement as tantamount to murder (23–6) and he evades the juristic issue of whether Eratosthenes is to be held responsible for a political execution that he did not condone but had not the courage to stop. In answer to the obvious plea of duress, Lysias follows the same oblique strategy he plotted against Agoratus: complicity will be treated as inseparable from the crime. From this principle the interrogation proceeds to the inevitable contradiction: 'Did you arrest him or not? . . . Were you present in council [when he was condemned]? . . . Did you argue to condemn him or did you oppose? . . . So you *spoke* against putting him to death but *took part* in the arrest for his execution!' The operative conceptions of planning and malice aforethought encompass those events where a defendant has acted without specific intent to kill but where any reasonable person would expect death or serious injury to result. And then as now, the fact that the defendant acted under a certain duress does not altogether exculpate him: it is the 'decision' or decisive act that causes the harm.[9]

This way of assigning guilt was integral to the Athenian way of justice; the framers of the new democracy tried to exclude such guilt by 'planning' in certain venues where it had become insidious. But guilt by complicity was practically a foundation of the new democratic thinking: the guilt of wrongs to the community is not just a matter of what a defendant did or ordered but what any concerned citizen would reasonably expect.

§2. Reinventing the Ancestral Law

It is Eratosthenes' decision that makes him guilty. Lysias' proof of this derives from the ancient rule that the 'planner' is as responsible as the perpetrator. But Lysias also relies upon a rule of great consequence for later legal thinking: guilty decisions are measured by the patterns of experience and the expectations of that quintessential creature of democratic justice, 'any reasonable person'. Proper remedies are not circumscribed by the letter of the law or dictated by special expertise; justice is open to the sense of right and responsibility that is accessible to all the people. Aristotle captured the principle as follows:

If the written law is against us, we must resort to the common law and principles of equity as the more just. . . . Fairness abides always and never alters, nor does the common law change—for it is according to nature—but the written laws are often revised.[10]

This justice in the abstract, Aristotle continues, 'is real and expedient' to the community, not simply 'a semblance' of what is just, as is the written law; 'for [the written law] does not do the [real] work of the law'—that remains for the judges to effect. The judge, after all, is 'like an assayer of silver': he must distinguish between false justice and the true. Such is the substantive rationalism, guided by social norms, that sprang up in the dicastic courts of

---

[9] The ancient causation has modern parallels: cf. Duff, *Intentionality*, 19, 53–4, regarding the case of a man (*Lynch*, 1975) compelled to drive a vehicle carrying IRA terrorists in search of their victim; it was held that his 'decision' involves some process of deliberation, hence intention. Duff himself defines 'decision' quite otherwise, pp. 44–7.

[10] *Rhet.* 1. 15. 4–5 (1375ᵃ).

fifth-century and grew into such weighty ramifications for the modern law. It was not a novelty in the time of Lysias; it was certainly not unknown to Aristophanes or Antiphon. It was rooted in the flawed foundations that Draco laid.

2.1 Draco's Law and the Discovery of the Mind

Draco inscribed into law the customary arrangement of self-help and private settlement that had evolved in the early *polis*. Intentionality was an acknowledged crux of homicide disputes, but Draco's aim was not to create special protections for unintentional killers; on the contrary, the old rules of automatic exile and self-help against trespass apply to all—*even if* a man kill *without malice*. Again, Draco evidently did not invent the court of the *ephetai*, and he does not appear to have altered the long-standing function of such tribal judges to decide liability in cases where the killer admits his involvement but denies that the guilt is his: for just such cases the lawgiver recognizes, 'guilty is the planner or the perpetrator'. The only profound innovation in this regard was the authorization of *ephetai* to intervene in those cases where there were no surviving kinsmen of the victim eligible to make settlement with the killer: in such cases—and only in such cases—the *ephetai* themselves would make a ruling on the separate question of the killer's intent; if they judged that he acted without malice, then they would appoint a board of phratry members to decide whether the killer might return to the community. Otherwise, so long as there were eligible survivors, the killer's intent was solely for the victim's family to weigh in determining whether they would deny or accept a settlement. Thus the question of the killer's intentions entered into the law, but it was not a question to be decided at trial until Solon made an issue of it.

Draco's secondary rules did little to resolve the structural divisions within Athenian society. Solon's legislation responded to the widening rift. His amendments to the Draconian code restricted self-help and reprisal with impunity (Dem. 23. 28), and it was probably he who enacted restrictions upon compensation (twenty head of cattle maximum) and exile (perhaps one to five years). And it was almost certainly Solon who assigned execution of the convicted murderer to officers of the state, thus removing one of the most divisive features of the ancient law. But of greatest

consequence were the reforms affecting the trial of accused murderers at the hands of the Areopagus. The reconstituted council
would now enlist all former archons, and these officers were henceforth elected by the people. Such was the body that would decide
those cases where the victim's family demanded that the killer's life
and all his goods be taken. This high court was to wield pre-eminent
authority by virtue of its popular empowerment, and such an
authority was evidently needed in those cases where the state would
usurp the ancient prerogatives of the victim's kinsmen. In sum,
Solon's reforms protected the community interests of the *dēmos*
against the most divisive disputes: he took the issue of the killer's
intent out of the hands of the families involved and put it to the
council.[11]

The weighing of intentions opened the door on the most essential devices of the classical rhetoric. The division of jurisdiction,
separating murder from the other issues, provided the first systematic model for defining the question at issue. This technical advance
began with the special jurisdiction for those cases where the victim's family demanded the extreme penalty for murder with malice
aforethought. And it was this otherwise inscrutable question of the
killer's intentions that led to reasoning from probabilities of motive
and circumstance.

The method for measuring guilty intentions was a product of the
social dynamics more than religious inspiration. Now it is sometimes assumed that religion first taught the Greeks to look beneath
the outward actions and probe the inner conscience, to show compassion to a kinsman of clan and cult who did not intend the harm
he did—as Gernet so persuasively argued. Along the same lines it
is often supposed that the cult of Pythian Apollo, with its hallowed
regime of purification, invented the rules of homicide jurisdiction,
dividing murder from manslaughter before Draco's time. Surely
there were some customary rules regarding ritual purification
going back before the lawgivers. But we can conclude with reasonable confidence that the division of jurisdiction between the
Areopagus and the *ephetai* was a product of Solonian reform, not an

---

[11] In the era of *Clouds* the Athenians may have been vague about the particulars,
but they firmly believed in the lawgiver's intent to safeguard the common man.
Thus Pheidippides exclaimed, 'Old Solon loved the people!' (1187), and on this
principle he would argue that the law was meant to be ambiguous so as to allow
debtors to evade their obligations.

ancient creation of gods and heroes as Demosthenes imagined. The religious sanctions were not originally embodied in the legal apparatus but functioned as an independent power of enforcement.[12] Thus defendants affirmed that they would not knowingly deceive the court since other forces of retribution ineluctably pursue the killer. In time miasma doctrine provided a popular rationale for rules surviving from the era of clan autonomy, but the statute law itself was not originally dictated by fear of miasma and avenging spirits.

The law was made to quell the wrath of vindictive plaintiffs, and for this reason the criterion of intentionality that emerged in the early law is not so much a measure of the inner conscience as a reflex of the outward acts. The plaintiffs who demanded the defendant's life and all his goods would have to swear upon their own conviction that he killed with malice aforethought—*pronoia*. This is a measure of the mind that they could readily swear to 'know well': the killer's preparations or prior involvement—bringing a weapon, waiting in ambush—were direct demonstrations that he undertook a course of action with fatal and foreseeable consequences. In the original reckoning of *pronoia*, there was no need to investigate the more elusive factors of probable motive: it was not a question of what he desired or intended but a matter of what he could reasonably expect. And as a criterion of the more grievous injury, *pronoia* also answers to the concerns of the original plaintiffs: regardless of what the assailant specifically intended, his preparations and prior machinations made the attack more lethal and more threatening. The survivors were likely to be more concerned with such demonstrations of calculated enmity than with the inner logic of why the killer would want to kill their kinsman.

Of course, this conception of forethought clearly prefigures reasoning from probabilities of means and motive, and it may seem to us a very short step from the outward demonstrations of malice to the inner intent. But murder trials in the age of Antiphon were still preoccupied with outward acts of preparation and planning and largely unconcerned with motives.

The conviction that the more grievous wrong lies in the inner motivation was strongly stirred by the crimes of civil conflict, and the procedural reforms of the amnesty tended, ironically, to

---

[12] See for instance the pronouncements of Wilamowitz, *Glaube der Hellenen*, ii. 36. Cf. Parker, *Miasma*, esp. 138–43.

reinforce this conviction. Indirect involvement in the proscriptions of the Thirty—complicity by 'planning', which would have been actionable under traditional rules—was excluded from homicide prosecution. But plaintiffs who could not put aside their grievances readily made use of other remedies. Summary arrest might still be invoked against those implicated in the killings, but this remedy involved its own legalistic calculus. Forcible arrest originally required that the immediate circumstances directly incriminate the accused as incontrovertibly as catching a thief with the goods on him. But such cases went to trial before ordinary juries of the people, and therefore, if the plaintiffs had no means of immediate incrimination in the strict sense, they might none the less seize upon the inner motives that everyman would recognize as the truest cause. Thus the people's juries were called upon to judge the wrong of guilty decisions and to weigh the defendant's intentions and expectations by the pattern of their own experience and in the interest of their community. Thus a procedure that originated as a Draconian instrument of self-help opened the door to a more substantive rationalism.

The special accountings, where Lysias lodged his indictment against Eratosthenes, gave full scope to this revolutionary justice. Here the citizen jurors are judges in their own case, on a charge of complicity in a murder that is more a crime against the community than a wrong against an individual or a family. The only formal 'evidence' on Eratosthenes' role in the murders is the interrogation, and in the absence of any other means of proof, the jury representing the community must judge by the events known to them all.[13]

2.2   Ancient Rationalism and Modern Law

There are relics of ancient customary rules, still in practice, which are utterly absurd . . . for instance, the law of homicide at Cyme, that if the prosecutor provide a majority of witnesses from among his own kinsmen, the defendant shall be liable for the killing.[14]

---

[13] Lys. 12. 33: τὴν ψῆφον, φέρειν, ἃ ἴσασι γεγενημένα τῶν τότε λεγομένων τεκμήρια λαμβάνοντας, ἐπειδὴ μάρτυρας περὶ αὐτῶν οὐχ οἷόν τε παρασχέσθαι. The witnesses later called (§§ 34, 37, 61) verify incidental points on Eratosthenes' role in the oligarchic movement.

[14] Arist. Pol. 2. 8. 20 (1269ᵃ). I cannot much improve on Barker's translation, 'relics of ancient custom . . . utterly absurd' (72).

Aristotle attests to the survival of a radically formalistic justice in some parts of the Greek world perhaps a hundred years after Antiphon's earliest cases. And roughly contemporary with Antiphon's early career is the inscription of the law code at Gortyn, where we find a similar persistence of automatic judgement on oath and prevailing witnesses (Ch. 2 §2). We should not find it surprising then that a certain formalism survived in the most conservative area of Athenian procedure, *dikai phonou*, where Draco's law prevailed into the fourth century BC. After all, even in Britain trial by battle was invoked in a homicide dispute on the eve of the Victorian era.[15]

But modern legal systems are generally guided by abstract rules embracing some concept of the greater good or quintessential fairness; specific applications of the law require interpretation of statute with reference to these overarching principles.[16] Such is the substantive rationalism that Weber described as the hallmark of the modern democracies. By contrast, the formal rationalism that the Athenians observed in their courts of homicide was guided by *external* requirements rather than inherent principles. The three speeches for *dikai phonou*—Antiphon 1 and 6, Lysias 1—centre upon overt processual acts: Have the plaintiffs properly sworn to their claim and availed themselves of all available witnesses? Has the defendant killer demonstrated by similar means his faith in the law? There is no juristic deliberation over the meanings of concepts, even though the concepts embodied in the law—planning, malice, and justifiable retribution—seem to cry out for clarification. The principals' oaths, the testimony of witnesses under oath and slaves under torture, the commandments contained in the law itself, are the chief means by which the judges are to decide the dispute.

These instruments are not adduced as 'irrational proof' in the strict sense, that is, with the expectation that gods and spirits will take a hand in revealing the truth and the judges should rule accordingly. A sign from the gods is occasionally mentioned in other procedures, but divine witnesses are nowhere indicated in the

---

[15] See Charles Rembar's very readable description, *The Law of the Land* (New York, 1980), 18–28: in Warwickshire in the year 1818 Ashford accused Thornton of the rape and murder of his sister, and Thornton demanded trial by battle; Ashford declined and Thornton went free.

[16] Dworkin's standard example is the principle that an offender should not profit from wrongdoing (*Taking Rights Seriously, passim*).

extant record of *dikai phonou*. Neither is there any vestige of ordeal outside of tragedy. But greatly impressed by the vows of tragic figures—to face trial by fire or sword and call the gods to witness—a generation of scholars were inclined to see the law as a child of religion much like medieval Germanic law. Such may be its remote antecedents, but the art of argument that grew out of Draco's law bears no resemblance to such *iudicia dei*.

On the contrary, alien as it may have seemed to us at first reading, the ancient trial by oaths and challenges to torture is not so remote from the 'burden of proof' in Anglo-American jury trials. In a modern criminal case, of course, it is not the victim's kin but the state that seeks redress for the killing as an injury to the community. But much like the ancient plaintiffs, the officers of the state must proceed with absolute conviction of their claim. There must be no rush to judgement. The prosecutors must show that they have undertaken every reasonable measure to validate the evidence and eliminate other theories—*beyond reasonable doubt*.[17] In meeting this criterion the *conduct* of the prosecution is as important as the evidence they have found. The jurors are *not* charged to find the defendant 'guilty or *innocent*', but 'guilty or *not guilty*'. The judge will instruct them that they need not determine on their own conviction that the defendant is innocent in order to acquit him. They are not asked to judge for themselves the objective reality of what happened, but to decide if the prosecutor has proved his case by all reasonable means.

Of course the modern jury is the trier of fact, and therein lies a sizeable distance between it and the courts of the *ephetai*.[18] But the *actual facts* of what happened or what was intended are as far

---

[17] On the whole nexus of issues related to burdens and presumptions, see now R. H. Gaskins, *Burdens of Proof in Modern Discourse* (New Haven, 1992), esp. 21–9. The requirement of proof 'beyond reasonable doubt' is a notoriously vexed phrase but it properly applies to the prosecution's burden of proof rather than the jurors' state of mind. Thus the judge will ordinarily instruct the jurors that reasonable doubt does not mean that they themselves can have no lingering suspicions, but they are to ponder more abstractly whether the proof is sufficient for a reasonable person to be convinced of defendant's guilt. The prosecution have the burden to eliminate any other theories short of far-fetched conjecture. In this respect the Anglo-American acquittal approximates the Scottish 'not proven'; it is not a determination of innocence.

[18] For the evolution from 'self-informing' peers of the community to triers of fact from the evidence presented, see Thomas Green's classic study 'The Jury and the English Law of Homicide 1200–1600', *Michigan Law Review*, 74. 3 (Jan. 1976), 413–501.

beyond certainty for the modern jurors as they were for the ancients. Both juries must settle upon a determination of *probable facts*, one that any reasonable person would share. And they must do so based upon the evidence that is put before them. Every precaution is taken to assure that the jurors do not rely upon extraneous material or their own peculiar beliefs. Whatever their own suspicions or certainties—for instance, that the woman scorned meant to poison her husband, or that the murderer of the wife is the abusive husband—the burden of proof rests with the prosecution. In this respect the modern jury remains much like the Draconian archetype: the jurors will render their verdict largely as a measure of the integrity with which the prosecutors have conducted their case.

Legal formalism has proved, as Weber remarked, a thing repugnant to democracy. And so we are likely to consign the formalistic justice of the Greeks to the infancy of moral conscience, before the growth of reason toward our own understanding. This complacent faith in progress would lead us to suppose that rhetoric evolved from naïve belief in the intrinsic meaning of the word or the deed and irrational faith in oath and ordeal. But the naïvety is ours if we forget that it is the rhetoric the Greeks devised that teaches us to construct a reality of probable facts and look there for justice, or if we deny the legacy of 'laws written in blood' in our own inherited assumptions. The prevailing proofs of malice and negligence are rooted in the old way of reckoning guilt by antecedent menaces or external conditions of fair choice. The legal discovery of the guilty mind began in the weighing of the blood price, and the difference between murder and manslaughter is still, as Justice Holmes observed, a precarious distinction.

APPENDIX

A Synopsis of the Athenian Homicide Speeches

(for quick reference, in order of the manuscript tradition)

The Corpus of Antiphon

ANTIPHON 1: traditionally titled *Against the Stepmother.*
Plaintiff charges the widow with malice aforethought in the poisoning of
her husband.
Evidence: Plaintiff (victim's son by another partner) swears to his
father's deathbed testimony and challenges his half-brother (*kyrios* for
the accused) to interrogate slaves under torture regarding a previous
attempt to drug the victim. The defender probably challenged plaintiff to interrogate slaves to substantiate his claim of the father's charge.
Court: Areopagus
Date: uncertain; probably before 420 BC.

ANTIPHON 2–4 = *Tetralogies* 1–3. Each *Tetralogy* includes two speeches
each for plaintiff and defence. Date and authorship uncertain.

Tetralogy 1
Victim was waylaid and murdered by unknown assailants.
Evidence: victim's slave, also injured in the attack, accused defendant,
then died. In his final speech defendant challenges plaintiffs to inter-
rogate his slaves regarding an alibi.
Intended Court: Areopagus.

Tetralogy 2
A juvenile defendant is charged with unintentional homicide in the
death of a boy whom he struck with his spear in athletic training.
Defendant's father speaks for him. Innocence of malice is not dis-
puted.
Evidence: None.
Intended Court: Palladium

Tetralogy 3
Defendant struck and injured an older and weaker man, who had
assaulted him in a drunken quarrel. Victim later died at the hands of

an incompetent physician. Defendant departs into exile before the final speech; his friends then defend him.

Evidence: Witnesses are called by the plaintiff to confirm the nature of the struggle, but they also reveal that the victim himself struck the first blow. Defendant invokes the law allowing superior force against 'the first to lay violent hands' on another.

Intended Court: Delphinium (or Areopagus?)

ANTIPHON 5: traditionally titled *On the Murder of Herodes*.

Defendant, a Mytilenean named Euxitheus, is charged in the death of Herodes, an Athenian who presumably occupied confiscated property on Lesbos. Herodes was on his way to Thrace, taking captives for ransom; he disappeared while their vessel was anchored in harbour on a stormy night.

Evidence: Defendant is implicated by the testimony of a slave under torture; the slave was apparently then put to death but recanted before he died. There is also testimony to a letter purportedly linking Euxitheus to a conspirator, Lycinus. A free man was also put to torture, but he did not implicate Euxitheus. Witnesses are called for these and other circumstances. The body was never found nor any weapon or signs of a struggle.

Date: *c.*420 BC.

Court: This case was tried by 'warrant and arrest' before a jury of Athenian dicasts (ordinary layman jurors).

ANTIPHON 6: conventionally titled *On the Choreutes*.

Defendant is charged with negligence in the death of a choirboy who was under his supervision for a public festival. The boy died from a drug given by defendant's subordinates, apparently without specific instructions. Defendant argues that the case is purely a means of obstructing political prosecutions that he has undertaken.

Evidence: Witnesses are called to confirm the various circumstances. Defendant challenged the plaintiffs to examine slaves under torture and witnesses under oath.

Date: winter of 419/18 BC.

Court: Palladium.

From the Corpus of Lysias

LYSIAS 1: conventionally titled *On the Slaying of Eratosthenes*.

Defendant, named Euphiletus, is charged in the death of the adulterer Eratosthenes, whom he caught in the act and killed. He bases his defence upon the laws against sexual violation. Plaintiffs allege entrapment.

Evidence: Defendant has witnesses to the killing and to the immediate circumstances. He cites text of various laws in evidence of legal cause. Plaintiffs apparently have no firsthand witnesses to prove entrapment and have not challenged defendant to examine a slave under torture.

Date: soon after 403/2 BC.

Court: Delphinium.

LYSIAS 12: traditionally titled *Against Eratosthenes*.

Lysias himself indicts the oligarch Eratosthenes for complicity in the death of Polemarchus (Lysias' brother) during the regime of the Thirty. The victim in Lysias 1 is presumably a kinsman of this elder Eratosthenes.

Evidence: Direct examination of the accused. Witnesses are called as to Eratosthenes' involvement and political motivation.

Date: soon after 403/2 BC.

Intended Court: special accounting of oligarchic principals (should they wish to return).

LYSIAS 13: traditionally titled *Against Agoratus*.

Plaintiff charges Agoratus with complicity in the deaths of certain officers by judicial murder under the oligarchic regime. Agoratus informed against the victims, and they then came to trial before a council sympathetic to the Thirty; the officers were condemned for conspiracy and executed.

Evidence: Plaintiff cites text of various decrees regarding the information given by Agoratus and condemnation of the officers. Witnesses attest to various circumstances regarding the role of Agoratus and his status.

Date: soon after 403/2 BC.

Court: This case was tried by summary arrest before a jury of Athenian dicasts.

BIBLIOGRAPHY

ADKINS, A. W. H., *Merit and Responsibility: A Study in Greek Values* (Oxford, 1960).

BARKER, ERNEST, *The Politics of Aristotle* (Oxford, 1946).

BARTLETT, ROBERT, *Trial by Fire and Water: The Medieval Judicial Ordeal* (Oxford, 1986).

BATEMAN, J. J., 'Lysias and the Law', *TAPA* 89 (1958), 276–85.

BAUER, FRITZ, and WALTER, GERHARD, *Einführung in das Recht der Bundesrepublik Deutschland*, 6th edn. (Darmstadt, 1992).

BIGNONE, E, *Antifonte oratore e Antifonte sofista* (Urbino, 1974).

BLACKSTONE, WILLIAM, *Commentaries on the Laws of England: Book the Fourth, Of Public Wrongs*. Facsimile of 1st edn., 1769 (Chicago, 1979).

BLASS, FRIEDRICH, *Die attische Beredsamkeit*, 2nd edn. (Leipzig, 1887–98).

BOEGEHOLD, ALAN L., 'Ten Distinctive Ballots: The Law Court at Zea', *CSCA* 9 (1976), 8–17.

—— *The Athenian Agora: Results of Excavations Conducted by the American School of Classical Studies at Athens*, xxviii. *The Lawcourts at Athens* (Princeton, 1995).

BONNER, ROBERT, *Evidence in Athenian Courts* (Chicago, 1905).

—— 'Evidence in the Areopagus', *CP* 7 (1912), 450–6.

—— and SMITH, GERTRUDE, *The Administration of Justice from Homer to Aristotle*, 2 vols. (Chicago, 1930–8).

BRICKHOUSE, THOMAS, and SMITH, NICHOLAS, *Socrates on Trial* (Princeton, 1989).

BRINKMANN, B., *De Antiphontis oratione de Choreuta commentatio philologa* (Jena, 1887).

BUSOLT, G., and SWOBODA, H., *Griechische Staatskunde*, 2 vols. (Munich, 1926) (= *Handbuch der Altertumswissenschaft*, 4.1).

CANTARELLA, EVA, *Studi sull'omicidio in diritto greco e romano* (Milan, 1976).

—— *Corso di Diritto Greco* (Milan, 1994).

CARAWAN, E. M., '*Akriton apokteinai*: Execution without Trial in Fourth-Century Athens', *GRBS* 25 (1984), 111–22.

—— '*Apophasis* and *Eisangelia*: The Role of the Areopagus in Athenian Political Trials', *GRBS* 26 (1985), 115–40.

—— '*Eisangelia* and *Euthyna*: The Trials of Miltiades, Themistocles and Cimon', *GRBS* 28 (1987), 167–208.

—— 'Thucydides and Stesimbrotus', *Historia*, 38 (1989), 144–61.

CARAWAN, E. M., 'Trial of Exiled Homicides and the Court at Phreatto', *RIDA* 37 (1990), 47–67.

—— review of R. Wallace, *Areopagos Council*, in *AJP* 111 (1990), 410–14.

—— '*Ephetai* and Athenian Courts for Homicide', *CP* 86 (1991), 1–16.

—— '*Νηποινεὶ Τεθνάναι·* A Response', *Symposion 1990* (1991), 107–14.

—— 'The *Tetralogies* and Athenian Homicide Trials', *AJP* 114 (1993), 235–70.

—— 'Tyranny and Outlawry: *Athenaion Politeia* 16.10', in R. Rosen and J. Farrell (eds.), *Nomodeiktes* (1993), 305–19.

—— review of S. Todd, *The Shape of Athenian Law*, in *AJP* 116 (1995), 140–4.

—— 'The Trials of Thucydides "the Demagogue" in the Anonymous *Life of Thucydides the Historian*', *Historia*, 45 (1996), 405–22.

CARTLEDGE, P. A., MILLETT, P. C., and TODD, S. C. (eds.), *'Nomos': Essays in Athenian Law, Politics and Society* (Cambridge, 1990).

CLARK, WILLIAM L., Jr., *Handbook of Criminal Law*, 3rd edn. ed. W. Mikell (St Paul, Minn., 1915).

COHEN, DAVID, *Law, Sexuality, and Society: The Enforcement of Morals in Classical Athens* (Cambridge, 1991).

—— 'A Note on Aristophanes and the Punishment of Adultery in Athenian Law', *ZSS* 102 (1985), 385–7.

—— 'The Athenian Law of Adultery', *RIDA* 31 (1984), 147–65.

—— *Theft in Athenian Law* (Munich, 1983).

COLE, THOMAS, *Democritus and the Sources of Greek Anthropology*, (Chapel Hill, NC, 1967; repr. as APA Monograph 25, 1990).

—— *The Origins of Rhetoric in Ancient Greece* (Baltimore, 1991).

COPE, E. M., and SANDYS, J. E., *The 'Rhetoric' of Aristotle*, 2 vols. (Cambridge, 1877).

DARESTE DE LA CHAVANNE, RODOLPE, *Recueil des inscriptions juridiques grecques* (Paris, 1895).

DAVIES, MALCOLM, *Sophocles* Trachiniae (Oxford, 1991).

DECLEVA CAIZZI, FERNANDA, *Antiphontis Tetralogiae* (Testi e documenti per lo stúdio dell' antichità 28; Milan, 1969).

DIAMOND, A. S., *Primitive Law Past and Present* (London, 1971).

DITTENBERGER, W., 'Antiphons Tetralogien und das attische Criminalrecht', *Hermes*, 31 (1896), 271–7 and 32 (1897), 1–41.

—— 'Zu Antiphons Tetralogien', *Hermes*, 40 (1905), 450–70.

—— *Sylloge inscriptionum graecarum*, 3rd edn., 4 vols. (Leipzig, 1915–24).

DODDS, E. R., *The Greeks and the Irrational* (Sather Classical Lectures 25; Berkeley, 1951).

DORJAHN, ALFRED, 'Anticipation of Arguments in Athenian Oratory', *TAPA* 66 (1935), 274–95.

—— 'On the Athenian Anakrisis', *CP* 36 (1941), 182–5.

——*Political Forgiveness in Old Athens: The Amnesty of 403 BC* (Northwestern Studies in the Humanities 13; Evanston, Ill., 1946).

DOVER, K. J., 'The Chronology of Antiphon's Speeches, *CQ* 44 (1950), 44–60.

——*Lysias and the 'Corpus Lysiacum'* (Sather Classical Lectures 39; Berkeley, 1968).

DRERUP, E., 'Ueber die bei den Attischen Rednern eingelegten Urkunden', *Jahrbücher für klassischen Philologie* (1898), 278–365.

DRIVER, G. R., and MILES, JOHN C., *The Babylonian Laws*, 2 vols. (Oxford, 1952).

DUFF, R. A., *Intention, Agency, and Criminal Liability* (Oxford, 1990).

DWORKIN, RONALD, *Taking Rights Seriously* (Cambridge, Mass., 1977).

——*Law's Empire* (Cambridge, Mass., and London, 1986).

EDMUNDS, LOWELL, *Chance and Intelligence in Thucydides* (Cambridge, Mass., 1975).

EDWARDS, MARK W., *The Iliad: A Commentary*, v, books 17–20 (Cambridge, 1991).

——and USSHER, STEPHEN, *Greek Orators*, i, *Antiphon and Lysias* (Warminster, 1985).

EHRENBERG, VICTOR, *Die Rechtsidee im frühen Griechentum* (Leipzig, 1921).

ERBSE, HARTMUT, 'Lysias-Interpretationen', in H. Diller and H. Erbse (eds.), *Festschrift Ernst Kapp* (Hamburg, 1958), 51–66.

——'Über Antiphons Rede über den Choreuten', *Hermes*, 91 (1963), 17–35.

——'Antiphons Rede (or. 5) über die Ermordung des Herodes', *RhM* 120 (1977), 209–27.

EVJEN, H. D., '*Apagoge* and Athenian Homicide Procedure', *Revue d'histoire du droit*, 38 (1970), 403–15.

FARRAR, CYNTHIA, *The Origins of Democratic Thinking: The Invention of Politics in Classical Athens* (Cambridge, 1988).

FIGUEIRA, THOMAS J., 'The Strange Death of Draco on Aigina', in R. Rosen and J. Farrell (eds.), *Nomodeiktes* (1993) 287–304 (= 'Draco and Attic Tradition', in *Excursions in Epichoric History* (Lanham, Md., 1993)).

FITTSCHEN, K., *Der Schild des Achilles* (= Archaeologia Homerica, Bd. II. Kap. N, Teil 1, 1973).

FREEMAN, K., 'The Mystery of the Choreutes', in *Studies in Honor of G. Norwood* (Phoenix Suppl. 1, Toronto, 1952), 85–94.

GAGARIN, MICHAEL, 'Self-Defense in Athenian Homicide Law', *GRBS* 19 (1978), 111–20.

——'The Prohibition of Just and Unjust Homicide in Antiphon's *Tetralogies*', *GRBS* 19 (1978), 291–306.

GAGARIN, MICHAEL, 'The Prosecution of Homicide in Athens', *GRBS* 20 (1979), 301–23.

—— 'Witnesses in the Gortyn Laws', *GRBS* 25 (1984), 345–9.

—— 'The Function of Witnesses at Gortyn', *Symposion 1985* (1989), 29–54.

—— *Early Greek Law* (Berkeley, 1986).

—— review of E. Heitsch, *Antiphon*, in *Göttingische Gelehrte Anzeigen*, 239 (1987), 56–64.

—— *The Murder of Herodes* (Frankfurt, 1989 (= *Studien zur kl. Philologie* 45)).

—— 'The Nature of Proofs in Antiphon', *CP* 85 (1990), 22–32.

—— '*Bouleusis* in Athenian Homicide Law', *Symposion 1988* (1991), 81–99.

—— 'The Ancient Tradition on the Identity of Antiphon', *GRBS* 31 (1991), 27–44.

GASKINS, RICHARD H., *Burdens of Proof in Modern Discourse* (New Haven, 1991).

GERNET, LOUIS, *Antiphon, Discours* (Paris, 1923).

—— 'Sur l'exécution capitale', *REG* 37 (1924), 261–93.

—— *Recherches sur le développement de la pensée juridique et morale en Grèce* (Paris, 1917).

GLOTZ, G., *La Solidarité de la famille dans le droit criminel en Grèce* (Paris, 1904).

GLOTZ, GUSTAVE, and COHEN, ROBERT, *Histoire grecque* (Paris, 1925).

GOEBEL, GEORGE, 'Early Greek Rhetorical Theory and Practice: Proof and Arrangement in the Speeches of Antiphon and Euripides' (diss. Univ. of Wisconsin, Madison, 1983).

GRAF, FRITZ, 'Apollon Delphinios', *MH* 2 (1979), 2–22.

GREEN, THOMAS, 'The Jury and the English Law of Homicide 1200–1600', *Michigan Law Review*, 74:3 (Jan. 1976), 413–501.

HANSEN, M. H., *Apagoge, Endeixis and Ephegesis against Kakourgoi, Atimoi and Pheugontes* (Odense, 1976).

—— 'The Prosecution of Homicide in Athens: A Reply', *GRBS* 22 (1981), 11–30.

HARDIE, P. R., 'Imago Mundi: Cosmological and Ideological Aspects of the Shield of Achilles', *JHS* 105 (1985), 11–31.

HARRIS, EDWARD M., 'Did the Athenians regard Seduction as a Worse Crime than Rape?', *CQ* 40 (1990), 370–7.

—— ' "In the Act" or "Red-Handed"? *Apagoge* to the Eleven and *Furtum Manifestum*', *Symposion 1993* (1994), 169–84.

HARRISON, A. R. W., *The Law of Athens*, 2 vols. (Oxford, 1968–71).

HART, H. L. A., *The Concept of Law*, (Oxford, 1961).

—— and HONORÉ, TONY, *Causation in the Law*, 2nd edn. (Oxford, 1985).

HAVELOCK, ERIC, *The Liberal Temper in Greek Politics* (New Haven, 1957).

HEADLAM, J. W., 'The Procedure of the Gortynian Inscription', *JHS* 13 (1892–3), 48–69.

HEITSCH, ERNST, *Recht und Argumentation in Antiphons 6. Rede* (Abh. Akad. Wiss. Mainz, 7, 1980).

——'Aidesis *im attischen Strafrecht*' (Abh. Akad. Wiss. Mainz, 1, 1984).

——*Antiphon aus Rhamnous* (Abh. Akad. Wiss. Mainz, 3, 1984).

——'Der Archon Basileus und die attischen Gerichtshöfe für Tötungsdelikte', *Symposion 1985* (1989), 71–87.

HOLMES, OLIVER WENDELI., *The Common Law* (Boston, Little, Brown, orig. ed., 1881; page ref. to repr., 1963).

HOMMEL, H., 'Die Gerichtsszene auf dem Schild des Achilleus', *Palingenesia*, 4 (1969), 11–13.

HORDER, JEREMY, *Provocation and Responsibility* (Oxford, 1992).

HUMPHREYS, SALLY, 'The Evolution of Legal Process in Ancient Attica', in E. Gabba (ed.), *Tria Corda: Scritti in onore di Arnaldo Momigliano* (Como, 1983), 229–56.

——'The Discourse of Law in Archaic and Classical Greece', *Law and History Review*, 6:2 (1988), 465–93.

——'A Historical Approach to Drakon's Law un Homicide', *Symposion 1990* (1991), 17–45.

INNES, D. C., 'Gorgias, Antiphon and Sophistopolis', *Argumentation*, 5 (1991), 221–31.

JACOBY, FELIX, *Die Fragmente der griechischen Historiker* (Berlin, 1923–58).

JANKO, RICHARD, *The Iliad: A Commentary*, iv, books 13–16 (Cambridge, 1992).

JEFFERY, L. H., *Archaic Greece: The City-States c.700–500 B.C.* (London, 1976).

KAKRIDIS, JOHANNES T., 'Erdictete Ekphrasen: ein Beitrag zur homerischen Schildbeschreibung', *Wiener Studien*, 76 (1963), 7–26.

KEIL, BRUNO, 'Antiphon κατὰ τῆς μητρυιᾶς', *Jahrbücher für classische Philologie* (= Fleckeisens Jahrbücher), 135 (1887), 89–102.

KENNEDY, GEORGE, *The Art of Persuasion in Ancient Greece* (Princeton, 1963).

——*Aristotle 'On Rhetoric': A Theory of Civic Discourse* (New York and Oxford, 1991).

——*Comparative Rhetoric: An Historical and Cross-Cultural Introduction* (New York and Oxford, 1997).

KÜHNER, R., and GERTH, B., *Ausführliche Grammatik der griechischen Sprache*, 2 vols. (Hannover and Leipzig, 1890–1904).

LÄMMLI, FRITZ, *Das attische Prozeßverfahren* (Paderborn, 1938).

LANGE, LUDWIG, 'Die Epheten und der Areopag vor Solon', *Abh. der königlich-sächsischen Gesellschaft der Wiss.* 7 (1874), 189–264.

LATTE, KURT, *Heiliges Recht. Untersuchungen zur Geschichte der sakralen Rechtsformen in Griechenland* (Tübingen, 1920).

LAVENCY, M., *Aspects de la logographie judiciaire attique* (Louvain, 1964).

LEAF, WALTER, 'The Trial Scene in *Iliad* XVII', *JHS* 8 (1887), 122–32.

LEISI, ERNST, *Der Zeuge im attischen Recht* (Frauenfeld, 1908; repr. New York, 1979).

LIPSIUS, J. H., *Das attische Recht und Rechtsverfahren* (Leipzig, 1905–15).

—— 'Ueber Antiphons Tetralogien', *Berichte der königlichen sächsischen Gesellschaft der Wissenschaften, Leipzig*, 56 (1904), 191–204.

—— 'Zu Antiphons Tetralogien', *Hermes*, 40 (1905), 450–70.

LLOYD-JONES, HUGH, *The Justice of Zeus*, 2nd edn. (Sather Classical Lectures 41; (Berkeley, 1983).

LOENING, THOMAS C., 'The Reconciliation Agreement of 403/402 BC in Athens: Its Content and Application' (diss. Brown University, 1981. (= *Hermes Einzelschr.* 53, 1987)).

LOOMIS, W. T., 'The Nature of Premeditation in Athenian Homicide Law', *JHS* 92 (1972), 86–95.

MACCORMACK, GEOFFREY, 'The T'ang and Ming Law of Homicide', *RIDA* 35 (1988), 27–78.

MACDOWELL, D. H., *Andokides On the Mysteries* (Oxford, 1962).

—— *Athenian Homicide Law* (Manchester, 1963).

—— *The Law in Classical Athens* (London, 1978).

—— 'Athenian Laws about Choruses', *Symposion 1982* (1985), 65–77.

—— *Demosthenes 'Against Meidias'* (Oxford, 1990).

MAINE, HENRY S. *Ancient Law: Its Connection with the Early History of Society and its Relation to Modern Ideas* (Boston, 1861; repr. 1963).

MARCH, JENNIFER, *The Creative Poet: Studies on the Treatment of Myths in Greek Poetry* (Univ. of London Inst. Classical Studies Bulletin, Suppl. 49; London 1987).

MASCHKE, R., *Die Willenslehre im griechischen Recht. Zugleich ein Beitrag zur Frage der Interpolationen in den griechischen Rechtsquellen* (Berlin, 1926).

MEIER, M. H., and SCHÖMANN, G. F., *Der attische Prozeß* (Halle, 1824).

MERITT, BENJAMIN, *The Athenian Calendar in the Fifth Century* (1928).

—— *The Athenian Year* (1961).

MEYER-LAURIN, HARALD, *Gesetz und Billigkeit im attischen Prozeß* (*Graezistische Abh.* 1) (Weimar, 1965).

MILLER, H., 'Drakon', in *RE* 5.2 (1905), 1648–62.

MILLER, STEPHEN G., *The Prytaneion: Its Function and Architectural Form* (Berkeley, 1978).

MOULINIER, R., *Le Pur et l'impur dans la pensée des Grecs* (Paris, 1952).

MUELLER, K. O., *Aeschylos Eumeniden* (Göttingen, 1833; trans. as *Dissertations on the Eumenides of Aeschylus*, Cambridge, 1835).

NILSSON, MARTIN, *A History of Greek Religion* (Oxford, 1925).

OBER, JOSIAH, *Mass and Elite in Democratic Athens* (Princeton, 1989).

OTTSEN, P. G., *De rerum inventione et dispositione quae est in Lysia et Antiphonte* (diss. Flensburg, 1847).

PARKE, H. W., *Festivals of the Athenians* (Ithaca, NY, 1977).

PAOLI, U. E., *Studi sul processo attico* (Padua, 1933; repr. Milan (Bibliotheca Iuridica 2), 1974).

PARKER, ROBERT, *Miasma: Pollution and Purification in Early Greek Religion* (Oxford, 1983).

PEARSON, LIONEL, *The Local Historians of Attica* (American Philological Assoc. Monographs, 11, Philadelphia, 1942).

PFLÜGER, H. H., 'Die Gerichtsszene auf dem Schilde des Achilleus', *Hermes*, 77 (1942), 140–8.

PHILIPPI, ADOLF, *Der Areopag und die Epheten. Eine Untersuchung zur athenischen Verfassungsgeschichte* (Berlin, 1874).

POTTER, H., *Historical Introduction to English Law and its Institutions*, 4th edn. ed. A. K. R. Kiralfy (London, 1958).

PRIMMER, ADOLF, 'Homerische Gerichtsszenen', *WS* 83 (1970), 5–13.

RADERMACHER, L., *Artium Scriptores: Reste der voraristotelischen Rhetorik*, *Sitz. Oesterreichische Akad. Wiss. phil.-hist. Klasse* 227.3 (Vienna, 1951).

RAUCHENSTEIN, R., 'Ueber die apagoge in der rede des Lysias gegen den Agoratos', *Philologus*, 5 (1850), 513–21.

REMBAR, CHARLES, *The Law of the Land* (New York, 1980).

RHODES, P. J., *A Commentary on the Aristotelian 'Athenaion Politeia'* (Oxford, 1981).

——'The Athenian Code of Laws 410–399 BC' *JHS* 111 (1991), 87–100.

RICKERT, GAILANN, *Ἑκών and Ἄκων in Early Greek Thought* (American Philological Assoc., American Classical Studies 20, Atlanta, 1989).

ROBERTSON, N. H., 'The Laws of Athens, 410–399 BC: the Evidence for Review and Publication', *JHS* 100 (1990), 43–75.

ROHDE, ERWIN, *Psyche: the Cult of Souls and Belief in Immortality among the Greeks*, trans. W. B. Hillis (New York, 1966; repr. of 1925 trans. from 8th German edn., 1920).

ROSEN, RALPH, and FARRELL, JOSEPH (eds.), *Nomodeiktes: Greek Studies in Honor of Martin Ostwald* (Ann Arbor, Mich., 1993).

RUSCHENBUSCH, EBERHARD, 'ΦΟΝΟΣ. Zum Recht Drakons und seiner Bedeutung für das Werden des athenischen Staates', *Historia*, 9 (1960), 129–54.

——ΣΟΛΩΝΟΣ ΝΟΜΟΙ. *Die Fragmente des Solonischen Gesetzeswerkes* (Historia Einzelschr. 9, Wiesbaden, 1966).

——*Untersuchungen zur Geschichte des athenischen Strafrechts* (Graezistische Abh. 4, Graz and Cologne, 1968).

RUSCHENBUSCH, EBERHARD, review of Gagarin, *Early Greek Law*, in *CP* 84 (1989), 342–5.

SAUNDERS, TREVOR J., *Plato's Penal Code* (Oxford, 1991).

SCHADEWALDT, W., 'Der Schild des Achilles', *NJb* 113 (1938).

SCHEIDWEILER, F., 'Antiphons Rede über den Mord an Herodes', *RhM* 109 (1966), 319–38.

SCHINDEL, ULRICH, *Der Mordfall Herodes* (Nachrichten der Akademie der Wissenschaften in Göttingen, Phil.-Hist. Kl. 9, 1979).

SCHÖMANN, G. F., 'Die Epheten und der Areopag', *Jahrbücher für klassischen Philologie*, 111 (1875), 153–65.

—— 'De Areopago et Ephetis' (Greifswald, 1833 (= Opuscula Academica 1, Berlin, 1856, 190–9)).

—— *Griechische Alterthümer*, 2nd edn. (Berlin, 1861; 3rd, unrevised edn., Berlin, 1871, trans. as *The Antiquities of Greece*, London, 1880).

SCHRADE, H., 'Der Homerische Hephaistos', *Gymnasium*, 57 (1950).

SCHÜTRUMPF, ECKART, *Aristoteles. Politik* (= Aristoteles Werke, ed. Flashar. Band 9), Teil 2 (Darmstadt, 1991).

SCHWARTZ, EDUARD, 'De Thrasymacho Chalcedonio', *Index scholarum in academia Commentatio Rostochiensi*, 1892: 3–16 (= *Gesammelte Schriften*. Berlin, 1956, 112–35).

SCHWYZER, E., *Dialectorum Graecarum exempla epigraphica potiora* (Leipzig, 1923).

SEALEY, RAPHAEL, 'The Athenian Courts for Homicide', *CP* 78 (1983), 275–96.

—— 'The *Tetralogies* Ascribed to Antiphon', *TAPA* 114 (1984), 71–85.

SHKLAR, JUDITH, *Legalism: Law, Morals and Political Trials* (Cambridge, Mass., 1964).

SMITH, GERTRUDE, 'The Prytaneum in the Athenian Amnesty Law', *CP* 16 (1921), 345–53.

—— 'Dicasts in the Ephetic Courts', *CP* 19 (1924), 353–8.

SOROF, MARTIN, 'Die Apagoge in Mordprocessen', *Jahrbücher für klassischen Philologie*, 127 (1883), 105–13.

—— 'Über die ΑΠΑΓΩΓΗ im attischen Gerichtsverfahren', *Jahrbücher für klassischen Philologie*, 128 (1884), 7–16.

STANLEY, KEITH, *The Shield of Homer: Narrative Structure in the 'Iliad'* (Princeton, 1993).

STEINWENTER, ARTHUR, 'Die Gerichtsszene auf dem Schild des Achilles', *Studi in onore di Siro Solazzi* (Naples, 1948), 7–20.

—— *Die Streitbeendigung durch Urteil, Schiedsspruch und Vergleich nach griechischem Rechte* (Münchener Beiträge 8, 1925).

STROUD, RONALD, *Drakon's Law on Homicide* (Berkeley, 1968).

—— *The Axones and Kyrbeis of Solon and Drakon* (Berkeley, 1979).

TALAMANCA, M., 'Δικάζειν e κρίνειν nelle testimonianze greche piu antiche', *Symposion 1974* (1979), 103–33.

THIEL, J. H., *Antiphons erste Tetralogie* (Groningen, 1932), 13–15.

THÜR, GERHARD, 'Zum δικάζειν bei Homer', *ZSS* 87 [1970], 426–44.

——*Beweisführung vor den Schwurgerichtshöfen Athens. Die Proklesis zur Basanos* (*Sitz. Oesterreichische Akad. Wiss. phil.-hist. Klasse* 317.1, Vienna, 1977).

——'Zum δικάζειν im Urteil aus Mantineia', *Symposion 1985* (1989), 55–69.

——'Die Todesstrafe im Blutprozess Athens', *Journal of Juristic Papyrology*, 20 (Warsaw, 1988), 142–56.

——'The Jurisdiction of the Areopagos in Homicide Cases,' *Symposion 1990* (1991), 53–72.

TOD, MARCUS, *Greek Historical Inscriptions*, 2 vols. (Oxford, 1946–8; repr. 1985).

TODD, S. C., *The Shape of Athenian Law* (Oxford, 1993).

TRAVLOS, J., 'The Lawcourt *ΕΠΙ ΠΑΛΛΑΔΙΩΙ*', *Hesperia*, 43 (1974), 500–11.

TRESTON, HUBERT J., *Poiné: A Study in Ancient Greek Blood-Vengeance* (London, 1923).

TULIN, ALEXANDER, *Dike Phonou: The Right of Prosecution and Attic Homicide Procedure* (Stuttgart and Leipzig, 1996 = *Beiträge zur Altertumskunde* 76).

VOLLMER, GERHARD, *Studien zum Beweis antiphontischer Reden* (diss., Hamburg, 1958).

VON DER MÜHLL, P., ' Zur Unechtheit der antiphontischen Tetralogien', *MH* 5 (1948), 1–5.

WALLACE, ROBERT W., *The Areopagos Council to 307 BC* (Baltimore, 1989).

——response to Thür, 'Jurisdiction of the Areopagos', *Symposion 1990* (1991), 73–9.

WEBER, MAX, *Max Weber on Law in Economy and Society*, trans. Max Rheinstein and Edward Shils from *Wirtschaft und Gesellschaft*, 2nd edn. (1925) (Cambridge, Mass., 1954).

WESTBROOK, RAYMOND, 'The Trial Scene in the Iliad', *HSCP* 94 (1992), 52–76.

WILAMOWITZ-MOELLENDORFF, ULRICH VON, 'Die erste Rede des Antiphon', *Hermes*, 22 (1887), 194–210.

——*Aristoteles und Athen*, 2 vols. (Berlin, 1893).

——*Die Glaube der Hellenen*, 2nd edn. (Darmstadt, 1955).

——'Die sechste Rede des Antiphon', *Sitz. Königlich Preussischen Akad. Wiss.* 21 (Berlin, 1900).

——'Lesefrucht CLXXI' (on Lysias 1), *Hermes*, 58 (1923), 57–61.

WILLETTS, RONALD F., *The Law Code of Gortyn* (Berlin, 1967).

WILLIAMS, BERNARD, *Shame and Necessity* (Sather Classical Lectures 57; Berkeley, 1993).

WOLFF, HANS JULIUS, 'The Origin of Judicial Litigation among the Greeks', *Traditio*, 4 (1946), 31–87.

——*Die attische Paragraphe* (Graezistische Abhandlungen 2, Weimar, 1966).

WOODS, MICHAEL, *Aristotle 'Eudemian Ethics'*, 2nd edn. (Oxford, 1992).

ZUCKER, FRIEDRICH, review of Solmsen, *Antiphonstudien*, in *Gnomon*, 12 (1936), 442–4.

ZUNTZ, GÜNTHER, 'Earliest Attic Prose Style', *C & M* 2 (1939), 121–44.

——'Once again the Antiphontean Tetralogies', *MH* 6 (1949), 100–4.

INDEX OF PASSAGES CITED

Aeschines
 1 (*Against Timarchus*)
  91 352 n. 71
 2 (*On the Embassy*)
  87–8 147 n. 12, 206
 3 (*Against Ctesiphon*)
  244 99 n.
Aeschylus
 Agamemnon
  1223–1634 258–9
 Eumenides
  429–32 11–12
  611–13 200
Alcidamas
 Ulixes (Radermacher B XXII 16)
  189 n. 45, 212 n. 78
Anaximenes (or Ps.-Aristotle)
 Ars Rhetorica
  4. 7–9 204
  14–17 21
Andocides
 1 (*On the Mysteries*)
  78 125, 160
  91 132
  94–5 127–30
Androtion (*FGrHist* 324)
 fragments 3–4 14
Anonymous
 Life of Thucydides
  6–7 114, 300–1
Antiphon
 1 (*On the Stepmother*) 187, 216–50
  3–4 196
  28 190
 2 (*Tetralogy* 1) 181–94, 245–7
 3 (*Tetralogy* 2) 177–80, 195
 4 (*Tetralogy* 3) 184, 196–203,
   259–60, 267, 301–8
 5 (*On the Murder of Herodes*) 23,
   314–50
  14 (= 6. 2) 1, 25, 320
  64–8 90
  87–9 (= 6. 3–6) 177, 326–7
  90 156
 6 (*On the Choreutes*) 251–81
  3–6 196 n. 58

 9 158
 18 188
 38–42 137, 153
 Fragments 68–70 (Blass) 175
Antiphon's Defence 189–90
Aristophanes
 Birds 755–9, 1337–9 373 n. 2
 Clouds 1421–4 373–5
 Ecclesiazusae 128 141
Aristotle
 Eudemian Ethics
  1226^b 30–1227^{a}2 39–40
 Nicomachean Ethics
  5. 8, 1135^{b}12–25 203
 Politics
  1268^{a-b} 85
  1269^a 386–7
  1274^{a-b} 16, 111, 146
  1300^b 27–30 102
 Rhetoric
  1354^{a}18–24 158
  1374^{a-b} 177, 204
  1375^{a-b} 302, 369
  1376^{b}8–13 368
  1401^a 208 n.
Aristotle or Ps.-Aristotle
 Athenaiôn Politeia (*Ath. Pol.* or
   'Athenian Constitution')
  3–4, 8 16
  3. 6 111
  39. 5–6 126, 131–2
  40. 2 130–1, 371
  57. 3–4 6, 104, 148–9, 162
  59. 6 143 n. 7
  63–7 158–60
 Magna Moralia
  1188^{b}29–38 113, 187, 226–7

Bacchylides
 Epinician
  9. 43–4 62

Demades
 fragment 23 (= Plut. *Sol.* 17) 2

Demosthenes
  20 (*Against Leptines*)
    157–8 88, 108–9
  21 (*Against Meidias*)
    70–6 202–3, 308–10
  22 (*Against Androtion*)
    2–3 152–3
  23 (*Against Aristocrates*)
    22–81 88–98
    22 89–91, 112
    28 77 n. 78, 90–1, 111, 150
    37 42, 77
    44 44, 77, 151
    51 82
    53–6 78, 92–4, 201–2
    60 76
    63–79: 12
    65–6 7
    67–8: 140
    69 148
    71 139
    72 18, 79, 117–18
    76–7 99–102
    80 163–4, 334–7
    82 44
  24 (*Against Timocrates*)
    7–8 152–3
    149–51 158, 161
  37 (*Against Pantaenetus*)
    59 = 38 (*Against Nausimachus*)
    22 153–4
  54 (*Against Conon*)
    25 224 n. 11
Ps.-Demosthenes
  43 (*Against Macartatus*)
    57 104, 159 n. 37
  45 (*Against Stephanus* I)
    81 352
  47 (*Against Evergus and Mnesibulus*)
    69–70 185–6
  58 (*Against Theocrines*)
    28–9 152
  59 (*Against Neaera*)
    10 145–6
Dinarchus
  1 (*Against Demosthenes*)
    50–5 163 n. 43
    87 10
Diodorus Siculus
  4. 31 3 n.

Empedocles (31 Diels and Kranz)
  fragment 135 198 n. 62, 208

Euripides
  Electra
    1050–1 200 n.
    1258–65 10
  Hippolytus: 12
  Medea
    37, 317 259
  Suppliants
    1165–94 62 n. 58
Eustathius (van der Valk)
  4. 236 53
  779. 60 151 n.

Gorgias (82 Diels and Kranz)
  Helen and *Palamedes* (F11–11a) 176,
    180–2, 212

Harpocration *Lexicon* (Dindorf)
  5. 6 (*s.v. hagneuete*) 175 n. 19
  115. 7 (*s.v. en Phreatou*) 104 n. 33
  128. 11–14 (*s.v. Prytaneion*) 100
    n. 23
  297 (*s.v. hypophonia*) 151–2
Hellanicus (*FGrHist* 323a)
  fragment 22 10–11
Hermogenes
  Peri Ideon
    B 399 171 n.2
Herodotus
  1. 45 47
  1. 96–103 64
  5. 71 4, 43
Hesiod
  Works and Days
    39 5, 58 n. 40
    265–6 258
Hesychius
  Lexicon (Latte)
    E 3450 (*s.v. en Phreatou*) 104 n. 33
Homer
  Iliad
    1. 152–6 43
    1. 536–43 58 n. 49
    3. 277–80 61–3
    4. 309–14 46–8
    6. 522–3 48
    8. 425–31 58 n. 49
    9. 85–120 46
    9. 338–9 63
    9. 632–36 46
    16. 387–8 58 n. 49
    18. 434 48

18. 497–508 52–7, 65
18. 526 38
19. 85–90 43
22. 255 63
23. 486–7 63
23. 573–85 48, 51, 56
Odyssey
2. 133 48
3. 214–15 48
3. 432–4 64
5. 363 38
8. 347–56 42–3, 55, 65
11. 547 58 n. 49
20. 17–21 249
22. 1–49 43, 46
24. 528–48 3
Homeric Hymns
  Hermes 22
  274–6, 382–3 43
  Selene
  1–2 61

Isaeus
4. 28 352
Isocrates
18 (*Against Callimachus*) 129
20 355 n. 74
51–7 144–6

Justinian
  Institutes
  4 1. 3 317

Lexicon Seguerianum
213 30–214. 2 333 n.
311 17–20 107
311 21–2 104
Libanius
  Declamations
  1. 1. 145 2 n.
Lycurgus
1.11–13 158 n. 33
Lysias
  1 (*On the Slaying of Eratosthenes*)
  284–99
  26–31 109 n., 157
  36 157
  37 200
  3 (*Against Simon*) 301
  28–43 39 n. 13, 114, 224–5
  46 158
  4 (*On Wounding with Premeditation*)
  4–11 39 n. 13, 143 n. 6, 223

Ps.-Lysias
  6 (*Against Andocides*)
  37–41 367–9
Lysias
  10 (*Against Theomnestus* I) 152
  8–13 373 n. 2
  12 (*Against Eratosthenes*) 376–82
  99–100 194–5
  13 (*Against Agoratus*) 126, 128, 132,
    354–70
  22 (*Against the Grain Dealers*)
  2 355 n. 75
  Fragmentary speeches
  Against Mikines 182–3, 246
  Against Lysitheus 39, 224

Maximus (Confessor)
  schol. Dionysius Areopagiticus
    (Migne *Patrologia Graeca*
    4. 167) 14–15

Pausanias
  1. 28 12, 100 n. 23
Philochorus (*FGrHist* 328)
  F 21 14 n. 21
Photius
  Lexicon (Naber) i. 236 (*s.v. ephetai*)
    159 n. 37
Plato
  Euthyphro 208, 311–12
  Laws
  859–76 206–8
  865d–e 196–7
  866d–867b 225, 235
  874c 95
  Seventh Letter
  336e–337a 129
Plutarch
  Pericles
  36. 4–6: 180–1
  Solon (Ziegler)
  12 4, 43
  17 2
  19. 3 110 n. 46
  19. 4 15, 50, 100
Pollux
  Onomasticon
  8. 106 62
  8. 118–19 12
  8. 125 14, 163
  9. 61 19
Protagoras
  Antilogies (80 Diels and Kranz, F5)
    174

Solon
  Laws (Fragments, Ruschenbusch)
    7 111
    9–12 19
    42 60
Sophocles
  Antigone
    264–7 23
    542 62 n. 58
  Oedipus Tyrannus 249
  Trachiniae 3, 248–50, 259

Thucydides
  1. 126 4
  1. 132 259

INSCRIPTIONS

Inscriptiones Creticae (*IC*)
  4. 9 60 n. 53
  4. 72 58–63
Inscriptiones Graecae (*IG*)
  I³ 76. 15 129
  I³ 102 357–8
  I³ 104. 10–20 33–43
  I³ 104. 26–9 42, 77, 106
  I³ 104. 30–1 77 n. 78
  I³ 104. 33–6 49, 70–1, 199
  I³ 104. 33–8 76–7
  I³ 104. 36–8 76, 150, 303
  I³ 104. 39–41 81 n. 84
  I³ 105. 36 355 n. 75
  II² 111. 58–60 129 n. 71
  VII 1179 62 n. 59

GENERAL INDEX

adultery 60, 287–91
  see also rape
agōnes timētoi 74 n. 73, 85
  see also *timēsis*
aidesis ('settlement') 34–5, 39, 108,
    117, 150–4
  see also 'pardon'
aitios ('guilty' or 'liable') 41–5, 55, 65,
    107
Alcmeonidae 4, 43
amnesty 125–32, 355–6, 367–72
  see also Plut. *Sol.* 19. 4, Andoc. 1. 78
Antiphon of Rhamnous 181 n. 28
Antiphon 'the Sophist' 171, 374
apagoge ('summary arrest') 81–2, 156,
    333–40, 363, 370–1
  see also *endeixis*
archon basileus 124–5, 137, 148–9, 278
Areopagus council and court 6–17
Ares' trial (foundation myth) 10–11
atechnoi pisteis ('non-technical
    proofs') 21–6, 271–5, 318–19

Babylonian Laws on homicide 60
basileis and *phylobasileis* ('tribal
    kings') 49, 69, 124–5
battle, trial by 387–8
bouleusis ('planning') 41–5, 116, 126–7,
    248–50, 379–82
  intentional 219–20, 231–3, 296,
    361–7
  unintentional 254–70, 305–6

circumstantial evidence, *see* probability
confiscation (*demeusis* and
    apographai) 148, 228–9
Chinese laws on homicide viii
Cylon 4, 43

Delphinium court 6, 12, 96, 118–25,
    282–4, 289, 300–1
  see also justifiable killing
deodand 99
dikazein ('give judgement') 49–69,
    112, 148–9
diomosia, see oaths
Draco, historical context 4, 33–6

Eleven (magistrates authorizing arrest)
    341, 362–6
endeixis 122, 164–5, 316–18
  translated 'warrant' 82 n. 86
enthymeme 20
ep' autophōrōi (immediate incrimina-
    tion) 165, 237–8, 316–17, 351–4,
    362–6
ephēgēsis (arrest by magistrate) 149 n.,
    337 n. 47
ephetai ('justices') 8–15, 34, 70–5, 115,
    133–4, 155–67
'error' as culpable (*hamartēma*) 200–6
Eupatrids 6, 114–15
euthydikia 84–7, 113
execution, by the state 112, 147–50
  summary execution 317

German law on negligent homicide
    233, 262–3
Gorgias 171–6

hekōn and *akōn* 37–41, 47–8
  see also *pronoia*
Heracles, punished for slaying
    Iphitus 3–4
Holmes, Oliver Wendell 99 n. 22, 236
    nn. 28–9, 300
hybris ('outrage') distinguished from
    aikia ('assault') 308–9
hypophonia (payment) 151
  see also *poinē*

impiety (*asebeia*) 152–3
inanimate objects as cause of death
    99
intention 36–49, 68–75, 112–14,
    358–61
  see also *pronoia*
istor 61–4

'justices', see *ephetai*
justifiable killing 78, 92–6, 198–208,
    291–2

kakourgoi 292, 333–5, 339, 363
  translated 'felons' 313–15

last clear chance 265–7
legalism 25

malice aforethought 235–8
  see also *pronoia*
martys /martyros ('witness') 62–4
mē mnēsikakein, see amnesty
mens rea 40, 66, 79, 123
metastasis (transferred blame) 178,
  206
miasma 17–19, 192–7, 378
'mischance' (*atychēma*) 200
'murder', origins of the English ix–x

'negligence' (*aboulia*) 233–6
  see also *bouleusis*, unintentional

oaths in homicide procedure 138–42,
  147
ordeal 23–4, 388
Orestes, tried for killing
  Clytemnestra 11, 119, 208 n.

Palladium court 6, 115–18, 147
paragraphē 85, 129–30, 332
'pardon', granted by phratry 34, 71–5,
  104–5
parricide 152–3, 373
Patroclus, in exile for homicide 46–7
perjury and false witness (*pseudo-
  martyria*) 143–7
Philippi, Adolf 8–10
phratry/*phratores* 34 n. 2, 75
  see also pardon
Phreatto court 102–8
'planning', see *bouleusis*
poinē 17–19, 150–1

poisoning (*pharmakeia*) 219, 251–2
probability (*eikos*) 20–4, 184–91,
  316–21
probable cause (or 'probable
  suspicion') 319–21
pronoia 37–41, 114, 223–7, 237–8, 324,
  385
Protagoras 174, 181
provocation 299–301
prytaneis 8, 14
Prytaneum 15–17, 99–101

rape 287 n. 6, 290

Schömann, G. F. 7–9
Socrates' trial 128, 212–13
Solmsen, Friedrich 21–4, 173, 239,
  271–2, 330
Solon's reforms 89–90, 110–15
stasis (defining the issue) 177, 284

technai (rhetorical handbooks) 172
Tetralogies, question of authenticity 171–6, 208–15
timēsis (penalty phase of trial) 337,
  340–2
torture and challenge to torture
  186–91, 221, 237–41, 274–5, 295,
  321–3, 343

Weber, Max 26–7, 375
Wilamowitz-Moellendorff, U. 22, 216,
  251–2
witnesses 191, 275
  see also *martys*
Wolff, H. J. 9, 15, 54–6, 332
wounding with intent to kill 223–4